Dreaming
of
Cockaigne

Pieter Bruegel the Elder, *The Land of Cockaigne*, 1567
Source: Munich, Alte Pinakothek.

Dreaming
of
Cockaigne

MEDIEVAL FANTASIES OF
THE PERFECT LIFE

Herman Pleij

TRANSLATED BY DIANE WEBB

Columbia University Press
New York

Columbia University Press
Publishers Since 1893
New York   Chichester, West Sussex

Translation copyright © 2001 Diane Webb
Copyright © 1997 Herman Pleij
First published as *Dromen Van Cocagne* in 1997 by
Uitgeverij Prometheus

Grateful acknowledgment is made to the Foundation
for the Production and Translation of Dutch Literature
for financial support for the translation of this work.

Library of Congress Cataloging-in-Publication Data
Pleij, Herman.
[Dromen van Cocagne. English]
Dreaming of Cockaigne / Herman Pleij ;
translated by Diane Webb.
p. cm.
Includes bibliographical references and index.
ISBN 0–231–11702–7 (cloth)
1. Cockaigne. 2. Civilization, Medieval.
3. Social history—Medieval, 500–1500.
4. Literature, Medieval. 5. Cockaigne in literature.
I. Webb, Diane. II. Title.

CB353 .P5413   2001
398'42'0940902—dc21   00–51916

Printed in the United States of America
Designed by Audrey Smith

c 10 9 8 7 6 5 4 3 2 1

Contents

List of Illustrations   vii

Part 1. The Forfeiture of Happiness: The Beginning

1. Paradise Lost   3
2. Contours of a Book   13
3. The Power of Literature   28

Part 2. Texts as Maps

4. Rhyming Texts L and B, Prose Text G   33
5. The Two Rhyming Texts on the Land of Cockaigne   45
6. Recitation and Writing   55
7. Oral Structures in Writing   62
8. The Existing Potential   73
9. The Prose Text on Luilekkerland   77

Part 3. Eating to Forget

10. Eating Habits   89
11. Hunger and Scarcity   100
12. The Topos of Hunger   107
13. The Intoxicating Effect of Fasting   118
14. Gorging in Self-Defense   128
15. Food in Motion   137
16. Literary Refreshment   147

Part 4. Paradise Refurbished

17. The Land of Cockaigne as Paradise   165
18. Never Say Die   182
19. Heavenly Rewards   191
20. Other Paradises   207
21. Lovely Places, Golden Ages   216

22. Wonder Gardens and Pleasure Parks 230
23. Dreams of Immortality 236

Part 5. The Imagination Journeys Forth

24. Geographical Musings 245
25. Real Dreamworlds 255
26. Wonders of East and West 263
27. Fanciful Destinations 281
28. Virtual Dreamlands 289

Part 6. Heretical Excesses

29. The Thousand-Year Reign of Peace and Prosperity 301
30. Heresies of the Free Spirit 311
31. Sex Adam-and-Eve Style 318
32. Low-Country Heterodoxy 325

Part 7. Learning as a Matter of Survival

33. Didactic Differences 337
34. Topsy-Turvy Worlds 352
35. Hard Times 365
36. Moderation, Ambition, and Decorum 372
37. Lessons in Pragmatism 384

Part 8. Dreaming of Cockaigne: The End

38. The Name Cockaigne 391
39. A Depreciated Cultural Asset 403
40. From Countryside to Town 413
41. The Necessity of Fiction 423

Appendixes

1. Middle Dutch Rhyming Texts on Cockaigne 431
2. Dutch Prose Text of 1546 on Luilekkerland 438
3. Dutch Poems Appearing in English Translation 443

Sources 451

Bibliography 489

Index 515

*I*llustrations

1. Beginning of the oldest Cockaigne text in Middle Dutch   4
2. Hugo van der Goes, *The Fall of Man*   9
3. The Fall of Man and the Expulsion from Paradise   11
4. The Expulsion from Paradise   14
5. The New Jerusalem descending from the heavens   17
6. Exuberant eating and drinking portrayed in *Graduale*   21
7. Courtly pleasure garden   24
8. Beginning of Cockaigne text B   29
9. End of oldest Cockaigne text in Middle Dutch   46
10. End of mock doctor's prescription   47
11. End of Cockaigne text B and beginning of mock doctor's prescription in prose   53
12. Title of the prose text on Luilekkerland   78
13. Lent and Carnival song   79
14. Woodcut by Erhard Schoen   82
15. A simple meal of broth and beer   91
16. A woodcutter's frugal meal   93
17. Cauldron of vegetable broth   94
18. Depiction of a copious supply of meat in a middle-class milieu   95
19. The sack of Jerusalem in A.D. 70   108
20. Famine in Jerusalem in A.D. 70   111
21. A man reduced to eating grass   113
22. Punishments awaiting gluttons in hell   115
23. Christ as food   121
24. Ritual meal before the Battle of Hastings   130
25. Edible portrayal of the siege of Jerusalem   139
26. Recognizable animals in a butcher's shop   143
27. *Battle Between Fish and Meat*   150
28. Circle of Pieter Bruegel the Elder, *Battle Between Lent and Carnival*   152

29. After Pieter Bruegel the Elder, *Battle Between Lent and Carnival* 153
30. *The Fat Kitchen* 154
31. *The Lean Kitchen* 155
32. *Tavern Scene* 156
33. Representation of paradise by Hieronymus Bosch 175
34. The healing well from the Gospel According to Saint John 183
35. *The Fountain of Youth* 184
36. Earthly paradise as a citadel 197
37. Courtly pleasure garden 217
38. Ideal garden outside the town walls 219
39. Lucas Cranach the Elder, *The Golden Age* 221
40. Simple fare in the golden age 223
41. Brawls common at the end of the silver age 225
42. Festivities at Binche in 1549 234
43. Title page of a book on the land of Prester John 251
44. "If two people walk in opposite directions. . ." 253
45. Monster races, from Hartmann Schedel's *Buch der Chroniken* 265
46. Monster races, from Jacob van Maerlant's *Der naturen bloeme* 266
47. Jan Mostaert, *Episode from the Conquest of America* 271
48. Skillful butchering of European intruders by cannibals 272
49. Title page of an account of Bartholomeus Springer's journey to India 275
50. Text on the title page of the account of Vasco da Gama's journey to Calcutta 277
51. Naked savages, depicted half "upside-down" 279
52. Archers 282
53. Winter as a person modeled of natural products 286
54. Chaining up the devil 304
55. Lollards shooting the breeze 315
56. Lustless sex in paradise 321
57. End of Luilekkerland text 338
58. Hans Lützelhüpsch comes from Luilekkerland 339
59. Race 341
60. Melting snowman next to a prayer 346
61. Male monkeys coupling beneath a prayer 349
62. Little man with his head between his legs 350

63. The upside-down world: animals acting as humans — 355
64. The topsy-turvy world: servants riding their masters' horses — 356
65. Beginning of satirical rhyming text about the hate-filled world — 359
66. Engraving by Pieter van der Heyden featuring the Blue Barge — 360
67. Unclean behavior engaged in by the inhabitants of the New World — 363
68. Drawing of *Desidia*, or Sloth — 367
69. Wine leads to lechery, anger, carousing, and foolishness — 373
70. Detail of engraving of *Gula*, or Gluttony — 374
71. Corpulence — 376
72. Drunkard — 377
73. Devilish personification of Gluttony — 379
74. Hell is a topsy-turvy world — 387
75. The song "Abbas Cucaniensis" from the *Carmina Burana* — 394
76. Pieter Bruegel the Elder, *The Land of Cockaigne* — 405
77. Title page of an eighteenth-century collection of popular texts — 409
78. Beginning of the *Lucidarius boeck* — 411
79. Shop selling precious stones in a city — 417
80. Title page of *Der Fielen, Rabauwen oft der Schalcken Vocabulaer* — 420

Dreaming
of
Cockaigne

Part 1

The Forfeiture of Happiness:
The Beginning

I

Paradise Lost

*E*VERYONE LIVING at the end of the Middle Ages had heard of Cockaigne at one time or another. It was a country, tucked away in some remote corner of the globe, where ideal living conditions prevailed: ideal, that is, according to late-medieval notions, and perhaps not even those of everyone living at the time. Work was forbidden, for one thing, and food and drink appeared spontaneously in the form of grilled fish, roast geese, and rivers of wine. One only had to open one's mouth, and all that delicious food practically jumped inside. One could even reside in meat, fish, game, fowl, or pastry, for another feature of Cockaigne was its edible architecture. The weather was stable and mild—it was always spring—and there was the added bonus of a whole range of amenities: communal possessions, lots of holidays, no arguing or animosity, free sex with ever-willing partners, a fountain of youth, beautiful clothes for everyone, and the possibility of earning money while one slept.

By the Middle Ages no one any longer believed in such a place, yet the stories about it continued to circulate around Europe for centuries. Apparently it was vitally important to be able to fantasize about a place where everyday worries did not exist and overcompensation was offered in the form of dreams of the ideal life. The stories about Cockaigne even competed with one another for the greatest entertainment value, incorporating contrasts—as absurd as they were grotesque—to combat the fear, sometimes driven to frantic heights, that this already wretched earthly existence would suddenly take a turn for the worse. These images thus linked the seriousness of the daily fight for survival with the humor of hyperbole to produce hilarious topsy-turvy worlds that proved to have didactic functions as well, supplying directives concerning desirable social behavior and the attainment of self-knowledge, as well as encouraging reflection on the nature of earthly existence.

No two stories of Cockaigne are alike, however; each varies according to time, place, and milieu. Things are further complicated by the problem of sources, for tales of the Land of Cockaigne belong preeminently to an oral tra-

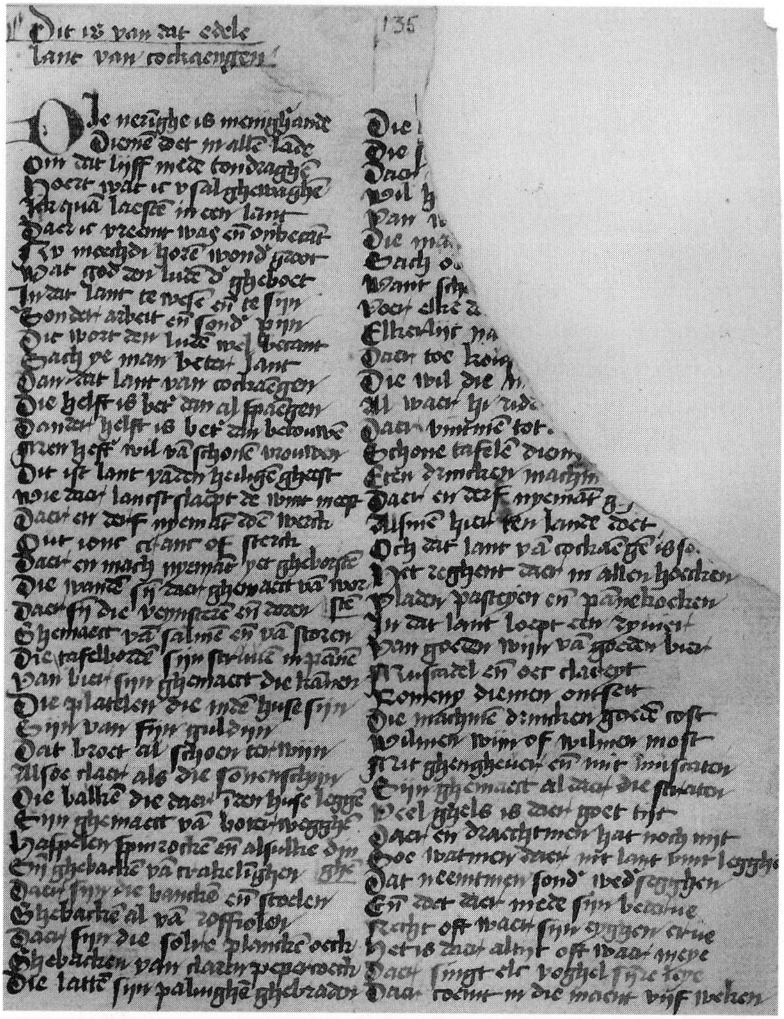

FIGURE 1

Beginning of the oldest Cockaigne text (L) in Middle Dutch, after 1458.

Source: London, British Library, MS Add. 10286, fol. 135 recto.

dition spanning generations. Tens of thousands of Cockaigne texts cropped up in the Middle Ages, in spontaneous adaptations full of new inventions as well as versions in which traditional motifs disappeared or were accidentally omitted. Once in a while an improvised version was written down—so as not to forget the dream (or, perhaps, its lessons)—to have on hand should the need arise. Countless Cockaigne texts circulated in the Middle Ages, but only a fraction of them were recorded in the vernacular of various countries.

Dreamworlds say a lot about those who devise them. Modern-day dreamworlds are the stock-in-trade of travel agencies: clever, custom-made products for typical holidaymakers in search of the ideal climate, unspoiled nature, cultural wonders, and forbidden sex. Even viewed over longer periods our dreamworlds display both common denominators and substantial differences. Present-day paradises are not marketed with promises of all you can eat or other exotic pleasures of the palate. Gorging oneself for a fixed price is little more than a weak echo of a Cockaigne that has deteriorated to the level of a corner café, soliciting the masses with their working-class dream of getting something for nothing. In the Western world food supplies are no longer an object of obsessive concern, which means that its Cockaignes do not culminate in eating sprees of disgusting dimensions. This certainly holds true for the average person. By medieval standards, modern-day Europe represents in many respects the realization of Cockaigne: fast food is available at all hours, as are climatic control, free sex, unemployment benefits, and plastic surgery that seemingly prolongs youth.

Nowadays Cockaigne, in the guise of Luilekkerland, is a child's paradise, with heaps of candy as high as houses and roof tiles made of pancakes. This Dutch phenomenon—a fairy-tale land whose name literally means "lazy-luscious-land"—is a mere shadow of the dazzling Cockaigne of the Middle Ages, now faded and relegated to the realm of child's play. This obstructs our view of the central place this dreamland seems to have occupied within the survival strategies of both peasants and townsfolk, and to a certain extent also of aristocrats and the clergy. Fantasies of Cockaigne offered a light-hearted counterbalance to the weighty obsessions of medieval existence, as experienced at all levels of society, by the laity and the clergy, men and women alike. Time and again, however, these fantasies linked up with images of other promising worlds, worlds that could claim a greater chance of fulfillment.

Cockaigne inevitably calls to mind an earthly paradise as frivolous as it is lavish, believed by many to be situated at some point on the globe and supposedly still boasting a fountain of youth, the most delicious food, and an everlasting spring. Didn't travelers recount tales of Atlantis, the Islands of the Blessed, El Dorado, and scores of other dreamlands with similar amenities that one could actually visit? And surely there was still the heavenly paradise, which also presented the prospect—after the Last Judgment—of eternal bliss for the laundered souls lucky enough to end up there. Finally, for the impatient, there was still the thousand-year reign of joy and prosperity foretold in the Bible as earthly compensation, which many believed would not be long in coming.

All these medieval dreamworlds bear strong similarities to one another. Some of their descriptions sound too real to have been dreamed up; perhaps they could better be called earthly idylls. The world was becoming more negotiable and more navigable all the time, while paradise and the hereafter also seemed to be getting closer, with specimens being cooked up and sampled here on earth. Cockaigne, no matter how unreal, conjured up such an alluring world that the necessity of dreaming was further stimulated rather than put in perspective.

This game was especially popular among the masses. Dreaming of Cockaigne was a means of alleviating the everyday worries of peasants and the lower middle classes, though it appears that the upper echelons of society were enticed by the image as well. The latter, however, always gave the impression of having less need for Cockaigne, given their ability to apply great inventiveness to the realization of their fantasies. After the sixteenth century, Cockaigne devolved into a diffuse Luilekkerland, a popular theme of graphic art, a multipurpose product hawked by peddlers as both boorish entertainment and a manual of etiquette for the young, before reaching its final destination: a fairy-tale candyland for today's toddlers.

First of all, however, Cockaigne was presented as a ready-made image designed to make the miserable circumstances of everyday life more bearable. Why, people asked themselves, was there so much suffering? It was difficult to find a satisfactory explanation for this and especially difficult to acquiesce in the answers offered by the church: such saintly forbearance is given to few. Nonetheless, the masses continued to torture themselves with never-ending questions about the origins of evil and indignation at the patent imperfections exhibited by humankind, themselves included.

Everyone knew, of course, that it had all begun with the Fall of Man. But why couldn't Adam and Eve's little faux pas be set to rights once and for all? If it were, the gates of paradise could be opened up again. The many portrayals of the first couple being driven out of paradise betray more impatience than acceptance. The huge numbers of texts, paintings, miniatures, prints, plays, religious processions, tableaux vivants, snowmen, tapestries, pottery, jewel boxes, combs, and what not, all of which record the painful beginnings of human suffering, are truly overwhelming. They seem to express incomprehension rather than resignation and certainly testify to constant demands for an explanation.

No parade or procession in the fifteenth-century Netherlands would have failed to present an enactment of Adam and Eve and their expulsion from paradise. The famous religious processions in the cities of Flanders and Brabant attracted thousands of spectators every year, not only from the cities themselves but also from much farther afield. There were often many dignitaries in attendance, even the king or prince, who would be feted at separate functions laid on by the burgomasters and town councillors. These religious processions were also instrumental in maintaining—as well as strengthening and expanding—relations between the municipal authorities and those on a regional or national level.

Starting in 1401 the Louvain city magistrates even insisted that the yearly religious procession open with a performance of Adam and Eve's expulsion from paradise, enacted on a float at the head of the parade. The expulsion was, after all, the point at which the notion of time had been introduced into the world, the moment when history had begun, so it was logical that the cart bearing its performance precede the others in the procession, with the actors—Adam, Eve, the angel, perhaps also a snake—performing at regular intervals along the route through the city. The sculptor Rombaut van Hingene and the carpenter Gorde den Draijer were commissioned to design and decorate a cart and to direct the spectacle. The performance proved to be such a successful overture to the procession that in 1462 the cart, with its backdrop of the earthly paradise, was given a complete overhaul. The result won the greatest admiration, this time from Duke Philip the Good and a whole train of prominent nobles and abbots.

The improvements continued, for in 1502 new costumes were made for Adam and Eve, and in 1531 the tailor André de Coster again supplied two new waistcoats and two pairs of stockings. Does this mean that the first couple was dressed for the performance? It is not inconceivable, given the forward march of civilization, which increasingly came to define nakedness as something unseemly that had to be suppressed. Or were the clothes (with con-

cessions made to contemporary fashions) meant to comply with the text of
Genesis, which says that after committing the evil deed Adam and Eve
attempted to hide their nakedness?

A depiction of this cart dating from 1594 has been preserved. The
accompanying rhyme stresses the joys of paradise, which Adam must now
exchange for a life of unremitting toil and hostility:

> Adam, the recalcitrant, is driven
> From blissful paradise, filled with delight,
> Because to God's command he did not listen.
> So daily toil is now to be the plight
> Of one who walked in heaven's peaceful light.

The depiction shows an angel with a flaming torch driving from the Garden
of Eden a naked Adam and Eve, who cover their genitals with their hands.
Perhaps they took off their clothes only for the performances. But it may
well be that their nakedness was shown only in this depiction, as it was
becoming increasingly unacceptable in reality.

In any case this annual enactment of the beginning of all earthly suffering must have been gripping indeed. This was the moment when we lost
everything, and there was no indication that the rather trifling error of judgment that caused it all would ever be forgiven and the doors of paradise once
again opened to the public. All bets now had to be placed on a rather uncertain hereafter, the sight of which was constantly being obscured by the devil.
And even these hopes would be dashed if it were really true—as so many people came to believe during the course of the fifteenth century—that as punishment for the schism existing within the church since 1378, with one pope
in Rome and another in Avignon, no one would be admitted to the heavenly
paradise ever again. It was also thought that since the schism the good souls
who had already died had been locked out of their waiting room—in the
form of an earthly paradise—which meant that all those souls were doomed
to wander about aimlessly as they awaited the Last Judgment.

The paradise—completely inaccessible—on the cart at the head of the
Louvain procession was fitted out as a Garden of Eden with beautiful trellis-
work, a splendidly decorated gate, a fountain, and a tree laden with fruit, a
sniggering snake twisted round its trunk. The very sight of it must have been

FIGURE 2

Hugo van der Goes (ca. 1440–1482), *The Fall of Man*, second half of fifteenth century.
Source: Vienna, Kunsthistorisches Museum.

unbearable. In the print a driver beats the horses that pull the heavy cart forward.

The scene is also colorfully spun out in the *Eerste Bliscap van Maria* (Mary's first joy). Starting in 1447 this play was performed once every seven years on the Grande Place in Brussels as part of a series of seven mystery plays, the finale of the so-called Great Procession. Adam and Eve cover themselves with a leaf in shame when God calls them to account. This awareness of their nakedness makes it clear that they have disobeyed God's command, and they are judged accordingly: Eve is condemned to painful childbearing and subservience to Adam, and Adam to toiling for his daily bread by tilling the earth, which will henceforth produce thorns and thistles as well as grain. This work promises to be difficult, and God condemns Adam to eat bread "in the sweat of thy face . . . till thou return unto the ground; for out of it wast thou taken: for dust thou art, and unto dust shalt thou return."

Then God asks his angel for the clothing he was supposed to sew for the fallen couple. Together they help Adam and Eve into their clothes, after which God banishes them from paradise for good. "For all eternity," he adds, just to make himself perfectly clear, which must have come as a great blow to those gathered on the square in Brussels. At last we know why new clothes were necessary for the procession in 1502. They were not intended to clothe Adam and Eve from the beginning but to be worn in their ex-paradisiacal life as mortals in the cold and transient world outside Eden. Before the gates of paradise God placed cherubim and a flaming sword, so that no one could ever again enter the garden and eat of the tree of life. And from that moment on paradise had been shut tight.

Locked out of the Garden of Eden, Adam and Eve lament their cruel fate. They have forfeited their chance of happiness by committing an act of unbelievable stupidity, as they now realize. Adam suggests begging God for mercy, but Eve continues to take the initiative, even though that idea she'd had about the apple had gone badly wrong and she was now supposed to be subservient to her husband:

> Beloved husband, stop, and take this spade,
> And with it start to work, and labor learn.
> Of toil and trouble life must needs be made,
> Disgraced, our daily bread we now must earn.

FIGURE 3

The Fall of Man and the Expulsion from Paradise. Miniature from
Flavius Josephus's *Antiquités judaïques* (fifteenth century).

Source: Paris, Bibliothèque de l'Arsenal, MS 5082.

And Adam concludes with a sigh that there had been no question of work in paradise, because God had willed the crops to grow of their own accord. So it was, "before he shut us out."

In the late Middle Ages in particular, such scenes were performed, portrayed, and viewed by the thousand. Any attempt to survey all the examples preserved inevitably reveals the nagging tone of melancholy informing them. Nowadays original sin seems to have been stripped of any existential meaning relating to the present, even for believers. The Fall is interpreted at most allegorically, and its images give less cause for reflection than for aesthetic and cultural-historical gratification. In the late Middle Ages, however, such displays seem to have had the impact—over and over again—of a scream or an accusation, inciting strong emotions, self-pity perhaps and certainly indignation at the devil, womankind, and mankind's pitifully weak nature. Here was fertile ground that gave rise to the search for compensation and a striving to restore the Garden of Eden.

The truth, presented in such a spectacular way, came as a blow to the masses, certainly in view of the drudgery and setbacks that many people endured in earning their daily bread—a much more time-consuming task in those days—not to mention the constant uncertainty as to the ready availability of food. The tension thus created must have cried out for both practical solutions and spiritual release.

2

Contours of a Book

IN THE MIDDLE AGES one of the most popular escape routes from earthly suffering led directly to the Land of Cockaigne, where, to begin with, one was immediately supplied with all one's basic needs. Paradise was shut tight, but Cockaigne was open to everyone, and all the known Cockaigne texts leave no room for doubt: work and exertion of any kind were absolutely forbidden there (Middle Dutch texts even claim this was the will of God). Food appeared from nowhere and in unimaginable quantities. The most beautiful clothes, including shoes and stockings, lay on everyone's doorstep, ready to wear. All this—instead of the miserable get-up that God ordered an angel to make for the first fallen couple!

But did Cockaigne really supply such clear answers? This dreamland certainly had a lot more to offer than the original paradise in Genesis ever did and—in its timelessness—supposedly still does. The countless portrayals of paradise dating from the Middle Ages display a tendency to spruce up the somewhat bare biblical paradise, inevitably lending it the character of a Cockaigne catering more to contemporary needs. These medieval paradises gradually took on the traits of a pleasure garden, a garden of delights, replete with feasting, music, and dance. And in this respect the images of Cockaigne and paradise began almost unnoticeably to mingle and merge into one. But whom did this benefit? And was this hybrid construct really permissible?

The most sensual picture of paradise was perhaps the one envisioned by Christopher Columbus. Over the years he became more and more interested in the precise location of the earthly paradise. During his third voyage (1498–1500) he even identified the Orinoco River as one of the four rivers of paradise. Moreover, in a letter sent from Hispaniola in 1498 he wrote that, according to his findings, the world was not so much round as pear-shaped, actually more like a woman's breast. Perhaps prolonged spells at sea had begun to take their toll on the stern, God-fearing Columbus. The nipple on

FIGURE 4

The Expulsion from Paradise. Miniature from a missal of 1482
preserved in the Bayerische Staatsbibliothek, Munich.

Source: Reproduced from J. Delumeau,
Une histoire du paradis: Le jardin des délices (Paris, 1992).

this breast was, in his view, the newly discovered land, with the earthly paradise at its center.

All medieval explorers went in search of paradise, or rather its immediate vicinity, whose prime location enabled it to take full advantage of the heavenly provisions stemming from this Garden of Eden. There, too, the weather was ideal, and fruit fell from heavily laden trees, while the healing waters of the four rivers of paradise carried spices and precious stones in their currents. Firmly convinced that such pleasant foreshadowings of paradise were actually within reach, travelers—as though on command—constantly reported sightings of such landscapes, modeling their descriptions on their own semiparadisiacal suppositions. In their turn the editors of these texts, from copyist to typesetter, all took a stab at heightening the effect.

Such voyages of discovery to the vestiges of paradise lost could also be projected onto one's own past, which must have begun with a golden age when everything was still perfect and humankind was still undefiled by lawlessness and discord. It is not only Christianity, however, that professes to have such immaculate beginnings of perfect harmony and abundance. The notion of an *aurea aetas*, or golden age, had been known since antiquity, and this classical image was eagerly seized upon by the humanists of the late Middle Ages, who wished to provide their own culture with a Germania or Batavia, peopled with honest and upright farmers and forest dwellers who profited—without any noticeable effort on their part and certainly with a blithe spirit—from the rich gifts of the earth. In those days the whole world was theoretically one big paradise, with pockets of local color that could assume the appearance of Cockaigne or Luilekkerland.

Even before this, however, medieval scholars had labeled the time between the Fall and the Flood as a period of positive primitivism that concerned itself as little as possible with the consequences of original sin. Such views were disseminated, for the benefit of layman and schoolboy alike, by the Antwerp magistrates' clerk and self-styled moralist Jan van Boendale. In his ambitious work with the unambiguous title *Der leken spieghel* (The layman's handbook), completed around 1330, he portrays the people living during this interim period as vegetarians. Inspired by the early Christian philosopher Boethius, he goes on to say that they drank no wine and slept in the open without bedding or pillows. They ate only dairy products and vegetables and did not dye their woolens; after all, God had not designed sheep in a range of fashionable colors. Purity and innocence were still the leitmotifs, functioning as a spiritual shield against all those worldly refinements that so often bore the mark of the devil.

The heavenly paradise, accessible to those recorded in the book of life, assumed in the Middle Ages the shape of the New Jerusalem, prophesied as a reward in the Old Testament. More influential still was the model in the Book of Revelation, which says that this city will descend from the skies to harbor the righteous. It appears to be a wondrous place, built of the most costly materials, including gold and precious stones. The *Sterfboeck* (Book of death), a widely known collection of teachings on life, described it in detail in the printed edition dating from 1491. Its aim was to teach patterns of behavior that would guarantee the attainment of the longed-for hereafter. Once again a comforting escape route from an increasingly appalling earthly existence was opened up, this time bearing a considerably more authentic hallmark than Cockaigne could ever offer.

In this New Jerusalem night and darkness are banned forever; gloom is shut out by the permanent light of God. Hunger and thirst no longer exist, neither do heat and cold, flood and fire, wind and rain, thunder and lightning, snow and hail. Just how much this heavenly Jerusalem was seen as a source of comfort and place of reckoning for all earthly suffering emerges from the negative formulations with which the attractions of the hereafter are described. There is no death, sickness, or frailty. No one is deformed, deaf, or dumb, and there are no hunchbacks or cripples. Nowhere are weeds to be seen, nor unclean animals such as worms and toads. Moreover, the most beautiful flowers and herbs grow everywhere, while the fruit is always ripe and everything blossoms forever. Each and every inhabitant is and always will be thirty-three years old, the age attained by Christ on earth. Angels make beautiful music, and everyone is in a permanent state of elation.

Here as well the dream of Cockaigne seems to have contaminated the heavenly paradise of the Bible; certainly, there was also singing and dancing to the music of flutes and trumpets in Cockaigne. The bond was strengthened by the sensational reports of the chosen few who actually visited heaven, hell, and purgatory. Their travels took the form of visions, and some of their accounts were so spectacular that they kindled the desire for quick and complete compensation for all the misery endured here on earth. Things started to get really dangerous when ideas arose of a utopia on earth, espe-

FIGURE 5

The New Jerusalem descending from the heavens.
Vision of John on Patmos. Side panel of Hans
Memling's *Mystic Marriage of Saint Catherine*.
Source: Bruges, Sint-Janshospitaal.

cially when they led to activities aimed at its actual realization. It appears, however, that the Cockaigne texts never had this goal in mind. Despite all its associations with plausible pictures of a better world, the completely fictitious nature of Cockaigne was never in doubt.

A utopia in the form of a thousand-year reign of Christ on earth is proclaimed in the Bible. Before the Last Judgment, Christ—together with the resurrected saints and martyrs—shall establish a kingdom of bliss and plenty on earth. In the Middle Ages it was thought that this act of miraculous restitution would not be long in coming. And although Augustine, long before the Middle Ages, had confirmed the church's standpoint, categorically stating that this thousand-year reign was actually an allegorical image of the church militant, its prediction continued to cause the poor and needy not only to believe in its swift coming but also to lend a helping hand in its establishment. At the end of the Middle Ages, especially in the Rhine valley and the Low Countries, there were loosely organized communities of lay brothers and sisters of the Free Spirit, who invoked the imminence of this promised thousand-year reign to justify their heretical visions of a perfect life that knows no sinfulness.

If we take a close look at the transgressions they allegedly committed against the orthodoxy of the church, practices come to light that appear surprisingly to involve a full-blown Cockaigne, no longer banished to an impossibly remote corner of the earth but now found beneath the smoke of Antwerp and along the banks of the Rhine. The Brussels Adamites, under the leadership of the priest William of Hildernissen, went very far indeed. Their name is already an indication of their striving to re-create an earthly paradise and put it into practice. They thought themselves capable of this because they had attained a perfection that placed them above every sin. Apart from that, they attempted to have celestial sex with the local Beguines, along the lines set forth by Augustine in his *City of God*. Adam, in complete control of his sexual organs, was permitted to experience a lustless erection, while Eve managed just as casually to preserve her virginity.

Perhaps the most remarkable aspect of these frequent heresies is that the Brusselers were let off so lightly. A lengthy trial in 1411 resulted only in reprimands and a couple of banishments. Did the authorities sympathize with what were perhaps only playful realizations of the Cockaigne dream?

Or were there simply too many priests and local notables involved in this far-reaching sex scandal for the authorities to inflict stringent punishments? At any rate, from the eleventh century onward, chronicles and court records eagerly reported instances of nudists bent on sex who were referred to not only as Adamites but also—much more tellingly—as Luciferans.

In the thirteenth century there was a report of men and women who assembled around midnight in an underground cave they called their temple. They came from all walks of life. A certain Walter said mass and delivered a sermon, after which a bacchanal erupted in the darkness, full of song, dance, and sexual diversions. According to the reporter, the Austrian abbot John of Viktring, the participants claimed to approach in this way the condition of Adam and Eve in paradise. Walter called himself Christ and introduced to the assembly a beautiful virgin who passed herself off as Mary. At the same time he proclaimed that all suffering was unnecessary in the light of the proper path to pleasure on earth. And fasting, he said, was completely pointless.

The Dutchman William of Egmont recorded similar re-creations of paradise in other places, though he was forced to draw upon German chronicles for his information. As usual, knowledge had been gained from hearsay. Again there were reports of a promiscuous Christ and an equally immoral Mary who indulged in underground excesses full of eroticism and nudity; the author even mentioned the "manner of pigs." And according to William, these sectarians made no bones about calling their den of iniquity a "paradise."

Many a monastery imagined it had resurrected paradise without the monks in question being suspected of any heresy. The Cistercians in particular, inspired by the infectious élan of Bernard of Clairvaux, combined ascetic ideals with the conviction that they were duty-bound to complete and perfect God's Creation. This meant they had to conquer, as it were, the most stubborn wilderness, founding their monasteries, gardens, and farmlands on the most intractable terrain they could find. The thorny bushes, bare boulders, and mud to which God had condemned Adam were transformed into farmland that supported a host of fruit-bearing plants, and treacherous and harmful animals had to make room for those useful to man.

Thus one returned to paradise, where everything was fertile and Adam had mastery over the animals. As late as the sixteenth century the Antwerp rhetorician Anna Bijns sighed that every convent was supposed to be an earthly paradise that banished all thoughts of the Fall of Man, where wisdom reigned and the trees provided food in abundance. This was how things were supposed to be, but in the closing line of her refrain she admitted how far reality in her day lagged behind the ideal: "It would be good if it were so, but I'm afraid it isn't." In the meantime it was also possible to receive an advance on eternal life, so to speak, by forming impressions here on earth of the heavenly paradise in store. It is no coincidence that the democratic religious practices of the Devotio Moderna suggested exercises for lay orders and laypeople alike to invoke as poignant and enchanting a hereafter as possible. To start with, one could conjure up a city built of gold and precious stones, with gates in its walls made of nothing but pearls. Such exercises in spiritual pleasure also allowed one to keep earthly evil at a safe distance.

All the same, the devil was not so easily put off. One of his undisputed talents was his ability to delude the senses, which he confounded from the inside out, as it were, conjuring up magnificent visions of virtual Edens that unsuspecting individuals thought they could not only see but also hear, feel, smell, and even taste. The important thing was therefore to focus firmly on God sitting on His throne in the middle of the heavenly paradise, for the devil was powerless to summon up the form of the Creator himself. It is hardly surprising, then, that the practices of the Devotio Moderna were aimed expressly at evoking such theocentric images of the hereafter.

Things could also be different, however. As early as the tenth century monastic communities and chapter churches created ingurgitative paradises—often lasting for several days—through celebrations of a rite of inversion known as the Feast of Fools. This religious festival, usually celebrated on Innocents' Day (28 December), was ruled by an alternative order that was a repudiation of the normal hierarchy, functioning not only as an outlet but also as a demonstration of the intolerable chaos caused by unrestrained guzzling and gourmandizing. In any case, the rite entailed a couple of days of feasting in the midst of unheard-of abundance, in stark contrast to the severe and sober existence dictated by the otherwise uninviting claustral life.

These ad hoc paradises in clerical circles also took the form of communal *caritas* drinking (and eating), an expression of the fraternal bonds within the monastic community. An excuse for these bouts of feasting and carousing in the name of brotherly love was found in religious holidays and some special Sundays, but they could also be precipitated by the abbot's birthday or the death of a fellow monk. Related to this was the practice of *minnedrinken*, which was widespread in the Middle Ages. This entailed proposing a toast while calling out the name of a particular saint, a custom that could easily degenerate into a brotherly booze-up.

It is hardly surprising that in courtly circles and also among the nobility suitable ways were found of experiencing paradise in the here and now.

FIGURE 6
Exuberant eating and drinking portrayed in *Graduale*, a monastic
manuscript by John of Deventer (also the illuminator), ca. 1500.
Source: Cuijk, Monastery of the Crosiers, MS M I 001, fol. 153 verso.
Photograph courtesy of Stichting Document en Boek.

Moreover, this enabled one to project the desired degree of grandeur, certainly one of the principal aims of such displays of opulence. Lengthy and spectacular banquets featured arrangements of richly garnished and varied victuals intended more to delight the eye than to satisfy one's hunger. Elements of Cockaigne's food fantasies were found here in concrete form. Tables were loaded with truly edible structures consisting of meat pies, pâtés, cakes, and ingeniously dressed animals. All this food had moving parts, and automatons even directed the antics of walking, fighting, and singing food. Inventive mechanisms also gave the illusion of animals, birds, and fish offering themselves up for consumption.

The court wanted only aristocratized Cockaignes, which in their own circles were intended to defy death with their surfeit of tangible elixirs of life while at the same time putting both country folk and townspeople in their place by permitting them to gape at all this provocative profusion. The Burgundians in particular were the perfect manipulators of such regalements, in no small part because they continually reached out to those gaping folk with offerings of beer and wine flowing from fountains mounted in female breasts or male genitals, which were an ever-present feature of every triumphal entry and royal banquet.

And then there were the gardens, modestly laid out along the lines of the enclosed garden of the Song of Songs and the monastic herb gardens based on its model, although they could also blossom into veritable pleasure gardens of love, based on the convention of the pleasance or *locus amoenus* of literature, where heavenly and earthly love are hopelessly intertwined. This connection is in fact quite concrete, for it is remarkable that in a milieu comprising an urban patriciate, the nobility, and the well-to-do middle class, pleasances and paradisiacal orchards inevitably take on a tinge of the erotic. Conversely, amorousness and sexual excitement invoke visions of dream-worlds.

The prose novel *Peeter van Provencen*, printed around 1517 for just such a public, is a good example. The beautiful Magelone lies sleeping in the woods with her head in the lap of the hero of the story. Peter cannot take his eyes off her and imagines himself to be in an earthly paradise. He gives vent to his emotions by bursting into song, a refrain based on a traditional literary recipe whose ingredients include praising her beauty from head to toe and uttering desperate exclamations of wonder at such loveliness. This only adds to his excitement, however. His desire begins to concentrate on her breasts, and he becomes even more convinced that he must be in some kind of earthly paradise, which causes him to emphasize, in spite of his arousal (remember the Brussels heretics), Magelone's virginity: "After sitting like this for a while, looking at her bosom and feasting his eyes on her virginal breasts, white as snow, which gave him such pleasure, he imagined he must be in an earthly paradise and that his joy would never end." A bit later he appears to think her good enough to eat—"thus touching and looking at his beloved's breasts"—but, alas, his pleasure is interrupted. One thing, however, is perfectly clear to Peter, Magelone, the author, and the reader: namely, that an idyllic spot conjures up erotic pleasures. Why, then, is there so little love in Cockaigne?

Pleasure gardens were to be found on the grounds of castles and in the gardens of rich townspeople. Humanists created gardens as allegorizing commentary on the act of creation, for the purpose of comprehending it better, which however did nothing to detract from their attractiveness as places in which to pass time and dally with lovers. At this time there also arose more worldly—perhaps more aptly described as earthly—variants in the form of zoological gardens and pleasure parks. The Burgundians excelled in this as well, demonstrating that Creation after the Fall did not deserve to be thought of only as the devil's playground, where the weak human soul was doomed to run the gauntlet between irresistible temptations. Nature, it was thought, was also there to satisfy human needs, as it had been in the beginning. Even in its corrupt state humankind must be capable of revering the unimaginable riches of God's Creation. Zoological gardens exhibited exotic species in paradisiacal surroundings, which meant not only amid a profusion of flowers and greenery but also in peaceful symbiosis. Moreover, taking in these sights could be passed off as an idle pastime, indulged in with no thought to the pressing needs of everyday life.

The pleasure grounds of the nobility testified to a creative impulse almost rivaling that of God. Nature was imitated by means of a deceptive backdrop built by a human hand that was able to guide so little in real life. Thus there arose elitist Cockaignes, such as the park at Hesdin Castle in northern France, where golden trees moved in the wind created by air conducted through an ingenious system of pipes. Birds were made to sing in the same way. The bewildered visitors were confronted with every type of

FIGURE 7

Courtly pleasure garden, or pleasance. Miniature from the *Roman de la Rose*,
illustrated by a Flemish master, ca. 1500.

Source: London, British Library, MS Harley 4425, fol. 12 verso

weather, be it hail, snow, rain, or sunshine. One might suddenly find oneself
in a hall representing outer space, with an azure firmament and twinkling
stars, while the next moment the unsuspecting visitor was boxed on the ears
by a mechanical doll. The ladies found themselves suddenly drenched by
streams of water sprayed under their skirts, while everyone was subjected to
other unexpected treatments involving soot and feathers. From 1299 onward
these attractions were continually expanded and perfected, but in 1553 the

entire park was destroyed, along with the town, by the imperial armies of Charles V. One would subsequently have to make do with the stylized Arcadias of literature.

The genteel amusements of the *jardin de plaisance*, zoological garden, or pleasure park could be shared by the majority of the population only from a distance. Once in a while someone caught a glimpse of one firsthand, but most information was hearsay. Cockaigne could take on earthly forms, however, when one was enticed into buying rejuvenation potions. Eternal life must, after all, be possible on earth. Death had admittedly come into the world through the devil's cunning allurements, but the original point of life on earth had surely been immortality. And the healing waters of paradise, which flowed into the world in four rivers, theoretically cured all ills and therefore put a stop to the deterioration of life itself.

Lots of streaming water, ultimately originating in paradise, was thus thought to cure all illness and fatal disease. And the closer one came to paradise, the stronger its effect. Travelers constantly reported the discovery of fountains of youth that washed away every wrinkle. Farces such as *Playerwater* (Phony water), dating from the first half of the sixteenth century, made fun of this apparently widespread belief in a fountain of youth. A wife bent on adultery sends her oafish husband far, far away to fetch her some *playerwater*, which was said to have miraculous healing powers. Only this water would be able to cure her of her feigned afflictions. But as soon as he disappears she opens the door to her lover—who else but the parish priest!

Physicians and alchemists nevertheless continued to search for natural means of thwarting the devil. In particular, the recipe for preparing the elixir of life—the *quinta essentia*—stood to make a big contribution to the science of survival and rejuvenation, even though it was clear that the first successful preparation had not yet been reported. Some even saw it as the devil's business. *De buskenblaser* (The box blower), a farce dating from the mid-fourteenth century, ridicules the desire to look young again. A devilish peddler hawks his wares, demonstrating how easy it is to tempt man in his fallen state. In an attempt to please his wife, as youthful as she is demanding, an old peasant lets himself be talked into buying a box of rejuvenating soot for quite a substantial sum. Following the instructions, he blows into it and ends up with nothing more than a black face, not to mention the bruises received from the beating his wife gives him, causing laughter all round.

The Land of Cockaigne here on earth: nearly every aspect of this dreamland, which no one actually believed in, appears to have had a concrete counterpart in everyday life. Or, to put it differently, it looks as though Cockaigne was experimentally tested and put into practice in all milieus throughout the Middle Ages and early-modern period. In addition, this dreamland continually featured in welcome yet unsolicited visions that had their worldly counterpart in the hallucinations brought on by the use of narcotics.

Little is known of intentional addiction in the Middle Ages, but times of scarcity frequently made it necessary to switch over to a diet of grasses and seeds. These substitute foodstuffs included hemp and poppies, which filled whole fields in parts of southern Europe. Hallucinations were stimulated in any case by the recurrent lack of certain nutrients. A constant deficiency of essential enzymes also weakened one's mental state, causing the mind to roam and automatically to dream up more pleasant circumstances. This physiological process was aggravated by the use of hemp seeds as a surrogate foodstuff. In this way Cockaigne was born again daily in hungry minds seeking hallucinatory compensation for everything the body was so painfully lacking. But could these hallucinated versions of Cockaigne really have played a part in the chance recording of the two Middle Dutch rhyming texts on which this study is based?

The escape to paradise—a golden age, Cockaigne, or El Dorado—belongs to all times and all cultures, and these dreamlands always reflect the private yearnings and ideals of their creators. Even in today's world this can give rise to bizarre excesses. Palestinian martyrs—responsible for suicide missions in Israel—and their families fervently believe that the perpetrators will go straight and unconditionally to the Muslim paradise. "My father is there, eating bananas and apples," said the five-year-old son of a blown-up victim. Less fanatic Muslims, on the other hand, accuse these young men of being too impatient, willing to sacrifice themselves partly because they can no longer wait for the erotic pleasures promised them in the heavenly garden of delights.

Throughout the centuries, however, all these dreamlands and pleasure grounds have had a lot in common, especially as regards eating and idleness. Such fantasies appear to span millennia and to encompass whole continents. This is remarkable, since it cannot be explained by mutual influence or borrowing, certainly not if one takes into account only written texts.

In addition to golden ages and blessed isles, Greek antiquity supposedly had its own Cockaigne. It was also acted out, for the notes preserved indicate that it was a theatrical performance. The country presented on stage had rivers full of tasty beverages and self-roasting birds that flew into open mouths when bidden to do so. Such motifs correspond directly to the medieval material and have remained a part of it till the present day. Were they part of an oral tradition? Or recorded in writing again and again? Or an idée fixe spontaneously generated by obsessions about hunger and drudgery? Or a combination of the above?

Cockaigne also appears to bear marked similarities to Celtic paradises, which became known in all of Europe through early medieval mariners' tales. Stronger still are the links with representations of the Muslim paradise, which since the Crusades has been an indispensable part of accounts of the hereafter. Cockaigne looms up in the worldly character of this paradise, which conjures up visions of a Christian hereafter with similar trappings: luxury foods for the taking, perpetually ripe fruit, precious jewels aplenty, and unlimited sexual pleasure with young virgins. Was a Western equivalent based on this immediate model devised to meet the existing needs in this part of the world?

All these dream notions of a perfect world lend the Middle Ages an atmosphere of restlessness, if not downright aggression. Medieval man seems to have been fed up with waiting for the hereafter. Hadn't Jesus himself said, in the Gospel According to Saint Mark, that the end of time was at hand? "Verily I say unto you, that this generation shall not pass, till all these things be done." Moreover, it was not at all certain—and preachers never tired of stressing this—whether one would in fact be admitted to that heavenly hereafter, considering one's state of sinfulness. The invention of purgatory as a purification plant was only partially satisfactory. It meant in any case an even longer postponement of eternal bliss, now coupled with incessant torture of an unusually painful nature.

Such a climate was highly conducive to the production of personal paradises, which had to be accessible and easy to imagine, with an abundance of everything that threatened to be lacking in everyday life. Or were these shortages indeed a reality?

3

The Power of Literature

$\mathcal{T}$HIS BOOK is about the status and significance of two Middle Dutch rhyming texts on Cocagne—the Land of Cockaigne—preserved in two manuscripts, one dating from the second half of the fifteenth century and the other from the early sixteenth century. A somewhat less important role is played by a later prose text concerning what is nowadays called Luilekkerland that is included in a printed anthology dating from 1600, though it was probably already available in 1546. These Dutch texts are enmeshed in a web of writings going back to antiquity that have been recorded in other languages as well.

Many questions concern the limitations arising from the necessity of working with written or printed texts that flourished in an age of oral traditions. Only by posing these questions, however, can we avoid the traps resulting from the tacit assumption of the existence of a written culture, which is often the pitfall of present-day scholarship. The ever-changing images of medieval Cockaigne, examples of which were occasionally committed to parchment or paper to guard against their being consigned to oblivion, seem to emerge primarily from a narrative tradition. The medieval texts all betray the need for comic relief, which is however eclipsed—and sometimes immediately contradicted—by an increasing tendency to moralize. Cockaigne's palette began to fade, even though its original colorfulness still shone through clearly. The mythical land could function as pleasure ground or school of life, and either could be activated at will by staging what was so popular at that time: a festive, topsy-turvy world.

Which function weighed most heavily for the intended audience or readership of these texts in the vernacular? Or was increased moralizing simply the price that had to be paid for converting oral material into reading matter? Literacy seems frequently to have had a contaminating effect, taking otherwise elusive images from mass culture and putting them to use in teaching and cultivating well-to-do townspeople and their children. In any

Beginning of Cockaigne text B, ca. 1500–1510.

Source: Brussels, Bibliothèque Royale, MS II.144, fol. 102 verso.

case, medieval Cockaigne developed into a place of exile for good-for-nothings, where otherwise decent youngsters could learn how *not* to behave in real life. But does this mean the disappearance of the liberating laughter induced by these madcap fantasies of revelry and sloth?

The Cockaignes recorded in these texts correspond to an extraordinary variety of idylls current among a broad public, from heretical utopias and pleasure parks to Christian and pagan paradises. The late medieval portrayals of Cockaigne were colored by great numbers of representations that had been part of the collective memory for centuries. This enabled Cockaigne simultaneously to assume the shape of the thousand-year reign of Christ on earth, the Muslim paradise, and the vision of a shrieking pulpit orator.

Part 1 has touched briefly on the dimensions of Cockaigne. The following chapters will assess its scope, thereby bringing the medieval Cockaignes and the early-modern Luilekkerland more clearly into focus. By the end of the Middle Ages, no one in the Low Countries really believed in the existence of such a place, yet the need to go on imagining it must have been shared by many, because of the indispensable help and consolation it offered. Is this perhaps the strength of what was later to be called literature?

Part 2

Texts as Maps

4
Rhyming Texts L and B, Prose Text G

RHYMING TEXT L

This is about the wonderful Land of Cockaigne

     Of livelihoods there are plenty, it seems,
     The world knows many and various means
     Of keeping body and soul together. Stay
     And hear what I have to say!
5   A country I lately chanced to see
     'Twas very strange, unknown to me.
     Now listen, for 'tis wondrous true
     What God commands those people to do:
     To come and abide in that blessed land,
10 Where toil and trouble are ever banned!
     They take this to heart, indeed they ought.
     Has anyone seen a better spot
     Than this Land of Cockaigne?
     Half is better than all of Spain,
15 The other half's better than Betouwen, I swear,
     For beautiful women are seen everywhere.
     This is the land of the Holy Ghost;
     Those who sleep longest earn the most.
     No work is done the whole day long,
20 By anyone old, young, weak, or strong.
     There no one suffers shortages;
     The walls are made of sausages.
     Windows and doors, though it may seem odd,
     Are made of salmon, sturgeon, and cod.
25 The tabletops are pancakes. Do not jeer,
     For the jugs themselves are made of beer.

Household plates and platters, I'm told,
Are all made of the finest gold.
Loaves of bread lie next to wine,
30 As bright and radiant as sunshine.
A fact I must not fail to utter:
The beams in the houses are made of butter.
Distaffs and spools, that kind of utensil,
Are made in that land of the crispiest cracknel.
35 The benches and chairs, I tell no lies,
Are all made of the best meat pies.
And all the attics overhead
Are of the finest gingerbread.
The rafters are grilled eels, what's more,
40 The roofs are tiled with tarts galore.
And a spectacle that never fails to delight
Are the rabbits and hares always bounding in sight.
One even sees wild boar and deer,
Sporting about throughout the year.
45 They can be caught with one's bare hand.
Has anyone seen a better land!
Nice clothes there are mighty cheap,
In front of each door lies a heap.
All may, to their own liking, choose
50 Some stockings and a pair of shoes.
Those who wish, don new attire,
Whether they be knight or squire.
There one finds in all the streets
Tables for all, piled high with treats.
55 They eat and drink the livelong day,
And no one ever has to pay,
As is the custom here with us.
That Land of Cockaigne is marvelous!
It also rains in those fair parts
60 Custards, pancakes, pies, and tarts.
Look at the river—what have we here?
Its currents flow with wine and beer,

Claret and fine muscatel,
Sherry one can drink as well.
65 For a pittance all may drink these,
New or old wine, sure to please.
Ginger and nutmeg, all one can eat,
Are what they use to pave the street.
No riches there, yet one lives well,
70 No hate or envy, truth to tell.
Things found lying around, unretrieved,
One takes without a by-your-leave
For one's own gain and no confessions;
One treats them as one's own possessions.
75 It's the month of May there all year long,
And every bird sings its own song.
Five weeks has every month, not four,
And no lack there of Sundays in store.
Four Easters a year, now what a provision,
80 Which surely means afterward four times Whitsun.
And four times a year the Feast of Saint John,
Which most folk surely count upon.
And four times Christmas, do you hear?
And fasting once every hundred years,
85 And the fast lasts only half a day.
Have you seen a better place to stay?
There's an even greater blessing there,
Which gladdens the hearts of many, I swear.
A Jordan runs through that very region,
90 The number of people who go there is legion.
For when its waters touch their tongue,
Old folk all start turning young,
Just as though they were twenty years old.
Believe it or not, it's a sight to behold.
95 To the music of pipes and the trumpets' sound,
They all make merry and dance in the round.
Their countless pleasures and revelry
Will last, I hope, for eternity.

So that those who go there, if and when,
100   Will truly be able to say: Amen.

RHYMING TEXT B

Narratio de terra suaviter viventium

There are livelihoods galore,
Folk will do any task or chore
To fill their stomachs. Just you wait,
And hear what I have to relate!
5   A country I lately chanced to see,
'Twas wondrous strange, unknown to me.
Astonished you'll be when I tell you
What God commands those people to do:
To abide always in that blessed land,
10   Where toil and trouble are ever banned!
This place we call the Land of Cockaigne,
And half is better than all of Spain.
The other half's better than Betavien, no wonder,
For beautiful women are seen in great number.
15   This land was made by the Holy Ghost,
For those who sleep longest earn the most.
No one works the whole day long,
Whether old or young or strong.
There no one suffers shortages;
20   The fences are of sausages.
The windows and doors, though this seems odd,
Are made of salmon, sturgeon, and cod.
Inside the houses, all the doorposts
Are made of carbuncles, 'tis no idle boast.
25   A fact I must not fail to utter:
The beams and joists are made of butter,
Which is why the attics overhead
Are of the finest gingerbread.

The benches and chairs, I tell no lies,
30 Are all made of the best meat pies.
Distaffs and spools, that kind of utensil,
Are woven there of the crispiest cracknel.
The rafters are eels, and I have proof,
While tiles of tartlets cover the roof.
35 And there one sees in all the meadows
Nothing but the finest hedgerows,
Woven of lampreys whose size astounds,
All dancing merrily in the round.
Rabbits and hares run round; what's more,
40 You also see wild deer and boar.
These can be caught with your bare hand
And led, untied, you understand.
Ladies' mounts and knights' fair steeds
Sport costly saddles, yes indeed.
45 Whether you gallop or just trot about,
You never need pay, of that there's no doubt.
This is the land that God holds dear!
Those who sleep longest earn the most here.
Things lying around in this country, 'tis true,
50 May be taken as though they belonged to you,
To do with freely as you like,
As though it were your perfect right.
Nice clothes there are mighty cheap;
In front of each house lies a heap.
55 Breeches, too, and pairs of shoes,
You may wear them, if you choose.
In all the streets there you will find
Tables with food of every kind.
On tablecloths of spotless white,
60 Bread and wine, oh what a sight!
And, moreover, meat and fish,
And everything that you could wish.
You can eat and drink the livelong day
And never even have to pay,

65 As is the custom here with us.
    Oh, that country is marvelous,
    For it rains there three times daily
    Custards, meat pies, eels aplenty,
    You'll find enough of everything
70 To satisfy your strongest craving.
    There you cannot help but thrive;
    The geese, they roast themselves alive.
    Meat, fish, fat capons, it's no ordeal,
    Cook themselves for the midday meal.
75 And other fowl all do the same,
    There in that Land of Cockaigne,
    Where a river flows whose currents
    Deliver wine and beer in torrents,
    And on the shores of that broad stream,
80 Bowls and plates of silver gleam.
    Its further reaches even swell
    With claret, sherry, muscatel.
    All drink freely, whether 'tis beer
    Or young wine that brings them cheer.
85 Ginger and nutmeg, all you can eat,
    Are what they use to pave the street,
    Vaulted with hides all sewn together,
    To lend protection from the weather.
    A custom there, much to be praised:
90 No one has enemies. Aren't you amazed
    That they are all each other's friend?
    On help and aid they can depend.
    Long and wide this land, whose clime
    Seems like eternal summertime,
95 As though 'twere April all the year:
    No discontented people here.
    And no one has to feel deprived,
    The months have not four weeks but five,
    And Easter comes four times a year,
100 And four times Whitsun, do you hear?

And four times Christmas, have no fear,
And fasting once every hundred years.
There's another bonus to be had,
Which cannot fail to make you glad.
105   Neither men nor women offer excuses,
There is no one who refuses
To sleep with another tenderly.
I tell you all this truthfully.
To the music of pipes and the trumpets' sound,
110   They all make merry and dance in the round.
Lovely women and girls may be taken to bed,
Without the encumbrance of having to wed.
Nothing sinful about it, no one feels shame,
For their custom in this is not to lay blame,
115   At least those who live there say this with pride.
But overcrowding is one thing they cannot abide,
So I would advise you, one and all,
If toil and trouble you would forestall,
Preferring feasts and drunkenness,
120   Philandering and wantonness,
Then why not just decide to leave?
In that rich land seek your reprieve!
No people go there, you will find,
Who have any occupation in mind
125   But drinking all day and eating their fill,
And never even paying the bill,
And seldom or ever paying their rent,
Not to mention all the time spent
In ignoring moneylenders' demands.
130   But here I'll leave things as they stand
And finish up with this last word,
Who knows if it will ever be heard: Amen.

PROSE TEXT G

This is about Luilekkerland, which is a most wondrous, exceedingly beautiful, and splendid place, filled with every pleasure and delight. It has just been discovered, in the year written as one thousand sugar cakes, five hundred custard tartlets, and forty-six roast chickens, in the grape-harvesting month when the meat pies taste wonderful. And it makes for very amusing reading.

> Eating and drinking and lazing around:
> These are three things that ought to have bounds.

Folk dare to claim, as untrue tidings, that an outpost has been discovered that goes by the name of Luilekkerland. Until now this land was unknown to all except those rogues and rascals who first discovered it. It is situated right in the middle of North Hommelen, catercorner to this
5   region and close by the gallows, three miles traveling through long nights. All those wishing to go there must be completely fearless and have a penchant for intrepid exploits, for the entrance to this land is formed by a very high and very wide mountain of buckwheat porridge, all of three miles thick, which visitors must eat their way through in order to gain
10 entrance. Then, however, they immediately find themselves in the aforementioned Luilekkerland, whose splendid riches, magnificence, and delights make it very well known and even renowned, especially among miscreants and all those who have turned their backs on honor and virtue.

All the houses there are normally roofed with delicious pancakes
15 and custard tarts, the walls are made of pancakes with bacon, the beams of suckling pigs, the doors and windows of sugar cakes, and the doorposts and window frames of very spicy gingerbread nailed together with cloves. Around every house stands a strong fence woven of fried liverwurst, mettwurst, or other kinds of sausage. Also to be found in that
20 country are a great many fine fountains spouting malmsey wine and all manner of sweet drinks, which flow by themselves into the mouths of all who wish to partake of them. Meat pies grow there in the same way as pine cones do in this country.

Tarts grow there on the oak trees and pancakes grow on birches, and anyone who's hungry, or just feels like it, can easily pluck them, for they hang low down in the trees. On the ash trees grow delicious pies. Sweet grapes may be plucked from the hawthorn, and cooking pears also grow in plentiful supply: they are very soft and extremely delicious, and when it snows in the winter they are sprinkled with sugar from the sky above.

Moreover, on the shores of the rivers there are willows on which white bread grows in abundance, and the rivers beneath these trees flow with sweet milk. The white bread constantly falls into their currents, so that all may eat to their hearts' content. There are also fish swimming in the water, all of which are wonderfully prepared: boiled, roasted, or grilled to perfection. And they swim so close to the shore that they may be caught with one's hand.

Chickens, geese, pigeons, snipe, and other fowl, all of them already roasted, fly just as obligingly over the whole country. And those people who are famished but too lazy to catch them just have to open their mouths, and these roasted fowl fly right in by themselves. Roast chickens, in any case, are not much valued there, for people simply throw them over the fence. Pigs thrive to such an extent that they walk around in the fields already roasted, with a knife stuck in their back. If one feels like taking a bite, one can straightaway slice off a piece of meat and stick the knife back in again. And there are just as many gooseberries lying around on the ground as stones.

Furthermore, farmers and farmworkers grow everywhere on trees, just like plums do in this country. And when the weather is fine they ripen quickly—one after another and each at the right time—and fall off the tree right into a pair of perfect-fitting boots, standing ready on the ground. Those who own a horse get rich quickly, considering that horses there can lay a huge basket of eggs in no time. Likewise the donkeys shit nothing but sweet figs, the dogs nutmeg, and the cows and oxen green pancakes.

Those who feel like eating cherries don't need to climb very high to pick them, for they grow as close to the ground as blackberries. Moreover, they're huge and as sweet as any kind of sugar. There are no hard pits in them either, but only a round, soft little stone that melts in

60 one's mouth. In truth, one could easily imagine it to be a sugared almond.

In that country there is also a wonderful and inviting fountain of youth, or rejuvenation pool, in which elderly people bathe and gradually regain their youth.

65 This land is in fact so filled with pleasure and delight that may be tasted of daily that there is no other place like it under the sun. For whether one's arrow hits the target or goes elsewhere, the winner is the one who shoots farthest from the bull's-eye. And when there are races, the winner is always the one who comes in last.

70 The winters in this country are just as pleasant and agreeable as the summers, for when it hails, sugared almonds fall from the sky, and the snow is nothing other than powdered sugar, which falls in abundance over the streets and fields, where folk then gather it up and eat it. Whenever it storms or there's a strong wind, a delicious smell settles over the

75 land that seems to come from violets, even in the dead of winter.

It is also very easy to earn money there, for those who are so lazy that they do nothing but sleep earn sixpence for every hour they spend sleeping. Those who can let a reasonable fart earn a half-crown. For belching three times or letting off a very loud fart (which feats are con-

80 sidered to be equal) one earns a whole sovereign. People who throw their money away, by shooting dice or gambling or other speculative methods, immediately get it back twice over. Those who sink heavily into debt or are remiss about paying back money are banished to a remote corner of the country where they are forced to stay for one

85 whole year, eating nothing but roast chicken, white bread, and suchlike, which they are given at no cost. And when the year is over they are free to return to their homes, where they are absolved of all their debts. If, however, they would rather pay off their debts but still have no money, they may return to their place of exile, to the innkeeper who gave them

90 lodgings the first time, who will point out to them three or four trees on which money grows in plentiful supply. There they may shake off as much money as they need to pay their debts, upon which they may return to their old friends in the heart of the land and resume their former lifestyle.

95 Likewise people in that country who are fond of drinking with

trusted comrades receive for each fair-sized drink a silver penny. Those who drink till it's coming out of their ears or till their eyes start to water receive a guinea for every drink they've imbibed. And anyone who can empty a whole tankard in one gulp, standing up and without taking a
100 breath, gets free drinks and a gold noble to boot. Bullies who tease and torment honest folk earn two shillings a day. Liars also earn good money there, for every lie earns them a crown, and the more skillful they are at lying and the more artful their lies, the more they earn.

Loose women are highly thought of in that country, and the more
105 wanton and frolicsome they are, the more they're loved. Even though it's said that lecherous whores are expensive to keep, this is certainly not the case in that land, where all sensual pleasures are readily available and at no cost whatsoever. One only has to say, or even just to think: Mouth, what do you want? Heart, what do you desire?

110 There is nothing more disgraceful in that country than behaving virtuously, reasonably, honorably, and respectably and wanting to earn a living with one's hands. Anyone leading such a virtuous and upright life is hated by everyone and eventually banished from the country. Likewise anyone who is wise and sensible is scorned and despised and
115 treated badly by everyone. On the other hand, those who are gruff, coarse, and foolish—and, moreover, either cannot or will not learn— such people are held in high regard. Whoever is found to be the biggest good-for-nothing, the most untrustworthy, rudest, most dull-witted, and moreover the laziest, most debauched vagabond and champion
120 rogue—such a person is proclaimed king. And whoever is merely coarse and stupid is made a prince. Those who like to horse around with the roast chickens and liverwurst, making a valiant stand amid the plates and platters in their efforts at stuffing themselves, these persons will be dubbed knights.

125 The biggest wine guzzlers or beer quaffers, who think of nothing but swigging and swilling and keeping their throats moist from dawn to dusk, will be elevated to the rank of count. And lazy day-dreamers who like nothing better than to sleep the livelong day are treated in those parts as refined noblemen. If here in this country
130 there are any prodigal children who intend to display such manners as those written of above—by abandoning all pretense to honor, virtue,

honesty, and civility, not to mention wisdom and knowledge—then these uncouth louts should go to that land, where, upon their arrival, they will undoubtedly be esteemed and respected. Above all else, 135 however, they should take great care not to steal, for they will then be hanged on the gallows that are close by Luilekkerland.

From the pen of old folk this tale has sprung,
To serve now as a lesson to the young,
Accustomed to a nice and easy life,
140   Where intemperance and laxity are rife.
To Cockaigne these youths must now be sent,
Till their excessive energies are spent,
And they acquire a taste for honest work,
For in their sloth a host of vices lurk.
145   *Finis.*

5

The Two Rhyming Texts on the Land of Cockaigne

THE OLDEST known text in Dutch treating only the Land of Cockaigne (referred to from now on as text L) is to be found in manuscript Add. 10286, preserved in the British Library in London. In this manuscript collection in folio format, containing eight texts of varying length and content (one of them is in Latin), the Cockaigne text occurs on the recto and verso of folio 135, with the following heading: "Dit is van dat edele lant van cockaengen" (This is about the wonderful Land of Cockaigne).

There are one hundred lines of verse in total, arranged in two columns on the recto but presented in only one column on the verso. It is possible that the copyist intended to use one page for the text but did not have a model text at his disposal that he could simply transcribe, though this must clearly have been the case with some of the other texts in the collection. Having arrived at the verso, he had already used up so much of his material that it was obvious he would have no trouble fitting the rest into one column. He then positioned this column in the middle of the page: using only half the left-hand column would have made the page seem rather unused, and neither the person commissioning the manuscript nor the copyist himself would have liked to see that in the middle of a book.

This wasn't necessarily the course of events, but such a striking way of dividing the text over both sides of the available page suggests that the transcription was not a straightforward procedure. At any rate, the two columns the copyist made on the recto did not always come out right, for several of his lines turned out too long. It is always possible, of course, that a scribe, whose work elsewhere in the manuscript looks relatively professional, here indulged his creative urge by writing down a text he knew only from hearsay. And it would not be so strange if he originally thought, hoped, or even feared that he might end up with more text than he actu-

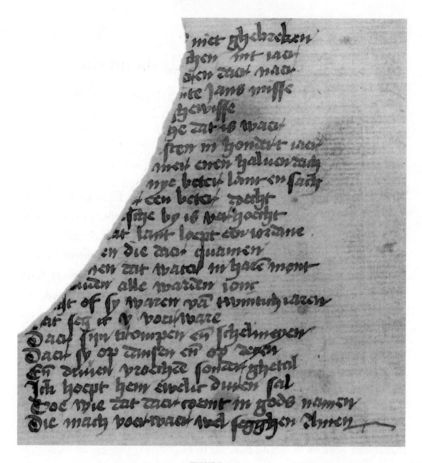

FIGURE 9

End of oldest Cockaigne text (L) in Middle Dutch, after 1458.
Source: London, British Library, MS Add. 10286, fol. 135 verso.

ally did, considering that the other Cockaigne text in Dutch is thirty-two lines longer.

Another possibility is that he did in fact have a written model, but because he possessed additional knowledge of the oral tradition surrounding Cockaigne, he improvised so much on his material that any planning he may have had regarding the mise-en-page simply proved to be inadequate. Perhaps this is assuming too much, however, and the copyist had an earlier

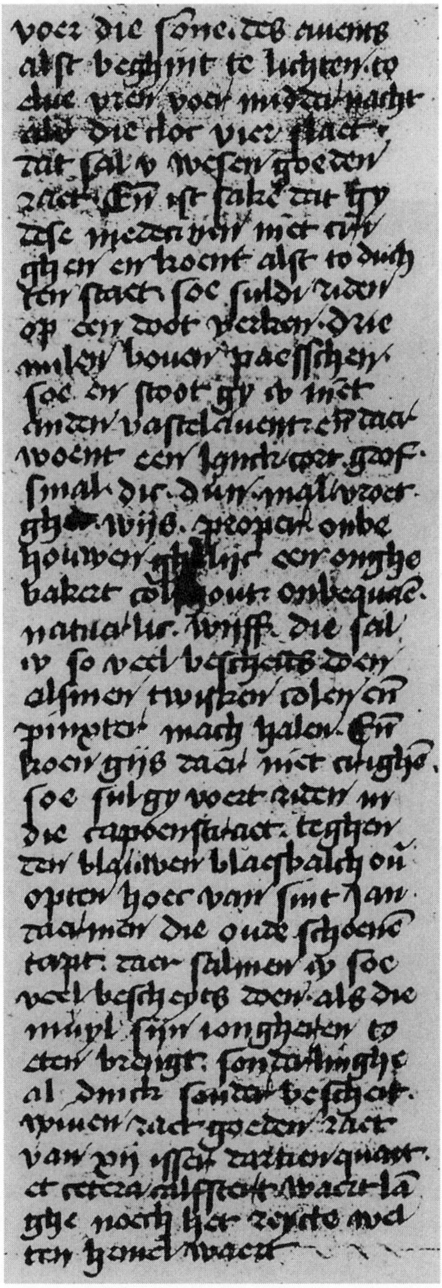

FIGURE 10

End of mock doctor's prescription.

Source: London, British Library, MS Add. 10286,
fol. 134 verso.

Cockaigne text as an example or an entire manuscript that also contained the Cockaigne text, and because he knew, or had happened to hear, that his next text (the Latin one) was supposed to start on folio 136, he draped the rest of the Cockaigne text as generously as possible over the verso of folio 135. In any case, this departure from the original model of two columns leads one to suspect that the text originated in the oral tradition. The previous page, folio 134, increases this suspicion, for it displays not only a similar division of text but also a similar sort of text emanating from the oral tradition: namely, a mock doctor's prescription.

Things are further complicated by the fact that the ravages of time have left their traces on this manuscript, on the very page bearing the Cockaigne text. A rather large piece has disappeared from the top right-hand corner of the page, which has caused quite some loss of text in lines 40 through 58 and 78 through 94. Some of these incomplete lines can be reconstructed with a fair degree of certainty, though elsewhere one can only make an educated guess—based on the other Cockaigne text—at the content of the missing lines. Other parts of the manuscript have also been damaged, as witnessed by the pages missing in various places. During restoration of the manuscript in 1974 a scrap of paper with several words on both recto and verso was attached to a page in the volume. The note on the end leaf, dated 30 October 1974, which maintains that this scrap was originally part of the Cockaigne text, is unfortunately incorrect. When deciphered, the text appears in fact to fit in perfectly with the *Sidrac* and must therefore have been part of the text on the missing folio 60.

The paper manuscript was finished sometime after 1458, as may be deduced from the occurrence of this date in a pilgrims' guide to Jerusalem that is also included in the manuscript. The language used bears traces of north-eastern or eastern Middle Dutch, though these hardly leave their mark on the manuscript as a whole, which, broadly speaking, reveals its roots to be in the area of South Holland. Its content generally consists of texts of a moralizing and didactic nature. The present volume opens with the *Sidrac*, widely known in Middle Dutch in both manuscript and printed form, which was an ency-clopedia presenting the Creation in a moral and theological light. It takes the form of a dialogue between a layman and a teacher, parts played in the text by King Boctus and the philosopher Sidrac. This is followed by a similar, equally popular didactic text, the *Lucidarius*, in which a teacher and his pupil engage in a comparable dialogue. Then there is a rhyming text about the hate-filled world, a mock doctor's prescription in prose to be used as part of the Carnival celebration, the text on *Cockaengen*, a Latin prose text elaborating on the evils of money, a pilgrims' guide to the Holy Land, and a rhyming text called *Sesterhande verwen* (Six kinds of colors), which discusses color symbolism.

It is important to reflect for a moment on this mixed bag of writings, which in our eyes could easily be seen as nothing more than a confused hodgepodge. The tendency to isolate the Cockaigne text and to pull it out of its curious context is almost matter-of-course. We have become accustomed to thinking of literary texts as strictly separate entities, different worlds even, that supposedly display a remarkable degree of autonomy, not only in relation to the existing world but also with respect to other texts, even though the recent focus on intertextuality has caused the notion of private domains to diminish somewhat in importance. This is why Middle Dutch texts of a literary nature have always been studied as autonomous, solitary entities, in spite of the fact that separate publication of literary texts as the result of commercial interest shown by printers did not come about until the end of the Middle Ages.

Before this time texts in the vernacular were presented, as a rule, in the company of other texts, so that Middle Dutch literature should actually exist more as a series of manuscript collections than as a string of separate titles. Each text should be viewed from the perspective of a number of other texts and should ultimately be studied in the light of these other writings. Their relationship to one another may have been established beforehand or suggested only as the text took shape. In addition, those who used the text and failed to notice any such connection would, while reading or listening to the other texts in the manuscript, automatically link up the separate texts, which are inevitably subject to comparison in such a context. In any case, the Cockaigne text in this manuscript is part of a revealing fabric of writings that may be classified for the time being as "world orientation."

At first glance it seems that two different hands are recognizable in this manuscript. One copyist, it appears, was at work on the *Sidrac*, while the other, starting with the *Lucidarius*, was responsible for the rest. Closer inspection reveals, however, that this manuscript was probably the work of one copyist and that the rather insignificant difference in handwriting may be explained by a certain amount of time having elapsed between the two projects, as well as by the adoption of another attitude—either physical or mental—during the writing process. This possibility is also suggested by the use of different inks. Over the course of several years even a professional hand undergoes certain basic changes. What appeared at first to be the work of two copyists more likely represents different phases in the career of one person.

For that matter, the professionalism of this copyist must also be called into question. He doesn't seem to have been highly educated, as evidenced by the mistakes that occur repeatedly throughout the manuscript. Sometimes there are incorrect or missing letters, as well as passages repeated by accident and sentences omitted, which were corrected on the spot with cross-outs and additions. In the pilgrims' guide, in a passage describing the grave of the well-known crusader Godfrey of Bouillon at the foot of Mount Calvary, he persists in speaking of "Godefridus van Beliren." He then goes on to identify him as one of the Nine Best of the past and a hero of the Holy Land, yet he fails to recognize (or neglects to correct) the mistaken name in his ledger.

Elsewhere in this text the copyist lacks the knowledge or alertness needed to spell the word *mosaic*. First he spells it "musike" and a short while later "musaike," apparently because this inlay work is unknown to him. Such mistakes, however, need not detract from his presumed professionalism. Copyists of texts in the vernacular were not always scholars by any means, and they were capable of producing the strangest slips of the pen, owing to the monotony of their exhausting work.

The second rhyming text on Cockaigne (referred to hereafter as text B) occurs in a manuscript collection comprising numerous songs, rhyming aphorisms, proverbs, fairy tales, calendar texts, satirical sermons, mock prescriptions, and riddles. This manuscript, also on paper but in a portable (octavo) format, is now preserved in the Bibliothèque Royale Albert I in Brussels under shelf mark II.144. The text appears on folios 102 verso through 105 recto and bears the title *Narratio de terra suaviter viventium* (A tale about the land of pleasant living), followed by a text of 132 lines of verse, ending with "Amen."

The oldest and principal part of this manuscript, consisting of folios 1 through 113, was written by one hand and can be dated to the first decade of the sixteenth century. The rest is more recent and was written some time during the seventeenth century. The language used in the first part (I do not discuss the rest) has a strong eastern or southeastern Dutch flavor and can perhaps be located more specifically in the southern part of the duchy of Gelre or the vicinity of Venlo in the present-day province of Limburg. The texts—apparently collected and adapted by the owner of the manuscript himself and possibly recorded for his own use in this small pocket-size volume—make occasional mention of place names that refer to the same area. In the calendar texts references are made to the place names Horst and Roermond (in present-day North and Middle Limburg, respectively), while the saints mentioned belonged to the diocese of Liège, whose authority extended over this region.

The best clue, however, is a suggestive song that opens with the words "Te Venloe all in dye goyde statt" (At Venlo, in that good town). Since other songs of this type make no mention of the actual location, it seems likely that the collector and transcriber of this lively, risqué song wanted to spice it up even more by introducing the name of his hometown in the opening line. The language employed, which leaves its personal stamp on the material inasmuch as texts known from other sources appear to have been rewritten in the transcriber's own regional idiom, is in keeping with that used in the area of present-day North Limburg and East Brabant, which at that time were part of the duchy of Gelre.

The copyist makes a scholarly impression, as witnessed by the Latin headings he gave to a number of the texts. It is unlikely that such announcements in Latin were part of earlier transcriptions: other known versions do not bear such titles, and this is true as well of the Cockaigne text. The language, structure, and content of the manuscript also give the impression that this is the basis of a private collection of texts suitable for celebrations and parties in a studentlike environment or perhaps even a monastery. The format—a pocket-size book—indicates its use in various venues: its portability was essential. Moreover, the copyist had a very personal hand that is difficult to read. It cannot have been his intention to supply others with easy-to-read texts, for that would have required him to use one of the more usual bookbindings. He scribbled his book (or loose sections in this handy format) full of texts that only he himself had to be able to read.

It is therefore questionable whether he should be called a copyist at all, even though I will continue to do so for the sake of convenience. Furthermore, a person acting in this capacity does not necessarily have to be seen only as a professional transcriber of other people's texts. One could also be one's own copyist, and the boundaries between copying, adapting, and rewriting were extremely vague. However, all these activities, which are often difficult to pin down, presuppose another text as the standard source or example, and the compiler of this manuscript appears not always to have had such material at hand. For the most part he recorded texts known from other sources, though he gave them a personal twist (the Latin titles, for instance), but it also seems that he simply wrote down a lot of things he remembered or wanted to remember.

This copyist was actually more of an author who worked with texts stored in his memory. If I continue to call him a copyist, then I must at least grant him the freedoms normally enjoyed by members of that profession. Comparison of his texts with other versions of the same material reveals that when writing things down from memory—or even when using written examples—he gave full rein to his own creative bent. This was not unusual for a professional copyist. There is continual evidence of his having adapted his texts to his own or someone else's needs, and in doing so he never shied away from intellectual acrobatics.

That this writer was most likely a student or former student is evidenced by the composition of the volume, which strongly resembles a modest variation in the vernacular of the *Carmina Burana*. He paid a great deal of attention to love songs, love poems, and erotic texts in general. Furthermore, the whole testifies to a particular penchant for parodies, with a special emphasis on poems about wine. Several of the latter display the so-called macaronic form, which is to say a humorous alternation—every line or half-line—between the vernacular and Latin. This form became popular in the vagabond verse of the High Middle Ages that found favor in university milieus. The manuscript even displays a direct link to this illustrious literature through the inclusion of the Latin student song "Meum est propositum in taberna mori" (My intention it is to die in the tavern), which is also included in the *Carmina Burana*. Finally, an ode to students leaves no room for doubt as to the milieu in which this collection was formed and the use for which it was intended: namely, students and scholars (successful or otherwise) and possibly clerics belonging to the minor orders.

All the texts in this collection were intended to be sung or recited aloud. Revealing in many respects is the fact that the Cockaigne text in this manuscript is accompanied by a mock doctor's prescription in prose, which was

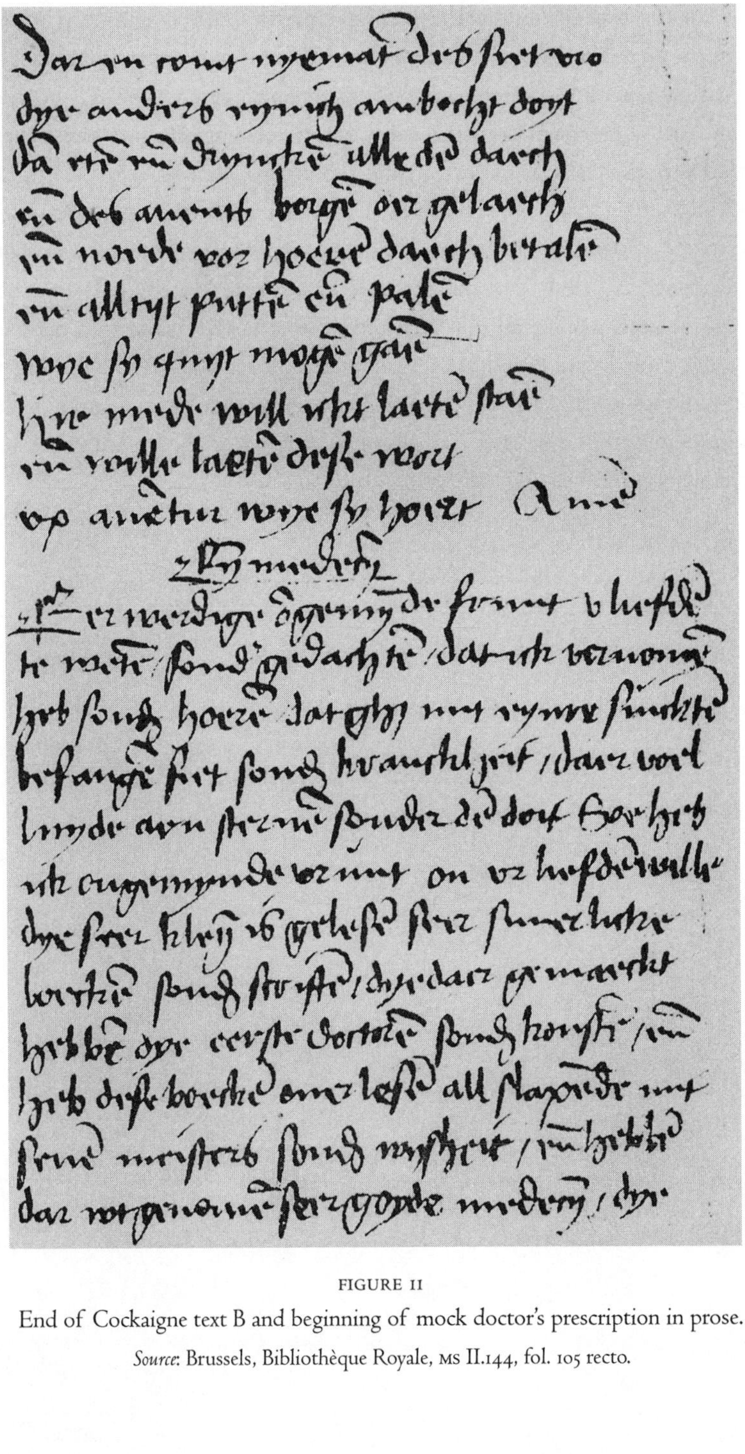

FIGURE II

End of Cockaigne text B and beginning of mock doctor's prescription in prose.

Source: Brussels, Bibliothèque Royale, MS II.144, fol. 105 recto.

one of the favorite pieces in the Carnival repertoire and was meant to be presented in public by a mock doctor in the midst of great hilarity. The rhyming text on Cockaigne is in good company here, and not only because the satirical representation of a topsy-turvy world fits in so well with these festive rituals. It appears in fact that the other Cockaigne text (L) in the London manuscript is preceded by just such a mock doctor's prescription in prose, also intended for humorous recitation during the temporary reign of Prince Carnival (and his personal physician). Moreover, both mock prescriptions display an oral relationship that is not unlike that between manuscripts L and B. There are, as a matter of fact, a great many similarities, and—just like the differences—these are difficult to explain by placing them within a written tradition that supposedly began with one and the same text.

6

Recitation and Writing

COMPARISON OF THE TWO Cockaigne texts reveals both similarities and differences that are quite striking. Approximately seventy lines correspond either exactly or quite closely, which means that well over two-thirds of text L also occurs in text B and that more than half of B is also to be found in L. But where do the huge differences come from? The lines of verse that vary do not in fact represent substantial variations; rather, they constitute completely new or different text. This makes it nearly impossible to assume the written transmission of a lost original (text X), via various routes, leading to text L and B, respectively. Thus text B does not represent, owing to its greater length, simply an expanded version of X (nor, conversely, does L represent a shorter version), considering that L contains a number of elements that are lacking in B.

The mere thought of an original text X leads to confusion. There were thousands of "original" Cockaigne texts in the vernacular that died away with the voices that recited, sang, and acted out these tales. The subject matter and motifs consisted more or less of semiformulaic lines of verse, stock expressions, and other familiar forms, the origins of which no one knew or ever will know. This common coin could be expanded, reduced, and adjusted at will. Through repetition and imitation some of these spontaneous changes acquired a formulaic status of their own, whereas others disappeared after being used just once. In addition, elements derived from the old, familiar material became worn out and were either replaced or disappeared altogether. The sturdiest components appear to be those making up the heart of the Cockaigne material: the motifs of eternal idleness, the superabundance of food, and the edible architecture. These images have even solidified into several proverbs and sayings, ultimately preserving these indestructible elements of Cockaigne in a much more enduring form.

With this reservoir of Cockaigne material upon which to draw, the engagement and talent of the reciter, his audience, and the circumstances of his performance determined which Cockaigne text was realized at any given time. It is indeed tempting to attribute the differences between texts L and B to a painstaking transcription of two different performances of one essentially fixed Cockaigne text, a text X in an oral form that could turn out differently every time it was recited. This assumes that the text was more or less set and included in the program of many a storyteller traveling around the Low Countries. Tall tales of a topsy-turvy world were favorites among professional entertainers, who did not hesitate to improvise upon their texts in accordance with the wishes and reactions of their audiences.

An audience judged the proficiency of a reciter by his ability to embroider skillfully on well-known material. In the written tradition, variations are viewed with alarm as possibly tainting the text, obscuring the view of a lost original presumed to be as authentic as it was accomplished. In an oral tradition, on the other hand, variants are the main attraction, and in the case of tall-tale telling, multiple recitations based on identical material could even involve a certain amount of competition to see who was capable of uttering the most outrageous nonsense in the most eloquent way.

In theory these speakers would have had to base their performances on a traditional text they had more or less memorized, which—owing to the above-mentioned variables—resulted in a new version each time. This course of events may easily be compared, in today's oral culture, with the telling of jokes, which are seldom told twice in exactly the same way. Rather, joke tellers attempt—often unconsciously—to adapt to the circumstances that prompted them to tell the joke in the first place. This means that any given joke exists in a fluid form in thousands of minds; a fixed or original form (X) is almost never ascertainable.

The genesis of texts such as those described above was fictionalized—and mocked—by Chaucer in his Canterbury Tales, in which he also appears as one of the pilgrims and tells a tale in his turn. Chaucer's "Tale of Sir Thopas" is rudely interrupted by the host, however, who cannot stand any more doggerel, whereupon Chaucer—apparently unwilling to take any more risks—suggests he present a story in prose of which various versions exist:

> I wol yow telle a litel thyng in prose
> That oghte liken yow, as I suppose,
> Or elles, certes, ye been to daungerous.

> It is a moral tale vertuous,
> Al be it told somtyme in sondry wyse
> Of sondry folk, as I shal yow devyse.

One should not think this strange, for was this not the case with the Gospel, of which four versions exist? And all four versions, despite their differences, tell the story of the Passion. Variation is simply a part of recitation, and Chaucer will do the same with his tale, for the special purpose of instructing and entertaining his audience:

> Therfore, lordynges alle, I yow biseche,
> If that yow thynke I varie as in my speche,
> As thus, though that I telle somwhat moore
> Of proverbes than ye han herd bifoore
> Comprehended in this litel tretys heere,
> To enforce with th' effect of my mateere,
> And though I nat the same wordes seye
> As ye han herd, yet to yow alle I preye
> Blameth me nat; for, as in my sentence,
> Shul ye nowher fynden difference
> Fro the sentence of this tretys lyte
> After the which this murye tale I write.
> And therfore herkneth what that I shal seye,
> And lat me tellen al my tale, I preye.

Differences in performed versions of a basic text learned by heart also occurred, of course, in repeat performances given by the same reciter. Research carried out in the twentieth century has shown that professional singers belonging to communities that engage primarily in oral communication cannot reproduce a text literally, even when urgently requested to do so, to a greater degree of accuracy than roughly 60 percent. Astonishingly enough, this concurs with the 50–66 percent correspondence between texts L and B. Things cannot be so simple, however. The singers in question were performing epic poetry that could go on for hours, whereas the Cockaigne texts have more the length of fairy tales, short stories in rhyme of not more than several hundred lines. Moreover, it is not at all clear how the copyists of L and B accomplished the recording of their texts. It is quite possible that text L is ordinary copywork, meaning that the text was adopted from another source and not written down as a result of a remembered perform- ance or a text learned by heart. On the other hand, this problem can easily be dealt with by directing all these questions to the written example of text L and assuming that its copyist has given us a faithful reproduction, marred only by the usual small mistakes any copyist might make. In any case, assum- ing that the texts are varying oral versions of the same basic text rules out the possibility that the copyists of L and B (or the recorders of their exam- ples) took them from dictation, and it is also rather unlikely that these texts represent versions performed by the copyists themselves.

The matter is complicated by the existence of three related French texts—products of the same basic building materials—that were all recorded in manuscripts dating from around 1300, although attempts have been made to prove their derivation from an "original text" that supposedly dates from the mid-thirteenth century. But this, too, is simply clutching at straws, assuming a written text transmitted along various paths that account for the sometimes considerable variations, the presumed corruption of the text, and the adaptations that have crept in. This narrow view of medieval texts is the price we pay for taking for granted the centuries of written cul- ture that followed, a culture that—certainly since the invention of the print- ing press—no longer takes into account the interference resulting from a rather long text being transmitted at one time or another in both the oral and written tradition.

The French material is just as malleable as the Dutch. Cockaigne must certainly have traveled around Western Europe for centuries before its real- ization in writing in the few examples we still possess in Old French and Middle Dutch. It is difficult to say whether the French texts are older than the Dutch, although it is clear that different traditions prevailed in the two regions, and these traditions are expressed mainly in the strikingly different framework in which the material is presented. While the Dutch texts refer in the opening lines—with their lament over the effort required to earn a liv- ing—to the Fall of Man and its consequences, the French choose instead to wrap up the material in a detailed allusion to the ritual diversion of chari- vari (a procession involving "rough music" played on pots and pans). These trappings may well have ended up in a written tradition in both regions, just as such frameworks resulted from the recording of the texts in the first place. Where literary texts in the vernacular are concerned, oral and written culture—especially in the case of realizations of the same material—continued to influence each other until after the Middle Ages. It is equally possible, however, for written and oral traditions to go their separate ways for a long time or even forever, though this does not appear to have occurred with the Cockaigne material.

In any case, the narrative skeletons of the French and Dutch texts have many formulaic elements in common. In addition, there is a great deal of new material in both texts, and some familiar elements have been added, subtracted, or recast in nearly unrecognizable form. It is indeed possible, in view of the steady stream of culture flowing from south to north in this part of Europe until well into the fifteenth century, that the semiformulaic elements floating around were first fixed in writing in the French-speaking region, undoubtedly to facilitate storage of the component parts. At any rate, the material—in all its elemental forms, including perhaps a written one—drifted across to the Low Countries, there to be given concrete form in the language of that region, with the simultaneous production of new set verses, the elimination or adaptation of others, and, above all, the introduction of a new setting. The latter makes it unlikely that the French texts served as the immediate example for the Middle Dutch texts, in view of their entirely different framework.

The supposition that the Cockaigne idea derives from an original French text is therefore based on a mistaken notion of the genesis of this kind of material. This by no means rules out the existence of oral and written traditions having developed around this material in both regions, traditions that continued developing on their own while at the same time influencing each other. Whatever the case, it is pointless to search for the ingenious author who came up with the original Cockaigne text. There were thousands of individuals, each of whom composed his own Cockaigne text by using the material available to everyone, which had been circulating in countless forms and in a host of languages since Hellenistic times.

Neither did things stop at the occasional recording of a Cockaigne text; written traditions also formed around this material. The Middle English *Land of Cokaygne* dating from the early fourteenth century, German texts treating Schlaraffenland datable to around 1500, and the Dutch prose text *Van 't*

Luye-lecker-landt of 1546 (known from an edition printed in 1600) were more likely to have been thought up by a writer seated at a desk. In contrast to the earlier incidental written recordings, these later texts—the product of a written culture—contain references, borrowings, and adaptations that exude the smell of ink, fresh from the pen or printing press.

The primary vehicle of an oral text—rhyming couplets—is preserved almost intact in text L, even though the loss of text through damage to the page prevents confirmation of this for its full hundred lines. Such oral characteristics long continued to nestle in written texts intended mainly for private reading. As far as the rhyme was concerned, however, it was important for texts meant to be read or recited to display a clever interweaving of end rhymes and internal rhymes throughout the poetical work. These visual accents lent the desired stress to texts that long continued to be read out loud. At the same time such patterns of sound created aesthetic effects that showed to advantage during recitation. A good example of this is the poetry of the rhetoricians, in which great importance was attached to ingenious rhyme schemes. Their rhymed morality plays and to no less extent their refrains are preeminent examples of the art of declamation.

In this respect the rhetoricians' art must be seen as quite distinct from the simple rhyming techniques of oral text transmission, such as those applied in both rhyming texts on Cockaigne. An even more important difference is that rhetoricians' works ultimately belong to the written tradition, despite their final destination in recitation. Their point of departure was a fixed text, devised by an author and committed to paper, whence it could be recited again and again, with no view whatever to deviations or improvisations. But in the oral tradition things are done differently.

If a text is written down primarily as an aide-mémoire, then rhyming couplets are the best-known expedient. More complicated forms of rhyme only make things more difficult. A textbook for laymen such as the *Natuur-kunde van het geheelal* (Physics of the universe), dating from the fourteenth century, refers right at the beginning to just such a mnemonic aid:

> I'll tell it you in fitting rhyme,
> Placed at the end of every line,
> So that your patience won't run out
> Recalling what it's all about.

Many Middle Dutch texts give the impression of purposely retaining oral characteristics, not only as an aid to memory but also with an eye to new renditions. This accords well with the work of the Anglo-Saxon poet Caedmon. Around 680 he dictated his texts to a copyist. With parchment in hand, reciters were then meant to breathe life into these texts in a theoretically infinite number of performances. The poems were recorded in writing through fear of text loss and to have them at hand when required. The written texts were not intended for private reading, either to oneself or aloud to others.

For that matter, it seems that not all the oral characteristics were recorded in any case. Texts were not meant to be recited verbatim. Whether imparting to his audience fictional stories or morality lessons, a professional reciter relied on familiar techniques and skills to compose the introduction, ending, improvisations and padding, additions, abridgements, and recapitulations. One thus did not have to include them when recording a text in writing, and so manuscripts contain only the bare blueprints of the oral versions. The only texts that were learned from memory were those intended for instruction or scientific learning, with a view to reproducing them word for word.

7
Oral Structures in Writing

THE ORIGINS OF Middle Dutch texts L and B are revealed in many features typical of the oral tradition. For more than twenty lines at the beginning the two Middle Dutch texts run nearly parallel, which is not at all unusual for texts stemming from the oral tradition. The introduction to a story ("Once upon a time") and the first statement of its narrative elements quickly provide the formulaic foothold on which a story as such is presented. The order of later lines and formulaic elements is less important than the more significant and sensitive opening lines. After these, memorized lines of verse lose their fixed place and may be inserted elsewhere, and free use is made of elements drawn from the personal and collective memory.

Such are the raw materials of Cockaigne, found not only in fixed lines of verse but also in the form of extracted submotifs, which both the author and reciter use freely, associating, adapting, adding, and abridging at will. Then repetitions start to occur—sometimes in exactly the same words—functioning as padding to keep the story going. This alternates with proverblike sayings that serve the same purpose, simultaneously condensing the truths presented into handy mottoes to live by. In this loose structure formulaic elements keep cropping up that appear in other realizations of the Cockaigne material, even those in other languages.

But first let us go back to the beginning. The opening is distinctly rhetorical, of course, in the original sense of the word: a storyteller calls his audience to attention with such phrases as "Stay and hear what I have to say" and "Now listen, for 'tis wondrous true." The narrator makes his presence felt throughout the text by uttering such solemn declarations as "Believe it or not" and challenging the audience with exclamations like "Has anyone seen a better land?" The narrator is most clearly visible, though, at the beginning and end of both texts: at the end of text B, for example, he actually addresses the audience and offers them his advice, yet another sign of the oral situation evidencing itself in the written text.

This orality is also evident in the other techniques used. Right at the beginning the audience becomes intrigued by having its attention drawn to a proverbial word of wisdom. This is such a commonplace truth, however, that the audience cannot help feeling that the only course now open to the narrator is to present them with a sharp contrast:

> Of livelihoods there are plenty, it seems,
> The world knows many and various means
> Of keeping body and soul together.
>
> (text L)

One can only nod in agreement: there certainly is a lot of drudgery in this vale of tears. On the heels of this depressing platitude, however, the story-teller hastens to add that he has just visited a strange and unknown land. This rather inconsequential announcement is straightaway followed by exhortations, entreating his listeners to prepare themselves for a miraculous story: "Just you wait / And hear what I have to relate," followed shortly afterward by "Astonished you'll be when I tell you . . ." (text B).

Now the truth comes out. God himself has commanded the inhabitants of that unknown land to cast all toil and trouble to the winds. A greater contrast to the opening is unthinkable. According to the narrator, there is one place on earth where a paradise—apparently inhabited by many—is in fact open to everyone. He has, after all, seen it with his own eyes. There must have been listeners who found these lines blasphemous, or were they used to the custom—as widely accepted as it was constantly criticized—of turning all kinds of occasions into topsy-turvy worlds? In any case, God—according to this text—has done something very remarkable indeed. In contrast to His punishment after the Fall, which required Adam and Eve—and their descendants, now in the audience listening to this story—to labor endlessly to keep themselves alive (echoes of this were heard in the opening lines), He has now supposedly issued the command, in force somewhere on the face of the earth, to avoid exertion of any kind.

So, a land exists where one does not have to do anything to stay alive; even better, one is not allowed to do any work at all. This is the heart of the Cockaigne myth. As a yardstick against which to measure the bliss in store, two well-known places are named that were believed to be delightful—Spain and Batavia (or perhaps Poitou)—neither of which could offer even half the attractions to be had in Cockaigne. This is followed by a list of its blessings, described in such succinct terms that they resemble the entries in an auction catalog: beautiful women are seen everywhere, the Holy Ghost is in charge, those who sleep longest earn the most, no one is required to do any work at all. Then begin the illustrative digressions, and this is the end of the rather strict parallelism between L and B.

The regularly recurring padding and other empty, stock phrases were also adopted from the oral situation. The reciter used these fixed, rhyming elements to keep things moving; he could, after all, toss them off casually and then continue on his merry way through the narrative. They also enabled him to emphasize certain points, to give himself time to think while his mouth kept moving, and to give the audience a break from concentration. The nature and number of such accents, pauses, and padding would vary from performance to performance, depending on the feedback from the audience.

But empty phrases are disturbing in a fixed, written text meant to be read—if perhaps aloud—by one person at a time. Such devices function only during improvised performances, when the reciter allows himself to be led by his own talent and his audience's reactions (or lack thereof). Compulsory formulas for pauses not prompted by the circumstances tend to backfire: people reading in private may choose for themselves what they read and how quickly they read it; their reading is disturbed by stock phrases and padding that are no longer relevant to the situation.

There is therefore practically no reason when recording a text in verse to make use of such oral cement; on the contrary, there is much to be said against it. When it does happen, however, there is every reason to assume that a written text in such auditory attire was intended for something other than reading or reciting in private. These texts must have been committed to paper as aids to memory, for oneself or others, which could be consulted at subsequent performances. Such texts report a recitation, turning it into a model for future use and storing it in written memory.

This presumed course of events does not contradict the previously mentioned "bare blueprints," which would have been used in similar situations, though they lack so many of the oral characteristics that presumably arose in the heat of the moment. The padded texts catered to the more primitive sphere of the occasional reciter and his target audience of spontaneous merrymakers; the blueprints presuppose the skill of the professional storyteller, who performed for an audience that came not only to hear the story but also to admire his talent and ingenuity.

Text B recalls in some respects a written recollection in full oral armor, whereas L gives the impression of a text intended for recitation. Not only are there fewer oral characteristics in L, but the scribe's hand and the other texts in the manuscript also point in this direction. And no matter how disturbing the remaining asides may seem, they could conceivably have aided the reciter in manipulating his audience. Who knows, he may even have succeeded occasionally in smoothing over, omitting, replacing, or even embellishing on them during the course of his recitation.

This is not to deny that many of these oral features have been retained, more or less automatically, in written texts meant for private reading. They seem especially at home in narratives. Still, the flourishing of a written tradition and a culture of private reading naturally meant that the stage directions began to disappear, only to return occasionally—up to the present-day novel—for the purpose of creating special effects ("Gentle Reader, hearken to my words"). There nevertheless seems to be reason enough to view L as a recitation text and B as the recording of a spontaneous performance, even though both texts have retained to a large extent the form of incidental realizations of the Cockaigne material. This cautious conclusion is based not only on the presence of the oral characteristics discussed above but also on the nature of the preserved manuscripts in their entirety.

In addition to the stock lines used to address the audience, text L is also padded with typical stopgap measures such as "truth to tell" and "believe it or not." Text B uses several others as well and also repeats them more often. Stock phrases, particularly those grafted on to the main motifs of Cockaigne, may also be counted as part of the oral filler. The texts vie with each other in this respect, for the following phrases occur in both: "where toil and trouble are ever banned," "old, [or] young, [weak], or strong," "they all make merry and dance in the round," "those who sleep longest earn the most," and "eat and drink the livelong day."

The padding and stock expressions flow naturally into the typical turns of phrase that describe the essential features of Cockaigne, thereby acquir-

[65]

ing a rather hackneyed character. In fact, these expressions form, on a small scale, the formulaic elements that also occur in a wider context as building blocks, whose formulations are less fixed. This applies to such elements as the edible architecture, the self-roasting animals, the rivers of wine and beer, the ever-present piles of food, and communal ownership of property. Some of these stock expressions have even acquired the nature of proverbs or sayings, and this certainly applies to the universal truths with which the texts begin. The references to houses roofed with custard tarts, the fences woven of sausages, and the roasted fowl that fly right into one's mouth have also taken on proverbial proportions, both through their inclusion in various contemporary lexicons of proverbs and through their appearance in Bruegel's famous and much-copied painting, *Netherlandish Proverbs*. This tendency of stock phrases to evolve into proverbs—a natural result of the strongly oral nature of the material in general—is perhaps most evident in Bruegel's *Land of Cockaigne*. This panel, painted in 1567, contains portrayals of at least sixteen proverbs.

An improvised text in which the reciter makes use not only of previously formulated material but also of techniques employed by professional storytellers inevitably has—apart from its constraining corset of rhyming couplets—a loose and untidy structure. There is little evidence, besides the end rhyme, of assonance or other sound patterns that could be of assistance in learning the pieces by heart. That these were not carefully written texts intended for reading but rather blueprints for—or records of—spontaneous performances is immediately evident in text L, as witnessed both by its very irregular line length and by the repetition of the word *daer* (there) at the beginning of so many lines in the original Dutch version. Neither does text B differ significantly in this respect.

Even though both texts have relatively few lines, such repetitions occur continually in both, especially in B. It must have been very easy indeed to memorize a fixed Cockaigne text of no more than several hundred lines— this is the length of the French texts—but that is not how things work with such material. Apart from the fact that a standard Cockaigne text—one that served as a fixed reference for variant models—seems never to have existed, this dreamland had already been part of the collective memory of the masses for thousands of years. Occasionally, however, some of the material seeped through to a culture of reading and recitation, enabling the establishment of a written text tradition. In the Middle Ages, however, the oral, do-it-yourself treatment of the Cockaigne material prevailed, and an endless number of texts treating this dreamland must have arisen. Texts L and B can provide insight into these, for they must contain a great many elements common to most realizations of this material.

Key concepts in B—such as "there no one suffers shortages/no one has to feel deprived," "eat and drink the livelong day/drinking all day and eating their fill," and "those who sleep longest earn the most"—are all repeated in the same or similar wording. Formulas drawing attention to Cockaigne's customs—"a custom there," "for their custom in this," and "as is the custom here with us"—are used three times in text B. Similarly, text L challenges the listener no less than three times to come up with a better place than the one being described.

All these repetitions are connected with the recurrence of a motif: text B, for example, with its handling of the theme of eroticism. Having first made the pronouncement that in Cockaigne "beautiful women are seen in great number," the author hammers the point home by reassuring the listener that total promiscuity is the custom, and this assurance of free sex is repeated again a short while later. These last two announcements are separated only by a bit of padding and a stock phrase regarding music and dance, which also occurs in text L. Did the narrator who looms behind text B get stuck at this point, or was he more or less finished with his story? After this he continues to stammer out filler phrases, stock expressions, and repetitions.

One can only conclude that he had no more to say and either hadn't yet realized it or didn't want to accept it. Only after rambling on for another ten lines or so does he wake up to the fact that he had better wrap things up and come to a conclusion, at which point he launches into a veritable epilogue, consisting primarily of exhortations to remember the lessons contained in his unambiguous tale of the Land of Cockaigne. From these recurring stabs at eroticism it emerges that sexual freedom does not occupy a distinct place in the Cockaigne décor as presented in text B, and in L the situation is not much different. This perfunctory summing-up of Cockaigne's delights—the superabundance of food, the edible architecture, communally owned property, self-cooking animals, the delightful climate, and the excessive number of holidays—has no clear-cut place for sex.

The marked closing of both texts also recalls the oral situation. The author of B says that he is finishing up and will just have to wait and see whether his words have been heard. He is not thinking of anyone but listeners. The categorical ending of both texts is also revealing: this was necessary for listeners but not for readers. In both cases the last word pronounced is "amen," which provides a definite and appropriate end to texts that opened with such proverblike phrases.

Both texts display examples of formulaic elements belonging to the basic material of Cockaigne, which the author uses at will in a longer or shorter version, a good example being the passage about tables that are always piled high with food, enabling one to stuff oneself all day long. The five lines treating this subject in L occur almost word for word in B, but the author of B added four lines specifying the way in which the tables are laid and the kind of food to be found on them. The copyist of L may have found these lines superfluous, or he may simply have forgotten to include them, though it is also possible that the copyist of B made an addition of his own, completely in keeping with his penchant for creative adaptation.

It nevertheless seems more likely that, rather than deserving praise for efficiency and conciseness, the copyist of L is guilty of sloppiness and forgetfulness, as evidenced by similar oversights elsewhere. His omission of the fundamental element of the self-cooking meat, fish, and poultry is nearly unforgivable. This motif is almost never missing from the European versions of Cockaigne and is a favorite feature of dreamworlds in general. Text B also mentions self-roasting geese and other animals that continually jump into the pan to cook themselves. It is difficult to think of a reason why this fixed feature of Cockaigne should have been purposefully omitted from text L. The copyist must have forgotten it, though it is hard to imagine a scribe copying a text and failing to correct such a glaring omission.

Some lapse of memory is actually quite natural when recording a text. Neither is the copyist of text B completely blameless in this respect, although he made fewer omissions. He also failed to make use of a common motif, at least as well-known as the self-cooking animals, namely, the fountain of youth, a theme that is omnipresent in dreamland material. According to L, Cockaigne, just like the Holy Land, has a Jordan that is capable of arresting and even reversing the process of aging. One sip of its water is enough to turn an old person into a twenty-year-old. The author of B must have forgotten this, for yet again it is impossible to think of any other reason for omitting this essential element. Forgetting fundamental motifs is a typical feature of oral text transmission, as are moving around lines within a passage and shifting formulaic elements within the text as a whole, all of which are evident in texts L and B. The assumption of a written tradition behind the recording of these texts makes such differences between the two very difficult to explain.

Other reasons may be put forth for the nearly total lack of sex in L. The only suggestive line—a variation of which occurs in text B ("beautiful women are seen in great number")—states that in Cockaigne "beautiful women are seen everywhere." This sobriety was more likely due to a conscious selection from Cockaigne's meager stock of material on this subject than to sloppiness. Eroticism is simply not one of the main attractions offered by these two texts. This was seen already in B: the remark about beautiful women is followed much later by two stray statements about free sex, which seem rather lost so close to the end. In no way does the author give the impression that carnal pleasures are anywhere near as important as idleness and overeating. Sex is apparently an incidental perk, elaborated upon only in later Cockaigne material.

Finally, B finishes up with a rather elaborate epilogue, stating in no uncertain terms a moral lesson based on the image of the topsy-turvy world. Nothing like this occurs in L, at least not explicitly. In B all those "preferring feasts and drunkenness, philandering and wantonness" are urged to go to Cockaigne, and this links the text to the popular genre of class satire, of which the best-known Netherlandish example—though by no means the only one—is the Carnival text relating the story of the Guild of the Blue Barge.

Here again the author of B makes a scholarly impression, for this genre—popularized by performances given during late-medieval celebrations of Carnival—belongs primarily to the written tradition, as evidenced by Latin satires dating from as early as the twelfth century, culminating later in humanist texts written around 1500 based on Sebastian Brant's *Ship of Fools*. In any case, texts of an explicitly moralizing and didactic nature seem more at home in a written tradition than in oral narrative. This is indicated by the explicatory nature of text B, where it is obvious that recording the irony evoked in a given narrative situation soon creates difficulties. Text L does not engage in such moralizing elucidation.

The three extant Old French texts on Cockaigne draw on the same material, though they display a framework of their own that does not occur as such in the Middle Dutch texts. The French texts begin with a rather detailed prologue, which seems to evoke the atmosphere of the charivari. During the pre-Lenten festivities in particular—but at other times of the year as well—the youth administered, with tacit permission from the rest of the community, an alternate form of justice. Their prime targets were solid citizens, especially those whose behavior deviated from the norms of marriage and acceptable family life: adulterers, couples who differed greatly in age, and hen-pecked husbands are examples of those singled out for such treatment.

Such circumstances must have provided the setting for the French texts. In this context old folk only *seemed* to be wise: true wisdom was not just a question of having a beard, otherwise goats would behave wisely. Unmarried young men, on the other hand, were considered in this topsy-turvy setting to be very sensible indeed.

Against this backdrop, irony immediately makes its entrance, for the narrator presents himself as an exile who has been sent on a penitential pilgrimage to Cockaigne. This already recalls the customs, prevailing at many festivals in northern France and the Low Countries, in which the dregs of society were heaped with ironic praise and subsequently expelled from the community in a boat or ship on wheels, sent on their way to places with such revealing names as Luilekkerland, Hell, Bread's End, and Hungery. The circumstances surrounding the penitential journey are recalled again at the end of the French texts.

The references to the Fall of Man and the patronage of the Holy Ghost that appear in the Dutch texts are lacking in the French versions, even though they do bear weak echoes of divine intervention in the pronouncement that God and all the saints have blessed this land more than any other.

Otherwise many similarities are evident in the treatment of the Cockaigne material, such as the basic law stating that those who sleep longest earn the most. Typical of the way Cockaigne motifs are used to construct a text is the fact that one of the French versions elaborates upon this point and actually specifies an hourly wage for earning while one sleeps. Similarities are also to be found in the edible architecture, the self-roasting geese, the fully laden tables, the rivers of wine, the frequent holidays, the tidal wave of warm custard pies, communally owned property, promiscuous sex, the fountain of youth, eternal spring, perfect harmony without hate or envy, and constant music and dance. Yet time and again the texts display differences, the French texts generally tending to be more detailed than the Dutch.

This is especially true of the passages about eating. While text B uses only one line to say that the geese roast themselves, the French text devotes four lines to the same geese, who walk the streets roasted and grilled, with white garlic sauce following on their heels. This stronger emphasis on food indicates yet again the most important reason for the existence of Cockaigne: the dream of outlandish amounts of food in curious combinations and extravagant displays.

The French texts are approximately twice as long as the Dutch texts, but this is due to their expansive digressions on food and not because they make use of more material. This makes the brevity of text L all the more striking, for its mere hundred lines nevertheless treat most of Cockaigne's main motifs. This text actually seems more like a synopsis of a Cockaigne recitation than a written recollection of a whole performance.

Nonetheless, text L occasionally contains details that occur in the French texts but are missing in B. One of the main attractions of Cockaigne is the greater frequency of feast days, and the French texts provide, as usual, more detail in this respect. The months have six weeks (stretching time is always a treat in Cockaigne), and Easter comes four times a year, as does the Feast of Saint John (24 June), the harvest festival, All Saints' Day, Christmas, Candlemas (2 February), and Shrove Tuesday. Fasting for Lent, on the other hand, is required only once every twenty years. Text B mentions only five weeks in a month, four times Easter, Whitsun, and Christmas, and fasting only once every hundred years.

It is precisely this tendency to vary numbers within more or less fixed formulas, as well as the spontaneous omission or addition of items in a list, that typifies oral text transmission. Text L has its own variation here, for it retains the Feast of Saint John. Even if L actually did specify five weeks in a month as does B (this information was most likely supplied on the missing corner), this was not part of a specifically Dutch tradition, as one of the French versions also mentions five weeks. The formulaic elements hovered in the copyists' minds, taking no notice of language barriers, and at each new realization of the text these elements were squeezed into place, the copyists making use of any adaptations, omissions, and additions they found necessary.

8

The Existing Potential

$\mathcal{T}$HERE IS NO REASON to doubt the existence in the Netherlands of story-tellers, both professionals and dilettantes, who worked in the way just described. Whether in someone's employ or as itinerant, freelance enter-tainers, they traveled from here to there, visiting royal courts, abbeys, and towns, making spontaneous appearances wherever there was something to celebrate. The accounts preserved by courts and municipal treasurers pro-vide extensive information concerning their names, behavior, and remuner-ation. Their status could vary considerably: Master Willem van Hildegaers-berch, for example, some of whose work is known, was a respected story-teller and a welcome guest in the better circles. It is highly doubtful whether he felt himself to be a colleague of the street poets and singers who roamed around in large numbers and often took a beating in the official literature of established authors such as Maerlant, Boendale, Bijns, and others.

Versifying vagabonds of this sort were apparently the reason for insti-tuting a disciplinary code in the Deventer hostel, a shelter for the homeless. The text, dating from 1418, takes these disturbers of the peace severely to task: "If they start making rhymes and telling stories, we shall forbid them to do so. If they go to bed and continue their banter, bandying a lot of words about, then they will be told to say their prayers and be still. . . . Later on, if they refuse to stop, we shall go to them again and say, 'Friends, you are not allowed to lie around making idle conversation and causing commo-tion and robbing others of their sleep.' "

Other sources also provide ample insight into these entertainers' narra-tive talents. One such person possessing a special gift was "Snelryem den spreker" (Quick-rhyme the speaker), whose fee was noted in records kept of a count's expenses over the years 1358–1359. He probably performed as an epi-grammatist, devising instantaneous rhymes on subjects suggested by the audience.

Another such reciter—this time a semiprofessional—was Pieter den

Brant of Geraardsbergen, a woodworker by trade, who also regularly gave public performances with a group of kindred spirits, for which the city magistrates paid him during the period 1427–1430. He also possessed a talent that was in great demand: the ability to improvise in rhyme, which was given as the reason for his high fee (though it is not clear how high it really was): "he is skillful in composing plays and rhyming texts, as well as epigrams, which he produces continuously." This calls to mind a more popular version of the thousands of lines of verse that—according to the Venerable Bede— the early medieval poet Caedmon could rattle off at the drop of a hat.

A brief testimony to Pieter den Brant's talent has been preserved in one hundred lines of rhyming text treating the characteristics of the four types of human temperament as defined by the medieval physiological theory of the four cardinal humors. This doctrine, which was general knowledge at the time, is expounded in an extremely simple rhyme full of empty phrases and padding, which not only suggests that it was written down the minute it was uttered but also gives the distinct impression of being intended only as an aide-mémoire for use in subsequent performances: the text is quite unreadable.

Writers and reciters who composed and performed texts from memory, based on their own skill and powers of recollection, were common in the Low Countries, and many a manuscript bears traces of their work. They must be distinguished from the more literary authors, who worked primarily in the written tradition. There is also a strong possibility that hybrid types also existed. This seems to apply in any case to the composer/reciter of *Van den IX besten* (Of the nine best), after the version in the so-called Geraardsbergen manuscript. In the introduction to this catalog of greats, he attempts to give an overview of the sources from which he drew his information about these exemplary figures:

> Because I store in my memory
> Rhymes, fables, and true history,
> The Bible, scholars, and chroniclers.

Before composing this work, he apparently studied the British-Celtic romances as well. Twice he impresses upon his audience the following: "I have seen the British histories with my own eyes" and "I have also read of

Arthur's heroic deeds." The compiler therefore maintained that he had a fixed body of works stored in his memory, which could be supplemented with written sources as the situation required. It is not inconceivable that this introduction was meant to appeal to as wide an audience as possible. On the one hand, he promised the attractions of a lively performance full of surprises; as a conscientious author, on the other hand, he was compelled to keep things in check with the reins of his erudition, which taught that the ultimate truth was to be found only in written sources.

This combination was a risky thing to offer. Serious authors generally did their best not to be confused with improvising street poets, which was probably what prompted a fourteenth-century reciter from Brussels, right at the beginning of his satire on the local artisans, to point to the fixed text in writing, which had been recorded by a learned clerk (perhaps himself). His words even suggest that he was reading directly from the parchment in question:

> Listen and take pains to understand
> What was written in Dutch by the hand
> Of a clerk on this parchment.

Such assurances indicate that there was a growing mistrust among authors and audiences alike of street poets who freely fantasized their fabulous tales. A good example is undoubtedly Jan van Boendale's outburst at such lying profiteers, which he included in a rhymed manual on the qualities and behavior desirable in the true author. The implication seems to be that by issuing a warning to patrons and potential customers to beware of all the deceptive imitations in circulation he was actually recommending himself. Versifying was not mere child's play (a sacred truth stated twice in his emotional plea). Neither was he the first to utter such serious warnings. The great Jacob van Maerlant, the father of all Dutch authors, had already pointed out the danger posed by the hordes of mendacious mock poets.

From these circles came the outrageous fabrication, which somehow ended up in writing, that Charlemagne once went thieving, which is, of course, ridiculous. It was also rumored that this king—the greatest Christian king of all time—was conceived illegitimately on a cart (*kar*), hence his name (Kar-el), which is even more ridiculous. Such nonsense came from the depraved sphere of the street poets, whose greed and penchant for sensationalism caused them to make up the craziest things just to earn a penny. Boendale pointedly corrected their meretricious misrepresentations by referring to an authorized, written tradition, at odds with all the lies and hearsay that one occasionally saw in print:

> May God cut short the life of the one
> Who thought up this deception
> And first gave it expression!

Lies, according to Boendale, belonged to the sphere of oral communication: they were "uttered," not written down—at least not immediately. He went on to offer a historical account of the actual circumstances surrounding Charlemagne's highly legitimate conception and impressive lineage, as testified to by the line "We read it thus." The supposed coupling on the cart was not, after all, to be found in any book.

The author of a version of *Tristan and Isolde* had already expressed a similar opinion, not while holding forth on the task of the poet but in the midst of his recital. Halfway through the story he complains about narrators who have the bad habit of giving a new twist to a story, referring to an oral tradition based on the same material. He would expressly like to distance himself from such storytellers as these, for they know nothing of the refined forms of courtly love underpinning the whole story: "But you should know, sir knights, that those narrators have altered and falsified the story. They thought up a lie because they could not understand the beautiful love that Marc always bore for the queen."

Clearly, texts L and B sooner represent the school of such accursed narrators than that of scholarly authors writing in the vernacular. Both texts bear traces of a lively oral tradition that has little or nothing to do with written literary traditions.

9
The Prose Text on Luilekkerland

PROBABLY AS EARLY AS 1546, but certainly in 1600, a Dutch text was published about a Cockaignesque country belonging to a completely different tradition. This was the prose text *Van 't Luye-lecker-landt* (subsequently referred to as text G), which was part of the popular and frequently reprinted volume *Veelderhande geneuchlycke dichten, tafelspelen ende refereynen* (Various agreeable poems, plays, and refrains). A copy of the first edition printed in 1600 is preserved in the library at the University of Ghent.

Most of the texts in this collection are certainly older, sometimes much older, and a few of them are known from earlier, separate editions. That text G must have been printed for the first time in 1546—or at least finished as a text in that year—may be inferred from the date contained in the descriptive title: "It has just been discovered, in the year written as one thousand sugar cakes, five hundred custard tartlets, and forty-six roast chickens, in the grape-harvesting month when the meat pies taste wonderful. And it makes for very amusing reading." Such a ridiculous date, written in the spirit of the text itself, would have been particularly topical and funny only in the year 1546. Why choose that year otherwise? For that matter, it does not say that the text was printed but that it was "discovered" in that year. This must be interpreted in the first place as referring to the discovery of this special country, although the term could also refer to the *inventio* of rhetoric, which would mean that the text was conceived in that year. And, finally, the expression also suggests so-called manuscript fiction, the credibility of which is seemingly heightened if the text suddenly appears out of nowhere. This, too, is only really funny if the text contains, as this one does, the most farfetched fantasies. All these possibilities undoubtedly play a role, but publication in that year is still the most likely reason for such a specific date.

Yet another indication of the previous existence of a separate edition is to be found at the end of the descriptive title: "And it makes for very amusing reading." This recommendation was commonly used on the title page or

FIGURE 12

Title of the prose text on Luilekkerland as it appears in *Veelderhande geneuchlycke dichten* (Antwerp, Jan van Ghelen, 1600), fol. G I recto.

Source: Ghent, University Library.

in the foreword of a printed text to arouse the curiosity of potential buyers or readers. When collecting various printed works and pamphlets to make this anthology in 1600, the publisher left the original presentations intact. Thirteen of the twenty-six texts still carry this recommendation, and three of them have actually been preserved in earlier editions.

The mock date belongs to the tradition of lying tales and satirical texts in general: these parodies of official ordinances, regulations, sermons, and doctors' prescriptions were popular amusements belonging to the traditional celebrations of Carnival. The incorporation of food in the date is another indication of its provenance. Carnival is first and foremost a celebration centered around excessive eating and drinking, a ritual intended to bid farewell to winter. This explains why the notation in a small manuscript, dating from 1517, of repertoire to be used at such celebrations shows musical notes composed of victuals. In addition, a German Carnival play dating from 1511 presents a mock charge (an address delivered by a bishop, archdeacon, or other ecclesiastical person at a visitation of the clergy under his jurisdiction), dated

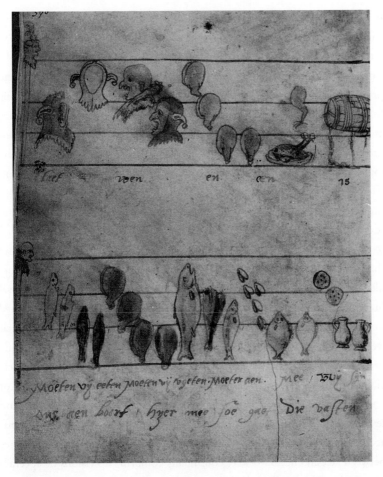

FIGURE 13

Lent and Carnival song, the musical notation consisting of suitable foods.
Reproduced from a repertoire manuscript originating in the vicinity of
Jutphaas in the diocese of Utrecht.

Source: The Hague, Museum Meermanno-Westreenianum, MS 10 C 26.

in the year "when one counted one thousand eggs, five hundred sausages on
an old walnut tree, and found a bladder worm in the eleventh pig." In this
play, moreover, Carnival and Luilekkerland are directly linked: further on, at
the close of the mock charge, there is talk of a place "where the peasants grow
on trees," an image that also occurs in the Luilekkerland text.

In this printed text, part of a "recital" book containing similar texts, the name Cockaigne no longer occurs. It is now Luilekkerland, a name that, unlike Cockaigne, was immediately familiar to a Dutch-speaking public from the sixteenth century onward. Luilekkerland was born on paper and propagated in that form by the printing press. This text, fixed in writing from the beginning, gave rise to other representations of Luilekkerland, such as songs and broadsheets, and it is quite possible that some of these in their turn ended up again in the oral tradition. The two Middle Dutch texts no longer played a demonstrable role in this new tour through the Low Countries of the Cockaigne material. The point of departure was now the printed prose text and possibly the model on which it was based, the Schlaraffenland text by the Nuremberg poet and playwright Hans Sachs.

There is no doubt whatever that text G originated at a writing desk and that it was intended for reading or recitation. The lengthy heading—more like an advertisement than a title—belongs to the tradition of printed travel literature and suspense literature in general. The "untrue tidings" mentioned in the first sentence of the text proper actually refer to the "true tidings" that were beginning to make headway in the 1540s. These forerunners of the daily press were popularized by printers specializing in this field. The commercially profitable passion for news and the equally lucrative reporting of unknown worlds were ridiculed right from the start by the Luilekkerland text of 1546. At that time the often bizarre and seemingly miraculous accounts of far-off lands—often exhibiting a not-so-delicate balance between fact and fiction—were continually conjuring up visions of spectacular lands of plenty in both East and West.

The text is written in prose form, with the exception of a two-line maxim at the beginning and a closing poem of eight lines that sums up the moral of the story. The prose form was not intended merely to make reading easier but also to strengthen the story's claim to truth—humorous as that may seem in this case—and to distinguish it from less serious-sounding rhyme. Furthermore, the prose consists of long and often complicated sentences, making the text rather unsuitable for verbatim recitation. In any case, it was not really intended for that purpose. Near the end there is yet another reference to "such manners as those written of above." In short, text G was born of a written tradition now availing itself of the printing press to provide material intended for reading only.

The text leaves no room for doubt: its primary aim is to moralize. The descriptive title is immediately followed by a rhymed maxim declaring that the behavioral norm in Luilekkerland is completely unacceptable. The first lines echo these sentiments. One really has to want very much to go to this place, for an enormous obstacle presents itself in the form of a mountain of buckwheat porridge that only very persevering individuals manage to eat their way through. Then, however, every possible delight is waiting, especially for miscreants and those who have left all virtuousness behind.

The verse at the end confirms once again the text's didactic intent, aimed especially at young people. The poem is intended for spoiled, good-for-nothing children: pack them off to Luilekkerland. This message, already proclaimed at the end of the prose text, is reiterated and reinforced by the closing verse. Such rhymed texts, which occur elsewhere in the volume as well, were probably intended for the untrained reader and offered by the compiler or publisher as helpful hints to prevent any confusion as to the meaning and implications of these mostly satirical texts. They also have a structural function, acting as an anchorman to "talk" the various texts together. The prose text itself closes with a warning to the "prodigal children," the usual term—based on the biblical parable of the Prodigal Son—used to refer to youths living in the lap of luxury. Elsewhere their privileged position caused them to be called "white-bread children."

The Dutch Luilekkerland text is a greatly expanded version of the rhyming text of *Das Schlaweraffenland*, written in 1530 by Hans Sachs and printed in the same year. Sachs's text in its turn is based on at least two older German texts dating from the early sixteenth century. While both these texts drew on the general Cockaigne material, they served to establish a typically German tradition comparable to those in France and the Low Countries. There is nothing to indicate, however, that the Dutch adapter had seen anything other than Sachs's text. His changes and especially his additions generally display the character of contemporary Antwerp realizations and other creative associations based on the material in Sachs's text.

Compared with its German example, text G is almost always more comprehensive, more detailed, and more inclined toward humor, which takes the form of private jokes that could only have been intended for personal enjoyment. In his own adaptation of the nonsense recipes underpinning all tall-

FIGURE 14

Woodcut by Erhard Schoen on a sheet dating from 1530 with the
Schlaraffenland text by Hans Sachs.

Source: Reproduced from M. L. Geisberg, *The German Single-Leafed Woodcut,*
1500–1550 (Munich, 1974), no. 1193.

tale telling, Sachs states that Luilekkerland is situated "three miles behind
Christmas." In text G this becomes "three miles through long nights," a
nonsensical translation that is noticeable only if one compares G with the
German text. But who would ever do such a thing?

Only occasionally does G omit a detail from Sachs's text, and this must
have been done consciously. The motif of sleeping on soft cushions is not
to be found in text G; neither are the two lines following this that Sachs
devotes to the only form of hunting practiced in Luilekkerland: the pursuit
of fleas, lice, rats, and mice. Perhaps the adapter of G found this kind of
behavior inappropriate to a dreamland, for it suggests the existence of
poverty and misery, as well as stench and filth. Moreover, it is possible that
the omission of these lines inadvertently caused the disappearance of the
preceding line.

Otherwise, nothing in Hans Sachs's text is missing from G. Submotifs
are repeatedly seized upon for use in associative expansions. The edible

architecture is augmented with nails of nutmeg. The ideal climate is further enhanced with snow in the form of sugar that garnishes the cooking pears. Neither are the other climatic fantasies, including the delicious smells, to be found in Sachs. The laconic description of the abundance of ready-to-eat food wryly adds that roasted chickens are held in such low regard that they are simply thrown over the fence. To the list of horses defecating eggs and donkeys shitting sweet figs (both found in Sachs) are added dogs' feces composed of nutmeg and cowpats consisting of green pancakes. There are also more subtle additions, however, and these include the sugary sweet cherries without pits, which have instead a soft little stone that melts in one's mouth like a sugared almond.

Remarkable indeed is the considerable attention paid to financial matters in text G. This subject already seems a bit out of place in Sachs's text, for why on earth would one need to earn—let alone borrow—money in Luilekkerland? This misunderstanding occurs already in the oldest Cockaigne material and contradicts the basic law, constantly repeated, of "earning while you sleep." Even such contradictions, however, are completely in keeping with literary treatments of the topsy-turvy world and lying tales, and were undoubtedly interpreted as humorous.

Text G takes this comic illogic to extremes, probably for the purpose of temporarily dispelling dreams of Cockaigne. Satire and moralizing steadily gained the upper hand as soon as the Cockaigne material began to settle down and propagate on paper, and by then the original concept of copious compensation for earthly discomfort may have faded into the background. Time and again the adapter of G loses sight of the prototype by letting the age-old dream of Cockaigne become enmeshed in a series of obsessions typical of the urban culture of late-medieval and early-modern times: the competitive spirit, the increasingly recognized need for self-preservation, and the striving for distinctive modes of behavior, all necessary ingredients for the middle-class morality prevailing at the time G was written.

In Luilekkerland these ideals are all turned upside down. Money is easily earned: for every hour spent sleeping one receives sixpence. "Earning while you sleep" is also one of the basic laws of Cockaigne, but there it is not embroidered upon. In G these topsy-turvy precepts are extended to include the rules of decorum obtaining among the elite. Anyone who can break wind convincingly earns a half-crown, and by belching three times or letting a very loud fart one can even pocket a sovereign.

This passage is followed—again only in G—by a long description of the treatment given to debtors and those defaulting on loans. People who gamble away all their money are immediately given twice as much in return. Those who are heavily in debt and make no attempt at repayment are banished to a remote corner of the country and condemned to eating nothing but roast chicken and white bread. This food is received at no expense. After a year these debtors are free to return from their "prison" and are then absolved of their debts. If they nevertheless insist on paying them off but still find themselves penniless, they must return to the landlord who gave them lodgings during their year of exile, who will then direct them to a couple of trees on which enough money grows to settle their debts, at which time they may resume their profligate lives.

This is not how things worked with real-life loan transactions, of course, as the citizens of Antwerp—a budding commercial center, striving at this time to become a new leader in world trade—must have been well aware. This extra item of topical interest says a lot about the new use to which the text was being put, as well as the middle-class milieu it was now meant to serve. This course of action is pursued further in the very next passage, which is limited in Sachs to a couple of brief statements. The tone has already been set in the section on monetary rewards for bodily noises, immediately preceding the treatment of the debtors, which in fact represents the beginning of a series of substantial elaborations by means of which the adapter of Sachs's text furnished Luilekkerland with local color and class-bound realia. Drinking is likewise remunerated according to a pay scale conceding the highest rewards to the most excessive displays of guzzling.

This absurd, inverse humor—something that Luilekkerland invariably invites—is then applied to new cultural ideals of the bourgeois elite by promising monetary rewards for what in real life is seen as undesirable behavior. For sneering at respectable folk one earns two shillings. The basic fee for a lie is a crown, with bonuses earned for the degree of artfulness employed. Although this source of income also occurs in Sachs, the additions following this passage in G seem to be directed at the situation in Antwerp in particular. Whores are held in high esteem, and "the more wanton and frolicsome they are," the more highly they are respected. The fact that they are expensive to keep should pose no problem in a place where everything is free and readily available, and this holds true for people, too. The obsession with whores in the metropolis of Antwerp emerges repeatedly in sixteenth-century literature, and the adapter of G does not hesitate to introduce this hot item into his text.

Finally, the conclusion of G is laid on even more thickly. The remark that prodigal children who want nothing to do with polite behavior should henceforth try their luck in Luilekkerland runs parallel in both Sachs and text G. The latter, however, adds rather cryptically that such good-for-nothings, when making their way to Luilekkerland, should take care not to steal, or they will be hanged on the nearby gallows. Is this a final reminder of the severe punishments dealt out in real life? At any rate, this warning fits in with the prediction that lack of "honor, virtue, honesty, and civility, not to mention wisdom and knowledge" will ultimately lead to the gallows, and Luilekkerland is, as it were, the harbinger of this message.

By the sixteenth century, Cockaigne had become a paradoxical place of instruction aimed at the acquisition of middle-class ideals. That this occurred within a literary tradition that made use of the printing press by no means implies that the humor in its absurdities had disappeared. Many of the comforting compensations that seem to form the basis of the Cockaigne material remained, however much the combination of schooling and moralizing began to obtrude, making for a rather dubious alliance. It is not clear whether the conversion of the oral Cockaigne material into written form gave rise to these new functions. Even though oral versions of the text could also be put to such use, it is obvious that the written texts, at the very least, made this new didactic intent more explicit and generally expanded and reinforced it. The freedoms that every reciter was allowed to take soon became compulsory on paper (though not always, as witnessed by text L). It seems clear that such moralizing did not occupy a fixed place within the material stored and transmitted in the collective memory, which is why the context of the two Middle Dutch rhyming texts differs from that of the three Old French texts.

The oral tradition passed on individual motifs and fragments of rhyme that were fixed firmly in many people's minds and did not stop at language barriers. It is possible that a more or less complete Cockaigne—without the moralizing—traveled around Western Europe, exploited at will for oral performances and written down every once in a while. This is also evidenced by the continual use of Cockaigne material in proverbs and texts about other subjects altogether. The German lying tale *Das Wachtelmäre* (The quail), which enjoyed a certain popularity and has been preserved in a manuscript datable to 1393, is a typical example of itinerant storyteller repertoire. It makes use of such freely available elements as houses roofed with custard tarts, fences made of sausages, roasted geese strutting about, and grilled swallows that fly into one's mouth. Other German and French texts emanating from the sphere of live entertainment also made free use of collective European memories of Cockaigne.

Hans Sachs and the adapter of G worked at their desks from the very beginning. They doubtless knew fragments of the Cockaigne material, which influenced them in structuring and furnishing Luilekkerland. The old formulations, however, which are heard so clearly in the Old French and Middle Dutch texts, made room for their own style of writing, translation, and adaptation. The bridge between the oral Cockaigne material and the Dutch text printed in 1600 is formed by the two, early sixteenth-century German texts that Sachs used. The Dutch adapter, as well as Sachs in his day, worked with written and printed material, and this seems somehow to have caused an increase in didactic content. Did the texts not seem worth writing down otherwise?

Part 3

Eating to Forget

10

Eating Habits

Cockaigne is first and foremost about eating, and in Luilekkerland things are not much different. In all three texts, 35 to 40 percent of the lines have to do with spectacularly displayed or magically mobile food. Only prose text G adds a new theme: descriptions as detailed as they are sarcastic of what one can earn with displays of extreme rudeness, failure at sports, and base behavior in general. This theme is largely missing from rhyming texts L and B, in which food occupies an even more prominent place. Text G, on the other hand, carries the eating theme to much greater extremes, not hesitating to add new and bizarre details.

The French Cockaigne texts are also chiefly about food. The Middle English *Land of Cokaygne* differs in this respect, for it pays much less attention to this primary need (or attraction). This is yet another indication that this idiosyncratic adaptation of the Cockaigne material belongs to a literary tradition of written texts intended mainly as monastic satire, which is why they play down the motif of what must still be regarded as compensation for the necessarily frugal life of country folk.

The most salient features of the Land of Cockaigne as presented in text B are the structures, enclosures, and interiors composed entirely of foodstuffs. The fences are made of sausages, the windows and doors are actually salmon and sturgeon, and the beams are made of butter. Furniture and household utensils consist of meat pies, cracknel, and even eels, while the roofs are covered with custard tarts. The hedgerows are woven of lampreys—a kind of fish—and the streets are even paved with spices.

Another attraction is all the delectable animals that simply let themselves be caught, such as rabbits, hares, deer, and wild boar. Better still, geese, capons, and other fowl, as well as meat and fish, all appear willing to roast or grill themselves. Laid tables are always piled high with food, and it even rains eels and meat pies three times a day. Various types of beverages, in unlimited quantities and free of cost, flow constantly in a river to which everyone has access.

Text L does not differ appreciably from the above-mentioned pattern in B. Text G also follows the same pattern, though it differs in detail and is more elaborate. One special feature is the mountain of buckwheat porridge one must eat through to gain entrance to Luilekkerland, where one finds growing on the trees food—already cooked or baked—such as pâtés, meat pies, cakes, pancakes, cooking pears, and white bread. Fish, fowl, and swine do not stop at self-preparation but offer themselves for consumption in a decidedly pushy way: roasted pigs even roam around with knives stuck in their backs. There are more examples of such particulars in G, but it is clear how things stand: everywhere there is food, everything is made of food, and all these edibles even fall out of the sky right into one's mouth.

It is not only the quantity, diversity, and constant consumption of all this food—some of it still alive—that is so remarkable. Rather, it is the total obsession with eating and the far-fetched fantasies surrounding food that immediately strike the reader of these lines. In addition to the ever-plentiful and self-replenishing supply of food, there is a vast variety of vegetable produce, meat, fish, and poultry, with no marked preference for food of a more exotic nature. Again and again, the point is hammered home that in these dreamlands no work of any kind is required in order to fill one's stomach. Not only are farming and cattle raising completely unnecessary, everything is there for the taking, growing on trees, walking around roasted, or simply falling into one's mouth from the sky. Finally, the inhabitants of Cockaigne even live in edible dwellings, every component part of their tangible world being composed of ready-to-eat bites of food.

Luilekkerland is associated with expensive delicacies, automatically giving the impression that all the spectacular food on offer must be luxury food or in any case food that is beyond the reach of the masses. This point is debatable, however. It is precisely these texts' emphasis on the constant availability, variety, and easy accessibility of all this food that suggests that it was these features—and not the food's exotic nature—that were for most people the main attraction.

There was a certain tendency in late-medieval and early-modern literature and art to think that peasants' fare was very simple indeed. This notion was not meant to be especially negative or denigrating—though this intention was not entirely absent—but followed logically from the fact that peasants

FIGURE 15

A simple meal of broth and beer. Pieter Bruegel the Elder, *Wedding Meal* (detail), 1568.

Source: Vienna, Kunsthistorisches Museum.

lived closer to nature, and this necessarily entailed austerity and a nearly ritual monotony based on the rhythm of the seasons. Within this framework, created by the ever-greater dichotomy between the notion of nature as the prototype of lost innocence and its conception as a diabolic morass of brutish folly, simple fare can just as easily symbolize utmost simplicity as sottish stupidity. Both, however, are idealizations at loggerheads with real-life experience and cannot therefore be viewed as evidence of such.

The "Kerelslied" (Peasants' song), dating from the end of the fourteenth century, has a refrain that reiterates how much time peasants spent stuffing themselves with buttermilk, bread, and cheese:

> Bread and cheese, curds and whey,
> The bumpkin eats the livelong day.
> That's why he's such a simpleton,
> He eats more than is good for him.

From this stinging attack on country folk it also emerges that they consume rye bread, gingerbread, and even wine at the kermis, or fair. This caricature is intended to show cultured townspeople the kind of behavior to be avoided at all costs. A much longer text in verse, *Van den kaerlen* (Of the peasants), which is at least as caustic as the "Kerelslied," maintains that the peasant's diet consists of buttermilk porridge, eggs, garlic, and beer. But several refrains found in the volume compiled by Jan van Stijevoort in 1524 declare that roots and vegetables are the peasant's standard fare, naming butter and cheese as occasional luxury items.

This last image began to predominate during the transition from the Middle Ages to early-modern times, as witnessed by class literature, which described for each social class not only the proper eating habits but also those to be avoided. Typical peasant fare was thought to consist of turnips, garlic, onions, and bread: in short, coarse fare for primitive beings. This was also codified in an exemplary woodcut—highly influential owing to its wide circulation—made in 1532 by Hans Weiditz, the so-called Petrarch Master. Opposite gluttony he portrayed frugality in the person of a poor woodcutter doing himself proud with porridge made of turnips, onions, and bread. In *The Harvest* of 1565, Pieter Bruegel the Elder—showing his appreciation of the idyllic moment—depicted peasants resting in the midst of the wheat, eating broth with bread and beer. Around 1600 his son Jan Brueghel the Elder also focused on the vegetable broth in his *Visit to a Farmstead*, placing it in an enormous cauldron in the center of the painting.

This nutritious, high-fiber swill for the masses endowed the lampoons enacted during the Carnival celebration with a special sort of fecal humor. Mock prognostications—parodies on predictions of the future that appeared in print every year—predictably wallow in this folkloristic filth by announcing that, especially in the winter, folk will often be on sentry duty in the outhouse, suffering from diarrhea as a result of their monotonous diet of beans, turnips, and onions.

The portrayal of the slaughtering month (November) in calendars and breviaries, however, indicates that other practices, though admittedly idealized, were undoubtedly just as prevalent in the countryside. From less suspect sources it emerges that sausages, meat, poultry, and fish were the last thing lacking on the menu of either peasant folk or the great majority of town dwellers. Although in the period from roughly 1000 to 1300 many peo-

FIGURE 16

A woodcutter's frugal meal. Woodcut by Hans Weiditz, the so-called
Petrarch Master, 1532.

Source: Reproduced from W. Scheidig, *Die Holzschnitte des Petrarca-Meisters zu
Petrarca's Werk "Von der Artzney bayder Glück"* (Augsburg, 1532; reprint, 1955), 204.

ple had to make do with little more than bread and beer, the fourteenth century witnessed the emergence of "carnivorous Europe"—as one modern
historian called it—a situation that prevailed until well into the sixteenth
century.

The picture most of us have of the Middle Ages is a rather sentimen-
tal one evoking gratuitous solidarity with the starving masses we imagine
were continually wandering along the highways and byways, knocking in
vain on the doors of abusive nobles, fat abbots, and ruthless extortionists.
The origins of this misconception can be found in medieval sources, not
infrequently based on biblical models, which exhibit a strong ideological
slant. It is remarkable to what extent the twentieth century—with its uncontrollable desire to come up with the greatest possible contrast to its own reality, regardless of whether that reality is highly valued or utterly abhorred—
continues to misconstrue this pseudorealism in literature and art, taking it
to be an eyewitness report produced by a superior form of journalism. The

FIGURE 17

Cauldron of vegetable broth. Jan Brueghel the Elder, *Visit to a Farmhouse*, ca. 1600.

Source: Vienna, Kunsthistorisches Museum.

reality of peasant life can only be inferred from the "information" supplied by songs like the "Kerelslied" or paintings such as Bruegel's, and this is also true of the eating habits of the masses.

Findings have shown that in the Low Countries in the fifteenth century and in Western Europe as a whole nearly a pound of meat per person was served up daily, with the exception of fast days, which were supposed to be meatless. This is considerably more than we are accustomed to eating. As far as the aristocracy was concerned, the daily serving could amount to as much as three or four pounds. The consumption of meat—especially pork and beef—and sausages in considerable quantities was therefore something quite normal. Such averages are highly suspect, of course, especially in view of the fact that the information available is rather arbitrary and amorphous. Nevertheless, it is clear that in Europe in the late Middle Ages the masses consumed meat, fish, and fowl with some regularity.

FIGURE 18

Depiction of a copious supply of meat in a middle-class milieu. Pieter Aertsen,
Butcher's Shop, 1551.

Source: Uppsala, University Museum.

Cockaigne therefore gives a literary answer to questions raised by literary images of what people should and should not eat. This would not be so very attractive, however, if all that food belonged in large measure to the daily regimen. Cockaigne, moreover, does not give the impression of having flourished within closed, literary circles but rather to have appealed directly to a real need felt by all segments of society for imaginative compensation. Of more importance than a comic correction of artistic images of common folk's alleged eating habits was the presentation of a pleasant contrast created by the suggestion of great variety and permanent abundance. In other words, the food itself was not so important as the fact that it was always available.

In any case, culinary Cockaigne is largely lacking in the typical dishes gracing the tables of the aristocracy. The preeminent food of the nobility—game—plays an indistinct role in this dreamland. Outside the context of exuberant ingurgitation, mention is made of small game like rabbits and hares frisking about, which are just as tame as the deer and wild boar, and all these animals may be caught with one's bare hand—presumably for the purpose of eating them, though this is not explicitly stated. Most likely there was a need to furnish Cockaigne as much as possible like the earthly paradise. Even then, however, potential consumption continued to play a role behind the scenes. When Adam gave names to all the animals he also acquired dominion over them, after which they existed to be eaten by humans. This provision, at least, had been made after the Flood, when God took so much pity on humankind—already so severely punished and degraded—that he permitted them to eat a bit of meat.

Even more striking is the total lack of fruit. This is a sore subject in a dreamland with paradisiacal pretensions, but Cockaigne serves up solutions based on rather blasphemous-sounding jokes treating the well-known Flood motifs. In this regard fruit would certainly present an opportunity not to be missed, but apparently there was something that made fruit undesirable in this garden of delightful debauchery. This conscious omission must probably be sought in the culinary association of fruit with courtly eating habits.

Members of the nobility who wanted to amaze their guests went overboard with fruit, more by displaying it than by eating it. *The Romance of the Rose*, the book of etiquette par excellence in Western Europe, which prescribed the correct courtly attitudes toward erotic love and other modes of behavior, offers a long list of summer fruit that supposedly causes women's resistance to melt away: apples, pears, walnuts, cherries, strawberries, plums, quinces, figs, chestnuts, peaches, oranges, grapes, mirabelles, melons, mulberries, blackberries, and raspberries. These also turned up, not surprisingly, on the tables of those who constantly tried to express their power in terms of dazzling displays of delicacies. Dishes combining different types of game were a popular tour de force, game being favored not so much for its taste as for the enticing possibilities it offered to dress it up in imaginative and exotic ways.

One of the banquets celebrating the marriage of Charles the Bold to Margaret of York at Bruges in 1468 exemplified this courtly tendency to overstep all boundaries. The following words were written by the renowned Anthonis de Roovere, town rhetorician of Bruges, who was involved in organizing the festivities, more specifically in decorating the route taken by the wedding procession. Once inside the palace, however, he feasted his eyes on all the delicacies and was even more impressed when he realized that it was only Monday and there were still many days of feasting to come: "At the banquet twenty-four dishes of roast game were served up, exquisitely garnished, along with about thirty-six desserts in the form of trees made of all sorts of fruit purée such as apples, pears, plums, and cherries. Next to each dish stood two male and two female dwarves with baskets, hampers, barrels, bowls, and straw bags, bearing a collection of all kinds of fruit from the various trees. These fruits were all soaked in sugar and deliciously candied."

Spices, generally one of the ingredients of refined, luxury food, are not lacking either. In Cockaigne the streets are paved with ginger and nutmeg. Such roads do not exist in Luilekkerland, but dogs defecate nutmeg, just as donkeys shit sweet figs and cows and oxen enormous pancakes. Although spices do not play a prominent role, they were apparently considered indispensable, not as a specific constituent of courtly fare but as an ingredient of costly food in general. Herbs and spices were imported in ever greater quantities from the Near East, which was in fact so far away that it was thought to be situated in the immediate vicinity of the earthly paradise, making it a dazzling and wondrous repository for all the intoxicating ingredients flowing out of the Garden of Eden, including the spices that washed up along the shores of the four rivers of paradise and their tributaries.

Jacob van Maerlant had already called spices the particular food of distinguished and worldly people, unsuitable for clerics and other servants of the soul, who were not supposed to eat "ginger or tansy, nutmeg, or other spices." And a certain Egidius—a singular name, perhaps the poet's stage name rather than his proper name—warns to what extent the table of a distinguished gentleman is likely to be plundered if he serves liqueur mixed with such spices as ginger and nutmeg, for when he can no longer afford to do so, all his congenial guests will surely disappear. Spices were obviously a status symbol of the highest order. In a sixteenth-century debate over food, enacted between persons presented as Lent and Carnival, the latter's trump card consists of the most exclusive and sumptuous food imaginable, namely "all things cooked with spices."

Cockaigne undoubtedly seasoned its offerings with a dash of these suggestions as to what the well-to-do should and should not eat. Their needs were constantly met in this dreamland, for Cockaigne also helped itself to the standard fare found on the tables of the rich. A sixteenth-century refrain tells of notables enjoying such heavenly produce as dates, almonds, and nutmeg, as well as more local luxuries such as white bread, mutton, geese, chickens, capons, young pigeons, partridges, and snipe. Still, this rhetoricians' text also testifies to regional fare that excels in abundance rather than choiceness. In previous centuries, too, the fantasized fare of wealthy burghers was more the object of Cockaigne's craving than the extravagant spectacles of the aristocracy with their courtly airs. This distinction is also made in *The Romance of the Rose*. Rich fare, though not particularly courtly, consists of pike, salmon, lamprey, eel, pastries, flan, cheese, spiced pears, young geese and hens, goats, rabbits, and pork rump.

As far as the quality of food in Cockaigne is concerned, this was sought more in the households of the rich and well-to-do in the immediate vicinity of both town and country than among the nobility. There was even a literary trend featuring appetizing descriptions of luxury peasant fare, which was supposed to make townsfolk's mouths water. Are we getting closer to Cockaigne and Luilekkerland? The farce *Hanneken Leckertant* (Hans the sweet tooth), written by the renowned Antwerp rhetorician Jan van den Berghe and winner of the "highest prize" at a festival held in 1541 in the town of Diest in Flanders, presents a fatso called Hans—as spoiled as he is fond of food—who is regarded with envy by a friend whose scrawniness puts him at a serious disadvantage. Hans goads him into feigning illness, so that he will be mollycoddled and fattened up: "So you'll have to eat to revivify, / Meat and pastry, pâté and pie." And so it came to pass: the supposedly sick child is also given sweet milk, rice, roast chicken and partridge, cakes, custards, meat pies, white bread, eggnog, beer, Rhine wine, and porridge. The farce is set either in the countryside or in a part of town full of recent immigrants from the countryside, who clearly hold fast to their rustic customs.

With regard to content, the dietetic dreams of Cockaigne and Luilekkerland fulfill the fantasies of luxury food entertained by the great majority of both country folk and townspeople. These dreams and fantasies, however, were realized on a regular basis during the frequent feast days and family celebrations, which almost automatically filled up the days remaining between the equally frequent fast days prescribed by the powers that be. So what exactly was the cause of all the excitement? It must be sought primarily in the ready availability—at the cost of neither money nor effort—of so much mobile food ad absurdum, the grotesque but edible edifices (but could you really sink your teeth into them?), the permanent supply of food and drink, and certainly also the great variety.

I might do well, in concluding, to stress that last point in the words of the doctor and moralist Jan de Weert. In his *Nieuwe Doctrinael* (New textbook), dating from the first half of the fourteenth century, he offered strict guidelines for life in the city, something that was new to many people, hence the title he gave to his instruction manual. He naturally warned his readers of the sin of gluttony, which gives rise to all other sins. Contrary to what one would expect, however, his main concern was not the iniquity of stowing away as much as possible but the constant shift between exclusive and less exclusive fare, indiscriminately consumed in a never-ending stream. The following is his description of the category "delicious," the sine qua non of a glutton's vocabulary:

> Sometimes boiled and sometimes roasted,
> Meat pies, pastries, tarts, and custard,
> Claret, beer, and malmsey wine,
> Ginger, also spices fine.

Now this, now that. In both Cockaigne and Luilekkerland all imaginable delicacies were available, both simultaneously and in perpetuity.

II

Hunger and Scarcity

IT SEEMS NATURAL to link these obsessive fantasies first of all to a periodic or perhaps even a permanent need to compensate for shortages of food, whether real or imagined. Such compensation took the form of escape into a dreamworld furnished with an abundance of everything lacking—or feared to be imminently lacking—in real life, this deficiency being experienced as a threat to survival. Such dreamlands also functioned as an outlet, enabling the constant worry caused by food shortages, real or otherwise, to vent itself in suggestions of abundance as bizarre as they were ridiculous.

These assumptions presuppose the existence of an initially agrarian society, later joined by that of the city, where the daily drudgery required to earn a living lent poignant emphasis to the prayer "Give us this day our daily bread." This immediately explains the contrast offered by Cockaigne and its ever-present variety of food: the Lord's Prayer, to be sure, mentions nothing but bread. Following this line of reasoning, the Cockaigne texts could only have functioned as mental antidotes, a means of bracing oneself for the horrors of famine, known both from experience and hearsay. It is generally assumed, after all, that everyone living during the Middle Ages must have experienced one or two periods of hardship in the course of his or her usually short lifetime.

Even though some chroniclers did their best to strengthen this impression, a picture nevertheless emerges of a Middle Ages in which the number of true famines was actually quite small. There was, however, a constant recurrence of periodic scarcity, causing broad segments of the population, including the upper crust of society, a great deal of suffering. Until well into the Middle Ages the provision of food was largely dependent on what the surrounding area could supply. When locally grown crops failed, there was no immediate alternative. Moreover, in those days an acre of farmland produced only a quarter of what is now considered a standard yield.

Food shortages were even thought to be a normal occurrence during the spring and summer months. The fasting required at Lent fulfilled in this respect a more earthly regimen, urging—if not compelling—one to undergo a period of cleansing sobriety precisely at a time when winter supplies were near depletion. If the church had not required a period of fasting at Lent, it would have had to be invented. Certainly the summer, just before the new harvest, was a time not only of scarcity but also of dietary monotony, which many people simply accepted as part of summer. In any case, it was certainly more bearable at that time of year.

The number of people who actually died of hunger, however, either directly or indirectly, represent only a fraction of what medieval chronicles and modern depictions of the Middle Ages would have us believe. Scholarship has also contributed—unwittingly, one may assume—to this image of spectacular contrast. From the viewpoint of present-day, Western prosperity, culminating in the welfare state and dominated—at least ideally—by peace, order, and well-regulated consumption, it seems almost inevitable that antitheses should be taken for granted and therefore created, either in the third world or in the most distant past that can still be linked directly to the present: the Middle Ages. Our understanding of the present is apparently increased if we assume that it was built on the ruins of its opposite. Or is this simply the compelling law of dialectics? Each victim of overconsumption in the West conjures up visions of his or her opposite starving in a third world of past or present.

This is perhaps why, since the Second World War, modern medievalists have populated their Middle Ages with devils, heretics, lepers, vagabonds, plague victims, witches, a lot of women in general, and great hordes of the hungry wasting away along the roadside. They need hardly stray from the truth, for that matter, for there are plenty of documents testifying to the existence of such victims, terrifyingly large numbers of them in fact. This image is intensified, especially in the case of food shortages, by the pictures now seen almost daily of hunger and famine on a massive scale in developing countries. They thrust the comparison with the Middle Ages upon us by offering a gruesome demonstration of what really can and does happen.

The problem, nevertheless, is not just the selection of these subjects, so pertinent to the discussion of modern welfare, but also the often indiscriminate application of medieval concepts that actually represent and propose something entirely different. Much has been colored by ideology; little handed down as neutral fact. This is true in particular of art and literature, which by their very nature reshape their subject matter, perhaps allowing them to provide even deeper insight into the underlying causes of people's actions.

In fact, famine in the Middle Ages was not that much of a problem. Hunger in the third world today is probably much more widespread and certainly more frequent, and the accompanying death rate inconceivably higher. To begin with, famine in the Middle Ages is difficult to verify. It was almost always accompanied by natural disasters such as floods and plague epidemics, making it difficult to determine the actual cause of death of many victims.

Hunger causes physical and mental deterioration and increased susceptibility to disease, paving the way for epidemics. While hunger and scarcity can have many causes, a high mortality rate seems to result only when the situation is aggravated by sickness or natural disaster. This is not the impression given by most chronicles written at that time, which paint terrifying pictures of emaciated famine victims driven by hunger to commit acts of desperation before giving up the ghost, their bodies being swept up and dumped in mass graves.

Hunger and scarcity almost always begin with very bad weather conditions. Protracted frost or unremitting rain, floods, and storms can cause a harvest to fail. A plague of grasshoppers recorded in Western Europe in 873 seems too biblical to be taken for the gospel truth, though there must have been some veracity in it. That such particulars were recorded at all makes it clear that natural catastrophes were interpreted at all levels of society as a just punishment by God, who was issuing the umpteenth warning before selling out and closing down Creation for good.

These natural causes were generally exacerbated by all kinds of profiteering and usurious practices. The best indications of scarcity and impending famine were strongly fluctuating grain prices, which could also point to profiteering. There are numerous records of this in the cities in the Low Countries. Bakers and grain merchants were always held responsible for food shortages, even when it was not at all clear how much they were to blame. The smallest disruption in the supply of grain could wreak havoc, leading to a vicious circle of imputations and speculations that could plunge a whole community into a state of turmoil. In 1532, for example, a rumor circulated in Brussels that a certain Jan Morre had driven up grain prices to exorbitant levels. His house was reduced to a heap of rubble, and he and other grain merchants were ignominiously dragged through the city.

This case is just one of thousands. Very revealing indeed is the treatment in sermons and literature of what was thought to be a basic evil. These homilies represent the collective anxieties of well-off burghers, anxieties fomented by such controversial authors as Willem van Hildegaersberch at the beginning of the fifteenth century and the Haarlem rhetorician Lauris Janszoon at the end of the sixteenth century. The popular hellfire-and-damnation preacher Dirk van Munster, whose congregations filled whole cathedrals and village squares, regarded usurers "who look forward to times of hardship" as transgressors of the Fifth Commandment: thou shalt not kill. A collective shudder must have gone through the masses when his words pounded from the pulpit, discrediting all those—from the baker to the merchant—who made their living from grain.

No matter how good their intentions (their championing of the masses is undeniable), these sermons—for example, the recitation text *Van den corencopers* (On the grain merchants) and the play *Van 't coren* (About grain)—instilled in people an intense and unfathomable fear of even the slightest disturbance in their daily diet. Such collective fears gave rise not only to a desire for retaliation but also to the need for release and escape. These fears were intensified considerably by the threat or outbreak of war, when anxieties increased at the first sign of plundering in the immediate area or upon hearing news of enemy forces closing off important supply lines. Again, the constant threat of such events could be just as disruptive as their actual occurrence.

There was always a war going on somewhere in the Middle Ages and early-modern period, and this led to fears that could take on dramatic proportions, even though actual occurrences of hunger and hardship were usually localized and of short duration. Waging war at that time was more a series of clamorous but short-lived disturbances than a question of protracted warfare, which is why its practical consequences for the food supply were usually very limited and always confined to certain regions. The masses, however, persisted in associating war, and especially the threat of siege or occupation, with the most horrific scenes of starvation, such as those continually recorded in chronicles, news pamphlets, and other historical works.

Reports of the fear of famine were considerably more frequent than indications of its actual occurrence. In the notorious period of hardship between 1000 and 1300, when many had to make do with little more than bread, there were nevertheless only three real periods of famine, that is, cir-

cumstances where over a wide area a substantial percentage of the population died as the result of what must have been a severe shortage of food.
This three-century span was followed, during the course of the fourteenth
century, by the arrival of meat-eating Europe, owing in part to improved
methods of agriculture, increased urbanization, and especially the explosive
development of trade. This period of relative prosperity in Western Europe,
however, was ushered in by what appears to have been the most horrific
famine in the whole of the Middle Ages, the famine of 1315–1317.

According to some, this was the only real famine and the only one to hit
all of Europe. Always given as one of its main causes, also by contemporaries, was the persistently bad weather of the preceding years. Not only did
this cause the harvests to fail, but it made the planting of crops difficult and
even impossible. Such weather was a frequent occurrence, however, though it
did not usually precipitate such immense catastrophes. There must therefore
have been unexpected and unfortunate complications, the outcome of which
was devastating. One contributing factor was undoubtedly the sudden spurt
of economic growth, which had given rise to irrepressible expansion without providing any of the safety mechanisms necessary in times of recession,
let alone those needed when natural disasters strike. And strike they did, hit-
ting the masses who were now packed together in rapidly growing cities,
whereas previously they had been spread out over the countryside, where
such life-threatening situations usually petered out, the less dense population and wider area eventually absorbing the brunt of the blow.

It must have been truly terrible. The reports came from all sides and
took many tones, all of which blend into one long, drawn-out cry of
anguish. Only in such terms could Jan van Boendale, Antwerp magistrates'
clerk and author of didactic treatises, write about the disaster. Still young at
the time, he must nevertheless have seen it with his own eyes. "All that moan-
ing and wailing, which one heard from the poor, could have moved a stone
to pity," were the emotional words recorded in his monumental work on
Netherlandish history, the *Brabantsche Yeesten* (Brabantian heroic deeds). He
had heard those groans himself, just as he had seen people starving with his
own eyes. One-third of the entire population was said to have died, though
these statistics are colored by a medieval lack of exactitude. In any case, great
numbers of people died, untold numbers, more than anyone had ever seen
before.

All the same, the following story, which underscores the seriousness of the situation, doubtless made an even deeper impression on contemporaries. The food shortage was in fact so severe that the king of France, Louis X, was forced to go hungry owing to lack of provisions during his four-day stay at the abbey of Saint-Martin at Tournai in present-day Belgium. This was unheard-of, a king not being received in style and given the food to which he had a royal right.

The 1315–1317 famine, with its many eyewitnesses, fostered a constant and sometimes overpowering fear of food shortages. This fear grew in intensity when it became clear that cities were especially vulnerable. There was no way back, however, and people were forced to devise emergency measures aimed at more effective regulation of the food supply, as well as spiritual escape routes to deal with their fear. The sight of thousands of dead being swept off the streets into mass graves at Bruges and Ypres in 1316 etched itself deep into the collective memory. People in the countryside started keeping a sharp watch on things, making sure that the pasturelands were not grazed bare and the soil not depleted by too much farming. Overworking of arable land was severely punished, and a watchful eye was kept on the threat of regional overpopulation.

Fears only increased, however. The aftermath of the terrible famine of 1315 meant a long period of general debilitation, which paved the way for the plague that struck at various times around the middle of the century. Moreover, the utilization of arable land produced yields that were entirely insufficient to cope with the tripling of the population and the transition to a market economy that took place in the late Middle Ages, both of which combined to produce an extremely unstable situation. The great fear of food shortages was based more on recollection than on reality, however, which is what makes it so unfathomable, for no matter how unsteadily Europe continued to plod on, it henceforth managed to stay firmly on its feet and even to avoid another widespread famine.

Local disruptions, however, continued to confirm the terrible memories of hardship. Indeed, more than once a generation severe food shortages were seen to wreak havoc in even the most prominent families. When all possessions had been sold, the only thing left was the beggar's staff, and then it was every man for himself. Prolonged hardship could mean the break-up of families and friendships. Again and again, horror stories made the rounds, telling of people forced to eat the most disgusting remains of animals as well as humans. Evidence for this is found in the so-called confession books: already in the early Middle Ages these books elicited confessions concerning the eating of mice, insects, and even the partially decomposed flesh of exhumed corpses. And, finally, there was the fear of dying alone and being left unburied, to be preyed on by carrion eaters. This fear was immense, especially as it was thought that this state of decay would mean exclusion from the Resurrection and Last Judgment.

Even if dying of hunger was not all that likely, faith in a minimum amount of security was at a premium. Everyone had heard stories of acquaintances who had been forced to become drifters. As late as 1492 Romboudt de Doppere of Bruges wrote in his diary that whole families had suddenly taken to vagabondage during a period of scarcity. Most of them chose, logically enough, the well-known pilgrims' routes, such as the road to Santiago de Compostela or Rome, where one was most likely to receive charity. The only problem was that so many other people had taken it into their heads to do the same thing.

To the misery of hunger was added the additional fear of an irate God, whose threat of scarcity was perhaps the harbinger of true famine. Everyone knew that the scourge of hunger was one of His favorite weapons, which he wielded whenever he wanted to remind corrupt creatures of His original plan. Wasn't this obvious from the many examples of such punishment in the Bible? Some thought that hunger was simply the ultimate punishment for original sin, while scholars and chroniclers generally placed hunger at the top of a long list of previous warnings sent from on high.

Galbert of Bruges took the famine of 1124–1125 as an example. First God sent an omen in the form of an eclipse, calling on people to repent and atone for their sins. When that didn't help, he followed this up with a food shortage that gradually assumed catastrophic proportions, intended to last until people repented of their sins. When repentance was not forthcoming, He punished humankind with death on a massive scale. This was the path taken by most discussions of food shortages in the Middle Ages, which usually included heated references to the relevant passages in the Bible that had prophesied it all. The gospels in particular viewed famine as a sign of the impending Judgment Day.

12

The Topos of Hunger

$\mathcal{A}$LL THESE MATERIAL and spiritual factors, which kindled and shaped ideas and experiences—or merely the threat—of scarcity created an immense fear of hunger that dominated the lives of a great many people. Cockaigne and Luilekkerland must be viewed first and foremost against this backdrop. It was liberating to imagine a situation in which such cares were totally absent. That famine was not actually such a threat made little difference. According to the chronicle by Galbert of Bruges mentioned in the last chapter, hunger was not really such a problem in the years 1124–1125; chaos nonetheless ensued, caused by the great fear people had of both God's wrath and an economic upheaval they could not comprehend.

This fear, as real as it was metaphysical, was not only fueled by the topos of hunger in chronicles: the chronicles actually produced the fear in the first place. Literature and memory detached themselves from a reality that God had shown he could bend at any moment to His will, putting people in their place as the incurable sinners that they were. Neither was there any indication that humankind was doing anything at all to mend its ways, which meant that the path to paradise must be paved with the most horrific famines.

Perhaps the most important source of medieval chroniclers' hunger topoi was the gripping account by the eyewitness Flavius Josephus of the Romans' destruction of Jerusalem in A.D. 70. Other models also existed, in particular biblical ones such as the prediction in Jeremiah that set the example followed by the chronicler John of Trokelowe when describing the catastrophe in England in 1315–1316. No account, however, was as comprehensive, detailed, and horrifying as that of Flavius.

The never-ending siege drove the Jews in their starved state to commit all manner of atrocities, which were taken to be an example of the extreme punishment inflicted by God on the murderers of His son, an exemplum that was cited with great approval throughout the Middle Ages. According to the *Boec van der wraken* (Book of vengeance), after the murder of Christ,

FIGURE 19

The sack of Jerusalem in A.D. 70. In the center foreground a mother eats her own
child. Ghent panel dating from the end of the fifteenth century.

Source: Ghent, Museum voor Schone Kunsten.

God waited more than forty years for the murderers to repent of their sin.
When atonement was not forthcoming He struck mercilessly. The desperate deeds of the Jews only proved to what extent such heathens were lacking
in Christian reason, knowing no restraints when it came to indiscriminate
displays of bestial behavior.

Horror stories of Jerusalem in A.D. 70 seem to have been immensely
popular. In all imaginable languages and forms, from sermons to epic songs
and from broadsheets to confession books, these stories continued to be
told far and wide until well past the Middle Ages, finding an enthusiastic
audience among all segments of society. The horrors were also among the
most popular subjects depicted on fifteenth- and sixteenth-century tapestries. When, after an extremely exciting pilgrimage in 1525, the Delft barber
Arent Willemszoon finally saw the holy city of Jerusalem from one of its
surrounding hills, he first recalled Jesus, who must also have viewed it from
this vantage point, only to have his thoughts turn immediately to the horrors of the year 70: members of the same family stealing bread from each

other, men consuming their wives, and mothers roasting their own children on spits and eating them.

These stories were narrated, acted out, and sung in two great traditions in Middle Dutch literature. The first is based on translations and adaptations of Flavius's *Bellum Judaicum* (*History of the Jewish War*), with the high point being Jacob van Maerlant's *Wrake van Jerusalem* (Revenge of Jerusalem). The latter in particular was used as the basis for new adaptations, such as the prose version brought out in Gouda in 1482 by the publisher and printer Gheraert Leeu. The other tradition stems from much more nebulous sources in numerous apocryphal works dating from the first centuries after Christ, which gave rise to great numbers of folk rhymes, ballads, epic songs, and prose texts, all of which testify to the frequency with which everyone was reminded of what Maerlant referred to quite simply as the worst famine of all time.

The points that never fail to occur in chronicles and historical surveys of the period include the following: the inhabitants of the besieged city first took to eating leaves, grass, and even the moss on the walls. Young men started chewing on the leather of their shields and shoes, after which they started stealing bread from one another. Indeed, the hunger was so acute that some did not hesitate to kill members of their own families for bread. Anything edible was immediately devoured raw, for fear it would otherwise be stolen. People soon began murdering others who had just eaten, cutting them open and gulping down their half-digested food. They also slurped up each other's vomit, and even human excrement didn't stay on the ground for long. Worst of all was the mother who butchered her own child, roasted half of the body on a spit and ate it and then salted down the other half to save for later.

These particulars were recounted and recorded thousands of times, in every way, shape, and form, taking on epic proportions guaranteed to captivate any audience. Master storytellers gave convincing proof of their narrative skills whenever they managed creatively to heighten current events by demonstrating parallels to the greatest famines ever staged by God. A good example is the mother who served up her own child: this detail is never left out of the Jerusalem horror stories, but it was also a popular way of drawing attention to the seriousness of famine elsewhere. Mother eats child: things can't get any worse.

The model for this story could be found in the Bible (2 Kings 6:24–30), but it was the wave of Josephus adaptations that brought the tale to life in the Middle Ages. Since then the story has cropped up in accounts of other famines, as well as recurring as a stock motif in folk tales and legends, though more generally in stories of parents nearly driven by hunger to butcher and eat their children. It is mothers, however, who really shine in this role. The Dominicans authorized by Pope Innocent VIII to eradicate witch-craft, Johann Sprenger and Heinrich Kraemer, embellished their witch-hunting handbook—the *Malleus maleficarum* (The witches' hammer), first published in 1487—with a story about women in the canton of Lausanne who cooked their own children and devoured them. Both these traditions, probably not directly connected at first, fed upon each other in the Middle Ages.

In his history of the world, the *Spiegel Historiael* (The historical mirror), Maerlant names two such cases on the authority of his source, Vincent of Beauvais. In Rome in the year 542, hunger reached such proportions that mothers could hardly restrain themselves from eating their own children. In "the German land" as well, in the year 851, there was a father who was so hungry he wanted to consume his own child. Is this a typical example of Maerlant's terseness, speaking in both cases of intentions and not of deeds? He gives the impression, at any rate, that the plans were not carried out.

Other historical accounts are less reticent. Regarding the appalling famine that swept across Europe from 1315 to 1317 (and lasted several years longer in some places), stories were continually told in far-flung regions of children disappearing into the stomachs of their parents. Whether it was Ireland, Poland, Silesia, northeastern or western Europe, everywhere parents were driven by hunger to eat their own children. Sometimes details were added that served less to strengthen the veracity of the story than to rouse public sentiment. During a period of great scarcity between 1437 and 1440, a woman was arrested who butchered small children—her own?—salted them down, and sold them at the market in Abbeville. She was burned at the stake on the site of her crime.

Panicky behavior caused by siege-induced hunger was described in terms of Flavius's diktat, particularly when it was displayed by reprehensible heathens. This model was still in use as late as 1535, when the Christian world attempted to put an end to the realm of the Anabaptists in the German city of Münster. In January the city was besieged, and by April the hunger had become unbearable. People began eating grass, moss, and the chalk from whitewashed walls, as well as animals such as dogs, cats, mice, rats, and frogs.

FIGURE 20

Famine in Jerusalem in A.D. 70, with a mother devouring her own child. Tournai
tapestry of ca. 1465–1475 (detail).

Source: Tournai (Belgium), Musée de la Tapisserie.

They gnawed on the leather of old shoes and finally stooped to eating the
meat of human corpses. Certain of these details were undoubtedly true, but
such reports were inevitably colored by what people had for centuries come
to expect in accounts of siege-induced famine. If such particulars were
omitted, the chronicler ran the risk of not being believed or of failing to
communicate the direness of the situation.

The points named in Flavius's elaborate account, already so neatly presented
in medieval chronicles, lent strength to the topos of hunger. Authors sometimes seized upon later events of a similar nature to revive these stock horrors and embroider upon them. Radulfus Glaber, the French chronicler and
visionary, not to say gossipmonger, was convinced there had been unimag-

inable famine in the year 1033 and went very far indeed to prove his point. Where God had apparently dropped a stitch in the fabric of the story, Radulfus took up the thread again. He could, after all, boast of first-hand impressions supposedly drawn from his own childhood experience. Exactly one thousand years after the death of His son, God should actually have let the world perish, for the thousand-year reign of harmony and abundance described in the Book of Revelation should then have come to an end. A couple of decades after the fact, Glaber launched the story of the world's near-ruin, which continued to make the rounds for centuries. As late as the nineteenth century a number of French medievalists were still reporting the near-disappearance of humankind in the year 1033.

Alpertus of Metz told of a famine in 1006 that allegedly claimed a huge number of lives the whole world over. This resulted, here and there, in rather sloppy clearance of the corpses, so that "people who were still breathing, even if they resisted with all their remaining strength, were buried along with the dead." Glaber mentions a wild man of the woods—a popular symbol of barbarism—who butchered and ate passersby who ventured near his hut in the vicinity of Mâcon in Burgundy. The gnawed-off heads of no fewer than forty-eight of his victims were eventually discovered in his dwelling. This savage was burned alive: Radulfus Glaber saw it with his own eyes. A more widely known story connected with the disastrous famine of 1033 concerns the wolf. Because many bodies remained unburied at that time, the corpses fell prey to animals, and not only to natural scavengers. It was supposedly at this time that wolves acquired a taste for human flesh and have preyed on us ever since.

Not only historical accounts and chronicles but also sermons, songs, romances of chivalry, and all manner of literature steer a middle course, more or less successfully, along a monotonous route of famine descriptions that we may now label as topoi. Their relationship to the historical reality of a certain time and place is generally difficult to ascertain, although each of the forms of behavior described undoubtedly occurred many times. The compounding of details in any one instance, however, seems aimed more at rousing public sentiment than at critical and factually reliable reporting. This procedure was more readily approved of then than it is now. In those days historiography was meant to reveal a higher truth, the outward form of events being a matter of secondary importance. And that truth was always the same: horrible, yes, but only what such sinners and humankind in general deserved.

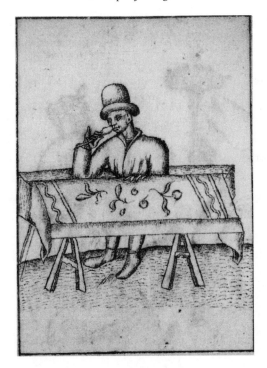

FIGURE 21

A man reduced to eating grass, reproduced
from *Proverbes en rime*, ca. 1485–1490.
Source: Baltimore, Walters Art Gallery,
MS W 313, fol. 65 verso.

The topoi occurring in nearly every description of famine sketch the following chain of events. For a long time, and against their better judgment,
people went on trying to make flour by diluting what was left of it with
sand, beans, straw, grass, wine lees, and even pig manure. When every last
grain of wheat, corn, or barley had been consumed, the auxiliary ingredients
were wolfed down on their own. People began grazing like animals, devouring anything that could be dug up or scoured off the earth, including car-
rots, herbs, grass, moss, tree bark, wild tubers, green corn shoots, and water
plants. This behavior seemed so natural that it even gave rise to various
adages. A French collection of proverbs dating from around 1485–1490, for

example, illustrates the sayings "Hunger makes people resourceful" and "Necessity is the mother of invention" with a drawing depicting a man eating a carrot and another of a man eating grass.

The next step in the process of degeneration was eating unclean and dead animals, sometimes even half-decayed or diseased by the plague. The animals in question were dogs, cats, donkeys, horses, and wolves, as well as frogs and snakes. Drawing blood from cattle for the sake of its nutritiousness was another regular occurrence, and this source of nutrition had the added advantage of not drying up instantly.

Foreign peoples were often accused of eating unclean beasts, just as they were often accused of doing everything that was taboo in the Christian West. And they didn't even have the excuse of scarcity. The point is continually stressed, and this is no coincidence, that only dire need drives people to such perverse behavior in this part of the world. Bestial behavior is undesirable under any circumstances, and descriptions of such conduct always convey the message that it is sinful. Moreover, by indulging in such behavior the hungry incriminate themselves even further, giving proof of the wickedness that apparently prompted God to punish them in the first place.

Let no one be in any doubt on this matter: in hell gluttons are condemned to eating all these unclean beasts. First the sinners—sitting at a bare table that proves, however, to be red-hot—are made to suffer such terrible hunger and thirst that they eventually beg for hay, dregs of wine, and finally excrement and urine. But even this is too good for them, because now the devils serve up the meal proper: "Raw and living toads are placed on the table before them, as well as snakes, dragons, and many another unclean beast. These they must eat in spite of themselves, for cruel devils stand over them and also sit on the table with large pincers and red-hot metal cudgels, to force the miserable souls to partake of this inhuman food." So it says in the *Boeck van der Voirsienicheit Godes* (Book of God's providence), a catalog of virtues and vices used in catechism and confession that was undoubtedly swallowed whole by Hieronymus Bosch, as evidenced by his depictions of hell, which he seems to have taken directly from this inventory of sins, transforming them into the most terrifying images any painter had created up to that time.

The fear of hunger took on a new dimension when one not only had to fear earthly death and the end of time but was also in danger of throwing away one's soul for all eternity. Hunger could lead quickly and almost impercepti-

FIGURE 22

Punishments awaiting gluttons in hell. Woodcut
appearing in the *Kalendrier des Bergiers*, 1496.

Source: Reproduced from E. Lehner, *Devils, Demons,
Death and Damnation* (New York, 1971), no. 72.

bly to the devil, propelling one along a path of ever more reprehensible forms of conduct. The most telling proof of this was cannibalism, dished up in many forms and a variety of cuisines as a last-ditch effort to stave off hunger.

In other, non-Christian cultures as well, cannibalism is considered a sign of absolute depravation, wholly alien to the indigenous culture. This model was already present in Livy's description of the ritual of the Bacchanalia, a rite of inversion during which one drank oneself into a stupor, ate insects and excrement, and abandoned oneself to total promiscuity and other forms of sexual debauchery. All order disintegrated, and complete chaos drove the participants to exact human sacrifices and consume human flesh. Later on, in the Middle Ages, such behavior would continually be imputed to foreign peoples, who functioned in the margins of Christian civilization like negatives, serving by way of contrast to bring Christian ideals more sharply into focus. In one's own circle as well, such behavior was ascribed, for example, to witches and heretics, in other words to all those who had already been possessed by, or taken into the service of, the devil.

In spite of all the warnings and punishments inflicted from above, humankind would inevitably sink to the most devilish depths imaginable, engulfed in absolute chaos and universal cannibalism, if God did not continue to intervene. He proclaims this Himself at the beginning of the morality play *Elckerlijc* (Everyman), which goes on to show, in precise and convincing terms, exactly how one can attain everlasting life:

> If I left the world much longer
> In this sad state, I fear at least
> That man would soon become a beast
> And on his fellows start to feast.

Any mortal could succumb to such behavior—the height of devilish inspiration—every time scarcity threatened. The many reported instances of cannibalism certainly seemed to imply that people quickly turned to it when forced by circumstances. Men and women were continually eating up their own and even other people's children, and there were also frequent reports of the reverse situation: children killing their parents to fill their stomachs. Neither was it unusual to dig up corpses to avail oneself of their nutritive value; to this end executed prisoners were also snatched from the gallows and the rack. Prisoners received even less to eat than ordinary hunger sufferers, which is why many newcomers to the jail were instantly murdered for the next meal. Numerous indeed were the reports of children who were lured away and kidnapped, travelers taken by surprise, and slaughterhouses set up to meet the demand created by the flourishing trade in human flesh, which could be passed off as pork when it was grilled.

The set pattern also included compelling descriptions of the terrifying sight of rotting bodies, their sheer numbers making it impossible to bury them all. The poor and sick were left to die along the wayside, and there was no longer anyone among the living with enough strength to give them a decent burial. Vast numbers are mentioned in this context: the cities and countryside appear to have been robbed of more than a third of their population. In Metz alone no fewer than five hundred thousand people were said to have succumbed to hunger in 1316. The medieval tendency to exaggerate figures is already familiar, but at any rate there were a great many victims, terrifying and unprecedented numbers of them.

No one living in the Middle Ages could have failed to recognize the truth of such stories, being convinced that such things could, did, and indeed were always about to happen. Fear kept all these topoi alive, and they in turn continued to feed the fear, constantly strengthened by the simple fact that something alarming always seemed to be disrupting the food supply. It was not until the breakthrough—after the Middle Ages—to more stable and better-regulated stocking and distribution of food that these age-old, existential fears could finally be laid to rest. Since then it has no longer been necessary to pray for one's daily bread, as though it were a blessing in danger of being withdrawn at any moment.

13
The Intoxicating Effect of Fasting

$\mathcal{A}$s LONG AS an intense fear of hunger persisted, there was a great need for comfort and moral support. Simply eating one's fill could not alleviate the fear, for it had nothing to do with palpable hunger but rather with the increasingly irrational and therefore unfathomable fear of famine. Daydreaming about a journey to the Land of Cockaigne or Luilekkerland was not the only answer, of course. A great many remedies were devised, so many, in fact, that they testify to the extent to which the fear of hunger kept all levels of society in thrall.

Oddly enough, simply not eating was one way of outwitting hunger as well as the fear of it. There were various ways of indulging in rigorous fasting, and—an added attraction—in a state of complete self-denial one was treated to the most wonderful visions. The unrivaled champions in this were the desert fathers of the first centuries after Christ, whose heroic deeds were emulated again and again. They were a rich source of inspiration for many, especially for devout women striving to lead a holy life.

The desert fathers excelled in sobriety and abstinence, thus lending support to their candidature for entry into paradise. The primal sin, after all, had always been gluttony, and it was thought one could atone for this by resolute fasting, even in a competitive context. Eating was a post-Fall indulgence and led to a fatal surplus of energy, causing people to gorge themselves even more, which in turn gave rise to feelings of anger and sexual arousal. Meat, in particular, was thought to stimulate sensuality. In addition, there was the conviction, supposedly based on scientific observation, that carnivores became what they ate, literally taking on the characteristics of the animals they consumed. For this reason a third-century church father forbade the eating of hares and hyenas, because these animals were known to be exceedingly promiscuous.

In Adam's day, even after the Fall, people had been vegetarians. Adam, still in easy circumstances, had set the example. In his original state he had a natural warmth that kept him alive, and he required sustenance only very occasionally. Owing to the well-deserved horrors obtaining since the Fall, God had allowed a small ration of meat as comfort and consolation. Since then, however, increasing sinfulness had caused meat eating to get out of hand, and it had become the driving force behind the decline of humankind. Everyone knew that gluttonous meat eaters stank more in their graves than did abstemious vegetarians.

Hence the action taken by the desert fathers, who were striving to regain Adam's natural state. Notable followers were also to be found among members of the Franciscan mendicant movements, who followed the example of their name giver (and through him the example of Jesus) and practiced mortification of the flesh by refusing all nourishment. Jacob van Maerlant—who around 1275 set the life of their founder to rhyme for the Friars Minor of Utrecht—painted the portrait of an unbending sufferer of hunger by vocation: whenever Saint Francis was given cooked food he would mix it with ashes or water to take away any hint of taste.

Excessive fasting was, of course, madness. In view of the frequently recurring periods of scarcity and especially the notorious fear of such recurrences, long-term, serious fasting was an act of true heroism for which only prospective saints could summon up the necessary courage. Hermits continually experimented with diets that brought them to the brink of death. From time to time—just to prove they were acting of their own free will (otherwise their fasting would be meaningless)—they gave public demonstrations of gorging to show that their ability to eat was still unimpaired.

As a token of recognition, those living a holy life received food directly from heaven, as witnessed by the story of a hermit inhabiting an island in the Celtic travel tales of Mael Dúin dating from the ninth century. Every day this hermit received half a loaf of bread, some fish, and water. Reminiscences of this are found in the widely told travel stories, possibly based on the tales of Mael Dúin, of the doubting monk Saint Brendan.

The need to work for one's daily bread derives from the sinful state of humankind since the Fall, from which time onward men and women were doomed to a life of toil. Even the noble savages, whose innocence enabled them to cling to a paradisiacal state of purity, obtained food effortlessly or could exist simply by inhaling the scent of spices or fragrant fruits. Apple sniffers crop up in all encyclopedic works with a section on exotic peoples.

Even Petrarch maintained that at the source of the Ganges there lived a people who nourished themselves with the scent of crab apples, nasty smells of any kind being intolerable to them.

The miraculous dispensation of food sometimes refers so explicitly to the Bible that it must have been clear to everyone to what extent the paradisiacal state was still attainable and worth striving for. After all, weren't there people known as the Camerini who received their daily bread in a shower from heaven? Even sniffing an apple a day in lieu of eating bread evokes pictures of paradise—a somewhat forced picture, admittedly, but nonetheless valid as long as one bears in mind that the apple on its own can cause no mischief.

Divine sanctions regarding fasting revealed themselves in even more sanctified emergency rations. Nuns given to extreme fasting appeared in the end to be living on nothing but consecrated wafers. The pinnacle of earthly abnegation, however, took the form of self-mortification inflicted by eating pus from the wounds of the sick. Conversely, one's own bodily fluids could also serve as nourishment and strengthening medicine for others. The suffering endured by Lidwina of Schiedam (1380–1433) is a bizarre example of such obsessions with food and fasting, though she was not alone in her languishment. There are many records of similar exercises indulged in by female saints and also, on a more modest scale, by many a lay sister from the circles of the Devotio Moderna in the IJssel region of the Netherlands.

Eating sanctified body parts and secretions, as well as feeding them to the sick and infirm, was inevitably associated with the Eucharist. Christianity cultivated a form of sacrosanct cannibalism, and this had been given its ultimate expression in the Gospel According to Saint John: "I am that bread of life. Your fathers did eat manna in the wilderness, and are dead. This is the bread which cometh down from heaven, that a man may eat thereof, and not die. I am the living bread which came down from heaven: if any man eat of this bread, he shall live for ever: and the bread that I will give is my flesh, which I will give for the life of the world." In the Eucharist the savior perpetually offers His body in the form of bread and wine. This food chain comes full circle when one achieves the state of perfection that makes all other nourishment unnecessary and also—to go one step further—repeatedly puts one's body at the disposal of the sick and weak, nourishing them in a supreme example of *imitatio Christi*.

FIGURE 23

Christ as food. Painting from the circle of Friedrich Herlin, 1469.

Source: Reproduced from C. Walker Bynum, *Holy Feast and Holy Fast: The Religious Significance of Food to Medieval Women* (Berkeley, 1987), plate 4.

The unrestrained manner in which the eating of Jesus' body was expressed and portrayed in the late Middle Ages—in images evocative of a caterer's paradise—indicate to what extent large segments of the population were bent on finding a definite solution to the problem of food shortages. The controversial lay preacher Johannes Brugman knew better than anyone how to stir up these sentiments in his sermons: in one magnificent example he treats the divine dispensation of food and its high point, the Last Supper. On this occasion Jesus provided "top-quality wheat, which was His holy body." This was then made into a pancake—the Holy Sacrament—and the following day "He was roasted on the cross."

Those who find this overly vulgar should remember that Augustine also used such imagery when he preached that His body was "sown in the Holy Virgin, fermented in the flesh, baked in the oven of the grave, and seasoned in the churches that daily distribute divine nourishment to the pious." Jan van Ruusbroec followed suit in the fourteenth century: "And on the following day the holy Lamb was tortured, killed, and roasted on the cross because of our sins, so that we could taste of it."

Since God himself had become food, food had—in one way or another—taken on a special meaning. By partaking of Him one also partook of the tortures His flesh had endured on the cross, thereby freeing oneself from all earthly cares. Such a state of perfect detachment is expressed in the earliest texts, one example being an Easter hymn dating from the fifth century, which is no less direct, judging by the now familiar terminology: "[We are] looking forward to the supper of the Lamb . . . whose sacred body is roasted on the altar of the cross. By drinking His rosy blood, we live with God."

During the first centuries of Christianity the faithful were accused by the Romans, on the basis of an intentional misunderstanding of their ritual sacrifice and its graphic expression, of cannibalism and sexual excesses. In their catacombs they allegedly consumed the flesh and blood of humans. It was said that when a woman became pregnant they waited until the embryo was large enough before aborting and eating it, though not without first seasoning it with honey, pepper, and other spices, as well as myrrh, to ensure that it would be palatable. Such stories are part of anti-Christian propaganda, which, later on, Christianity itself let fly—with just as little discernment—at so-called pagan peoples such as Jews and Muslims.

Taking place on the sidelines was a spiritualization of Roman banqueting traditions, which also helps to explain why such ideas and practices were so quick to capture the Western imagination. Priapus, the Roman god of virility, was often molded into a dessert. Sometimes his impressive genitals sufficed to create a delectable priapic pastry, as described by Martial in an epigram: "If you want to satisfy your hunger you can eat my Priapus; you may gnaw his very groin, yet you will be undefiled." A culture therefore arose that not only expressed and depicted the partaking of Christ in very graphic terms—as a means of obtaining consolation, protection, identification, and divine perfection—but also transformed the bodily parts of saints into delicacies. In the Franciscan monastery at Nicosia there lay, still intact, the body of the crusader Jan van Montfoort, a follower of the greatest Christian hero of all time, Godfrey of Bouillon. His body, impervious to decay, was visited daily because of the miracles it allegedly brought about. Joos van Ghistele, however, on his way from Ghent to the Holy Land in 1481, was dismayed to find that a bit of flesh was missing from the arm of the centuries-old corpse. Upon inquiry it appeared that a descendant had taken a bite out of it, after being denied a relic of his hallowed forefather.

Saint Lawrence also tried until the bitter end to bestow his blessings on the heathens. Condemned to being burned alive, he lay bleeding and sizzling on a red-hot griddle, attempting nonetheless to convert his tormentors to the true religion. When at last the only thing he had to offer was his roasted body, "he asked the tyrant if he wanted to eat his flesh, for he was nearly cooked through, and the meat was beginning to fall off the bone."

Perhaps the great desire for relics must also be seen in this light, as illustrated by a story Sir John Mandeville told about the burial customs of an exotic people living in the isles adjacent to the land of Prester John:

> In this land it is a custom everywhere that when any man's father is dead and his son wants to honor him, he sends for all the kinsfolk, his good friends, priests of their religion, minstrels and others; and they carry the body to a hill with great solemnity and great rejoicing. When they get there, the most important priest strikes off the dead man's head and lays it on a great platter of silver, or of gold if he is a rich man, and gives it to his son. And then all his friends sing and say many prayers, and then the priests and religious men

of their cult hew the body into small pieces and say many prayers. And birds of that land, familiar with this custom, gather there and hover around them—vultures, eagles, ravens, and other raptors; the priests throw this flesh to them, and they carry it a little way off and eat it. . . . Then the son boils his father's head, and the flesh from it he distributes among his special friends, giving each one a little bit, as a dainty. And from the cranium of the head he has a cup made, and he drinks from it all his lifetime in remembrance of his father.

If fervent fasting did not lead directly to paradise, and if one suspected that this long road of self-inflicted deprivation was only the harbinger of eternal fasting in the hereafter, there were interim gratifications to be had in the form of sneak previews, which were classified as full-fledged visions. As was only to be expected, these usually provided an idea of the culinary delights on offer in the hereafter. It is interesting to speculate whether in those days people even wanted to understand that such mirages of heavenly fare were a joint product of mind and body. Constant food shortages and chronic deficiencies of vitamins, glucose, and enzymes easily lead to hallucinations, reduced coordination, and severely diminished powers of reason and discernment. In short, starvation leads to a radical narrowing of consciousness. Add to this the fervent desire for heavenly rewards for earthly abstinence, and steaming platters of food soon start looming up—food no longer wrapped up in problems of procurement or self-imposed prohibition.

Modern insight of this sort is not called for here, however. Even those desert fathers, emaciated nuns, and macerating monks received their just deserts. There's no reward for insufficient suffering, as evidenced by the otherwise rather obscure abbot Apollonius and his companions, who were visited in their cells by angels and given a taste of the pleasures of the heavenly paradise. In a vision they saw huge apples, enormous bunches of grapes, exotic fruits, and warm loaves of white bread. Extreme heat and cold had given way to the balminess of fragrant breezes that caressed the fruit trees. Fasting not only quells the fear of hunger to the extent that one is practically immune to the need for food, but it also has spiritual rewards, glorifying fine food in the proper way: Cockaigne, in other words, with the Supreme Being's own seal of approval.

The dreamworlds arising from less far-fetched circumstances have a more impromptu nature. In preindustrial Europe a large part of the population was thought to be walking around in a half-drugged state much of the time. The reason for this was not only lack of food, which produced hallucinatory dreams, but also the necessity of eating nutritional substitutes with bewitching effects. An overdose of spoiled food, leaves, bran, and fermented drinks could easily give rise to protracted fantasizing.

This process was speeded up by eating—out of sheer necessity—mushrooms, toadstools, and grasses of all kinds. It must have been incredible, the sight of an entire community betaking itself to the poppy fields for want of anything better to eat. Such behavior was reported in early-modern Italy, where people also deliberately sniffed salves and lotions in the hope of sailing away on a cloud of bliss. In the rest of Europe as well, there had been reports in preceding centuries of bread made of poppy extract and even of hemp-seed flour being used to make bread dough.

Such diets inevitably gave rise to distorted visions of reality that could be so terrifying that hunger sufferers, in their quasi-delirious state, readily transformed them into nirvanas of nourishment, although afterward it appeared that such experiences were only fit to be passed on by word of mouth. Even so, the dreams continued to live on as compensation. The effect of this physiologically induced dream factory, which certainly did much to sow hallucinations and visions during periods of scarcity, was not unknown at the time. In his treatise *The Praise of Folly*, Erasmus based his satirical treatment on the assumption that his readers were familiar with narcotic drugs, even if their knowledge had been acquired through hearsay. His protagonist, Folly herself, was born in the Fortunate Isles (which some presume to be identical with the Islands of the Blessed and others maintain are something altogether different), a paradisiacal dream of antiquity that the Middle Ages readily adopted and situated in the Canary Islands. There she was taught while still in the cradle to sniff hypnotic herbs that made her crazy as well as forgetful. Laughing, she forgot all her cares and felt young again, though talking gibberish and continually taking leave of her senses were the unfortunate side effects. Herein, of course, lay the source of all Folly.

In the West one also heard rumors of the feared Turks, whose madcap courage was attributed to their use of opium, which "made them happy and not at all afraid to die, and made it seem as though they'd taken leave of their senses, or as though they were half drunk." These were the words used in a graphic description of the Turks' behavior distributed as a scandal sheet by the press in 1542. This passage was nearly lost in an avalanche of rabble-rousing recitals of similar sentiments, which deluded more minds in all of Europe than noxious weeds were ever capable of doing.

Reports of the hallucinatory effects of recurring malnourishment, the use of alternative foodstuffs, and the conscious use of intoxicating substances are generally negative. Only pious fasting and its accompanying visions could count on admiration and imitation, affording—in contrast to folly and stupidity—glimpses of an attainable perfection. Moreover, hallucinations of lavish meals in luxurious surroundings could even bear the heavenly hallmark, though it appeared that no material means were allowed in achieving this, so that there was nothing to do but sit back hungrily and wait.

The preeminent teller of travelers' tales Sir John Mandeville found an attractive means of bridging the gap between proper and improper daydreaming by telling tales of unheard-of amenities in lands with a surprisingly unobjectionable form of proto-Christianity. Halfway to Ethiopia is the land of Job, where one's daily bread falls from the skies like manna from heaven. This food resembles dew, for one can scrape it off the plants and shrubs, and when eaten it appears to have a soporific effect and also to ward off melancholy. Administered daily, this heavenly intoxicant keeps the devil at bay, who would otherwise seize upon a melancholic state to bring humankind to rack and ruin. In that land a narcotic drug of divine making creates a paradise on earth: not only is the devil banished forever, but work is banned as well, because everything one needs simply rains down from the skies.

Many people were later surprised by the numerous visions and other spiritual vistas opened up in the Middle Ages to endow earthly existence with an added dimension. Scores of theological and salvational explanations have been sought for this, which in themselves are not without merit, though they fail to explain why so many people so frequently ventured on these devotional dream trips. Or should we say delivered themselves up to them? The question is even more pressing in those cases in which the devil succeeded in perverting dream journeys to serve his own purpose, providing yet more proof of the popularity of such hallucinatory trips, which were undertaken with impunity in spite of their apparent hazards.

One must nonetheless bear in mind the uncertain outcome of these excursions, even though all those saints and hermits, as well as a whole army of enthusiastic monks and nuns, would like us to believe otherwise. Rigorous fasting could be a conscious choice, but the consequences were unpredictable. Much has been written in recent years about the possible causes and effects of extreme eating disorders among women. Connections with deep-seated beliefs in the necessity of suffering, linked by some to syndromes such as anorexia nervosa, have found widespread recognition, also as an explanation for past events. Lidwina of Schiedam, intentionally starving and slowly dying from wounds sustained in a skating accident in 1395, has at last found a sympathetic following. She, too, was rewarded with appetizing visions of saints dining in the heavenly paradise—a practically inevitable result of her constant refusal of all nourishment.

This physical factor—automatically stimulated by surrogate foodstuffs in times of scarcity and consciously sought by those who craved the effects of intoxicants—deserves greater attention in the study of the medieval mind in general. Where did the penchant for mysticism come from otherwise? Communion with the Most High was wrested, as it were, from feverish dreams, with an impatience and deep disdain for earthly imperfection that could inspire unbelievably fine literature. The human condition was dependent in the Middle Ages on a food supply so fickle that it could not help inciting illusions of a better world. There was more to it than mere dreaming, of course, but Cockaigne was born and reborn from illusions kindled again and again in the minds of pious young women, fasting clerics, and fearful hunger sufferers.

14
Gorging in Self-Defense

*I*N CONTRAST to the strategy of not eating, with its accompanying dream trips, a more earthly variety of resistance consisted in gorging while the supplies lasted. Both tactics could dispel vague fears of hunger or at least banish them temporarily. "When the belly is full, the head is happy" are the words of a proverb, various versions of which graced the pages of many a manuscript. Belly worship apparently took on such extravagant proportions that the church was forced to launch an antigluttony offensive. Jan de Weert, the physician and moralist—an especially happy combination in this context—declared that the only God many people knew was "their own putrid paunch." With these words he was paraphrasing the apocryphal evangelist Thomas, who—through Saint Paul—prompted the medieval exegesis of viewing gluttons as violators of the First Commandment. Didn't they worship another God, namely, their bellies?

Many priests and lay preachers repeated the words of Jan de Weert. One turned one's belly into God, and one's kitchen into the house of God. The "Aernout brothers"—the term used for a so-called brotherhood of drifters—also had an ironical rule that taught belly worship. This rule was best observed at the courts of the nobility, where, in the consecrated kitchen, one flattered and praised the personnel, adopting prayer and song in the service of mouth and stomach. The only worry known to this congregation of spongers was filling one's belly, and their only sacred duty the demonstration of complete idleness.

Eating is a sign of decadence. The Roman Christian Tertullian accused those compatriots of his who persisted in being heathens of indulging in disgusting, gluttonous marathons, emphasizing by way of contrast the absolute sobriety of those sharing his religious beliefs: "The air turns sour from the belching of all those patricians, senators, and politicians. When the Salius family sits down to eat they have to take out a bank loan. . . . And the fire brigade hurries to the scene when they see the smoke produced by a dinner for Serapis." In the central panel of his triptych *The Adoration of the Golden Calf,* Lucas van Leyden underscores unbridled gluttony in particular. It is the fat, sybaritic individuals who, despite their dancing and flirting, appear to be bent on guzzling and gorging. In the center is a table with an enormous leg of ham, gripped by a man of massive proportions, while a chubby child sits on the lap of its shapely mother and munches on food clutched in its fat little hand.

Blowouts, unmistakably hedonistic in character, are un-Christian rituals that attempt to disavow death by temporarily keeping it at a safe distance. Gregory of Tours recounted pagan practices of this sort that took place in the sixth century, telling of peasants in Auvergne who betook themselves on certain days to a large lake, into which they threw all kinds of textiles, as well as cheeses, beeswax, and masses of bread of all sorts, baked in all shapes and sizes: "With cartloads of food and drink they went to that spot, sacrificed animals, and gorged themselves for three whole days." As usual, it took only one priest to convert them all. The plain truth of Christianity was an easy match even for dozens of demanding deities.

Pagan religions are populated by a variety of gods demanding, as well as bringing, nourishment. William of Auvergne describes a female demon called Satia "who brings plenitude to the houses she visits." He believes her name to be derived from *satietas* (satiety), and she is also known as Lady Abundia (*abundantia,* or abundance). She consumes whatever she finds in the houses she visits, but the quantities of food and drink are in no way diminished by this, especially if the pots and pans have been intentionally left open for her. Where there is no food to be found, however, she brings bad luck. Pre-Christian peasant rituals such as this also betray a fixation on a food supply that might be disrupted at any moment.

Throughout the whole of the Middle Ages there were eyewitness reports of panic-stricken binges, which seem to have been on the increase toward the end of this period. Every opportunity was seized to stuff oneself to the gills, as though death by starvation were just around the corner. Galbert of Bruges recounts that people, staring the specter of hunger in the eye, devoured as much bread in one sitting as they usually ate in two days, and in Ghent the Lenten fast was broken when meat suddenly appeared to be available but no bread. This attitude was aptly expressed by Till Eulenspiegel—Howleglas in the first English translation, which appeared around

FIGURE 24

Ritual meal partaken of by the Normans shortly before the Battle of
Hastings (1066). Detail from the so-called Tapestry of Bayeux.

Source: Reproduced from J. M. van Winter, *Van soeter cokene: Recepten uit de
oudheid en middeleeuwen* (Haarlem, 1976), 49.

1560—who offered his starving mother a stolen loaf of bread with the
words, "Eat now, when you have it, and fast when you don't have any."
Indeed, a very sensible approach to life.

This attitude did not arise from any lack of piety but was born of a
pragmatism necessitated by the constant fear of a sudden food shortage.
One ate to excess whenever possible and preferably in company, since communal feasting suggested a ritual surfeit designed to banish all thoughts of
scarcity. During the early Middle Ages in particular, banqueting had a nearly
sacred significance, implying bonds of friendship and solidarity capable of
keeping all evil at bay. Later on, the face of such all-out feasting changed as
it increasingly came to be used as a display of princely power.

The original function of avowed solidarity in the struggle for survival
actually spans the entire Middle Ages, manifesting itself in the various
names used to describe a multiplicity of festive meals, such as the
convivium—a meal of reconciliation at which formerly feuding parties swore

friendship to one another—the kermis feast, the harvest festival, Easter dinner, Christmas dinner, and all the other meals that marked important events in life, including the seasonal feasts following the slaughtering of animals in November or celebrating the spoils of the hunt. The triumph of life was celebrated time and again, a life that not only refused to surrender to death but also challenged it by extravagant eating in an unbeatable collective.

Among the ancient Franks the big eater was a veritable cult hero. Charlemagne, according to medieval notions the most renowned king of all time, swung back and forth between the Christian doctrine of temperance and the Frankish tradition's macho model of the glutton, the latter usually being the winner. According to Jacob van Maerlant, Charlemagne's daily rations included a quarter of a sheep or two capons, a whole goose, a joint of beef, a peacock, and a crane or a hare, depending on what he felt like. The prototype, however, came from the world of Germanic myth, in which ruffians reigned who were capable of stowing away huge amounts of food. In the *Younger Edda* (also known as the *Prose Edda*)—written by the Icelandic poet and historian Snorri Sturluson around 1222–1223—Loki challenges onlookers to compete with him in wolfing down a gigantic plateful of meat. Logi accepts the challenge and wins by "polishing off all the meat, the bones, and even the dish." Heroes of this ilk are frequently found in Germanic mythology, as well as in many a romance belonging to the Carolingian epic.

In the *Chanson de Guillaume* the main character retreats from the fray, disappointed in the outcome, his only consolation a joint of wild boar, a roast peacock, a large loaf of bread, and two cakes. His wife then remarks that anyone whose constitution allows him to eat so much food should not be forced to admit defeat. Just before this scene, she serves her husband's nephew a huge meal that he loses no time in devouring, which all goes to show that he is destined to become a great warrior and a worthy member of her husband's family.

In stark contrast to these big bruisers—who drag themselves, belching and farting, across the battlefield—is the courtly hero of the British-Celtic romances of chivalry, who flies the flag of temperance. In the German story *Erec*, a knight comes to take part in a tournament, having fortified himself with only three bites of chicken. Moreover, according to Gottfried von Strassburg, in their *minnegrot* Tristan and Isolde were able to exist on nothing but love.

Huge blowouts and fantasies thereof were not only the result of worries about food shortages and the fear of famine. Another stimulus was the sharp contrast they provided with the austerity and abstinence of the many days of compulsory fasting. The church stipulated no fewer than 140 to 160 fast days that demanded total abstention from meat. Compensation for this was sought in the equally numerous holidays of a national, regional, and local nature, which provided the opportunity for culinary excesses that would dull the memory of all those days of fasting, after which one was hungrier than usual anyway.

The rhythm of the peasant's life also brought about a natural contrast in patterns of consumption. Winter was a time of excessive eating. The work had been done, the animals slaughtered in November, and the provisions laid in. Plowing and sowing would not begin until the spring, which meant that in the dead of winter work on the land came to a standstill. One turned to eating and celebrating, which coincided almost automatically with the great number of holidays during the transition from winter to summer. The high point was the long, drawn-out celebration of Carnival, which not only culminated in veritable pig-outs but also in the ritualized fantasies of such. Afterward, spring and summer were ushered in with purgative fasting. By then the food supplies had been depleted, and once again there was hard work to be done, calling for a soberness that would not be rewarded until the late autumn.

Clerical discipline, festive ritual, and the peasant life found themselves locked in a pattern determined by a compelling dialectic of enforced frugality and equally obligatory indulgence. This does not mean to say that the church kept its distance from such compensatory celebrations. Since the early Middle Ages it had also had its own Feast of Fools and Carnival celebrations, which were certainly not without their share of food and drink. In addition, there was the more exclusive form of *minnedrinken*, which underscored solidarity within the monastic community by means of festive gatherings during which dining—not to say gluttonizing—was the main motif. Excuses for these banquets were found several times a year, usually on Christian feast days, though the abbot's birthday or the death of a fellow monk could also provide the occasion for festivities. In particular the *Johannesminne*, or toast to Saint John, often turned into an extravagant banquet, certainly related to the exuberant folk festivities taking place on his birthday, 24 June.

Related to this was the custom of *caritas* drinking, whereby every toast proposed in honor of a saint called for the draining of one's cup. These practices are often seen, not without reason, as the Christianizing of pagan libations to the gods and the dead, of which the drinking that took place upon the death of a monk is certainly reminiscent. The Land of Cockaigne links up with such ritual revelry at the end of line 81 in the London text with "the Feast of Saint John." The words preceding this disappeared with the missing corner, but Cockaigne must have offered four Feasts of Saint John every year—at least that is what the text must have said, going by the context of holidays in multiples of four: four celebrations of Easter, Whitsun, and Christmas, as opposed to fasting only once every hundred years. This offered a considerable increase in the number of opportunities for inordinate indulgence.

Quite apart from the feasts ordained by liturgical and ritual calendars, Western European clerics were known for their capacity to eat. The call for moderation and even absolute abstinence as a typical Christian ideal was a matter of some note within the church. According to the Roman Curia, priests in the north of Italy—in spite of the order to eat "normal amounts"—actually ate Pantagruelesque portions. As late as 1059, reminders were issued at the Lateran Synod of the apparently unforgettable excesses that had taken place at a church conference in Aachen in 816. Was it the great Charlemagne himself, with his Frankish gulosity, or only his spirit that had haunted the gathering? At that time the canons had really overindulged, consuming gigantic portions that seemed "more suited to the greediness of cyclops than to Christian moderation."

Yet the priests were no competition for the nobility. Though the Frankish champions of consumption give us a taste of things to come, truly lavish entertaining—with tables as long as airport runways, filled to overflowing—had yet to get off the ground. By the thirteenth century, however, the spadework had been done: in courtly circles, banqueting had become the preeminent means of social distinction. From its function as a community gathering, the simple knightly feast had gradually taken on the proportions of a sumptuous banquet, intended to exhibit wealth and might. The heirs to power decked themselves out as extravagantly and regally as possible to show that they would bow to no one. Royal households were all fully equipped to mount ostentatious displays of grandeur. Townspeople in particular had to be put in their place, for they dared to camouflage their covetousness with the artificial pomp of the nouveaux riches. Having blue blood meant giving oneself over to extravagance and noisy demonstrations of affluence, leaving no room for doubt as to one's aversion to all forms of bourgeois small-mindedness.

This determination to astound the bourgeoisie could take on very concrete forms. At a banquet in Bologna in 1487 the various dishes, before being served, were shown one by one to the commoners outside. This calls to mind the teasing remark made by the prologue speaker in the Latin school play *Aluta* dating from 1535, written for the Carnival celebration by the school rector Macropedius (Joris van Lancvelt) and intended for performance by his pupils. He announces that the most magnificent banquet will be seen onstage, but—he hastens to add—the pheasants, geese, pigeons, thrushes, and meat pies will not fly into your mouth, though just the sight of all that wonderful food may be enough to make you feel comfortably full. Macropedius was undoubtedly referring to Cockaigne and knew that his pupils were just as likely to be thinking of it, too. Moreover, he shrewdly pointed out that such displays of abundance could function as compensation for appetizing food that is out of reach.

This lavishing of food also included public fountains that spouted various sorts of wine and sometimes beer as well. It had all started at the table, though the fountain fad soon took on unmanageable proportions that sometimes required its spurting antics to be removed to other parts of the banqueting hall and even out of doors. In the thirteenth century the table fountain made its appearance, functioning more as a game than as a practical way of dispensing drinks. Sometimes its possibilities were confined to the washing of hands, but most table fountains spouted drinks of various kinds. Some were mounted with wheels that set little bells in motion, and it was not unusual to deck them out as ships.

Above all, these fountains were useful for practical jokes, spouting unexpectedly in equally unexpected directions. Another source of amusement consisted in replacing the wine with another substance, whereby the most vulgar effects were probably not shunned. The medieval sense of humor is perhaps the furthest removed from our present-day forms of behavior. The infliction of serious injury and the loss of control of bodily functions were at that time considered humorous high points, whereas today we endure them silently and with consternation. Moreover, education and background played no role in such behavior. On the contrary, it was precisely nobles and aristocrats, as well as members of the higher clergy, who were wont to indulge in fun and games of this kind.

In addition to such dubious uses, however, table fountains were also wrapped up in symbolism and allegory, having an obvious connection with the fountain of youth. This dream also occurs in Cockaigne, in the London manuscript.

At the wedding of Anthony of Burgundy and Elizabeth of Gorlitz in Brussels in 1409, the reception hall featured a mermaid who spouted red wine from one breast and white wine from the other. This miracle was also shown to the people outside, to impress them as well as to win their allegiance. From around 1380 onward, such wine spouters were never lacking at triumphal entries of royalty and other noble festivities in France and the Low Countries, though it was not always clear whose generosity they were meant to reflect, that of the sovereign or that of the local aristocracy.

On the occasion of the triumphal entry of Philip the Good in 1440, the city of Bruges made various arrangements, including a pillar bearing a stone statue of a youth who constantly urinated a fragrant wine called hypocras. The marketplace was supplied with a fountain spouting both red and white wine and, in addition, a statue of a young woman whose breasts flowed continually with milk. What greater vision of charity could one imagine? At the court something even more artful had been devised: an imitation camel mounted by a Saracen holding a bottle from which wine constantly flowed.

When it was its turn in 1458, the city of Ghent did things in even grander style, no doubt intentionally, for the cities tended to vie with each other in such matters. The efforts were aimed not only at currying favor with the duke but also at displaying a pomp and circumstance—equal to his— that commanded respect of its own accord. Here a large fountain was installed from which various wines flowed, with no less ambitious an aim in mind than evoking the fountain of life in paradise, from which four rivers flowed forth to water the earth. There was also an elephant—naturally somewhat larger than the Bruges camel—equipped with a handy spout in the form of its trunk, which trumpeted forth an uninterrupted stream of wine.

In 1468, however, Bruges hit back hard on the occasion of the wedding of Charles the Bold and Margaret of York and yet again for the triumphal entry of Charles V in 1515. At that time statues were actually erected of three women standing back to back who spouted red wine, white wine, and milk from their breasts. The spectators could not believe their eyes: the statues were so lifelike that people were convinced they must in fact be real women with magical powers.

At any rate, certain aspects of both Cockaigne and Luilekkerland were continually being brought to life. Dispensing free wine and beer was not unknown at medieval festivals, whether indoors or out, whether staged by the nobility or by burghers eager to make an impression. The provision of drink in real rivers lends these fantasies a touch of the grotesque that went too far for everyday life and therefore granted these make-believe worlds their right to exist.

The demonstrative battle against hunger and death (and in fact any kind of earthly decay) by means of endless feasting that was also intended as an advertisement of power took on such spectacular proportions at the end of the Middle Ages that the results were truly mind-boggling. To begin with, the amounts of food that were stowed away are almost inconceivable. The food consumed at the Pheasant Banquet in Lille in 1454—where the host, Philip the Good, toyed for the last time with the idea of undertaking a crusade—included nine thousand loaves of white bread, forty-eight hundred gourmet breads, six barrels of Germolian wine, twenty-four barrels of Beaune wine, two barrels of hypocras, eight hundred chicken pies, sixteen hundred roast pigs, sixteen hundred pieces of roast veal, and sixteen hundred legs of mutton—these figures give the impression that everyone was meant to eat one of each of these items—four hundred pieces of wild fowl, six hundred partridges, fourteen hundred rabbits, four hundred herons, thirty-six peacocks, and six horses laden with confectionery. This display, too, was doubtless meant to teach the bourgeoisie a lesson: feast your eyes, for this is the proper way to eat.

15
Food in Motion

THE MAIN CAUSE of excitement at these banquets was not the amount of food consumed. The most important aspect was the artful arrangement of all those delicacies, some of which were geared to take part in animated spectacles. Whole battles, abductions, sieges, hunting parties, and shipwrecks were portrayed in, through, between, and with the help of food. A special form of table humor consisted in rendering the ingredients unrecognizable, masking tastes, and molding meat to look like fish, fish like fowl, and fowl like meat. Surprise courses and disguised dishes were among the high points of aristocratic dining pleasure. What could be more fun than a rabbit made of dough, especially when a hungry knight bit into it? Serving up a giant egg made of a pig's bladder could also do a lot to raise the guests' spirits.

A well-known number was the seemingly live peacock, roasted and carefully sewn together again, with lit camphor and wool in its beak to make it spit fire. Another popular treat was a variation on this theme using a pig: when it was cut open it spewed forth an avalanche of blood sausages, each one wreathed in an array of tiny sausages. At the wedding of Charles the Bold in 1468 there was also a wondrously large whale, from whose mouth singing mermaids and dancing sea knights unexpectedly appeared. The effect created by hidden attractions was also extremely popular. As early as the twelfth century there are stories of enormous cakes in which little birds were enclosed. When the cake was cut open the birds escaped in a chirping swarm, but order was quickly restored by pygmy falcons let loose in the hall.

Edible architecture of epic proportions began to make its appearance on banqueting tables, offering an almost immediate realization of what one could only dream of in Cockaigne. Starting in around 1200, cookbooks began to offer descriptions of how to make these edible structures, which, it must not be forgotten, were also meant to tell a story. For example, there is a recipe for the portrayal of a fight between a snake and a dove in an arena of cake, which in its turn is encircled by entrails stuffed with delicacies. The recipe does not, however, specify whether the fighting animals are real or whether they, too, consist of baked goods.

In practice things were carried to even greater extremes. One of the entremets—side dishes, or in-between courses—served at a banquet given by the French king Charles V in 1378 consisted of a representation of the siege of Jerusalem during the first crusade. As I have already noted, mentioning Jerusalem and siege in the same breath invariably conjured up the most shocking visions of extreme famine, which means that this ingeniously modeled display of delectables must have been highly spiced with irony. The representation was dominated by models of the crusaders' ships, which also served to hold the silverware and tasting utensils used by a special functionary to determine whether it was safe for the rest of the company to tuck in.

Ships were an especially popular element in these epic displays of edible architecture. The main table at one of the banquets marking the marriage of Charles the Bold displayed six ships, each of which bore an enormous meat dish with the name of one of the territories under Charles's rule. Around these ships sailed sixteen smaller vessels, each accompanied by four boats filled with spices and fruit. The great ships, painted in gold and azure, were even supplied with coats of arms and other devices. The cities in Charles's territories had to be satisfied with cakes bearing their names and coats of arms.

One of the most amazing examples of edible architecture with a narrative element was undoubtedly the representation displayed (and, one hopes, consumed) at a banquet given on the Tuesday of the weeklong wedding festivities in question. The masterpiece represented the Tower of Gorcum (a town, still famous for its brick tower, in the present-day province of South Holland). I give the floor to the previously mentioned Bruges rhetorician Anthonis de Roovere, who certainly knew the ropes as far as celebrating was concerned, though here he appears to have been little more than a gaping burgher. It even seems as though he wanted to distance himself from amusements of this kind:

There were goats playing the shawm and the trumpet, imitation donkeys singing, wild boars playing large flutes, and bears playing lutes, all performing one after the other. There was also a watch-

FIGURE 25

Edible portrayal of the siege of Jerusalem served at a banquet given by Charles V
of France in 1378. Miniature appearing in a chronicle dating from ca. 1380.
Source: Reproduced from J. M. van Winter, *Van soeter cokene: Recepten uit de oudheid en middeleeuwen*
(Haarlem, 1976), 50.

man on the tower who recited an appropriate rhyme between each
performance. At the end a troupe of monkeys appeared, who performed morris dances, causing a great deal of laughter. At the
tower the monkeys met a hawker who was asleep, and they subsequently robbed him of his mirrors, hairpins, and combs and gave
these to the young ladies, all of which combined to produce a thoroughly idiotic spectacle.

One should always bear in mind that this aristocratic variety show was packaged in food and partially—in the case of the animals displaying human behavior—made of food. Comestibles were transformed into theatrical displays and "consumed" as such. Until well into the sixteenth century scenes were staged that featured mobile food normal people would probably have refused to eat, though perhaps consumption was no longer the point.

If the word *decadence* now springs to mind, then it must be mentioned that Roman cuisine went to even greater lengths, with deceit being the touchstone of culinary art. Roman decadence took the form of meat modeling that gave rise to a whole industry of adulteration. The "art" consisted in taking inferior ingredients and transforming them, at least as far as form and taste were concerned, into costly foodstuffs. Sauces were naturally an important instrument of camouflage in this game. Petronius tells of a famous chef who conjured up a whole range of dishes from parts of a pig. He made, for example, a fish from a pig's uterus, a wood pigeon from bacon, a turtle dove from ham, and a chicken from a pig's shank. Another chef served up entire meals consisting of nothing but zucchini, the dishes appearing to be everything from fish and mushrooms to black pudding and sweet pastry.

Roman cuisine seemed to be based entirely on deceit. The most highly renowned chefs earned their reputation by virtue of their mastery in falsifying foods. In Pompeii, too, bronze baking molds have been found in the form of poultry, pigs, and rabbits. Less talented cooks could fill these with ingredients that at least took on the form of the desired animal. A spicy sauce could also remedy a host of evils as regards taste.

Representations of medieval eating spectacles were also expressed in other ways. The human behavior displayed by animals in a topsy-turvy world, which was the source of such hilarity in 1468, was repeatedly portrayed in literature and particularly in the margins of illuminated manuscripts. Above all, it appears that edible architecture was not limited to the world of dreams or fairy tales but was also a regular feature in a long culinary tradition of the affluent aristocracy. Even though the image of inhabitable foodstuffs took on various forms, they all sparred with similar weapons in their efforts to combat the fear of food shortages by conjuring up an overabundance as ridiculous as it was fanciful.

In the make-believe world of lying tales, to which the Cockaigne and Luilekkerland texts certainly belong, such alternative architecture occurs in myriad forms. Even weapons could consist of food. Around 1550 the Bruges rhetorician Eduard de Dene described in a humorous refrain in his *Testament rhetoricael* how peasants storming a castle were armed with weapons made of pastry. A French tall tale lays it on even more thickly, recounting the story of "la grande confrarie des soulx d'ouvrer" (the great brotherhood of those who are fed up with working) dating from the time of Rabelais. Details are related of a marvelous castle, its walls made of creamy Milanese cheese speckled with tiny diamonds. The battlements and windows are made of fresh butter, melted cheese, and sugar; the drawbridges are paved with head-cheese, and the chains holding them consist of sausages and black pudding.

These table games closely resemble depictions in literature and the visual arts, also—and especially—where texts about other dreamlands are concerned. For example, a number of the attractions on offer in Cockaigne and Luilekkerland also feature in long traditions of dreams and blessings portrayed elsewhere. This is certainly true of the animals offering themselves in consumable form, sometimes with cutlery in their beaks or knives sticking out of their backs, as well as the birds willing to fly into one's mouth.

This all applies to the animal world, but sometimes plants have a contribution to make as well, and these evoke even stronger associations with paradise, which are often projected onto the exotic realm of travel stories. According to Genesis, in the Garden of Eden food was freely available, and no effort was required to obtain it. The early Christian writer Papias transferred this blessing to the heavenly paradise, which, during the course of the Middle Ages, increasingly came to be associated with rewards in the form of food as delicious as it was abundant. In Papias's version of heaven the grapes prayed to be picked.

Imputing animals with a willingness to be eaten is more than just a flight of fancy. According to medieval exegesis, when Adam was permitted by God to name the animals, thus acquiring dominion over them, this meant that people were henceforth allowed to make use of them in any way they saw fit. No less a person than Thomas Aquinas interpreted this to mean that animals existed primarily for human consumption, which was why fish obligingly swam in schools: the better to catch them.

It is important to bear in mind that when the consumer became acquainted with these animals, birds, and fish, they were generally in a recognizable form and not infrequently still alive. In today's society this is a rare occurrence, and there is an unmistakable tendency to avoid such confrontations. The animal product on one's plate often consists of an unrecognizable part of the beast in question. In the Middle Ages, however, no one bought a pig in a poke. Most animals arrived at the butcher's while still alive and were butchered on order. Many kinds of fish, such as eel and lamprey, also traveled live from the fishing grounds to the shopkeeper. This situation, coupled with the prevailing ideology, made it as easy as it was agreeable to think that animals knew full well what was expected of them, namely, the satisfaction of human cravings.

It is not inconceivable that, during the course of the late Middle Ages, an increasing distaste for slaughtering animals in public acted as a stimulus to dreaming of animals offering themselves for consumption. What was becoming less permissible in practice was perhaps forced to live on in dreams. Were the texts on Cockaigne and Luilekkerland recorded at a time when the first slaughterhouses were moved out of town? Things could not have been so simple, though such tendencies could easily have provided an added incentive to dream of Cockaigne.

Finally, there is the important factor of the consumption of Jesus' body when receiving Holy Communion, whereby He offers himself with complete submission to the purified sinner. I have shown how graphically this was depicted in the Middle Ages, not just to move the humble masses but also to touch the right chord among the elite. Furthermore, the most concrete culinary concepts were not shunned in giving expression to this most sacred of self-sacrifices.

The dream of food spontaneously offering itself is part of the yearning for paradise lost. This is recalled by a very well known proverb, which gives apt expression to the frustration at this loss: "Plums will not drop into your mouth." Another expression in this vein is "The larks fall there ready roasted." Similar sayings occur in all of Western Europe and even have parallels dating back to classical antiquity. Various classical authors also dreamed of consumable beasts. In a dish conjured up by Trimalchio's cook, Petronius saw fish swimming: "On the sides of the dish there were four little images that spouted a relishing sauce on some fish that lay near them as

FIGURE 26

Recognizable animals in a butcher's shop. Colored drawings from the *Chronik des Konstanzer Konzils, 1414–1418*, by Ulrich Richental, in a manuscript of ca. 1465.

Source: Konstanz (Germany), Rosgartenmuseum.

in a canal. We also seconded the shout begun by the family and fell merrily aboard this." Elsewhere in his gormandizing *Satyricon*, Petronius speaks of better worlds, always the object of envy, owing to "the pigs walking round already roasted." We met up with these in Luilekkerland, but that is not the only place they wander around. For the painter Jan Mandyn, schooled or perhaps bowled over by the work of Hieronymus Bosch, such edible surprises belong to the list of delusions of which the devil routinely avails himself. In his attempts to tempt Saint Antony, Satan tends to pull out all the stops, inspiring Mandyn to paint a roasted pig with a knife in its back. In this way the devil tries to entice this supersaint into committing two sins at once, namely, gluttony and sloth.

Examples of the divine dispensation of food are offered by the Bible not only in paradise but also in the form of manna falling from heaven and even in the quails that "came up and covered the camp" of the children of Israel. These manifestations were always interpreted, not without reason, as expressions of divine intervention and heavenly reward, intended to prove that humankind was not meant to toil and go hungry but had only itself to blame for such deprivations.

Exotic worlds with their portents of paradise also retained this necessary ingredient, namely, the acquisition of food by both providential and natural means. Alexander the Great, approaching paradise by traveling upstream along one of the rivers flowing from it, saw the world reversing itself, reverting from corruption to innocence, as it were. He observed fish grilling themselves in the water and swimming through fire, their flesh willingly falling off the bone.

The situation is even more clear-cut on the island of Calanok, of which Mandeville wrote. There all kinds of fish swim ashore and remain lying on the beach for three days, where people may help themselves to as many as they want. The inhabitants attribute this marvel to a gift of God, who has chosen this method to honor their king, a world-champion begetter of children on his countless wives. Every night he sleeps with a different woman for this very purpose and has already produced hundreds of descendants, whose numbers are constantly on the increase. The king can therefore be pointed to as a role model for those striving to obey God's command to go forth and multiply. An annual miracle involving so many self-sacrificing fish is the least that can be expected in return. Mandeville borrowed this story from Odoric of Pordenone, a Franciscan friar who claimed to have seen with his own eyes that which biblical exegesis and popular imagination had been dictating for centuries. The Celtic travel tale of Mael Dúin also mentions a dream island where enormous salmon throw themselves on the beach, many more than needed for the inhabitants' daily consumption. Clearly, fish are dying to be eaten.

The upside-down world of exotic lands also harbors the opposite of everything that is considered civilized in the Western world, a prime example being cannibalism. Barbarian patterns of consumption could force white people to offer themselves up as food as spontaneously as animals do in the Land of Cockaigne. This was the fate of a German, Hans Staden of Homburg (in Germany's region of North Hessen), who was held for years in captivity by Brazilian Indians. His sensational account of this experience, published in 1557 in Marburg, was hugely successful in all of Europe. A Dutch edition of his book appeared as early as 1558, published by Christoffel Plantijn in Antwerp. Although Staden was nearly eaten again and again, each time his pleas for postponement proved successful. In the meantime, he was constantly forced to present himself to the natives as a potential source of nourishment. At one point he was taken off, captive, to a village where he was required to call out to the women in their huts that he was hereby presenting himself for the purpose of being eaten. The natives apparently placed great value on such formal introductions. Later on, his legs were tied together, and he "had to hop around among the huts with his feet pressed together, which caused a great deal of laughter, and the people kept saying, 'There's our food hopping past!' "

Paradises are sooner found in exotic lands than close to home. Mandeville, the most important source of knowledge regarding countless exotic worlds, reported that on the island of Thalamass (which some call Pathen: it must be situated near Borneo) there grow trees that bear flour instead of fruit. This flour, obtained without the added complication of growing wheat, was used to make delicious white bread. Just as simply, the grape was dispensed with, and wine was produced directly by trees. This simple procedure was described by Mandeville in the following words: "And if you want to know how the trees bear flour, I tell you that one cuts with a hatchet round the bole of the tree near the ground in many places, so that the bark is pierced; then a thick liquid flows out, which they catch in a receptacle and set in the sun to dry. When it is dry they grind it in a mill, and it is then fine white meal. And wine, honey, and poison are drawn from the trees in the same way and kept in pots." As is so often the case with Mandeville and the accounts of other travelers, the forcefulness of these dreams lies in their connection with a perceivable phenomenon, which is then confirmed in the accounts of subsequent travelers. In this case the story embroiders upon the blessings of the sago palm, whose pith yields an edible starch resembling flour.

Creative trees that supposedly produce birds and beasts are also encountered in these tales. According to Mandeville, in the kingdom of Cadhilhe (Kao-li), which possibly refers to Korea, "there grows a kind of fruit as big as gourds, and when it is ripe men open it and find inside an animal of flesh and blood and bone, like a little lamb without wool." These were apparently delicious to eat. Mention is also made of trees bearing "fruit that became birds that could fly," also nothing to turn up one's nose at, for "there is good meat on them." Also belonging in this category are the "bernakes," or barnacle geese, written of by Vincent of Beauvais and others, which were presumed to grow from the stalked barnacle.

The above-mentioned French lying tale of "the great brotherhood of those who are fed up with working," published before 1540, pokes fun at all the kamikaze comestibles reportedly seen in exotic lands and other dreamworlds. Here as well, parodying paradise meant underscoring the fact that food could be obtained effortlessly. In the brotherhood's wonder castle, one could take a seat at the dining table and find everything in exactly the right portions. At the smallest sign, pieces of meat even sprang into one's mouth. In the orchard outside, ready-to-eat birds and beasts grew on the trees. This is how things were meant to be, and if reports were true, this is how things still were in the Far East and West. In order to make the paltry provisions of one's own civilization more tolerable, it was best to acquire detailed information about the existence of abundance elsewhere. Dreaming also helped, dreaming about delicious food that cost nothing to obtain and required no effort to prepare. This desire, too, had found expression in a proverb: "The cat would like a fish to eat / But not if it has to get wet feet."

16
Literary Refreshment

O<small>NE CAN ALSO</small> indulge one's uncertainties and fears on parchment and paper. In such examples, anger and fear, self-mockery and irony are alternately highlighted and often found in one and the same text. There is more than just humor in these writings, however, no matter how much their oft-repeated utterances have degenerated into tasteless and vulgar jokes.

The texts are quite frequently connected with the standard repertoire of public celebrations, led, of course, by Carnival. This connection is suggested by all the crazy enumerations of humorously distorted dishes, which are twice as funny when proclaimed at the top of one's voice. Such mad performances were the heart of the Carnival celebration, voiced by the pseudoauthorities—the prince, the judge, the preacher, the doctor, and the astrologer—responsible for providing their temporary mock kingdom with a suitable mock infrastructure.

The humorous enumerations were literally eaten up by listeners reduced to nourishing themselves with words and visions instead of food. This kind of humor is in fact as old as sudden scarcity itself. Classical antiquity had its own brand of kitchen humor, several examples of which have already been sampled in this book. Starting in the thirteenth century, German literature even displays a separate genre that could be called the literature of eating and drinking (or gorging and guzzling), which is related to the above-mentioned kitchen humor, though it actually goes much further. Within the framework of the courtly epic, such texts served as didactic tracts, intended to teach proper etiquette to young uneducated knights by showing them how *not* to behave. This resulted in cannonades of crazy culinary nomenclature, a good example of which is *Gefraess* (Voraciousness), written by the German knightly poet Neidhart von Reuenthal (ca. 1185–1245), in which no fewer than forty-two dishes are listed. Neidhart may have written this text especially for Carnival, for what better occasion was there for a diverting romp in the kitchen?

Carnival, coming at a time when winter was waning, offered the most suitable occasion to stuff oneself silly, as though the opportunity would never present itself again. In a certain sense this was true, considering what the future held in store: a period of scarcity and enforced frugality prevailing until the next harvest. The literary estate of the Bruges rhetorician Eduard de Dene, which he himself compiled, included a separate section with various texts suitable for use by Carnival celebrants, whom he addressed in his own inimitable idiom as "Epicurean idlers, gormandizing gulpers," flabby servants of Epicurus, the classical philosopher who, de Dene thought, had specialized in culinary pleasures. These servants scoured the tables, talking of nothing but eating and drinking. They dined until late at night but rose early the next day, ready for the morning meal. They were accused of belly worship, the usual reproach—with a biblical basis—aimed at medieval gluttons. De Dene, however, did not seem to object to them so strongly. Rather, he seems to have been seeking a suitable classification for behavior of a temporary nature that, considering his own lifestyle, he did not disapprove of in the slightest.

In the mock sermon in particular, which proclaimed the topsy-turvy morality obtaining during the reign of Prince Carnival, strict rules for behavior prescribe what one should and should not do when indulging in culinary excesses. A sermon expounding the virtues of the holy Saint Nobody, who appears to be related to Sanctus Drincatibus, states "that one may reach the heavenly kingdom by boozing / For those who guzzle too much beer or wine / Release a soul from purgatory every time." Drink as much as you can, therefore, to save your own soul and those of others. This is followed by a ludicrous list of personifications of food, some of which would not appear on the table till Easter and some that either should or should not be served during the coming Lenten fast: Peter Ox, Gerard Cow, Jeffrey Hare, Paul Sheep, and John Capon; their adversaries Harry Halibut, Peter Shellfish, John Lox, Lance Carp, and Joseph Salmon; as well as the more vegetarian-minded Cal Olive, Gertrude Apple, Trish Fig, and Bev Raisin.

It was considered especially funny to graft the obsession with hunger and overindulgence onto dramatic narratives about sainted martyrs. Presented as part of a mock sermon, the suffering of a goose or herring being roasted or grilled for dinner became an object of pious contemplation. This tradition stems from the Latin satires in the *Carmina Burana*, such as the "Song of the Roasted Swan":

> So in the pan for you I fry,
> A bird that can no longer fly,
> With pain I'm racked,
> I'm turning black,
> Of fire that scorches there's no lack!

Such texts were undoubtedly performed during the religious Feast of Fools, for which (and of which) the above-mentioned volume contained quite a sampling of repertoire. These festive outlets organized by the church were subsumed into predominantly urban celebrations of Carnival that also adopted and adapted much of the original text material. A fifteenth-century mock sermon on Alijt the Goose fits into this pattern. It was probably composed for the celebration of the Feast of Saint Martin on 11 November, which traditionally marked the opening of the series of rites of inversion, or festivals enacting the *mundus inversus*, celebrated during the winter and leading up to Lent. On Saint Martin's day, of course, one invariably ate roast goose.

The *Legende van Sinte Haryngus* (The legend of Saint Herring), recorded in the mid-sixteenth century, was also modeled along these lines. Solemnly, it recalls how the hero had managed quite selflessly to fill the stomachs of the masses during Lent by giving freely of his own body. Despite this, he had been pursued and captured in the most underhand way, and this had been followed by an extremely gruesome martyrdom, which the preacher then disclosed in elaborate detail. His jaws were cut open and stuffed with salt. He was then stowed away in a barrel and subsequently grilled over a fire and hung up, by means of a wire stuck through his head, to dry in the smoke. And as though that were not enough, his skin was even peeled off, his stomach cut open, and his guts removed. After this he was stuffed full of butter and mustard, and still it was not enough: he was put in a tub of flour and turned over and over until he was whiter than snow. Finally, this king of the sea was thrown into boiling hot oil. Only then was he ready for a revolting eating spree indulged in by the masses, who gnawed away at him until at last they were stuffed, throwing the remains of his noble body to the cats and dogs.

What had he done to deserve such cruel treatment? May he nonetheless

FIGURE 27
Battle Between Fish and Meat. Woodcut, ca. 1530.
Source: Oxford, Ashmolean Museum.

remain well disposed toward us for all eternity, intoned the preacher, that he and his subjects may go on feeding us (the subjects then being recollected in a long list of names). The Carnival celebrants—alas—had to nourish themselves on the names alone, and the pastor finished in style by blessing them all with smallpox, scabies, boils, pleurisy, and the runs.

An eighteenth-century echo of this stock humor referring to ingurgitation at the Carnival celebration has been preserved in three mock documents intended to accompany the festivities. There is every indication that they fully reflect late-medieval rituals. The whole celebration, deeply rooted in fertility rites, purification, and ritual inversion, has here been reduced to a confrontation between stuffing oneself to the gills and the devout austerity of the subsequent Lenten fast. According to an age-old tradition, the opposing parties consist of meat and fowl on one side ranged against fish on the other. Lent is represented by the "Emperor of Abstinence," who announces in a mock decree that he rules over the fishing grounds and all the fish therein, which are subsequently enumerated in a never-ending list. He also rules over fruit, vegetables, and everything "to do with plain cooking."

The object of his decree is the immediate banishment from his kingdom of all meat and fowl, the declaration of which is followed by another long list of personifications of all the wonderful food from which one must now abstain: Roland the Bull, his uncle Dick the Ox, his wife, Henny, and many others. This proclamation was made in the city of Great Hunger, in a year whose date appears to be an obscure game based on the Carnivalesque number eleven and signed by the clerk Walter Pompous-Paunch.

Such texts treating debates and brawls between leaders of Lent and Carnival, typically containing long lists of food incarnate, have been preserved in great number in northern French literature of the late Middle Ages and early-modern period. These are always performance and recitation texts, which offered ample opportunity for rhythmic recitation and the humorous representation of armies of food parading past, marching to face each other on the battlefield. A few of these texts take the form of plays written out in full.

There are enough traces of such material in Dutch to indicate that the genre was well known. There is a dispute, for example—composed in the form of a rhetoricians' farce—between Carnival, dressed up as a peasant, and Lent, who appears to be a Beguine. Typical Carnival fare is also the subject of discussion: "custard pies, waffles, pancakes," to which are added "eggs, spices, chicken, meat pies, partridges, and capons." It can be no coincidence that we here recognize much of Cockaigne and Luilekkerland's edible architecture, especially the baked goods. There were, of course, reasons enough to resurrect these dreamlands during Carnival.

The clearest evidence, however, of the popularity of fights between food, as well as fighting food itself, is to be found in the visual arts. Everything is eclipsed, of course, by Bruegel's *Fight Between Carnival and Lent*, painted in 1559, eight years before his *Land of Cockaigne*. Here everything revolves around food, in arrangements that literature has meanwhile made familiar to us. A fatso standing on a barrel of beer or wine brandishes a meat skewer— full of such edibles as a grilled pig's head and a roast chicken—at a woman, as wan as she is skinny, whose weapons consist of nothing but a breadboard bearing two lean stockfish and some cracknel and bread rolls. Other edibles trot alongside the glutton, including an enormous ham with an inviting knife stuck in it, eggs, waffles, white bread, and pancakes.

This tub of lard armed to the teeth with food, who portrays the proverbial knight with a full stomach, turns up repeatedly in literature, the visual

FIGURE 28

Circle of Pieter Bruegel the Elder, *Battle Between Lent and Carnival,* second half of sixteenth century.

Source: Copenhagen, Statens Museum for Kunst.

arts, and festive entertainment. He frequently appears in prints armed with his usual attribute—the lethal meat skewer—carrying hams, suckling pigs, and capons. In Poperingen in West Flanders, in the late Middle Ages, there existed a society of fools, led by a crazy knight called Ghybe or Gib. It was probably a social organization whose members played the fool on festive occasions like Carnival. Despite his obscure name, Ghybe's outward appearance in the drawing preserved of him leaves no room for doubt that he is the personification of the gormandizing behavior called for on such occasions. He is armed with a meat skewer and wears pots and pans as armor; he uses spoons as spurs and sits backward on his donkey, beating on a large stone with the puzzling weight of eighty-three pounds. There is much to suggest that this informal organization later grew to be the chamber of rhetoric known as the Stone Heads.

The grossly fat stock figure representing Carnival recurs as an inde-

FIGURE 29

After Pieter Bruegel the Elder, *Battle Between Lent and Carnival,* ca. 1600.

Source: Antwerp, Museum Mayer van den Bergh.

pendent motif in another painting attributed to the circle of Pieter Bruegel the Elder that bears the rather confusing name *Battle Between Lent and Carnival.* There are several copies and adaptations of both paintings, dating from the time of Bruegel or immediately thereafter. The last-mentioned painting (fig. 28) shows a round, fat boy's face being bitten into by what is perhaps the emaciated head of a man, half-covered by the gaunt profile of a woman. Did Bruegel (or one of his pupils) intend to portray a variation of the Dutch saying "Eating the ears off someone's head"? Related to these are the pendants, also produced in great number, representing the lean kitchen and the fat kitchen, engraved after Bruegel's design by Pieter van der Heyden in 1563. These depict rival eating habits and, in particular, the various foods on offer in the two kitchens.

FIGURE 30

The Fat Kitchen. Engraving by Pieter van der Heyden after
Pieter Bruegel the Elder, 1563.

Source: Brussels, Bibliothèque Royale, Print Room.

Another striking element in all these Carnival representations, both literary and visual, is the standard getup of the merrymakers, who are fond of
decking themselves out in kitchen utensils. They even make music with meat
skewers, grills, serving forks, pokers, ladles, and pots and pans. There was
obviously a strong need for public presentations of contrasting pictures of
scarcity and abundance, not just at Carnival but also at other times of the
year, as witnessed by the above-mentioned Poperingen fools' society and
their paunchy master Ghybe. In Dendermonde in Flanders, starting in
1561—just after a notorious period of hardship—the yearly procession featured a performance with the title "Mr. Lean's New Stick Stirs the Food,"
the formulation of which seems strongly related to the print after Bruegel.

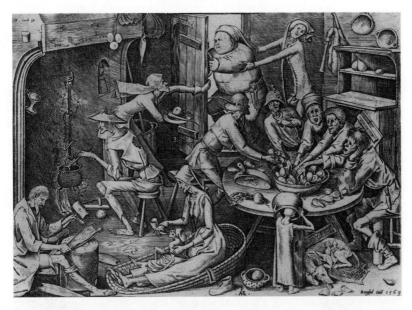

FIGURE 31

The Lean Kitchen. Engraving by Pieter van der Heyden after Pieter Bruegel
the Elder, 1563.

Source: Brussels, Bibliothèque Royale, Print Room.

Carnival is all about food, and Carnival songs were even written down in musical notation composed of food. A festival program presented in 1517 in Jutphaas in the diocese of Utrecht featured, in addition to a mock charge—the
previously mentioned address delivered by a bishop to the clergy under his
jurisdiction—and numerous beautifully painted escutcheons of the mock
dominions, a Carnival song with staves of music filled with fools' caps, hams,
capons, geese, eggs, and a barrel of wine or beer. This is followed by a song
for Lent, the tone of which is set by notation consisting of stockfish, plaice,
mussels, and jugs (no doubt of water). The accompanying texts offer similar
enumerations. Festive songs embellished in this way were evidently not
unusual, for a painting dating from Bruegel's time depicts revelers in an inn
singing from an open songbook that also displays staves of edible music.

The key to understanding the representation of all this food is the con-

FIGURE 32

Tavern Scene, featuring songbook with musical notation consisting of food, second half of sixteenth century.

Source: Budapest, Museum of Fine Arts; reproduced from E. Szmodis-Eszláry et al., *Middeleeuwse Nederlandse kunst uit Hongarije* (Utrecht, 1990), no. 15.

cept of exaggeration and caricature, the forms of humor most effective in combating hunger. They typically belong to the arsenal of artistic forms that intentionally distort reality with specific objectives in mind. Where food or the lack of it is involved, magnification in every conceivable form is the most effective method of presentation and the right moment is the pre-Lenten festival of Carnival, which presents the entire body and especially the bodily functions cloaked in ridiculous forms and performing ridiculous activities. This serves to ridicule and exorcise all the behavior that, in everyday life, is considered undesirable or even the devil's doing. Literature is not the only medium in which this occurs: Bruegel also follows suit. The engraving *Gula* (Gluttony) (fig. 70), known also in a drawing, portrays this deadly sin by means of figures consisting almost entirely of bloated mouths and bellies that immediately catch one's eye among the company of over-stuffed caricatures. The above-mentioned prints of the fat and lean kitchens show the same picture of strongly exaggerated leanness and obesity, further strengthened by the "enumeration" of figures all cast in the same mold, contrasted with a visitor from the opposing camp whose appearance at the door is certainly no coincidence.

Literature gladly makes its contribution as well. The Latin *Ysengrimus* by Master Nivardus, written around 1149 in Ghent, focuses on the incredible gluttony of the wolf Ysengrim by making constant reference to his jaws, which begin to take on a life of their own. When he closes his jaws, it sounds like the action of a loom or like a sheet of iron being struck on an anvil. His teeth are also viewed under a magnifying glass and likened to pickaxes or scythes. Altogether, this wolf commands a considerable arsenal of destructive machinery, which can easily devour eight cakes as well as the dish containing them. As far as gorging is concerned, however, Reynard the Fox can vie with his uncle in this story. When they really go at it, their stomachs swell up like balloons, until, in the end, the fox can no longer see his feet and—what's worse—cannot use them, so that he has to roll instead of walk. He is reduced, quite simply, to a huge gluttonous ball, as wide as he is tall.

These overdone representations of food and human digestion have a long history, beginning with the Celtic and Germanic traditions, where it is immediately clear to what extent eating to survive governed one's existence in the ancien régime and how often the imagination was called upon—for lack of anything better—to provide solace and escape. In Celtic mythology a major role is played by Mac Datho's pig, pork being the most important source of meat in the Middle Ages. This swine is a gigantic beast that has been fed for seven years on the milk of sixty cows. When he is finally served up for dinner, he is garnished with no fewer than forty oxen.

Germanic lore has an enormous wild boar, Saehrimnir, that provides an inexhaustible supply of meat to the dead war heroes in paradise. Snorri Sturluson's *Younger Edda*, in which this boar occurs, also mentions the cow Audhumla "from whose udders four rivers of milk flow." The correspondences to heavenly rewards of nourishment as well as to the four fertile rivers of the earthly paradise can be explained as examples of Christianizing—the stories were generally recorded by monks—but also as authentic elements belonging to all paradise material that many cultures molded to suit their own needs. In any case, we recognize in the gluttonous warriors the Germanic hero, who was constantly forced to prove himself by demonstrating his prowess as a bulk consumer.

It would be going too far to list here all the incidences of culinary rough-and-tumble in medieval literature. The choice of that theme and its burlesque treatment, certainly during those days specially devoted to ingurgitation, are revealing enough in themselves. I will thus give only a few more examples that fall within the period examined in this book, the late Middle Ages and early-modern period.

Colorful indeed is the black humor permeating several facetious dialogues found in Italian literature of the early sixteenth century. To drive away the feared enemy, Hunger, various solutions are put forward. One can, for example, stop up one's body with a plug in one's behind, keeping the muck inside and the intestines full. Someone else indulges in autophagia—self-devourment—and calls out that he has finally conquered Hunger, now that he will die replete and satisfied. This technique was not unknown: the triumph seemed to lie in the victory itself, even at the cost of one's life.

Autophagous orgies are suggested in the clever decorations of initials in illuminated manuscripts and in related figures adorning the capitals of pillars in churches and monasteries. Monstrous people and animals bite not only each other but also themselves, thereby referring to their complete inhumanity, typical of heathens and other marginal figures who no longer, or never did, believe in God. On 24 June (the Feast of Saint John) in the year 1500, the miracle play *Van den heilighen sacramente van der Nyeuwervaert* (Of the Holy Sacrament of Nyeuwervaert) was performed in Breda in the duchy of Brabant. A consecrated wafer, found in the mud and apparently bleeding, was able to perform all manner of miracles. A skilled lawyer from the diocese of Liège came to test the wafer's authenticity, piercing it five times, upon which the wafer started to bleed again. Distraught, the man fled, biting off his hands and, according to reports, eating them.

This lawyer was not suffering from real hunger. At most, he was a victim of spiritual hunger, since he had dared to doubt God's omnipotence. Most instances of autophagia, however, are indicative of extreme gluttony, transformed in literature into a weapon, at once comical and efficient, to combat hunger. Literature is not its only venue, though, for art can also dictate reality. Indeed, it appears to have made a contribution to the hunger topos of the preindustrial era, as evidenced by a chronicler who prefaced his account with assurances of first-hand reporting ("we would not dare to say it if we had not seen it with our own eyes, for it caused such horror"), stating that in seventeenth-century Picardy in northern France there were starving peasants who "ate their own arms and hands and died in despair." In particular, the avowal of having been an eyewitness to something so unbelievable arouses the greatest suspicion, recalling the traditional images that the fear of hunger and scarcity not only kindled but were also meant to justify.

Precisely at a time when the Low Countries were experiencing bouts of serious food shortages that fanned the flames of fear, such obsessions were counterbalanced and exorcised by a farcical play that was performed at the rhetoricians' festival held in 1561 in Antwerp. It was thought up by someone from the chamber of rhetoric "'t Heybloemken" (The heath flower) in Turnhout, probably the factor himself, who acted as artistic director and generally supervised the literary productions intended for public performance. The actors were undoubtedly also members of this chamber. The play took a satirical sideswipe at the hordes of wandering mercenaries, who were greatly feared, not only for their plundering but also for their official confiscations. In retrospect, the direct influence of war on scarcity and famine proved to be rather negligible, but the masses felt otherwise at the time.

In the Turnhout farce almost nothing happens. The action focuses on the presentation of a long series of mock figures, whose names and appearance are nothing but caricatures of various eating habits. In this respect the text of the play bears some similarity to the German *Reihenspiel*, a distinctly Carnivalesque text in which a number of figures heap ironic praise on themselves. The Dutch Carnival play has a long list of actors, including a whole regiment of potential mercenaries. The plot consists of little more than their recruitment, ostensibly to serve in the army of the count of Schockland, a country where one can *schokken* or, in other words, eat like a trooper.

During the enlistment procedure it emerges that all the candidates are eminently qualified to defend such a country. LongGut can wolf down twelve bowls of porridge in one gulp. HollowBelly recently downed fifteen plates of beans. BigPlate masticates on a permanent basis, priding himself on the fact that he never stops eating. In one go he can stuff down ten plates of peas, or more if necessary, with a couple of hams and twenty pounds of bread on the side. Just recently SwallowChunk consumed a whole sheep and fifteen pounds of bread, and afterward he still felt hungry. SeldomFull can drink the contents of a whole wine cellar, and MakeEnough thinks nothing of eating a whole feeding trough full of gruel.

This crazy name game is a late echo of typical Carnival amusements. The difference between these ironical nicknames and modern parlance is actually not so great as one would think. People have always given each other nicknames based on the most embarrassing physical or behavioral traits, and in the past these were recorded in official registers with the greatest of ease. In a document from the abbey of Ter Doest in Flanders, for example, a certain Daniel "alias the Glutton" is recorded as having acted as a witness in 1269.

These and similar mock names connoting hunger and gluttony—also occurring in the form of toponyms gone wrong—are encountered repeatedly in fifteenth-century festival repertoire. They not only serve to allay fears of both hunger and overindulgence by ridiculing and satirizing them but also teach a lesson based on the irony of the topsy-turvy world. Eat and drink yourself silly on the pilgrimage to Saint Have-Not, which is undertaken in the Ship of Poverty. During the voyage the ship naturally puts in at Hungery, Bread's End, and Empty-Purse, which is not at all what one intended, having been headed for Taphouse, Beerberg, and Wetfields.

There is no end to such games, especially when one considers that these texts were only occasionally written down, destined to lead a new life as a text for private reading, or recitation in small circles, or even as simple souvenirs. It is also possible that they continued to be used, in the form of inexpensive printed matter, at Carnival celebrations, which slowly but surely went underground during the course of the sixteenth century, eventually becoming home entertainment. A group of related texts tells of a mock order or brotherhood of wandering scroungers, the so-called Arnoutsbroeders, presumably named after Saint Arnoldus, the patron saint of beer brewers, although another Arnold with the reputation of a wastrel may also have been their founding father. This brotherhood lived according to the Law of Saint Lean, the Holy Have-Not, and the names of the brothers testify to this: HollowJaws, GreatHunger, DryPot, NoFat. On their journeys this merry company meets up with such cheerful passersby as William Worry, Sam Spotless, and LeanMan, the latter personifying either Hunger or the Grim Reaper himself.

These are the vestiges of hunger-fighting texts, which must have given rise to hilarious performances occasioning peals of laughter and much-needed relief, welcomed by both the actors and the audience, who thus found themselves mercifully thrown together in a protective community. Indeed, the decibel level of the peals of laughter provoked by this collective ritual can be used to gauge the seriousness of the situation, and in view of the similarities exhibited by these texts in both treatment and characters' names, it appears that mass culture used such means for at least a century, if not longer, to come to grips with what they perceived as a life-threatening predicament. Related texts, such as the prayer parodies *Sotte Benedicite* (Sottish benediction) and *Sotte Gratias* (Sottish grace) choose other methods, in which the humor consists in substituting the usual devotional content with a supplication for God's blessing of all manner of delicacies. Here, too, the tone remains combative. The latter text concludes by giving thanks to all suppliers of food and drink "for all that is cooked, or roasted, or conquers hunger."

The dream of an abundance of food in an alimentary paradise was not something that died away at the dawning of the modern age. Instead, it was directed at the New World, which had been considered a gastronomic paradise since its discovery at the end of the Middle Ages. After the Second World War, fervent yet vain hopes of discovering in North America the land of milk and honey were kindled in emigrants from the occupied territories in Europe, including of course the Netherlands. Only a short time before, these survivors had endured a "medieval" experience of acute hunger and its accompanying inhuman behavior. While the hunger was quickly suppressed, the fear remained, and many Europeans sought to allay this fear by emigrating to what they perceived as the promised land.

Hunger is something we know only from pictures of the third world, which portray its terrible consequences with unbearable visual immediacy. What it means to be possessed by the permanent fear of hunger is something we cannot imagine. At a safe remove in newspaper photographs and television documentaries, hunger is shown to be a more or less normal phenomenon, seemingly giving rise not so much to fear as to apathetic dying or, at best, acquiescence in one's fate. We are, however, dependent on the news we are given: never do we see pictures of exuberant feasting in that same world, treasured moments in which the mortal enemy is temporarily laid to rest. Neither do we know anything about fantasies entertained there of dreamworlds and paradises featuring—and even built of—fantastic food-stuffs or harboring immense beasts destined for consumption. Come to think of it, do people in the third world ever engage in defiant fasting?

Information on this score is certainly obtainable, though it does not belong to the pictures we are bombarded with in the Western world, which is why it takes so much effort to comprehend the seriousness and need expressed in images like Cockaigne and Luilekkerland. Our incomprehension is increased because we delude ourselves into thinking that we know what it means to suffer acute hunger, even though all we see is the emaciation and the flies, not the arsenal of behavioral forms and cultural expressions used by the hunger-struck to combat it. Only when we have armed ourselves with such knowledge will we be able to make enlightening comparisons.

Panicky and compulsive eating is now known as a disorder, not as a weapon. This aberration is one of the few taboos of modern society, and one necessarily indulges in it only in complete isolation. In the Middle Ages, however, the point was to confront in all openness humankind's greatest enemy on earth, next to the devil. Eating pleasure now consists of culinary tours de force that do not seek justification in traditional images of communal feasting or the alleviation of fear. The latter-day gourmet expects an imaginative sequence of small dishes along the lines of a *menu de dégustation*, and this, paradoxically, has given rise to an entirely new fear: the dread of ruining one's health with an excess of rich food.

Gulping down food and glorifying gluttons belong to a time of all-pervasive fears of death by starvation. Acute and widespread famine, however, was not a frequent occurrence in the Middle Ages, and the very fact that these fears were unfounded makes them all the more unfathomable and more in need of a pretext—or, better still, justification—in constantly repeated stories about bizarre experiences of hunger. On the other hand, there was just as great a need for escape, consolation, and compensation, and these were provided by such places as Cockaigne and Luilekkerland.

All this refers continually to paradise, and that is how the Cockaigne texts begin: a land where one is condemned to a blissful life of enforced laziness. Time after time, when the discussion turns to edible rewards and definite solutions to the problem of provisions, paradises are quickly conjured up, and in this context Cockaigne seems simply to be a worldly—as opposed to an earthly—paradise.

Part 4

Paradise Refurbished

17

The Land of Cockaigne as Paradise

$\mathcal{T}$HE LAND OF COCKAIGNE is a paradise on earth. Just as the true earthly paradise, it can be found in a specific place; according to texts L and B, it is even accessible, though with difficulty. This, however, points up an important difference from the earthly paradise, which was utterly inaccessible. The impenetrable walls surrounding the earthly paradise had only one gate of entry, and that was guarded by an angel with a flaming sword. Some even thought a whole curtain of fire hung in front of the entrance. The Land of Cockaigne, on the other hand, was open to all who could find it. The entrance to Luilekkerland, however, was more problematic: one had to want to get in very badly indeed and even be willing to perform an incredible feat to gain entrance. Text G discloses the necessity of eating one's way through a mountain of buckwheat porridge in order to gain access. Other texts tell of mountains of Parmesan cheese or nearly unfordable rivers of dung.

These striking variations immediately place Cockaigne and Luilekkerland in the realm of salutary fantasy, whereas the geographic reality of the earthly paradise was not doubted by anyone living in the Middle Ages. This explains why Cockaigne could be provided at will with more worldly and contemporary furnishings, so lamentably lacking in the description of paradise in Genesis. That paradise, after all, is rather boring, what with all that greenery and only a bit of fruit. A certain monotony is immediately apparent in Middle Dutch accounts of the Garden of Eden: "In paradise all the trees are the same shape and size, with erect branches bearing no twigs." It goes on to say that they are forever in blossom and grow with no abnormalities. While it was inevitable that paradise should be a paragon of the perfect harmony ordained by God in His Creation, it was also evident that harmony, however agreeable, soon becomes boring—quite apart from the fact that Eden was now off-limits and likely to remain so.

According to medieval notions, the food in paradise was not up to scratch, either. Of course, one was well aware that Adam and Eve did not trouble themselves much about food in that garden of delights. As vegetarians, they could easily exist on water, sweet smells, and the occasional piece of fruit. But times had changed. Their sin was the reason one now had to slave away on an earth that had become the devil's playground, yielding up food only at the cost of blood, sweat, and tears. And that was when times were good, for things could easily go wrong, and then God would let fly with one of His punishments. Pity had moved Him to permit people to eat a bit of meat, but there could be no talk of regular provisions, so that one now had to live with the constant fear of natural catastrophes, inclement weather, drought, floods, sickness, intractable land, and all manner of earthly disruptions that had destroyed heavenly harmony. But the principal fear, and one not to be shaken off, was the fear of hunger and scarcity.

The Land of Cockaigne provided an instantaneous paradise full of medieval attractions. At the same time, this dreamland was no less a parody than ironic censure of the standard sins and vices prevailing in society, and it achieved this stance by focusing on modes of behavior as desirable as they were praiseworthy. We do not have to search far for proof of this. The Middle English text *The Land of Cokaygne*, recorded at the beginning of the fourteenth century and undoubtedly the most literary of all the texts, opens with a comparison at once provocative and parodic: "Far in the sea, to the west of Spain, there is a land we call Cokaygne." The parody is evident right from the start, for the earthly paradise was generally believed to be situated in the East. The beginning of the text runs as follows:

> Fur in see, bi west spayngne,
> is a lond ihote cokaygne.
> þer nis lond vnder heuen-riche,
> of wel, of godnis, hit iliche;
> þoȝ peradis be miri & briȝt,
> cokaygn is of fairir siȝt.
> what is 'er in peradis
> bot grasse, & flure, & grene ris?
> *oȝ 'er be ioi & gret dute,
> þer nis met bote frute;
> þer nis halle, bure, no benche;
> bot watir, man-is 'urst to quenche.

[Far in the sea, to the west of Spain,
There is a land we call Cokaygne.
Under God's heaven no other land
Has such wealth and goodness to hand.
Though Paradise be merry and bright,
Cokaygne is yet a fairer sight.
For what is there in Paradise
But grass and flowers and green rice?
Though there be joy and great delight,
There is but fruit for the appetite;
There is no hall, no room, no bench,
Just water, man's thirst for to quench.]

Paradise's lacks are extremely well provided for in the Middle Dutch Cockaigne texts, in which Cockaigne is primarily a paradise of eating and drinking, catering to the most outlandish dreams of medieval gourmands. Luilekkerland portrays the same picture from a slightly more distant vantage point, more distant because the opening lines of both rhyming texts underscore the parodic nature of this paradise, giving it at the same time an added dimension. Everywhere on earth one has to toil to earn a living, but somewhere there exists a land where God has commanded the people to avoid work of any kind. What a wonderful place!

In medieval times not even a child could have failed to see this ironical reference to the Fall of Man, at which time God issued a warning that henceforth humankind would be condemned to a life of toil. Apparently He has now made an exception, and this is the wondrous news with which the narrators of texts L and B begin their story. Everyone knows they cannot be talking about paradise, because the narrators tell of a place they've seen with their own eyes. It will soon become clear, however, that they must be talking about a subsidiary of Eden that combines the usual paradisiacal accoutrements with the most bizarre dreams of earthly abundance.

Cockaigne's similarities to biblical paradise are abundantly clear and would have been immediately obvious to every listener. In the Middle Ages representations of paradise were part of the common cultural heritage, often connected with the creation of Adam and Eve or the Fall, not infrequently appearing as part of a series (of prints, for example) or simultaneous portrayals (such as tableaux vivants). This gave rise not only to miniatures, paintings, sculptures, and other works produced by the most divergent branches of the applied arts but also to numerous descriptions in the vernacular, appearing separately or included in larger volumes of writings, whether intended for recitation, portrayal, or performance. The high points were the tableaux vivants and plays enacted on floats during and after religious processions, at which time thousands of people had the fact drummed into them that they had forfeited their once-in-a-lifetime opportunity of attaining paradise, a paradise now parading past them, so close they could reach out and touch it. At the same time these portrayals kindled the desire to experience that paradise once again in its sublimated, heavenly form, and the flames of this desire were further fanned by the hope that a world traveler like Sir John Mandeville would one day discover a negotiable route to this place so much nicer than one's own sullied surroundings.

The animals in Cockaigne and Luilekkerland are reminiscent of their species in paradise: they exist in order to serve humankind. In Genesis it is declared repeatedly that all animals, fish, and fowl are subordinate to humans and must function as a source of their food. It is typical that these rather abstract remarks from the Bible are made much more concrete in Cockaigne. Its rabbits, hares, deer, and wild boar are tame and readily caught with one's bare hands. Text B takes this theme one step further, having the animals cook and serve themselves. But although this one-sided interpretation of animals' servitude—viewing them solely as a source of nourishment—may have some biblical basis, it is certainly not the only possibility the Bible has to offer. The prophecies in Isaiah of a new paradise also predict the existence of tame animals that function not as easily caught food but as a sign of perfect harmony that knows no discord between living beings. Strictly speaking, text L does not specify what one is supposed to do with any captured animals, but the context and situation, as well as the elaboration in texts B and G, leave no room for doubt: the point of catching these animals is to eat them.

Gold and precious stones are connected with paradise in various passages in the Bible. One of the four rivers of paradise in particular, the Pison, carries precious stones in its currents. In the Land of Cockaigne, the "bowls and plates of silver" lying on the shore of "that broad stream" in text B are perhaps reminiscent of their biblical example. Moreover, the stray carbuncle (a kind of ruby or garnet) that crops up in text B's edible architecture (the doorposts) might also be explained along these lines. This precious stone is included in the recollection of paradise and the Fall in the Book of Ezekiel, and I shall soon show how the presence of this mysterious carbuncle can provide the key to a more exact interpretation of the whole Cockaigne myth.

A certain embellishment of paradise along biblical lines took place on a large scale in the Middle Ages, and this was coupled with elaborately allegorical interpretations of the biblical story of paradise. Cockaigne ignored these possibilities completely, however. The dream of Cockaigne was conjured up again and again in an attempt to satisfy more material longings, which is why the texts contain no apparent allusions to the idea that paradise is actually the church, that the four rivers stand for the four gospels, that the trees represent the saints, with Christ himself as the tree of life, and that the tree of the knowledge of good and evil refers to man's free will.

The underpinnings of these material furnishings of paradise were provided by existing biblical exegesis, itself the interpreter of contemporary needs and fantasies that one would naturally graft onto one's personal vision of paradise. First and foremost, however, the attractions of the enclosed garden, with which the author of the Song of Songs compares the body of the beloved, functioned as a reservoir of elements necessary for assembling the desired décor, supplying fruit, spices, and wonderful fragrances, as well as honey, milk, and wine. The related tradition of the *locus amoenus*, or "lovely place," of classical rhetoric, as well as the idyllic spots and dreamworlds of other cultures, also exerted a noticeable influence.

The *locus amoenus* certainly has a history extending back to antiquity. Influenced by this tradition, early Christianity transformed paradise into the "lovely place" par excellence, as presented by Bishop Avitus of Vienne (ca. 460–518). Neither the cold of winter nor the heat of summer has to be endured in this paradise, where it is always spring. Rain never falls—only dew—and the grass is always green, the trees always have leaves, and flowers are omnipresent. The rivers, moreover, carry jewels in their currents.

Refurbishing paradise in this way began already with Pseudo-Basil, of the fourth century. His paradise has a balmy wind and equable temperatures, with no thunderstorms, hail, ice, or drought. Flowers never wilt, and there is a constant flow of milk and honey. The meadows are permanently green, and the roses have no thorns. Above all, there is no trace of care or sorrow. It is clear that, in addition to the Song of Songs, the Old Testament prophecies play a role here with their promises of a better world for the tribes of Israel. This better world recurs constantly in these early descriptions, which furnish paradise with an orchard supplying delicious food and drink. The Syrian Christians in particular carried on in this tradition, exhibiting these amenities in a material and sensual form that must have been a source of inspiration for the almost voluptuous paradise of Islam.

These furnishings intersect the representations of the golden age, the *aurea aetas* of antiquity, and there is practically no civilization that is lacking in a similar idealization of its own past. It seems to have been the natural answer to the unacceptable conditions under which one was forced to live. There must have been a mistake somewhere along the line, a fatal mistake—even a whole series of them—that had necessitated the forfeiture of that golden age or paradise. Classical antiquity could also point to certain places, most of them islands, where this golden age had existed and where it was thought to survive still, though sometimes in a rather rudimentary form.

Bearing in mind that the desires of the Greeks, Romans, and Christians had many points in common and that earthly misery was much the same the world over, it is no wonder that during the first centuries after Christ descriptions of the golden age were difficult to distinguish from those of paradise. In other words, the ideal past was furnished with the attributes at hand. Saint John Chrysostom (ca. 347–407), for example, speaks of paradise in terms of typical *aurea aetas* concepts. Admittedly, he situates it in the East, specifically India (officially recognized as a garden of delights since the time of Alexander the Great), but otherwise his paradise is dominated by the *locus amoenus* elements that are highly conspicuous in descriptions of the golden age.

In Chrysostom's paradise there is no sickness or poverty, everyone is young and beautiful (nevertheless attaining the age of at least four hundred), work is unnecessary, and cunning and deceit are nonexistent. The days are spent laughing and playing in flower-filled meadows, while a chorus of song-birds sings sweet melodies. The trees urge their fruit on passersby, as it were, by letting their branches bend toward the ground. Representations of the heavenly paradise certainly play a role here. Pleasure and bliss in another world—whether on earth or in heaven, whether still to be attained or once upon a time—all these are on offer in the Middle Ages in a cocktail brimming over with fantasies, fed by scores of cultural currents, but ultimately guided by the frustrations arising from the daily drudgery endured in one's own miserable surroundings.

In the first centuries of the first millennium, however, these unremitting projections created so much confusion that the church was finally forced to restore order, resulting, among other things, in a codification of paradise in the encyclopedia called *Etymologies* compiled by Bishop Isidore of Seville (ca. 560–636) at the beginning of the seventh century. Backed up by the weighty authority of Augustine's work of two centuries earlier, Isidore determined the actual nature of the earthly paradise. To begin with, it lies in the East. Its name means garden, *eden* in Hebrew. (Knowledge, as far as Isidore was concerned, meant defining things on the basis of their etymologies.) This garden contains all sorts of bushes and fruit trees, including the tree of life. It is always springtime. The fountain is present, as are the four rivers. Since the primal sin, this part of earth has been decidedly inaccessible, for an angel guards its entrance with a flaming sword. This, according to Isidore, was the inescapable truth, and every right-minded Christian had to learn to live with it. Indeed, medieval encyclopedists following Isidore took careful note of this basic plan but nevertheless felt compelled to elaborate upon it, justifying their embellishments by pointing out their well-intended and fervent desire to improve on the standard furnishings. Nonetheless, the extent to which the *locus amoenus* of antiquity and biblical representations of paradise became entangled in the Middle Ages emerges from the influential codification in Isidore's encyclopedia: summing up, he refers to paradise quite simply as a "lovely place."

A second yardstick of great importance was provided in the thirteenth century by the Franciscan scholar Bartholomaeus Anglicus (Bartholomew the Englishman), who lectured in divinity at the University of Paris. His famous encyclopedia *De proprietatibus rerum* (*On the Properties of Things*) was also known from a Dutch edition published in 1485 by Jacob Bellaert of Haarlem. This nineteen-volume encyclopedia carried unparalleled authority in the medieval world, as witnessed by its immense popularity in various vernaculars. Bartholomaeus was a scholar *pur sang*. He considered it his calling not only to ascertain the nature of the earthly paradise but also to weigh existing and previous notions of it, specifying where they were to be found and how they should be judged. Thus originated one of the earliest scholarly discourses in the Middle Ages, in this case with references to Isidore, at the head of the list, followed by a certain Petrus Damascenus (perhaps intended as a reference to Peter Damian), Augustine, the Venerable Bede, Pliny, Saint Basil the Great, and Ambrose, as well as a number of anonymous authors. He quotes, as his point of departure, Isidore's central characterization of paradise: "It is the garden of pleasure and delight."

This was enough to keep medieval man going. Clearly, this standpoint, which exerted widespread authority in the vernacular, also formed the starting point for dreaming of Cockaigne and Luilekkerland. Bartholomaeus followed this quotation with the usual ingredients, recalling that Elijah and Enoch live in the earthly paradise, whence they were translated that they may remain immortal, as their services will be necessary to preach against the Antichrist on Judgment Day. Later on in the Middle Ages, the earthly paradise also came to be thought of as a waiting room for those who, after the Last Judgment, would be allowed to proceed directly to heaven—an idea, by the way, that was not without its opponents. Distancing himself somewhat from this notion, Bartholomaeus cites the supposition of Pliny—shared by Isidore—that the Islands of the Blessed harbored the earthly paradise. Clearly, he did not believe this for a moment, but his maturity as a scholar, as well as his respect for the great scholars of the past, forbade him to question their standpoint openly.

For people living in the Middle Ages, both Isidore and Bartholomaeus depicted paradise as it was meant to be, but the rather emotional accounts in the vernacular describing the attributes of this lost paradise clearly expressed a need to color and clarify the facts. Trees, fruit, flowers, birds: these things were all specified, as well as the lovely fragrances, the fountain, the rivers, and what have you. In this context, the prose text *Dit is 't bescrive van den eertschen paradijs* (This is a description of the earthly paradise), intended for reading aloud, provides a revealing development, not only by clarifying that one may—under certain conditions—again reside in paradise but also by stating that paradise contains something for everyone. One should not assume that paradise meant being at the mercy of divine generosity, for there were all kinds of possibilities to upholster paradise with one's own choice of material, as it were. The fountain and four rivers, for example, were supposedly "obedient to those living in paradise, taking on the desired proportions and velocity according to the residents' personal wishes, so that the rivers may be directed collectively as well as individually, to the satisfaction of everyone."

The certainty that people could in fact inhabit paradise, as well as the suggestion of the do-it-yourself nature of one's pleasurable stay there, are present in many late-medieval representations of the earthly paradise. Its characteristics are increasingly interwoven with the prospect of heavenly rewards in the hereafter, sometimes resulting in a complete merger of both heavenly and earthly paradises. It must again be emphasized that these ideas invited one to imagine an attainable paradise entirely of one's own making. Everyone's desires would be fulfilled, for that pleasantly topsy-turvy world—the true world, according to credulous Christians—was in no way troubled by conflicting interests. This point should be borne in mind when searching for inducements to dreaming of Cockaigne and Luilekkerland. The dreams were not caused by bread alone. In the Middle Ages, paradise was brought closer to, and was more readily connected with, one's own existence, sometimes in such an attractive and compelling way that it inevitably began to resemble the Land of Cockaigne.

There are, to be sure, close correspondences between representations of the two paradises. Another Middle Dutch text mentions two summers and winters per year, not because of the weather (which is always mild) but because of the resulting double harvest. This dream, also known from stories of the golden age, indicates the shortsighted, earth-bound nature of these paradisiacal projections. Two harvests a year can hardly be an attraction when one requires almost no sustenance and the trees perpetually bear fruit. The dream of abundance, however, knows no limits, and this may be traced to the direness of the real-life situation. Such avid multiplications are dealt with more thoroughly in Cockaigne, where every month has five weeks, and every year four Easters, Whitsuns, and Christmases, along with a reduction in fast days to one every hundred years. Text L even adds multiple Feasts of Saint John.

The above-mentioned Middle Dutch description of the first paradise, which mentions the paradise dwellers Elijah and Enoch, also displays the compulsion to spruce up paradise with some appealing exotica, sought in particular in a greatly expanded bird population. Beautiful swans now swim in the fountain, storks stand on the shores of the rivers, and other beautiful birds strut around as well, such as splendid peacocks "who stand with their tails spread, glittering so beautifully in the sunshine that it is an extraordinary sight." Nightingales, singing wonderfully, also perch in the trees near the fountain. The author of this text, obviously well aware of paradise's deadly monotony, hastens to add that, even though the landscape is covered with plants of the same variety, fortunately "they may be distinguished from one another to such an extent that the earth has everywhere such a charming appearance that it is well worth viewing."

It still sounds sparse, but apparently the author did not dare lay a finger on the perfect harmony that was the essence of the earthly paradise. Half a century later, Hieronymus Bosch would not feel the least bit inhibited by this orthodoxy, fusing all the traditions with renewed and truly fantastical fantasy—in the most literal sense—into his *Garden of Delights*, which may be molded into any paradise, even one fitting the description of Cockaigne.

One or two things have already been said about the location of the earthly paradise. No one doubted that it could be pinpointed to a specific place on earth. Genesis, after all, stated this quite clearly. Moreover, no matter how allegorically one played around with this explanation, the point of departure nonetheless remained the nearly palpable presence of a place on earth—according to some, a place of considerable size—where the original conditions of Creation still obtained. This was what made it possible to go in search of it.

Though he is loath to admit it, the earthly paradise is one of the few places Sir John Mandeville failed to visit. To be sure, he organized his geography book in such a way as to enable him to take his readers by the hand and lead them past scores of exotic lands and peoples. No one, however, was able to set foot in paradise, not even Mandeville. He therefore had to depend on assertions: it is said, he begins cautiously, that it lies on a mountain in the East, where "the earth begins." It is in fact "so high that Noah's flood could not reach it, though it covered all the rest of the earth."

Mandeville gives a most meticulous description of paradise:

FIGURE 33

Representation of paradise by Hieronymus Bosch. Detail of
The Garden of Delights, ca. 1503–1504.

Source: Madrid, Museo del Prado.

Paradise is encircled by a wall; but no man can say what the wall is made of. It is all grown over with moss and with bushes so that no stone can be seen, nor anything else a wall might be made of. The wall of Paradise stretches from the south to the north; there is no way into it open because of ever burning fire, which is the flaming sword that God set up before the entrance so that no man should enter. In the middle of Paradise is a spring from which come four rivers, which run through different lands. These rivers sink down into the earth inside Paradise and then run many a mile underground; afterwards they rise up out of the earth again in distant lands.

With regret, Mandeville must concede that no living man may enter this earthly paradise:

By land no man can go thither because of the wild beasts in the wilderness, and because of the hills and rocks, which no one can cross; and also because of the many dark places that are there. No one can go there by water either, for those rivers flow with so strong a current, with such a rush and such waves that no boat can sail against them. . . . Many great lords have tried at different times to travel by those rivers to Paradise, but they could not prosper in their journeys; some of them died through exhaustion from rowing and excessive labor, some went blind and deaf through the noise of the waters, and some were drowned through the violence of the waves. And so no man, as I said, can get there except through the special grace of God.

Dispirited, Mandeville ends his story of the earthly paradise and turns, reluctantly, to descriptions of "the isles and lands" he has been privileged to see. Or so he says.

This and similar accounts of the earthly paradise, weighed in the balance by Isidore and Bartholomaeus, recur constantly in texts in the vernacular. Some of them have the tendency to embroider upon its specific location and dimensions. The mountain in the East then reaches to the heavens, even to the point of touching the moon, offering at the same time a meteorological explanation for the ideal weather conditions: at such heights there is no longer cold or ice; neither do clouds and rain have any business being that high. The most far-fetched description stems from a vision—in which anything goes—beheld by a virgin called Petrissa, who saw and experienced the immenseness of paradise, as well as its inaccessibility. According to her, an impassable strip of land approximately two hundred miles wide separates paradise from the rest of the world. It is, of course, impossible for a human being to negotiate a desert, high mountains, sharp rocks, deep valleys, thorny bushes, impenetrable forests, and deep water. Practically the only path left to her was to travel there in a vision.

These problems of utter inaccessibility were the first to be solved in Cockaigne. This dreamland is easily reached: the narrator can attest to this, having just returned from a visit there. The closing lines of both rhyming texts imply that a visit to Cockaigne may be freely undertaken by anyone. Even before mentioning its location, the text on Luilekkerland comments ironically on its striving to provide an education in middle-class morality. "Until now this land was unknown to all except those rogues and rascals who first discovered it." This statement is followed by mention of Luilekkerland's nonsensical position on the map, opening as it does into a huge mountain of buckwheat porridge no less than three miles wide. All those managing to eat their way through this obstacle, however, will truly find their bread buttered on both sides. Luilekkerland is therefore freely accessible, providing one has the audacity—not to mention the voracity— to behave like a morally myopic mole.

There is not much to be said about the fare on offer in paradise. No real problems exist on this score: the accent here is not so much on permanent abundance as on the need for any food at all, let alone a great variety of it. In medieval society, the need for excessive amounts of food was thought to be symptomatic of the decadence that had crept into the world after the Fall of Man. As I've noted before, even after their expulsion from paradise, Adam and Eve were vegetarians, as were their descendants, until the time of the Flood. They required hardly any sustenance, merely some water and per- haps some fruit. The *Sidrac*, a popular didactic manual for laypeople, states that there was only fruit, yet this fruit assumes a remarkably multifunctional character. In one instance, it guaranteed resistance to disease, while in another it was capable of bestowing immortality on those who ate it. It could even ensure that one was never hungry again.

This is the meaning of the Bible's near silence on the subject of food in the earthly paradise, and this was just as hard to stomach as all those other monotonies of paradise that were so quickly replaced in the Middle Ages by elements derived from other dreamworlds, onto which were projected one's own time-bound fantasies. In her vision, the virgin Petrissa saw whole baskets of fruit, full of apples, pears, figs, and much, much more, all of it delicious and, of course, extremely nutritious. Upon eating some, she instantly noticed how much stronger she felt. And luckily all that fantastical fruit had the power to remain permanently fresh.

There was not much more to it than this. The trees were always dripping with ripe fruit, which cured all evils. Hunger did not exist, and eating was scarcely necessary. Gluttonous fantasies, fed by the permanent fear of hunger and scarcity, were difficult to deal with in an earthly paradise of a biblical nature, the scholarly explanations of which did not permit any occurrence of El Doradean belly worship. A wider range of possibilities presented itself when outfitting the heavenly paradise, about which the Bible remained agreeably vague. Here, in any case, was a blatant challenge to come up with a more adequate solution based on the medieval situation. That Cockaigne and Luilekkerland readily accept this challenge is abundantly clear. It is even possible that this lack in the Bible was an important stimulus to the spirited development of a Cockaigne based on the existing dreamland material stemming from classical antiquity.

The prevailing paradisiacal weather conditions were certainly no cause for dispute in the Middle Ages. The Bible kept silent on this point, apparently because it was taken for granted that—as emerges from nearly every description of paradise—the weather there was indescribably mild and invariably pleasant. The implications of this assurance can best be measured against the threat to survival posed by the unstable weather conditions prevailing in the Low Countries. Protracted hot spells and drought could be bad enough, but persistent rain and unrelenting frost were even more devastating, continually disrupting the more or less well-ordered lives of many people. Things could become serious when one was long deprived of one's normal source of income, which meant dependence on one's family or on charitable institutions and not infrequently the loss of one's home. Above all, however, weather conditions exerted a profound effect on the food supply, and the permanent fear of hunger was automatically fed by the fear of bad weather.

This is why paradise has a permanently mild climate: not too warm, not too cold, not too dry, not too humid. During the Renaissance, when paradise was refurbished, taking on the aspect of a garden of delights with the inevitable characteristics of a *locus amoenus*, its weather was given the quality of eternal springtime. So it had been during the golden age, which still caused a balmy breeze to caress the Islands of the Blessed. Spring as the key typification, however, occurs already in the writings of the earliest Christian authors. The vernacular versions of reports from paradise occasionally try to introduce some tension into the story by means of a negative comparison: not how good the weather in paradise is, but how bad it isn't. And at least it is not subject to unexpected changes.

In a society that experienced constant variability as a threat, the qualities of constancy, stability, and harmony meant infinitely more to people than they do now. But even though these feelings arose as a result of practical experience, they were still founded on the theology of the Fall. To be sure, it was then that inconstancy—and with it transience—had come into the world. Paradise in medieval garb was in no way less monotonous: it still displayed a rather boring mixture of harmony and stability. Its new clothes were merely intended to make it less drab and more up-to-date.

A climate characterized by sharp contrasts was viewed in the Middle Ages as the scourge of humankind. In horror-struck terms, Mandeville describes such weather in the land of Tartary: "That land is seldom without great storms. And in summer there are great thunderstorms, which kill a lot of animals and people. The air temperature changes, too, very quickly— now great heat, then great cold—and so it is a bad place to live." Clearly, such a land can be no good, and its defects have rubbed off on its inhabitants: "They are a very foul folk, cruel and full of ill will." Paradise, of course, is the other extreme, where there are no seasons, no wind chasing the clouds, likewise no burning sun and no wintry cold. Clearly, such constancy was Creation's original intention.

Just how important the assurance of stable weather was is apparent from the weather reports broadcast from the heavenly paradise. Weather, just like hunger, generated unfathomable fears that called for reassurance.

The *Sterfboeck* (Book of death) of 1491—contrary to what the title suggests, a practical guide to the behavior most likely to guarantee one's admittance to the hereafter—leaves no room for doubt as to the absolutely ideal circumstances obtaining there: "There is no heat or cold, water or fire, wind or rain, snow or lightning, thunder or hail. Neither are there storms. Rather, there is eternally fine, clear weather, much nicer and more pleasant than scholars will ever be able to imagine. It is always a wonderfully agreeable May." Columbus, who never wavered during the course of three voyages from the opinion that he was frequenting the immediate vicinity of paradise, always described ideal weather conditions in terms of spring in Andalusia or elsewhere in Spain. For him, too, the most important things were balminess and constancy.

At the end of the Middle Ages, the weather in paradise became more and more attuned to the month of May, at which time everything displays the most ideal stability and temperateness, at least in Western Europe. With the increase in the appreciation of nature and the accompanying developments in courtly revelry, May became the ideal month in which to indulge in cultured entertainment. The cultivation of such pleasures became so much the norm that it gave rise to a Dutch proverb: "It isn't always a May evening," meaning, of course, that the world at its best can resemble paradise only once in a great while.

It is not surprising, then, that it is always May in text L, a provision borrowed directly from what had meanwhile become the normal weather prevailing in paradise. The "eternal summertime" in text B—"as though 'twere April all the year"—suggests in a subtle way that ideal summer temperatures are actually those typical of spring, which summer in the Low Countries often resembles. Furthermore, these slight variations again show how text L realizes the mainstream of Cockaigne material in a straightforward way, whereas text B exhibits a number of cerebral twists and turns in the recording of its version.

Cockaigne's precipitation mostly takes the form of foodstuffs. There it rains custard tarts, pancakes, meat pies, and—according to text B—even eels. This was a chance not to be missed in a belly-worshiping paradise. The fear of catastrophic weather naturally leads to a fear of scarcity, which is why it rains food in Cockaigne, ridding the inhabitants of two obsessions in one go. The prose text about Luilekkerland is less active in this respect. The weather is not described as such, but the precipitation now consists only of sweetness. Text G mentions that the snow is like powdered sugar, while hailstones appear to be sugared almonds. Even in its proffering of such details, this text betrays its orientation toward youth, who get a good dressing down at the end of the text and are severely reprimanded for their tendency to display such lazy, candy-crazed behavior.

The Land of Cockaigne also has a miraculous river, flowing with beer and wine of every description. The inspiration for this provision, which did not require a lot of imagination to come up with, does not have to be sought far afield. Milk, honey, and wine are the basic ingredients of every promised land in the Bible, including the enclosed garden of the Song of Songs. The golden ages of antiquity, as well as the Muslim paradise, were also brimming with these nutritious and noble drinks.

Some of these predictions of future rewards have a tendency to vary their outpourings. The earthly paradise that the doubting Saint Brendan visited—to see with his own eyes just how factual the Bible was—possesses, perhaps for this very reason, more attractions of this nature. His account, after all, had to sound especially convincing. In any case, in the Middle Dutch version of his voyage there is an abundance of balsam, syrup, olive oil, and honey. The dreamland visited by the Celtic traveler Mael Dúin, from which Saint Brendan's earthly paradise was probably derived, displays a multiplicity of blessings with the distinct nature of rewards. There is, for example, a spring flowing with water, though it pours forth milk on Sundays and wine and beer on important Christian holidays. In Cockaigne one may partake forever of wine and beer, at no cost whatsoever, and the wine is of the very best quality. Cockaigne goes no further than this, and neither does Luilekkerland, in which this attraction is not emphasized at all. Indeed, there was no credit to be gained by doing so, as all the known paradises and dreamworlds were already overflowing with the most delicious drinks. Cockaigne could, of course, vie with them, but its potational possibilities were nothing more nor less than an accurate reflection of late-medieval tastes.

18

Never Say Die

IN TEXT L there is yet another river, unhesitatingly called "a Jordan," that offers rejuvenation, "for when its waters touch their tongue, old folk all start turning young." This means that in Cockaigne, just as in paradise, immortality is the rule, and aging is simply an ailment that can be cured. In essence this puts Cockaigne on a par with the Holy Land, for both have a miraculous river at their disposal.

As far as the real Jordan was concerned, there was no doubt as to its miraculous nature. Saint John Chrysostom, a Christian of late antiquity, had already noted the healing powers of its water, while as early as the sixth century pilgrims betook themselves to the Jordan to take advantage of its curative properties. Such hagiographic texts as *Van den heilighen driën coninghen* (Of the three holy kings), dating from the early fifteenth century, give detailed confirmation of its medicinal properties. The lame, the blind, and the sick bathed naked and were washed in the Jordan, after which many of them were restored to health. Pilgrims never failed to fill a bottle—and sometimes a whole barrel—to take home with them, where the sick who drank of it were often healed. Cockaigne's Jordan can do even more, namely, what the fountain of life in paradise is also considered capable of doing: bestowing one with eternal life.

All cultures report instances of springs, fountains, lakes, and rivers that have a miraculous effect on human health. Their wondrous properties usually boil down to their lending protection against sickness and death, often by taking the person in question back to a much younger age. This ailment-free age is, not infrequently, the presumed age of Christ at the time he was crucified: thirty-two or thirty-three years old. Sir John Mandeville lost a great deal of credibility by maintaining not only that he had seen such a fountain of youth at the foot of the mountain Polumbum but that he had also drunk from it: "I, John Mandeville, saw this well, and drank of it three

FIGURE 34
The healing well from the Gospel According to
Saint John. Miniature from *The Book of Hours of
Catherine of Cleves*, ca. 1440.
Source: Reproduced from J. Plummer, ed., *The Book of
Hours of Catherine of Cleves* (New York, 1975), no. 86.

times, and so did all my companions. Ever since that time I have felt the
better and healthier, and I think I shall do until such time as God in his
grace causes me to pass out of this mortal life. Some men call that well the
fons iuventutis, that is, the Well of Youth; for he who drinks of it seems
always young. They say this water comes from the earthly paradise, it is so
full of goodness."

In particular, pilgrims' accounts and guides to the Holy Land point out
springs and fountains with spectacular healing powers, often in biblical settings. Practically no one fails to mention the pool-cum-bathhouse at the
sheep market in Jerusalem, told of by John the Evangelist. In the five porches
of this pool "lay a great multitude of impotent folk, of blind, halt, with-
ered, waiting for the moving of the water. For an angel went down at a certain season into the pool, and troubled the water: whosoever then first after
the troubling of the water stepped in was made whole of whatsoever disease
he had."

FIGURE 35

The Fountain of Youth. German woodcut, ca. 1535.

Source: Reproduced from *Die Welt des Hans Sachs* (Nuremberg, 1976), no. 153.

Dominating all other fantasies, however, was the dream of achieving immortality simply by taking a sip of water. The starting point, of course, is that unfortunate matter of having forfeited eternal life in the Garden of Eden, where immortality was made manifest by the blessings of both the tree of life and the fountain, which could bestow one with eternal life. The earthly paradise, however, was so far away as to be unreachable, while the achievement of the heavenly paradise was anything but certain. There, too, provision had been made for eternity, in the form of a river flowing with the water of life, which rose beneath the throne of God and His Son and subsequently flowed down the middle of the heavenly city's main street. On its shores stood the trees of life, with their rather redundant healing powers. Moreover, this dream is as old as life itself, for in Babylonian legend there already occurs a wondrous spring lying at the source of rivers that can heal all illness.

The yearning for immortality also sought satisfaction closer to home, giving rise to a remarkably large number of fantasies during the transition from the Middle Ages to the early-modern period. Neither is it at all clear how literally one should take these playful presumptions of life-lengthening methods. Such fantasies could also be deadly serious. Death had become an intolerable prospect, and the cures for dying were many and various. In fact, there were so many supposed cures for dying that it seems as though people thought death could be outwitted by sheer inventiveness. Moreover, speed was of the essence. Humanity's persistent sinfulness seemed to be leading to a gradual worsening of man's mortal state since the Fall. Life spans were getting shorter all the time. In spite of everything, one used to be able to count on reaching the age of eight or nine hundred years. According to the *Lucidarius* in the manuscript containing text L, Adam—sins and all—had lived to be 980. In Abraham's day life expectancy had already been reduced to around two hundred years. And because people were hell-bent on persevering in their sinfulness, things had only gone downhill since then. David stated in his psalms that in his day life stopped at eighty. And the author of a late-fourteenth-century didactic manual in prose, the *Ridderboek* (The knight's handbook), wrote in dismay that it had since dropped to sixty years, with many people dying even younger.

Clearly, there was no time to lose. Before long everyone would be dying in the cradle. Virgil, presented in the Middle Ages as a heathen sorcerer who nonetheless possessed a great deal of useful knowledge, had found a remedy. Or so it seemed. In a story published around 1525 by the popular press, the Dutch version of this internationally circulated news flash tells that Virgil first gave orders for his body to be cut into four pieces. His remains were then salted like a herring and put in a barrel, with his heart on top. Every day for the next nine days his servant was required to drip the oil of a lamp over him. Unfortunately, the servant was disturbed while performing this task on the seventh day, causing the whole experiment to backfire and putting an immediate end to the story.

Well-known methods of rejuvenation were based on the idea that making people was comparable to baking bread. The weary, sagging dough could simply be kneaded into shape again, and out of the oven would come a rebaked, reborn, and, most importantly, rejuvenated person. This is referred to in sixteenth-century German broadsheets, as well as in the folklore of Eeklo in East Flanders, where legend has it that heads undergoing this procedure were temporarily replaced with cauliflowers.

Five hundred years ago, this fantasy sounded slightly less absurd and considerably less childish than it does now. Did not the wonder of the Eucharist imply that the body of a god could be constantly transformed into dough and back again? Neither was bakers' terminology shunned in discussions of this phenomenon. Being born again or undergoing extreme rejuvenation, as well as the recovery of immortality, were realistic expectations for many people. The church also spoke in these terms of the true life that would begin only after earthly death.

These immortalizings were subsequently projected onto other crafts as well: rejuvenation by being ground in a mill, for example, or pounded on the anvil of a smith. Here as well a craft was chosen that could transform raw material of a coarse nature into newer, rejuvenated forms. In this respect, the young smiths of Deventer compared themselves to the Creator Himself. On Shrove Tuesday of the year 1546—the very year in which Luilekkerland was conceived—they enacted on the public square in front of the town hall a farce in which they demonstrated how "to forge a young woman from an old one." The text has not been preserved, but it is easy enough to imagine the peals of laughter that must have reverberated around the square. Plenty of prints and paintings reveal the seedy manner in which women were generally portrayed, their bodies seemingly crying out for revitalization.

Of course, the increase in the number of witnesses of actual rejuvenation did anything but dispel these implausible fantasies. It was obviously necessary to be able to dream, at least occasionally, of a situation where death did not exist. At the same time science was doing its work, for the belief in rejuvenation or immortality was not merely a question of the masses letting themselves get carried away. Renowned explorers reported seeing fountains of youth and successful rejuvenation cures, the attainment of extremely old age, and even death by choice. One did not necessarily have to die, as evidenced by the inhabitants of an island where, according to Celtic tradition, one could simply decide that one had had enough. It was then necessary to travel by boat to another island, where dying was a possibility. As usual, the Christian paradise is dimly visible through the fabric of this story, for there, too, it was—and is—impossible to die.

From a completely different source—alchemy, which was practiced only by a chosen handful of modern scientists of the day—reports came of the steady progress being made in the production of the *quinta essentia*. One swallow of this primal liquid, actually containing the secret of human life itself, was enough to make old folk forty years old again. On the threshold of the modern age, one could therefore expect a breakthrough on all fronts, providing definitive reversal—finally granted by God to humankind—of the punishment endured since the Fall.

Most hope, however, was directed at the miraculous waters of paradise, which flowed into the world directly from the fountain of life via four wild rivers. Regaining one's youth and keeping it went hand in hand: all one had to do was find the source by retracing these rivers, which branched out endlessly to bring fertile and healing waters to every place on earth. Moreover, the closer one got to the source, the more powerful the effect of the water. In theory, any stream could lead to its discovery. The French knightly epic poem *Huon de Bordeaux* contains a story about a brook in the garden of the emir of Babylon that supposedly came straight from one of the rivers of paradise. Whatever its source, it brought health to the sick and youth to the old.

Many other texts praise such blessings in other parts of the world. The story that tops them all, of course, is that of the land of Prester John, according to hearsay a proto-Christian country in the neighborhood of Ethiopia. This land, where a pocket of pure Christianity had apparently been preserved, reaped considerable benefits from the water flowing out of nearby paradise. Dying was no longer possible. While young, one was required to drink this healing water three times, after which one was never ill and stopped aging once one's years reached the auspicious number of thirty-two.

The stories that appeal most to the imagination, however, are those surrounding the Nile, which was thought to be one of the four great rivers flowing out of paradise and was also the best known among medieval pilgrims, merchants, and explorers. Jean de Joinville, in his account dating from 1306 of the seventh crusade, describes his attempts to find the source of the Nile, in order to prove that by going upstream one would necessarily arrive at paradise. For the time being, though, no one had managed to penetrate farther than the border of Egypt. Where the Nile entered the country, nets were thrown out to fish up the well-known wares flowing out of paradise, especially rhubarb and ginger, cinnamon, and other spices. Even the mud along the Nile's shores was known for its great fertility, which was thought transmittable to animals and especially to women, who could use it to cure themselves of barrenness.

Felix Fabri, a Dominican from southern Germany who traveled around Egypt in 1483/1484, noted in his diary that the insalubrious sludge along the banks of the Nile was responsible for both local overpopulation and the huge numbers of animals. Adornes of Bruges, as enlightened as he was keen on traveling, ascertained that the water of the Nile was very soft and fragrant—certainly proof of its paradisiacal origins—as well as being nutritious, an aid to digestion, and—last but not least—healing. After drinking it, one broke out in such a sweat that all illness was expelled from the body.

A halt had to be put to all this dying, and if that should prove impossible, then at least something had to be done about the continual reduction in life expectancy. This was possible only by scientific or fantastical means, and in the late Middle Ages methods proposed by both these approaches were working in full swing. Everyone was striving for a permanent age of thirty-three years, after which all change would come to a standstill and one would enter a permanent eternity. This was how things were meant to be in the earthly paradise, and that is how things still were in heaven. Such assurances were provided by popular didactic manuals such as the *Sterfboeck* (Book of death) and the *Boeck van der Voirsienicheit Godes* (Book of God's providence).

With a method for achieving stasis established, one would only have to get through the interim period of the first thirty-three years. The word of deliverance could come at any moment, bringing news of a fountain of youth accessible to everyone or an herb seller with an affordable recipe for an elixir of life. Perhaps Sir John Mandeville had already discovered the means of salvation. And what should one think of the news sent home by the great Christopher Columbus? His travels, at any rate, had taken on a much more tangible nature since the appearance of his letters in 1493. Reports had it that he was forever seeing paradise on the horizon.

In the meantime, dreams and fantasies offered a substitute both pleasant and useful. In Cockaigne one could stuff oneself to the gills and sip water that endowed one with eternal life and the chance to start anew. This is something altogether different from the kind of eternity that ascetic hermits strove after by means of strict abstinence and mortification of the flesh. In Cockaigne one ate and drank in order to stay young. That was how things were supposed to be, and that was why Cockaigne existed. As already mentioned, literature and the visual arts also opened up many other paths: texts, paintings, miniatures, prints, tapestries, mirrors, ivory statues, and stained-glass windows all testify to the many ways leading to earthly immortality by means of simple rejuvenation cures. Even the Carnival parades took part in this: in Nuremberg the pre-Lenten procession invariably included a fountain of youth, suitably enough, for the renewal of life on earth in the form of a spring cleaning was one of the main motifs of late-medieval Lenten rituals.

Medieval representations of paradise have the tendency to transform it into an apothecary's shop offering efficacious remedies for all common ailments, including death. Paradise is equipped with facilities designed to put an end to the daily inconveniences of hunger, thirst, and sickness, as well as the fear of these bothersome things. The *Elucidarium*, by Honoré d'Autun, dating from the twelfth century, unhesitatingly gives the following answer to the question of what paradise is: "It is a place where various kinds of trees are planted to combat all possible discomfort." Lest anyone mistake the meaning of this, for the laity there was a rhyming adaptation of this text, called the *Dietsche Lucidarius*, which spelled this message out in verse:

> In the midst of Paradise
> The tree of life He planted
> And the strength and power granted
> To bear choice fruits, which were to be
> Good health and great longevity.

These medicines clearly consisted of nothing but fruit, which could be a remedy for anything and everything, while the tree of life specialized in healing old age, sickness, and dying.

In the late Middle Ages, this text served as the layman's handbook par excellence, enjoying widespread application in education. Versions appeared in nearly all the vernaculars, including several in Middle Dutch. This is also true of the *Sidrac*, admittedly stemming from a courtly French milieu but later just as widely read as the *Elucidarium*. Versions of these treatises on the *ars vivendi* occur in the London manuscript that includes text L, revealing the close proximity of this pragmatic vision of paradise, taught even at school, to Cockaigne. In the *Sidrac* this close relationship is brought just as clearly into focus. In paradise "there are various sorts of trees that are good for healing any complaint; for there is a fruit that, when eaten, prevents one from feeling hunger ever again. And another fruit, called the fruit of life, prevents one from growing older or falling ill or dying."

The shelves are always stocked, full of every possible fruit, large or small, in any taste, smell, or color. The earthly paradise dares go no further. Everything revolves around fruit, while the drinks on offer are usually limited to water, although occasionally extended to include milk and honey as the standard beverage of promised lands. Cockaigne, though, does not exchange these lost blessings for more worldly and immediate desires. For there was also a paradise in heaven, and that paradise was perhaps more likely to lend itself to worldly furnishings.

19
Heavenly Rewards

*H*EAVEN HELD THE FUTURE. In theory it was accessible to everyone, though unfortunately only after death. One could, however, take heart from the central message of Christianity, which said that life did not truly begin until then. The main thing—and this was no small matter—was to take care not to forfeit the right to everlasting bliss during one's brief stay on earth. Even if one managed to arrive safely at death's door, there was still a long wait until the resurrection and the Last Judgment, and only after that would it finally be possible to sample the delights of heaven.

Everything that happened in the meantime was a source of great disagreement in the Middle Ages. Were the good and righteous given some interim rewards? Were the good-for-nothings subjected to a bit of preliminary torture? It was nice to think of the righteous parked temporarily in the earthly paradise, waiting for the Lord to pronounce judgment, but in 1329 Pope John XXII condemned this idea as heresy, though this did nothing to deter the masses from believing it anyway.

One way or another, after death decent folk deserved some kind of reward, which could only be enjoyed in full and for all eternity, however, when one finally arrived in heaven for good. Semirespectable folk were not excluded, but they would be arriving a bit later, after compulsory purification in purgatory. The nature of one's defilement, as well as help from below in the form of masses said for the dead, determined the length of the treatment, but purgatory had only one egress, and that led directly to heaven.

If the earthly paradise was generally thought of as unspoiled nature, the heavenly paradise assumed more the shape of a city. This distinction arose primarily from the need to distinguish between these two biblical places by bestowing them with different outward appearances. That the heavenly paradise was portrayed as a city, the New Jerusalem, stemmed from the need— strongly felt by Christians—to see a truly resurrected Zion that could blot out the accursed memory of the ground defiled by the Jews' heinous deed. Hadn't the earthly Jerusalem's walls and houses been rightly reduced to rubble again and again? Reconstruction in the concrete sense also dominated the spirit of the crusades, frequently giving rise to visions that connected or even identified a New Jerusalem on earth with its heavenly counterpart. Hadn't Pope Urban II himself, when making his appeal for a crusade at the Council of Clermont in 1095, declared that Jerusalem was the navel of the world, situated in an extremely fertile land?

The most immediate cause of this merging of heaven and Jerusalem lay in the messianism of the Jews, testified to by Jehovah in various places in the Book of Isaiah, which speaks of the New Jerusalem in terms of a promised land, built literally of the most dazzling treasures: "Behold, I will lay thy stones with fair colors, and lay thy foundations with sapphires. And I will make thy windows of agates, and thy gates of carbuncles, and all thy borders of pleasant stones." Elsewhere in Isaiah Jerusalem is praised as the final stopping place of this miserable life on earth, which is destined to culminate in unimaginable glory. The emphasis here is on comforting food, provided in true maternal fashion in ever-flowing abundance: "Rejoice ye with Jerusalem, and be glad with her, all ye that love her: rejoice for joy with her, all ye that mourn for her: that ye may suck, and be satisfied with the breasts of her consolations; that ye may milk out, and be delighted with the abundance of her glory.—As one whom his mother comforteth, so will I comfort you; and ye shall be comforted in Jerusalem. And when ye see this, your heart shall rejoice, and your bones shall flourish like an herb."

The most important role in medieval images of heaven, however, was played by the conversion of the Jerusalem prophesied in Isaiah into the form manifested in the New Testament's Book of Revelation, also known as the Apocalypse. During the whole of the Middle Ages and afterward, this most cryptic of biblical books gave rise to extremely diverse interpretations of messianism and its proclamation on earth. It describes how Saint John the Divine is shown the holy city of Jerusalem from atop a high mountain, at the moment it descends from heaven. It glitters with the precious stones from which it is built. Its contours are marked by a high wall with twelve gates, guarded by as many angels and bearing the names of the twelve tribes of Israel, while the foundations of the city walls bear the names of the twelve apostles.

This heavenly city is built according to ideal plans, in which its length, width, and height are always equal, everything being based on the number twelve. Its walls are made of jasper and its gates of pearls, and the foundation consists of twelve kinds of precious stones, all of which are mentioned by name. The city itself is of pure gold. Night never falls, for God's light shines eternally. A river full of the water of life flows through the city after rising under the throne of God the Father, seated next to His Son. On either side of this river grow trees of life, which bear fruit twelve times a year and have foliage with healing qualities. "And there shall be no more death, neither sorrow, nor crying, neither shall there be any more pain."

The heavenly Jerusalem is the sublimation of the earthly paradise, the characteristics of which it adopted wholesale. These were subsequently expanded to include a variety of rewards, such as those eagerly awaited by various sections of medieval society. Perfect harmony reigns, above all else. It is precisely these promises, held to be true, of rewards accruing in the near future that Cockaigne incorporates into its more earthly dreams of the blessings on offer in a land with paradisiacal dimensions. A fountain of youth, a constant supply of food, rivers full of delicious drinks, silver vessels lining the shores, and much, much more: all these things correspond to the standard images of heavenly rewards.

Even the stray carbuncle in the edible architecture described in text B could have fallen from the structures of precious stones seen in the New Jerusalem. In any case, the somewhat cryptic statement in B—"long and wide this land"—is now more comprehensible. This line should probably be interpreted as "this land is as long as it is wide," which provides the earthly counterpart of the ideal dimensions of the heavenly Jerusalem.

The much-admired harmony in heaven is given an earthly translation in Cockaigne in the heartily acknowledged friendship and helpfulness shown by all to one another. Enemies no longer exist. The complete complaisance in sexual matters could also have been inspired by the unceasing display of mutual affection by which inhabitants of heaven practically cuddle each other to death. Furthermore, according to the ideas of Augustine, there would certainly have been sex in the earthly paradise if only Adam and Eve had not sinned so quickly—after only seven hours in residence—and consequently been driven out. If everything had gone according to plan, they would have indulged in procreation in the Garden of Eden and with no fear of interference from the devil, who did not turn the human genitals into mere instruments of pleasure until after the Fall. Such notions of celestial sex, of course, are readily adopted by Cockaigne.

Isn't the invitation in text B to "sleep with another tenderly" a reference to these passionless forms of intercourse? In Cockaigne sex is a tender activity, as it ought to be, engaged in without the brute fury introduced by the devil. And who else should one have sex with but friends, for only kindred spirits reside in heaven or Cockaigne. Those who think these visions of coupling have something modern about them—namely, respect for one another—will be happy to have their opinion seconded by the Bruges rhetorician Anthonis de Roovere. Around the time the Cockaigne texts were recorded, he described how one should copulate tenderly and lovingly, using the word *friendly* to typify the procedure. It was not his intention, though, to remove sex to a more acceptable and heavenly sphere. He recommends tenderness toward the woman with the assurance that this will considerably increase the man's pleasure in bed. Clearly, this makes friendly intercourse an interesting option for Cockaigne.

The blueprints for medieval descriptions of the heavenly paradise lay in both the earthly paradise and the New Jerusalem, both found in the Bible in the form of testimony and prediction. Haste was necessary in obtaining assurances regarding the arrangements in heaven, for it was thought that the earthly paradise must also be subject to decline and decay, inevitable ingredients of earthly existence.

A favorite method in these descriptions was the use of the negative comparison, which actually offers a long list of all the earthly suffering that does not exist in heaven: "There is neither hypocrisy nor dissembling, deceit, flattery, strife, discord, neither hate nor spite nor envy. There no one suffers hunger or thirst, heat or cold, sickness or pain, disease or fear or worry, dejection or suffering." So it says in *Somme le roi*, a popular didactic manual offering guidelines for conduct, translated by William Caxton as the *Royal Book* (1484) and by a later translator as *The Book of Vices and Virtues*. Similar formulations are to be found everywhere, sometimes embellished with descriptions verging on the spectacular, such as that found in the *Sterf-*

boeck (Book of death) of 1491: "There no one is lame, cripple, or blind, no one cross-eyed or mute, there are no people with scabies or pimples; neither are there deformed people; rather, everyone exhibits a beautiful perfection in all parts."

Interminglings of the earthly and the heavenly paradise occur already in Jewish apocalyptic literature dating from around 200 B.C., which develops the idea that the earthly paradise should also serve to harbor the righteous after death, either as a waiting room for the resurrection or as a resting place for all eternity. Other cultures also produced similar blends of the promised hereafter with the lost paradise. In the Egyptian realm of the dead, the souls of the deceased linger in the Milky Way, a happy place where both the sun and the moon shine simultaneously, flooding everything with bright light. Balmy breezes also blow there, and one can reap the most bountiful harvests, this last attribute being more characteristic of the earthly paradise. On the other hand, the construction of the realm of the dead bears a resemblance to heavenly architecture: thick walls offer protection from evil spirits, and a palace is situated right in the middle of the Milky Way.

The Bible furthers this confusion in a number of places. The Book of Ezekiel reminds us that man used to reside in the Garden of Eden and calls him to account: "Thou hast been in Eden the garden of God; every precious stone was thy covering, the sardius, topaz, and the diamond, the beryl, the onyx, and the jasper, the sapphire, the emerald, and the carbuncle, and gold." It is precisely this display of precious stones that will later determine the aspect of the heavenly Jerusalem.

Some texts in the vernacular give descriptions of both paradises in terms that are completely confused, sometimes quite intentionally. The city in heaven may then be overgrown with greenery, as witnessed by a sermon given by Johannes Brugman around 1470, in which he presents himself as a reporter giving an account of every nook and cranny in heaven. In search of the souls of deceased monks and nuns, he finally finds them in the midst of nature: "I then saw them sitting over yonder in a beautiful orchard, in which all kinds of flowers were to be found. There was the loveliest columbine. Words cannot express how they stood there; and the most beautiful things of all were the lilies." The *Sterfboeck* (Book of death) of 1491 turns heaven into a nature reserve, full of delightful flowers and herbs, perpetually ripe fruit, and ever-present greenery. The opposite is also possible. In such descriptions, the well in the middle of the Garden of Eden grows into a fountain, which in the late Middle Ages provided the inspiration for great architectonic representations that grew increasingly to resemble urban edifices. The prose text *Dit is 't bescrive van den eertschen paradijs* (This is a description of the earthly paradise) presents in the middle of the garden an enormous fountain-cum-temple made of precious stones, large enough to contain all humanity of the past, present, and future. Precious stones stream out of the temple in the four rivers that rise there, and the ground underneath this paradise is composed of the purest gold dust.

Elsewhere, too, the urban design of the hereafter exerted some influence on the living arrangements in paradise. These assumed the shape of all manner of buildings, as discovered by the monks in the Middle Dutch version of *The Voyage of Saint Brendan*. Saint Brendan is forced to journey with his companions across the seas to see with his own eyes the wonders of God's Creation on Earth. One of the stops is the earthly paradise, where the travelers land on a beach of golden pebbles and brightly shining carbuncles. They see at once a castle with walls of gold and gateposts made of carbuncles. Otherwise, the place matches the usual description of the Garden of Eden, but then they see a second castle, more beautiful than the first, and at last it is revealed to them that this is the earthly paradise, even though its appearance is more reminiscent of the heavenly Jerusalem.

This contamination is exacerbated by the negative image that cities had in classical antiquity and the Middle Ages. The first founder of a city on earth (Enoch) was the fratricidal Cain, and Rome was founded by Romulus, who murdered his twin brother, Remus. Cities were generally considered dens of iniquity, full of narrow streets where one could hide from God's view. Tacitus cursed the city for opening its doors to all the evil of the world, though ironically enough he based his judgment on the widening acceptance of Christianity as evidence of humankind's increasing wickedness.

Desert fathers and hermits fled the cities, which threatened to blind them to the sight of God. A late medieval rhyming text from Bruges gives direct expression to this fear in a dialogue between a hermit and a youth, the latter calling out enthusiastically:

FIGURE 36

Earthly paradise as a citadel. Detail from the so-called Walsperger Map of 1448.

Source: Reproduced from A. Verrycken, *De middeleeuwse wereldverkenning* (Leuven, 1990), 99.

Of fasting, sir, I take no heed,
And neither do I tend to read;
But revelry, friends, and roistering
Made me go on wandering.

. . . .

Father, I live inside the town,
But if I lived outside like you,
I'd surely take more care, that's true.

Moreover, the twelfth-century abbot Rupert of Deutz declared unequivocally that "God does not like cities or citadels."

This, however, was exactly what the heavenly Jerusalem looked like. Man,
on the other hand, was permitted to build nothing more than temporary
dwellings on earth, not such immense constructions designed for extreme
durability. Wasn't the Bible full of such ill-starred cities as Enoch, Jericho,
Babylon, Assur, Nineveh, Sodom, and Gomorrah? A fire in the town of Deutz
in 1128 was interpreted by the above-mentioned Rupert as a sign of God's
wrath, because not only had the place begun to develop into a center of trade,
it had even welcomed this change and taken steps to accommodate it.

This is part of the reason why greenery was cultivated in the heavenly
Jerusalem, appearing in the form of orchards, flower-filled meadows, and a
profusion of trees, fruit, and plants. Replacing the urban character of heaven
with a more castlelike ambience was an attractive idea in an age whose imagination and sense of romanticism were closely bound up with fortresses and
castles. That the presence of a castle or stronghold had so often been the very
reason for a town forming around it seems to have been ignored in this case.
Another way of blurring the dimensions of a city consisted in projecting the
heavenly blueprints on churches and cathedrals, whereby everything was compared with the ideal proportions obtaining in the heavenly Jerusalem. These
dimensions became the basis for symbolism of staggering detail: the gleam of
gold and precious stones was imitated by trompe-l'oeil painting on walls and
pillars, while the rays of sunlight piercing the stained-glass windows automatically conjured up colorful, gemlike patterns on the floor.

Heaven was thus brought to earth, and earth likewise determined the aspect
of heaven. Cockaigne comes even closer to these paradises if one includes

the descriptions of heaven stemming from visions. Such revelatory experiences were recorded throughout the Middle Ages, curiosity and a desire for sensation often leading to their widespread publication in all Western languages. These visionary offerings consequently appeared as separate texts, as well as being included in larger volumes of writings, and were just as likely to be found in mass culture as in the literature of the elite. The entire genre is crowned by Dante's *Divine Comedy*.

Reports of visions frequently recounted the experiences of blessed or privileged people who were taken while asleep on inspection tours of the hereafter. Upon returning, these people could describe the horrors of hell and purgatory and the rewards of heaven, the whole reported to earthly mortals in the form of cautionary tales that nonetheless made for addictive reading. One could no longer claim ignorance of the situation, now that the final destination, including the stopover at purgatory, had been presented—repeatedly and in such graphic detail—to the sinners on earth. At last people knew where they stood.

These popular accounts invited impressive elaboration. The Bible described the heavenly paradise in far less hospitable and certainly less recognizable terms than it did the earthly paradise, which left more scope for fleshing it out. To this end, the greenery of the earthly paradise was the first thing to be transplanted to the heavenly version. Happily populated meadows and wonderfully fragrant flowers became standard attributes, as did music and dance. Instead of two people at the most, this heavenly paradise harbored countless masses, and new inhabitants were arriving all the time. These people had to be given something to do that by medieval standards would represent the ultimate pleasure. For this reason eating was supplemented with cultured entertainment, provided by musicians in the form of heavenly choirs of angels.

In particular, the question of who was likely to be up there stirred the imagination, and this was something the visions gladly recounted in detail. Everyone in heaven was dressed in brilliant white. Saints, apostles, and martyrs, placed in order of rank, were usually sitting at table. At the highest table sat God the Father and God the Son. Lesser souls were to be found in the lower echelons, their greatest joy consisting in viewing God, His family, and the saints. Ordinary righteous folk actually resided in a kind of waiting room, presented as a market square, until Judgment Day, when they would be admitted to heaven for all eternity, but this seemingly uncomfortable position in no way diminished their pleasure at beholding heaven's permanent inhabitants.

It should come as no surprise that early on, and in ever-increasing measure, banqueting—in appropriately toned-down lavishness—became one of the favorite pastimes in the heavenly paradise. As I have described in earlier chapters, this obsession with food (or the lack of it) affected all levels of medieval society, especially when dreamworlds and rewards were the topic of discussion. It also explains why heaven so quickly acquired agrarian attributes, such as a rapid succession of superabundant harvests. Papias, bishop of Hierapolis in Phrygia, was the one who started this trend. Writing around A.D. 130–140, he filled the hereafter with an unprecedented abundance of food and drink.

Lidwina of Schiedam—bedridden and starving, her wounds festering on her way to sainthood—also had visions. Indeed, her daily regimen made it medically impossible not to have them. According to a chapter heading in a highly successful account of her life, she was granted a glimpse of the earthly paradise, but the event as described in the text reveals that her soul was actually transported temporarily to heaven. In fact, she described companies dining, though the food at their banquet was remarkable not so much for its abundance as for its undiminishing supply. One could only dream of such a miracle on earth, and that is, of course, what continually happened.

Lidwina was highly gratified to see, lying on the table, the alms she had so generously distributed to the poor. Furthermore, all the food and drink continually increased in amount, though the beer was no longer in earthenware jugs but in crystal carafes served along with the fried fish she had given the poor. Elsewhere she saw the saints sitting at table, and now her vision appears to have contained a glimpse of the future: the saints were being served by Lidwina herself, and afterward she was permitted to eat and drink with them.

Even the ultrasober Lidwina could not avoid being associated with the medieval obsession with eating. Her bizarre self-mortification by means of absolute abstinence from all nourishment was contrasted with the heavenly opposite as a reward, providing yet more evidence of the fervent desire for inexhaustible and self-replenishing supplies of food. Heaven, it was thought, must be organized along these lines. Indeed, in one of his sermons Johannes

Brugman gave a comprehensive summary of heavenly eating habits. Each type of inhabitant was assigned to a separate dining room, with the patriarchs in the main dining hall and the prophets in the wine cellar. Everywhere, however, eating and drinking was in evidence: "I then saw a splendid cellar room . . . with a laid table! There were barrels of sherry and malmsey wine. Jesus was seated in their midst as the prophet of prophets. And he began to serve and pour, so they could drink until they burst." When Brugman asked who the banqueters were and where they came from, they answered that as prophets they were now profiting from Jesus' teachings in his Sermon on the Mount: "Blessed are they which do hunger and thirst after righteousness: for they shall be filled."

This very literal translation of the heavenly blessing into bouts of eating and drinking in the heavenly hostel of the Lord occurs frequently in late medieval literature. Like the graphic description of the Eucharist, such vivid portrayals stem from mysticism, especially from its more democratized forms. Dirk van Delf, the erudite chaplain of the court of Holland, offered a scholastic counterbalance which taught that the truth should be interpreted allegorically. His view was that God in heaven laid the table of virtue, upon which lie the foods of reward and bliss. There was no talk of real food, which, of course, was unnecessary in the heavenly paradise.

On the level of mass worship—where there was more scope for developing one's own personal, mystical vision of heaven and one's relationship to the Holy Family—the penchant for heavenly banqueting only increased. A well-known exemplum tells of a dead knight in the hereafter who is visited by his still-living cousin on earth. Here, too, what is indicated as the earthly paradise actually seems to refer to the heavenly variety. In any case, its only attraction is a huge blowout, in which the visiting knight is allowed to participate. He enjoys the exquisite food, afterward admitting that he has never dined so well in his entire life. Such exempla were known far and wide, not only because they were recounted again and again and used as illustrative material in sermons but also because they inspired literary elaborations of the highest quality.

One of the permanent attractions of paradise is music, song, and dance. The angels are supposed to be the musical trendsetters, but among the dead souls there are also reputable musicians who play a major role. Brugman described in a sermon how King David, during the prophets' meal, actually made a spectacle of himself: "And there sprang David with his harp in front of the tables, just as though he were their court jester." According to other texts, David was able to produce a sound that carried so far one could hear him anywhere.

The Meditations on the Life of Christ by Bonaventure (ca. 1217–1274), a widely known devotional text in Latin dating from the late thirteenth century, provided another boost to David's reputation. When Jesus enters paradise with the freed souls from the gate of hell, all the souls begin to sing. David accompanies them on the harp, while others also play harps or tambourines. David then begins to dance, and it all ends in a celestial jam session filled with song, music, hand-clapping, and cheering.

It became standard in all the longer descriptions of paradise to include a detailed enumeration of all the musical instruments played in heaven. According to the *Sterfboeck* (Book of death) of 1491, the angels played organs, wind instruments, lutes, violins, harps, psalteries, cymbals, zithers, trumpets, and trombones and also knew how to produce a host of other sweet sounds. This heavenly orchestra was a permanent part of the repertoire of such great painters as Hans Memling, Jan van Eyck, and Rogier van der Weyden.

If the earthly paradise must be thought of as heaven's waiting room, the people ending up there must be entertained in some way. Here both paradises imperceptibly flow together: some descriptions speak of an angel in each of the four corners of paradise, a quartet that produces a wondrously sweet sound by flapping their wings. This mingles with the sound of trombones played by two other angels. According to Dirk van Delf there is also music in the earthly paradise. The leaves of the tree of life are hard, and when the wind moves them they make the sound of strings. Angels, schooled in this art, play the tree like an instrument.

This fantasy is not as far removed from reality as it seems. In Dirk's time there existed in various places in northern France and elsewhere pleasure parks built by the nobility. Part of their standard equipment consisted of metal trees, the twigs and leaves of which could be set in motion mechanically by bellows. The result was a wonderful jingling that was meant to be taken as heavenly music. Dirk undoubtedly knew of these musical trees, and it is not inconceivable that he actually visited such a park—the one in Hesdin, for example—in the retinue of his employer, the count of Holland.

The Bible often refers to musical settings of this kind. Isaiah draws a connection between the end of time and the restoration of paradise in the destroyed Zion: "For the Lord shall comfort Zion: he will comfort all her waste places; and he will make her wilderness like Eden, and her desert like the garden of the Lord; joy and gladness shall be found therein, thanksgiving, and the voice of melody." Moreover, it is well known that angels like to make music, and they are among the permanent residents of the heavenly paradise. The pleasure garden, based on the model in the Song of Songs and the *locus amoenus*, could not exist without music either, although there, of course, the angels were replaced by professional musicians. Andreas Capellanus, the author of a manual of instruction in courtly love, places musicians in a garden of love, where he has them playing every imaginable instrument. In addition, *The Romance of the Rose* names in this context flute players, drummers, singers, dancers, and castanet players.

Music and dance—on earth at least—were considered suspect. They were generally thought to be the instruments most often employed by the devil to tempt people into idleness, especially at times when they were supposed to be performing religious duties. On his way to the Holy Land, the Delft pilgrim Arent Willemszoon passed a village in Switzerland, or at least the ruins of it. It had been destroyed by God in 1517 "because the folk were dancing on Christmas Eve. And what happened? God ordered a mountain to hurtle down, unforeseen, which buried all the people of the village beneath it. Only one house was left standing, which is still standing today, so that one may clearly see that only one family was saved."

Dancing, in particular, was thought to be the root of many evils. Literature and the visual arts seized upon the example of the Jews dancing around the golden calf to underscore their cautionary elements. Another example, apparently just as attractive, was the worldly life of Mary Magdalene, portrayals of which inevitably featured musicians and drummers, with lots of dancing in the background. Literary and artistic treatment of the seven deadly sins generally entailed portrayals of music and dance, which Hieronymus Bosch depicted, for example, being performed by a pandemonium of truly devilish figures. Opposite these devils is a depiction of heavenly music being performed by angels in white robes.

The medieval debate between good and evil never actually came to a head, however. As happened so often in the late Middle Ages, people read-ily admitted—loudly, frequently, and often tastefully—in confession books, literature, and paintings that they knew perfectly well how to behave, only to turn around and indulge in the very behavior they supposedly found so objectionable. These double standards allowed the nobility, townspeople, and country folk to dance with a vengeance, not only on holidays but when-ever an occasion presented itself.

It goes without saying that there is music and dance in the Land of Cockaigne, not only on special occasions but always. Neither is it likely to be just any old worldly custom that is immortalized in Cockaigne but rather a copy of the customs obtaining in the heavenly paradise, whereby the pleas-ures of the hereafter are amplified and given a worldly counterpart. This is something that occurs continually: both the instruments (trumpets and pipes) and the choice of words (dancing in the round) point to scenes staged in heaven, as they were repeatedly described and portrayed. When, for exam-ple, the popular encyclopedia of vices and virtues *Somme le roi* speaks of danc-ing in the heavenly paradise, it is always in terms of "dancing in the round."

In Luilekkerland, on the other hand, things are quiet: there is no talk of music or dance. Text G stems from another tradition and is much further removed from the fantasies of paradise that were a strong stimulus to the ideas behind Cockaigne. The prose text, based on Hans Sachs's example, also lacks the direct reference to the lost paradise that opens both Cockaigne texts. That paradise no longer plays a role in text G, although the baby seems to have been thrown out with the bath water, for music and dance should not be lacking in Luilekkerland. This makes it just as likely that the omis-sion of music was simply a slipup. However much text G is the product of a written tradition, the author undoubtedly made a rather spontaneous adaptation of his material, without serious contemplation and without con-sulting other sources. This spontaneity links him to the transcribers of the two Cockaigne versions, who also gave little thought to what they were doing, consequently forgetting one thing and another, such as the sweet smells wafting through every paradise. These fragrances were not omitted in Luilekkerland, however.

The agreeable quadrupling of holidays in Cockaigne, contrasted with fast-ing only once every hundred years, appears to be an expansion of heavenly time telling. In paradise time does not exist, so that one day may seem like a thousand years and a thousand years like just one day. This is what it says in the Bible, which provided the basic fabric on which several medieval authors embroidered. The Brussels manuscript containing text B also includes a little rhyme, based on a passage from the Bible, describing the miraculous experience in store for us:

> Oh what joy has come our way,
> A thousand years is but one day!
> And we can have no cause for tears,
> For one day is a thousand years!

Within this framework summers and winters are doubled (furthermore, the winters are mild), and the harvests are also multiplied, not so much because this is necessary in the heavenly paradise but to indicate how rapid repetition is able to erase the memory of earthly deprivation. Luilekkerland does not participate in this aspect either, perhaps owing to its greater distance from the medieval dreams of paradise.

Other, smaller details also provide a direct link between the heavenly paradise and earthly Cockaigne. Text B states that piles of nice clothes, including breeches and shoes, lie in front of every house, and that "you may wear them, if you choose." Surely this is reminiscent of the angels who dress the resurrected souls in the most beautiful robes.

A similar connection seems improbable in the case of the boots in Luilekkerland that stand at the ready, waiting for the farmers who grow on the trees to fall into them. As there is only mention of footware, it seems more likely to refer to the pre-Christian outfitting of the dead with traveling requisites, including, at the top of the list, shoes to ensure their successful passage to the hereafter. Remains of this ritual recur in visions and exempla that are often contaminated by folk traditions from other cultures. The peasant Gottschalk had a vision in 1189 that took him on a journey through the realm of death, where he had to cross a thorn-studded plateau. Luckily, however, just before it he saw a linden tree whose branches were blossoming with shoes. One could only pluck a pair of shoes, however, if one had done enough good works on earth.

It is unlikely that the farmers in Luilekkerland were given their boots for this reason. The peasants grew on the trees as a source of free labor, falling at "birth" into the necessary working clothes. Nonetheless, there is a slight similarity with the visionary shoes of Gottschalk. Like the thorny field, Luilekkerland proves to be a prickly place of sins, where good-for-nothings are supposed to learn how *not* to behave. And one hopes that these wayward youth will find—just like the peasants in Luilekkerland—the means to give them a surer footing on such dangerous ground.

20

Other Paradises

$\mathcal{E}$VERY CULTURE has its own paradise that was forfeited through an act of naive pride. As early as the turn of the seventh century B.C., the Greek epic poet Hesiod told of a significant incident that caused humankind to forfeit its place in the ideal world, since which time Zeus has kept the secret of this beautiful life hidden. His wrath was caused by Prometheus, who stole fire from the gods to give to humankind. Zeus's punishment for this act of pride was to degrade life on earth to a sorrowful existence, filled with worry and pain. Before this time there was no exertion or sickness, only joy, and one day of work was enough to provide one with food for an entire year.

It's always the same old story. All this misery cannot possibly be the point of life. Someone must have made a mistake somewhere along the line that infuriated the powers that be, and this mistake must be set to rights. Perhaps by doing penance one will be rewarded with the recovery of ideal life, no longer tormented by pain, toil, or dying. The Greek geographer Strabo (b. 64/63 B.C.) situated such a lost paradise in India, already in his time an exotic garden of delights, the first glimpse of which had been granted to Alexander the Great. At one time the whole area had been an alimentary paradise: all the fields were permanently covered with barley and wheat. In addition to the water flowing from the springs, there were rich streams of milk, honey, wine, and olive oil. This abundance, however, had made the people overconfident and godless, which caused Zeus to withdraw all their privileges, with the result that life there had been filled with pain and toil ever since.

Such notions of sin, punishment, penance, and reward are universal, and not at all bound to a certain time, place, or milieu. They belong to the cultural baggage of every society, and it is not necessary to assume a common source in order to forge links of mutual influence. On the other hand, such influence certainly exists, especially as regards the outward forms taken by these fantasies. Nevertheless, correspondences in this sphere occur even between cultures that could never have come into contact with each other. The fear of famine and dread of senseless drudgery are timeless horrors, constantly creating visions of remedies that may conjure up stable spring weather, healing water, spontaneously growing food, or delicious drinks for the taking but may just as well have to do with blessings of perfect harmony in human affairs or the complete absence of all suffering.

Mutual influence and spontaneous adoption were inextricably entwined in the minds of those who gave oral or written shape to their desires for a better life. Outsiders living centuries later are certainly in no position to make any distinction between the two. Just because Greek comedies written long before the Christian era present self-cooking geese and self-roasting pigs does not mean that these motifs have undergone a complicated oral or written text transmission in order to nestle, twenty centuries later, in the mind of a clerk recording his version of Cockaigne. Neither is it necessary to search for Indian folk tales of even more remote origins that might be able to explain what possessed the Greek writers of comedies to invent such amusing details. It is quite possible that these myths and motifs were transmitted as a matter of course, being adopted spontaneously as elements common to the primary survival strategies of all cultures.

The Indo-Germanic cultures of Eurasia, at any rate, have produced an astonishing number of paradises, golden ages, and blessed isles, all of which bear remarkable similarities to one another, both in outward appearance and underlying motives. Researchers are forever announcing that they have found links, as compelling as they are conclusive, between various elements within this body of material. It has been fervently maintained, for example, that the Muslim paradise was the immediate source of inspiration for the development of Cockaigne in the West. The Muslim paradise exhibits a decidedly worldly character, bridging the gap, as it were, between Christian paradise and Cockaigne. But while it is true that this idyll of the Islamic hereafter exerted a stimulating influence on realizations of Cockaigne in the Western world, it neither lay at Cockaigne's origins nor paved the way for its genesis.

The certainty of this is immediately apparent from the major role played by erotic love in the Muslim paradise. It is precisely this element that plays only a marginal role in Cockaigne and Luilekkerland and was more likely added as a concession to time-bound and milieu-related obsessions that do not belong to the main body of the Cockaigne material. In any case, sex plays a very modest role in Western dreamlands. This is also true of the Christian paradises, however much the store of eroticism in the Song of Songs lay ready for plundering. Christian asceticism and awareness of sin stood in the way of any positive appreciation of erotic love. Free love and promiscuity belong to the dreamlands of other cultures, though some of these bear a very close resemblance to Christianity or even belong to its early phases.

The Celtic realm of the dead does make provisions for free sex in surroundings that are otherwise strongly reminiscent of the heavenly Jerusalem. A dream island occurring in the journeys of Mael Dúin, for example, appears to be inhabited only by women, and each traveler spending the night there is assigned one. The golden age of antiquity also displays a natural promiscuity, which Jean de Meung dutifully mentions in his *Romance of the Rose*. The Middle Dutch adaptations of this romance deleted this passage—though this cannot be said with certainty in the case of one version, which is incomplete—as if that ancient paradise might still pollute their own Garden of Eden. Nonetheless, the desire for a definite solution to jealousy and longing in relations between the sexes is real enough, as is the masculine dream of unbridled sex with ever-willing women. The gratification of these desires, however, is found in the Christian hereafter primarily in assurances that no bodily appetites will torment the soul ever again. A solution to the need for exuberant fulfillment of these desires is simply not one of the things on offer in paradise. Or does *Somme le roi*, that popular encyclopedia of virtues and vices, toy for a while with this idea? Heavenly pleasures are made much of in this text, which says that in paradise "one sees loving glances going from lover to lover." This must refer to more worldly modes of behavior between the sexes, something highly unusual in heaven. Oddly enough, it appears to be an addition made by the Dutch adapter of the original French text. Was this finally a frivolous move in the opposite direction?

From the very beginning the Muslim paradise was well known in the West through widely circulated descriptions in Latin translations. At the same time there were the reports sent home by growing numbers of travelers to the East. Merchants, pilgrims, and crusaders heard and read of unimaginable delights, made notes of their supposed findings, and told their stories over and over again back home. A lucky few were even permitted a glimpse of the kind of imitation paradise that graced the court of many an Eastern potentate.

The representations of paradise in the Koran were strongly influenced by the first centuries of Syrian Christianity. The most important exponent of what are quite sensual notions of paradise was Ephraem Syrus (ca. 306–373)—theologian, poet, doctor of the church, and author of *Hymns of Paradise*. Mohammed has been reproached fairly often for seeing salvation only as the unlimited fulfillment of highly primitive and sensual desires. The source of such ideas, however, is to be found in Eastern Christianity, which had little success in persuading its own flock of their validity but exerted a great deal of influence in its immediate geographical surroundings.

Around 1106 Pedro Alfonso, a Jewish convert of Byzantium, described for the first time in Latin the Muslim garden of delights. Life there was filled with endless and unrestricted pleasure, a superabundance of fruit was always ripe for the picking, and one's every desire was satisfied. These desires are mainly sensual pleasures, as is abundantly clear from the translation of the Koran commissioned in 1143 by Peter the Venerable, who found the text to be completely lacking in Christian spirituality. The deepest impression, however, was made by the *Liber scalae* (Book of the ladder), about Mohammed's trip to the heavenly paradise, which was known in a French version dating from 1264. The walls of paradise were apparently made of rubies and the doors of pearls. Lovely virgins of indescribable beauty lay waiting, singing glorious songs. There were also pavilions made only of precious stones such as rubies, pearls, and emeralds. Fountains spouted water—surely a precious commodity there—and wine. Everywhere fruit hung within easy reach, and tables were laid with everything one could possibly crave in the way of food and drink.

The Muslim paradise entered the Western world in the form of a cocktail composed of Cockaigne and the heavenly paradise of Christianity, seasoned with the additional and immediately overwhelming flavor of unbridled sex. In this paradise the virgins on call were doled out to the male contingent of faithful souls. Moreover, this garden of delights—unlike the West's own paradise, no matter how much it came to be influenced by its Eastern counterpart—appeared to offer the absolute fulfillment of all earthly desires of a sensual and material nature, with gastronomic delights, costly apparel, free sex, and all other bodily pleasures vying for the leading role.

This picture was also propagated by the influential history of the world by Vincent of Beauvais, the *Speculum Historiale* (ca. 1245). It should come as no surprise that here again it was the erotic aspect that received the most attention. Sir John Mandeville viewed this unequivocally as the high point of the Muslim paradise: "Every man shall have four score wives, who will be beautiful damsels, and he shall lie with them whenever he wishes, and he will always find them virgins." Not only are there virgins to spare, but the potency to possess them all continually is also part of the bargain, with self-perpetuating female virginity thrown in for good measure.

Other Christian travel writers generally made do with furtive sniggers, contenting themselves with innuendoes aimed at the erotic pleasures to be had in the Saracens' paradise. In general, however, they reported on conditions that strongly recall the circumstances prevailing in Cockaigne. Again, one is warned not to jump to conclusions. These authors' descriptions of the Muslim paradise—based on other texts and hearsay, all of which emphasized the fulfillment of earthly desires—were inevitably colored by their own knowledge of the Cockaigne material. Later on I will discuss how the discoverers of the new worlds in the West also based their rapturous descriptions of the climate and the bounty of these worlds on a picture seen through the rose-colored glasses of Cockaigne. This, too, makes it extremely difficult to draw conclusions based on the existence of similarities between two or more dreamlands. These travelers, as well as the readers of their tales, actually wanted to go on discovering the same thing, as long as the misery and drudgery of everyday life persisted.

In 1486 a knight called Gruenemberg traveled from Konstanz in southern Germany to the Holy Land. At the end of the account of his pilgrimage, he added some information about the beliefs of the Mohammedans, closing with a paraphrase of what Mohammed said about paradise: it is very large and covered with greenery and flower-filled meadows. Such profusion, by the way, must have made a bigger impression in the East than in the damper countries of Western Europe. The earthly paradise of Christianity, with all its lushness, is the merest of sublimations of the hedgerows and fields of Ireland, the Low Countries, or Normandy and Brittany. Paradise in this guise must therefore have been the invention of desert folk who knew only sparse oases of green.

The Muslim paradise, according to Gruenemberg, also has this lush aspect. Milk and wine flow freely, the lakes are teeming with fish, grapes and apples are ripe for the picking. Wild animals are just as easy to catch as tame cattle, and birds can either be a source of food or of beautiful song. Moreover, the cities enjoy a superabundance of food, laid out on tables under the trees complete with drinking vessels of gold inlaid with precious stones. Wine also gushes out of rocks, beehives drip with honey, sugarcane bursts with sweetness, and spices simply fall from the trees. Huge quantities of gold, silver, and precious stones lie around in piles. Young girls and boys dance to all kinds of music, and, finally, mention must be made of the surfeit of sexual satisfaction, for everyone is always ready and willing to take anyone as a partner.

This paradise of Islam gave rise to an infamous imitation, which many travelers did not hesitate to mention. Marco Polo was the first to report in detail on the Old Man of the Mountain, who lived in a huge castle south of the Caspian Sea. The Old Man acted as leader of a heretical Islamic sect that had been founded in the eleventh century. His followers viewed him as God's deputy. To increase and consolidate his power, he required the blind faith of a select troop of young men who undertook suicide missions to help him reach his goals. To get them to agree to this, he had a paradisiacal garden laid out, which provided miraculous offerings by means of a sophisticated system of conduits and fountains. Everywhere there flowed water, milk, honey, and wine, and beautiful women were on hand to satisfy these young men's every erotic fancy.

The Old Man's methods were also described by Mandeville:

> Then this rich man gave these youths a kind of drink [actually hashish] which quickly made them drunk; then they were more blinded than before, and thought they had indeed been in bliss. He then told them that if they would put themselves in danger of death for his sake, when they were dead they would come to his Paradise and would evermore be of the age of the maidens, that they would evermore live with them and have pleasure and dalliance with them and they should still remain always virgin. . . . Thereupon they all agreed to do what he wanted.

These misguided, murderous youths gave rise to the French word *assassin*: originally meaning a user of the drug derived from hemp, *hash-shahsin*, led by his intoxicated state to commit murder.

There were also more innocent variations of an imitation Muslim paradise, comparable to the pleasure parks of the nobility in the West. The pilgrim Joos van Ghistele of Ghent, who undertook a long journey through the Middle East and North Africa starting in 1481, described various examples of such pleasure grounds, which always made him think of the earthly paradise. Sometimes he took an area of unspoiled nature to be such a garden, like a valley in the vicinity of Bethlehem where it was always green and the trees always bore fruit. Again, observations of this kind made by Van Ghistele and others mean that we have come full circle: the Christian Garden of Eden was inspired by valleys and oases such as those in the Middle East.

Near Boulac in Egypt Van Ghistele came across orchards with summerhouses where rich merchants relaxed in the company of other powerful leaders. Sometimes their recreation sessions lasted ten or twelve days in a row, in the midst of tents, pavilions, and other ad hoc architecture. They laid on debauched banquets that included indulging in sexual excesses with hordes of women. Van Ghistele sighed and remarked that it seemed like the earthly and the heavenly paradise all rolled into one, a sure sign of the priorities of his own personal paradise.

As close to home as Venice, the pilgrim Arent Willemszoon of Delft ran into an imitation Eden that had more the character of a casino-cum-brothel in verdant surroundings. He and his fellow travelers visited a splendid courtly garden in which all worldly pleasures could be viewed or practiced in a setting of trees and fragrant herbs. Among the attractions were games of chance, offering the opportunity to win the most precious prizes of velvet, damask, and silk. The games included one that must have been a variant of skittles or bowls and another involving the casting of dice. The pilgrims, unfortunately, lost all their money, though they gladly let themselves be distracted by young men and maidens feasting and simultaneously making music with string instruments, drums, and trumpets. They also surrendered to sensual pleasures, adds Arent Willemszoon somewhat cryptically (or perhaps blushingly). Many people were dancing, and in dark corners they seized whatever opportunity presented itself. Now it is clear what the author meant. He did not want to leave anything out but balked at giving a more explicit description of the delectable details. On the other hand, there is nothing to indicate that he or his companions were disapproving witnesses of these diversions. This is made plain by the frank conclusion of his passionate account: "I would almost like to call it Venus's Garden, for I never saw the likes of it before."

Other dreamworlds, dream eras, and paradises from the West and Near East have been mentioned in passing. The Celtic paradise, owing to the Christian tradition rich in source material on this subject, flows almost imperceptibly into the paradises of Christianity, as already evidenced by the examples cited from the Middle Dutch version of *The Voyage of Saint Brendan*. Whether in the land of Multum Bona Terra or on Mount Zion, the traveler is always confronted with an abundance of food requiring no effort to obtain, as well as fountains and fantastic castles made of precious stones.

The Celtic myths of paradise are strongly connected with the geography of the sea voyages of the heroes who inspired this mythology. Paradises are continually encountered on islands to the West in the open and endless waters of the ocean. When the Middle English *Land of Cokaygne* begins by locating itself on an island somewhere in the West, past Spain, this text places itself in the tradition of Celtic representations of the hereafter, a paradise that was said to be scattered over various islands. There everyone enjoyed eternal youth, and there was no sickness. Jealousy, hate, and envy were unknown, and everyone lived in peace. Celebrations with song and dance were held in the midst of flowers and fruit, and sex was indulged in without restraint. The Celtic paradise also contained elements that were quite specific to its particular setting: the cows were white with red ears, and the horses were sky blue.

Bartholomaeus Anglicus—apparently quite near, though by medieval standards just as far away from the marginal country of Ireland as was the rest of Europe—added some particulars with a supposedly scientific basis. One had to try very hard to die there, and returning "unto dust" was nearly impossible. The whole of Ireland seemed to him to be a magic underworld, where the boundaries between living and dying had become blurred. It was known, for example, that "in Hybernia [Ireland] the dead neither decompose nor decay." Moreover, there was supposedly an island in the vicinity where one could not die even if one wanted to, a feature it shared with paradise.

The existence of the earthly paradise and the heavenly Jerusalem together on an island in the West, as occurs in a traveler's tale by Godfrey of

Viterbo (1125–1192), clearly indicates to what extent such representations could influence each other in the gradually Christianizing Europe of the early Middle Ages. In Godfrey's story, British monks make a journey across the sea, in other words, westward. At the end of the ocean they spy a golden mountain that appears to shelter a powerful city. The city walls and the houses are all made of gold, as is a statue of Our Lady and the Child. Two old men, Enoch and Elijah, explain that the island is guarded by a crack corps of cherubim and seraphim. Angels also sing there, food is delivered from heaven, and one day lasts a hundred years.

As already mentioned, practically all medieval conceptions of paradise are rolled into one in *The Voyage of Saint Brendan*: Irish-Celtic myths of the hereafter, the Christian iconographic tradition of the earthly and the heavenly paradise, and reports of wonders stemming from folk tradition, all of which blended into the original Latin text recounting the voyages of the Irish abbot Saint Brendan. At the suggestion of a fellow monk, Brendan goes in search of God's promised land. In the Dutch tradition this widely known story took on the character of a penitential journey: Brendan doubted God's miracles and was condemned to see them with his own eyes.

In the Middle Dutch version of this story, Brendan and his companions, nearing the end of their travels, approach an island of mysterious beauty and abundance. Its special nature is announced already on the bottom of the sea, visible through the crystal-clear water. Here the sea bed has changed into sand of fine gold, in which many carbuncles and other precious stones glitter. Then a castle looms up with golden halls and pillars of carbuncle. Four rivers gush forth from a fountain, their currents carrying balsam, syrup, olive oil, and honey. There are beautiful trees everywhere, and the island is also covered with grapevines and spices. The next castle can also boast of the appropriate climatic conditions: no frost, snow, cold winds, or rain. All those who have meanwhile lost their way in this labyrinth of traditions and cultures are set straight by the closing line: "So that was the earthly paradise."

21

Lovely Places, Golden Ages

$\mathcal{A}$LL THESE paradisiacal pleasure grounds belong to the tradition of the *locus amoenus*, or "lovely place," that was a fixed topos of antique literature, usually used to glorify rural life or to portray the nostalgia of a lost Arcadia. The "loveliness" is concentrated in a garden or orchard, one of the oldest examples being the garden of Alcinous, the father of Nausicaa, in *The Odyssey*. His garden consists of "a large orchard of four acres, where trees hang their greenery on high, the pear and the pomegranate, the apple with its glossy burden, the sweet fig and the luxuriant olive. Their fruit never fails nor runs short, winter and summer alike." There were also vineyards and vegetable gardens, the whole being watered by two springs.

This idyllic orchard recurs repeatedly in epic literature of the Middle Ages, where it forms the perfect backdrop for courtly modes of behavior between men and women, not infrequently providing the stimulus for passionate declarations of love. During the Middle Ages the *locus amoenus* merged with the gardens and promised lands of the Bible, in particular the enclosed garden in the Song of Songs. A similar convention for portraying idealized nature as a setting for love was not only practiced but also formally laid down in the medieval *artes poeticae*. These rules for writing literature in Latin also provided examples of how to treat certain subjects. One of the best-known textbooks in the field, the *Ars versificatoria* by Matthew of Vendôme, written around 1175, gives just such a sample description of the *locus amoenus*, consisting of no fewer than sixty-two lines of verse. Its essence, however, can be summed up in a couple of lines: "Here blossoms bloom sweetly, herbs grow vigorously, trees leaf profusely. Fruits abound, birds chatter, streams murmur, and the gentle air warms all."

Paradise was conceived from the very beginning as a garden, which displays its relationship not only to the enclosed garden in the Song of Songs but also to the places of refuge held out to the people of Israel: "And it shall

FIGURE 37
Courtly pleasure garden, or pleasance. *Roman de la Rose,*
Flemish manuscript, ca. 1490–1500.
Source: London, British Library, MS Harley 4425, fol. 14 verso.

come to pass in that day, that the mountains shall drop down new wine, and
the hills shall flow with milk, and all the rivers of Judah shall flow with
waters, and a fountain shall come forth of the house of the Lord, and shall
water the valley of Shittim." The notion of paradise providing such abundant gifts of nature must have arisen from the oasis yearnings of desert
nomads, inspired in particular by the fertile valley of Mesopotamia between
the Tigris and the Euphrates. These rivers were understandably thought to

carry in their currents the blessings of the now unreachable paradise, which must be a sublimation of this valley.

The *locus amoenus* also recurred in the healing herbal gardens of monasteries and convents. It was precisely nature's curative properties that underscored recollections of paradise. Moreover, the cloister as such could also be thought of as an earthly paradise, and indeed the Benedictines even assumed this to be its purpose. This ideal seems to have been imitated most successfully at the Benedictine abbey at Cluny. In a letter to Abbot Hugh written in 1063, Peter Damian stressed how struck he had been by the similarities. He had seen "a paradise" in Cluny, watered by the four rivers of the gospels and overflowing with spiritual virtues. There was much more to his outpourings, though, than the mere allegorizing of monastic life. Wonderful roses and lilies sprang up to meet him, and he was also captivated by the fragrance of spices. Having said that, he again abandoned himself to metaphorical musings on the monastery's fertile fields, which yielded such rich harvests.

Just like the nobility with their paradisiacal pleasure parks and menageries, ordinary burghers also built recreational resorts that were just as intent on re-creating nature in its ideal state, with its original Arcadian character. Outside the town walls these burghers created enclosed gardens full of trees, flowers, and other plants, and these lush pieces of paradise grew into playgrounds for all kinds of amusements. In concentrated form these little Edens could also be driven around town on floats in parades or religious processions or figure as part of the spectacle surrounding the triumphal entry of a prince. The young Charles V was received in Bruges in 1515 in a pleasance, or pleasure garden, featuring Orpheus playing the harp in the midst of beautiful trees and flowers, complete with swarms of birds flying in to make an appearance. Spectacles involving such sleight of hand were nothing out of the ordinary on such occasions.

These Edens of entertainment probably stemmed from the concept of castle gardens, the ideal arrangement of which was described in detail by the learned Albertus Magnus in the thirteenth century. Remarkable indeed is his assurance that these gardens were not to be exploited with an eye to yielding any fruits of the land but existed instead for the sake of pleasure pure and simple. This was the reason for the great profusion of greenery: to please the senses of sight and smell. Perhaps the carefully composed pleasure gardens in humanist circles were more direct heirs to the medieval concept of

FIGURE 38

Ideal garden outside the town walls. *Spring,* engraving by Pieter van der Heyden
after Pieter Bruegel the Elder, 1570.

Source: Reproduced from E. de Jong et al., *Aardse paradijzen: De tuin in de Nederlandse kunst,
15de tot 18de eeuw* (Ghent, 1996), no. 106.

castle and cloister garden architecture. An elegantly worked-out model is
given in Erasmus's *Convivium religiosum,* a long colloquy dating from 1522.
Finally, the luxuriant garden—besides being a source of pleasure—also gave
rise to the most spiritual of allegorizations.

Lost paradises may also be part of one's own past. There is no culture that
has not created for itself an ideal starting point. For the Greeks and Romans
this was a golden age, which was not only discussed repeatedly in the Middle Ages but also colored medieval visions of the *locus amoenus.* It even became
the model for golden ages of other European cultures and dynasties, which
began to take shape within the framework of growing nationalism in the
early-modern period. Once upon a time everything had been perfect, but
pride had put an end to all that. Worse still, there had been almost no sign

of repentance since that first indiscretion, causing the whole of Creation to plod along on a downward path that could only end in the depths of misery.

In classical antiquity as well, this lost ideal age, the possibility of its continued existence at a specific location on earth, and the future idyllic home of the blessed became inextricably entangled. This is already evident in the confusion over the earthly and the heavenly paradise. Again and again, the desire to dream of a more carefree and beautiful existence seemed to transcend the actual need for the dream in the first place.

The golden age, the Islands of the Blessed (often identified as the Canary Islands), and the Elysian fields all merged in antiquity to form one big garden of delights, no longer subject to earthly laws. According to Hesiod, people lived like gods in those days. They were always in good spirits, kept their youthful appearance, and died peacefully in their sleep. The earth spontaneously produced an abundant harvest, while people lived peaceably in the midst of their riches. On the Islands of the Blessed this *aurea aetas* was thought to flourish still. Horace peopled them with the pious and God-fearing. Everything grew by itself: wheat, vines, and fig trees needed no tending, and neither did cows or goats. The climate was unparalleled. Related to this antique paradise is the island of the Hyperboreans, supposedly situated to the north of Gaul. It was inhabited by very happy people who benefited from a climate both stable and temperate, as well as reaping the benefits of two harvests a year.

It has been continually emphasized that in all these places no effort whatsoever was required to earn a living and the climate was invariably mild. In other respects, too, the similarities between these antique paradises and the medieval dreamworlds colored by Christianity are striking. Virgil seems to have been referring simply to the heavenly Jerusalem when he bathes his hereafter, Elysium, in a blinding light, where the souls happily surrender themselves to sports, song, and dance. The mention of sports is the only thing that lends his paradise a touch of the antique.

Perhaps things are better expressed the other way around. It is rather the heavenly Jerusalem that continues to build onto the palaces and dreamworlds of antiquity. Related to the Islands of the Blessed was, a bit further on, the immense island of Atlantis, mentioned already by Plato in the fourth century B.C. It is rather remarkable to see how both the ancients and the

FIGURE 39

Lucas Cranach the Elder, *The Golden Age*, ca. 1500.

Source: Munich, Alte Pinakothek.

Celts tended to seek their paradises in the West. Atlantis also displayed a great abundance of flora and fauna, as well as two wonder fountains. But that was not all. There were also palaces and mountains of gold, and the landscape was graced by the temple of the sea god Poseidon, to whom the island was said to belong. This building had an ivory roof and walls of gold, and its structure contained other precious metals as well, the whole gleaming with inlaid precious stones.

All these visionary landscapes, offered with great claims to authenticity, had in fact been called into doubt already in antiquity. Pythagoras, for example, viewed all talk of Atlantis as sheer fantasy, and later on Lucian, in an uproarious parody, mercilessly attacked those who were credulous enough to believe in such idyllic places.

Naturally these golden ages of the past were still alive and well in medieval times. This myth of humankind's origins functioned as an attractive key to the comprehensibility of classical history and consequently the significance of subsequent events as well. People were still making mistakes, perhaps more and more all the time, gradually decreasing their chances of attaining eternal bliss. Redemption was possible, however, thanks to the unremitting grace of God and the resolute but touching pleas made by Mary at her Son's tribunal. Moreover, there was always Fortune, who, at God's urging, was forever giving a new twist to fate.

The most important transmitter of the *aurea aetas* to the Middle Ages was the early Christian philosopher Boethius (ca. 480–524). He offered a vision of a golden age swallowed up by man's inability—since the Fall—to practice self-restraint according to Christian reason that may nevertheless be restored to mankind in one fell swoop by the vagaries of Fortune. Of course, this must be interpreted allegorically. Boethius was undoubtedly referring to the heavenly paradise, though he attempted to link heathen concepts stemming from the beginning of earthly history to the Christian doctrine of salvation. Many texts written in the vernacular adopted his vision of the golden age, primarily in the historical sense, as one of the stages in the pre-Christian past of antiquity. In particular, Jan van Boendale's *Der leken spieghel* (The layman's handbook) and *The Romance of the Rose*, both dating from the fourteenth century, were responsible for the dissemination of this body of ideas at once depressing and optimistic.

Boethius's principal work, *De consolatione philosophiae* (*Consolation of Philosophy*), was reprinted frequently and supplied with commentary throughout the whole of the Middle Ages. One example, immense and impressive in other ways as well, is the edition containing extensive notes by an anonymous scholar, whose commentary was published along with the original text in 1485 by Roland de Keysere in Ghent. He translated Boethius's text into verse, though he continually interrupted it with detailed commentary, which in the main follows an earlier commentary by Renier of Sint-Truiden.

Boethius conceived his text on the golden age as a criticism of the times, painfully in keeping with the circumstances surrounding the genesis of his masterpiece, which he wrote in King Theodoric's dungeon in Pavia while awaiting his execution, which was carried out in 524.

The golden age, according to Boethius, was characterized by great aus-

FIGURE 40

Simple fare in the golden age. Detail from Lucas Cranach the Elder,
The Golden Age, ca. 1500.

Source: Munich, Alte Pinakothek.

terity. One ate only raw acorns and apples, which sufficed to quell one's hunger. Wine was not mixed with honey or other sweet-tasting substances, clear spring water served as the daily drink, and clothes were not dyed. At night one slept in the tall grass, and during the day one lay in the shadow of pine trees. There was no mercantile shipping, and neither were there any wars. This blissful time came to an end, however, with the discovery of gold and precious stones, when greed got the better of people. If only those days had never passed! If only they could be exchanged for the present!

Boethius follows this description with a historical sketch of a civilization slipping further and further into decline. The simplicity of the golden age was followed by a silver age. People formed families, settled down, and started to till the land. The Bronze Age following this period was marked by increasing egoism and discord. Finally, in the present-day Iron Age—from Boethius's perspective—neither laws nor rights obtained, and people were rotten through and through. He finishes by lamenting that in the golden age people and wild animals coexisted in perfect harmony. These ideal circumstances were generally thought to have survived in certain regions of Scotland and Ireland, remote corners of the world at that time and—as marginal areas—representatives of an upside-down order. Usually such distant lands come off badly in comparison with one's own, idealized civilization. For Boethius, though, society was completely corrupt, which meant that original purity was only to be found in areas that had never, or scarcely ever, come under its influence.

The whole passage is permeated with a fervent desire for a better life, which had once seemed possible. Perhaps for Boethius, with the death sentence hanging over him, it would be possible in the hereafter. The late-medieval commentary underscores Boethius's extraordinary restraint. The author of the commentary then discusses a few examples of admirable behavior displayed in more recent times, which he views as a sort of reversion to the primeval past. He mentions, for example, Diogenes, who drank water from a cup made of tree bark until one day he saw a child drinking from his cupped hands. He instantly threw his cup away "and discovered that nature had given him both his hands to use as a dish or cup in order to drink." Nowadays, on the other hand, gluttony prevailed, giving rise to another of the cardinal sins, namely, that of sloth.

The commentator dwells in detail on nature's spontaneous provision of

FIGURE 41

Brawls common at the end of the silver age (?). Lucas Cranach the Elder,
End of the Silver Age (?), ca. 1500.

Source: London, National Gallery.

food in the golden age. Sowing and reaping were unheard-of in those far-off days, just as were plowing, harrowing, and raking. Another bonus was the complete lack of personal possessions and the absence of all authority. Everything belonged to everyone: people could not be robbed of their money or goods, as the concepts of "yours" and "mine" did not exist. This last notion was anything but new in the Middle Ages. In the thirteenth century it had already been passionately expressed in the vernacular by Jacob van Maerlant, completely in the spirit of the mendicant movements inspired by the Franciscans. His work remained highly popular until the end of the Middle Ages, leading not only to its wide dissemination but also to frequent imitation.

The Land of Cockaigne reverses this golden-age austerity by opening up possibilities for humorous overindulgence. The fantasies of food offering itself up for consumption are the same, but Cockaigne significantly supplements primeval vegetarianism with a healthy ration of meat. This ties in with the idea that wild animals coexist peaceably with humans and are apparently conscious of their subservient position, which means that they willingly submit to being eaten. Even more striking, however, is the correlation of the notions of communal ownership of property, especially the similarity of the formulations used to express these ideas. In this respect Cockaigne corresponds down to the last detail with the views put forward in the vernacular in the contemporaneous and scholarly commentary on Boethius, in other words—those of text L to be exact—"things found lying around, unretrieved, one takes without a by-your-leave for one's own gain and no confessions; one treats them as one's own possessions." The relationship between the two texts is revealed precisely in the similar, accidental nature of the finding. Both authors voice the same desires in similar words. Only the framework is different.

This does not mean to say that any direct relationship between these authors and their texts is presumed to exist. In a certain sense these dreamlands and golden ages are property common to all of Europe, not only the subject matter but also the way in which it is expressed. It is important to stress how passionately these views were held and how often they were uttered, over and over again, at all levels of society and in all languages. The French *Romance of the Rose* adds to its elaborate treatment of the Boethius passage another detail concerning the golden age, namely, that free love also existed at that time. All people, men and women alike, could have any part-ner of their choosing. This detail is missing from both Middle Dutch ver-sions of the romance but not from Cockaigne. There the concept of com-munal property is extended, just as in the *Rose* text, to include each other's bodies. It has already been pointed out that these passages in the Cockaigne texts give the impression of last-minute additions, compared with the age-old core of the Cockaigne material. This addition stems from the *Rose* tra-dition, which places for the first time erotic love and free sex in the dream-lands written about in the vernacular. Cockaigne remains a cocktail. But can't this be said of all the other texts as well?

Other peoples in Europe also assumed a golden age to have been part of their past. The German-speaking territories began more and more to iden-tify with the Germanic peoples portrayed by Tacitus in his *Germania*. Espe-cially after the distribution of this text in print in 1473, the picture of posi-tive primitivism it presented—contrasted with the decadence of the civi-lization of ancient Rome—was received with great enthusiasm by the descendants of the people it portrayed. These ideas were still exerting an influence in the twentieth century, as witnessed by the Third Reich's *Blut und Boden* (Blood and Soil) theories, which continued to plead the racial purity of the Germanic folk, contrasting it with the corruption of peoples else-where.

Above all, the Germanic peoples liked to view themselves as having been a forest people, in close communion with nature. At that time, culture and civilization had not yet sown the seeds of their own destruction, meaning that humankind had not yet distanced itself from nature. It was culture, after all, that had debased nature in order to satisfy its decadent needs. In the beginning, though, people had simple diets, lived in harmony with wild ani-mals, and knew neither discord nor strife. Personal possessions did not exist. And by appealing to Tacitus, one could even augment these Germanic virtues with a naturally hospitable nature, a strong sense of what can only be described as Christian charity, and chaste obedience to strict rules of mar-riage.

This borrowed golden age, derived by the Germans from Tacitus, took a different turn in the Low Countries at the end of the Middle Ages. They gave their ideal past a name—Batavia—and the historiographers of the sixteenth century would proclaim it an exemplary model of the ideal society. Emphasizing the primarily rural nature of life at that time was also a way of curbing the growing supremacy of the cities. That cities were especially corrupting was a piece of wisdom widely believed since classical antiquity.

None other than Erasmus began with the upgrading of the coarse and uncivilized image evoked by the Batavians, who, he insisted, had been an upright and earnest folk, living in a beautiful and prosperous country, rich in forests, lush meadows, fish-filled waters, and beautiful villages. This sunny myth was turned into a political pamphlet by the humanist Cornelius Aurelius, who projected contemporary ideals onto the exemplary society of that time. His *Divisiekroniek* (Division chronicle), published in 1517, gave a picture of the conditions obtaining in the good old days, when Batavia had been populated by free fishermen and farmers, and women had still been subservient to men. (Unfortunately, in Aurelius's day this was no longer the case, and sometimes he could not restrain himself from voicing his criticism.) Adultery did not exist in those days, and the men had proven to be brave soldiers when the need arose. Every month they assembled—and the States of Holland would do well to follow this example—after which the ruling prince made decisions based on their advice. There was no trace of a corrupt city. One could get along very well without importing that article from Rome.

This idealization of nature appeared to catch on even within the town walls. When an Italian humanist praised Rotterdam to the skies in 1514, he seemed to turn it into an earthly paradise overgrown with buildings. The heavens were undeniably clear, a soft breeze was always blowing, there was an abundance of flowers, and even the willows gave off a sweet smell. This praise, by the way, was inspired chiefly by the fact that Rotterdam had been the birthplace of Erasmus.

It is not inconceivable that the Cockaigne texts refer to this idealized Batavia. Near the beginning, the excellence of Cockaigne is compared with that of two other lands, neither of which is half as good. These lands could not have served as a basis of comparison if they had not been recognizable to a late medieval audience. Spain is not a problem, but that other country is less convincing. Text L has "Betouwen," while B has "Betavien." Both forms could easily pass for corrupt spellings of "Batavia," whose eminently desirable primal state would make an excellent comparison. One objection is the difficulty of ascertaining whether the concept of Batavia had become widely enough known by the second half of the fifteenth century to be able to function in this capacity, nor is it known whether Batavia was a particularly cherished myth in the eastern part of the Netherlands, where the origins of both Cockaigne manuscripts must be sought. There is however another possibility: the names could have been derived from Poitou, a wine-growing region in the Low Countries that supplied the popular *petauw* or *betouw* wines.

22

Wonder Gardens and Pleasure Parks

*P*ARADISE COULD ALSO be imitated. To start with, the model architecture of the heavenly Jerusalem was also to be found in churches and cathedrals, and occasionally cities were even built with the same ideal proportions and resplendence. In the twelfth century the abbot Philip van Harvengt compared his Paris with Jerusalem, where theological scholarship was thought to have flourished. The clergy flocked there in great numbers "so that they would presently outnumber the many laymen who inhabited the city. . . . Fortunate indeed is the city where so many eminent teachers live and where theological scholarship is of such a high standard that one may indeed call it the city of the belles lettres!"

More materialistic appreciation is voiced by Charlemagne in the French romance of chivalry *Aymeri de Narbonne*, more or less a sequel to the Old French epic poem *The Song of Roland*. From a hill he looks down on the city of Narbonne: "The city was nicely surrounded by walls and pillars. Twenty towers of shining stone loomed above it. In the very center another tower caught my eye. It was crowned with a massive golden ball, which had been brought from overseas. Inside it lay a ruby that glittered and gleamed with a splendor that made one think of the rising sun."

Such dazzling dream architecture, modeled after the heavenly Jerusalem and dripping with gold and precious stones, is found repeatedly in medieval chivalric literature. The power and courtly refinement of a prince were judged on the basis of his creativity and the wonders his court could offer. Very similar to this is the citadel encountered by Saint Brendan and his monks (in the Middle Dutch version of Saint Brendan's travels) on so-called Mount Zion. It has walls of crystal, containing animals—cast of copper and bronze—that move and make noises. A broad river flows right through the middle of the castle. The walls display animated hunting scenes. The illumination is brilliant, and the floors are made of snow-white glass through which golden specks gleam, while songbirds hide in the profuse green of the trees. There are no fewer than six thousand towers. Moreover, everywhere costly, decorated cushions lie at the ready. And all this is repeated in another palace in the middle of the citadel, built entirely of precious stones.

Heavenly indeed are the arrangements at the palace of King Wonder, which are taken advantage of by the severely wounded Walewein in the romance of the same name. He is laid down on a golden bed, with golden pillars and ivory bed boards, next to which stand four angels, also made of gold, singing beautifully in clear voices. The sound appears to be produced mechanically by a system of underground pipes and bellows. Each angel carries a sapphire in one hand and a carbuncle that sheds light in the other. The bed has a healing effect, causing Walewein to wake up completely recovered and able to do his host a favor in return. He proposes to do no less than free the beautiful Ysabele, whom King Wonder loves to distraction, from the castle of the evil King Assentijn. There she languishes in a little paradise with a golden tree with a golden bird sitting on each branch and a golden bell hanging from every leaf. Wind is piped in through the roots and the trunk, causing the birds to sing and the bells to tinkle.

Similar wonders were also reported by the court chaplain Dirk van Delf, though he was referring to the sweet music of paradise, also produced by wind caressing the acoustically attuned leaves of the tree of life. Even the tomb of Floris and Blancheflur features—in the text of the same name—dream architecture complete with automatons. On the pseudotomb built of crystal and marble are displayed birds, beasts, and fish made of precious stones. At the head stands a marble statue inlaid with gold and silver, the hand of which functions as a sundial. In the middle of the tombstone stand golden statues of Floris and Blancheflur themselves. Wind blowing through hidden pipes sets the figures in motion, causing the lovers to kiss, embrace, and caress each other to their hearts'—as well as to their stage manager's—content.

These worldly imitations of the Jerusalem of the Book of Revelation were not limited to literature. In reality as well, pleasure parks and paradises were built along the lines of their heavenly example and supplied with the requisite automatons that were set in motion by wind and steam conducted through invisible pipes. Here, again, the aim was to ensure—already on earth—the necessary satisfaction, consolation, and relaxation to those from the upper walks of life who seemed to think that such bonuses were their God-given right.

In any case, these ingenious imitations of natural phenomena were exceedingly popular in the Middle Ages. A model book by Villard de Honnecourt has been preserved, for example, that contains instructions for making such automatons, referred to as *mirabilia*, or marvels. With the help of this manual, one can make a bird that drinks out of a fountain spouting wine, as well as a rotating angel that keeps its face turned toward the sun. Extant examples of such automatons are practically nonexistent; we know only designs and instructions for use. Several fire spewers have been preserved, however, that blow hot steam by means of an ingenious system of conduits. Another design offered a variation of this, whereby the steam escaped from a larger-than-life-size male member, though this was already known from the writings of the antique architect and engineer Vitruvius, whose designs and theories of proportion found a new following in the Middle Ages.

Apparently these wonders were first conceived in the Islamic world; the literature gives good reason to think so. The wonder garden of Ysabele in the *Walewein* was situated in India. More famous still are the pleasure grounds of the emir of Babylon (in the Middle Dutch version of *Floris ende Blanchefloer*), where the whole of Creation and the universe are portrayed. The above-mentioned pseudotomb with its wondrous automatons is also to be found in the Orient, at the court of Floris's heathen parents.

Such artifices were mentioned by Sir John Mandeville as well. He tells of magicians at court in far-off China—everything in the East was strange and marvelous—who could delude spectators into thinking they saw the most curious and fantastic worlds. These artificers could produce the illusion of a sun and moon in the sky that shed a light so bright spectators could hardly see each other, and they also knew how to conjure up beautiful women, jousting tournaments, and hunting parties.

Of the wonder gardens that did in fact exist, the best-known was that of Caliph Haroun al-Rashid, who ruled in Baghdad at the time of Charlemagne. In the midst of a pond stood a silver tree with golden branches, upon which sat gilded birds that were mechanized to move and sing. Many crusaders later claimed to have seen such gardens. By way of the Sicilian court of Frederick II, where there was a great deal of interest in mechanical timepieces, this automated garden architecture was said to have made its way to the West.

In Western Europe the first report of such a wondrous paradise garden occurs in an account of a January 1249 visit by Count William II of Holland to Albertus Magnus at Cologne, generally regarded as the greatest scholar of his time. The distinguished party was asked to wait in the reception room of the monastery, where it was bitterly cold—it was the dead of winter—to the great annoyance of the Dutchmen. The great Albertus himself then appeared barefoot, wearing a summer habit. The Dutchmen were dumbfounded to hear him announce that the meal would be served outside. The visitors' indignation was boundless, having interpreted this move as a demonstration, as bothersome as it was impertinent, of misplaced asceticism.

In the cloister garden, however, it appeared to be as warm as a summer day. The flowers were in blossom, the trees were fully laden with ripe fruit, and birds were warbling. In such climatic conditions the food could not help tasting wonderful, and the company left in the best of spirits, flattered by their truly regal reception. Clearly, Albertus had made use of little-known techniques from the Orient, which would later undergo further development at many a noble's court. Lodewijk van Velthem appears to have been well informed of these developments. Writing half a century later, he described such spectacles as a kind of "playfulness" of which he had often heard.

In the vicinity of the Netherlands, the most well-known pleasure park was that of the castle at Hesdin in northern France, which had been famous since the end of the thirteenth century. Heaven and earth, paradises, Jerusalem: all were to be found in ingenious constructions, intended first and foremost to provide humorous entertainment. Indeed, the magnitude of such spectacles and their increasing fame on the continent induced the English printer and man of letters William Caxton to go and have a look for himself. Caxton had begun as a merchant and commercial agent for his country, first in Cologne and then in Bruges, where he set up a press, by means of which he provided an English elite with his own adaptations of current literary successes from the circles of the French aristocracy. Later he moved to Westminster and continued to run his prosperous business there. In the foreword to his 1477 edition of *Jason*, containing the stories of the Golden Fleece so popular in Burgundian circles, he recalls a personal visit to the gardens of Hesdin. He had feasted his eyes on the spectacle, especially impressed by the lightning, snow, rain, and storm machines, but it was undoubtedly the tapestries with their scenes of chivalry that sprang to mind

FIGURE 42

Festivities at Binche in 1549. Food on tables rotating out of the wall; fountains
spouting drinks from the other wall. Colored pen drawing.

Source: Brussels, Bibliothèque Royale, Print Room.

as he was writing his foreword, for there hung in Hesdin a series devoted to
Jason's capture of the Golden Fleece.

Similar to the spectacle mounted at Hesdin, which was eventually razed
to the ground in 1553 by the troops of Charles V, were the wonders in and
around the pleasure castle of Binche in Henegouwen (Hainaut, in present-
day Belgium). A year later it was destroyed as well, another victim of mili-
tary force, this time on the part of the French. On the occasion of a mag-

nificent celebration held on the evening of 30/31 August 1549, the castle had been completely transformed into a wonder palace. The focal point of the festivities was a series of spectacles presented in the so-called Enchanted Chamber that were attended by a highly select group of nobles, led by the future Philip II. Constellations moved across the firmament and personifications of planets paraded past on floats. Everywhere were lamps burning sweet-smelling oil. There was also a mechanism that enabled richly laid tables to be lowered from the ceiling on invisible cables. Truly, this was food offering itself up for consumption! There followed an imitation storm with thunder and lightning, after which it hailed sugared almonds—just as in Luilekkerland—and drops of orange blossom water and other perfumes rained down on the guests. Food and drink could be taken from the tables that slowly moved past; wine sprang forth from a rock in the wall and also spouted from fountains.

Measured against such megaproductions, bourgeois versions, such as that mounted by the wealthy Jacques Duché of Paris, tended to look like cheap imitations. Around 1400 he had a commoner's palace built for himself in Paris. The walls of his study were inlaid with precious stones and fragrant spices. Furs lay everywhere, the sheets and tablecloths were embroidered in gold, and the rooms were full of gilded statues.

There is something touching about this rather pathetic attempt to compete with the lavish animated spectacles of the nobility. It is clear, nevertheless, that people not only sought and found Cockaigne in their imagination but also attempted to construct it in reality. Based on the model of the heavenly Jerusalem, diversions of a more worldly nature were designed in an attempt to give concrete form to the promises of joy and abundance in paradise. Eating and making music were prime examples of these joys, and apart from one or two paltry attempts made by the bourgeoisie, it was undoubtedly the elite, celebrating in style with no holds barred, who set the tone for the realization of these blessings. Such opulence is very far removed from both Cockaigne and Luilekkerland, but they all fed upon the same source: the lost paradise. Despite such biblical underpinnings, however, these re-creations of paradise were naturally viewed by the church as nothing less than the work of the devil.

23

Dreams of Immortality

$\mathcal{P}$ARADISE WAS NOT really lost. After purification in purgatory it could be found again in the heavenly Jerusalem. Even the earthly paradise was not necessarily so inaccessible as many people maintained. Surely Alexander the Great had not lied to us; many seemingly reliable accounts reported that he had been in paradise. Moreover, paradise had proved not to be empty, as Enoch and Elijah had been waiting there for the end of time. Seth, Adam's son, had also been permitted a glimpse of paradise, when his dying father had sent him there to fetch a healing oil. The angel guarding the entrance had not let him in, but he was allowed a quick glance. He saw and smelled everything, according to *Dat boec van den houte* (The book of the wood [of Jesus' cross]), which was so well known, instructive, and probing that it was repeatedly attributed to the great master of such texts, Jacob van Maerlant.

The many medieval descriptions of paradise are informed by tremendous optimism, secure in their knowledge that this miserable life on earth could not possibly be the true destiny of humankind. Moreover, earthly suffering could even be seen from a positive angle, now that some accounts of paradise were saying that the greater one's suffering on earth, the greater one's blessings in the hereafter. As an advance on those eternal rewards, the followers of the Devotio Moderna were urged to perform meditative exercises in the viewing of the heavenly paradise. At the end of the fourteenth century, Gerard Zerbolt of Zutphen (1367–1398) produced, as part of a larger work, instructions in Latin with a view to achieving this goal. A Middle Dutch translation has been preserved, the title of which gives a description of its contents: "A general method of forming an image of the kingdom of heaven, with the purpose of becoming so inspired as to yearn for its attainment." This text conjured up the well-known picture of the heavenly Jerusalem, followed by a strong recommendation to keep it firmly fixed in the mind's eye. Great joy would result, again and again, especially if one also tried to imagine what it would be like to reside permanently with God, His Son, and Mary, along with the angels, prophets, patriarchs, apostles, and martyrs.

This exhortation closes with the assurance that all earthly suffering would then be a thing of the past. Never again would one have to be afraid of missing the boat: having inherited the kingdom of heaven, one could never be thrown out. Neither would one ever again be plagued by carnal desires, surely a great comfort in that tightly packed community of ambitious young men. The devil and his artful enticements could no longer get a foot in the door. There would be complete freedom, purity, and joy, in addition to friendship, honor, and love: "Everything you want you shall have, and everything you cannot have you shall not want." In such a paradise man is practically equal to God.

All these medieval paradises were furnished according to the tastes of the times. There was an abundance of food, plenty of music, no lack of song and dance, and Jesus was up there performing the duties of a generous host, carving the meat, slicing the bread, and pouring the wine: in short, this was a heaven with the contours of Cockaigne. The hereafter could not escape being a Luilekkerland, even though hedonistic gorging and guzzling would never get the upper hand in images of lost paradises or deserved hereafters.

Except, of course, where children were concerned. At the end of the sixteenth century the Lutheran preacher Johannes Mathesius recommended talking to children about the hereafter in just such Cockaignesque terms, undoubtedly inspired by a remark made by Luther to his son. Children should be presented with a picture of the hereafter as a heavenly playground, to be enjoyed by those who have behaved piously in life. In this children's paradise sugared almonds and many more delicious snacks grow on trees, and springs flow with nothing but malmsey wine. The houses are roofed with custard tarts instead of normal tiles, and children may all hop about on their own hobbyhorses complete with skirts of gold.

These are the appropriate terms in which to tell children of the hereafter. Heaven and Luilekkerland have finally merged into one, for children at least. Even before this, however, Luilekkerland had struck off on its own didactic path aimed at youth education.

Unfortunately, the devil also availed himself of these well-intentioned and agreeable images. One of his shrewdest ploys was the derangement— from the inside out—of the human senses, causing one to see, hear, feel, smell, and taste things that had been not God's doing but his own. Augustine called this the devil's specialty. His most cunning trick was to insinuate himself into a person's mind, "whether he was asleep or awake," and summon up "various fantastic images."

The senses, thus deluded, could also conjure up visions of paradise, causing the person in question to give himself over to wildly unchaste behavior. He had been deluded, after all, into thinking that his original state of purity had been restored to him, meaning that he could no longer sin and was now being rewarded for all eternity.

Commentaries on the First Commandment were seized upon to serve as warnings against such devilish visions. Explanation could also be sought in numerous exempla, which recounted the tallest tales about pleasure grounds within easy reach. Some catechistic works simply reported that God had forbidden one to believe in dreams, now that the devil had proved so adept at imitating them. Responding to these developments, priests hearing confession began asking questions designed to pry out of people whether they attached any significance to dreams.

Frequent mention was made of a Mount Venus, where every human wish was fulfilled, yet this proved to be nothing but lies and devilish deceit, designed to bring ruin upon humankind. There was, moreover, a knight who could testify to this. More than once had he set foot on that mountain, where women catered to his every desire, until once he suddenly awoke and found to his dismay that he was lying in a pit with a revolting dead beast. He realized immediately that he had been taken for a ride by the devil.

The lay preacher Stephen of Bourbon warns in an exemplum against such tricks played by the devil and his cronies, who were thought to wander about in packs, posing as the dead souls of one's ancestors, who apparently had lots of unfinished business on earth. This notion, fiercely adhered to by simple folk, was vigorously resisted by Stephen. He told of just such a horde of devils, calling themselves "Arthur's retinue," of all things, who maintained that the great King Arthur was alive and living on the island of Avalon. The members of this gang dragged a simple peasant into a cave beneath Mont Chat in Savoie. This credulous man found himself "in a huge and noble palace where ladies and gentlemen were playing and dancing, eating fine foods and drinking." All of which proved to be a delusion, of course.

Another exemplum, taken from a huge collection titled *Der sielen troest* (The soul's comfort), tells the story of a competition between a group of devils and a hermit. Anyone living a life of self-abnegation could inspire a devil to devise tricks of the utmost cunning. The devils therefore decide to tempt the hermit with sex. The holy man is led away under false pretenses to an orchard, filled with the loveliest and most fragrant flowers, where nightingales are singing. There is also a splendid canopied bed, and after the hermit is tied to it, a beautiful, naked woman appears and begins to fondle him in a most improper way. Meanwhile, the holy man has realized into whose clutches he has fallen, and with his last bit of willpower he manages to spit his bitten-off tongue in her face.

The devil's greatest success consists in deluding people into thinking they are actually in heaven. There were so many reports of such devilish ruses that their signs soon became easily recognizable. The *Biënboec* (The book of bees), a very popular anthology of exempla after the original Latin text (*Bonum universale de apibus*) by the Dominican moralist Thomas of Cantimpré, contains the story of a Dominican friar whose expertise tells him that something is the matter when he is invited to go on a little excursion. Though he smells a rat, he gladly accepts the devil's challenge. To be on the safe side, however, he arms himself with a consecrated wafer, which he carries in a little container next to his heart. In a mountain cave he is shown a magnificent palace, bathed in a clear, bright light, which immediately reminds him of the heavenly Jerusalem. The interior contains furniture of pure gold, upon which distinguished people sit enthroned, illuminated in the radiant light. The Dominican is mistrustful, however, and offers up the host: "The light went out, and it quickly became so dark that the brother and his guides could barely find their way out of the mountain."

Such warnings also permeate epics of chivalry. In the various versions—both rhyme and prose—of the popular romance *Margarieta van Lymborch*, devils conjure up a castle out of thin air, probably counting on recognition of the way in which the heavenly Jerusalem descends from the skies in the Book of Revelation. Inside the castle Margarieta's father appears to wield the scepter, though he is actually a devil in disguise. The hellish household makes further attempts to lure Margarieta inside by providing a concert of truly divine music, played on harps, lutes, and flutes.

Margarieta, roaming around the area with a merchant, hears the heavenly music from far away, and the merchant, who recoils at first at the sight of the castle—merchants have a traditional dislike of castles—can no longer be restrained. Without bothering to knock, they enter and make their way through the castle. Margarieta takes the devil to be her father and lets him give her a tour of the castle, all of which she finds beautiful, a veritable "earthly paradise." Only when she and the merchant are seated at table and start to say grace does the truth come out: "But when they thus blessed the table, there was a great commotion among the devils. Each one took a torch from the castle, and some of them also took food and drink. And together they departed, leaving behind an awful stench that seemed to come from all the filth of the world."

Not all paradises were the same, however. Many medieval texts in the vernacular sweep both the earthly and the heavenly paradise into one pile and call it simply "paradise." There we find dreamlike nature and wondrous architecture all mixed up, banquets with servants and vegetarian self-service, a lot of music and hordes of people. Some texts emphasize the possibility of self-styled eternal bliss, and visionary dreams show how this can and should be achieved. At the same time, instructions are provided on how to prepare oneself mentally for the hereafter. All these promises and inducements practically compel one to design one's own transcendental happiness. Building it all a bit closer to home might not be a bad idea, either. Indeed, there were those who even built their paradise in their own backyard, resulting in the construction of complete wonder gardens and pleasure parks. Constructing Cockaigne is a human necessity. And where's the harm in it? There are building materials in abundance, especially in heaven.

This yearning for a paradise on earth is undoubtedly an unconscious mode of human behavior, no matter how consciously these dreamworlds are constructed with building elements bound to time and place. The only variable is their outward form. Modern society now has at its disposal an unprecedented variety of paradises, characterized by ready accessibility and their ability to compete in revitalizing facilities.

In the Middle Ages, on the other hand, one was struck by the relative monotony of both lost and promised dreamlands. Roughly speaking, there were only two types, which were—not coincidentally—each other's opposites. Neither one existed in a pure form, but their conceptualization can serve to clarify our thoughts on the matter. First there was the spiritual dream of complete immunity from all earthly defilement, which attempted to reduce existence to a permanent state of unthinking passivity, exemplary of the greatest possible austerity. The reward for this was to be had in heaven, where any interference from the devil was unthinkable. Diametrically opposed to this was the fantasy of wanton overexploitation of one's most earthly desires, serving as a distinctly aggressive protest against the misery of daily life. Between these two extremes lay the reality of an endless series of ad hoc constructions, which drew upon Eurasian material displaying remarkable similarities and spanning all of twenty-five centuries.

Only the breakthrough to the early-modern period and the coming of the industrial welfare state put an end to these relatively unchanging and persistent dreams. Present-day paradises are tailor-made to suit the individual customer. This idea seems to be lurking in some of the portrayals of the heavenly paradise dating from the Middle Ages: eternal life should be lived in a setting of one's own choosing. Heaven, however, was far away and anything but certain, which explains the need to discover paradises and lingering golden ages at the edges of one's own civilization and beyond. Inspired by Mandeville and sometimes even with his book in hand, intrepid travelers left in swarms, ultimately finding, of course, what they had set out to find.

Part 5

The Imagination Journeys Forth

24
Geographical Musings

*T*HE LAND OF COCKAIGNE is presented as a concrete place situated somewhere on earth. Texts L and B both begin with a first-person narrator who announces that he has just been to a country previously unknown to him. This land was full of wonders that he was apparently able to see and experience himself. It is precisely this reference to "wonders" that establishes a connection between Cockaigne and the well-known *mirabilia* of the Orient, which were common knowledge already in classical antiquity, undergoing continual enlargement and elaboration as they made the rounds of a broad lay public until late in the Middle Ages.

Only text B takes up the suggestion of travel again at the end, by urging all good-for-nothings to betake themselves to "that rich land." The prose text G develops the travel parody within the still-young tradition of "tidings," the forerunner of the newspaper, which was proving to be an ever more lucrative source of income for Western European printers. Straightaway in the title it is mentioned in passing that Luilekkerland was discovered in 1546, the date being stated in a way typical of lying tales, spelled out in corresponding quantities of appetizing food. Such stylistic principles, characteristic of this genre, will continue to form the guidelines for the parodic technique evident in the rest of the text.

Both these frameworks—tidings and tall tales—come together in the opening sentence of the text proper, which typifies itself as "untrue tidings" in exactly the place where this perfect medium for the reporting of imaginary travelers' tales invariably praises itself as being absolutely true. This is followed, in keeping with the tradition of lying tales, by a description of the travel route, along with the hardships one must endure before arriving at one's destination. At the end there is a recommendation—not dissimilar to the one in text B—urging "prodigal children" to betake themselves to this land without delay.

All the dreamworlds discussed so far, including the earthly and the heavenly paradise, have a geographical aspect. Even in the case of Christian paradises, such a geographical connection has been created in a telling way by depicting human existence as a pilgrimage from the Garden of Eden to the heavenly Jerusalem. Whether one has been driven from paradise, is trying to rediscover it, or thinks oneself worthy of attaining it, the result it always the same: a peregrination involving a more or less direct route toward a fervently desired objective believed to have a concrete location. This conviction is strengthened by the popular visions, in both Latin and the vernacular, that recount visits to heaven, hell, and purgatory and strongly resemble a special kind of travel literature with the unmistakable characteristics of nascent journalism.

More particularly, the road to the hereafter was likened to a journey, which could be expedited by the deceased's next of kin not only by saying prayers and masses but also by depositing in the grave realia in the form of shoes and other travel requisites. Such burial offerings stem from pre-Christian and non-Christian traditions but were unquestionably assimilated into certain Christian forms of lay piety, such as those expressed in exempla.

Any distinction between the worlds described in travelers' tales and the above-mentioned dreamlands is inevitably somewhat arbitrary and to a certain extent the result of modern projections on the distant past. This problem becomes acute when examining the case of the earthly paradise. Although the Garden of Eden was enthusiastically allegorized throughout the Middle Ages, this in no way prevented one from being certain of its earthly existence. Even though the earthly paradise, the intended beginning and end of Creation, had meanwhile been hermetically sealed to keep out the descendants of Adam and Eve, it was nevertheless certain that Eden continued to exist in its original form somewhere on earth. Theoretically, therefore, it must be possible to travel to this place, even if only to view it from a distance.

Nonetheless, a certain practical grouping along historical lines is justified if one wants to take a closer look at these dreamlands and pleasure spots. A substantial number of them pose as real places, which were discovered or described at a given time by a given person. In such cases there is the strong implication that both the land and its supposed discoverer do in fact exist, which means that idyllic spots are not the only sort being discussed here. Exotic countries may be presented in either a positive or a negative light and are often observed from both perspectives in one and the same text. Unbiased descriptions, on the other hand, are far less common.

The claims to reality and moving disclosures of eyewitness reports that characterize these fabulous travelers' tales are in themselves an indication of the suspicion—justifiable or no—that such writers could let themselves in for. In any case, not every travel account was taken at face value in the Middle Ages, and these doubts had manifested themselves already in classical antiquity, as witnessed by the tendency to poke fun at this genre. One example of this is Lucian's classic *True History* dating from the first century A.D., which so thoroughly and aptly mocks all fantastic descriptions of strange peoples that every travel story written thereafter seems to refer more to his parody than to any possible reality.

Examples of this kind of satire, though admittedly less spectacular, are also to be found in the Middle Ages. It is not inconceivable that the Cockaigne and Luilekkerland material also functioned as a parody or satire on the sometimes overdone and extremely fantasized travel stories. This notwithstanding, much of what we have meanwhile come to know as unquestionable fantasy—if not downright deceit—was accepted in the Middle Ages as the bewildering truth about a world whose boundaries were becoming more blurred every day. A growing public eagerly seized upon Sir John Mandeville's elaborate and exciting account of his travels to the Holy Land and subsequently Africa (at that time a designation for an Orient that also encompassed Asia) as much-needed information about the sadly unknown dimensions of the globe. (That the world was a flat surface one could fall off was something almost no one believed anymore.)

Nowadays we are certain that Mandeville could not possibly have made the journey he pretends to have made. Some are even convinced that his name is the nom de plume of a cunning compiler who strung together a number of fairly popular travel stories and inflated them into a breathtaking tale of the extreme forms of behavior exhibited in far-off lands. In addition, Mandeville demonstrated an extraordinary feeling for what the fourteenth-century market demanded, namely, the ultimate contrast with the way of life experienced and thought desirable by the reader: in other words, an antithesis that could serve a number of illustrative purposes. One thing is certain, however, and that is Mandeville's ability to write, which he did in such an evocative way that no translation or adaptation has been able to detract from its significance. Starting in the fourteenth century the text enjoyed widespread popularity and was regularly reprinted until well into the sixteenth century.

Mandeville's text therefore belongs to that group of dreamland texts suspected of being an impromptu potpourri, although perhaps his work should actually be viewed from a different perspective. It is possible that we have shown too little understanding for a type of text that steers a middle course between personal observation and tacit copying of other sources and drawing upon hearsay—an admittedly unacceptable compromise in view of the present-day penchant for so-called truthful reporting—that represented for his contemporaries a spectacular new genre: a geography book based on partly simulated travels. Modern research has suggested such an assessment, making a justifiable comparison with Dante's technique in *The Divine Comedy*, in which the writer lets himself be led through the landscape of the hereafter. Dante's account of this journey thoroughly acquaints the reader with the joys, sorrows, and architecture of the other world. Although for the intended readers and listeners this world largely represents a reality—literally of the highest order—it is also clear that the poet himself could only have made this journey in his dreams.

According to this enticing viewpoint, Mandeville (or whoever it was who appropriated this name) actually produced a realistic picture of the world, centered around a first-person narrator whose experiences were not necessarily the same as the author's in every respect. Above all, Mandeville offers a compendium of world knowledge based on many oral and written sources, the first part of which (his journey through the Middle East to the Holy Land) is founded on personal experience. The second part, "Africa," is also based on experience, though of a more vicarious nature, consisting not so much of personal observation as of a literary journey through his sources.

The whole nevertheless remains a personal undertaking, the account of which was made with great concern for the failings of Christianity, which, according to the author, had not succeeded in retracing its steps after straying from the true path after the Fall. Worse still, Western man seemed to be wandering even further from the straight and narrow. The confrontation Mandeville offered with the lost Holy Land and with numerous disparate lands elsewhere in the world was meant to persuade people of the error of their ways.

These contrasts showed, roughly speaking, two ways of life. There were, first of all, peoples who—as a result of the failure of Christianity to convert them—were sinking further and further into uncontrollable wildness and bestiality. These would inevitably become the accomplices of the Antichrist at the end of time. On the other hand, Mandeville met people who had preserved their original purity from the beginning of Creation. They had not—or not yet—been corrupted by pride and dubious book learning, which was causing the Christian world to sink deeper and deeper into a morass of sin. Somehow they knew naturally how to avoid all sin, while they just as naturally observed the greatest moderation in eating, drinking, and expressing their emotions, as well as in exhibiting all those other forms of human conduct that in Mandeville's eyes could so easily deteriorate into reprehensible behavioral excesses. He repeatedly described such folk as the Brahmans: "In this land are no thieves, no murderers, no prostitutes, no liars, no beggars; they are men as pure in conversation and as clean living as if they were men of religion. And since they are such true and good folk, in their country there is never thunder or lightning, hail nor snow, nor any other storms and bad weather; there is no hunger, no pestilence, no war, nor any other common tribulations among them, as there are among us because of our sins." Moreover, these Brahmans fasted daily and excelled in following the Ten Commandments, for they knew no cardinal sins. They were all equal and cared nothing for earthly possessions. Best of all, they died of old age and not of disease.

This amalgam of Western paradises and golden ages was projected onto a remote corner of the earth and presented as the gospel truth. In the Middle Ages heaven and earth were indissolubly linked, as were finiteness and eternity, life and death. Mandeville wrote a textbook with a geographical basis, setting forth the behavior necessary if humankind was to save itself. Everything in it is "real," but earthly reality is more easily understood because it is apprehensible to the human senses in their earthly condition. Consequently, when we concern ourselves with places on earth that were thought discoverable in the Middle Ages, then distinguishing them from supernal realities of a timeless nature (including the paradisiacal precinct) is not only possible but also justifiable.

How does the text about Prester John—stemming as it does from a semi-written tradition—fit into this pattern? From the twelfth century onward, this story was widely distributed in many languages, also as a separate text, retaining its popularity into the age of the printing press. But from which sources was this experience gleaned? Or was it an imagined dreamworld? Here as well, very few doubts were actually voiced about the existence of this ideal Christian realm located immediately beneath the ether of paradise. Certainly, in this case, all suspicions must have been dispelled by the overwhelming amount of detail on offer in this ethics textbook based on personalized morsels of global geography.

Once in a while, however, Mandeville failed to make an impression, or perhaps—in the opinion of Willem van Rubruck, at any rate—he had simply gone too far. This Franciscan friar, who started out in Palestine and traveled around the Middle East from 1252 to 1255, was one person who thought the stories about Prester John grossly exaggerated. Disagreeing with him, however, were many supporters of equal stature. Even a serious traveler such as the patrician Joos van Ghistele, who set out late in 1481 from Ghent, resolved after his visit to the Holy Land to go in search of the country of Prester John. And the printed versions of his detailed account, published with great success for the first time in 1557, did not detract from the dubiousness of this reckless plan.

Van Ghistele and his traveling companions did not decide to seek out Prester John on impulse. With a view to such a venture, the pilgrims had taken with them costly rings and jewels, which they had personally imbued with luck by rubbing them against the relics preserved in Cologne (in this case the bones of the Three Kings). As it happens, Van Ghistele had been given to understand that all Christians from the Low Countries who were supplied with such validated treasures would be particularly welcome guests in Prester John's country. The only problem was how to find the kingdom—thought to be near the equator—of this archpriest and champion of a brand of proto-Christianity that had somehow managed to retain its purity.

The travelers only knew that Prester John resided somewhere in Africa, perhaps in the vicinity of Ethiopia. To complicate matters, Ethiopia was also called Abyssinia, which according to some meant simply Africa, which most people also took to include Asia. At the end of the Middle Ages it was possible for world travelers, lacking topographical information and stan-

Van die wonderlicheden en costelicheden
van Pape Jans landen des.

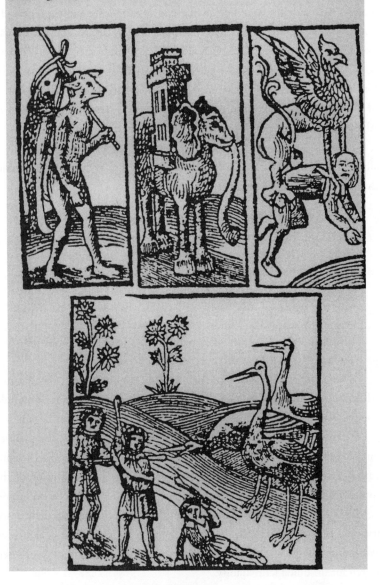

FIGURE 43

Title page of a book on the land of Prester John, ca. 1506.

Source: London, British Library, C.32.h.6.

dardized place names, to misjudge their positions by whole continents. Only Columbus's confusion has become really famous, however, when he mistook America for India and was surprised to find it inhabited by copper-colored natives. At least they were not as black as expected, Columbus repeatedly noted with a sigh of relief. This misunderstanding added another dimension to the terminological jungle, however. The Delft barber Arent Willemszoon, writing in 1525 about his pilgrimage, lapses into incomprehensibility for this very reason. When naming the seven Christian sects of the Church of the Holy Sepulchre, he specifies the last one as that of the "Indians or Abyssinians. . . . And these Indians are all as black as Moors."

From a geographical viewpoint, the country of Prester John was literally an upside-down world. In Mandeville's view at least, it lay exactly under the feet of Western Christians:

> And understand that to my way of thinking the land of Prester John, Emperor of India, is exactly below us. For if a man were to go from Scotland or England to Jerusalem, he would be going upwards all the way. For our land is in the lowest part of the West, and the land of Prester John is in the lowest part of the East. They have day when we have night, and night when we have day. And however much a man climbs when he goes from our country to Jerusalem, he must descend as much to the land of Prester John. The cause is that the earth and sea is [sic] round.

After Jerusalem, therefore, one simply had to keep on walking. But would one really notice when the upward climb ended and the descent began?

Having arrived in Mesopotamia, Van Ghistele and his companions questioned a merchant from the East. What was the best way to Abyssinia, where Prester John ruled? They were then given a detailed description of the route, which unfortunately did not produce the desired result. By no means, however, did Van Ghistele blame this on the illusory nature of their destination. Discord and setbacks had kept the pilgrims from their goal, as well as—some thought—a guilty conscience, which stood in the way of their search for unsullied Christianity.

Questioning the reality of the destinations described in such travelogues is little more than an expression of modern-day realism, which has skeptically distanced itself from spiritual travels with ethical aims that

FIGURE 44

"If two people walk in opposite directions
across the face of the earth, they will meet up
again: the earth is round." Miniature in
fourteenth-century manuscript of the *Image
du Monde*.

Source: Paris, Bibliothèque Nationale, MS f. fr. 574,
fol. 42 recto.

become more elusive every day. Grave doubts have even been cast on the authenticity of one of the greatest exploratory expeditions of all time, that of Marco Polo. Indeed, there are serious grounds for these reservations. Not only was his method of reporting extremely dubious (the events were supposedly recorded by a clerk in prison), but a much more significant factor is the popularity such texts had begun to enjoy at that time, causing accounts based on this pattern to be churned out by the dozen.

This literary assembly line made more use of traditional dreamland material than of real-life experiences that were difficult to verify, which were likely to deviate drastically from the prefabricated models. Moreover, the observations made by world travelers often underwent literary treatment when being recorded, bringing the reported exotica in line with attractive fantasies and cultural ideals. To go one step further, it may be said that Western dogmas of the ideal existence—forfeited in the past and redeemable in the future—immediately colored the observations of travelers who were convinced that traces of that pure life were still to be found somewhere on earth. The best evidence for this is provided by the close similarities shared by the descriptions of paradises, golden ages, other dreamworlds, and exotic lands, all of which influenced one another.

Cockaigne also takes part in this competition, for scores of its attractions are reported to be everyday occurrences in other parts of the world. Any European living in preindustrial times would have been moved to remember Cockaigne or Luilekkerland when, traveling abroad, he suddenly felt a balmy breeze, or saw trees sagging under the weight of their fruit, or heard exotic birds singing, or detected the fragrance of spices, or tasted strange and delightful food for the first time. In many travel accounts Cockaigne appears to be a reality, though sometimes a rather far-fetched one.

Between the observation of exotica (or stories thereof) and the publication of their description lay many opportunities for adaptation or recasting. The genesis of such travelers' tales was always a dubious procedure in itself. Other sources describing these wonders were often lacking, at least contemporary sources not stemming from the same tradition. If we are to believe what we are told, these reports were usually based on one or more letters written by the explorer to his patron, previously published excerpts from his diaries or ship's log, or simply a recorded version of a report from his own lips. In all cases there was serious doubt as to the reliability of the sources, while the biased adaptations seem to speak for themselves. Starting in the late fifteenth century, printed "tidings" began to appear on the scene, which referred to the same sources for their veracity. When the European press as a whole seized upon these travel stories, there was no stopping them, and the texts were further developed into spectacular, sensationalized stories, illustrated with equally spectacular woodcuts.

25
Real Dreamworlds

THE DREAMWORLDS and idyllic places occurring in travelers' tales are more or less distinguishable from other dreamlands in that they may be pinned down to an earthly time and place. They were discovered by someone who then reported the discovery to the Western world, paving the way for others to seek out the described location. The ideal places and golden ages mentioned earlier in this book are in any case less tangible, not to be visited without difficulty (or perhaps not at all) and very far removed in time.

Nevertheless, journeys were regularly made to the earthly paradise, even after the Middle Ages. The stimulus for such undertakings stemmed not only from the conviction that such a place must still exist on earth but especially from the growing certainty that there must be an entrance somewhere, considering the supposed presence of Enoch and Elijah, who had been stationed there to help combat the Antichrist at the end of time, as well as this paradise's presumed function as a wondrous waiting room for honest souls expecting to enter the heavenly paradise.

Various medieval travelers—such as the Utrecht priest Jan Witte van Hese, who set off in 1339 for the Holy Land—reported having stood at the moss-covered but sky-high wall of paradise. There was even a legendary account of a tedious trip to paradise that had nevertheless been crowned with success. This *Iter ad Paradisum* (Trip to paradise), recounting the journey made by Alexander the Great, had no trouble establishing itself among the medieval canon of material on Alexander to be found everywhere and in all languages. Alexander eventually achieved his aim, after almost being snuffed out by the most thundering of the four rivers of paradise, which, of course, had to be negotiated by wading upstream. As proof of having reached his goal, Alexander had ever since carried with him a dazzling jewel that was too heavy to have been washed downstream by any of the rivers.

The way to paradise was also paved with consolation prizes. According to reports, the immediate vicinity of paradise was steeped in paradisiacal comforts, as it naturally would be considering its close proximity. The four rivers and their branches washed over the whole world and saw to it that the rest of the earth was fertile enough to thrive. Everyone took it for granted that these rivers carried in their currents precious stones, seeds, plants, and especially spices, great quantities of which were thought to lie along the shores for the taking. The Tigris, Euphrates, Nile, and Ganges (sometimes also the Donau) were thought to represent the four rivers of paradise. The closer one came to their source, the closer one was to paradise, and the richer the harvest of spices, precious stones, and gold. Was it not written in Genesis that "a river went out of Eden to water the garden; and from thence it was parted, and became into four heads. The name of the first is Pison: that is it which compasseth the whole land of Havilah, where there is gold; and the gold of that land is good: there is bdellium and the onyx stone."

The learned Dirk van Delf, chaplain of the court of Holland at The Hague, explained to his lay public that in addition to precious stones, the Pison and the Euphrates and one of its branches carried medicinal herbs out of paradise. The Euphrates also supplied the aloe, which was known to be a medicine at once healing and intoxicating. By ingesting the juice of this plant, one sank into a soporific state imbuing one with the certainty of immortality, which is why the dying Adam had his son Seth fetch some of this cheering balsam from the gates of paradise. The assurances given by the Bible that death and dying were not on the paradisiacal agenda were often demonstrated to the lay public by pointing out the existence of this herb and other rejuvenating and healing substances that the rivers of paradise brought directly from their source.

For many a person, therefore, it was a simple fact that paradise put its temperate climate, its abundance of all-weather fruits, and even its spirit of unspoiled purity at the disposal of neighboring regions, where civilization, with all its corrupting influences, had not been able to establish a foothold. This had even given rise to the thought that the way to the East (which could also be reached from the west, south, or north) automatically led to abundance, harmony, and eternal springtime, all of which presented themselves very gradually as one drew nearer to paradise.

It is difficult to imagine Columbus's continued obsession with the idea of finding paradise, or a rough equivalent of it, in India. This remained his firm intention, in pursuance of orders he insisted were received directly from

God. On his third voyage in 1498 he sailed up the Orinoco River directly into the Amazon forest, certain that he was on one of the four rivers flowing out of the earthly paradise. As soon as he saw that the forest was inhabited by naked savages, he broke into a song of praise, commending the innocence and natural goodness of these people, who did not appear to have been corrupted by civilization and, as a result, could easily be shepherded into the Christian fold. At the same time their presence was interpreted by Columbus as a sign that paradise must be close by.

Columbus thought that only about one hundred and fifty years remained before the end of time, providing three conditions were met: the discovery of India via the West, the conversion of all savages and other non-believers to Christianity, and the conquest of Jerusalem. He also believed that he had been appointed an instrument of divine providence, responsible for bringing about the fulfillment of these goals. He was convinced he had already discovered India through the divine agency of the Holy Ghost, paving the way for preaching the gospel to the heathens. This is why he rated the convertibility of the natives so highly. He remarked repeatedly that the natives he encountered seemed to glow with a natural goodness, even though they did not appear to adhere to any religion. Their conversion could therefore take place with the greatest of ease.

Great wealth had to be amassed for a new and last crusade, meant to liberate Jerusalem once and for all from the infidels. Riches to sponsor this goal were there for the taking, he thought, now that he found himself in India in the immediate vicinity of paradise. This was another reason compelling him to pursue his objective: all those precious stones would be even easier to find the closer he got to the source. This glittering mirage would, in time, give rise to a gold rush, based on the assumption of the existence of complete lands of gold.

In fact, the El Dorado of classical antiquity took on such concrete shape in the early-modern period that it precipitated the wildest expeditions. The travel literature is fairly glutted with their descriptions. The tone was set by Columbus's account of his first voyage, in which his obsession with finding gold was recorded almost daily. Antonio Pigafetta—traveling between 1519 and 1522 with Magellan, the first to sail around the world—seems to have lost his head upon arriving in the Philippines near the end of their voyage: "This chieftain told us that lumps of gold had been found on his island that were as big as walnuts and even as big as eggs; they were extracted from the ground with the help of a sieve. He told us that all the drinking vessels, barrels, and ornaments were made of gold." Pigafetta then began to suspect the presence of gold everywhere. A man offered him a bowl of rice and some figs but refused his proffered gold ducats, choosing instead a knife. Another native traded a large bar of gold for six strings of beads made of glass. Magellan immediately put a stop to this bartering, for otherwise the inhabitants would notice how much the newcomers coveted all that gold. On Borneo, Pigafetta could not take his eyes off the gold and precious stones with which the warriors decorated their bodies. They wore, for example, belts of gold brocade, gilded daggers inlaid with pearls and precious stones, and gold rings on practically every finger.

Long before Columbus, the most famous land thought to be situated in the immediate vicinity of paradise was the kingdom of Prester John. Straight through this country ran a river coming directly from paradise that carried precious stones in its currents. There were also rivers of milk and honey, another direct derivative of the Old Testament prophecies of paradise. In addition, the Garden of Eden's ability to generate spices had been passed on to this kingdom, as witnessed by the forests that produced an abundance of pepper. There was, moreover, a fountain of youth, which barred all disease and guaranteed a constant age of thirty-two years. The supply of food was inexhaustible, and the fish willingly offered themselves for consumption. Sin was unknown, and all lived in perfect harmony. The whole country was dominated by a magnificent palace made of gold, crystal, carbuncles, and other precious stones.

All these voyages of exploration—whether completed, cut short, or simulated—of the late Middle Ages and early-modern period brought dreams of comfort, riches, and salvation, intended either to recover the lost paradise or to pave the way to heavenly fulfillment. Not infrequently these desires merged, as in the case of Columbus. The thirst for action impelled by a yearning for consolation appealed to the imagination of many a traveler. Moreover, such a spirit of enterprise produced an infectious optimism once one seemed firmly on the way to a better life. Apart from the riches for the taking, one could learn from the "savages" how to negotiate the dangerous path to be taken on earth.

In the New World, in particular, paradise lay ready for a private viewing. There, people lived in their pure and natural state in perfect harmony,
inhabiting lush surroundings that were stocked directly from paradise. The
longing for unimaginable material comfort, however, meant that any high-
flown ideology with which explorers started out was repeatedly pushed to
the sidelines. During the course of the sixteenth century, the New World
came to represent no more than a warehouse full of untold treasures, existing only to be efficiently exploited in the true commercial spirit.

The collection of treasures presented to Cortez in 1519 by Emperor
Montezuma was exhibited in the following year by Charles V in Brussels.
Albrecht Dürer, on a trip through the Netherlands, saw it and made detailed
notes in his diary about the treasures "from the new golden land," El
Dorado. Especially in the trading metropolis of Antwerp the idea was
eagerly put forward that such riches should be well looked after by someone
with both business acumen and a noble spirit. During the *landjuweel*, or literary contest, held in 1561, at which chambers of rhetoric from the whole of
Brabant competed in singing the merchant's praises, the prologue play presented by the Diest chamber pointed out the possibilities of such previously
unheard-of expansion. Vespucci and Columbus had pointed the way, and
the Antwerp traders followed suit, so that now "the whole of Europe
gleamed with silver and gold."

All these high hopes of riches and salvation, hope and comfort, meant
that the travelers (and their scriptwriters) could see little beyond what these
dreams promised them. One discovered what one expected to discover and
described what one was expected to report, and if necessary the copyists or
publishers gave the material a helpful push in the right direction. In addition, the uncertain and meager food supply, as well as deprivation—sometimes lasting for months at a time—of the more usual forms of sexual gratification could steer the observations reported by pilgrims and ships' crews
in highly compensatory directions. It is remarkable, for example, how often
and in what a caricatural way excesses of food and willing women figure in
these texts.

The ideological framework of this dream geography was first laid down
in numerous descriptions of paradise, including all its regional elaborations
and variations. One's background and degree of literacy also determined the
color of the glasses through which one's observations were made. Nonethe-

less, quite a few chroniclers of the early-modern era portrayed the New World in colors corresponding very closely to those of a golden age.

In this context, dreams of Cockaigne also seem to play a role. Otherwise it is difficult to explain why Cockaigne continued to crop up at various places on the globe, albeit under different names. The similarities are always found in unmistakable details. During his curious travels, for example, Alexander the Great found himself in a forest where the world had been turned upside-down to the extent that food spontaneously appeared from nowhere. This did not occur according to the pattern found in mythic paradises or nostalgic recollections of golden ages but along the lines of Cockaigne: the fish were seen to be swimming in fire and grilling themselves in the water.

More widely known and therefore more difficult to trace to one exclusive source yet just as replete with the fulfillment of very worldly desires are Marco Polo's repeated descriptions of tribes who practiced adultery and openly indulged in promiscuity with ever-willing women. According to him, there was even a tribe that placed the most value on brides who had versed themselves before marriage in numerous modes of intercourse. He even urged young men between the ages of sixteen and twenty-four to pay this land a lengthy visit to take advantage of the ample opportunities it offered for training in this field. This seems like a direct link to the moralizing ends of texts B and G. The rhyming text in particular addresses itself to young good-for-nothings, who gladly abandon themselves to "wantonness," an unmistakable reference to sexual pastimes.

Direct influence is not very likely, however, though perhaps it is better to say that it was not really necessary. Although Marco Polo's text was known in many parts of Europe around 1500—also in Latin, thanks to the Gouda printer Gheraert Leeu—such commentary, whether or not intended ironically, belongs to the stock-in-trade of describers of dreamlands and other frivolities. Moreover, a moralizing implication is nearly always to be found. The point is that quite apart from the writers' intentions, in these travelogues the reader can always recognize Cockaigne as the ultimate destination of all possible yearnings, even when they have been parceled out to different places on the map.

This overpowering obsession with Cockaigne is demonstrated by Columbus's experiences during his third voyage, from 1498 to 1500. Thanks to long quotations from his lost letters to the king, published in a book written by his admirer Bartolomé de Las Casas, we know that Columbus was seriously worried about the nature of the Cockaigne in which he had landed. These worries were also pointed out by Las Casas in his commentary. In his letter Columbus had asked the king for religious support in the form of specialized missionaries, not for the necessary conversion of the Indians but in order to keep the whites in line. Instead of urging their beliefs in *imitatio Christi* upon the natives, they themselves had started to adopt the behavior of the Indians, who lived—by European standards and certainly those of the zealot Columbus—in just as much luxury as sin. Apparently there was an irresistible excess of all kinds of food, not only meat and bread but also grain, chicken, and pigs. The only things missing were wine and clothing: "But otherwise it is a veritable Cockaigne!—I'm not in the least happy about local customs, nor about their practice of eating meat on Saturdays or any of their other bad habits, unworthy of good Christians."

Each white person from his company had meanwhile acquired two or three Indian slaves and just as many hunting dogs. The women were very beautiful, and though Columbus (and Las Casas) did not elaborate upon the effect this had on his crew, in the light of his general worries it is easy to imagine what was going on. Furthermore, Columbus could have had only one reason for calling them beautiful, certainly in a letter addressed to the king. Their devilish beauty obviously constituted a serious danger to the spiritual welfare of his men.

To this negative approach to Cockaigne Las Casas added, by way of explanation, that Columbus had maintained in various letters that he had discovered the richest and most fertile land on earth. Unfortunately, this made it the perfect setting for a life of bliss, which exerted an irresistible attraction on sinners and good-for-nothings. This suggests a direct connection to the moralizing conclusion of text B and the prose text on Luilekkerland: idyllic places were meant to be both edifying and character building.

The northern part of the New World continued to be described as a Luilekkerland, even after it had become the United States of America. This tone had already been set by the very first European emigrants to that new promised land in the West. In their eyes it was truly a Garden of Eden, a place fulfilling their primary needs and answering their every fantasy. The partridges were said to be so well fed they could no longer fly, and the turkeys were apparently as fat as sheep.

Filled with similar ideas about paradise, the golden age, and the human condition in general, Amerigo Vespucci wrote about his exploration of the coast of Suriname and Brazil between 1499 and 1502. Whiffs of Cockaigne continually waft through his account as well, and these were gratefully inhaled by his eager readers in turbulent Europe. Everywhere he saw lovely landscapes, covered with tall trees that never lost their leaves, always gave off delicious scents, and were permanently laden with ripe fruit both healing and nutritious. Vast pasturelands were dotted with fragrant flowers, and everywhere birds of the most diverse description filled the air with song. Vespucci thought he must be very close to paradise, and this he dutifully recorded.

In such ideal circumstances people would naturally grow to be much older than in time-worn Europe. Vespucci estimated the natives to be on average between 130 and 150 years old. The people in the New World were seldom ill, and the pure air carried no contagious diseases. If once in a while someone did fall ill, the best herbal medicines were rushed to the rescue. Antonio Pigafetta, Magellan's scribal companion, came up with a similar estimate for the age of the Brazilian Indians: 125 to 140 years. His explanation emphasizes yet again the narrow framework in which these travelers' thoughts were confined: Pigafetta based his estimate on the fact that the natives had managed to retain something of the original state of innocence of Adam and Eve.

26

Wonders of East and West

$\mathcal{T}$HE GEOGRAPHY of the fulfilled promise, however, took a long time to manifest itself. The first world traveler to cause a furor in the Middle Ages was none other than Alexander the Great, who was shamelessly accepted as the perfect embodiment of what modern times would later prefer to cover up: discoverer and conqueror, the latter interpreted in the Middle Ages as vital to the necessary task of converting the heathens, which for Alexander simply meant civilizing them. Through his eyes we see the wonders of the East, which gave rise throughout the Middle Ages to more and more elaborate stories and depictions of India as a magic garden.

There, in the Far East, Alexander had reached the edge of the earth, close to the paradise that he would also set foot in. One way or another, these margins of the world granted nature more freedom. It was there that the most marvelous exotica flourished of their own accord, as the learned Franciscan Ranulf Higden (ca. 1280–1364) stated with great authority in his Polychronicon: "Note that at the farthest reaches of the world often occur new marvels and wonders, as though Nature plays with greater freedom secretly at the edges of the world than she does openly and nearer us in the midst of it." According to Jacob van Maerlant—the renowned disseminator of any knowledge that could possibly be useful to layfolk—India was the first country to be inhabited by people. By this he undoubtedly meant that Adam and Eve, after being driven out of paradise, simply went to live next door, as it were. At any rate, he also informed his readers that India was located close to paradise.

India, according to Maerlant, was immeasurably large and incomparably rich. Silver, gold, and precious stones were to be found in abundance, as well as a profusion of flora and fauna. It was also blessed with two harvests a year. One shouldn't think, however, that it had no cities: on the contrary, an expert had calculated that there were at least five thousand, of which the smallest had no fewer than nine thousand inhabitants (in keeping with medieval norms). The place was also teeming with the most wonderful beasts, such as three-hundred-foot eels and whopping big snakes.

The medieval encyclopedias of the world, in Latin and the vernaculars, all contained a standard section called "Exotica" or "Strange Peoples" that paid particular attention to the so-called monster races. Chroniclers were especially fond of this subject, as it provided a good opportunity to raise the tension in the story to unbearable heights. This section was usually found at the beginning of the encyclopedia, near the discussion of the Creation and the division of the earth after the Flood among the three sons of Noah. Remarkably, these descriptions present all these misshapen folk as a people without a history, not unlike the treatments of the animals, which were considered equally timeless. Somehow they seem to have gotten stuck in their natural state, which either makes them evil beyond redemption or else serves to protect their innocence but in any case ensures that they are completely lacking in historicity. This makes them an appropriate subject for static descriptions at the beginning of historical surveys. Only Europe had a history, which could be treated in depth, and its evil at least showed some sign of abating (but for how long still?), thanks to the powerful message of salvation.

Even before Columbus and Vespucci started gallivanting around the New World, there had been keen interest in the wonders of the West. The point of departure had been the mysterious Atlantis, an immense island far away in the ocean to the West, a "fact" known already in antiquity. Just like the Islands of the Blessed and the slightly more northern islands of the Hesperides, this island was generously endowed with golden-age attributes, which were enjoyed to the full by nothing but happy people.

Nevertheless, the West as a place—or rather a point on the compass— where wondrous things could happen first took shape in the paradisiacal pleasure spots told of in Celtic travelers' tales, which became known in all of Europe through the story of Saint Brendan. This generally led to a revaluation of the remote country of Ireland. Until the early Middle Ages Ireland had been treated as a typical example of negative marginalism. The Greek geographer Strabo, for instance, accused the Irish of being incestuous cannibals living in absolutely bestial conditions. Slowly but surely, however, this picture changed, undoubtedly owing in part to the early, almost mirac-

FIGURE 45

Monster races, portrayed in Hartmann Schedel's *Buch der Chroniken*, 1493.

Source: London, British Library, IC.7458.

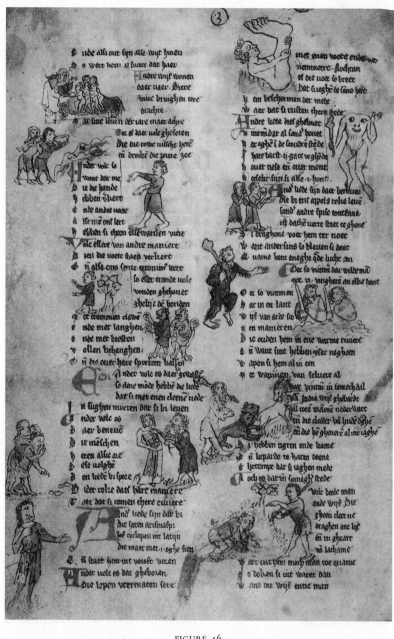

FIGURE 46

Monster races, portrayed in Jacob van Maerlant's *Der naturen bloeme*,
manuscript ca. 1325.

Source: London, British Library, MS Add. 11390, fol. 3 verso.

ulous Christianizing of the country and subsequent missionary work in the rest of Europe. Ireland then came to be known as the umpteenth promised land, flowing with milk and honey and blessed with such a mild climate that there was no need for animals to be stabled in the winter.

Neither did Ireland have any snakes, those accursed descendants of the primal tempter in the Garden of Eden. Ireland's increasingly compelling image as a subsidiary of paradise led many to believe that it even had a fountain of youth. This aura of enchantment also extended to the islands off the Irish coast, on one of which, it was said, it was impossible to die even if one wanted to. Nevertheless, the negative connotations also live on in the adaptations in the vernacular of antique and early-medieval sources.

The Middle English *Land of Cokaygne* also situates its idyllic place within this tradition of Western dream islands, and this was done not only as a parody on the well-known location of paradise in the East. Cokaygne is situated, says the text, even farther away than the most western part of Europe, which was Spain. Its western position meant that Spain—which according to medieval notions stretched far out into the ocean—was also privy to those wonders of the West and therefore must have had mysterious charms of its own.

Bartholomaeus Anglicus had already offered an explanation of Spain's prominent location based on the etymology of its name. Spain had supposedly been named after the evening star, Ysperia, "which is westward." Furthermore, according to this learned Englishman, Spain formed a sort of bridge between Europe and Africa, whose mere mention conjured up visions of divine blessings. The sky was always clear, and the earth was fertile and rich in gold, silver, precious stones, and metals—information that Bartholomaeus had gleaned in part from Pliny.

That Spain could serve in the late Middle Ages as a basis of comparison with Cockaigne is due to this fairy-tale image. Both rhyming texts try to sketch the contours of their dreamland by announcing, right from the start, that "half is better than all of Spain." There are also indications that an idyllic picture of Spain was etched in the collective imagination. There is, for example, the frequent occurrence, from the fourteenth century on, of the expression "to build castles in Spain," which in English also means to build castles in the air, a very direct reference indeed to the ultimate dreamland full of imaginary attractions and therefore highly suitable for comparison with the illusory Cockaigne.

The implications of these descriptions of exotica from both East and West are generally clear: the point is always to depict striking contrasts that serve to boost the image of one's own culture and to encourage reflection and reform. Such efforts often come across as an automatic reflex occurring every time exotic peoples are described. Mandeville informs us that somewhere in India there grows an abundance of powerful grapes, the wine of which is drunk only by women, the men being completely abstemious. This immediately leads to conjecture as to the relationship between men and women, which, in view of the new division of labor taking place in the family at the end of the Middle Ages, gave rise to all manner of commentary.

Positive primitivism may have served as the immediate example, but perhaps one's own ideals and intentions were brought more clearly into focus by concentrating on their opposites, as exemplified by the barbarities that took place on the edge of the world. Model peoples nevertheless cropped up in all travelogues and other surveys of the time. This had begun already in the early Middle Ages with the Camerini, a people living somewhere in Africa who were fed spontaneously by food falling from the sky, their nourishment requiring no effort of any kind on their part. They lived in a state of nature and knew no evil in their lives. Completely happy and already lying in a sarcophagus made of aromatic wood, each breathed his or her last at the age of 120, and since all of them died at this age, no parent ever had to mourn the premature death of a child. Moreover, their land was covered with precious stones, which also explains why they were so virtuous: jewels were thought to incite such behavior.

Especially appealing to the imagination were the previously mentioned Brahmans, who lived in India. During his long journey Alexander the Great reportedly heard of their existence, which prompted him to exchange letters with their king, Didimus. Upon being asked by Alexander to explain the Brahman way of life, Didimus complied, emphasizing however that they had no need for Alexander's "civilizing" interference. These widely known stories warned—if not constantly, at least with regularity—of the corrupting influence of culture and learning, which cultivate the pride that will ultimately lead to the ruin of the human species in the finale of the piece whose overture was played by Adam and Eve.

The Brahmans, according to medieval notions, knew no riches or luxury, and neither did they engage in trade or wage war. They were chaste, ate only fruit and honey, and lived to a ripe old age. They would be model Christians, if only they were baptized. In the Middle Ages they represented the ideal type of noble savage, instinctive proto-Christians of the purest kind. They did not work, as work only fostered avarice. They lived according to the laws of nature and made no effort to resist them. Rhetoric, philosophy, and even education in general were not practiced, for such activities had a pernicious influence on the natural order of things.

It is odd, on the face of it, to find this story being told with enthusiasm by such a luminary of Middle Dutch letters as Jacob van Maerlant. What must this paragon of popular pedantry have thought when translating the relevant lines from Vincent of Beauvais's Latin world history for inclusion in his own *Spiegel historiael*? Was education yet another evil influence? Perhaps people in the West already viewed themselves as too far gone—Maerlant never tired of emphasizing this point—and the only way back was to acquaint oneself with everything that had gone wrong before. Knowledge, for these teachers, meant learning to live according to God's plan by taking note of all the wrong turns taken in the past. The Brahmans were certainly not in need of such education, as they had never been tempted to use knowledge to wield power, either over each other or over other peoples.

Every traveler or historian could produce examples of such pure and natural lives, which might be called more Christian than any behavior displayed by disciples of the mother church. Full of admiration, Mandeville tells of Indian pilgrims who "believe that the more pain they suffer here for the love of that idol, the more joy they will have in the other world and the nearer God they will be. And truly they suffer so much pain and mortification of their bodies for love of that idol that hardly would any Christian man suffer the half—nay, not a tenth—for love of Our Lord Jesus Christ."

In a letter to the cardinal of Salzburg, Maximilianus Transsylvanus displayed similar feelings of envy when reporting on Magellan's alleged discovery of the Moluccas in 1511. The people there apparently fought only in self-defense and even then begged instantly for peace, which was considered an honorable action. Indeed, it was thought disgraceful not to beg for peace, even if one was attacked without reason. They possessed nothing but their spices, yet they were always at peace among themselves. This lifestyle contrasted sharply with that of greedy Christians: "We are driven only by greed and the desire for valuable spices in this unknown and peace-loving world." The true Christian spirit was embodied by the Moluccans, who by nature always turned the other cheek on evil.

Even the visual arts managed to keep pace. In the mid-sixteenth century Jan Mostaert made one of the first paintings meant to depict the New World. Although its interpretation is still a matter of controversy, it seems primarily to depict the cruel disruption by Christian soldiers of a primitive but pure society deserving of esteem. The painting shows naked Indians being attacked by heavily armed men. A woman attempts to restrain her husband from joining the fray. Unsuspecting cows and sheep go on grazing tranquilly against a backdrop of cannons, heightening the sense of an unspoiled paradise threatened with destruction by an arrogant civilization.

This does not mean to say, however, that the negative aspects of marginality did not predominate. "Savages" had one great failing, which was that they were lacking in Christian reason. This explains the acceptance in their societies of behavior that is considered bestial in the Christian world: cannibalism, incest, the eating of unclean beasts, and nudity. The fourteenth-century *Boec van der wraken* (Book of vengeance) offers examples of the behavior imputed to the Jews. This textbook, with its treatment of sin and death, informs the reader that although Alexander the Great had succeeded in locking these people up, they would soon manage to break out again:

> Those wretched folk, I'll tell you then,
> Would stoop to eating flesh of men,
> And drink the blood of beasts, they would,
> And even find it very good.
> It is their nature to partake
> Of scorpion and even snake,
> And carrion, wherever found,
> They eat right there upon the ground.
> Adders, snakes, I tell the truth,
> All things degrading and uncouth,
> They'll eat, although they be defiled.
> And women who are great with child
> They're not afraid to open up

FIGURE 47

Jan Mostaert, *Episode from the Conquest of America*, ca. 1520–1530.

Source: Haarlem, Frans Hals Museum.

And on the unborn babe to sup.
The land they shall destroy and plunder,
Leave befouled and torn asunder.
And no one will be brave enough
Their base behavior to rebuff.

These unclean peoples were supposedly descended from Gog and Magog, whose names are mentioned in the Book of Revelation as culprits in the Battle of Armageddon. They, too, were said to eat dogs, mice, snakes, and human embryos.

At the end of the Middle Ages, following in the footsteps of Columbus, the Western world began to take more pointed action against these marginal folk, hordes of whom were now within reach of Christianity. In 1493 Pope Alexander VI divided the world up between the two leaders in unlocking its secrets, Spain and Portugal, thereby signaling the official start of the creation of sanctioned order in these newly recognized outlying ter-

FIGURE 48
Skillful butchering of European intruders by cannibals in the New World.
Divi Caroli.V victoriae, 1556, plate no. VI of 1530.
Source: London, British Library, G.2674.

ritories. By relieving the natives of their possessions (gold) and turning them
into slaves ("servants")—Columbus writes that they were very well suited to
this job—the conquistadors could cause these savages to be born again, as it
were, and eventually to grow into free Christians. During the golden age, the
combination of unbridled greed, the presence of precious metals, and the
lack of guidance had caused decline to set in. Only Christianity could arrest
this process. The implementers of the plan were not entirely in agreement
on the issue of enforced slavery, but the rest of the program seemed a solid
starting point for imposing the necessary order and civilizing influence.

This framework with its dichotomy of good or bad, naturally pure or innately savage, began to lose its usefulness during this period, clouded by the rapidly increasing body of information on the Indians of the New World. They appeared to be beasts, because they brushed God aside, yet they maintained fully fledged societies that in some respects could function as an example to the Christians. In fact, their way of life could at least be called an attractive alternative to what passed for an acceptable existence in the Christian world.

In all honesty, one had to admit that Indian societies seemed to be superior to white societies on many counts. Partly as a reaction to the doubts cast on European culture, there developed during the course of the sixteenth century large numbers of political utopias that seriously toyed with the idea of total reform and radical changes in traditional values. A powerful force behind the conception of these utopias was the growing awareness that on many occasions—far too many, in any case—Christian societies prompted bad and sinful behavior. Jean de Léry, who spent some time in Brazil in 1557, was angered by the nakedness of the savages, asking himself at the same time whether all the fashionable wigs and décolletages of European women were not actually more titillating. He also found cannibalism hard to accept, but was it any worse than the practice of usury in his own country? Usurers sucked the blood of widows, orphans, and poor folk, leeching the life out of them with excruciating slowness. Perhaps, he thought, it's better to take a human body and kill it and eat it right away.

These grave doubts about Christian fellowship, as well as the utopian blueprints for a better society, have little or nothing to do with Cockaigne and Luilekkerland, although they are sometimes lumped together. Not only were these dreamlands patently nonexistent, but they did not even aspire to existence, and every reader or listener was well aware of this. Cockaigne offered only spiritual compensation for the acute discomfort suffered by humankind, which had however brought some of its troubles upon itself. Creation as such was inviolable. There was nothing wrong with Creation, it was humankind that fell short, and even this was something Cockaigne and Luilekkerland taught us, by wielding the weapon of irony when the situation called for it.

A much closer connection exists between Cockaigne and countless geography books, encyclopedias, pilgrims' guides, and travelogues. Even in the sixteenth century, these were still inspired more by dreams of a better life, including the one that had been forfeited in Eden, than by attempts at recording first-hand observations. The reality content of such dream geography was at first heightened by having the exotic inhabitants of the land recount in letters the facts of their ideal living conditions. In this way the Brahmans could have their say, and Prester John was able to address us, even though they only wrote what the inhabitants of Europe dictated, impelled by their own fears and frustrations, dreams and desires.

This all involved ordinary wishes and rather simple dreams, so simple that they could easily be fulfilled in a dream landscape, complete with confirmations supplied by the imaginary inhabitants themselves. We find the letter form again in the accounts written by the first travelers to the New World. Columbus and Vespucci wrote to the kings in whose service they sailed, but even though this situation is in itself highly authentic, there was a world of difference between their original letters and the versions ultimately published in many languages. The original reports were conceived from the beginning under the influence of Western prejudices and then finely honed by clerks, copyists, typesetters, and publishers, as well as by friends and descendants. Vespucci's letters certainly underwent such treatment. The Dutch edition published around 1507 by the Antwerp printer Jan van Doesborch not only did away with the letter form but also crossed out Vespucci's name. The book appeared with the simple title *Van der nieuwer werelt* (From the New World).

As already mentioned, desires and frustrations could receive an important impetus from long isolation at sea or in the vast regions of the steppe or the desert. Wild fantasies about unusual forms of eroticism and violent longings for—as well as fear of—willing women were written about frequently. Or were these episodes simply colorful accents added by money-hungry publishers who managed around 1500 to create a lucrative market for spectacular travel tales? The above-mentioned book on the New World dwells repeatedly on the unbridled lust of the natives. They gave in to every urge and were more interested in satisfying their carnal desires than in practicing a trade or occupying themselves with science or art. Being always naked, they were constantly prepared to engage in the most forthright copulation with anyone at all, for they indulged in complete promiscuity and

Die repse vā Lissebone om te varē na d;epladt
Ragnaria in groot Indien gheleghen
voor biCallicuten en Guischi dair
dpe stapel is vander specerie
Daer ons wonderlijcke di
gē wednaren zn.endair
wpveelghesē heb
bē/als hier na
ghescreuē
staer.
Welcke repse gheschiede
door dē wille en ghebode des alder
doo:luchtichstē Cōns vā Portegale,Emanuel

FIGURE 49

Title page of an account of Bartholomeus Springer's journey to the west
coast of India, printed in 1508 at Antwerp by Jan van Doesborch.

Source: London, British Library, C.32.f.26.

incest. The women in particular were said to be overcome by uncontrollable sexual desires, and at this point the writer—to his regret—has something scandalous to relate: "There is another vile and shocking practice, which has nothing human about it whatsoever. Because the women there are very hot-blooded and lecherous, they know of a trick to make a man's penis swell up enormously by means of the venom of poisonous snakes. If these men do not seek a remedy, their manhood falls off and they are 'unmanned.' The women do this, however, not in order to bring men to ruin but purely to gratify their hot-blooded nature and to quench their sexual thirst, as it were."

There was no stopping this writer. His embarrassment at his own outpourings betrays itself a bit further on, when he tries nonetheless to endow these fearsome women with some attractive traits, subsequently attempting to bestow them with a modicum of Western modesty and decorum: "These women, although they wander about in their hot-blooded state, unchaste and naked, nevertheless have pure and clean bodies. Some think that because they are fat they must be ugly, but this means instead that their female parts are less conspicuous and more covered up."

Neither do their bodies suffer as a result of pregnancy: "Even when they have borne children, they have no sagging breasts, or wrinkles, or ruptures, or other flaws, or anything to distinguish them from virgins. On the contrary, every part of their body is equal to a virgin's, though modesty forbids me to write any more about this. And when these women are able to come to us Christian folk, they cast aside all feminine feelings of shame and seek to gratify their desires with us wherever they have the chance."

Compared with these repeated fantasies, the other idyllic projections seem rather like a perfunctory enumeration of stock delights: a mild climate, an abundance of food, communal property, practically no disease, and a long life span.

By trampling on the natives the author acquaints us with himself, his cronies, his copyist, and the biases of Western ideology, one of which was its firm belief that savages could be easily converted to Christianity. This was already evident in the case of Columbus. The expression of such hopeful expectations probably served more to alleviate the writer's own fears than to point to the establishment of real contact. The cannibalism observed—an essential part of any description of primitive societies—was condemned

FIGURE 50

Text on the title page of the account of Vasco da Gama's journey to
Calcutta, printed ca. 1504 at Antwerp by Willem Vorsterman.
Source: London, British Library, C.32.f.37.

by these Europeans in no uncertain terms, and if we are to believe their
reports, their condemnations had immediate results: "And we did our best
to warn them seriously that they should give up these ill-mannered practices.
And they promised us they would."

It was repeatedly suggested that one should not condemn the savages
out of hand but rather credit them with having a certain decency. This no
doubt led to the observation of their presumed propriety, which served to
strengthen the Westerners in their conviction. Moreover, the moral upgrading of the savages made the women, and perhaps also the men, considerably
more attractive in Western eyes. The Dutch edition of the account of Vasco
da Gama's second voyage to India in 1502–1503, which was published—hot
off the press—in 1504 in Antwerp under the title *Calcoen* (Calcutta), reports
constant sightings of nakedness on the African coasts. In Quiloa on the East
African coast, however, things improved somewhat: "The king and all the
people walk around naked (men and women alike), although they wear a
cloth over their private parts and wash themselves every day in the sea." At
least these people had clean bodies, which they did not put completely on
display, unlike many other tribes, who had not yet progressed this far. The
more naked, the more primitive, at least in Western eyes. In Guinea no part
of the body was covered, and this fact was blamed as the reason the women
there lorded it over the men and kept them like house pets (monkeys, to be

exact). Those naked savages seemed unable to distinguish between good and evil.

The question remained, of course, whether these natives even understood why it was considered more decent to wear a loincloth. They were, after all, extremely—if not completely—deprived of reason. Columbus had a positive attitude nonetheless: "Men and women walk around naked, just as they came out of their mothers' womb, though the women wear a little cotton cloth, big enough to hide their most intimate parts but nothing more. They nevertheless display very modest behavior." Antonio Pigafetta's experience was quite different, however. On a voyage with Magellan, he described a tribe in Central America whose only clothing consisted of a belt of parrot feathers, the only part of the body that was covered being the buttocks, "which caused us to laugh at them and ridicule them." A savage was a savage, he seems to be saying, even when he did his best to appear civilized.

The dream geography of these voyages, however, has everything to do with Cockaigne and Luilekkerland. Thousands of travelers' tales bore witness to their existence, which in turn had a stimulating effect on the fantasies. Moreover, the centuries-old Cockaigne material could be touched up with colorful accents derived from more or less real-life observations. More particularly, the East became a rich source of decorative material for Cockaigne, as may be inferred not only from the frequent mention of wonders but also from such details as the streets paved with spices and overhung with animal skins. For pilgrims and other travelers, this last detail was a characteristic feature of every city in the Middle East, while spices generally evoked pictures of the world of Islam.

It is remarkable that the mere mention of spices conjures up visions of Cockaigne's edible architecture, whereas the hide-covered street has no such connotations. Here reality breaks through, affording a glimpse of the East, in itself enough of a fairy tale to supply Cockaigne with a backdrop. The popular history of the Three Kings, known in Latin and many vernaculars by the end of the Middle Ages, tells of just such a covered street in Bethlehem: "For they were in the habit of shading them [the streets] from the heat of the sun, as is still customary in that land."

Otherwise the connections between the East and Cockaigne are primarily a question of one-way traffic. The marginal world with all its positive and negative models is scarcely detectable in the conception or realization of Cockaigne representations. A weak echo of the contrastive input of strange places is present in Luilekkerland, however. Near the beginning of text G the marginality of this "civilization" is indicated by calling it an "outpost." This contrast is also present in its internal structure, just as it is in the kingdom of Prester John, in which there also existed wild and remote corners of the country where one found all the evil that had been banished from the heart of the land. In Luilekkerland, however, the tone remains mildly sarcastic, and it is only the pattern that has been transposed. Anyone who sinks heavily into debt is banished for a year to "a remote corner of the country," later being allowed to return to their homes in "the heart of the land."

The other similarities are rather superficial: frequent good weather, an

FIGURE 51

Naked savages, depicted half "upside-down" with respect to the civilized world. Portrayed in an account of Bartholomeus Springer's journey to India, printed in 1508 at Antwerp by Jan van Doesborch.

Source: London, British Library, C.32.f.26.

abundance of food, sanctioned laziness, and eternal life. Beastly evil does not raise its ugly head in Cockaigne, not even ironically. The same is partly true of the pure proto-Christianity of rigid temperance and chastity, which in a sense actually enters the picture via the didactic principles of the topsy-turvy world.

Cockaigne is a dead-end sidetrack on the road from the earthly to the heavenly paradise, with stopovers at the golden age, the Islands of the Blessed, the wonders of India, and the New World itself, all explored untiringly in the Middle Ages by people from every walk of life. Perhaps for this reason it might be good to stop for a while and rest the imagination. From this angle, too, longed-for salvation is clearly visible. Sometimes it even seems as though the somber realities of lost paradises, as well as those paradises recoverable via increasingly sensational dream routes, can be brought more sharply into focus by viewing them from the vantage point of Cockaigne.

27
Fanciful Destinations

ONCE OR TWICE the idea has suggested itself that Cockaigne and Luilekkerland are actually poking fun at the torrent of medieval accounts of paradises, golden ages, and travels to parts unknown. The parallels are sometimes so striking that it seems certain these texts were also meant to be interpreted as parodies. One thing remains indisputable: neither medieval Cockaigne nor sixteenth-century Luilekkerland claim to have anything at all to do with reality. This is in stark contrast to the vehement assertion of reality voiced by all the other texts, which in itself was enough to invite the invention of mocking imitations. In the face of so many sham similarities between essential points, the possibility of satire and parody must have suggested itself to readers and listeners, especially of prose text G.

This is certainly not the raison d'être of Cockaigne and its realizations. Yet the extent to which the parodic element was sensed by the public is particularly evident in the similarities between Cockaigne and scores of other so-called travelogues and descriptions of idyllic places in which the creation of fiction with satirical intent seems to be of overriding importance. Moreover, all three Dutch dreamland texts display characteristics of various text types that together established a tradition of nonsense verse in the European literature of classical antiquity, the Middle Ages, and even later periods: the *fatrasie* (from *fatras*, meaning trash: a communication that is nonsense despite the intelligibility of its component parts), the *ballade à l'impossible*, and lying couplets, all of which are closely related to one another. The *rederijkers* (rhetoricians) in particular became skilled at producing mendacious nonsense texts. These were related to the tradition of social criticism, in which one described the plain truth as though it were a lie, such typifications often turning into nonsensical outpourings in rhyme or prose.

If one attempts to compile an overview of European texts mocking fantasy lands and dreamworlds from classical antiquity onward, then depictions of

FIGURE 52

Archers, in an engraving after Pieter Bruegel the Elder, *The Kermis at Hoboken*
(detail), 1559.

Source: Brussels, Bibliothèque Royale, Print Room.

Cockaigne, presented under a variety of names, appear to belong from the
very beginning to the literary game of parody and satire. Implicit criticism
of contemporary society usually played a role as well, whether or not it was
part of the text's original intention.

A problem arises, however, when trying to determine, especially in the
case of antique literature, whether a text was intended primarily as satire or
as an attempt to describe reality. Such questions are raised by a story written by Diodorus Siculus (first century B.C.) that appears in his very serious
Bibliotheca historica, which tells of a man called Iambulus who travels from
Ethiopia to an island near the equator. There he meets gigantic people with
two tongues, which enable them to carry on two conversations at once. This
island also enjoys a mild climate and an ample supply of both warm and
cold water. Nature produces everything in abundance. The inhabitants never
fall ill and are still in excellent shape when they reach the ripe old age of 150,
after which they die peacefully in their sleep. Promiscuity is the order of the
day, taking place always in complete harmony. Meat and fish are eaten on

alternate days. Much of this information is entirely plausible, though such things had already been repeated and recorded so often before Diodorus's time that the whole story inevitably carries an undertone of parody. It is also possible, however, that this interesting information was embellished only at the outset with the facetious mention of the two-tongued beings, perhaps in order to draw the reader's attention to the story.

In any case, toying with the idea of an obviously nonexistent dreamland is as old as literature itself. This must mean that the Cockaigne material belongs to the oldest of oral traditions, otherwise it would not have been written down as soon as man started wielding the pen. Evidence for this is found in the earliest traces of Cockaigne, which occur in the Attic comedies of Pherecrates and Teleclides of the fifth century B.C. The fragments that have been preserved contain the main motifs that also determine the shape of Cockaigne and Luilekkerland. The writings of these ancients suggest dreamlands in which absolute peace reigns and no one is tormented by either fear or disease.

Above all, there is a surfeit of all one could possibly wish for. Food appears spontaneously, wine flows in the creeks, white and brown bread compete for the honor of being the first to enter one's mouth. Fish force their way into people's homes, grill themselves, and personally serve up their tastily prepared bodies. A permanent stream of soup carries on its waves chunks of meat and spoons with which to ladle it all up. Spicy sauces are provided via a system of irrigation ditches. Roast fowl and pastries fly into one's mouth or nestle on one's chin, awaiting their turn. The edible nature of things even extends to children's toys, which are manufactured entirely of delicacies. Scarcity is an impossibility, as everything is endowed with the gift of self-replenishment: anything one eats or drinks immediately reduplicates itself.

This early evidence in writing of an already abundantly present Luilekkerland is an important indication that such dreams of plenty inevitably belong to the fantasies of humankind in its earthly condition. Their ingredients—consisting of formulaic elements, individual motifs, and stock themes—are part of a widespread oral culture that has continued to the present day. In addition, details of this oral tradition continue to crop up in written literature, which then forms its own traditions, sometimes—but not necessarily—interacting with the oral transmission of these same stories. For example, when the Roman satirist Petronius wrote in the first century A.D. about a blessed land where the pigs walked around already roasted, this seemed already at that time to be a commonplace occurrence.

This idea is strengthened by a satire published a century later by the Greek author Lucian. His *True History*, as it was called, takes a culture of gluttony—apparently already existing in elaborate form—and hauls it over the coals in imaginary travelers' tales telling of enticing dreamlands. The detailed text is a typical product of the written tradition, as emerges already in the introduction, in which Lucian argues in favor of a release that even intellectuals are in need of. His text, which at the time undoubtedly functioned as a parody on numerous fantastic travelers' tales, formed at the same time a model for the genre of lying literature in general. Later on, humanists such as Erasmus were fond of referring to such texts, but it is also possible that, starting in the tenth century, there was a resurgence in their popularity.

The objective of the voyage recounted by Lucian is the discovery of the Islands of the Blessed. Along the way a monster tries to devour the boat, but luckily it reaches the calmer waters of a milk sea. (As an aside, it must be mentioned that such motifs also occur in the Celtic travel stories of the early Middle Ages, culminating in *The Voyage of Saint Brendan*. The narrators of those stories, moreover, must have drawn upon the same oral sources as did Lucian.) On the island itself a fragrant breeze is blowing, and the place appears to be a natural pleasure ground. Pastures dotted with flowers alternate with forests full of singing birds. One may quench one's thirst at springs spouting water and honey, and, to top things off, it is always spring.

In the middle of the island a golden city rises up, with walls of emerald and streets paved with ivory and precious stones. There are thirteen harvests a year, with the exception of grapes, which may be plucked from the vines only once a month. On the stalks of wheat grow freshly baked loaves of bread, while crystal trees bear bowls of fruit of various kinds. One may also pluck cups that immediately fill themselves with wine. There are a total of 365 springs of water, seven rivers of milk, and eight rivers of wine. Music and dance can be enjoyed everywhere and at all times of the day. Eroticism exists in any form desired, for both homosexuals and heterosexuals.

This picture contains pretty much everything, including overtones that any man of learning could not help hearing. Representations of the golden age and the Islands of the Blessed, as well as of the heavenly paradise, are first ridiculed and then coated for good measure in a caricatural frosting of dreams of plenty. Striking indeed is the catering to specific fantasies that would have appealed to the imagination of those in Lucian's milieu. This explains the attraction of the great number of springs containing only water (as opposed to other drinks) and especially the possibility of unlimited homosexual enjoyment.

As far as detail and breadth are concerned, Lucian's writings remained unsurpassed in the Middle Ages. By that time, travel parody and dreamland description had developed into a permanent subgenre of satirical literature, generally taking the form of farce, mock sermons, and tall tales in general. Aimed directly at imaginary voyage literature in the style of Mandeville and the compulsory section of exotica in chronicles and encyclopedias is an absurd story told in the *Farce des coquins à cinq personnes* (Farce of scoundrels for five people). One of the characters tells of a valley in which gold grows, while the inhabitants have eyelids made of apples, eyebrows of frozen cabbages, and eyes of peeled onions. In addition to parody, this farce presents the ultimate picture of humans as part of the food chain and as such invulnerable to food shortages. If need be, one can always eat oneself or those like one. This thought is whimsically expressed in the portraits painted by Arcimboldo, which are composed of food and other natural ingredients.

It is important now to establish the extent to which late-medieval Western Europe was awash with more or less fixed formulas, all of which contained parts of the Cockaigne material. "More or less fixed" is the most that can be said of these formulas, however, because each realization testifies to the matter-of-course injection of a bit of local color. Every country's version of Cockaigne features roast geese flying into one's mouth, but while German geese may offer themselves with pepper, French geese prefer to serve themselves with garlic sauce, and Dutch geese have no more to offer than their own grilled drumsticks. The motif remains the same, however, and belongs—just as do the roof tiles of custard tarts and the fences woven of sausages—to the realm of the imagination of preindustrial man, which could be endlessly exploited, varied, and augmented.

In this context the visionary literature that was so popular must also be taken with a grain of salt. In another French farce dating from the fifteenth century, the *Farce de Jenin Landore,* the main character, thought to have died,

FIGURE 53

Winter portrayed as a person modeled of natural products. Painting by
Arcimboldo, 1563.

Source: Vienna, Kunsthistorisches Museum.

miraculously returns to life and claims to have been in paradise. He proceeds to describe the hereafter in terms both vulgar and barbarian, the whole of his story being on a par with the craziest of lying tales. He had seen, for example, Saint Lawrence, whose martyrdom entailed his being roasted on a red-hot griddle. His heavenly reward now consisted in roasting the Swiss mercenaries who had threatened to overrun paradise. According to Jenin's story, it was just like watching someone roast sausages in front of an inn. Here the notion is ridiculed that the saints, both as patrons and intercessors, were experts in the affliction to which they had succumbed. This Saint Lawrence, however, does not appear to excel in the healing or treatment of burns but in roasting itself, to which he vindictively subjects others, choosing heaven of all places as a setting for such unsaintly behavior.

The constraints placed on these stories and representations of the earthly paradise and heavenly rewards were not the same for everyone. The general agreement that characterized the belief in the certainty of earthly and heavenly joys did not extend to the form these joys would take. On the contrary: on this point much skepticism and incredulity came to the fore. One way to air these doubts was ritual playacting, in which the texts mentioned here could have played an important role. The big advantage of such performances was—and still is—the possibility, when treating a delicate subject, to distance oneself from it, to step back from the action in order to point out the aloof nature of fiction. One could continually turn one's back on the play and return, chastened, to the reality of everyday life, having repented for the umpteenth time.

An example of this is the popular performance and recitation text *Aucassin and Nicolette*, which originated in the first half of the thirteenth century in northern France. Its most important feature is its use of the motifs of the upside-down world to voice serious social criticism. The male protagonist, Aucassin, immediately declares that he hopes not to end up moldering in the earthly paradise until the Last Judgment, because it must be populated by the old and infirm. He would much rather go to hell, which is surely full of young and beautiful people who know how to have a good time.

Together with Nicolette, Aucassin finds himself in the land of Turelure, where everything is upside down. Its very name carries the audience off to the world of Carnival, where they hear the sound of bagpipes, played by the peasants who are the best-loved personification of the fool, the most distinguished inhabitant of the temporary mock kingdom of Carnival:

> See the pipers marching in,
> Their bagpipes wail till day is done.
> Aye, listen to the awful din,
> And hear the frenzy of their fun!
> The yokels jig and skip about,
> Beards flapping in their gladness.
> They never cease to dance and shout,
> May God cut short such madness!

Bagpipes, of course, have the shape of caricaturally enlarged genitals. That, along with the sound they produce, makes them symbolic of the boorish, beastly sexuality thought to be typical of country bumpkins. Any land named after the riveting, suggestive sound of the bagpipes (in Dutch the sound they make is rendered as "turelurureleruut") is bound to be marked by topsy-turvy sexuality and role reversals. And, indeed, this seems to be the case: the women wear the pants here. Aucassin is told upon arriving in Turelure that the king has just given birth, while his wife is out on the battlefield. This makes our hero furious, and he gives the king hell, making him promise to set things to rights by swearing that no man will ever again have to submit to such ignominy.

The satire is unequivocal on this point. Aucassin promptly puts a stop to what was thought of at the time this story originated as a very real danger: the inauspicious approach of role swapping between men and women that had already been witnessed among so many exotic peoples, in both ancient and contemporary cultures. Hadn't the Greek geographer Strabo spoken of men who behaved like women in childbed? This must be a sign of the world's downfall, for only the Antichrist could be responsible for such an insidious inversion of the order established by God.

28

Virtual Dreamlands

THE LIBERATING MOCKERY of dreamlands, which the increasing influx of travel stories had made more tangible and easier to localize, experienced a heyday with the appearance of several printed texts in French starting in 1500. This was done by making use of the Cockaigne material, so that these texts even seem to sneer at the various versions of Cockaigne and Luilekkerland, though this is difficult to prove, as the material, borrowed to achieve other aims, may have been contaminated in the process. Things are complicated by the fact that Cockaigne itself, still very much alive in the collective imagination of sixteenth-century Europe, had already become an intentionally ludicrous caricature that could be used for a wide variety of purposes. In addition to the possibilities these dreamworlds offered for cathartic compensation, there was also ample opportunity for moralizing. On the surface, too, there remains the snubbing of all those claims to truthfulness made by popular travelers' tales, which had also conquered the world of the printing press. Finally, there was the not insignificant matter of the mockery of the readership, who swallowed tall tales whole and could not get enough of the sensational literature churned out by the press.

The title of *Le Disciple de Pantagruel* of 1538 refers directly to Rabelais, in whose work one would naturally expect to find the description of a fullblown Cockaigne, though this does not occur. The writer does, however, offer constant evidence of his familiarity with the material, every detail of it. At one point he tells of a semiparadisiacal place where one is rewarded for snoring as well as sleeping. This motif recurs repeatedly in the French and Middle Dutch Cockaigne texts, none of which the author of *Le Disciple* necessarily knew in their fixed forms. Such submotifs were the common property of countless Europeans in the late Middle Ages and early-modern period.

The text dating from 1538, however, seems to have made up for the lack of a signed Rabelaisian Cockaigne by offering one with an oblique reference to his name. It is, after all, not very likely that Rabelais is the author of this text. At any rate, without ever mentioning it by name, *Le Disciple* portrays a gigantic Cockaigne. The central concern of the dreamworld described is never in doubt: its landscape is dominated by enormous edible edifices. The reader is introduced to a group of worn-out heroes, constantly doing battle with monsters, who are finally enjoying a well-earned rest thanks to the blessings on offer in this archipelago completely isolated from the rest of the world.

The description of the ups without downs of this island draws upon very well-known ingredients that, since Mandeville, a broad public had come to connect with existing countries and exotic peoples at the edges of the earth. These lands are difficult to reach, and they have wondrous trees, great quantities of food on offer, mild climates, and inhabitants who are ensured of eternal youth. The author deploys all the satirical weapons at his disposal by citing such authorities as Pliny, Lucian, Strabo, and Mandeville, which only serves to underscore his parodic intentions.

Everything in this text is bound up with food, burgeoning everywhere and running rampant until this Luilekkerland is completely overgrown with victuals. First the travelers arrive at the Islands of the Blessed, where they see an island consisting of a mountain of butter, awash in a river of milk. In the distance they see another mountain made of flour. There is also a fountain that spouts hot peas and bacon, as well as sausages made of salted chitterlings. The trees on the river bank, besides being forever green, bear immense legumes containing fried sausages. In the milky river swim eels, lampreys, and other fish. Its inhabitants call this island the land of Coquardz, a term of abuse for tramps that possibly carries overtones of Cockaigne.

This provides the framework for the subsequent descriptions. Everything Cockaignesque occurs more frequently and in considerably more grotesque form than in its land of origin. On other islands warm meat pies, tarts, and puddings grow on bushes. Roasted larks fly into one's mouth. Elsewhere cranes, completely grilled and stuffed with bacon, may be grabbed as they fly past. The trees produce cakes, cracknel, Brussels sprouts, cheeses of various kinds, and also bottles in which to catch the wine flowing in the rivers. Rain, hail, and snow consist of all kinds of candy, almond pastry, pats of butter, fish, poultry, meat, and game.

This is no longer a spontaneous recording and not even a distant echo of tried-and-true formulations that had served for centuries to allay fears with a liberating laugh. *Le Disciple de Pantagruel* is without doubt a product of the written tradition. Its point of departure is the genre of travelers' tales, with Mandeville in the lead, seized upon here for the purpose of parody. The current representations of Cockaigne and Luilekkerland supplied the instruments used in producing the exaggerated caricatures and blow-ups so typical of lying tales. The ground of the dream islands in *Le Disciple* is so fertile that everything grows to fabulous sizes. Placed in the middle of Paris, the heads of lettuce and the Brussels sprouts would supply enough shade for the entire city.

These printed travel parodies form a literary tradition to which the Luilekkerland text of 1546 finally links up, albeit via a German route. One of the first of these parodies immediately offers itself as alternative "tidings," derived from the previously coined genre *nouvelles*, a designation applied to short, entertaining prose stories. The book in question is called *Nouvelles admirables* and dates from 1495. The rest of the title announces that the crew of a galley blown off course was carried by the winds to strange parts and exotic islands, where they saw cows giving wine, chickens laying boiled eggs, sheep falling roasted from the skies, and other examples of spontaneous food dispensation. The influence of Lucian is also noticeable, providing yet another indication of a tradition of written literature only vaguely connected with the orally transmitted tales of Cockaigne.

The pioneer in this genre is undoubtedly a novella from Boccaccio's *Decameron*, a volume of stories that was immediately exploited, also in translation, by the printing press. In nearly perfunctory fashion Boccaccio presents a travel parody in the sermon of Fra Cipolla (Friar Onion). This friar is searching for relics, to which end he leaves Venice and travels in the direction of India. Boccaccio pokes fun in particular at the highly fantastic tales told in growing numbers by travelers, with monks in the lead. This genre would remain popular throughout the sixteenth century (and even afterward), especially in the form of novellas published individually.

Related to this new kind of text is *La grande confrarie des soulx d'ouvrer et enragez de rien faire* (The great brotherhood of those who are fed up with working and keen on doing nothing). This prose text, printed between 1520 and 1540 at Lyons, stems from another tradition, namely, that of the mock charge (episcopal address) and monastic parody. This text features a pseudo-order or mock brotherhood of monks whose community exposes abuses existing in the church and the world at large. The patron saint of these gluttonous, boozing brothers is a certain Saint Lax. Such representations, performed or recited, were popular at the church's annual Feast of Fools and later on in urban celebrations of Carnival. Examples of this genre may be found in the twelfth-century *Carmina Burana* and also in theater repertoire such as *Van den covente* (Of the convent) and the text about the Guild of the Blue Barge.

The relationship of the *Confrarie* text to travel parodies becomes evident when the other customs and practices of the brothers come to light. Their communities are often situated in remote corners of the world. That such different points of departure as travel parody and monastic parody could coalesce into one text is shown in the Middle English *Land of Cokaygne*, where a Luilekkerland (literally a "lazy-luscious-land") is portrayed in the guise of a community of monks living on a far-off island.

There is practically no end to the insane fantasies portrayed in the above-mentioned *Confrarie*, in which precious stones, silk, damask, and other wonderful things, such as scents and music, play an architectonic and decorative role. The art of such description became a literary game in itself, scarcely concerning itself with realities or emotions outside the fantasy being treated. The author attempted to excel in inventive tours de force, focusing on the chosen theme but not hesitating to exploit to the full all his ready knowledge of earthly and heavenly paradises, golden ages, and blessed isles, parodying them in one big, wild orgy. This all-encompassing bacchanal is highly spiced with grotesque exaggerations, although there are fewer of them than one would expect. Much of their fantasized content is an innate part of the existing framework. For example, on this island only one day seems to pass when listening for a whole year to the heavenly orchestra of organs, tambourines, flutes, and other instruments. This, however, is a rather conventional demonstration of heavenly time telling and occurs as well in more serious travelogues.

Dutch material of this nature does exist, though it is less effusive. A travel parody is included in *Twee bedelaers* (Two beggars), by the Protestant rhetorician Lauris Janszoon of Haarlem. In this simple *tafelspel* (literally a "table" play, which actors performed while the audience dined) two professional beggars exchange information on the best place to ply their trade. The first has just come "from Italy, where I truly thought the houses were roofed with warm pancakes and held together by sausages," though it turns out he was deceived. Lauris Janszoon made use of a well-known proverb to this effect, which had been part of the Cockaigne material for centuries. Of more recent origin is the satirical presentation of Italy (or Rome) as a pleasure ground, especially popular among followers of Erasmus and other rebellious spirits fond of exposing the humbug in which the Catholic Church was generally thought to excel. Echoing the sentiments of the beggars, everyone in the audience would have to admit that something had gone wrong with all those biblical promises of lands of milk and honey.

Italy is also mentioned in a lying song from a text printed in 1597 with the title *Drie Eenlingen* (Three loners):

> That's why we sailed to Italy, where the geese did speak.
> From grindstones I saw parrots made, heard tales
> Of heaps of fine gold made of whales.
> Shiploads of nuggets lined the street,
> Where Amsterdam has mud and sand.
> I saw there apes that tilled the land,
> On hedgerows milk and wine to hand.

This booklet was based on Sir John Mandeville, whose ever-popular work was still in print, although publishers now addressed themselves to a lower and broader sort of readership that had to be sought in the countryside as well, as witnessed by the considerably less expensive editions and sloppy treatment of the text. The author opens with a reference to this downsized Mandeville, only to state immediately afterward that his own travels were much more extensive and considerably more spectacular. He has been, not surprisingly, in paradise—we recall, of course, Mandeville's regret at having failed to see it—and even claims to have been borne there on the back of a grasshopper. There he met Enoch and Elijah, who gave him warm whole-wheat bread to eat, and he even succeeded in meeting Prester John, who had just sat down to eat with twelve thousand bishops, cardinals, abbots, priests, and deacons of the church.

Of a different nature entirely are the sometimes distant similarities between Cockaigne and the political utopias of the sixteenth century, including the satires on them. I broached this subject at the end of the last chapter, when I noted how little Cockaigne and Luilekkerland have to do with creative fantasies involving a better and more just society. Within this tradition, which may be traced back to Plato, solemnity and mirth are not always easy to distinguish from one another. Things are complicated by the fact that, at the end of the Middle Ages, humor in no way precluded a serious objective. On the contrary, it often served to drive home a serious message in an entertaining yet convincing way.

Such texts focus on suggestions for a totally different organization of society, sometimes presented as a critique or satire of the existing order, though always in terms of an inevitable revolution. This is certainly not true of Cockaigne, where there is no suggestion whatever of new laws or an alternative order but rather the hope of being allowed to wallow in ideal circumstances of abundance and idleness within the existing system. In a utopia this situation can at best be the result of other structures, the establishment of which are more likely to require austerity, moderation, and chastity.

Above all, it must be clear that Cockaigne and Luilekkerland are concerned not so much with satire—and certainly not with revolution—as with cathartic compensation aimed at allaying fears arising from the existing order, without any thought of doing away with that order. On the contrary, the possibility of temporary escape is precisely what makes the daily yoke more bearable, and this seems to prove the necessity of such release in continuing to bear up against the troubles of the world. Even if Cockaigne and Luilekkerland present an ironic institution of learning, teaching one how *not* to behave in the real world, the result is the same: confirmation of the existing order by portraying in a playful way the total chaos brought about by the lack of that order. In essence, utopias, at one end of the spectrum, and Cockaigne, at the other, are striving toward totally different goals.

The few similarities that do exist result from the occasional coincidence of their using the same remedies to treat the same symptoms. Utopias propose the implementation of another structure to remedy evils that Cockaigne compensates for temporarily by supplying their opposite. The absence of private property and the acceptance of communally owned possessions are an example of this, just as is promiscuity. In Cockaigne these are simply pleasant thoughts, in conformance with the cult of promised pleasure prevailing in that dreamland. The inhabitants have at their disposal everything imaginable in the way of goods and amenities, including the unlimited fulfillment of their naughtiest sexual fantasies. In the utopias, on the other hand, the new laws are intended to call a halt to inequality and adultery, which are bringing the world closer to ruin every day. Possession, even the possession of a woman, is corrupting. Unfortunately, it was jealousy that seemed to be holding society together in the Middle Ages, and the golden age was regarded wistfully as a time when people had not yet shown an interest in personal possessions.

The utopias belong to the literature of the elite in Latin and the vernaculars. While stemming from a strong antique tradition, they underwent decided revitalization with Thomas More's *Utopia*. This text, published at Louvain in 1516, gave the name to a genre that would once again flourish in the eighteenth century, only to disappear from view in modern times owing to its subsumption under the rubric of science fiction.

This antique tradition—having entered the Middle Ages by way of Trogus Pompeius, Valerius Maximus, Vincent of Beauvais, and the *Gesta Romanorum*—is still to be found in an exemplum contained in *Dat kaetspel ghemoralizeert* (The cat's play moralized). This didactic text, based on an allegorization of a well-known sport practiced at that time by the elite, was written in 1431 by the jurist Jan van den Berghe and has been preserved in a number of manuscripts and early printed editions. It is therefore quite likely that the text was well known in the Netherlands until the mid-sixteenth century. It tells of a noble who established eleven stringent laws that he himself obeyed to the letter but the people found much too severe. When they pressed him to have them repealed, the noble devised a cunning plan. He said that the laws had been issued not by him but by Apollo. He was, however, fully prepared to go to the oracle at Delphi and ask if the laws could be suspended. But for the duration of his absence strict obedience was of the utmost importance, to show their unquestioning faith in the commandments of this god. And so it came to pass: the noble, who never returned, even arranged for his bodily remains to be disposed of at sea, so that they, too, could never return. And the laws remained in force ever after.

What were these laws exactly? They imposed, to begin with, absolute austerity. They also forbade the glorification of gold and silver, because of the possibility of inciting jealousy and greed. War and trade were to be engaged in only by pious and wise citizens, whose deliberations took the form of a parliamentary democracy based on representation. There were also laws restricting the kind of clothing worn, with a view to eliminating envy, and prohibitions were imposed on child labor and the marrying off of daughters for financial gain. One was also obliged to honor old people because of their wisdom, as opposed to rich people because of their ostentation.

An idealized society such as this exemplifies the striving for a Christian utopia on earth, by reinstating the pure Christianity existing in the first centuries after Christ, the most important characteristics of which were extreme austerity and simplicity. In fact, it does not resemble Cockaigne in the slightest, except for the fact that both are fictitious lands that try to alleviate feelings of dissatisfaction with life. The exemplum in the *Kaetspel* seeks to remedy matters by effecting structural changes in a spirit—presumed to be pure—of true Christianity, whereas Cockaigne provides a platform for the instant gratification of one's most worldly desires.

Further comparison with More's *Utopia* is therefore rather pointless. More's text was a frontal attack on everything that had gone wrong in old Europe. Moreover, it attempted to right these wrongs by means of a completely new political system, which it presented in highly ironic fashion. Was the author implying that he knew in his heart of hearts that his proposals never had a hope of realization? Here, too, a few accidental similarities to Cockaigne crop up, such as the abundance of food, proletarian shopping, and community ownership of property. Otherwise Utopia is founded on principles of moderation and austerity, and this imposes constraints on the use of material inducements to happiness.

At most it can be said that a certain literary fashion existed that attempted to evoke an imaginary or exotic land in a remote corner of the world, which could then function as the basis for social criticism or satire directed at one's own community. This literary trend became in turn the object of derision and parody, as evidenced by such texts as the German *Lalebuch* of 1597. This jolly prose text with an anecdotal character begins by describing the destiny of the Lalen folk of Laleburg, part of the kingdom of Utopia. The wisdom they initially demonstrate eventually degenerates into a foolishness that leads to their ruin.

These texts are most likely a reaction to actual attempts to reform society, such as those undertaken in Europe throughout the sixteenth century. This desktop devising of utopias—a game generally indulged in by intellectuals—and actual attempts at reform, as well as the literary fun poked at both, would cause the concept of utopia to flourish for centuries, reaching new heights in the eighteenth century. This is a completely different path from that taken by Cockaigne and Luilekkerland, which inevitably point to rural life and the children's nursery, another reason why these imaginary lands, unlike the utopias, were never taken seriously in modern times. There is nevertheless something very rebellious lurking in these so pointedly antirevolutionary texts, something, in fact, that could almost be called heretical.

Part 6

Heretical Excesses

29

The Thousand-Year Reign of
Peace and Prosperity

BOTH COCKAIGNE TEXTS contain several rather direct references to the creative and inspiring work of God and the Holy Ghost. This immediately places the world of Cockaigne in a paradisiacal perspective, because God has ordered its inhabitants to do the opposite of what he commanded Adam and Eve to do. The inhabitants of Cockaigne are not permitted to expend any energy whatever on work, though this is the very opposite of the punishment meted out to humankind after the Fall.

Shouldn't this be interpreted as blasphemy? And doesn't the whole text exude what for many must have been reprehensible hedonism? It is difficult to deny that the warm recommendation to indulge in unrestrained sexual gratification sounds very inviting indeed. Or was it meant as a warning? One could also interpret the apparent mockery of God's intentions as an indication that such topsy-turvy behavior has no place in the real world. A statement such as "this is the land that God holds dear" is a more innocent, commonplace expression with little power to evoke the actual presence of the Supreme Being.

Finally, the mention in text L of "a Jordan" with rejuvenating properties refers unmistakably to Christ's baptism in that holy river, which also endowed him with eternal life. But making a mockery even of this should not be taken too seriously, as there was more scope for such devotional banter in those days. Jokes of this sort were made with the best of intentions, certainly during celebrations of the kind of festive rituals in which the Cockaigne texts were probably performed.

Innocence may well be missing, though, when the subject of the Holy Ghost crops up. Text L says that "this is the land of the Holy Ghost" and text B that "this land was made by the Holy Ghost." There is no question here of a commonplace expression. At the beginning of both texts is an assertive declaration regarding the raison d'être of this intriguing land: the

Holy Ghost is responsible for it in the most all-encompassing way. But what is He doing here? And how blasphemous is this dominion of His?

These questions become more pointed when one discovers that the French Cockaigne material has no such ties to the Trinity. This is obviously a special feature of Middle Dutch Cockaigne realizations, which nevertheless go no further than the two rhyming texts representing the oral tradition of the Cockaigne material. Prose text G presents a Luilekkerland lacking any divine dimension whatsoever, while the echoes of heavenly blessings have become almost inaudible. This seems to be the result of its roots in the written tradition—the written or printed word is much more permanent and therefore more perilous—as well as being a sign that times were changing.

The year 1546 falls in an especially difficult period as regards the use of ambiguous, dubious, or blasphemous references to the godhead. Efforts were continually made at this time to catch out the smallest unorthodoxy, in literature in particular, and this could have far-reaching and dangerous consequences for many rhetoricians and other purveyors of the word. In the morality plays presented at the rhetoricians' festival in Ghent in 1539, outspoken utterances of a reformational nature caused the highest authorities to impose severe limitations on the freedom of speech. Not only bona fide poets but also the singers of street songs were warned to stay away from obvious religious themes and even to refrain from alluding to any material remotely related to religion.

The mere mention of the Holy Ghost as the architect or custodian of worldly pleasures forged in the medieval mind an unmistakable link with the most fundamental heresies of the Middle Ages, collectively termed millenarianism or chiliasm. These refer neither to a concrete movement nor to a subversive and insidious sect, though many people in the Middle Ages believed that was the case. Rather, they are convenient generic labels for numerous, localized groups, all of which propagated—under various names—a fervent belief in the imminence of a thousand-year reign of prosperity and harmony on earth. Such hopes and convictions were regularly looked upon as a chance to put theory into practice, not only as an advance on future pleasures but also as a means of effecting a concrete realization of this kingdom.

The basis for such beliefs lay in the Book of Revelation, or the Apocalypse, as well as in the many explications and commentaries provoked by this most obscure of biblical texts. In all these expectations of salvation on earth, unbridled pleasure generally plays the main role, and the name of the Holy Ghost is linked to this from the beginning. During the course of the Middle Ages these bonds would only be strengthened, until He came to be designated in certain circles as the ruler of this thousand-year reign, which caused the greatest suspicion on the part of the church. When a pleasure land like Cockaigne is placed under the regime of a Holy Ghost of this ilk, the texts take on the added dimension, both piquant and perilous, of heresy. Certainly in the southern Netherlands such heretical pleasure seeking appeared to be especially popular in the fifteenth century, giving rise to ideas and practices that far surpassed mere blasphemy. Or were these instead simply playful efforts at mocking these ideas?

According to the Book of Revelation an angel will descend from heaven to put the devil in chains "and cast him into the bottomless pit, and shut him up, and set a seal upon him, that he should deceive the nations no more, till the thousand years should be fulfilled." At this point the earth will be transformed into a messianic kingdom, where Christ will reign amid the martyrs and saints, who will be given their first taste of everlasting bliss. "And when the thousand years are expired, Satan shall be loosed out of his prison, and shall go out to deceive the nations which are in the four quarters of the earth." In other words, the devil will be given one last chance to lead man into temptation, though this will result in his final defeat, as the evil peoples whom Satan has gathered together to fight on his side will be devoured by a fire sent down from heaven by God. "And the devil that deceived them was cast into the lake of fire and brimstone, where the beast and the false prophet are, and shall be tormented day and night for ever and ever." The righteous, however, will find an eternal resting place filled with love and joy in the New Jerusalem, which will descend from heaven and provide them with a place to live, ruled over by the Holy Ghost: "Behold, the tabernacle of God is with men, and he will dwell with them, and they shall be his people, and God himself shall be with them, and be their God."

Strictly speaking, this entails both a temporary and an eternal kingdom of joy, only the second of which (the heavenly paradise or the New Jerusalem) is connected with the Holy Ghost. The obscurity of the text, however, and the confusing fact of the New Jerusalem's descent from heaven

FIGURE 54

Chaining up the devil; in the background, an angel points out the New Jerusalem
to Saint John the Divine. Woodcut by Albrecht Dürer, 1498.

Source: Reproduced from W. Kurth, *The Complete Woodcuts* (New York, 1963), 120.

caused both of these heavenly kingdoms to become mixed up and to merge into one. Such visions typically invoke, in terms at once impatient and aggressive, the general image of an earthly utopia. Moreover, the kingdom of the saints on earth was not just for the martyrs but for everyone and, according to some, more particularly for the poor.

Hopeful predictions for the recovery of the earthly paradise are voiced repeatedly by Old Testament prophets. After being punished and purified by famine, thirst, war, pestilence, and captivity they will enjoy an age of peace and prosperity, with all manner of food and drink, as well as joy and gladness. This was interpreted by some as a confirmation of what would be exacted at all costs, namely, the fulfillment of God's promise of a better life to be enjoyed already here on earth.

Nonetheless, it could never have been the intention of the author of the Book of Revelation to encourage such high hopes of a better life. Augustine was already intent on squashing all literal interpretations of the coming of a kingdom of God on earth. He was probably so keen on stressing a spiritual-allegorical reading because he was also fighting against the millenarianism he had subscribed to in his youth, which he continued to find fascinating in spite of himself. The millennium, Augustine was now saying, must have begun with the birth of Christianity, and its aims could be forwarded by no better institution than the church militant. The thousand-year reign of Christ and the saints must therefore refer to the present church, he maintained, and this interpretation continued to be official church dogma until the end of the Middle Ages.

This by no means prevented both the genuinely destitute and the voluntary poor to rise up, biblical predictions in hand, to proclaim and enforce the establishment of the kingdom of God on earth. Inevitably, they also paved the way for a whole procession of would-be saints and messiahs, as inspired as they were crazy, who often demonstrated consummate skill in leading the hordes in any direction they wanted. Furthermore, these pseudo-saints were nurtured by the predictions—presented with much scholarly aplomb—made by Joachim of Fiore (1145–1202). This Calabrian monk, whose writings—together with a body of work attributed to him—were read throughout Europe in the centuries following his death, proclaimed with the arrogance of the true scholar that he had found the key to interpreting the predictions of the future contained in the Bible.

This typological pattern—proclamations made in the Old Testament that are subsequently fulfilled in the New Testament—should in its turn reveal, directly and in great detail, what the future has in store. According to Joachim this produced, roughly speaking, a division of history into three successive eras, with one of the persons of the Trinity presiding over each stage. The first age was that of God the Father, the time when the old law prevailed. This was succeeded by the time of the Son or the Gospel. Finally, there was the age of the Holy Spirit, which would be like high summer compared with the winter and spring of the preceding eras. On the basis of careful calculations, Joachim reckoned that this last era would dawn precisely in the year 1260.

This third age of the near future was loudly hailed by Joachim as an era that would put an end to the darkness of the first age and the uncertainty of the second, in which humankind still found itself. If under the old law there was only fear and servitude and under the Gospel only faith and submission, the coming age of the Holy Spirit would be filled with love and gladness, bringing with it a well-earned rest. The world would be as one big monastery, in which all people would give themselves over to mystical ecstasy, living as contemplative monks and singing the praises of God. This kingdom of the saints, according to Joachim, would continue until the Last Judgment.

This immediately calls to mind the Middle English *Cokaygne* text. Again it is instantly apparent that this is the work of a learned author, who with the greatest of ease was able to take Celtic voyages, travel parodies, monastic satire, and now the Joachite prophecy of a kingdom of joy and combine these with the European Cockaigne material. Cokaygne is situated on an island inhabited by monks who reside in a wondrously beautiful monastery. In this sense the text also reaches out to the millenarian dreams of its time, without however mentioning the Holy Spirit in so many words or attempting to explicate any other connection. *Cokaygne*, which reveals its playfulness right from the start in its use of the vernacular, is an entertaining jigsaw puzzle for intellectuals.

Joachim's vision had such a great impact because he succeeded in relating these optimistic predictions of the future to the abject misery of his own time. All that wretchedness and despair was thought to be a hopeful sign of the impending arrival of the thousand-year reign. Each of the three eras had supposedly been preceded by a period of worldwide catastrophe, which was meant to effect the necessary cleansing. Evidence both of the church's corruptness and of humankind's persistence in pursuing earthly pleasures were taken as signs of the imminent arrival of this third era.

In the Low Countries Jacob van Maerlant was the interpreter of such thoughts. This did not necessarily mean that he was familiar with the work of Joachim, for the body of thought attributed to him had meanwhile been widely disseminated and had found broad acceptance. Perhaps Maerlant needed no more than Paul the Apostle, whose words in the Second Epistle to Timothy he refers to: "This know also, that in the last days perilous times shall come. For men shall be lovers of their own selves, covetous, boasters, proud, blasphemers, disobedient to parents, unthankful, unholy, without natural affection, truce breakers, false accusers, incontinent, fierce, despisers of those that are good, traitors, heady, high-minded, lovers of pleasures more than lovers of God." More than once Maerlant connects the barbarity of his own days to the coming of the end of time, and he does this the loudest in the prologue to his *Sinte Franciscus leven* (Life of Saint Francis), which opens with a reference to the epistle of Paul quoted above. This biography, written for the Friars Minor of Utrecht, undoubtedly provided a convenient opportunity to allude to the passionate devotees of millenarianism among the friars belonging to the order of Saint Francis of Assisi. The spiritualistic branch of the Franciscans both professed and practiced extreme poverty and expected in return to be among the first to sample the blessings of the thousand-year reign.

Like the Franciscan Spirituals, Maerlant saw the third age as a period of divine harmony, to be enjoyed in a state of complete self-denial and contemplation. Any pleasure promised to be of a purely spiritual nature. The pursuit of earthly pleasure had wreaked havoc on earth, and humankind had turned the world into a kind of Cockaigne—Maerlant did not use this word, however—where the odious needs of the body were catered to so exclusively that the soul had been completely forgotten. This is why he begins his life of Saint Francis with the words "The end of the world is nearing apace / as it seems to me, in great disgrace." People had become so foolish that they no longer loved anyone but themselves and were completely preoccupied with amassing property and possessions:

Two things we love most, to our shame,
And the devil himself is the one to blame:
Our bodies and our property,
Dressed well and shod properly.
Food and drink and sleep most pleasant
Are pastimes loved by priest and peasant:
Thus, you see, we love ourselves.

The explosive material in the Book of Revelation was eagerly seized upon by the truly destitute of the Middle Ages. Together with the dregs of urban society and the scum of the countryside, their ranks swelled by renegade monks and failed students, these poor people rose up from time to time in an attempt to install the thousand-year reign, if need be by means of anarchy and revolution. Leaders and seers continually sprang up in their midst, men with a messianic allure who had generally been members of the lower clergy. Whipping up popular passions with their sermons, they proclaimed the dawning of the kingdom of joy and prosperity. Although there was some amount of squabbling as to just how near at hand it was, there was one thing they all agreed on: this kingdom would bestow them with earthly delights. And these would be granted on earth and not in some remote corner of heaven, where one would end up, after a perhaps terrible death, living out eternity in God only knew what kind of condition.

The violence inherent in the idea that the thousand-year reign must be gained at all costs—even by force if necessary—crops up again and again. This aggression was probably aggravated by the proclamation that wealth and abundance could only come about after a period plagued by calamitous events. A certain Commodianus, a Latin poet presumably of the fifth century, advocated taking up arms in order to establish this kingdom. It is no coincidence that such would-be messiahs and prophets most often surfaced during times of natural catastrophes, epidemics, and food shortages. They were highly successful in the Rhine valley in particular, even after the Middle Ages. Until well into the fifteenth century, however, the southern Netherlands and northern France also proved to be fertile ground for the growth of spectacular delusions of instant gratification.

In the north of France the dramatic increase in population was accompanied by sweeping changes in the existing socioeconomic order. The smallest setback meant that large groups of people were forced to endure such extremities of poverty and suffering that they had no choice but to take to the road, a floating rural proletariat that also converged on the cities with some regularity. Between the eleventh and the fourteenth centuries, there grew in medieval society a volatile lower stratum that found itself in a permanent state of fear and frustration. In such a climate every disturbance was seized upon as an opportunity for more massive rebellion. Not infrequently, this took the form of identification with a group of chosen people, led by a so-called messiah, who attempted to transform hopes of salvation into an actual kingdom of unparalleled prosperity.

This happened in times of famine or plague or after any disruptive event, such as the death of a ruler or a summons to a crusade. Would-be messiahs then set their sights on the New Jerusalem, which would not only endure forever but was also meant to descend from the heavens sometime soon. This was the Jerusalem that the poor were convinced was intended for them: a city filled with peace, equality, and plenty, in other words, everything that was so sorely lacking in their own lives. Dressed as pilgrims or soldiers, they went in search of the place in the holy city of Palestine where the Savior had already taken upon himself the guilt and suffering of all humankind. And there was no time to lose, for the gates of the New Jerusalem might be opening at any moment.

In the minds of all these distraught poor, the promised city was confused with the existing Jerusalem, and despite the church's interdictive warnings against heretical ideas of an earthly Eden, the displaced poor continued to demand the right to a better world, egged on by the unrelenting stream of prophecies uttered by aggressive lay preachers who based their teachings not only on the Bible but also on the writings of such theologians as Tertullian. In the first years of the third century Tertullian had reported that in Judea every morning for forty days in a row a walled city had been seen in the clouds, which had faded away during the course of the day. Surely this was an omen presaging the proposed landing of the heavenly Jerusalem on that very spot, an occurrence that everyone believed to be imminent.

One thousand years after the death of Christ—1033, to be precise—was thought to be a likely time to expect the appearance of this paradise. Or a timely moment to mobilize one's forces? Everywhere destitute hordes (*pauperes*) were pushing on across Europe on their way to Jerusalem, pilgrims possessed of the firm conviction that their suffering would be assuaged and they would be showered with unimaginable blessings. This army of fortune hunters, as greedy as they were militant, was whipped up at the end of the eleventh century to undertake a true People's Crusade to free the Holy Land. To earn some travel money and also to bolster their fighting spirit before embarking on their mission, these crusaders—in particular those from the Rhine valley—set about massacring whole communities of Jews, sparing only those who converted to Christianity. For the other descendants of Christ's murderers, however, there was no place in the new paradise being claimed by the poor.

Reckless and impatient, the poor sewed an emblem on their sleeves to show from the start that they were the chosen inhabitants of the New Jerusalem, which they themselves would create by driving out the infidels. At the sight of every town looming on the horizon one of them would call out, "Is this Jerusalem?" There were also continual sightings of a mysterious city in the clouds being stormed by an army of thousands. Most got no further than the Balkans, however, succumbing on the way to exhaustion, contagious diseases, malnutrition, the murderous impulses of fellow crusaders, and the aggression of the local population. Those who finally felt the hot sand of the desert beneath their feet proved to be no match for the ruling Seldjuk Turks. These poor few died with the walls of Jerusalem reflected in their eyes, blissfully happy nonetheless, now that a heathen's scimitar had given them—on this very spot—their passport to heaven.

The dream of the heavenly Jerusalem persisted, however. The earthly Jerusalem, once freed, would be an idyllic place, the exact opposite of the shocking scenes of starvation caused by the siege of the Romans in the year 70. After all, Pope Urban II himself had said—at least in the words put into his mouth by a monk reconstructing the pope's appeal at the Council of Clermont a century after the fact—upon summoning the people to a crusade, that Jerusalem was "the navel of the world, the land fruitful above all others, like another paradise of delights." And this veritable garden of delights, unlike the sealed-off Garden of Eden, would be readily accessible to all who deserved to enter. The Bible itself said so—repeatedly—and who would be so presumptuous as to doubt it?

30
Heresies of the Free Spirit

IN THE LATE Middle Ages these solidly founded and passionately pursued expectations of salvation on earth assumed the form of what is broadly referred to as the heresy of the Free Spirit. This conviction—perhaps better referred to as a mentality—may be seen as a democratized mysticism that got out of hand. This spiritual exercise essentially aimed at personal communion with the divine, whereby the traditional means offered by the church played a subordinate role or even none at all.

The adherents of the so-called Free Spirit movement fervently believed in the possibility of attaining a state of perfection. Once this state was achieved, one was no longer capable of sin and was in fact free to do whatever nature dictated. The moral norms of Christianity, on the other hand, were the standards by which sinners should be judged. Thus, in order to make it quite clear that one had attained a state of perfection, it was necessary to violate all the moral precepts commonly held to be the desired norm, particularly the highly restrictive Christian principles governing sexuality and chastity. This climate of antinomian beliefs—which held that faith alone was enough for salvation, releasing one from the obligation of adhering to moral laws—meant that promiscuity was often the sin chosen on principle.

The position of these adepts of the Free Spirit can be compared with that of Adam and Eve before the Fall: the difference between good and evil did not yet exist in the Garden of Eden. The first pair could do whatever nature dictated, including openly coupling, assuming they found the time for it, for according to medieval calculations they were in paradise together for a mere seven hours. After the Fall, however, they were forever polluted by the devil, who would henceforth be capable of leading them and their offspring into temptation. From then on they would have to live in a world full of sin, from which one could escape only by means of divine grace and Christian penance. None of this applied, however, to those who had already managed to attain the primal state of paradisiacal perfection. Moral and ethical laws were not meant for them, for no matter what they did, they were not capable of sin.

The perfect person is therefore equal to God and completely filled with God. Confirmation of this state of sinlessness and permission to follow the dictates of nature were found by adherents to this doctrine in the First Epistle General of John, with its key sentence: "Whosoever is born of God doth not commit sin; for his seed remaineth in him: and he cannot sin, because he is born of God." This meant that anything was permissible, which adepts of the Free Spirit interpreted as the right to engage in unbridled mating. For this reason Jean de Meung's continuation of *The Romance of the Rose* was constantly presumed to present arguments in favor of this, because it bluntly urged one to follow unconditionally the demands of nature and to indulge freely in sexual gratification, unimpeded by the unnatural constraints imposed by marriage.

The striving for and attainment of such a state of perfection was another matter entirely. The whole process could be expedited by embracing a life of poverty, which often led to violent renunciation of all things worldly. This could entail extreme mortification of the flesh or the attempt to keep oneself alive on an absolute minimum of nourishment. Flagellation and self-mutilation could wreck the body in no time, making it susceptible to hallucinations that in turn led to convenient illusions of the desired state of perfection. Finally, reduced by such barbaric asceticism to the depths of poverty and physical deterioration, it was no longer possible to sin. The poorer one was, the easier it was to indulge in carefree eroticism, spurred on by the thought that all the rich people of the world were already doomed to eternal damnation.

Around 1230 in Antwerp a certain Willem Cornelis, who died in 1245, was active in propagating these ideas and attempting to put them into practice. He himself was "wholly given up to lust," but his greatest obsession was with ideals of poverty. He maintained that the self-discipline of poverty could eradicate all sin. Consequently, a poor whore was better than a virtuous rich woman. Carnal desires were not sinful when indulged in by the poor, and therefore a woman who prostituted herself out of poverty could never be considered a sinner.

The story of Willem Cornelis's scandalous heresy is recounted in detail in the *Biënboec* (The book of bees), a popular collection of exempla compiled by Thomas of Cantimpré and widely distributed in manuscripts and printed editions. In this work the doctrinal core of the entire body of Free Spirit thought is imputed to Cornelis, for he supposedly said, "Just as rust is consumed by fire, all sins are obliterated in the eyes of God by poverty."

It is tempting to assume that an early tradition of millenarianism existed in Antwerp, as witnessed by the stories surrounding the activities of a preacher named Tanchelm around 1110. Perhaps there was only a tradition in tumult, however, for as usual the limited sources are all supplied by the opposing party. In this case practically the only evidence is a letter from the chapter of Utrecht to the archbishop of Cologne. The canons of Utrecht would not write a letter unless they had something spectacular to report, and in this case they tell of Tanchelm, a preacher of compelling eloquence, who traveled about Flanders, Brabant, and Zeeland with a throng of disciples, finally making Antwerp his base of operations. He condemned clerics, the taking of the sacraments, and the church as a whole. He proclaimed himself equal to God, as he was possessed of the Holy Spirit in the same measure as Christ. In addition, he abandoned himself to the zealous pursuit of sexual intercourse with a wide-ranging clientele, though this did nothing to deter his becoming engaged to a statue of the Virgin Mary.

This self-image and behavior concur with much of the body of thought adhered to by adepts of the Free Spirit, at least in rudimentary form. This is also true of the promiscuity practiced by Tanchelm's followers. His closest disciple, a smith called Manasses, founded a brotherhood of twelve men who called themselves "the guild" and professed to represent the apostles. In their midst was a woman—called Mary, of course—who slept with each of the guild members in turn. Their God was Tanchelm, whom they revered so much that they distributed his bath water among his masses of followers, who drank it, convinced it was holier than the Eucharist.

First and foremost, however, Tanchelm was a millenarian. According to his teachings, which continued to exert a great deal of influence for quite some time, a thousand-year reign of prosperity and justice was at hand. In propagating this notion he proved himself to be a true folk messiah, capable of bringing masses of the poor and needy under his sway.

Another ringleader of the Free Spirit movement was Marguerite Porete, a pious Beguine from Valenciennes, who was burned as a heretic in Paris in

1310. According to one chronicler, Marguerite held that a soul that had become one with God could and should do anything the body desired. Such individuals were not subject to moral laws, and this again evokes the heresy of the Free Spirit. In fact, believers such as Marguerite Porete—she was not the only one by any means—were opposed to the mechanism of negotiating salvation through the doing of good works and the arrogant undertaking of conspicuous acts of virtue. Such practices eventually degenerated into competitive conceit and were primarily indulged in with a view to soliciting a prominent place in heaven. Notions such as these seem to have been shared by many. One salient fact is that the text for which Marguerite was burned at the stake had been known—without her name attached to it—for quite a while, though it had never before called attention to itself as a distinctly heretical work.

The great mystic Meister Eckhart, a German Dominican, has also been pointed to as the father of the Free Spirit movement on the basis of sermons and texts attributed to him. This opinion was shared by Jan van Ruusbroec, as evidenced by the fierce attacks directed at Eckhart by van Ruusbroec's diligent pupil and housemate Jan van Leeuwen. The reasonableness of such imputations is questionable, however, considering the dubious origins of many of the Middle Dutch translations of Eckhart's texts. In this form they do in fact give cause to suspect far-reaching heresies of the Free Spirit.

The numerous texts attributed to Meister Eckhart that circulated in the Netherlands demonstrate how one can become a paragon of perfection by voluntarily undergoing the greatest humiliations. Various exempla served to make this religious sleight of hand appealing to people. One text presents a lay brother, for example, who visits a hermit, whom he astounds by demonstrating the high degree of perfection he has attained. Upon being asked how he managed this, he explains that he achieved it through complete destitution and boundless humility. This has erased his shortcomings, causing him to be absorbed completely by God: "I have united my will with that of God, who cannot and may not act effectively without me." It was texts like this one—intended, of all things, as inspiring intermezzos during sermons—that provoked accusations of heresy.

It was probably the total disregard for the sacraments that was the most difficult for the church as an institution to stomach. Moreover, although the practice of higher mysticism promised (and presupposed) a freedom of

Lolbardi lollant vt nummos vndiq3 tollant.
At reynbart volucres ficlolbart fallit mulieres

FIGURE 55

Lollards shooting the breeze; the text reads "Lollards spout nonsense to fill their
own pockets. / As Reynard does to the chickens, the Lollard outfoxes women."
Woodcut from prognostications printed for the year 1488.

Source: Reproduced from *Truwanten, Een toneeltekst uit het handschrift-Van Hulthem*
(Groningen, 1978), 96.

spirit that did not necessarily lead to vulgar excesses, in practice things usually turned out differently. With only a few exceptions, the emphasis
appeared to be on self-mortification and denial of all things worldly. Austerity, as opposed to immersion in all earthly pleasures, is the trademark of
orthodox mysticism, which was more in search of spiritual perfection than
heretical excesses. Besides, there was a practical side to arguments in favor of

more sexual tolerance, which also occur in literature and by no means only in *The Romance of the Rose*. It was no coincidence that the Averroists, followers of the twelfth-century Spanish-Arabian philosopher Averroës and condemned as heretics by the bishop of Paris in 1277, rather reasonably maintained that complete abstinence from sexual acts in a sinful world is unbearably trying and can actually pervert virtue.

The heresy of the Free Spirit was a loosely organized movement with adherents in countries ranging across Europe. The belief in the existence of such a community arose from a list of so-called heretical doctrines, which were subsequently attributed to every heretical and unorthodox movement in the church. This is why the descriptions of heretical practices in different parts of Europe display close similarities. These seeming correspondences are more the result of tracking down people answering to a composite description of a heretic than of the existence of any coordinated activity among the various regions. Moreover, it is highly doubtful whether the people and groups named in this context actually led the amoral lives that these lists suggest. Rather, the church used the heresy of the Free Spirit as a label to describe any form of unorthodoxy thought to pose a threat to its hegemony. This holds true as well for the accusations aimed at Marguerite Porete and Meister Eckhart, both thought to have been founding members of and great sources of inspiration to the "movement."

The alleged adherents were most frequently called Beguines, Beghards, or Lollards, all of whom were essentially representatives of semireligious lay movements. From the very beginning, they aroused the greatest suspicion, and the honorable nature of their intentions was called into question, for they did not live according to a rule recognized by Rome and were therefore not subject to any supervision. In particular, they were accused of unrestrained restlessness and said to commit all manner of fraudulent and deceitful acts in the course of their wanderings. Indeed, the Lollards owe their name to this reputation: their name—derived from *lullen*, which means "to shoot the breeze"—is a term of abuse denoting the drivel they supposedly deployed in duping well-intentioned burghers and peasants, to whom they poured out stories glorifying the ideals of their professed poverty. In addition, there were constant rumors of their insatiable sexual appetites.

In particular, the so-called *Ad nostrum*, a decree issued by the Council of

Vienne in 1311, both defined the heresy of the Free Spirit and explicitly imputed it to "an abominable sect of malignant men known as Beghards and faithless women known as Beguines in the kingdom of Germany," who were thought to form the core of the Free Spirit movement. The decree consists of a list of eight errors commonly imputed to Beghards and Beguines, which together form an identikit picture of a heretic. The first tenet is the most important: the belief in perfection. These heretics thought it possible to attain a degree of perfection in earthly life that would make them incapable of sinning. Fasting and praying were no longer necessary, as anything done by such people was necessarily perfect. Such enlightened persons could therefore do anything they wished (this conviction being the second tenet).

Human obedience to the word of God was no longer considered necessary, and neither was listening to the laws of the church. This third tenet was justified by referring—wrongly, of course—to the Bible: "Now the Lord is that Spirit: and where the spirit of the Lord is, there is liberty." Virtuous deeds were for imperfect people. All acts of virtue were a sign of sinfulness, whereas those who had attained perfection simply did what nature told them to do, which had been God's original plan in paradise. According to a statement issued by the inquisition at Strasbourg in 1317, these heretics even objected to strong, healthy men engaging in bodily labor, as work was considered to be punishment for those who had forfeited their chance of paradise and the Free Spirits no longer wished to be counted among those original sinners.

For centuries these notions of the heresy of the Free Spirit continued to be a strong influence throughout Europe, forced into the limelight again and again by the notorious persecution of Beguines, Beghards, and others who had been condemned by the dogmatic pronouncements of the Council of Vienne. Furthermore, literature seized upon these collective slurs and slandered images, both by supporting—whether or not intentionally—such presumably heretical ideas (as witnessed by *The Romance of the Rose*) and by contributing to the endless rounds of accusations and mockery to which the Beguines in particular were subjected.

31
Sex Adam-and-Eve Style

PERFECT PEOPLE do exist on earth: in theory anyone can attain a state of perfect sinlessness, and many have already done so. It is important to realize that in the Middle Ages this fact was accepted with the same unshakable belief with which we nowadays maintain that such convictions are merely a conceit. The whole story bears a close resemblance to the persecution of witches, an undertaking that took on a systematic character late in the fifteenth century. Evidence was sought to confirm what one already believed, and witches were a reality for a broad section of society, including men of letters.

Adepts of the Free Spirit did not believe in personal property, or, rather, they regarded all things as up for grabs. One of their favorite sayings was, "Whatever the eye sees and covets, let the hand grasp it." In the light of their orientation toward sexuality based on paradisiacal precepts, it was only natural that they should hold Adam in special reverence. Everywhere there were reports of ritual nakedness that frequently degenerated into sexual orgies.

Obviously, the opponents of heretical ideas of perfection would attempt to discredit them by spreading stories of the adepts' wanton behavior. The assertions of Sir John Mandeville undoubtedly played a role in this as well. He was reputed to have seen Adamites of the purest sort, whom he found in a country called Lamory to the northwest of Sumatra: "In that land it is extremely hot; the custom there is for men and women to go completely naked and they are not ashamed to show themselves as God made them. They scorn other folk who go clothed; for they say that God made Adam and Eve naked, and men ought not to be ashamed of what God has made, for nothing natural is ugly."

Owing to their natural sinlessness, the inhabitants of Lamory lived in complete promiscuity, justifying this by referring to God's command to "be fruitful, and multiply." "In that land there is no marriage between man and woman; all the women of that land are common to every man. . . . When women are delivered of a child, they give it to whom they want of the men who have slept with them. And in the same way the land is common property." Mandeville's description thus far fits the picture of the noble savage who has retained the original purity of Creation as it still existed during the golden age of European civilization. In this case, however, praising such a society would also mean open praise for Free Spirits and Adamites, especially as Mandeville also portrayed these savages as proto-Christians who knew, believed, and followed the biblical story of the Creation. He therefore felt compelled, after drawing this much of their portrait, to make it quite clear that these people were not true Christians.

The decisive factor in determining their underlying un-Christian nature was a bad habit that Mandeville goes on to describe as follows: "But they have an evil custom among them, for they will eat human flesh more gladly than any other. . . . Merchants bring children there to sell, and the people of the country buy them. Those that are plump they eat; those that are not plump they feed up and fatten, and then kill and eat them. And they say it is the best and sweetest flesh in the world." By reporting this Mandeville was distancing himself from any form of Free Spirit heresy, even though his words carry an unmistakable undertone of yearning and nostalgia for the openness and candor of the primal state of innocence he describes.

Allegations concerning Adamites also made the rounds in Europe. Titillation and fear, frustration and rigid orthodoxy gave rise to reports, from the eleventh century on, of Adamites everywhere, all of whom were denounced in very similar terms. They were said to run around naked in an attempt to resurrect paradise, engaging in nocturnal orgies full of wild and totally promiscuous sex. For help in identifying Adamites, one could turn to the writings of Augustine and the encyclopedia of Isidore of Seville. Both authorities had cataloged the characteristics of these heretics, and throughout the whole of the Middle Ages and even afterward reports of Adamites continued to be based on their descriptions.

The ideological violence inflicted on alleged Adamites—by leveling imputations at them, producing false evidence that took on a life of its own until it became a self-fulfilling prophecy, and making them the subject of compelling literary representations—nevertheless leads to the conclusion that such practices were indeed rife in the Rhine valley, northern France, and the southern Netherlands. One of the more direct pieces of evidence for their existence is provided by a movement in Brussels formed by members of both the lower clergy and the patriciate, which became known around 1400 as the Homines intelligentiae, or "Men of Intelligence," "*intelligentia* being, in the terminology of medieval mysticism, that highest faculty of the soul, which makes mystical ecstasy possible." These enlightened people—for these Homines included some women—strove to reenact the Creation up to the time of the Fall by setting up a true paradise. The second time around, however, the focus was on sex in the here and now.

With the help of the local Beguines, these Brussels Adamites merrily set about training themselves in the raising of their members—not lustfully, we are given to understand, but voluntarily, as one would raise a finger—all the while assuring their partners that their virginity would remain intact. Sin and lust had not existed before the Fall, and they, comfortably situated in their pre-Fall paradise, could not therefore be guilty of it. Augustine continued to be the voice of authority on this matter, with the church seconding his pronouncements. The extensive records of the trial of the Homines intelligentiae, which took place in 1411, provide a detailed account of what these Adamites actually believed, put into practice, and eventually confessed. Although much of the story remains vague, it is nonetheless true that for many people this trial finally provided definite proof of the existence of such practices. Those found guilty actually got off lightly: the main culprits were sentenced to banishment, and the Beguines were publicly reprimanded.

It is remarkable to what extent both Middle Dutch Cockaigne texts dare, from the very first line, to broach such a highly stigmatized subject. This is done not only by promising a land where God has commanded the people to dismiss all thoughts of work but also by referring explicitly to its leader: that champion of material millenarianism, the Holy Ghost. In fact, the whole lifestyle enjoyed by the inhabitants of Cockaigne seems to correspond exactly to the sins constantly being imputed to heretics of the Free Spirit, namely, gluttonous overconsumption, the denial of the existence of private property, and unbridled promiscuity.

From the very beginning, the abundance of food and its willingness to serve itself up also filled the dreams of the millenarians. One of the first was Papias, born around A.D. 60, who is thought to have been a disciple of John

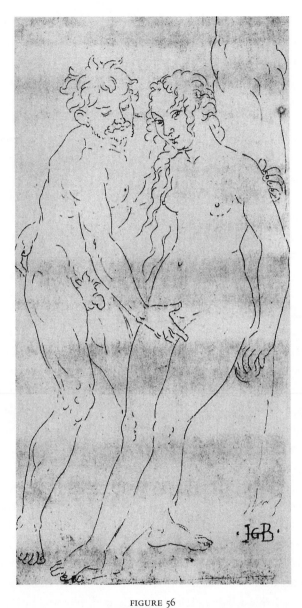

FIGURE 56

Lustless sex in paradise as indulged in by Adam and Eve.
Drawing after an engraving by Hans Baldung Grien, first
half of sixteenth century.

Source: Reproduced from J. Bernhard, *Hans Baldung Grien*
(Munich, 1978), 283.

the Evangelist and propagated Christ's teachings on the basis of first-hand accounts that he himself collected and preserved. Wielding this authority, he attributed the following prophecy to Christ: "Likewise [the Lord] said that a grain of wheat would bear ten thousand ears, and every ear would have ten thousand grains, and every grain would give ten pounds of the finest flour, clear and pure; and apples and seeds and grass would produce in similar proportions." In addition, food—in this example, bunches of grapes—offered itself up, even to the extent of thrusting itself on people, a feature that is also one of the amenities of the thousand-year reign of peace and prosperity: "And when any one of the Saints shall take hold of a bunch, another bunch shall cry out, 'I am a better bunch, take me; bless the Lord through me.' "

Such fantasies surrounding food and erotic pleasure constitute the core of the picture most people conjured up when imagining the thousand-year reign of Christ on earth, and this picture became a matter of some urgency to those seriously deprived in this life. In 1251 a movement began to form that quickly coalesced into the Crusades of the Shepherds. Their army included many peasants from Picardy, Flanders, Brabant, and Hainaut, but they were soon joined by thieves, murderers, whores, apostate monks, and other down-and-out drifters, all of whom now made their way to the Holy Land. One of their companies was led by a renegade monk called Jacob, who was known as the "Master of Hungary." In his preaching, he railed against the great orders of monks, accusing them of arrogance and hypocrisy. He himself compared his messianic powers with those of Christ. He announced to the novice crusaders that they would never be short of food and drink, for any food or wine set down before them would not be diminished by their partaking of it; instead, the supplies would only grow. This, too, is an expression of the fervent wish to sample in advance the blessings of the New Jerusalem they soon hoped to conquer.

Many a would-be prophet or surrogate messiah, proclaiming humankind's definite deliverance from all misery or even claiming to be the instrument of this deliverance, lent strength to his promises by holding out the prospect of huge amounts of food and drink. The brothers and sisters of the Free Spirit were continually exacting food handouts that they said were being "transmitted to eternity," such forced generosity guaranteeing the giver a comfortable place in the hereafter. And any money given them naturally took the same route to heaven.

The most important similarity between Cockaigne and the millenaristic Free Spirit movement, however, is the reverential attitude demonstrated toward their leader, the Holy Ghost. Appointed by Joachim of Fiore as the ruler of the blessed and blissful third age, His dominion in the following centuries was transferred to the thousand-year reign that was thought to be identical with the third era. Starting in the fourteenth century, His name was generally connected with sects and societies that imagined themselves to be enlightened, chosen, and perfect. A letter written in April 1313 by Pope Clement V to the bishop of Cremona informs the latter of numerous cells of Free Spirits in the valley of Spoleto and elsewhere in Italy and asks if he would please be so kind as to extirpate them. The members of these sects, consisting of clerics and laypeople alike, did whatever they liked and justified this attitude by pointing out that their leader was the Holy Ghost.

The Holy Ghost also provided a shining example for the Brussels Homines intelligentiae discussed above. In the reports of their trial, He is without doubt the protagonist. One of the sect's leaders was the elderly Aegidius Cantor, an illiterate layman whose name suggests that his role in church life could have been that of precentor. Perhaps he was presented as a layman because one of the heresies most typically objected to was a member of the clergy presenting himself as completely bereft of all worldly goods and spiritual qualities. This Aegidius claimed to be illuminated by the Holy Ghost, which gave him the license to indulge in the most shocking sexual excesses. He deemed himself already to be living in the thousand-year reign, and in these new surroundings—and in his perfect state of sinlessness—he had been entrusted with the task of propagating the very opposite of official church doctrine regarding poverty, chastity, and obedience.

The other leader of the Brussels sect, William of Hildernissen, at first denied any involvement, though he later appeared—according to records of the proceedings—to be completely conversant in the language of these radical mystics. He, too, persisted in naming the Holy Ghost as the source of inspiration for the clerical freedoms he had enjoyed.

A certain Hans Becker told of the spectacular nature of his conversion to the community of the Free Spirit. Shortly before Whitsun in the year 1442, he was praying in a church in Mainz when the Holy Spirit suddenly hurtled down, creating a terrible clamor and gripping him with a fierceness that caused a great pain inside him. Since that time the Holy Spirit had often borne him away, illuminating him to the extent that he could distance himself completely from the church and its sacraments. His church was now inside him, and he had been forced to mock the church of sinners: "during the elevation of the host in the Cathedral of Mainz and other churches the Holy Spirit compelled him to stick out his tongue." In 1458 he was sentenced to death and burned. A salient feature of Becker's trial was the fact that his prosecutors presented the Holy Spirit—both His behavior and His inspirational powers—as a devil. They were of the opinion that Becker had been the victim of a particularly contemptuous caper of Satan.

One must not lose sight of the fact that these are vindictive interpretations offered by ambitious heretic hunters. After all, the Holy Ghost had brought spiritual illumination and inspiration to the world as God's messenger on Whitsunday. Columbus, too, had first received inspiration from the Holy Ghost, who had actually given the initial impetus to his voyages, placing the discovery of the New World in a millenarian perspective. His son Ferdinand maintained that his father's name also gave expression to this passion: his name was derived from *columba*, meaning dove, the symbol of the Holy Spirit.

In the Low Countries as well, the Holy Ghost was warmly embraced as the bearer of generous gifts. Around 1400 the famous storyteller Willem van Hildegaersberch, who was permitted to use the title of "master," made the rounds of royal households with his own texts written to suit any occasion. In *Van den zekeren hope* (In the certain hope), he says that the Holy Ghost is a bringer of comfort who will be sent by God to earth after His resurrection. And so it came to pass, giving rise to the miracle of Pentecost. In the late Middle Ages the name of the Holy Ghost was certainly connected with the bringing of comfort, inspiration, and enlightenment, opening up new vistas of rewards to be had in the near, yet everlasting, future. In the meanwhile, His name was given to all manner of charitable institutions, from almshouses to hospitals, that had taken it upon themselves to alleviate the acute afflictions of the needy in this world.

32
Low-Country Heterodoxy

*I*N THE TERMS OF the Brabant mystic Jan van Ruusbroec, the inhabitants of Cockaigne are perfect heretics, people who act purely on instinct, satisfying their every desire and doing whatever nature dictates. In no way do listeners and readers of the Cockaigne texts or the work of Ruusbroec find themselves in disparate worlds. Everyone knew Cockaigne, while Ruusbroec's ideas were circulated in lay sermons and catechism, as well as in the simple books intended as an aid to private devotion that were so popular in the fifteenth and sixteenth centuries.

Heretical ideas and Cockaigne also share a use of the vernacular. Inquisitors were continually pointing out the subtle propaganda at work in broad segments of the population, surprising the populace by issuing warnings to this effect in their own language. One should also bear in mind that the communication of these texts was a public occasion: they were recited aloud to an interested audience. The combination of the vernacular and religious subjects—meaning the dissemination of God's word among the masses—was in any case highly suspect. Even the translation of a sacred text like the Bible aroused the greatest suspicion. Jacob van Maerlant complained of this when adapting Peter Comestor's historical Bible as his own *Rijmbijbel*, a Bible in rhyme. The Franciscan Gilbert of Tournai wrote to the pope to complain that many Beguines were guilty of distorting religious doctrine and that their translations of the Bible into the vernacular were full of heresies.

The Middle Dutch Cockaigne texts, whose moralizing implications bear witness to all manner of serious objectives, flirt dangerously with a millenarianism that was far from dead. It is precisely the didactic turn that the material took in written form, however, that indicates how such unambiguous coquetry with the realm of the Holy Spirit was more likely to be interpreted as ridicule of such thoughts and practices than as a recommendation to embrace them or as an attempt to poke light-hearted fun at an explosive subject of current interest.

It is also quite possible that fun was being made of the extremely rigid millenarian views of the ascetic Franciscans of the thirteenth century, known as the Franciscan Spirituals. These mendicant fundamentalists, whose aim was to be more destitute than the poorest of beggars, viewed the thousand-year reign as the terrain of the Holy Spirit, where the whole of humankind would abandon itself in perfect harmony to prayer and mystic contemplation against a background of voluntary poverty. Compared with this, a Cockaigne created by the Holy Spirit represents an upside-down world, whose lavish abundance and excesses make a complete mockery of the Franciscan extremists. Perhaps the hypocrisy of their pursuits was also the object of ridicule, for many a friar's dream was a far cry from reality, if we are to believe the reports of countless contemporary sources.

The question that still remains is to what extent the Cockaigne texts, as well as other unknown realizations of the Cockaigne material in general, may be brought in line with what has been called the transition from yearning for a golden age to the active pursuit of its restoration, spurred on by the predictions of the swift coming of the thousand-year reign. These developments are often attributed to the years around 1380, a time of extraordinary waves of violence in the cities of Flanders, Brabant, and northern France, though it is highly doubtful whether such a massive change in mentality can ever be pinned down to a precise period.

Clearly, Cockaigne was never seen as inviting revolution and could never have served to stir the masses to action. Cockaigne does not exist in either the past or the present. It was never anything other than a playful image that could be conjured up for a variety of purposes. Moreover, its various functions—which included ridiculing existing institutions, alleviating fear, and providing moral instruction—may have worked for many people simultaneously. Its very nature, at once humorous and fictional, made it impossible for it to function as an incitement to revolution.

It is more likely that the Middle Dutch rhyming texts on Cockaigne introduced a topical element of satire by presenting time-honored Cockaigne as the land of the Holy Ghost. This mocked, with the stroke of a pen, all those dreams of a thousand-year reign and a blissful state of sinlessness in which anything goes. The recorded Cockaigne texts were intended, above all, as moralizing and satire, which were expressed by taking a firm stand against any form of total immorality, supposedly to be enjoyed on earth as an advance on rewards in heaven.

The erotic fantasies of Cockaigne have the same objective. As already mentioned, these passages seem a bit out of place and certainly do not belong to the core of the Cockaigne material. Such additions, grafted on to the age-old yet ever-current themes of excessive eating and slothful living, contain supplementary material of a topical nature. That this refers in particular to popular ideas about the promiscuity thought to be rife among Beguines and Beghards, or the brothers and sisters of the Free Spirit, is an obvious inference, considering Cockaigne's audience. In particular the Beguines, or lay sisters, who were not required to obey any officially recognized vows, were thought to be very keen on having sex with any man who presented himself.

The Beguines were a permanent target of erotic satire whenever overly eager women were the subject of discussion. Their status as single women made them the frequent butt of jokes and the subject of wild stories about sophisticated pleasure seeking. Their innate hedonism had supposedly prompted them to maneuver themselves into a position outside the control of Rome, the better to satisfy their desires while appearing to lead a life as chaste as it was holy. As late as the sixteenth century it was still common to hear erotic platitudes regarding Beguines, and the scholarly compiler of the Brussels manuscript containing Cockaigne text B willingly contributed to this tradition. Among the numerous proverbs and sayings he collected as a sign of his worldly-wise nature was one that read: "God better us all, the Beguine softly said, and she had the monk's breeches up over her head."

Generally speaking, heresy was associated in particular with an undue and peculiar predilection for sex. Bernard of Clairvaux succeeded in strengthening these convictions with his violent outbursts against heresy. The pretense of the perfect life—he uses other terms to describe it—is only a license to indulge one's most scandalous desires. Moreover, by repudiating marriage, Free Spirits opened up the door to adultery, incest, masturbation, homosexuality, and other excesses that in his eyes were equally reprehensible.

The obsession with sexuality in the heresy of the Free Spirit, whether alleged or real, is a ready excuse for the inhabitants of Cockaigne to take a fancy to each other whenever they are overcome with the urge to mate. Even in the strict sense, Cockaignesque practices correspond closely to alleged heretical beliefs on this point. According to the "confession" of a fourteenth-century Beghard by the name of John of Brünn, those who had attained perfection made their desires known to one another through a series of signs. The signal that one desired intercourse always met with a positive reaction, because giving oneself over to eroticism indicated that one was free in spirit and therefore in a state of complete sinlessness no matter what one did. For this reason brothers and sisters were always ready and willing to comply with each other's demands on this score, even if a brother should request intercourse from a sister who had just been to communion. Moreover, he was even urged to go at it forthwith and to satisfy her "with vigor, two or four times."

Elsewhere the view is expressed that women exist first and foremost to sleep with brothers of the Free Spirit. That this involves the innocent sort of sex encountered in paradise is underscored by the assurance that the woman's virginity will nonetheless be preserved. What's more, a woman who has long since passed this stage can count on her virginity being restored to her after coupling with a brother who has attained perfection.

In Cockaigne there are many beautiful and willing women. In text B, moreover, beautiful women and virgins are available to everyone, "nothing sinful about it" and "no one feels shame." This expresses the heart of the Free Spirit movement. Woman is by her very nature meant for intercourse, and man in his enlightened state is completely free of sin and therefore incapable of doing anything scandalous. In short, everyone should simply follow the dictates of his or her nature. In this way Cockaigne comments on current views of these heretical practices, which were attributed in particular to the Beguines and Beghards in the audience's immediate surroundings.

The satirical connection between the Free Spirit movement and Cockaigne appealed even more to those who were aware that the state of perfection could only be achieved through strict fasting. Bizarre stories circulated on this score, most of which involved women living in semireligious communities. Cockaigne ridicules this as well: its inhabitants experience the greatest pleasure, after all, by eating and drinking to excess. This reaction is not dissimilar to the mocking of the ideals of the Franciscan apostles of mendicancy, who also justified their fervent self-denial with the imminence of the millennium.

Here as well there are striking similarities. In a sermon in Middle Dutch attributed to him, Meister Eckhart, one of the alleged leaders of the movement, says that Free Spirits enjoy a special dispensation that enables them to come closer to God by displaying slothful behavior and gorging themselves on mountains of food. While others fast and keep vigil, they are privileged to stuff themselves and sleep, and these are also the main activities indulged in by the inhabitants of Cockaigne, as repeatedly stressed by both rhyming texts.

Only the Dutch Cockaigne material is directly connected with the heresy of the Free Spirit, which seems to be due to the wide dissemination of these ideas in the southern Netherlands and lower Rhine valley. Tanchelm, Willem Cornelis of Antwerp, Bloemardinne of Brussels, and especially the Homines intelligentiae, who also operated and were sentenced in that city, were generally seen as the spearheads of the Free Spirit movement, not to mention the countless communities of Beguines.

In Europe, Brabant had a reputation as the preeminent breeding ground for heretics. The Englishman Walter Map mentioned a heretical movement in his country that Henry II drove out in the second half of the twelfth century. This sect consisted of drifters, robbers, swindlers, and apostate monks, all of them from Brabant. Moreover, the opponents of the well-known heresies suggest the existence of a certain tradition within the duchy of Brabant. Around 1410 the bishop of Cambrai appointed two inquisitors at Brussels, charging them with extirpating the remaining members of the sect of Bloemardinne. These are the facts, at any rate, as presented by a later account. The bishop's action resulted, among other things, in the legal proceedings taken against the above-mentioned Men of Intelligence.

Bloemardinne is supposedly the heretic named by Ruusbroec's rather unreliable biographer, Pomerius. The daughter of a Brussels patrician, she lived from around 1260 to 1335 and, according to Pomerius, developed daring ideas about the spirit of freedom and carnal love. She was worshiped by numbers of zealous followers, who presented her with a silver chair. This vague picture leaves a lot in darkness, but the little that is known about her points unmistakably in the direction of Free Spirit thought. She apparently enjoyed the full confidence of the clergy in Brussels, for around 1316 she founded a hospice in that city. It must be borne in mind that the adherents of the Free Spirit movement who were persecuted in 1411 also maintained close contact with local notables and members of the clergy. In any case, even before Pomerius wrote about her around 1420, Bloemardinne was a typical sister of the Free Spirit, which lends weight to the assumption that the movement had existed for centuries in Brussels and Brabant, making it apparently worth the while of someone of Jan van Ruusbroec's stature to oppose it.

There are further indications that these heresies enjoyed a certain fashionableness among the population at large; in Brabant, at least, they received a lot of attention over the course of two centuries. This emerges not only from the remarkably mild sentences following the trial in 1411 but also from the hostile attitude of the people of Brussels toward the inquisitors. One of them was the victim of an assassination attempt, and a mocking song in the vernacular was sung about him in the streets.

An important indication of the enormous amount of interest taken in the heresy of the Free Spirit in Brabant is also to be found in a passage added to the widely known confession manual *Somme le roi*. Jan van Rode, working in 1408 in a Carthusian monastery on his translation of the French original, could not restrain himself when he arrived at the treatment of free will and true freedom of spirit. In a frenzy, and undoubtedly spurred on by what he perceived to be a very real problem, he expanded the text to include an attack on those who wrongly interpreted such freedom, referring to them as "poor, deceived Lollards" in a way that presupposes that everyone knew about whom he was speaking. These Lollards' freedom of spirit depended on their denial of the existence of dirty, vulgar sins, as well as on their assumption that they could bodily indulge in the greatest lechery while their spirit remained untainted.

After these somewhat sympathetic words, however, Jan van Rode lashed out strongly against the Free Spirits, his language degenerating into a torrent of abuse. These idiots, he maintained, believed in an "evil, ugly, devilish heresy," and it was scandalous that such "dirty, deceitful peasants" should be tolerated in any country. God grant that they should burn in hell, so that simple folk should no longer fall victim to their evil practices. To add the crowning touch to this outburst, he ended his tirade with a verse: "Such folk are the work of devilry, / Though Free Spirits they profess to be." Only afterward, when his passion had subsided, did he again take up his work with renewed dedication and explain what true freedom of spirit was, his explication rightly based on his French example.

The most important references to the agitation in Brabant resulting from the heresy of the Free Spirit are to be found in the work of Jan van Ruusbroec, who seems to have waged constant battle in his own sphere of influence against both real and alleged adherents of Free Spirit thought, including the mother superior of the movement, Marguerite Porete. Some reservation is called for, however, as he never mentioned names or titles of works. Even so, the content of his complaints, which he expounded repeatedly, refers unmistakably to the body of thought associated with the heresy of the Free Spirit as expressed by Porete in particular. According to his pupil, Jan van Schoonhoven, Ruusbroec was especially intent on eradicating the "sect of the Free Spirit" that was flourishing in Brabant.

Ruusbroec certainly gives the impression of treating a topical matter with which he was constantly confronted. Above all, he strongly disapproved of the idea that the Holy Spirit was the inspiration behind the movement: heretics maintained, for example, that only the Holy Spirit, and not God, had any effect on their actions. Ruusbroec also condemned in no uncertain terms their assertions that they were in a state of total spiritual poverty and consequently no longer liable to classification in categories such as good and evil.

In the north of the Low Countries it was Geert Grote who carried the torch, proving himself to be at least as formidable a heretic hunter as Ruusbroec. He was also especially intent on extirpating Free Spirits such as those who had made their way to the Low Countries via the German territories, staging spectacular processions featuring wild dancers and flagellants. It is no coincidence that spiritual leaders like Ruusbroec and Grote became such outspoken critics of these heresies: it was an essential part of the reputation they hoped to acquire and that was posthumously attributed to them. Of importance is the fact that it was always the heretical ideas of the Free Spirit movement that caused them to take up arms, and this shows that such obsessions—whether they were justified or not—apparently disturbed the peace of mind of many people in Brabant and elsewhere.

If Cockaigne does in fact ridicule the enthusiastic and long-standing fantasies of the attainment of the kingdom of the Holy Spirit that would open the floodgates of abundance and erotic love, then it must also include parody and provocation directed at the extreme self-mortification practiced by adherents of the Devotio Moderna. The context remains the same, for the heresy of the Free Spirit maintained that a state of sinless perfection could be reached only if one succeeded in eliminating all material and spiritual burdens of body and mind. Though the brothers and sisters of the Brethren of the Common Life did not wish to go to such extremes, their democratized lay mysticism nevertheless bespoke their dreams of rewards in the form of heavenly blessings full of spiritual riches.

Elevation to a life free of sin is achieved in the Cockaigne texts by means of boundless gorging, guzzling, idleness, and sleeping around. Adherents of the Devotio Moderna achieved the same by trying to excel in the most bizarre forms of abstinence and self-torture. Manuscripts containing biographies of these brothers and sisters were in circulation, and these provided extremely exaggerated examples of such behavior. Standard descriptions of female adherents' self-inflicted suffering include the constant asking of forgiveness (especially when one has been falsely accused), kissing the feet of all the sisters in the refectory, and cleaning the latrines with one's bare hands. It was possible to distinguish oneself only by making periodic confessions containing huge exaggerations and even sins of one's own invention.

A highly placed individual could also gain distinction by performing the most humble tasks. The prior of Marienborn, for example, decided to help the brothers clean out the cesspit and had therefore asked not to be disturbed. By accident, however, he was surprised in this nasty work by the entire town council of Deventer, and when asked what he could possibly be looking for, he was happy to call out, "The kingdom of heaven! The kingdom of heaven!"

The most impressive spiritual exercises, however, consisted in ignoring the body's natural need for food, drink, and sleep. The early ascetics of Christendom, known as the desert fathers, based their behavior on the conviction that any surrender to these requirements of nature meant playing into the hands of the devil. Too much food and drink aroused sensual desires, which caused the cunning tempter to jump into action. Following in this tradition, the first hermits and monks attempted to outdo each other in their displays of the most thoroughgoing self-abnegation. Their inspiring examples continued to shine with unabating brilliance throughout the Middle Ages.

Sister Liesbeth Gisbers, who died in 1442, never lost any time in claiming the most unappetizing food for her own plate, and if a like-minded sister got there before her, she was downcast, as though a great wrong had been done her. One of her tasks was watching the fire by which the sisters warmed themselves day and night. In tending the fire she regularly reached with her bare hands into the glowing embers, an act that never failed to shock the other sisters. Ever pious, she only laughed and said she didn't feel anything, because her hands had been hardened by unremitting labor. Another example was Brother Thonis, who fought his natural urge to rest at night and refused to sleep for more than two hours. When sleep threatened to overcome him, he went to stand by an open window, thereby staying awake through fear of falling out.

During the course of her thirty-eight-year sickbed Lidwina of Schiedam outdid everyone in her denial of earthly pleasures. She was convinced, as no other, that the refusal of nourishment could free one from any bodily dependence and earthly involvement in general. She finally attained a condition of anorexia sacra, her wounds festering disgustingly and hordes of worms plowing their way through her ravaged body. A medical horror of this magnitude, caused by self-inflicted torture of the most unimaginable kind, was never surpassed in the Middle Ages. Clearly, there was a public eager to hear such stories. Three manuscripts and four printed editions telling in the vernacular the story of her sacrosanct suffering have been preserved, all of which originated within a space of less than two decades around the year 1500.

According to eyewitness reports, between 1414 and 1421 Lidwina no longer ate anything and slept less than two nights in total. She vomited pieces of intestine, lung, and liver. Huge holes developed in her body, and these were covered with bandages soaked in eel or poultry fat, honey, flour, and cream to draw out the worms that otherwise threatened to eat her alive. Lidwina herself hung the pieces of vomited intestine on a rack next to her bed, continuing the while to beseech God for new ordeals.

Exciting stories such as that of Lidwina circulated in many forms at the end of the Middle Ages, recounting devotional acts of heroism that gripped the masses. Behind these stories lurked the conviction that earthly suffering was meaningful and that self-abnegation was the true path to eternity. Nevertheless, these spiritual exercises involving fasting and self-mortification contained a certain degree of arrogance, and this did not go unnoticed. It was even criticized by the ascetics themselves, who at last had something to confess. In contrast to such haughtiness, the Cockaigne texts provide a satirical alternative by urging one to indulge in unlimited drinking and relentless gorging, this being one plausible interpretation of both versions.

Stronger still is the explicit connection between the Middle Dutch Cockaigne texts and the millenarian dreams entertained by the masses, who were waiting with bated breath for the advent of the thousand-year reign of equality, harmony, and abundance. Cockaigne was placed under the protection of the Holy Ghost, and this must have made it for many people the dreamworld repeatedly conjured up not only by the dregs of society but also by priests and Beguines, causing the Land of Cockaigne and the thousand-year reign to intermingle and merge into one. According to the records of the trial that took place in Brussels in 1411, the condemned adepts of the Free Spirit were convinced that in their realm they should practice the opposite of what the church taught regarding poverty, abstinence, temperance, self-control, and obedience. Moreover, it is this blithe denial of earthly constraints that the topsy-turvy world of Cockaigne succeeds in mocking mercilessly.

Part 7

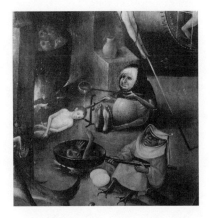

Learning as a Matter
of Survival

33
Didactic Differences

$\mathcal{A}$s I HAVE SHOWN, the Middle Dutch texts on Cockaigne and the prose text on Luilekkerland also had moralizing intentions. This tendency is self-evident in texts B and G, especially as the texts themselves explicitly reveal their intentions. The closing passage of text B urges one to betake oneself to Cockaigne posthaste, though this recommendation is not aimed at every-one. The only people who need follow this advice are those with an aversion to work, who like to horse around and squander their money. People not fit-ting this description are barred entrance, for otherwise Cockaigne would suffer from overcrowding. It seems obvious that these closing remarks are meant ironically and that the image of Cockaigne is here cast in the didac-tic role of the upside-down world. As I have noted, this principle was very popular in the literature and visual arts of the late Middle Ages and was put into practice during the celebration of various festivals, the most exuberant of which was Carnival.

This didactic and moralizing aspect is expressed in even stronger terms in prose text G, dating from 1546, which fires a warning shot at the begin-ning in the form of the couplet offered as a motto after the long descriptive title preceding the text proper: "Eating and drinking and lazing around: / These are three things that ought to have bounds." This could be interpreted as irony, were it not for the fact that the end of the text offers more lines of verse that are just as unambiguous in condemning the excesses so warmly recommended in the text they close. This serves to affirm the text's place in a time-honored tradition and also to emphasize its didactic function as a manual of instruction for young people given to sloth and dis-sipation: they should cure themselves of such uselessness in Luilekkerland, where they will learn that no good can come of such behavior.

The conclusion of the prose portion of text G also points in this direc-tion. Here—in a manner similar to text B—the "prodigal children" of the world are called upon to betake themselves to Luilekkerland: that is, if they

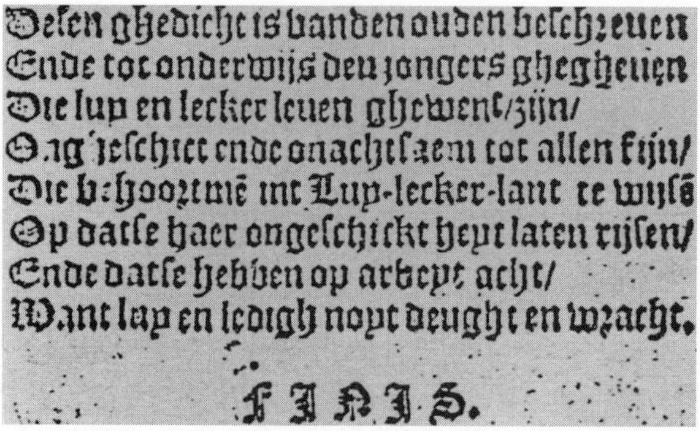
Desen ghedicht is vanden ouden beschreven
Ende tot onderwijs den jongers ghegheven
Die luy en lecker leven ghewent zijn/
Mag 'ieschiet ende onachtsaem tot allen tijn/
Die behoortmē int Luy-lecker-lant te wijsē
Op datse haer ongeschickt heyt laten rijsen/
Ende datse hebben op arbeyt acht/
Want luy en ledigh noyt deught en wracht.

FINIS.

FIGURE 57

End of Luilekkerland text (G), with eight-line verse treating the text's moral implications.

Source: Veelderhande geneuchlycke dichten (1600), fol. G4 recto.

want to continue to live like the inhabitants of that land, with no regard for honor, virtue, courtesy, wisdom, and cultural refinement, in which case they will be highly esteemed there.

In these presentations one recognizes the tradition of class satire, which occurs in many texts and rituals dating from this period. One praises the opposite of the message one hopes to get across, whereby the words uttered and the behavior displayed take on something of the ridiculous. When, in addition to taking this tongue-in-cheek detour, pains are taken to make one's actual intention more explicit, it means that such texts—in this case B and G—account for the possibility that their messages will go unnoticed if the texts are presented only in their recorded form. If one were simply to read the text and commit it to memory, it is conceivable that the reader would fail to see the irony in it and interpret the pleasures described simply as an endorsement of building castles in the air. Nonetheless, this compensatory function is never actually absent, remaining as an undercurrent in the recorded texts for those who are looking to alleviate their fears and frustrations.

Outside the Low Countries as well, the Cockaigne material was used for didactic purposes in the late Middle Ages and early-modern era. The French texts play around with the practices of charivari (the "rough music" rituals

FIGURE 58

Hans Lützelhüpsch comes from Luilekkerland, as
indicated by the owl perched on his hand and the
brothel on his nose.

Source: Reproduced from P. Vandenbroeck, " 'Jheronimus Bosch'
zogenaamde Tuin der Lusten. I," *Jaarboek van het Koninklijk Museum
voor Schone Kunsten te Antwerpen*, 1989: 103.

surrounding the people's tribunal) and the amusements of a topsy-turvy
world, both of which have strongly moralizing—perhaps better described as
disciplinary—tendencies. Such didactic intentions are displayed in a German print dating from around 1520, published even before Hans Sachs's text
of 1530, which served as the model for text G. The print shows a laughing
man with clothing and attributes that indicate he is a depraved good-for-
nothing who fritters away his time with loose women at the public baths-

cum-brothel. The accompanying text informs us that his name is Hans Lützelhüpsch—Hans LittleHandsome—and that he comes from Schlaraffenland, which is full of people like himself.

These moral implants in the Cockaigne material take the shape of irony, which means that a sizable part of the audience must have been familiar with the implications of portrayals of an upside-down world. There is everything to indicate that it would have been difficult, in the late-medieval cities of the southern Netherlands, to find someone who had no notion of such connotations. And if occasionally one was unsure of oneself, there was always the reciter, or a fellow listener, or another reveler whose explanations would leave no room for doubt as to the meaning of the text, performance, or ritual.

Such an entourage is missing when one finds oneself alone with a written or printed text. In this case the consumer alone is responsible for figuring out the meaning of the product in hand. When trying to convey their meaning, authors and adapters can only trust to the adequacy of the signals they have committed to paper, as well as to their judgment of the worldview and frame of reference of their intended readership. The latter variable cannot easily be changed, but the signals can be strengthened and explained more fully, and this is what appears to have happened as soon as the Cockaigne material left the oral tradition and entered the sphere of the written word, being committed to paper in the form of version B.

Rhyming text L has fewer problems in this respect. Here the moralizing implications remain beneath the surface and can only be brought to life by means of a reciter, listener, or reader. Rhyming text B and prose text G, on the other hand, leave no room for doubt as to their purpose. Moreover, at the time text L was recorded, around 1460, urban celebrations of Carnival were at their height, whereas by the time text B was recorded around 1510 and text G in 1546, such festivities were on the wane, having been affected by elitist encapsulations, legal prohibitions, and a general suppression of everything reeking of popular culture. In other words, the sixteenth-century public had begun to lose contact with such festive rituals, which had been so effective in plumbing the depths of the upside-down world, serving to underscore moralizing irony and to flush out camouflaged criticism.

Whether the Cockaigne material as such—in its raw state, meaning when it was not in the process of being recited or performed—contains moralizing implications is a question that cannot be answered. Such impli-

FIGURE 59

Race. Woodcut by Hans Weiditz, the so-called Petrarch Master, 1539.

Source: Reproduced from W. Endrei, *Spiele und Unterhaltung im alten Europa* (Hanau, 1988), no. 129.

cations were dependent on each performance or written record, as well as on the times, circumstances, and audience, and in any case we have only recorded or printed texts to go by. Putting something in writing generally means adapting it to the milieu that desires or requires the text in written form. In practice this boils down to oral material being contaminated with other designs and ideas, undergoing adaptations meant to make old material attractive to a new audience or readership, perhaps a public living elsewhere and at a later date. This notwithstanding, much of the old material remains visible and apparently also serviceable when put to new uses.

This process of hybridization resulted in the prose text of 1546, an exemplar of a still-young literary tradition making use of the medieval Cockaigne material. Luilekkerland is a topsy-turvy world where everything happens that is not supposed to happen in the normal order of things, such as gorging, guzzling, sleeping around, belching, farting, and refusing to do useful work of any kind. The biggest louts and muttonheads are king and emperor, while the dullest fools are declared champions because they come in last in races and shoot their arrows widest of the mark. From this the young may learn, concludes the text, how *not* to behave in the real world.

In Luilekkerland, however, elements of the Cockaigne material have been preserved that can easily be put to other uses. The weather in Luilekkerland is wonderful: it snows powdered sugar, it hails candy, and storm winds smell of sweet violets. This makes a slyboots of Luilekkerland, for these features actually make it very attractive indeed, even to people who have no use for belching, gorging, flexible sexual mores, and all the other amenities of the fringe.

Two essentially opposite applications collide here in what is, to my way of thinking, a rather unacceptable way. How can these satirical exaggerations, meant to induce liberating laughter as compensation for dissatisfaction with actual living conditions, function at the same time as an incitement to avoid such behavior? In the Middle Ages, however, such opposing functions coexisted quite happily and even served to reinforce one another. Humor and instruction were a duality firmly founded in clerical humor, which the church used as a lubricant to get its message across more smoothly. Any informal intermingling of the most holy and the most banal must be understood in the light of this practice, which was put to use with great success from the thirteenth century onward by such mendicant orders as the Friars Minor, who described the height of heavenly rapture in terms of divine drunkenness, manifested in extremely earthly forms.

In particular, the marriage at Cana, where Jesus turned water into wine, provided ample opportunity for trivializing the religious mysteries for the masses in a way at once instructive and humorous. A guest capable of performing such a miracle would be welcome anywhere, as a sixteenth-century wedding song remarks:

> The Lord Jesus came to the wedding;
> From water he made jugs of wine,
> So that we'd have a merry time.
> Wine, come now, down the hatch,
> Come on, wine, now, down the hatch.

A pious drinking song seems strange in our day and age, and it is even stranger to learn that it was such exalted mystics as Hadewijch writing in the thirteenth century and Jan van Ruusbroec in the fourteenth who introduced the image of spiritual drunkenness as representative of the greatest ecstasy. To our mind humor and seriousness should be kept quite separate, especially in the case of religious matters, otherwise the greatest misunderstandings are likely to arise. Admittedly, seriousness may sometimes have a touch of irony, and humor sometimes bears an implicit message, but the intermingling in equal measure of coarse humor and purifying religious events, which thereby serve to strengthen each other, seems to us like pure blasphemy and actually quite denigrating.

A popular variation of this curious combination—serious teachings couched in humorous terms—consisted in contrasting the message proper with the opposite extreme, the latter therefore representing an upside-down world, often presented as a blissful place where one was permitted to wallow in the most exquisite sin. Literature, the visual arts, and traditional festivals such as religious rituals of inversion, fertility rites, and Carnival celebrations all show to what extent this cultural principle became the method employed by more and more people to make their existence more bearable.

The cities in particular overindulged in such festivities, the burghers seizing every possible opportunity provided by the religious calendar to stage festivities involving masks and disguises and rites of inversion. Starting in the twelfth century and peaking in the fifteenth, the towns and villages of the southern Netherlands repeatedly immersed themselves in festivals that seemed at first glance to dissolve into general chaos, only to prove upon closer inspection to be serious yet humorous rituals designed to cleanse society and give it a fresh start.

During the course of the sixteenth century, however, these collective celebrations largely died out. Early-modern society was splitting up according to a multitude of sharply divided ideas about the social order, as witnessed not only by the divisions within the church resulting from the Reformation but also by the increased interest in utopias and the small-scale attempts made here and there to establish them. These ideological divisions diverted attention from—and lessened the need for—the temporary establishment of such ritual inversions as an upside-down world.

In the Middle Ages, however, a stable point of reference did dominate the religious life of most people, who believed that God had created a fixed order on earth that had been translated in practice into the tripartite model of society based on the three estates. This formula prescribed that peasants, preachers, and warriors govern the world through their concerted efforts, paving the way to a common end ushered in by the Last Judgment. This would signal the end of time and also the end of earthly order, which would be replaced by an egalitarian eternity. Considering the nature of this vision, it is no coincidence that the first satires of a topsy-turvy world appeared in the eleventh century, when the church launched its first offensive aimed at clarifying this divinely inspired class order.

The humor with which such serious ideas were driven home threatens to obscure our view of the grave implications of these rituals. Those who failed to meet the late-medieval requirements of a planned civil order with its accompanying middle-class morals of hard work, frugality, and especially individual self-preservation, were roundly ridiculed as fools and invited to go on living their good-for-nothing lives of dissipation in a temporary mock kingdom erected especially for this purpose. When the festivities came to an end, however, the ship of fools set sail, bearing off its cargo in a gesture meant to drive home the fact that there was no place in normal society for those displaying such foolish behavior. Moreover, accusing one of foolishness or madness—the total lack of any Christian reason—seems to have been the obvious means of ridiculing unproductive members of society (including the elderly, infirm, and deformed), for whom there was no place in the new order.

One problem is that many of the late-medieval caricatures of a brutish, immoderate life that populate the upside-down world have been viewed as faithful reproductions of a reality at once yearned-for and abhorrent.

A popular and persistent notion still informs a picture of the Middle Ages based on the conviction that people in those days let themselves be caught in the act of living their daily lives and that literature and the visual arts were intent on depicting such lives as realistically as possible. And, thanks to all those eyewitness reports from writers and painters, we think we can now gauge the exact extent of their awareness of the intensity with which life was supposed to be lived.

In those days, it seems, life was lived a great deal more intensely than it is now: people were not subject to inhibitions or other spiritual constraints; they displayed complete submission to the earth or to God; they gave themselves over to self-flagellation or copulating in the mud, drinking themselves into a stupor whenever nature prompted them to do so, sleeping off their hangovers, screaming in agony, and roaring with laughter. It is quite possible, however, that we should interpret this evidence of so-called medieval realism as a satirical construct designed to ridicule such utter earthiness. And surely this also serves to present a contrast, as vivid as it is enlightening, to the ideal world God had intended in the beginning, which humankind had proved incapable of putting into practice.

It is this world of ultimate depravity and base impulses, the opposite of how things were meant to be, that is depicted in scenes of drunken and brawling peasants, sexual excesses, scatalogical folklore, hulking amazons, and animals acting like people. And not infrequently, all this was portrayed next to the ideal, heavenly world ruled by love and harmony. Time and again medieval man sought the contrast of the *mundus inversus*, the better to focus on his own world in its ideal state.

Confrontations of such seemingly incompatible material within one and the same text can be very disconcerting indeed. In the margin of a late-medieval prayer book there appears next to a very solemn verse about Jesus' suffering a picture of a snowman, which by modern-day standards seems highly inappropriate, if not blasphemous. He sits on some kind of stool with his back to the reader, gazing at us over his shoulder with a look of dismay, perhaps because he is warming his buttocks over a brazier. He even wears a silly hat on his head, as if his droll appearance in such a place isn't already bad enough.

Snowmen were a well-known phenomenon in the Middle Ages, even more so than now. As soon as kneadable snow fell, towns were filled with snowmen or, rather, snow sculptures that rivaled ordinary sculpture both in technique and subject matter. The streets were filled with biblical representations, mythological stories, medieval heroes, animals, and folk figures, and people came from far and wide to take walking tours past all these works of art. Spectacular examples of such snow festivals took place in 1434 at Atrecht and in 1511 at Brussels.

Just how well known such spectacles were emerges from François Villon's famous ballad about the renowned women of yesteryear, with its refrain "But where are the snow [figures] of old?" This is a direct reference to the portrait sculptures modeled in snow—probably made during the severe winter of 1457/1458 in Brussels—of the women whose praises he had once sung and whose images had melted long before.

FIGURE 60

Melting snowman next to a devout prayer in rhyme.

Source: The Hague, Royal Library, MS KA XXXVI, fol. 78 verso.

The snowman in the manuscript seems a bit primitive compared with all those beautiful but short-lived sculptures that were so often reported. But what is he doing next to a religious text? This prayer in rhyme, intended for meditation and private devotion, is about the so-called *arma christi*, the traditional instruments of the Passion. This page also displays a depiction of the sponge on a reed and its accompanying vessel of vinegar, with which Jesus was tortured shortly before His death. The text also records it thus: "Lord, you gave up the ghost shortly after uttering the words, 'It is finished.' " And next to this sits the shocked, melting snowman.

Here again we are confronted with a didactic and emotive technique that has become alien to us: namely, the shocking combination of earnest piety with vulgar humor of the basest sort. However, while it is generally true that religious instruction can be transmitted by the most profane means, here there is more than meets the eye. The ideal world designed by God, for which he even sacrificed His Son, is repeatedly elucidated and praised by contrasting it with the transience of earthly life since the Fall.

This confrontational technique gives rise to what are by modern standards bizarre effects. We also encounter it in churches and cathedrals, where gargoyles have been sculpted into evil monsters and misshapen freaks who have usurped the power of Creation. Inside, the choir stalls are decorated with depictions of sinful behavior in grotesque situations, with no shying away from eroticism and excrement.

Even more closely related to the contrastive marginal illustrations in illuminated manuscripts are the decorations on capitals such as those preserved from a monastery in Toulouse. As recorded in the Gospel According to Saint Matthew, Christ revealed his divinity to His disciples, and this is depicted around three faces of the capital. On a strip parallel to this, however, and around all four sides of the capital are depictions of sports and games, such as wrestling, music making, casting dice, playing trictrac, and high jumping. The poses of the figures also offer the greatest possible contrast with the elongated, self-effacing figures below. These antitheses serve to contrast the world of earthly pleasure with the ideal life within the cloister. Again and again, the ideal world is juxtaposed with a degenerate world, the opposite of what God intended, a *mundus inversus* ruled by the devil, who never tires of laying traps for weak and gullible humankind.

It is confusing for us to see the upside-down world so frequently depicted alongside the ideal world. In religious processions with devotional aims, for example, the world was also represented by hobbyhorses and sword dancers, as well as by monstrous devils led on long leashes like true hellhounds, who cleared the way for the procession with their screams. They also played a role in this beguiling combination of instruction and pleasure that seems so strange to us.

By portraying the horrors and depravation of the counterworld as realistically as possible, the radiance and bliss of the ideal world came more strongly to the fore. Once in a while, however, things got out of hand. The town of Sint Lievens Houthem near Ghent was notorious for the debauched scenes that invariably followed hot on the trail of its religious processions. This caused the town council of neighboring Mechelen to issue a stern warning to the organizers of the Procession of the Holy Cross, stating in no uncertain terms that there were to be "no displays of tomfoolery."

In the above-mentioned manuscript with its rhymed prayers there appears, across from the description and portrayal of the holiest moment on earth— Salvation—a depiction indicative of the ultimate in transience: a melting snowman. Such references to snow and frost occur repeatedly in literature and biblical commentary. In Middle Dutch an added attraction is a pun on the word *dooien*, meaning "to thaw." Dying means the melting away of all things earthly, including one's sins. Jan Smeken, a Brussels rhetorician, thus ends a poem written in 1511 on the occasion of a local snow festival that found its natural end when the thaw set in:

> God grant that we may die like this
> And cause our sins to melt away.
> May we rejoice in heavenly bliss,
> Devoid of all death and decay.

The contrast between everlasting heavenly life and short-lived earthly existence was probably enhanced by having the snowman wear a Jewish skullcap, or yarmulke. This served to recall the contradistinction between *ecclesia* and *synagoge*, which was often invoked in the Middle Ages to set off the true faith from the allegedly pagan beliefs of the Jews.

This confrontational technique proves to have been a popular device, as

FIGURE 61

Male monkeys coupling beneath a devout prayer in rhyme.

Source: The Hague, Royal Library, MS KA XXXVI, fol. 69 recto.

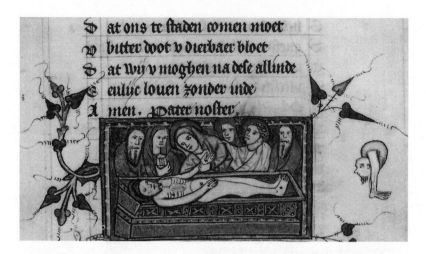

FIGURE 62
Little man with his head between his legs next to the laid-out body of Christ.
Source: The Hague, Royal Library, MS KA XXXVI, fol. 98 recto.

evidenced by other pages in this manuscript. The holy highlights of the everlasting life undergo ironical elucidation by being contrasted with the most bizarre antitheses. This is most effective on the page where the rhyming prayer describes the essence of the spiritual love that binds the Father, Son, and Holy Ghost into the Trinity. Under this, in the lower margin, is a depiction of two copulating male monkeys, serving to contrast the highest possible form of love with the most extreme opposite to be found on earth: brutishly bestial and homosexual, there was nothing more sinful.

Elsewhere a miniature displays an extremely elongated body of Christ in the grave, confronted in the margin with a comical, convoluted little fellow, turning into himself, as it were. This bodily opposition in posture readily lends itself to interpretation as the greatest willingness of the Savior to place Himself at man's disposal, as opposed to the earthly introversion of sinful creatures. There is also a funny little man who stares out at the reader in amazement from behind the frame of a miniature depicting the Holy Cross. Is this not the ultimate expression of human incomprehension when confronted with an event as laden with significance as Jesus' death on the Cross?

[350]

Many marginalia, here and in other manuscripts, are less directly associated with the texts they accompany. All of them, however, represent a counterworld full of coarse, everyday banalities and exaggerated scenes referring to the upside-down world. This didactic technique is more difficult to pin down in literature, where the ideal world designed by God is only implicitly present or cursorily sketched and where all that remains is in fact the portrait of the upside-down world that is so tempting to interpret as a realistic portrayal of medieval life.

34
Topsy-Turvy Worlds

ONTRASTING THE WORLD God intended in His Creation with the hard
reality of the existing world, ruled by the devil and his cohorts, is one of
the chief stylistic principles informing medieval literature and art. The
model for these contrasts between heavenly ideal and earthly reality was
supplied by Augustine. Juxtaposing the *civitas terrena* (earthly state) with the
civitas dei (divine state), he argued that the blissfulness of everlasting life
could only be proven through the saddening portrayal of the depravation
of earthly life. God had known that evil would emerge in the world: it was
part of his design, and therefore it had meaning. Only by contrasting it
with evil could the beauty of Creation become apparent. In other words,
without the badness the goodness would remain invisible. And, according
to the eleventh-century chronicler Radulfus Glaber, the Bible even said:
"There must be heresy in order to distinguish those who truly believe."

Augustine derived his notion of the efficacy of contrarieties from classical
rhetoric, the art of eloquence that was the basis of his education. Herein lies
the foundation for the portrayal and description of all those seemingly realistic excesses and scabrous caricatures: they were intended to make the opposite
stand out with that much more brilliance. Augustine's own words to the effect
read: "So, just as beauty of language is achieved by a contrast of opposites in
this way, the beauty of the course of this world is built up by a kind of rhetoric, not of words but of things, which employs this contrast of opposites."

Augustine found the models for the revealing opposites by means of
which he defined Creation and eternity primarily in the Bible. The Book of
Ecclesiastes in particular explains the necessity of sharp contrasts. Mortality consists in riding out the bumps on the way to eternity:

> To every thing there is a season, and a time to every purpose under
> the heaven: a time to be born, and a time to die; a time to plant,

and a time to pluck up that which is planted; a time to kill, and a time to heal; a time to break down, and a time to build up; a time to weep, and a time to laugh; a time to mourn, and a time to dance; a time to cast away stones, and a time to gather stones together; a time to embrace, and a time to refrain from embracing; a time to get, and a time to lose; a time to keep, and a time to cast away; a time to rend, and a time to sew; a time to keep silence, and a time to speak; a time to love, and a time to hate; a time of war, and a time of peace.

This ties in with the concept of *concordia discors* (unity in discord) from the ancient art of rhetoric. Nature itself engendered opposites, for only through contrast with its opposite can a thing of quality survive and contribute to the order and beauty of the whole. And in spite of recurring discord, all-encompassing unity survives unscathed.

Rhetoric is by its very nature antithetical, for the orator assumes the existence of adversaries whom he must persuade with his counterarguments. Following the Bible and the art of rhetoric, the medieval *ars poetica* points out the special possibilities inherent in portraying topsy-turvy worlds, which literature in particular is well suited to doing: "Art . . . can almost work magic and is able to represent things so beautifully that the last becomes the first, the future the past, the remote near; the indirect direct; thus uncouth things become refined, the old changes into new, public into private, black into white, and sordid into precious." Hadewijch offers elaborate proof of this in a fifty-line poem that attempts to capture the essence of spiritual love, whose true nature emerges from the misery it evokes. The tone is set in the very first line and reverberates throughout the long list of paradoxes:

> Love is most sweet when it takes one by storm;
> The depths of despair its most beautiful form;
> Losing one's way brings one close to the goal;
> Starving for love is a feast for the soul;
> Mistrust of it is knowledge sure;
> Love's sorest wound is its own cure;
> To die for it brings life eternal.

This model may, of course, also be used to describe everlasting pleasure, whereby negative components are denied existence, causing the positive qualities to come more strongly to the fore. This is the method employed in many Middle Dutch descriptions of heaven, an example of which occurs in *Sinte Augustijns hantboec* (Saint Augustine's handbook): "O spirited life, O eternal life in everlasting bliss: there reigns gladness without sorrow, rest without toil, dignity without fear, riches without loss, health without sickness, abundance without want, life without death, eternity without mortality, bliss without misery." Similar reasoning and writing techniques are ridiculed— and consequently also given recognition—in lying tales that juxtapose highly unusual opposites in a seemingly logical connection. As already stated, the travel literature of classical antiquity and the Middle Ages also dealt with things in this way, and it was considered no small feat to parody the differences between one's own world and that of an exotic people by presenting absurd contrasts.

Of perhaps even greater importance to the medieval application of these techniques is the tradition established by the Book of Revelation and the commentaries it provoked, in which opposites provide an overpowering structural principle, aimed at characterizing—once and for all and as convincingly as possible—the final struggle between good and evil. Evil is described again and again as the opposite of good or even as its absence. Referring to Augustine, Thomas Aquinas underscores this notion of the necessity and significance of evil, which has its own place in the order of things, its main purpose being to highlight all things good: "Hence many good things would be taken away if God permitted no evil to exist; for fire would not be generated if air was not corrupted, nor would the life of a lion be preserved unless the ass were killed. Neither would avenging justice nor the patience of a sufferer be praised if there were no injustice."

The upside-down world enters literature chiefly in the form of a *Zeitklage*, or complaint on the times. Since the Fall, Creation had degenerated to the extent that it now found itself spiraling downward toward total domination by the devil. When that finally happened, God would intervene. In the meantime, all earthly activities—which in any case had always been an expression of humankind's mortal state and the punishment suffered since the Fall—represented the upside-down world in the spirit of Augustine's *civitas terrena*. This world of opposites often appears, for example, in a pictorial

FIGURE 63

The upside-down world is frequently portrayed by means of animals acting as humans. Print from Gotha, ca. 1533.

Source: Reproduced from M. L. Geisberg, *The German Single-Leafed Woodcut, 1500–1550* (Munich, 1974), G.1195.

tradition featuring depictions of peasants working the land and pictures of hard-working townsfolk divided into various occupational groups. One must exercise caution in interpreting such depictions, however, especially those produced at the end of the Middle Ages. While they are undoubtedly rooted in the tradition of portrayals of post-Fall doom and transience, later on the revaluation of nature and the recognition of the necessity—not to mention joys—of hard work caused these activities to be viewed in a more positive light.

That the visual arts did not hesitate to use the weapon of satire in portraying a revealing *mundus inversus* to counter Augustine's heavenly state has already been seen in the marginal drolleries in illuminated manuscripts, the gargoyles on churches and public buildings, and the decorations on choir stalls and capitals. Woodcuts and engravings contributed to this visual deluge as well. In 1486 Hans Vintler included in his printed *Buch der Tugend* (Book of virtue) woodcuts meant to illustrate his teachings on virtue with

FIGURE 64

The topsy-turvy world: servants riding their masters' horses. Appearing
in Hans Vintler's *Buch der Tugend*, 1486.
Source: Reproduced from *The Illustrated Bartsch*, gen. ed. W. L. Strauss
(New York, 1983), no. 23.713.

a series of funny examples of topsy-turvy worlds. A bishop spins a top, a
monk gets on his high horse and practices with the crossbow, nuns ride in a
wagon to court, a man sits at a spinning wheel, a child downs a beer, and servants ride fine horses while their masters walk along behind.

Medieval literature confined itself almost exclusively to the weapon of
satire in its attempts to expose the misery of everyday life. Things got even
more complicated when, during Carnival celebrations, the existing world in
idealized form was turned upside-down, and the opposite of desirable
behavior and the virtues normally aspired to were loudly extolled. An early
example of this is Bishop Adalbero of Lâon in the eleventh century, who
attempted, during the course of such festivities, to explain the tripartite
model of society based on the three estates. Humankind had failed, he said,
in fulfilling its class-bound tasks, and the world was certainly doomed now
that peasants walked around with crowns on their heads, kings did nothing
but pray, and bishops trudged along behind the plow.

In the same period or shortly thereafter, the songs of the *Carmina Burana* offered an elaborate treatment of the same theme, indicating that in Latin satire of the High Middle Ages a genre was growing that aimed to explain, above all, the necessity—indeed, the urgency—of strict adherence to the class model imposed on society. Complaints about students failing at their studies and leading lives of dissipation provoked attempts to sketch a world headed straight for the end. In these songs, biblical and classical figures, church fathers and popes all live in an upside-down world. Martha slouches around, while Mary slaves away keeping house. Lucretia stands at the street corner ogling men as though she were a whore, and church fathers such as Jerome and Gregory the Great hang around alehouses gambling and drinking.

The presentation of a topsy-turvy world, whether or not depicted alongside the ideal world, was very popular in Middle Dutch literature. The objective was invariably to point a stern finger at those thought responsible for the deterioration of everyday life. A song from the Bruges Gruuthuse manuscript dating from the second half of the fourteenth century begins with the desperate cry: "I don't have any idea how to behave!" This is followed by the reason why: "The world has been turned upside down / Unfaithfulness waxes where faith wanes."

The storyteller Boudewijn van der Luere rails against the depravity of his times in his story in rhyme called *Van tijtverlies* (Of lost time). Every virtue has been contaminated by vice, the holy church appears to be a hotbed of usury, preemption, and simony, shame goes before honor, youths rule the world, women walk around in men's clothing, and promiscuity is rife. Boudewijn needs dozens of verses to criticize his contemporaries who are helping the world toward rack and ruin. That is where things are headed, he maintains, for God will not go on forever warning the world with plagues and devastation and floods, not to mention fires and epidemics. This was all child's play compared with what his sword of justice would do shortly.

The text is exemplary, not only in its contrastive design but also in its treatment of the sins and vices, as well as the people who have transformed society into a topsy-turvy world. There are striking similarities, for example, with a strophic text from the Jan Phillipszoon manuscript compiled in Leiden around 1470. The pattern occurs everywhere, however, and was also a favorite of the Bruges rhetorician Anthonis de Roovere.

Neither is such a text missing from the London manuscript containing the Middle Dutch Cockaigne text L. The fifty-two-line rhyming text immediately precedes the mock doctor's prescription and the Cockaigne text, making the relationship of these three texts all the more obvious. The upside-down world is first satirically identified with the degenerate contemporary world, then cloaked in the Carnivalesque genre of lying tales, and finally presented ironically as a place of higher learning.

The poem immediately offers itself as social critique:

> Behold, this world with hate is filled!
> Do me good, I do you ill;
> Help me up, I cast you down;
> Honor me, my scorn abounds.

This complete degeneracy is the result of truth dying out and justice being suppressed. Deceit and indecency reign; faith, humility, and kindness have lost the battle. Hate and envy germinate at a fully laden table, for as soon as the food runs out, the friendship will be over as well. Money rules the world.

The closing passage also forms a link to the text following the mock doctor's prescription and the Cockaigne story, causing the two intermediate texts to become even more closely bound to their neighbors. The text following Cockaigne is a satirical treatment in Latin of the penny and some rather loosely structured rhymes about the omnipotence of money. Cockaigne and the mock doctor's prescription therefore seem to be surrounded by satires on the wickedness of existing society, whereby the contrastive function of the upside-down world plays a decisive role.

Ironical lessons are generally linked to celebrations of Carnival, typical examples being the mock charter that lays down the rules for membership in the Guild of the Blue Barge and the mock sermon on Saint Nobody. This kind of text, of which several dozen examples from the fifteenth and sixteenth centuries have been preserved, commended new modes of behavior to members of developing urban society by praising to the skies their exact opposite. This took place by inviting the masses, according to set rules in a ritualized game, to band together as a guild and join the ranks of the lazybones, prodigal sons, and adulterers. The ritual ended with the banishment

FIGURE 66

Engraving by Pieter van der Heyden after Hieronymus Bosch, featuring the
Blue Barge, 1559.

Source: Brussels, Bibliothèque Royale, Print Room.

of those embodying such blameworthy conduct, which the city no longer
wished to tolerate. This served not so much to affirm the existing order as
it did to propagate new values, especially those of self-preservation, personal
responsibility, and decorum.

The Guild of the Blue Barge sought its membership among spongers
from all sections of society, including the clergy, alleged wastrels, and reput-
edly loose women, who were assured they would be allowed to carry on
quaffing and whoring till the end of time. This immediately incriminated
the needy of late-medieval society, for it was often the case that those sum-
moned to join the guild either found themselves in a distressing position
through no fault of their own or were on the verge of landing in such a situation. But the text, composed as a parody of guild rules and regulations,
simply suggests that it is all their fault, adamantly decreeing that in the new
society one should be able to take care of oneself. Moreover, the ironical

tone is abandoned twice at the end of the text, in order to offer a straight-forward explanation of the intended message, thereby leaving no room for doubt as to the meaning of these apparently light-hearted recommendations to fritter one's life away.

Membership in the Guild of the Blue Barge is reserved for representatives of accepted social groups, who then overindulge in frivolous and licentious behavior that is heartily applauded. Excluded from membership are murderers, arsonists, thieves, pirates, traitors, cutpurses, and vagabonds, who are all past saving and in any case do not display the kind of behavior that a city can proclaim to be ideal in a simple rite of inversion or period of temporary misrule. Their likes should be done away with. The guild conscripts are assured that they will be released from membership as soon as they wise up, get married, or become rich, and this confirms the makeup of the new order.

In the mock sermon on Saint Nobody, the faithful are urged to do the following:

> Take pains to understand me well,
> The ranks of the heavenly kingdom swell
> With drunkards and wastrels, I must explain.
> So, dearest, if saving your soul is your aim,
> Then spare neither goods nor legacy,
> Though your children might starve in misery.
> Swig and swill at each opportunity.

This message was repeated again and again by the mock preacher: blow all your money, and drink yourselves under the table.

These texts, a number of which also take care to conclude with an explanation of the moral of the story, are directly connected with the rhyming texts on Cockaigne and the prose text on Luilekkerland. All three—both rhyming texts meant for recitation and performance and the prose text intended for private entertainment (reading to oneself or reading aloud to others)—preserve the memory of the festive ritual of the topsy-turvy world, which seems to have only a vague connection with the original ritual of inversion. The increasing obscurity of this connection is seen in such collections as *Veelderhande geneuchlycke dichten* (Various amusing poems), first printed in 1600, which contains many texts of this kind dating from the previous two centuries. Even the earlier edition of text G, presumably printed in 1546, dates from a time that has said farewell to the ritual inversion of the upside-down world and at the very most looks back on it with nostalgia.

Examples are legion of topsy-turvy worlds characterized by role swapping between the sexes. The most famous in this respect was the kingdom of the Amazons, whose existence was confirmed by many medieval scholars. These women had banished all men from their midst and were as cruel as they were pugnacious. With a view to procreation they enjoyed fleeting contact once a year with the men of a neighboring island. The male babies resulting from these unions were immediately beaten to death or sent away, while the female babies started receiving their education in the art of warfare while still in the cradle. Later on these female offspring had one breast burned off, the better to handle their weapons. Their savagery was said to have enabled them to subject a large part of Asia to their power. This dominion of women in an upside-down world still had repercussions on late-medieval satire in both literature and the visual arts, which warned of the threat of women coming to power in an increasingly urban society.

Power was not the only thing subject to topsy-turviness: emotions could be turned upside down as well. There was said to be an island in the Great Ocean where the women were very sad when a baby was born and extremely happy when one died. Sir John Mandeville thought this demanded an explanation, and he sought one in an orthodox Christian notion that had scant hope of acceptance in his own wicked world. The inhabitants of this island apparently realized that this earth was nothing but a vale of tears and that true life began only after death: "The cause why they weep and sorrow at the birth of their children and rejoice when they die is that when they are born into this world they come to sorrow and trouble, and when they die, they go to the joy of Paradise, where rivers of milk and honey and plenty of all kinds of good things are, and a life without sorrow." Mandeville hereby confirmed that the topsy-turvy world in fact represented life as it was in the West, having been corrupted by Christian society, while some exotic peoples had managed to preserve the ideal world in its original paradisiacal purity.

Von der neüwe Welt

vmß welches wille wir dannzemal nit wenig belustiget gewesen. Von welcher leüt sitten (da wir sie haben gesessen/ hond wir die seitmal die bequemlicheit sich begibt/ auch vnderweil herein wöllen ziehen.

Von ire leben vnd sitten

FIGURE 67

Unclean behavior (urinating in public, adultery, cannibalism) engaged in by the inhabitants of the New World. Title page of the book *Von der neuwe Welt*, I. Grüninger, Strasbourg, 1509.

Source: London, British Library, G.6540.

Such marginal civilizations thus proved to supply an immediate example of how things were really meant to be.

This sometimes bizarre mixture of nostalgia for pure Christianity, xenophobia, and self-promotion was not confined to the often primitive-sounding scraps of information in travel tales and chronicles but also colored the vision of Columbus and other modern explorers. I have already reported how, during his third voyage, from 1498 to 1500, Columbus was seriously worried about staying in the Cockaigne they had discovered and the effect it would have on his crew. That lawless land of plenty was suitable only for sinners and good-for-nothings. This, too, was the conclusion of both Cockaigne text B and the prose text on Luilekkerland. Not only on paper but also in the flesh Cockaigne appears to be a school for gluttons and idlers, who are condemned to remain there until they come to their senses and realize how much chaos and depravity are ultimately created by such utter godlessness.

35
Hard Times

*I*F THEIR EXPLICATION and place within the didactic framework of the upside-down world have already made clear to what extent Cockaigne and Luilekkerland may serve as educational institutions, then such purposes must also be inferable from particulars in the texts themselves. What do these texts actually teach us, and how do the attractions of these dreamlands serve to draw our attention to these teachings?

First of all, take idleness, a feature that completely dominates both Cockaigne and Luilekkerland. It is not necessary to expend any energy whatever to obtain the most delicious food. That this is the cornerstone of the dreamland is evident from the opening of both Cockaigne texts. Everyone has to work hard to earn a living: this is the consequence of the Fall of Man. The texts then proceed to introduce Cockaigne as a land where God has banned all toil and trouble. Food and drink present themselves for consumption, even in the form of roasted animals who thrust themselves upon one, complete with the necessary eating utensils. Moreover, everything in this land is so topsy-turvy that one can earn the most simply by sleeping.

Text G develops these fantasies of obtrusive food much further. In Luilekkerland all manner of delicacies grow on trees, always within easy reach. Fish, boiled or grilled, purposely swim so close to the shore that one can simply grab them out of the water. Roasted birds of every kind fly through the skies right into one's mouth, if it happens to be open. Pigs walk around with knives sticking out of their backs, and donkeys and horses lay eggs and pancakes.

The accent is not so much on the strange behavior of all this mobile food but rather on the fact that the consumer need do practically nothing to obtain it. The only thing left to do is chew and swallow, and even that may prove to require too much effort. Beneath a print of *The Land of Cockaigne* made after Bruegel's painting of 1567 is the following inscription: "The idler crosses his arms and finds it difficult to bring them toward his mouth."

Laziness generally receives even more attention in text G, chiefly because the name of the dreamland is now, for the first time, Luilekkerland: "lazy-luscious-land." Anyone who wants to earn a living with his hands can count not only on the enmity of his fellow countrymen but also on eventual banishment. The biggest lazybones, who do nothing but sleep and daydream, are looked up to as nobles.

Such fantasies raise the question of work and consequently one of the seven deadly sins: acedia, or sloth. Originally this sin was defined as negligence or failure to discharge one's religious duties, especially in the case of monks and other clerics. This was a much graver oversight in the Middle Ages than it is now, and thus this sin—nowadays somewhat forgotten—was in medieval times every bit as sinful as the other, more spectacular cardinal sins. In particular, members of the lower clergy were continually in danger of becoming sleepy and dozing off as a result of constant prayers, study, and contemplation. Repeated occurrences of this could lead to melancholy, and this was just what the devil was waiting for, for a man in a state of melancholy was easily led into temptation.

This situation is not referred to in the texts, which are apparently more concerned with the necessity of hard work in everyday life. Starting in the fourteenth century, a growing need was felt to exhort people to work, even—and especially—by presenting, in a manner as funny as it was effective, the picture of a topsy-turvy world. Surely it was necessary to combat the idea, still rooted firmly in people's minds, that toil and trouble were the just punishment received by Adam and Eve when they were driven out of Paradise. This was stated in no uncertain terms by Jan van Boendale:

> Then God spoke to Adam:
> For complying with your wife's demand
> And paying no heed to my command,
> From now on you will have to learn
> With sweat and tears your bread to earn.

The new urban economy could not thrive if work was not viewed in a more positive light. Luckily there were a lot of biblical passages just waiting to be brought to light for this purpose, as well as the possibility, alluded to in Genesis, that God had in fact required some work to be carried out in Paradise

FIGURE 68

Drawing of *Desidia*, or Sloth, by Pieter Bruegel the Elder, 1557.

Source: Reproduced from L. Münz, *Bruegel: The Drawings* (London, 1961), no. 133.

("And the Lord God took the man, and put him into the Garden of Eden to dress it and to keep it"), though this could be taken to mean at most a bit of hoeing and raking on a regular basis. The *Spiegel der sonden* (Mirror of sins), however, turned this quite plainly into the following: "God placed Adam, the first man, in Paradise in order to work." And the rhyming *Dietsche Lucidarius*, also to be found in prose form in the London manuscript containing Cockaigne text L, presents a similarly distorted picture, this time with the added assurance that Adam actually enjoyed the work assigned him by God:

> From the place of his creation
> God took Adam and carried him
> Into Paradise, because the first man
> Should labor, according to His plan;
> Not that he should toil beyond all measure
> But rejoice in work as well as pleasure.

Some commentators went so far as to interpret the passage from the Bible as an incitement for man to complete Creation himself. A more positive image of work is barely conceivable.

According to this guided change in mentality, work was not to be seen as punishment. The punishment the first couple endured after the Fall consisted only in a change of the secondary terms of employment, and this must have been what was implied in the verse from the *Dietsche Lucidarius* quoted above. If Adam and Eve had previously gone off to work whistling, now they set off in trepidation, knowing their toil would cause blood, sweat, and tears. The necessity of work, however, and its positive effect on society was no longer in doubt, which is why sloth was henceforth ridiculed, the better to get this message across. Idlers were now seen as good-for-nothings or failures, who belonged in Cockaigne or Luilekkerland. And acedia, or sloth, came to stand both for neglecting one's work and for idleness in general.

Promoting the desirability of hard work was necessary for urban society. Many people lived by begging or ate regularly in poorhouses. Militant monks and millenarian fortune hunters chose, on the basis of loudly stated principles, the path of poverty, which meant in any case the forsaking of all work. Work, after all, was corrupting, as it invariably led to the accumulation of possessions and the sin of pride. There is no question here of extreme fundamentalist viewpoints. Encyclopedias of morals—such as the *Sidrac*, widely distributed until well into the sixteenth century—did not hesitate to pay tribute to such ideas, and it is therefore hardly surprising that all attempts to restore paradise on earth promised, as their most important feature, that one would no longer have to work.

A Middle Dutch text attributed to Meister Eckhart complains about such devotionally inspired but unproductive members of society. Work is healthy and protects one from sin. Moreover, it is necessary for the preservation of society that everyone earn his own living. Laypeople should avoid too much religious devotion at all costs: "They should not spend all day idling in church and giving themselves over to sloth. And they should not go to Communion too often."

Other texts also allude to the practice of devotion as a cover for a simple disinclination to get one's hands dirty, a trait thought to be second nature to members of the clergy. Jan van Boendale's view of work primarily as a punishment to be endured nevertheless meant that this work should be duly carried out as a true "service to God," which, to his way of thinking, consisted not so much in tarrying in church as in getting on with one's daily work.

When *The Romance of the Rose* also lends its support to such sentiments, it must mean that a growing lay public was beginning to share this point of view. It was argued that Paul the Apostle made it clear that one had to work for one's daily bread and the other necessities of life: "Begging was forbidden them, / he said: 'Work with your hands, / Do not disgrace yourselves by scrounging.'" Later he himself refused to take money from the people he was addressing:

> Good folk, keep your kind gifts to me,
> On my own work I get along,
> My own hands are extremely strong,
> There's no need for your charity.

In general, however, everlasting idleness in paradisiacal conditions in some remote corner of the world was presented as a desirable beginning or ending to life, which one might also wish to strive for while still alive and enjoying good health. Neither the golden ages of the past nor the heavenly delights of the future entailed work of any kind. The lay preacher Johannes Brugman made such enticing remarks to this effect that his congregation probably couldn't wait to leave all that earthly toil behind: "What will we do in the everlasting life? There we will not toil or carry out any work. What will we do then? There we will do nothing but gape and marvel." Dutch proverbs such as "an untilled acre seldom yields good grain" figure prominently in this context. This saying seems like an open door, and, indeed, at the end of the fifteenth century it could be seen either from the perspective of the long-standing and oft-revived tradition of fields spontaneously supplying crops or as an exhortation to carry out the necessary work many people deliberately neglected. Both attitudes rebel against the age-old connection between food and work: food is the reward for work, representing humankind's daily victory over the constant threat of death by starvation.

Both Cockaigne texts open with a saying that underscores this profound truth—or should we say curse?—only to surprise us by proclaiming an exception to this basic law. During the course of this study, yet more exceptions have come to the fore, from the lost but perhaps recoverable paradise to the new worlds in the Far East and West. One way or another, there remains a deep desire for food with no strings attached. There are numerous proverbs that give expression to the desire for a source of food requiring no effort, such as a saying found in a collection printed in Kampen in the east of the Netherlands in 1550: "It will be put in your mouth and prechewed for you." This is exactly what the lazybones depicted in the *Cockaigne* print want when they wait with crossed arms for food to be put in their mouths.

Work is promoted by warning against idleness, which was said to be related to the search for release and relaxation in a natural setting. Such warnings required one to take a firm stand, for at the end of the Middle Ages masses of people had begun to discover that nature, which had traditionally been distrusted, could also be a source of pleasure, bringing comfort and even a cure for the illness of melancholy. The way to such pastimes is shown by the personification of Idleness in *Dat boeck van den pelgherym* (The book of the pilgrim), printed in 1486 but known from earlier manuscripts. On his journey across earth to the heavenly Jerusalem, a pilgrim is continually led astray by a host of sins and vices appearing in human shape, who have the most surprising and wonderful things up their sleeve. Idleness presents itself as a beautiful maiden standing at the beginning of a wide road with no obstacles whatsoever, in contrast to the narrow path full of stones, boulders, and potholes that Work guards over. The beautiful maiden, however, appears to be the daughter of Sloth: "I am in fact the gatekeeper of many beautiful paths. I lead the people who come here straight into the greenery and lovely landscape, where they can pluck splendid roses and other flowers. I take them to wonderful places where they find comfort and pleasure. There I let them sing to the music of harps, lutes, and other instruments." The warning is obvious: we are meant to choose the straight and narrow, whose entrance is guarded by Work. Only in the heavenly paradise will there be music and dance, for it is there we will be given eternal rewards. Such diversions have no place on this earth. This message is also implicitly present in Cockaigne, whose inhabitants may dance and make music to their hearts' content.

The compiler of the Brussels manuscript containing version B of the Cockaigne text also takes part in this work offensive. Rather solemnly he records—closing with a Latin aphorism—that work is meant to be the foundation of society. Moreover, one should always bear in mind that a verse like this is already connected with the Cockaigne text merely by the fact of its having been recorded in the same manuscript by the same copyist:

> *Notabile.*
> He who sleeps when it's time to sow,
> Will have at harvest time nothing to show;
> He who sleeps when he should beg and pray,
> Will receive no alms when they're given away;
> He who sleeps when he should eat to survive,
> Will have nothing in his belly to keep him alive;
> He who sleeps when it's time for hard labor,
> Will have to fast when it's time for his dinner.
> *Qui timet deum nihil*
> *negliget.*

36
Moderation, Ambition, and Decorum

THE RECOMMENDATION to exercise moderation in eating and drinking appeared to be gaining acceptance in both courtly and middle-class milieus, even if many people did not actually practice what they preached. At any rate, moderation in eating—with respect to both the amount of food consumed and the number of meals per day—is a fixed theme in the confession manuals that warn against the sin of gluttony (*gula*). When the Cockaigne material was finally recorded at the end of the Middle Ages, the texts automatically conjured up an upside-down world that showed how one was *not* supposed to behave, and this was done by means of a procedure extremely familiar to city folk. In other words, in an urban context Luilekkerland's themes were inevitably seen in the light of discussions concerning moderation and within the framework of Christian teachings concerning gluttony.

An overwhelming amount of attention was paid to gluttony (including addiction to drink) in late-medieval and early-modern society. Gorging and guzzling came more and more to be associated with the highest forms of pleasure and were at the same time likened to the total lack of restraint characteristic of animals. Moreover, most people believed that gluttony was the mother of all sins. Drunk and replete, one was more likely to succumb to the devil's temptations and abandon oneself to everything that God had forbidden. Thomas of Kempen gave a vivid description of this in his *Imitatio Christi*: "When the belly is full to bursting with food and drink, debauchery knocks at the door." According to the author of the *Ridderboek* (The knight's handbook), a popular didactic manual written between 1412 and 1415, gluttony gives rise to lechery, aggression, and slothfulness in carrying out good works, as well as promoting such wicked diversions as dancing, gambling, and games like bowling.

Practically no confession manual missed the opportunity to catalog these sins, which were set in motion as soon as one's blood was stirred up by too

FIGURE 69

Wine leads to lechery, anger, carousing, and foolishness. German woodcut, 1528.

Source: Reproduced from *Die Welt des Hans Sachs* (Nuremberg, 1976), no. 28.

much food and drink. The widely known story of John of Beverley probably appealed most to the late-medieval imagination, as witnessed by its
occurrence in many forms in the Western European treasure trove of narratives. The hermit John, who excels in self-abnegation, is punished by God
for his pride, though at first he does not realize he is being punished. God
appears to send an angel to him, who forces him to choose one of three sins:
getting drunk, raping a woman, or committing a murder. The instigator of
this wickedness later proves to be the devil, who practices the advanced art
of temptation on hermits simply because he finds their lonely struggle
against the sins of the world so provoking. John, of course, chooses to get
drunk. In his drunken state, however, he rapes his sister, whom he subsequently murders. This, then, serves as a graphic and convincing illustration
of the dangers of gluttony.

Moderation had already been claimed as one of the ideals of courtly

society, where this virtue was extolled as the prime weapon in the never-ending battle against the devil, who had so successfully confounded man's senses
since the Fall. In towns and cities, this striving for moderation was directed
chiefly at the consumption of food, supplies of which had to be regulated
in a sensible and practical way in view of the constant threat of food shortages, which could have a catastrophic effect in crowded urban areas. In this
context, moderation with respect to food consumption remained a mode of
behavior by means of which the urban elite could distinguish itself.

Gluttons were seen as violators of the First Commandment in that they
chose to worship another God: namely, their own bellies. Belly worship had
already been remarked upon by the evangelist Matthew. The learned Dirk
van Delf offered a creative elaboration of this comparison, mentioning in

FIGURE 70

Detail of engraving of *Gula*, or Gluttony, by Pieter van der Heyden after Pieter
Bruegel the Elder, 1558.

Source: Brussels, Bibliothèque Royal, Print Room.

passing the idea of gluttony as the mother of all sins: "Then there is gluttony, whereby one worships one's own belly. The temple is the kitchen, the altar serves as dining table, the deacon as head butler, cooked and roasted foods form the offertory, and the choral accompaniment is the quarreling, fighting, and backbiting going on during the meal."

Attempts to regulate food consumption more stringently and to reduce social tension more effectively led to a government ban on excessively sumptuous meals—both at home and in public—which were condemned as nothing but displays of undesirable and gluttonous behavior. In 1531, for example, Charles V issued a decree designed to "call a halt to the uncontrolled gluttony and addiction to drink to which the people in our region abandon themselves daily in many an alehouse, tavern, and inn." Laws were enacted forbidding more than twenty people to sit down to a wedding dinner, and the accompanying festivities were not permitted to last longer than noon the following day.

Perhaps the terrifying results of too much food and drink are more obvious when literature, the visual arts, and festive entertainment all have a hand in showing that such behavior does not have a place in polite society. Bruegel revealingly portrayed Gula, the female personification of gluttony, riding backward on a pig. In the topsy-turvy world of Carnival, however, excessive eating and drinking were of paramount importance, and it was precisely these ritual celebrations that provided the occasion for the wild festivities that were a frequent feature of life in the city. Here as well compensation for the frugality practiced during the rest of the year exists side by side with blatant moralizing.

Hieronymus Bosch's *Ship of Fools* is jam-packed with food and drink. The barrel, cups, and pitchers, the huge ladle functioning as a rudder, the ham being bitten into, and also the vomiting man on the afterdeck all evoke superabundance. The image is crowned by the mast, a fertility symbol of the wrong kind, for a bad omen in the form of an owl lives in the masthead. A plucked chicken is tied to the top, causing the mast to resemble the *mât de Cocagne*, which had been known in France since 1425. This consisted of a tall pole with all kinds of delicacies tied to the top, the point being to lay one's hands on this delicious booty. The pole, however, was smeared with tallow or soap, so that many people not only tried their luck in vain but also made

FIGURE 71

Corpulence. Engraving by Hans Weiditz, the so-called Petrarch Master, 1532.

Source: Reproduced from W. Scheidig, *Die Holzschnitte des Petrarca-Meisters zu Petrarca's Werk "Von der Artzney bayder Glück"* (Augsburg, 1532; reprint, 1955), 302.

spectacles of themselves in the process. The reveler in Bosch's painting has been more successful: he has managed to get near the chicken and tries to cut it loose with a meat cleaver.

The leader of the feasting legions is often an extremely obese man, draped with food, who sits atop a barrel of beer and brandishes a spit full of roasted meat at the gaunt personification of fasting. The Fatso as the exponent of gluttony, contrasted with the Skinnybones as the symbol of frugal living, is also to be seen in Bruegel's design of 1563 for engravings of *The Lean Kitchen* and *The Fat Kitchen*. Related to these are prints dating from 1532 by Hans Weiditz, the so-called Petrarch Master, that were used repeatedly as book illustrations and frequently imitated. A very fat man and woman sprawl at a table laden with food and drink. The man plays a guitar. In the background one sees another fat man. The engraving illustrates how idleness, loose living, and intemperance lead to corpulence. The pendant of this engraving depicts

FIGURE 72

Drunkard. German engraving, ca. 1521.

Source: Reproduced from Geisberg (1974), no. 511.

a lean man sitting at a table and eating simple food, the attributes of his active life as a woodcutter displayed conspicuously next to him. A grotesque contrast is formed by the enormous beer belly of the drunkard portrayed in a German engraving dating from around 1521. He is forced to convey his oversized and protruding paunch on a wheelbarrow.

The plays performed during this period at the Latin schools of the humanists featured the Parasite and the Sponger, types based on antique models that were now revived to confront a contemporary actuality of which the young had to be warned. All day long the Parasite is plagued by his gluttony, for life consists of nothing but trying to think up ways to fill his stomach. The skill required to do this raises parasitism to an art.

The rhetoricians' art, which was actually little more than humanism in the vernacular, shows a similar interest in the figure of the Sponger. Two of these are portrayed in *Twee bedelaers* (Two beggars), by the Haarlem rhetorician Lauris Janszoon. These beggars also bemoan their horrible hunger, their complaint taking the form of artfully rhyming verse:

> Zounds! My stomach is a gaping hole,
> My belly's like jelly, my cheeks too sleek,
> My legs thin as pegs . . .
> My bowels utter growls, there's just no describing
> Their clamorous crying.

Related to this is the lament of a poor father in the farce *Van Onse Lieven Heers minnevaer* (Of Our Lord's journey of love), from the same pen. This man's children have such huge appetites that they eat him out of house and home:

> In the morning before dawn, with stomachs insistent
> And so upset, like wagons rumbling on their way,
> Two or three loaves they eat in an instant.
> They all eat two or three rye breads a day,
> In order to keep their hunger at bay,
> Their stomachs are a bottomless pit.

This obsession with gluttony, which threatens to shake the foundations of polite society, is also highlighted in parts of the Cockaigne texts, which

FIGURE 73

Devilish personification of Gluttony. Detail from Pieter Bruegel the

Elder's *Dulle Griet,* 1562.

Source: Antwerp, Museum Mayer van den Bergh.

correspond inversely to the detailed prescriptions of etiquette in the confession manuals. In both Middle Dutch versions a great deal of fuss is made about the tables standing at the ready day and night in all the streets of Cockaigne, laden with bread, wine, meat, and fish. These few lines conclude with the observation that one can "eat and drink the livelong day"—rather obvious, it would seem, and therefore a superfluous comment, to my way of thinking. In version B this attraction is expanded to include meat pies and eels raining down from the skies, as well as self-roasting geese and other forms of self-cooking meat.

[379]

A late-medieval audience would inevitably interpret such amenities as particularized warnings against the cardinal sin of gluttony. In other words, this amenity in the topsy-turvy world of Cockaigne has been fine-tuned to represent the exact opposite of what is desirable in the real world.

The didactic manuals that cataloged virtues and vices preached that a layperson should not eat more than twice a day and then only at set times. This is how things generally were in practice. The first meal of the day was taken at the end of the morning, between eleven and twelve o'clock, the second at the end of the working day. Breakfast in the modern sense was not customary. Eating more than twice a day, or eating at other than these set times, was considered a sin, and according to Jan van Boendale this made one a beast, the usual term for those lacking in Christian reason. On the other hand, eating only once a day was a sign of self-abnegation, and this was deserving of the highest respect:

> He who sets his mind, they say,
> On having but one meal a day,
> Leads the life of a true saint;
> And he who, though with less restraint,
> Eats twice a day, at noon and dusk,
> He surely lives like most of us;
> And he who eats three times at least,
> Can be no better than a beast.

The hero Renout van Montalbaen of the knightly poem of the same name can therefore atone for his sins by eating only one frugal meal a day while working as a laborer building a church:

> Each day he ate at a fixed time
> Barley bread and that was all;
> Spring water he drank, as I recall.

Bread and water, "at a fixed time." This discipline is also laid down in the *Boec van het kerstene leven* (Book of Christian living), which distinguished between five kinds of gluttony. The first type mentioned consisted in eating at inappropriate times: "The first, whenever one eats or drinks before the appointed time."

Exotic peoples could, of course, be presented as a contrastive element in this respect. Some reports of the land of Prester John tell of people eating once a day—ordinary people, that is, and not just the clergy. In the land of Tartary, only princes ate once a day, making the ability to exercise restraint a characteristic of the elite. The marginal cultures in remote areas of the world, however, provided contrasts that could be variously judged as either favorable or unfavorable.

Mandeville records the negative example of the country of the Great Khan, where the people had no table manners at all.

They eat dogs and lions, mares and foals, mice and rats, and other beasts both great and small, excepting pigs and other animals forbidden in the Old Law. And they eat every bit of the animals except the dung. . . . And when they have eaten, they wipe their hands disgustingly on their clothes; for they use neither tablecloths nor napkins except in lords' houses. . . . They eat only once a day, and then very little. A man of this country eats more in one day than two of them do in three. And if a messenger comes from a foreign land to the Emperor, he will have food only once a day, and then very little.

Respectable people, according to Mandeville, are meant to eat twice a day, but what seems to anger him even more is these peoples' refusal to display courtly behavior to guests from the Christian world.

The offensive that had been launched against unlimited and continual eating, though, was unaffected by comments such as Mandeville's that pointed out the uncourtly and meager nature of some foreign eating habits. Evidence shows that the campaign against excessive eating was gaining ground, and this fact makes Cockaigne's constant food supply seem like a polemic challenge, a warning issued in the language of the upside-down world. It is tempting to think that this added value came about as a result of the tale's being set down in writing. An even more likely possibility is that each scribe made a personal choice only at the moment of recording the Cockaigne material, at which time the necessity arose to explicate some of its messages, all of which tied in with the development of middle-class morality.

It is, moreover, not impossible that the ironical warnings against eating more than the usual number of meals at other than the usual times were already part of a certain literary tradition. Evidence for this is found in a passage in a piece of Anglo-Norman monastic satire dating from around 1300 that displays a certain similarity to the Middle English *Land of Cokaygne*. This satire features an abbot who urges the monks "to eat well and copiously three or more times a day."

Prose text G on Luilekkerland lacks this detail, though it gives ample treatment to the problem of gluttony, even more so than the two rhyming texts on Cockaigne. Moreover, text G contains even more items belonging to the repertoire of urban culture, such as humorous concerns about decorum and stimuli to the competitive spirit. In Luilekkerland, of course, these themes are turned upside-down for inclusion in the list of attractions. Competition and rivalry are praiseworthy phenomena in an urban society, especially that of Antwerp in the sixteenth century, as this city was rapidly acquiring the characteristics of an international center of trade and commerce. Praising the competitive spirit was in keeping with the fight against acedia, or sloth, and the development of a more positive attitude toward work in general. Text G's praise for these developments, however, does not go beyond a sly dig and a couple of feeble jokes aimed at athletic under-achievers.

On the other hand, a much greater accent is placed on polite behavior, propriety, and respectability, for those who get ahead in Luilekkerland are those who excel in the opposite of the above-mentioned virtues. Breaking wind always earns one a certain amount of money, but a huge fart is worth considerably more, as is belching loudly three times in a row. Bankrupt gamblers and other debtors are treated in the most amiable way imaginable. Drinking is also a well-paid activity, but getting drunk pays much more. Mockers and liars also earn good money: the bigger the lie, the better the pay. The Dutch text even adds a special category not found in Hans Sachs's text, the example on which it was based: in the Middle Dutch version whores are also held in especially high esteem.

Furthermore, wisdom and common sense are despised and scorned, whereas coarse and foolish people—unable or unwilling to learn anything—are highly respected. The worst person of all—the biggest, laziest greedy-guts who is, moreover, the most outrageous liar and cheat imaginable—is proclaimed king. The other rungs in the social ladder are determined by one's degree of coarseness and ability to drink to excess.

Text G gives precise indications of the qualities necessary for inclusion in this hall of fame of uncultivated louts. Anyone wishing to forsake all respectability, good manners, and wisdom should depart at once for Luilekkerland. There such clodhoppers could learn how *not* to behave in a society that was beginning more and more to attach importance to modes of behavior designed to distinguish one from the masses. This civilizing movement also figured in cultural life, where attempts were being made to elevate bourgeois ideals by presenting contrasting caricatures of boorish peasants.

The inhabitants of Luilekkerland may also take a place in this parade of antimodels, though a bit on the late side, considering that this text did not appear in print until 1600. By then the battle of the urban elite had been fought and won, leading to the definite suppression of popular culture. The outcome of this battle was doubtless a foregone conclusion already in the year 1546, and text G is therefore more likely to be but a nostalgic recollection of the militant weapon the upside-down world once was. The Luilekkerland text largely treats a matter that is no longer of current interest. What remains are increasingly feeble jokes, which require some effort to translate into the stinging provocations of yesteryear.

37

Lessons in Pragmatism

IN THE SIXTH CENTURY Boethius described a golden age of the greatest soberness. According to the Middle Dutch translation made around a thousand years later, in 1485, hunger at that time was stilled with fruit and thirst quenched with spring water. Trade was unknown, for the earth offered more than enough for survival. The discovery of gold and precious stones, however, meant the birth of greed, and the world had been burdened with sin ever since.

These lines by Boethius were elaborately discussed by the translator, who compared the ideal situation obtaining during the golden age with the boundless greed of his own day. People were now eating and drinking much more than the body required and doing so whenever they felt like it. Moreover, they displayed a contemptible craving for costly and exotic foods. This outburst of indignation was followed by a long treatment of gluttony, the mother of all evil, whose favorite children were sloth and idleness.

Together with quotations from a selection of authorities, this scholarly commentary must have made a big impression, owing as well to its formidable volume. It included the famous quotation from the Epistle of Paul to the Romans: "For they that are such serve not our Lord Jesus Christ, but their own belly." The author then deals at length with the earth's capacity for spontaneous regeneration, which makes human labor unnecessary in ensuring a supply of food: "In those days the people had no knowledge of sowing and reaping; they knew no other fruit than the fruits of the earth, and they had never heard of the plow, rake, or other tools." He closed by expressing the hope that the golden age would flourish again in this era dominated by extreme gluttony, which people would have to suppress if they were ever again to please God. Greed was, after all, the mother of all sins. In this commentary, gluttony (*gula*) and greed (*avaritia*) mingle unobtrusively. Together they represent the greatest threat to the well-being of humankind.

This commentary, however, divulges even more. The readiness with which the opportunity was seized to teach and moralize in a scientifically sound way in the vernacular may be inferred from a strange turn of phrase with which the commentator refers to Boethius's source text. This text maintains that the people living in the golden age were vegetarians, a point of view shared by other writers as well. The writer of this commentary, however, does not accept this standpoint lock, stock, and barrel. Besides eating fruit, the commentator maintained, those people also caught wild animals for the dual purpose of eating the meat and using the hides as clothing.

This requires an explanation. The author had already set the tone by voicing his doubts about the commonly held notion that eating meat was a stimulant to sin. This had been asserted by none other than Bernard of Clairvaux in his commentary on the Song of Songs (quoted by the author of this commentary on Boethius), though the great churchman had been mistaken in this. The point, said the translator and commentator, was not the nature of the food but the quantities in which it was consumed, and he substantiated this opinion with many references to well-known stories from the Bible: Adam ate no meat but only fruit from the tree of the knowledge of good and evil; Esau did not bargain away his birthright for meat but for a plate of lentils. Such examples may also be taken from the trials and tribulations of Jonathan, Elijah, and Abraham. The moral of the story is therefore that it would be better to eat a modest amount of meat than to gorge on vegetables and gruel.

Why did the commentator take this provocative stand? His whole work forms one of the earliest examples of a scholarly treatment of ethics in the vernacular that challenges, continually and explicitly, such authorities of the Latin world of scholarship as Bernard of Clairvaux. This author was a pragmatist, a down-to-earth person who hoped to prevent those of his own time and milieu from sinking further into the morass of gluttony and greed. He knew there was no point in trying to resurrect the vegetarianism of the golden age, which is why he tried to remedy things by warmly recommending moderation, the key to earthly salvation that had been tried and tested by courtly culture and the rules of etiquette of the urban bourgeoisie. It was all right to go on eating meat, but only in the proper amount and at the proper time, with due regard for the days of fasting laid down by the church. Our forefathers in the golden age had been guided by these principles, and they had never been judged to be wrong. At least not according to this commentator, and he was probably the first to say so.

In a middle-class milieu Cockaigne seems to function well as a didactic treatise. It was generally thought that urban society was the cause of many evils, including greed, usury, laziness, and gluttony. Indeed, it seemed as though the city had created for its inhabitants a Cockaigne where one could wallow in abundance. In *Der leken spieghel* (The layman's handbook) Jan van Boendale has a young nobleman who is criticizing the son of middle-class parents plainly state that city dwellers in fact practice the things that Cockaigne promises:

> Eating, drinking, too much sleeping,
> Waiting in the hope of reaping
> Profits large, vast rates of interest,
> Townsfolk like these things the best.
> Preemption, extortion, and usury
> And myriad forms of skulduggery,
> Burghers jump at every chance.

This corresponds closely to the Cockaigne texts: the theme of getting rich while you sleep, for example—stressed in version B in particular—with which Boendale begins the outburst quoted above. The Luilekkerland text also displays similarities to the more straightforward instructions issued by the moralists. At the same time, text G exudes the urban odor of corrupt morals, which pervert pleasure by turning it into a source of income.

A late-medieval audience was schooled, above all, in the art of unmasking evil with the aid of opposites and contrasts. These were supplied by the Bible, taught by Augustine, propagated by literature, and confirmed in urban festive rituals. The upside-down world and social criticism belonged together, and a long tradition with antique, biblical, and Germanic roots testified to this. During the course of the sixteenth century, when the world was starting to disintegrate even further owing to differing notions of social order, the principle of the topsy-turvy world began to lose ground, eventually being relegated to the realm of inexpensive prints sold by hawkers to rustic householders. The latter became further and further removed from the urban hotbeds of social change, and it

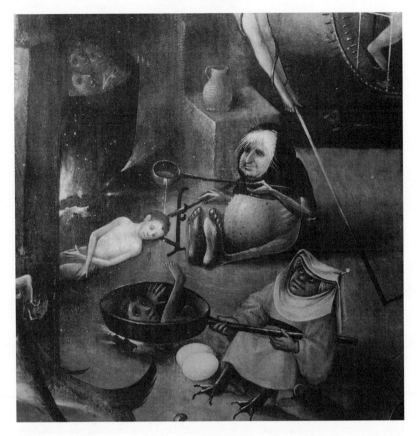

FIGURE 74

Hell is also a topsy-turvy world, where being eaten is one of the special punishments inflicted on gluttons. Detail from Hieronymus Bosch's triptych

The Last Judgment.

Source: Vienna, Akademie der bildenden Künste.

is no coincidence that Luilekkerland flourishes in this day and age exclusively in the children's nursery.

It seems natural to connect the explication of the message of texts B and G with the erosion—perhaps better described as the gradual extinction—of this previously widespread cultural principle. This need to supply moralizing explanations would merge at the end of the Middle Ages with a more general tendency to supply worldly material with a moral or at least to incorporate into it some sort of spiritual element. This nonetheless seems not to have been the most important reason for underscoring the things that listeners and readers were not allowed to miss. Even in the mid-sixteenth century the element of social criticism contained in these fictitious dream-worlds must have been obvious enough, at least when they were transmitted through recitation or performance.

It is more likely, then, that the act of recording them led to the moral of these stories being stressed in such a way, especially in light of the fact that a lay public was probably not accustomed to taking in such texts individually and in isolation. Although reading in private cannot be said to have caught on in the sixteenth century—a lot of evidence shows that people continued for a long time to read fiction in the vernacular aloud to one another—printers understandably felt compelled to lend a helping hand in promoting the new habit of reading silently to oneself. This also explains the need to explicate a moral couched in irony, the meaning of which might otherwise remain hidden for a lonely reader lacking the support of professional entertainers, reciters, or fellow listeners. This, then, is the pedigree of this type of bastard text, formerly intended for oral completion and explication, whose new trappings were due not so much to its new surroundings as to its exposure to a new and different method of communication.

Just like the golden age described by Boethius, Cockaigne and Luilekker-land offered an escape route to better worlds. These dreamlands, however, represented the very situation the Boethius commentator denounced as the harsh reality of the late Middle Ages. Via their images of a topsy-turvy world, Cockaigne and Luilekkerland drew a satirical picture of excessive consumption and a total lack of productivity that no longer had a place in the modern world. Both types of behavior appear to have been under fire in an inchoate urban society that depended for its very existence on strict adherence to the precepts of moderation and the work ethic. The compensatory dream of the olden days, still present in unabridged form in the Cockaigne material, was now used as a didactic method, especially valuable in educating the children of the rich and other good-for-nothings.

Part 8

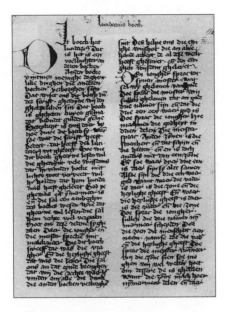

Dreaming of Cockaigne:
The End

38

The Name Cockaigne

ATTEMPTS TO DISCOVER the derivation of the name of Cockaigne have not been lacking, though no satisfactory answer has yet been found to explain the origins of the French-sounding word Cocagne. There is, however, much profit to be gained from examining the muddle of proposed explanations, for many of the solutions put forward undoubtedly reveal what contemporaries experienced upon hearing the name Cocagne. The fact is that the word conjured up—in the various languages in which it occurred—a wealth of associations with the attractions and lessons that Cockaigne had on offer. This perhaps explains the highly exportable nature of the term, which found its way not only into such Romance languages as French, Spanish, and Italian but also into Germanic languages such as Dutch and English.

Somewhere, sometime, the name Cocagne was first used as a suitable epithet for a dreamland inundated with delicious food and immersed in everlasting idleness. As was customary in the Middle Ages, the spelling of this mock toponym varied greatly from language to language; even within the same language one repeatedly finds variant spellings, owing to the lack of spelling norms, even in the case of toponyms. Moreover, names transmitted orally were especially susceptible to variation, and it is well known that Cockaigne traveled around for a long time in this manner.

It is therefore all the more striking how consistent the spelling is in Middle Dutch version L. The same spelling (Cockaengen) occurs in the heading and in lines 13 and 58, which means that for the copyist of the manuscript this term was fairly well established and matter of course. Is this also the reason why he refrained from offering explanations of the message as the recorder of text B did? That he (or she) was capable of taking a more lackadaisical attitude toward names was shown earlier in the corrupt spelling of Beliren for Bouillon in the pilgrims' guide contained in the same manuscript. This was meant to refer to the famous crusader Godfrey of Bouillon, who was buried in Jerusalem and subsequently admitted to the medieval heroes' hall of fame.

Cocagne, however, was no problem for the copyist of text L, though the compiler of the Brussels manuscript had more difficulty with it. He spelled it Cockanyngen in line 11, an unusual form, especially in view of its international reputation. Apparently he found it necessary to twist the word *Cocagne* into what was for him a more acceptable toponym with the more usual suffix *-ingen*. This proves to have been so important to him that he even spoiled—or failed to use—an obvious rhyme in his text. The natural partner would have been Hyspanien, easily rhyming with Cockaenien. It would also have been possible to use the alternate form of Hyspanien—Spaengen, as in text L—rhyming with Cockaengen. Apparently, however, the copyist succumbed to the overpowering urge to make something logical out of it, finally arriving at the toponymic fantasy Cockanyngen. Here as elsewhere, honoring the oral structure of the rhyming couplets proves to have been low down on this copyist's list of literary priorities.

Another indication that this name said little to him emerges from his obvious avoidance of the name Cocagne in places in his text where one would expect it and where text L does in fact use it. He chose Latin for the heading, for example, in keeping with the studentlike feel of the whole manuscript. In doing so, however, he did not translate Cockaigne into the form used in Latin satire—Cucania or Cucaniensis—but sought refuge in a descriptive title: narratio de terra suaviter viventium (a tale about the land of pleasant living). In line 66 he again avoids mentioning the name Cockaigne, whereas the parallel passage in text L (line 58) does mention it: "Oh, that country is marvelous," as opposed to "That Land of Cockaigne is marvelous!"

The word *Cocagne* did not appeal much to the copyist of version B. In the Low Countries in his day—around 1500—the term seemed slowly to be making way for Schlaraffenland, which was invading the region from the east. In the area of Venlo—assuming this is where the manuscript originated—this influence must have been noticeable early on. Yet he neither opted for a related equivalent nor chose to adopt the new term. Only in 1546 did the adapter of Hans Sachs's text (G) find a suitable translation with his Luyeleckerlant, literally, "lazy-luscious-land."

Except for three times in text L and once in text B, the word Cocagne is not to be found in any Middle Dutch writings. This confirms the typically oral nature of the material, as well as the isolated position that these two versions—incidental recordings of essentially oral material—continue to occupy. Even in written form the Cockaigne material exerted little influence on literary traditions in a written culture. In the oral tradition, however, the name remained current for a long time. Long after the Middle Ages and even now and again in modern times, Kokanje (or Kokinje) occurs in typical folk narratives and portrayals.

The name of Luilekkerland, on the other hand, has been a child of the written tradition since its conception. This designation, transmitted by the printing press, ended up in a tradition of reading (and reading aloud) that has stood its ground up to our time, even in new applications; it now serves, for example, both as the name of a restaurant and a contemptuous label for the initiative-killing Dutch welfare state.

The word *Cockaengen* is best explained as a Middle Dutch toponymical translation of the French place name Cocagne. This name occurs repeatedly in several Old French fabliaux known from manuscripts dating from the end of the thirteenth and the beginning of the fourteenth century, though the name must have taken root before this time as the designation for a dreamland. In the early-thirteenth-century romance *Aymeri de Narbonne* occurs the saying "cuidier avoir cocaigne trovee," which boils down to "believing in the possibility of having all your dreams come true." This sequel to the *Song of Roland* belongs to the genre of courtly literature, from which it may be inferred that Cockaigne must have been known for quite some time in that milieu as well, since sayings and proverbs do not appear out of the blue. Furthermore, this expression is also used in other romances of chivalry dating from the same period. In the thirteenth-century romance *Joufroi de Poitiers* the references to this dreamland certainly seem to have a self-evident character. The protagonist of this humorous romance presents himself as the duke of Cocagne and also uses this name as a battle cry in a tournament.

It seems quite likely that the origins of this name lie in the sounds and associations produced by French or Provençal words having to do with cooking and a special kind of honey cake (*cocanha*). Echoes of such a provenance can also be heard in the other languages in which one or more Cockaigne texts were recorded. It has even been suggested that the French word *Cocagne* was derived from the Low German word *kokenje*, a word meaning honey cake that lives on in the Dutch word *kokinje* (sugarplum). Such a source of inspiration is rather far-fetched, though, as Provençal dialect itself already provides a ready link.

At any rate, the most appealing possibility is to assume that the name Cockaigne is derived from a word designating a delicious food. The greatest excitement in Cockaigne stems from the spectacular superabundance of food that offers itself up for consumption in every imaginable form. Naming the land after culinary copiousness and alimentary acrobatics would be in keeping with this priority. Cockaigne must therefore refer first and foremost to the land of honey cakes, a kingdom where cooks and their cuisine rule the roost.

The assumption of such origins does not exclude the possibility that in the process of being recorded a number of other associations were created that did at least as much—if not more—to advance the name's fame. The most important association derives from a tradition of literary games played by an intellectual elite that zealously wielded the weapon of satire both inside and outside the church.

A short song—dating from around 1164—from the *Carmina Burana*, which begins with the line "Ego sum abbas Cucaniensis," features an abbot who spends his time exhorting his brothers to drink and gamble, thereby bringing them to rack and ruin:

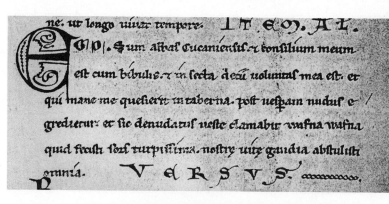

FIGURE 75
The short song of the "Abbas Cucaniensis."
Source: Reproduced from *Carmina Burana*, facsimile ed., 2 vols., ed. B. Bischoff
(Munich, 1967), fol. 97 verso.

I am the abbot of Cockaigne,
and I take counsel with my drinking companions,
and my persuasion is that of the gambling fraternity,
and if anyone consults me in the tavern at matins,
come vespers, he'll have lost the shirt off his back:
and being thus fleeced of his raiment will cry—
"Save me! Save me!
What have you done, god-forsaken dice?
Now you've made me sacrifice
all I knew of paradise!"

This is a popular theme, well known not only from this collection of songs
but also from satirical Latin poetry written during the High Middle Ages
that gave rise to an extraordinarily forceful and varied train of sequels in the
vernacular. The key apparently lies in the word *Cucaniensis*, undoubtedly a
humorous corruption of well-known and apposite names and concepts, for
this is one of the standard ingredients of such satirical poetry, written especially for celebrations marking the church's Feast of Fools.

For men of letters the association with Cluny must have been practically unavoidable, for it was there that the most famous abbot of all
Christendom resided, and what could be more fun than accusing him of
gross negligence and overindulgence? There was exactly enough difference
between *Cucaniensis* and *Cluniacensis* to produce the desired humorous effect,
and this was achieved by steering the names to be mocked in the direction of
a negative association. The negative image here is the cuckoo (*cuculus*), an
exceedingly unpleasant bird that tries to take advantage of everyone, chiefly
by moving in with other birds and then egoistically singing its own name.
This was a perfect image to throw in the clergy's face, all compactly
expressed in that one word: *Cucaniensis*.

This verse about the abbot of Cockaigne does not stand alone. Two
other texts dating from the thirteenth century, from the same sphere as the
Latin satires, tell of an abbatissa Cacunacensis and a Gugganiensis gulescopus. Humorous bastardizations and purposeful ambiguities—the gulescopus is a subtle combination of *gulosus* and *episcopus*, in other words, a gluttonous bishop—play around with an apparently familiar expression for the
personification of the most extreme hedonism as the spiritual leader of

Cucania. This fits in with a derisory expression in Spanish, recorded around 1340 by the priest Juan Ruiz, who speaks of an "escolar goloso compañero de Cucana," a lecherous (or greedy) fellow student from Cucana.

Was the Middle English *Land of Cokaygne* derived from the Vulgar Latin? Linguistically there seems to be no objection to this derivation, which would then have taken place via Old French. From the angle of cultural history this provides further confirmation that the oral Cockaigne material was generally given a moralizing slant when put in writing, for if one gives such a name to a dreamland, that land instantly turns into a platform for what is in fact undesirable behavior, traditionally linked through satire and critique to the conduct of the clergy. Two pieces of supporting evidence now spring to mind. The Middle English text of around 1300, which has no clear connection with the French fabliaux or the Dutch rhyming versions, is rather curiously set on an island with a monastery complete with an abbot, gluttonous monks, and biddable nuns. Surely this is the result of the influence exerted by medieval Latin satires on the clergy.

The second piece of supporting evidence is derived from the connection established in the Dutch material between Cockaigne and the coming of the millennium in the Book of Revelation. In was in the thirteenth century that Joachim of Fiore developed this idea in his famous and influential vision of the end of time. According to Joachim, the thousand-year reign of prosperity and justice would begin at the latest in 1260. It would be the dominion of the Holy Ghost, and all men living in this blessed era would be called monks. Preceding this would be a period of chaos and sin during which the devil would be especially active. The rather aggressive way in which Joachim's ideas were disseminated—declaring the dawn of a new age of salvation in which monks would live in luxury who were now behaving like beasts—may have evoked new associations with the name of Cockaigne, derived from these anticlerical satires emanating from the clerical sphere itself.

The Latin song of the depraved abbot is thought to stem from the second half of the twelfth century. Rather than being the product of an oral culture, it seems to be part of its own literary tradition. Written sources confirm that shortly after this the name Cocagne was circulating in a common saying in the French vernacular, so the name was not necessarily coined in Latin. It is more likely that in such a semischolarly milieu a new application had been discovered, which in turn fed a literary tradition from which the Middle English *Land of Cokaygne* seems to have profited as well.

Perhaps this traditional name is much older, having started already in the earliest realizations of the Cockaigne material in Greek comedy dating from the fifth century B.C. The possibility cannot be ruled out that in the Middle Ages students and learned monks were familiar with Latin translations and adaptations of these plays. It is therefore conceivable that literary elaboration by means of a play on words—a favorite pastime in such circles—directed at an expression like Cockaigne that was already current in the vernacular was further stimulated by Aristophanes' *Birds*, written in 414 B.C. This comedy features a plan for an immense city of birds suspended between heaven and earth that will give the birds dominion over man and the gods. This place is called Nephelokokkygia, the original Cloud-cuckoo-land.

These sounds, combined with the references to a dream city and the exploitative behavior of the cuckoo, could have provided an additional impulse to transform the vernacular Cocagne into the Cucania that led to the abbas Cucaniensis. There is perhaps an even more direct connection to the Middle English *Land of Cokaygne*, whose monastic satire links it more strongly to the tradition of the *Carmina Burana*. In the Middle English text Cokaygne is an island inhabited by a community of monks. These monks have a habit of taking off and flying, a pastime the younger monks find particularly exciting. This recalls not only Aristophanes' birds but also a more general tradition found in the dreamworlds of antiquity, which often feature people who fly. The best evidence for the firm anchoring of such submotifs in texts of this kind is provided by Lucian's *True History*, which also parodies this motif.

The abbas Cucaniensis text and the Middle English *Land of Cokaygne* both point to the existence of an intellectual and literary tradition of punning on the term *Cocagne*, which may well have roots in Hellenistic culture. The name itself, however, derives from a traditional recipe based on cake, cooks, and cuisine.

The strong influence of representations of the Muslim paradise on the Cockaigne material and its realizations has already been discussed. This influence could also hold true for the name. Assuming that the suffix *-agne* is used in French to indicate a country (as in Espagne and Allemagne), then Cocagne could be understood to mean "the land of the coc," or rooster. A rooster is named as the guardian of the Muslim paradise in the *Liber scalae* (Book of the ladder), a translation from the Arabic that includes a description of Mohammed's journey to paradise. Starting in the thirteenth century or slightly earlier, this work became known in Europe, and a French version dates from 1264. In this account the prophet Mohammed sees a rooster of enormous dimensions. The rooster, an angel of God and gatekeeper of paradise, is described in some detail, which means that the association of this paradise with a rooster could have been known throughout Europe from the thirteenth century onward.

The above explanation, however, deals with a literary tradition of the elite that could have been responsible for coining the name of Cocagne only after 1264. It is in fact highly unlikely that Cockaigne originated in this way. The French vernacular tradition, the stock expressions in the Latin satires, and the place name Kokkengen in the diocese of Utrecht (discussed below) all point to the likelihood of Cocagne having been known for a long time by that name. Moreover, a provenance in the narrative tradition, based on the cornerstone of the dream—food—is much to be preferred. Here as well, the possibility exists that associations with the rooster gatekeeper of the Muslim paradise developed at a later time, certainly in view of the similarities discussed earlier between this extremely worldly paradise and Cockaigne. The name must have existed already at that time, and—who knows—the *coc* therein may have automatically led many a Frenchman to the world of Islam.

What should we think of the place name Kokkengen in the province of Utrecht? No one doubts that this name is a modernized version of Cocagne or Cockaengen. It has been asserted that it refers to colonists settling in the peat bogs to the west of the city of Utrecht who attempted to establish a utopia of which only this toponymic trace remains.

It seems more logical to seek an explanation for the name Kokkengen in a humorous trend taken up by the Utrecht clergy, who bestowed a number of colonies of peat cutters to the west of the river Vecht with the names of great European kingdoms or mock kingdoms. The humorous element consisted in the grotesque contrast between these kingdoms and the bleak and windy spots named after them, mostly a handful of farms, sheds, and huts that barely managed to rise up out of the mud on which they were built. At any rate, it is remarkable that places with such names as Demmerik (Denmark), Spengen (Spain), Portengen (Bretagne), Kamerik, and Kortrijk (literally meaning "short of funds")—the latter two places being Cambrai and Courtrai in present-day Belgium—are all located so close to one another.

The name Kokkengen belongs to this family, referring to the dreamland with a French name. The village dates from the twelfth century, though the name Cockenge (also written as Cockange and Kockange) was first recorded in 1326. The other fantasy names were first recorded in the twelfth and early thirteenth century. Land reclamation to the west of the river Vecht and the river Aa had already begun in the tenth and eleventh centuries, and the area was fully cultivated around 1200.

The interpretation of Kokkengen as a mock name is supported by the existence of a place to the southwest of the above-mentioned region called Bonrepas, "good meal"—situated above a place with the equally revealing name of Schoonhoven, or "beautiful gardens." Recorded as early as 1253, Bonrepas straightforwardly states the principal pastime in Cockaigne. The present-day town of Gieltjesdorp—which used to be called Gheliken dorpen, meaning "equal villages"—situated near Kokkengen also fits into this scheme of things. This name, recorded for the first time in 1297, could be a playful reference to the egalitarian ideals prevailing in Cockaigne and so many other medieval dreamworlds. This idea must have occurred in any case to the people living in the vicinity of Kokkengen.

It has also been suggested that these place names in the province of Utrecht—assuming they are in fact toponyms—could actually indicate the country of origin of the foreign workers who were recruited by the count of Holland and the bishop of Utrecht to colonize the area. Moreover, Demmerik (Denmark) supposedly recalls the latter years of the Vikings, when their days as brutal robbers were over and they were more likely to assume the role of emigrants. This idea is not inconceivable, but judging by Cockenge and possibly also Gheliken dorpen, these imaginative names had humorous connotations even in those days.

It is also possible that there is a direct link between recorded Cockaigne material and certain place names in the Utrecht peat district. Spengen is close to Kokkengen and was previously a hamlet within that municipality. These names correspond to the fairly set rhyme Cockaengen / Spaengen in text L, which also occurs in another spelling in text B, even though the latter version displays a reluctance to use this name. It is very tempting to assume that the Utrecht clergy, consciously and somewhat humorously, bestowed this barren land and its humble dwellings with place names eminently capable of stimulating the desire for a better life. For one thing is certain: realizations of the Cockaigne material were widely known by this time.

This humor perhaps had an inspirational effect on Kokkengen. The praises of this little place were sung until well into the eighteenth century, as emerges from the following description dating from 1759: "It is very cheerful and amusing in itself, no less so than the surrounding countryside, owing to lots of healthy air and the variety of fruit with which the inhabitants of this Village and Seigniory are blessed." The text goes on to say that this paradise also has several noble industries by means of which the rural inhabitants earn a good living. Among these are a brewery with delicious, healthy beer "and two breweries making honey-sweet mead, which was invented here and which is very much in demand in many places." Indeed, Kokkengen is a honey-sweet oasis in the bare plains of the Utrecht polder landscape.

All these applications of Cockaigne, not only as a dreamland but also as a shelter for good-for-nothings and a school for youths gone astray, are confirmed by new associations with the name. Its moralizing function in Middle Dutch is strengthened by echoes of *kockinen* (*coquin* in French), a much-used term of abuse for fools, rogues, and rascals, who could be considered the permanent residents of Cockaigne, especially when one hears the characterization of them given by Jan van Boendale: "Today one finds many rogues, who neither work nor take pains to learn but are simply idle."

This also holds true for the *cockaert* in the farce *Drie daghe here* (Lord and master for three days), a term of abuse for a fool and a henpecked husband. It is indeed striking how many words in Middle Dutch start with *coc-* and invariably denote fools, drifters, and swindlers, as well as rambunctious revelers. In addition to *kockijn* and *cockaert*, *coc* has also been recorded as a term of abuse for a man, *cocxskin* as a synonym of coquette or flirtatious girl, *cockelueris* and *cockuwe* meaning a twit and probably a cuckold, *cocketoys* indicating an evil spirit, *cockuut* to mean cuckoo and consequently also exploiter, *cokelaer* (stemming from *joculator*) for clown as well as crook, *cokerellen* for merrymaking, especially at Carnival time, and *cocorul* for doggerel.

It has already been pointed out that Cockaigne seems to live on as a name in a folk ritual recorded from the late Middle Ages onward in France, Italy, and Spain. Delicious food was hung at the top of a mast or in a tree-top, and the sport consisted in trying to get it down. The pole, however, had been rubbed with tallow or soap and was therefore slippery. This *mât de Cocagne* is clearly recognizable in the masthead in Hieronymus Bosch's painting *The Ship of Fools*.

As far as explanations of the name Cockaigne are concerned, the possibilities are neither easily linked nor readily ranged in opposition. New associations were continually at work here, conjured up by the enticing name of a dreamland where abundance and amply rewarded idleness were the order of the day. We are doing things backward if we view these new utilizations of the name as explanations of it. In particular, the broadening of its connotations resulting from Cockaigne's assumption of the role of moralist opens up new vistas as regards the interpretation of its name.

Nevertheless, somewhere, sometime, the name must have been uttered for the first time. The early occurrence of a French saying in which Cockaigne is called the land where all one's wishes are fulfilled leads to the assumption that the name was first uttered in Old French. This also means that the cornerstone of this dreamland was spontaneously turned into a toponym based on the greatest delicacies in the baked-goods sector. Remarkable indeed is the lightning career of this popular concept once it found its way from a primarily oral tradition into the Latin literature of the elite. Via the pun on Cluny and the cuckoo, Cockaigne in the form of Cucania appears henceforth to have taken on a life of its own in the written tradition of monastic satire, which in turn had repercussions on literature in the vernacular. Both traditions became so widespread and compelling that they could move the Utrecht clergy to baptize a swampy village in the peat bogs with the name Cockenge.

From the moment that Cockaigne first appeared in recorded form, satire and social criticism became inextricably linked to the wide range of comforts on offer as compensation for this wretched life. All these possibilities are implicit in the Old French and Middle Dutch versions of Cockaigne, while the material continued for a long time to invite new associations. Even after the Middle Ages, Cockaigne was put to such diverse uses as satirizing an idle life of abundance and stimulating the desire for a better world. This poses intriguing questions as to the origin of the distinguished family of Cockayne, recorded as early as the twelfth century in the English county of Derbyshire, and their reasons for assuming the name of this dreamland.

39
A Depreciated Cultural Asset

WHY MUST WE pay so much attention to what is at first glance such instantly recognizable and easily understood humor? Indeed, there's no need to: this seems to have been the answer given by Dutch literary historiographers from the very beginning. The Cockaigne and Luilekkerland texts were simply not allowed to compete for their attention, as witnessed by the interest shown in them, which—then as now—is practically negligible.

This neglect has been due only in part to these texts' supposed lack of aesthetic merit, a nineteenth-century notion that has retroactively caused much damage to medieval literary stockpiles, giving rise to a canon of its own invention. This literary-historical creative process, dominated by ideals of timeless beauty, does in fact bear most of the blame for the flat dismissal of what has often been regarded as awkward versifying and foolish banter focusing on humankind's basest impulses.

The sophisticated literary aesthetes of the nineteenth century, however, also had an eye for more popular forms, which the Middle Ages were thought to supply in abundance. Yet Cockaigne and Luilekkerland appear not to have met the requirements for inclusion in this genre either. Are these texts not folksy enough? They share this neglect with popular festival repertoire and in some cases with burlesques and fabliaux. Once upon a time, folksiness in literature was considered acceptable only in terms of an original purity of form and ideas, not unlike the notion of the noble savage that medieval man projected on the distant past and exotic peoples. Book learning was considered a corrupting influence; the language and modes of expression of anonymous unlettered folk were thought to be uncontaminated by the perverted preciosity of semiliterate authors who earned their living twisting beauty and truth, armed with the misleading and devilish art of rhetoric. Folk songs (especially Christmas carols) and ballads dating from the Middle Ages were thought to preserve a great deal of this presumed purity, which many people found echoed in the Middle Dutch language itself.

Our Cockaigne texts are not considered pure enough to be eligible for the literary qualification of "popular." Their language, form, and the tradition in which they were handed down to us appear to have been unacceptable. The folio bearing text L is missing a sizable piece from the upper-right-hand corner, and this obviously did not appeal to the romanticism informing the notions guiding popular aesthetics. The language of text B has a strong eastern Netherlandish flavor, which probably prevented it from looking sufficiently Dutch. Text G does not even enter into the picture, as prose did not count at all as far as popular culture in the Middle Ages was concerned.

The failure to be awarded folk culture's seal of approval, however, must chiefly be due to the texts' content, which probably gave the impression of being a light-hearted recommendation to satisfy one's most vulgar desires. In addition, the words of warning addressed to the young could do nothing to prevent unhealthy high spirits from ruling the roost, and in such a base way as to give a youthful public completely the wrong idea. Child's play, therefore, but child's play that had become so dangerous it was no longer suitable for children, who had meanwhile become familiar with the fairy tale of Luilekkerland, a watered-down fantasy that could scarcely serve as the vehicle for wise messages of an educational nature, answering more the need to satisfy the sweet tooth—now considered a charming attribute—of the dutiful offspring of upper-class families.

Cockaigne and Luilekkerland fall between two stools. For a long time—up to now, in fact—they were not considered socially acceptable enough for inclusion in the carefully marked out domains of traditional literary studies, historiography, and folklore. In the meantime, however, the barriers dividing these disciplines have fallen in the course of many cultural-historical studies, and an all-out search has begun for sources that can provide new insight into popular and collective mentalities of an anonymous nature. In this context, of course, so-called low literature may again take part, and its well-advertised ribaldries have become more of a recommendation than an obstacle, the new danger being that the caricatures of the upside-down world will now go unnoticed.

It is perhaps more important to understand that recorded texts such as both Middle Dutch versions of Cockaigne seem to be capable of providing insight into a written tradition in the making, a process that even in the fif-

FIGURE 76
Pieter Bruegel the Elder, *The Land of Cockaigne*, 1567.
Source: Munich, Alte Pinakothek.

teenth century had not nearly gained the upper hand from the oral tradition. Such texts as L and B stand out among the thousands of Cockaigne texts that never made it to paper or even aspired to do so. Their existence affords us a closer look at the process of oral text transmission—listening, improvising, changing, cutting out, adapting—that guided, supported, or frustrated the lives of so many.

Folklorists and art historians were the first to subject the Dutch Cockaigne and Luilekkerland material to systematic examination. A fascination for adages, proverbs, and sayings, as well as an interest in the field of genre painting of the early-modern period, seems to have come together in the work of Pieter Bruegel the Elder, whose painting *The Land of Cockaigne*, dating from 1567, put him at the cutting edge of sixteenth-century trends. This painting, based on an engraving by Pieter Balten, may be directly linked to the prose text of Luilekkerland dating from 1546. That text must have provided Bruegel with enough ideas for his portrayal of the theme, which underscores the proverbial motifs of idleness and gluttony, now pointedly imputed to representatives of the various social orders: a warrior, a peasant, a scholar, a merchant. (It is doubtful, however, that Bruegel's choice of this constellation was actually his way of taking a stand on the events leading up to the Dutch Revolt, an idea that has recently been put forward, not for the first time.)

During the course of the twentieth century, Cockaigne has been caught up in the greater interest shown for revolutionary utopias, in keeping with the ideological confrontations that were such a conspicuous part of the last century. One Marxist even spoke of Cockaigne as "a feudalistic, rural, folkloristic social utopia," while another saw the Middle English *Land of Cokaygne* as the expression of the deepest desires of the revolutionary masses. This interpretation completely ignores the text's ingenious jesting and monastic satire, as well as its parody of travelers' tales in general.

Appropriation of the Cockaigne material, which was given shape in the late Middle Ages and early-modern period, to serve modern interests such as those mentioned above completely distorts its original intentions and primary functions. As previously shown, these texts did not aim at reversing the existing social and political order, and it is just as far-fetched to assume the existence of contemporaries who thought they had found in these dreamlands a pretext for their revolutionary aims. Insofar as these texts offer compensation, their function is more like that of a safety valve, reducing social tension to an acceptable level. Within this framework, however, rebelliousness certainly manifests itself in the form of aggressive and highly imaginative hyperbole, which pits itself against the often intolerable scarcity and misery of everyday life by defying it with a superabundance so exaggerated as to be provoking.

To what extent the Dutch texts reveal the mentality of the masses is a question that has not been posed in this book, and this book has therefore made no attempt to answer it. The point of departure was the discovery of the functions and meanings these texts may have had during the transition from the Middle Ages to the early-modern era. How did they come about, which material was used, which techniques were employed in the process, were these most common among certain groups of people, and how did the material and its stylistic principles correspond to the body of thought one hoped to express by such means? Questions like these may also be asked of more widely recognized and esteemed texts of the past that enjoy a certain literary reputation. Such investigative instruments have only recently found acceptance in this field of study, however, and there has been scarcely any attempt to apply them to texts of the Cockaigne sort, which have for so long been found wanting and even offensive.

In any case, Cockaigne's humor seems at first glance to be of a kind requiring little commentary, as evidenced by its easy comprehensibility even after a lapse of five centuries. Why waste words on what must have been at the time no more than entertaining nonsense? Such thoughts are further stimulated by the fact of recognition, by jumping to the tempting conclusion that humor is timeless, a pitfall that even experienced scholars find difficult to avoid.

It seems natural to blame the lack of interest in Cockaigne and Luilekkerland on the relative meaninglessness of their supposed message and their traditional relegation to the sphere of light entertainment. The fact that in the Netherlands the whole concept of Luilekkerland ended up in the children's nursery surely proves that it is nothing but a naive image capable of fulfilling only the most primitive of children's dreams. This fact in itself is undeniable: Luilekkerland has indeed become children's literature, entertainment for toddlers in the form of picture books. It proves its current usefulness by acting as a name for Dutch pancake houses and for a factory that mass-produces pâté— pâté, of course, of the very finest quality.

The path to a younger readership was taken already in 1546, when prose text G began its career as a cautionary tale, addressing itself to young men in particular while at the same time increasing the attractions on offer for those with a sweet tooth. In any case, the designation *gesunkenes Kulturgut*—a depreciated cultural asset—is highly appropriate here. Even though "depreciated" seems like a rather negative way to describe this facet of mass culture, it cannot be denied that the Cockaigne material in its Luilekkerland guise has given rise to simpler and certainly more superficial versions that have severely limited the uses to which the image can now be put.

Other medieval texts share a similar fate, reduced to the status of cheap wares in severely watered-down form. The process of deterioration has continued in a certain sense through the making of contemporary musicals— *Camelot*, for example—and a variety of films like *Robin Hood*. The flip side of the coin—a cultural asset appreciating in value—is much less common, though it does occur, an example being the creative treatment of individual medieval texts for inclusion in the literature of the elite. One well-known example of this is Goethe's *Reineke Fuchs*, and an example of this occurring in another sphere is Carl Orff's setting of the *Carmina Burana*.

Cockaigne and Luilekkerland have continued to decline in importance. They became superfluous when their central concerns lost their topicality and urgency. Increased control of the food supply, a more accessible job market, and a universally accepted work ethic have caused a corresponding decrease in the fears and frustrations surrounding food and work, only to make way for new fears engendered by that same change in lifestyle. The undermined ritual designed to alleviate hunger and drudgery survived for centuries in much more superficial fantasies, however, one side effect being the rekindling of old resentments in people with good memories. It is no coincidence that Luilekkerland long continued to flourish in the countryside, where the collective memory of large-scale natural catastrophes of yesteryear was the strongest.

Moreover, the old Cockaigne has been tacitly put into practice in modern-day Western society, which is why there is no longer any need for an oral or written surrogate. Cockaigne may now be found in a colorful collection of vacation spots and supermarkets that supply a tailor-made Cockaigne to every customer, some of whom (in the Netherlands) do not hesitate to describe their favorite food or vacation spot whole-heartedly as a Luilekkerland, completely ignoring the didactical and satirical nature of the image in its original sphere of use. The recycling of texts and motifs says little or nothing about their earlier intentions and functions. At most it is proof that the material, whether or not in newly adapted form, is so supple that it is able to retain its attractiveness in new situations and milieus.

Humor, however, is never merely superficial. It is one of society's most important lubricants, making an important contribution to the smoothing over of current fears. Just like social conventions and existing frustrations, the nature and significance of the forms of humor employed at any given

Het af-vaaren van het vol en zoet geladen SCHIP

ỈINT REYN-UYT,

Zeylende met een altyd goede Wind naar de aangen.ame Contreije van

LUY-LEKKER-LAND.

Met een befchryvinge desjeive Lands.

Gedzuckt booz het tegenwoozdige Jaer.

FIGURE 77

Title page of an eighteenth-century collection of popular texts
that includes an adaptation of the *Luilekkerland* text of 1546.
Af-vaaren (ca. 1700).

time are changeable. In the late Middle Ages, for example, humor was used as an effective means of instructing the masses, alleviating fear, and dispelling life-threatening melancholy. Such conditions not only justified the frequent use of humor in texts and performances, they also determined the nature of the texts themselves.

Fears and frustrations in particular were combated with what by present standards must seem to be very coarse and violent joke making. As we are no longer capable of recognizing these distressing situations, let alone able to understand or share in them, it is easy for us to find such humor blunt and childish. This attitude is especially applicable to the endless stream of jokes about feces, sex, the devil, and hunger. The people of the Middle Ages must have been children, we think, if all they could do was display such childish behavior.

This viewpoint precludes the existence of any historical variability, leading to the tacit acceptance of current standards in judging what is beautiful, ugly, filthy, common, or immature. However, the use of humor in texts and presentations can be just as apt, penetrating, and effective as the presentation of abstruse ideas. It is therefore unreasonable to dismiss such humor out of hand as an outdated derivative of childish joking, especially as it was not removed from the culture of the elite until after the Middle Ages. In the short films made in the 1920s, Stan Laurel and Oliver Hardy quelled the fears of middle-class Americans, who dreaded the rise of a matriarchy, by having bullying battle-axes tyrannize their sheepish husbands. No moviegoer thought of himself as such a schlemiel, and even these motion-picture caricatures of hen-pecked husbands often succeeded in outwitting such overbearing matrons.

Finally, Cockaigne also ridicules—for those able to detect the irony—the very act of fantasizing about a dream place filled with sensual delights. Such fantasizing was recommended in all earnestness to adherents of the Devotio Moderna as a stimulating exercise designed to prepare oneself for the true life in the hereafter, and this recommendation was accompanied by warnings to beware of the devil, who sometimes deluded the senses of those performing such exercises, thereby leading to their undoing. Dreaming on earth of fulfillment and happiness was obviously asking for trouble, which meant that the exercises practiced by the Brethren of Common Life also had to demonstrate the superiority of the true Christian to the devil, to the same

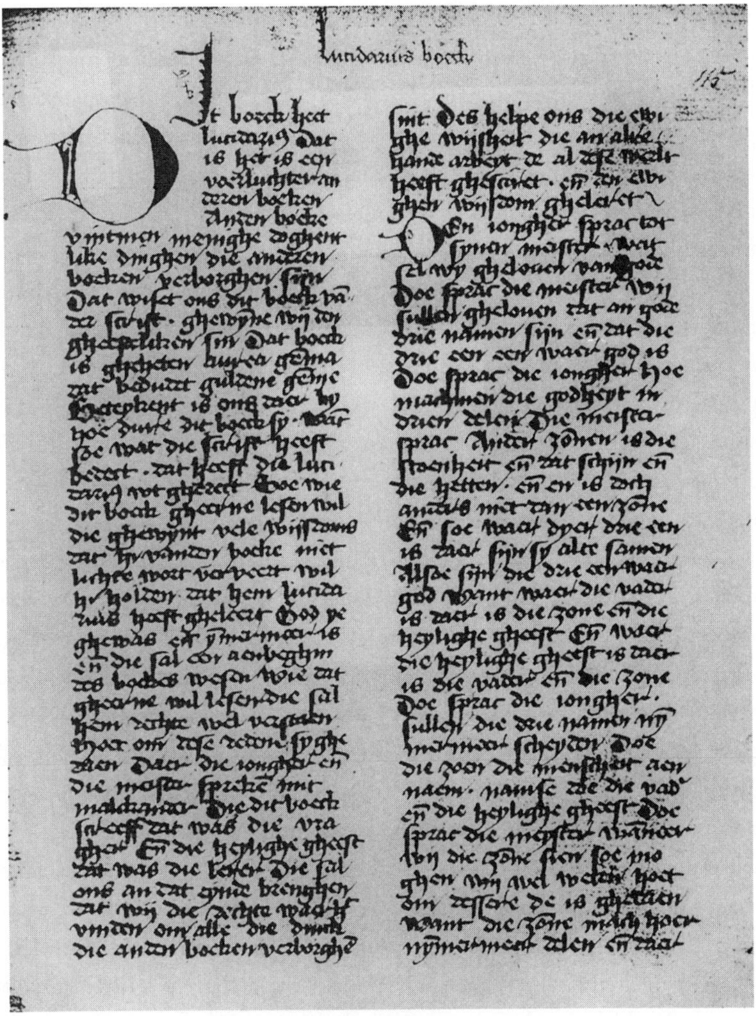

FIGURE 78

Beginning of the *Lucidarius boeck*.

Source: London, British Library, MS Add. 10286, fol. 115 recto.

extent that hermits attempted to demonstrate this by means of self-abnegation. An altarpiece dating from 1488, now in the municipal museum in Regensburg in Germany, gives expression to the uncertain path taken by people whose heads are filled with joyous fantasies of the hereafter. Portrayed in this altarpiece are things that should definitely not be on one's mind while praying, such as avarice in conducting trade, undue attachment to earthly possessions, eroticism, drinking, and physical beauty.

On the basis of all these functions and meanings, the two Middle Dutch Cockaigne texts are not at all out of place in the collections that contain them. Version B is completely at home in the midst of an endless potpourri of student mirth and mild seriousness, expressed in the form of songs, fairy tales, sayings, and other assorted texts. All explain the world and attempt to exercise control over it, straightforwardly or in a topsy-turvy manner, by whichever means was convenient at the time.

Version L only *seems* to be out of place, surrounded as it is by longer didactic texts for the laity, such as the *Sidrac* and the *Lucidarius boeck*. On closer inspection, however, the description given earlier of the contents of the entire manuscript—"world orientation"—proves tenable. The technique of the upside-down world presented in Cockaigne, as well as the mock doctor's prescription, serves just as much to elucidate the world and the road to salvation as the more directly didactic texts, such as the treatise on color symbolism and the satires on money and corruption. Moreover, the mock texts wield the weapon of humor against the feared illness of melancholy, which the devil was always quick to use as a means of exterminating those whom he considered too well versed in spiritual matters. Finally, the tenor of the whole manuscript was well served by including a short pilgrims' guide to Jerusalem, which supplies the theoretical objectives of the manuscript with the ultimate in practical directives.

40

From Countryside to Town

To what extent are the Cockaigne texts and the prose text on Luilekker-land actually the product of simple folk and their traditions? The concepts of folksy, common, and popular have all been used in conjunction with these texts to designate the anonymous masses. These masses may also include members of the clergy, lay brothers and sisters, and members of the minor orders, none of whom has a name outside his or her immediate sur-roundings. Above all, however, the masses consist of laypeople who never rose above the level of peasant or artisan, their anonymity remaining absolute owing to their lack of title, office, blue blood, or leading position in civic organizations of a religious or cultural nature.

The very act of recording the Cockaigne material must have led to an increase in its moralizing content, which had been present from the very beginning in performances of upside-down worlds for the intellectual elite. Cockaigne's rustic décor is well suited to such a framework. Late-medieval burghers were fond of peopling their instructive topsy-turvy worlds with caricatures of peasants that were meant to portray extreme brutishness, irra-tionality, and foolishness, in other words, the opposite of polite behavior. Cockaigne presents a rustic image. Everything happens out of doors. The edible architecture covers at most a village, for it comprises nothing but houses and fences. There are also animals running around wild, and the "dancing in the round" engaged in by its inhabitants refers to typical peas-ant behavior expressed in words and imagery current at that time.

It is not likely that this rural character was an ingredient added to Cock-aigne when it was first written down. Its rusticity was at most embroidered upon, but the countryside remains the basic setting for fantasies first per-petuated in oral form. These dreams were continually reborn and handed down as comfort and compensation, their satire and morality being valuable by-products that finally came into their own when the texts were at last recorded and allowed to enter the written tradition. As such, the annotated version can never be direct evidence of popular culture, which is at most dimly visible between the lines, shining more brightly where the main themes make their appearance, bearing hilarious tidings of compensation for the fear of food shortages and grueling work.

There are also more tangible indications that the Cockaigne material was contaminated at the time of writing by visions and constituent parts of other cultural milieus. For example, the golden plates and platters in text L and the bowls and plates of silver in text B, lying on the shore of a river supplying wine and beer, seem somewhat out of place. After all, in these texts opulence and abundance are translated into absurd quantities of food and drink appearing in every conceivable—and inconceivable—form, not expressed in a wealth of precious metals suggesting another milieu. The best evidence of contamination, however, is provided by those details that came about accidentally, resulting from the copyist's attempt to record the oral material as he thought fit. This includes such details as small corrections or adjustments that the adapter introduced into his material without a moment's thought.

Is it a milieu-bound slip of the pen, for instance, when the author of version B interrupts the edibility of his architecture by introducing doorposts of carbuncles? The detail is striking: this variant is missing from the other Middle Dutch version, which makes no mention of doorposts; neither does it have an equivalent in the Cockaigne material recorded elsewhere. After mention of the fences made of sausages and the windows and doors of salmon and sturgeon, the Cockaigne recipe is varied to include the following:

> Inside the houses, all the doorposts
> Are made of carbuncles, 'tis no idle boast.

This is followed by twelve verses that conform to the old pattern: the beams are made of butter, the attics consist of gingerbread, a variety of furniture is made of meat pies, spinning implements are made of cracknel, the rafters are eels, the roof is covered with custard tartlets, and the hedgerows are woven of lampreys, a kind of fish.

As early as classical antiquity the carbuncle was seen as a diffuser of bright light. It was originally thought to be a mythic stone belonging among the typical furnishings of paradise. Isidore of Seville described it as crimson on the inside and black as coal on the outside. Bartholomaeus Anglicus adopted this description from Isidore and again stressed the bright light given off by the stone at night. Sir John Mandeville also made a point of describing its function in the bedchamber of Prester John: "The pillars in his chamber are of gold set with precious stones, many of which are carbuncles to give light at night." It became customary to identify the carbuncle with the ruby to make it more recognizable.

It is difficult to imagine the word *carbuncle* being used to mean a boil in this context. Neither is it likely that another connotation of the word was intended, namely, a reference to a kind of cabbage—possibly available in the sixteenth century but certainly no earlier—as this would hardly be appropriate in a list of food considered varied and luxurious by both burghers and peasants. Why, then, did the author of version B suddenly start talking about precious stones at this point? In the corresponding place dealing with edible architecture in prose text G, the adapter mentions only doorposts of gingerbread, which fit in perfectly with the traditional pattern.

The adapter of Cockaigne text B must have been familiar with another kind of architecture that had become commonplace in knightly epics and travelers' tales, namely, wondrous castles built completely of gold, silver, and precious stones along the lines of the heavenly Jerusalem. Descriptions of such architecture follow the same pattern as those of the edible houses in Cockaigne and Luilekkerland, the only difference being that all the component parts consist of various precious metals and stones. The author actually appears to have been acquainted with these castles, as witnessed by a song describing the citadel of paradise appearing elsewhere in his collection:

> There stood an ivory citadel
> In an orchard, and all told
> It had nine doors of carbuncle,
> Topped with crowns of gold.
> Its turrets were all made of coral:
> That castle, it was said, shone bright,
> Much clearer than a crystal.

Did one of the building materials used in these constructions manage to slip unnoticed into Cockaigne, simply because the author was momentarily overwhelmed by his knowledge of bejeweled castles? This is quite likely the explanation. The plot thickens when we find that carbuncles, as well as other precious stones, are a prime building material in paradise. According to the Bible, the New Jerusalem will have carbuncle gates, and this specification is repeated in Middle Dutch texts. One of the paradisiacal places visited by Saint Brendan and his fellow monks (in the Middle Dutch version) even features a castle with windows and doorposts made of carbuncles. The special affinity the Cockaigne texts have for the house and garden architecture of paradise could easily give rise to the accidental contamination of meat and fish with precious stones.

Accidental? We must reserve a place for the assumption that the author of text B—presumably a student or former student but in any case a man of letters—has here permitted himself a playful allusion to Cockaigne's indebtedness to representations of paradise. He was not the only one to adopt this procedure. The wonder castle in *La grande confrarie des soulx d'ouvrer et enragez de rien faire* (The great brotherhood of those who are fed up with working and keen on doing nothing) has walls made of creamy cheese from Milan dotted with diamonds. Here as well the precious stones refer to other conventions in the description of fantasized structures, for the rest of the castle is built of food.

The strongest piece of evidence for conscious pleasantry, however, is to be found in the plan followed by the author of the Middle English *Land of Cokaygne*. This learned monk imagined his dreamland to be a worldly annex to paradise, which on its own he found rather colorless. He demonstrates in exemplary fashion a conscious blending of various traditions in his description of the wondrous architecture on this dream island. The abbey is first portrayed as a product of the original recipe for edible architecture. The walls are made of meat pies, various other kinds of meat and fish, and an abundance of other dishes, all of them made of the most costly foods available. The roof tiles consist of cakes made with the finest flour, while nails are made of fatty sausages. Then, however, this display of food makes way for buildings made of precious stones. The cloister has pillars of crystal, while pedestals and capitals consist of green jasper and red coral. In this description the interweaving was done consciously and with a distinct feeling for harmony.

In any case, the carbuncles in text B betray a certain amount of contamination from a different milieu at the time the text was recorded. Other-

FIGURE 79

Shop selling precious stones in a city. *Platearius* manuscript, fifteenth century.

Source: Paris, Bibliothèque Nationale, MS f.fr.9136, fol. 344 recto.

wise what are we supposed to think of those heavenly jewels wedged between the sturgeon doors and the butter beams? Moreover, well-to-do burghers in the late Middle Ages were beginning to display a passion for precious stones, which served to show how wealthy they were, thereby compelling the respect of the upper crust of society.

Cockaigne remains the story of the continual interweaving of oral material with more intellectual, written traditions. During the High Middle Ages, monastic satire and the church's Feast of Fools, with their portrayals of a *mundus inversus*, combined to elevate Cockaigne to the level of Cucania, an idyllic spot that also functions as an example of how things should and should not be done in the real world. At the same time, however, Cockaigne continued to circulate outside this contaminated zone in the minds of many who had no use for Latin metaphor and ritual. But as soon as someone actually wrote down his own version, a text came into being that bore the traces not only of the author and his milieu but also of the literary traditions of which he was inevitably a part.

There is even indirect proof that Cockaigne flourished chiefly amid the rural population, where it acquired many of its themes and set formulas. Consider, for example, the near absence of sex in the oldest versions, including the French and English texts. While one would expect that a surfeit of food and idleness would give rise to thoughts of uncomplicated erotic diversions, there is little evidence of this in Cockaigne. This is indeed strange, especially because exempla and confession books do not refrain from warning one of the three-pronged evil of idleness, gluttony, and sex, which exacerbate one another as the widely known story of John of Beverley so compellingly proves. The prose text of 1546 on Luilekkerland pays more attention to this aspect, and it is not difficult to detect later additions emanating from other frustrations in other milieus.

Does the absence of humorous and suggestive obscenities point to peasant folklore as the primary source of these texts? If so, the same holds true for fairy tales, which are also thought to have taken shape in early rural society. It is well known that verbal exercises regarding the excesses of the lower part of the body were a favorite form of entertainment in courtly, monastic, and urban milieus, where sexuality bred feelings of unease. The court tried to compensate for the consequences of awkward marriage policies with its obscene culture of riddles and fabliaux, the monastery made the denigration of marriage and sexuality the main subject of its Feast of Fools, and the city tried to vent its displeasure at the pressure the church brought to bear on marriage in a long series of merry portrayals of shabby behavior performed during the protracted pre-Lenten festivities.

The above-mentioned relationship shared by idleness, overeating, and eroticism in Christian teachings on morality already leads one to assume that compensation in the form of unlimited gorging and laziness in idyllic surroundings must have developed outside the confines of these teachings. This also focuses attention on early medieval peasantry, whose daily lives were known to have been determined by myriad manifestations of their belief in nature. Is it not logical to assume that the one thing people could in fact deal with in those days was sexuality? The church had not yet begun to meddle in the matter, and it was therefore unnecessary to vent one's frustrations in a dreamland.

Sexuality was rarely seen as a problem during the first centuries after Christ. In their battle against sins of the flesh, the desert fathers were not fighting against temptations of an erotic nature but against those of meat and wine. They strove for total self-abnegation by forgoing nearly all nourishment and giving themselves over to rigid regimes of abstinence. This opened up possibilities for bizarre competitions in this field, compared to which sex must have seemed like just another trifling problem.

Neither did dynastic interests play an important role in rural society, though later on they would prove to be a nearly insurmountable obstacle to love, severely curtailing one's chances of marrying for love or longing. It seems as though the natural rhythm of the seasons automatically encompassed the human rhythm in a free and natural way. Normal sexual satisfaction met with few restrictions imposed by the church or other authorities, so that the need to compensate for frustrations on this score was slight.

This line of reasoning is less gratuitous than it seems and has serious methodological underpinnings. In 1547 *Der Fielen, Rabauwen oft der Schalcken Vocabulaer* (Dictionary of riffraff, rascals, and rogues) was published in Antwerp. Both entertaining and informative, it was a handbook describing the practices of professional beggars. It contained a vocabulary list of medieval thieves' slang, based on genuine reports of this argot recorded around the middle of the fifteenth century in Basel. This internationally known jargon was also current in the Low Countries, as witnessed by its inclusion (and reprintings) in the beggars' handbook. Almost none of the two hundred words recorded have anything to do with sex. Instead, nearly everything has to do with the primary needs of vagabonds, who had to make a living on the road. The daily struggle for survival was made easier by using a private language that pointed out dangers and discomforts and defined them in terms of acquiring food, drink, and clothing, as well as serving to smooth over contacts with the sheriff and courts of law. Sexuality was not a problem, for the people in this milieu encountered no difficulties on this score with the outside world.

The supposition of an early rural culture as the source of compensatory fantasies finds support in the extremely persistent motif of edible

Der Fielen / Ra

báuwen/oft der Schalcken Vocabu er/der
de beuepsde manieren der bedeierten oft he
delerssen daer nienich mésche deur hedioget
wort/wort hier geleert / op dat hen, elck dart
voor wachten mach/ eñto seer r···r ende
profijtelijck om lesen hoor
alle menschen.

℃ Ghedruct Thantwerpen by Jan de Lae
in die Rape. Xnno. M. D. xriij.

FIGURE 80

Title page of *Der Fielen, Rabauwen oft der Schalcken Vocabulaer*
(Dictionary of riffraff, rascals, and rogues), from the
1563 edition.

Source: Ghent, University Library.

architecture. This building method is a central issue in the oldest Cockaigne texts and is also found in fairy tales and myths, the most famous being the gingerbread house in the fairy tale of Hansel and Gretel. If one accepts the assertion that such material—despite the infelicities of the versions recorded since romanticism—contains the oldest traces of the emotions and ideas prevalent in society, then this is another indication of Cockaigne's origin in—or in any case eager adoption by—an early manifestation of peasant folklore.

Such indirect indications may also be deduced from the absence of wonderful fragrances in Cockaigne, whereas the much more literary Luilekkerland does boast this attraction. According to text G, a pleasant scent—reminiscent of violets—settles over the whole country whenever the wind rages, and the delicious fragrance remains even in the dead of winter. Such intoxicating scents are part of the standard delights of both the earthly and the heavenly paradise, where the smell is said to be so penetrating that one can stay alive just by breathing. A similar means of survival was also attributed to an exotic people who were supposedly fortunate enough to be stuck in paradisiacal surroundings: these folk nourished themselves merely by sniffing apples. In addition, a few saints depended on divine dispensation for their food supply: after all, their home on earth was already halfway to heaven.

The focus on taste and smell also grew to become an important mark of culture, increasingly brought to bear by the elite in their attempts to civilize both courtly and urban culture. This was why devils also took to availing themselves of this weapon, but in their case the point was to delude such haughty folk with sweet fragrances. Mandeville gives repeated evidence of his obsession with delicate odors, which comes to a head in his account of the land of Prester John. This priest-king is so refined that "every night he has burning in his chamber twelve vessels of crystal full of balm, to give a good sweet smell and drive away noxious airs."

Also revealing in this respect is Mandeville's reference to a story concerning the four kinds of wood used to make Jesus' cross. The foot was made of cedar, which does not rot, for "they wanted it to last a long time. And because they thought Christ's body would stink, they made the upright, on which His body hung, of cypress, for it is sweet smelling, so that the smell of His body should not be offensive to men who came by." Such considerations only come into play in a society with a heightened sensitivity to odors.

In the late Middle Ages the cities began to take more stringent measures to banish stench from their midst. At the very least they strove to limit the nuisance—apparently experienced more intensely now—and to bring it under control. From the podiums used by the local rhetoricians for their performances pleasant smells were spread about, an attraction that aimed to add luster to the unveiling of the tableaux vivants that served as interludes during morality plays.

This refinement of smell as a means of distinguishing oneself was brought to new heights in French and Burgundian courtly culture, where securing a paramour was of the utmost importance. Italian courts were a major source of inspiration in this respect. Distinguished ladies were instructed to wear gloves made of soft Spanish leather perfumed with extract of violets. At the end of the fifteenth century this fashion was the newest of the sophisticated techniques aimed at arousing a man's senses through his nose. Kissing a hand dressed in this way was said to drive an infatuated lover to distraction. During the course of the sixteenth century yet more aromatic substances were added to this olfactory arsenal, including the sperm of civets, with which Catherine de' Medici dabbed her wrists.

Subtle niceties of this kind play as minor a role as sex in the compensations and dream surroundings sought by the peasantry, who in any case would have been especially indifferent to sweet, life-giving fragrances. Such notions clash with the primary image of Cockaigne as a place where massive quantities of food are devoured daily. This is why Cockaigne does not smell, that point apparently being of so little importance that it never even led to cursory additions in the recorded versions. Only text G, the product of a written tradition, betrays its entirely new purpose by ensuring that nice smells are not lacking in Luilekkerland.

41
The Necessity of Fiction

*M*EDIEVAL RURAL CULTURES were not only in search of compensation; they also sought weapons for use in acts of physical and spiritual resistance. If hunger was the scourge of God, the umpteenth punishment for breaking His commandments, then stuffing oneself silly testified to rebelliousness, as did fantasies of such behavior. "Take what you can get, for tomorrow you may die." This attitude, already detectable in the Germanic culture of the early Middle Ages, was expressed in a proverb recorded in 1550: "He stuffs himself as though he'll hang tomorrow." And this decisiveness was in keeping with gorging as an expression of self-confidence and power, as demonstrated not only at royal banquets but also in the streets during Carnival celebrations.

Given the food situation at the time, it is also tempting to assume the existence in the early Middle Ages of a first wave of more specific realizations of dreamland material, leading up to a medieval Cockaigne. The fifth and sixth centuries, after all, were apparently ravaged by protracted food shortages in the whole of Western Europe. This distressful and seemingly hopeless situation cried out for consoling images and moral reinforcements.

It is equally tempting to date the first Old French and Middle Dutch written records of the Cockaigne material to the period roughly between 1000 and 1300, when for many the food situation was dominated by the numbing monotony of consuming almost nothing but bread, which must have cried out just as hard as did food shortages for spectacular forms of relief, if only in the imagination. This explains the enormous variety of food in Cockaigne: it provides the greatest possible contrast to compulsory monotony, the unbearableness of which explains in turn why simple variety was preferred to a range of luxury foods. In particular, the period shortly after 1315–1317—the only true famine on a massive scale experienced in Europe during the whole of the Middle Ages—provided the perfect breeding ground for prospects, which multiplied with a vengeance, of a land of culinary abundance lasting for all eternity.

Nonetheless, these assumptions are no more than fortuitous guesses that might not be out of place in a coarsely painted history of humankind from its very beginnings until now but decidedly go one step too far in this context. Cockaigne is timeless: even its name does not necessarily indicate specifically medieval origins. Orality and literacy—or oral and written cultures—both helped themselves to the Cockaigne material, influencing one another while at the same time going their own way. The oral tradition acted as a continual enticement to new inventions, embroiderings, and adaptations that were again reflected in the written versions. The latter formed, admittedly, their own tradition, these written texts being more set and therefore guaranteeing the Cockaigne material a certain orderliness. But within the scope of this tradition, the hallucinations of a drugged famine victim provide unexpected outpourings that represent not so much Cockaigne's raison d'être as a recurring source of wild manifestations of the material.

More particularly, the Middle Dutch texts offer insight into the worries and dreams of an urban population, this being the obvious purpose of the Old French texts as well. The focus on money and earning a living—concepts actually quite alien to a land where everything is readily available at no cost whatsoever—indicates all the more forcefully that we are dealing with the cares and concerns of townsfolk, these motifs having been deposited in the Cockaigne material only when the texts were put down in writing. Further evidence of this is the exaggerated attention paid to money and the discharging of one's debts—a most illogical element—in the prose text on Luilekkerland. This text dating from 1546 betrays its urban interests in other elements as well.

Remarkable in this context is the attention paid by the author of text B to honoring the wishes of each inhabitant in a strictly individual manner. Cockaigne can be tailor-made to suit anyone. The tables are laden with huge quantities of food and drink, "and everything that you could wish," making it clear that everyone is allowed to make his or her preferences known. Typical of recorded texts that are still quite close to the oral tradition is the assurance, a few lines later, that "you'll find enough of everything to satisfy your strongest craving," again stressing the possibility of individualized satisfaction of one's needs. The fact that such accents are lacking in text L makes these personalized particulars in text B even more significant.

Apart from underscoring such elements, the texts generally promote the interests of the masses, at the same time injecting them with a dose of moral teaching in line with urban aspirations. Even this cautionary element, however, need not conflict with Cockaigne's overwhelmingly popular character. The comment that the French Cockaigne is not intended or suitable for the rich must surely be seen as compensation for the anonymous, nondescript masses, who are allowed to reside anywhere, even in Cockaigne. Further in the background, the irony of the topsy-turvy world again plays a role: the poor are safely tucked away in a nonexistent land and therefore excluded from normal life. In the Middle English *Land of Cokaygne*, which also has strict rules governing admittance, this exclusion is used at the same time as a satirical poke at both the exploiters and the idle monks.

In terms of compensation and escape as well, the Middle Dutch Cockaigne texts respond primarily to the needs of broad segments of the population, who are sooner found in the countryside and the city than in a courtly milieu. The dreamworld of the nobility consisted in the ideal development of courtly norms in the form of self-discipline, moderation, and beauty, practiced and portrayed in veritable pleasure grounds of their own making. Moreover, lavish displays of food were a regular feature of banquets that were as playful as they were self-congratulatory. This world was at odds with the dream of Cockaigne, where the mere fact of unbridled consumption in the midst of bizarre abundance was meant to allay one's fears, the trappings of this abundance being of no importance whatsoever. Via a detour, the more prosperous burghers managed to come into their own by embracing courtly modes of behavior based on the instructive inversion of the rustic rewards of Cockaigne, eventually arriving at the same destination, adopting the same virtues of moderation and a passion for hard work.

Why was Cockaigne necessary? In the Middle Ages there was certainly no lack of compensatory, didactic tracts, some serious, and some availing themselves of humor in portraying a topsy-turvy world and other dreamlands. There was even a superabundance of paradisiacal fantasies and spectacular reports of exotic peoples and newly discovered lands. In addition, every milieu had its own representations of pleasure grounds, whether they consisted in townspeople viewing performances and tableaux vivants during religious processions or the nobility feasting at royal banquets and dallying in pleasure parks. Finally, pious members of the laity were constantly betaking themselves to dream spots along the perilous path of mysticism. Sometimes these idyllic places were acted out on earth by those who had become adept in such techniques, and this often resulted in far-reaching accusations of heresy. A safer route was taken by those who traveled to their dreamworlds in visions, the more sensational of which sparked off a bombardment of moral teachings.

Escape routes, weapons, compensation, and lively lessons aplenty. Why, then, the need to create a Cockaigne that so strongly resembled what one already harbored in the imagination or sought in reality? The answer must lie in the fictional character of Cockaigne. At the end of the Middle Ages, this dreamland could be deployed to combat many a vexation and to pursue all manner of pleasures, always in the secure knowledge that it was all just a game, putting no one under any obligation whatsoever. All those other escape routes were true and tangible, claiming to exist in reality or to be palpable, inasmuch as cardboard imitations or raked-over idyllic nature spots were palpable.

Cockaigne was a lie from beginning to end and as such was never imitated under that name. This was also true of the sixteenth-century Luilekkerland, and its inimitability appears to have been a comforting thought. Paradise, heaven, the New World: these were all burdened with a genuineness that could overwhelm one, strike fear into one's heart, and make one a slave to their attainment. Cockaigne was a fantasy with no strings attached. Neither confessing one's sins nor undertaking a dangerous journey was a prerequisite to reaching it, and this is why it was so easy to deliver oneself up to Cockaigne: it didn't really mean anything.

Neither is Cockaigne a viable utopia. While utopias suggest the possibility of ideal living conditions for everyone, no one seems to have believed in the imminent realization of such dream societies. Still, utopian patterns of living were continually devised that were quite plausible and seemed anything but imaginary. It has been pointed out repeatedly that the societies found in the New World were an important source of inspiration for the establishment of such utopias in the sixteenth century. In any case, they functioned as a touchstone for the reorganization of Europe's own social climate. But it was precisely Cockaigne's strictly fictional and unreal nature that gave everyone the license to search for a maximum of satisfaction, and this is why the quest for spiritual weapons and compensation in this dreamland and no other could have such a great impact on one's personal well-being in everyday life. None of it was true anyway. Why should anyone get worked up about the amusements on offer in Cockaigne? It didn't even exist! And this, of course, is why it had to be invented.

Footloose fantasizing is a most stubborn survival strategy. It cannot be eradicated in one body, for it lives on in a thousand others, being passed continually from one to the next. A spiritual weapon of this kind cannot be laid down until the enemy has definitely retreated. Cockaigne was therefore brought to its knees only in the early-modern period, when hunger was gradually defeated in the Western world. When, in the chivalric romance of the same name, the comical knight Joufroi of Poitiers adopts "Cocagne!" as his battle cry, it is to be understood as a bittersweet protest against the perennial threat of hunger, whose humorous note would not resound until long after the Middle Ages.

The price paid for this victory over hunger and the fears it inspired was the destruction of a unique dream, a dream that had made the lives of many thousands of people more bearable by raising their spirits to hilarious heights. Not even in the guise of Luilekkerland did Cockaigne ever again find such an appreciative audience.

Appendixes

Deſen ghedicht is banden ouden beſchreuen
Ende tot onderwijs den jongers ghegheuen
Die lup en lecker leuen ghewent/zijn/
Ong ieſchict ende onachtſaem tot allen fijn/
Die behoortmē int Lup-lecker-lant te wijſē
Op datſe haer ongeſchickt heyt laten rijſen/
Ende datſe hebben op arbept acht/
Want lap en ledigh nopt deught en wracht.

F I N I S.

Middle Dutch Rhyming Texts on Cockaigne

TEXT L

Dit is van dat edele lant van Cockaengen

Die neringhe is menigherande,
Die men doet in allen lande
Om dat lijff mede t'ondraghen.
Hoert, wat ic u sal ghewaghen!
5   Ick quam laesten in een lant,
Daer ic vreemt was ende onbecant.
Nu moechdi horen wonder groot,
Wat God den luden daer gheboet:
In dat lant te wesen ende te sijn
10   Sonder arbeit ende sonder pijn!
Dit wort den luden wel becant.
Sach ye man beter lant
Dan dat lant van Cockaengen?
Die helft is beter dan al Spaengen,
15   D'ander helft is beter dan Betouwen.
Men heft er wil van schonen vrouwen.
Dit is 't lant van den Heiligen Gheest.
Wie daer lancst slaept, de wint meest.
Daer en derf nyemant doen werck,
20   Out, jonc, cranc of sterck.
Daer en mach nyemant yet gheborsten.
Die wanden sijn daer ghemaect van worsten.
Daer sijn die veynsteren ende doren
Ghemaect van salmen ende van storen.
25   Die tafelborden sijn struven in pannen,
Van bier sijn ghemaect die kannen.

Die platelen, die in den huse sijn,
Sijn van fijn guldijn.
Dat broet al schoen ter wijn,
30 Alsoe claer als die sonnenschijn.
Die balken, die daer in den huse leggen,
Sijn ghemaect van boterwegghen.
Haspelen, spinrocken ende alsulke dinghen
Sijn ghebacken van crakelinghen.
35 Daer sijn die bancken ende stoelen
Ghebacken al van roffiolen.
Daer sijn die solreplancken oeck
Ghebacken van claren pepercoeck.
Die latten sijn palinghen ghebraden.
40 Die h [uise syn gedeckt mit vladen],
Die s [yn geflochten, sonder waen].
Daer [lopen hasen ende conynen],
Wil h [erten ende everswynen]
Van w [?]
45 Die ma [ch men vangen mitter hant].
Sach o [yt iemant beter lant]!
Want sch [oen kleyder syn daer oeck goitkoep].
Voer elke de [ur licht er eyn hoep],
Elkerlijc na [synen sin].
50 Daertoe kous[en ende schoen]:
Die wil, die m [aech se aendoyn],
Al waer hi ridd [er ofte knecht].
Daer vint men tot [allen straeten gespreit]
Schone tafelen, die m [en nyemant wederseit].
55 Eten, drincken mach m [en alle den dach].
Daer en derf nyemant gh [even ghelach],
Als men hier ten lande doet.
Och, dat lant van Cockaengen is so [goet]!
Het reghent daer in allen hoecken
60 Vladen, pasteyen ende pannekoecken.
In dat lant loept een ryvier

Van goeden wijn, van goeden bier,
Muscadel ende oec clareyt,
Romeny die men ontseit.

65 Die mach men drincken goeden cost,
Wil men wijn of wil men most.
Mit ghenghever ende mit muscaten
Sijn ghemaect aldaer die straten.
Veel ghels is daer goet tijt.

70 Daer en draecht men hat noch nijt,
Soe wat men daer in 't lant vint legghen,
Dat neemt men sonder wedersegghen
Ende doet daermede sijn bederve,
Recht of 't waer sijn eyghen erve.

75 Het is daer altijt of 't waer meye.
Daer singt elc voghel sijnre leye.
Daer coemt in die maent vijf weken
[?] niet ghebreken
[Ende .iiij. Paes]chen in 't jaer,

80 [Ende vier Pinxte]ren daernaer
[?] nte Jans misse
[?] ghewissen
[Ende .iiij. Kersdag]he, dat is waer,
[Ende eynen va]sten in hondert jaer

85 [?] mer enen halven dach
[?] nye beter lant en sach.
[Noch is dae]r een beter doecht,
[Daer elck myn]sche by is verhoecht.
[In d]at lant loept een Jordane

90 [?] en die daer quamen
[?] men dat water in haren mont
[?] ouden alle worden jonc,
[Re]cht of sy waren van twintich jaren.
[D]at seg ic u voerware.

95 Daer sijn trompen ende schelmeyen,
Daer sy op dansen ende op reyen,

Ende driven vroechden sonder ghetal.
Ick hoep 't hem ewelic duren sal.
Soe wie dat daer coemt in Gods namen,
100 Die mach voerwaer wel segghen: Amen.

TEXT B

Narratio de terra suaviter viventium

Die nerynge is mennigerhande,
dye men doit in allen landen
om dat lijff mede te belgen.
Nu hoert, ick sall u wat geseggen!
5 Ick quam lesten in eyn lant,
dat my vremde was ende onbekant.
Ghy sult hoeren wonder groit
wat Got dair geboit:
in dat lant altoes te syn
10 sonder arbeit ende sonder pyn!
Het is dat lant van Cockanyngen.
Dye eyn helft is beter dan all Hyspaniën
ende dye helft dan all Betaviën,
want men heft dar vill van schonen vrouwen.
15 Dat lant maeckden dye Heylige Geist,
want wye 't langste slaept, dy heft meist.
In dat lant doyt nyemant werck,
is hy alt, jonck off sterck,
ende dar en mach nyemant yet ontbrecken.
20 Dar syn dye tuyne gemaeckt mit worsten.
Die vinsteren ende dye dueren
syn gemaeckt van salm ende stueren.
Die stender in den huise staen
syn all van carbonckel, sonder waen.
25 Dye balcken, dye in den huyse liggen,
syn all gemaeckt van botterweggen.

Darom syn dye sulderplancken oeck
gemaeckt van claeren peperkoeck.
Bancken ende stoelen
30   syn all gebacken van roffiolen.
Haspelen, spinrock ende sulcke dyngen
syn all geflochten van krakelyngen
ende dye laeten van palingen.
Ende dye huise syn gedeckt mit vladen.
35   Dye tune, dye up den velde staen,
dye syn geflochten, sonder waen,
mit groten schonen lampereyen
darup dansen ende ryngen.
Daer lopen hasen ende conijnen,
40   wilde herten ende everswynen.
Dese maech men vangen mitter hant
ende leyden ewech sonder bant.
Dar syn oeck rosen ende rosijnen,
gedeckt mit kostelicken gesmijden.
45   Wilt hy seer draven, houwen off lopen,
dye en darff hy tegen nyemant kopen.
Dit is dat lant dat Got mynt!
Dye daer 't langste slaept, dy 't meiste vynt.
Ende wat men in dat lant vynt liggen,
50   dat maech eyn yegelick upnemen sonder seggen
ende doyn darmede syn bederven,
recht off waer syn eygen erve.
Schoen kleyder syn daer oeck goitkoep,
want voer allen huyseren licht er eyn hoep
55   ende dartoe haesen ende schoen.
Dye will, dye maech si aendoyn.
In allen straeten vynt men gespreit
schoen taeffelen, dye men nyemant wederseit,
mit witten laecken onbeflect:
60   broit ende wyn daerup gesett,
ende dartoe vische ende vleysche,
egelick nae synen heysch.

Men mach daer eten ende dryncken alle den daech
daer en gilt nyet gelaech
65 als men hir te landen doit.
Och, dat lant is soe goit,
want het regent .jjj. werff 's dages vladen,
palingen ende pastien gebraeden.
Men vynt van alles genoich,
70 elick mynsche nae syn gefoech.
Daer en bleyff nymant onberaeden,
want dye gansen gaent hemselven braeden.
Vich, vleysche ende vette capunen
koecken hemselven tot allen nonen,
75 ende dye vette vogelen mede:
het is dar des lants sede.
In dat lant loupt eyn revyr
van goyden wyn ende bier.
Aen beyden syden van den over
80 liggen silveren schaelen ende grote cover.
Ende eyn lutter vort loept klaereyt,
muscatel, romenye dye men nymant wederseit.
Dar maech eyn yegelick dryncken sonder kost,
wilt hy wyn, bier off most.
85 Mit gingfer, mit notenmuschaeten
syn daer gemaeckt dye straeten,
ende mit pellen overhangen,
dat men daronder mach gangen.
Dar is eyn goyde castuyn in 't lant:
90 nyemant en is daer des anderen vyant,
elick is daer des anderen vrunt,
dye hem gern helpen ende dyent.
Dit lant is lanck ende wyt,
ende is daer altoes sommertyt,
95 recht off 't waer in den apprill.
Dar en heft nyemant synen onwill
ende daer en maech nyemant yet ontbrecken.

Elick maent heft vyff wecken.
ende .iiij. Paeschen syn daer in 't jaer,
100 ende vier Pinxten, dat is waer,
ende .iiij. Kersdagen, waeren,
ende eynen vasten bynnen hondert jaeren.
Noch is daer eyn ander duecht,
daer elick mynsche is aeff verhoecht.
105 Daer en roept wijff noch man,
dye den anderen geweygeren kan
om eyn fruntelick slaepen gaen:
dat segge ick u all sonder waen.
Dar syn trompen en scalmeyen,
110 daer syn nae dansen ende reyen.
Schone vrouwen ende jonfrouwen,
die mach ellick hebben all sonder truwen,
sonder sunde ende sonder schande.
Het is daer dye sede van den lande:
115 dat seggen sy, dye vandaer comen.
Dat lant en maech nyet te voll wonen.
Hiromme raede ick allen uckyngen,
dye noede arbeyden ende pijnen,
ende gerne eten ende dryncken wael,
120 ende gerne dryven lodderspoel,
dat sy hir laeten staen
ende in dat ryck lant gaen.
Dar en comt nyemant, des siet vro,
dye anders eynich ambocht doyt
125 dan eten ende dryncken alle den daech,
ende des avents borgen oer gelaech,
ende noede vor hoeren daech betalen,
ende alltyt putten ende palen
wye sy quyt mogen gaen.
130 Hirmede will ick 't laeten staen
ende wille laeten dese wort,
up aventur wye sy hoert: Amen.

Dutch Prose Text of 1546 on Luilekkerland

Van 't Luyeleckerlant, 't welcke is een seer wonderlijck, overschoon ende costelijck landt, vol van alder gheneuchten ende wellustigheeden. Ende is nu eerst ghevonden in 't jaer doe men schreef duysendt suyckerkoecken, vijfhondert eyervladen ende sesenveertich gebraeden hoenderen, in de wijnmaent doe de pasteyen wel smaeckten. Ende is seer ghenoechlijck om te lesen.

> Luy en lecker en veel te meughen,
> Dat zijn drie dinghen die niet en deughen.

Men wil seggen voor onwaerachtige nieuwe tidinghe hoe datter gevonden is een hoecklandt, hetwelcke genoemt wort het Luyeleckerlant. Dit landt en is tot noch toe niemant bekend geweest dan alleene den deughnieten, die 't aldereerst gevonden hebben. Ende het is gheleghen recht in Noort-Hommelen, dwars op dese syde naby die galghe, drie mijlen door lange nachten. Alle diegenen die daerhenen willen trecken, die moeten gantsch onversaeght zijn ende wel gemoet tot groote dinghen te bestaen. Want vooraen dit lant is gheleghen een seer hooghen ende langhen bergh van boecweytenbry, wel drie mijlen breet oft dicke, daer zy voor eerst moeten dooreeten, aleer zy in 't lant comen. Ende alsdan so sijn se terstont in een ogenblic in dit voorseyde Luyleckerlant, 't welcke om zijn costelijcke rijcdommen, heerlijckheydt ende gheneughelijcheyt seer welbekent ende vermaert is, sonderlinghe by den onverlaten ende dengheenen die alle deugt ende eerbaerheyt te rugghe ghestelt hebben.

Want die huysen zijn daer ghemeenlijc al tesamen met leckere pannekoecken ende vladen ghedeckt, de muyren ende wanden ghemaeckt van speckstruyven, de balcken van braetverckens, de deuren ende vensters van suyckerkoecke, ende de stijlen ofte posten van de deuren ende vensters van welgekruyde peperkoecken ende met muscatennaghelen t'samengheslaghen. Om elck huys staet eenen stercken tuyn, de sommighe van ghebraden leverworsten ende sommighe van metworsten ofte andere t'samenghevlochten. Item, in dit lant zijn seer veel schoone fonteyne van malvesey ende alderhande soete dranck, die eenen yeghelijcken als men 't begeert vanzelfs wel in den mondt springhen. De roffiolen wassen daer in sulcker manieren, ghelijck als hier te lande de pijnappelen.

De taerten wasschen daer op de eyckebomen ende de struyven op de berckenboomen. Ende wie daer appetijt oft lust toe heeft, die mach se lichtelijck afreycken, want zy hanghen niet hooghe. Op de esscheboomen wasschen leckere pasteyen. De soete wijndruyven die pluckt men daer van den haeghdoorn. Ende die braetpeeren wassen der overvloedigh, heel murwe ende lecker. Ende 's winterdaeghs als 't sneeuwt, soo worden sy vanboven uyter locht met suycker bestroyt.

Item, op de willigen die aen de kanten van de rivieren staen wasset het wittebroot seer overvloedigh. Ende de rivieren die daeronder heenlopen zijn van enckel soete melck. Daer valt dan het wittebroot ghestadigh in, soodat een yeghelijck zijn gheneught ende lust daeruut krijghen ende eeten magh. Oock so dryven de visschen daer in 't water ghesoden, ghebraden ende lecker gebacken, ende wel toeghemaeckt. Sy coomen oock wel soo na by de kanten, dat men se gemackelic met de handen vanghen mach.

Desgelijcx soo siet men daer over alle 't lant in de lucht de hoenderen, gansen, duyven, snippen ende ander ghevoghelte vlieghen. Ende zijn al t'samen wel gebraden. Ende isser yemant soo luy dat hij se niet vangen en mach, so vlieghen sy dien wel vanselfs in de mondt, indien hy zijn mont opendoet ende daerna gaept. Nochtans en zijn der de gebraden hoenderen niet veel geacht, want die werpt men wel over den tuyn. De verckens die groeyen daer alsoo seer in 't landt, dat zy met hopen oock al wel ende lecker ghebraden hier ende daer overal in 't veldt loopen. Ende hebben een mes op de rugghe steken. Ende isser yemant die daeraf lust te eeten, die mach terstont met dat selve mes een stuck daervan snijden ende steken dan 't mes daer weder in. Oock wassen daer de kruyskaesen soo overvloedich als de steenen.

Item, de boeren ofte boulieden wassen daer overal op de bomen, ghelijck hier in dese landen de pruymen doen. Ende wanneer 't schoon weder is, soo worden sy al haest rijpe ende vallen dan d'eene voor ende de ander nae metter tijdt van de bomen, elck in een paer leersen, dewelcke daer onder de bomen op de aerde al bereyt staen ende passen juyst elcken nae haer benen. Die daer in 't landt een peerdt heeft, die wort terstont wel een rijck meyer, want die peerden leggen daer wel in corten tijt een groote corf vol eyeren. Desgelijck de esels schiten daer anders niet dan soete vijghen, ende de honden muscaten, de koeyen ende ossen groene pannekoecken.

Heeft yemant lust om kerssen te eeten, die en darf daer niet hoghe om climmen om te plucken, want sy wassen der soo lage als stekelbesien. Ende sy zijn heel groot ende soo soet als eenighe suycker. Daer en sijn oock geen stenen in dan alleene een ront murw steenken, 't welcke soo haest als men de kerssen etet terstont in de mont smeltet. Jae, het is te gelooven dattet een suyckerboone is.

In dit selve lant is een schoone ende heerlijke jeuchden-fonteyne ofte -bat, daer die oude lieden in gaen baden ende allencxkens weder jong en jeuchdigh werden.

Dit landt is also vol gheneuchten ende vreuchden die daer daghelijcx ghebruyct ende ghehanteert worden, dat diergelijcken niet vonden en wort onder die zonne. Want als men daer in de doele schiet ofte anders, so wie dan alderveerst van 't wit is, die wint het spel. Ende als men een weddeloop loopt, so wint altoos die leste.

Des winters is 't immers soo geneuchlijc ende lustigh in dit landt als des somers, want als het haghelt, dat en zijn niet anders dan suyckerboonen. De snee is anders niet dan gheschaefde broodtsuycker, die alsdan heel overvloedich ende met grooter menighten van der straten ende velden wert opgeraept ende opgeslickert. Als 't stormt oft die wint harde wayt, soo comt er soo gheneuchlijcken reuck over alle 't lant, alsof het niet dan fiolen en waren die dan in 't lant is, ooc in 't hardtste van den winter.

Voort soo is daer in 't landt seer lichtelijc geldt te winnen, want soe wie daer soo heel luy is dat hy gaet ligghen slapen, dien geeft men van elcke uyr dat hy slaept een stuyver. Ende wie eenen passelijcken scheet kan laten, die verdient een stooter. Van driemael te respen oft eenen harden scheet te laten, 't welc daer alleens is, verdient men eenen enckelen daelder. Ende isser yemant die zijn geldt soo gantsch ende al in den grondt verspeelt, verdobbelt, vertuyschet ende om den hals gebracht heeft, die ontfangt het terstont dubbelt wederomme. Maer isser yemant die veel schulden ghemaeckt heeft ofte quaet van betalinghe is, die wort daer terzijden af aen eenen hoeck van 't lant ghebannen, daer hy hem een jaer lang moet onthouden ende eeten niet anders dan gebraden hoenderen met wittebroot oft dierghelijck, 't welcke hem daer ghegheven wort om niet. Ende als nu 't jaer om is, soo mach hy vrylic weder in 't landt comen. Ende dan moet men hem alle die schult quijtschelden. Oft wil hy liever de schult betalen ende nochtans gheen geldt en heeft, soo mach hy desen hoeck daer hy ghebannen is gheweest gaen tot deselve weert daer hy ter herberghe ghelegen heeft. Die sal hem drie ofte vier bomen wijsen daer geldts ghenoegh op wasset. Ende daer mach hy sooveele afschudden als hy behoeft om sijn schult te betalen, ende comen dan weder by sijn oude gheselscap middenin 't landt, ende doen weder nae als voor.

Item, wie in dit landt geerne drinct met goede gesellen, die ontfangt voor elcken passelijcken dronck eenen braspenninc. Is 't dat hy drinct dat hy pruyst oft dat hem die ogen tranen, die verdient wel een snaphane van elcken dronck. Maer is 't, dat hy heel kannen vol met een teughe can uytdrincken, al staende sonder snuyven, dieselve heeft vry ghelagh en daertoe een nobel in die handt. Isser een spotvoghel die goeden luyden honen ende bespotten kan, die verdient des daeghs twee schellinghen. Een leugenaer die verdient daer groot geldt, want van elcken leugen heeft men daer een kroone. Ende hoe men behendigher ofte subtijlder lieghen kan, hoe men meer verdient.

De vroukens die van lichter munte zijn, die worden in dit lant seer hoogh geachtet. Ende hoe dat se luyer ende leckerder zijn, hoe men se daer liever heeft. Want al is 't dat men seyt dat leckere hoeren veel costen te houden, 't selfve en is nochtans in dit landt soo niedt, omdatter alle gheneughlijcke leckerheyt soo overvloedich wasset, die men lichtelijck sonder eenighe koste krijgen mach. Men en derf maer seggen ofte dencken: mondeken wat meught ghy? Herteken, wat begeert ghy?

Daer en is gheen meerder schanden in dit lant dan dat hem yemant deuchdelijck, redelijck, eerbaer ende manierlijc hout ende met sijn handen geerne zijn cost winnet. Wandt die hem alsoo deughdelijc ende eerlijck aenstelt, die wort van alleman gehaet ende ten lesten uyt den landen gebannen. Desgelijcx die wijs ende verstandich is, die wort vooral veracht ende versmaet, ende wort van niemant vriendelijck onthaelt. Maer die plomp, grof ende onverstandich is ende niet leeren en kan noch en wil, die wordt aldaer tot grooter eeren verheven. Want wie dat men bevint dat die alder onnutste, onverlateghste, groofste, plompste, daertoe oock de alderluyste ende leckerste truwant ende alder schalcken meester is, dieselve wort aldaer in 't lant tot eenen coning ghemaeckt. Ende die alleene plomp ende onverstandigh is, die wort tot eenen vorst ghestelt. Maer wie aldaer geerne vechtet met die ghebraden hoenderen ende leverworsten, ende weert hem aldermeest in de schotelen gelijck een vraet, die wort daer een ridder geslagen.

Ende die aldermeeste wijnsuyper of bierleerse, die niet en denct dan nae gulpen ende gieten, ende zijn kele te netten van den morgen toten avont, die wort aldaer tot eenen grave ghemaeckt. Ende wie datter een luy daghd-roomer is die niet en begheert dan te slapen, die is daer te lande voor een fijn edelman gheacht. Oft hier nu in desen lande yemant van den verloren kinderen ware, die nae dese voorschreven oft diergelijcke manieren zijn leven aenstellen wilde ende alle eere, deughde, eerbaerheyt ende beleeftheyt, ooc wijsheyt ende conste, achter rugge stellen, die mochte daerhenen in dit lant trecken. Hy soude ongetwijfelt als hy daer quame wel gesien ende gheacht wesen. Maer hy moeste hem bovenal wel neerstigh wachten ende toesien dat hy niet en stele, want hy soude aldaer aen der galghe ghehanghen worden die daer ontrent by het Luyeleckerlant staet.

> Desen ghedicht is van den ouden beschreven
> Ende tot onderwijs den jongers ghegheven,
> Die luy en lecker leven ghewent zijn.
> Ongheschict ende onachtsaem tot allen fijn,
> Die behoort men in 't Luyleckerlant te wijsen,
> Opdat se haer ongeschicktheyt laten rijsen
> Ende dat se hebben op arbeyt acht,
> Want luy en ledigh noyt deught en wracht.
> *Finis.*

Dutch Poems Appearing in English Translation

[p. 8]
Adam, als den wederspannighen, wordt verjaeght
Uijt dat lustich Paradijs, vol soeticheden,
Omdat hy naer Godts gebot niet en heeft gevraeght.
Dus moet hij zijnen tijt in arbeijt besteden,
Die tevoren wandelde in grooter vreden.

[p. 10]
Gheminde man, hout, nemt dees spade,
Daermede soe moetti wercs beginnen.
Met bitteren arbeide ende met smade
Soe moeten wi onsen nootdorst winnen.

[p. 60]
Ic sal u segghen in vraeyen rimen,
Elc gheset op sine linien,
Om dat ghij 't te bet onthouden sult
Ende niet daerin en sijt verdult.

[p. 74]
Omdat ic hebbe in mine memorie
Rime, favelen ende vraye ystorie,
De biblen, auctoren ende croniquen;

[p. 75]
Nu hoert alle ende werct u werc
Wat geschreven heeft een clerc
In dietsche, op dit parchement.

[p. 76]
God die gheve hem onlanghe lijf,
Die dese loghene dachte
Ende eerst in plaetsen brachte!

[p. 91]
Wronglen, wey, broot ende caes,
Dat heit hi al den dach.
Daeromme es de kerel so daes:
Hi hetes meer dan hij 's mach.

[p. 99]
Nu ghesoden, nu ghebraden,
Nu pasteyden, nu tarten, nu vladen,
Nu maleviseye, nu bier, nu wijn,
Nu ghingebaers of specie fijn.

[p. 116]
Want liet ic die werelt dus lange staen
In desen leven, in deser tempeesten,
't Volc soude erger worden dan beesten
Ende sou noch d'een den anderen eten.

[p. 149]
Zo lig ik voor U in de pan,
een vogel die niet vliegen kan,
O, welk een smart,
thans ben ik zwart,
't vuur dat zengt mij veel te hard!

[p. 189]
In de middewaert vandien,
Soe plante Hi des levens hout,
Dat heeft die cracht ende die wout
Dat het groten vrucht mach geven,
Gesonde ende lange leven.

[p. 198]
Van vastene, heere, dan pleighic niet;
Ic pleghe ooc cume te lezene yet;
Maer waken, brasseeren, gheselscap goet,
Dat es dat mi nu wandelen doet.
. . . .
Vader, ic wone al binder stat,
Woond' ick er buten alzo ghi,
So zoudix ooc wel hoeden mi.

[p. 205]
Och, wat vrouden daer wesen maech,
daer dusent jaer is eynen daech!
Vort is te wesen daer,
daer eyn daech is dusent jaer!

[pp. 270/271]
Dat quade volc, wildij 't weten,
Sal vleesch van menschen eten
Ende van beesten drincken d'bloet:
Dat sal hen duncken harde goet.
Si selen eten in haren doene
Beyde serpente ende scorpioene.
Ende dode corren, daer si se vinden,
Selen si eten ende verslinden.
Adren, slanghen, sijt 's gewes,
Ende dat onmenschelijc es,
Selen is t'etene bestaen.
Vrouwen, die met kinde gaen,
Selen si opdoen sonder ducht
Ende eten die ongheborne vrucht.
Die lande selen si struweren
Ende al in vulecheden keren.
Ende nieman en sal wesen so coene
Daerjeghen iet te doene.

[p. 288]
Dan comt de grote cornemuse
Ende pijpt hem turelurureleruut.
Ay, hoor van desen abuze!
Dan maec si groot gheluut,
Dan sprinc si alle overhoop,
Dan waecht haer langhe baert.
Si maken groot gheloop,
God gheve hem quade vaert!

[p. 293]
Vandaer seylden wy naer Italiën, daer die gansen spraken.
Daer sach ick van wetstenen papegayen maken,
Van walvisschen bergen fijn van gouwen.
't Gout lach daer by der straten, by hulcken en braecken,
Ghelijc 't slijc t'Amsterdam voor mannen en vrouwen.
Scheminkelen sach ic daer landen bouwen.
Melck en wijn lach daer op hie heggen.

[p. 308]
Twee dinghen minnen wi alremeest,
En tat leert ons die quade geest:
Dat 's ons vleesch ende ons goet,
Wel gecleet ende wel ghescoet.
Wel eten, drinken, zochte slapen,
Dit minnen leke metten papen:
Dus minnen wi ons selven dan.

[p. 342]
Heer Jesus in der bruyloft quam;
Van water maeckten hij wijn,
Omdat wij souden vrolijck sijn.
Wijnken en nu gaet in,
Nu wijnken en gaet nu in.

[p. 348]

God gheve dat wi so doyen moeten,
Smelten en de te nieute doen ons sonden,
Dat wi in den hemel verfroyen moeten,
Daer nemmermeer doot en wort vonden.

[p. 353]

Dat suetste van minnen sijn hare storme;
Haer diepste afgront es haer scoenste vorme;
In haer verdolen, dat 's na gheraken;
Om haer verhongheren, dat 's voeden ende smaken;
Hare mestroest es seker wesen;
Hare seerste wonden es al ghenesen;
Om hare verdoyen, dat es gheduren.

[p. 358]

Merket hoe die nydighe werlt staet!
Doe mi goet, ick doe di quaet;
Help my op, ick werp di neder;
Ere my, ick schen dy weder.

[p. 361]

Pijnt doch wel te verstane,
Dat hemelrijcke es te winnene
Met droncken te drinckene, ic moet verklaren.
Dus mijn beminde, wilt doch hulieder ziele bewaren
Ende en sparen goet noch eerve,
Al sauden u kinderen van hongher sterven.
Drijnct vrij altijts waer gij muecht.

[p. 366]

Doe sprac God tote Adame:
Om dattu dijns wijfs wille dades
Ende du mijn ghebod versmades,
So staet di dijn broot t'etene
Met pinen ende met zwetene.

[p. 367]

God droech Adaem van der aerden,
Vandaer hine gemaect hadde werde,
In 't paradijs, omdat hi woude
Dat hi daerin werken soude;
Niet dat hi pinen soude door noot,
Maer ghenoechte hebben groot.

[p. 371]

Notabile.

Wye slaept, als men seyen sall,
dy en heft geyn frucht, als men meyen sall;
wye slaept als men bidden sall,
dye wort geweygert, als men geven sall;
wye slaept, als hy sich erneren sall,
dye mist, als hy verteren sall;
wy slaept, als hy wercken sall,
dy sall vasten als men eten sall.
Qui timet deum nihil
negligit.

[p. 378]

Gans plaech! mijn maech is heel gespleeten,
Mijn buyck is sluyck, mijn wangen verstrangen,
Mijn beenen vercleenen . . .
Mijn dermen die kermen, 't is niet om weten,
Hoe sy grayen en crayen.

[p. 378]

's Morgens, eer 't dach is, es die maech al gespleeten
En soo onstelt, daer sou een waghen in hollen;
Een broot twee of drie is soo haest versleeten.
Elcxs behoefde wel 's daeghs twee of drie roggebollen,
Sout men haer buyck tot boven toe vollen,
Haer maech moet geen gront hebben . . .

[p. 380]
Men seit, die hem daertoe set,
Dat hi eenwerf 's daghes et,
Dat hi gheestelike leeft;
Ende wie hem daertoe gheeft,
Dat hi tweewerf et daghelike,
Dat hi leeft menschelike;
Ende die driewerf et ofte mee,
Dat hi leeft alse vee.

[p. 380]
Elx dages ad hi tere tijt,
Een gerstijn broet ende niet el;
Borre dranc hi, dat wet wel.

[p. 386]
Eten, drincken, langhe slapen,
Altoos wachten ende gapen
Na wasdom ende na ghewin,
Daertoe staet der poorters sin.
Voorcoop, perseme ende scalke neringhe
Ende vele ongheloofder dinghe
Hantieren poorters ghaerne.

[p. 415]
Stonde eyn borch van alpenbeynen
in eynen bomgart schoyn;
negen dueren van karbonckelsteynen,
darup eyn gulden croen.
Ende alle dye tynnen weeren eyn corall:
die borch, sy solde verlichten
vil clarer dan eyn cristall.

Sources

All translations into English are Diane Webb's unless otherwise specified.

The subject of this book has been tested out in several articles written over the space of some years, though my articles are no longer recognizable as such in this study. Only my original purpose has remained: to discover the meaning of the two Middle Dutch texts on Cockaigne (referred to as L and B, indicating London and Brussels, the places where the manuscripts are preserved) and the prose text on the related Luilekkerland (referred to as G, indicating Ghent, where a copy of the printed book with this text is preserved). Over a period of eight years I have discussed questions concerning these texts with many students at the University of Amsterdam; my greatest reward was getting so much fruitful feedback. Many of my students offered detailed and inspiring suggestions, and the same holds true for several colleagues who helped me with problems I could not solve myself. At the request of my publisher, Marieke van Oostrom made a whole series of critical remarks, often accompanied by suggestions for clarification or improvement, of which I gratefully made use.

The texts that form the point of departure for this book appear in English translation in chapter 4. The original Middle Dutch texts appear in appendix 1. The brackets in the original of text L indicate text that must have been on the missing corner of the folio. The correspondence between the line numbers in the original and those in the translation make it possible to ascertain where the translator filled in a plausible version of the missing text. Appendix 2 contains the original Dutch text on Luilekkerland. The Dutch originals of the poems appearing throughout the book are to be found in appendix 3; the page numbers refer to the places in the text where the English translations appear.

This book has no footnotes. Acknowledgment of the sources used and the visions of others adopted in this book are listed below by chapter.

PART I. THE FORFEITURE OF HAPPINESS:
THE BEGINNING

1. Paradise Lost

As noted, the English translations of the Dutch texts appear in chapter 4; all related information is given in chapters 5 and 9. Everything known up to the early-modern period in the way of Cockaigne texts and Cockaignesque texts in European literature has been gathered together in a German translation with commentary and references in two surveys, published at the same time, that are remarkable in the amount of overlapping information they contain: Müller (1984) and Richter (1984); additional bibliographical information is supplied by Bolte (1918) and Wunderlich (1986). Kasper (1992/93) could no longer be included in this book, but this wide-ranging article, based on Pleij (1991), also has a bibliographical character. A great deal of information and numerous references to the religious processions taking place in the Low Countries are to be found in Ramakers (1996b); for the Louvain procession, see van Even (1863), 19, 26, 27, 29, 31, 36, 39, and 50 and plate 5, an illustration of the cart in question; cf. Boonen (1880), 245. For similar carts elsewhere, see Ramakers (1996b), via the index; de Burbure (1878), 2, 7; Autenboer (1962), 40; van Gassen (1949), 135; van Lantschoot (1930), 22; and de Potter (1870), 30, 32, 34, 37, and cf. Hummelen (1968), 214. On the occasion of the royal entry preceding the marriage of Charles the Bold and Margaret of York in Bruges in 1468, there was also an elaborate performance of the Expulsion from Paradise, which apparently provided an attractive contrast to the unimaginable lavishness of the feasting that went on for days: see chapter 14; see also de Roovere (1866), 26–27. An example of a series of tapestries portraying this fundamental theme appears in Duverger (1973). The supposed phenomenon of souls being refused admittance to heaven as a result of the schism was expounded by the renowned chancellor of the University of Paris, Johannes Gerson (1728), col. 920–21. Regarding the *Bliscappen van Maria*, see Ramakers (1996a) and Pleij (1988b), 170–4, 264–65; the quotations are taken from *Die eerste bliscap* (1973), lines 371–4 and 379, respectively, and from the modern translation in *Maria* (1995), 16. Ramakers (1991/92) treats the emotive effect of performances at religious processions; cf. Pleij (1991/92).

2. Contours of a Book

Attractive anthologies containing Middle Dutch descriptions of paradise were compiled by de Vooys (1906) and Endepols (1909). A concise survey of this theme in the visual arts is to be found in van de Velde (1982), and Delumeau (1992) offers a general overview of Western visions of paradise. Columbus's vision is to be found in Greenblatt (1992), 78, and his belief that the Orinoco was one of the rivers of paradise in Cook (1977), 32. The idea of a golden age is also treated in a short survey by Delumeau (1992), 15–20. Regarding Germania, see Silver (1983) and Schama (1995), 75–134. Tilmans (1988), 121–66, deals with the myth of Batavia. Boendale (1844–1848), part I, ch. 31, bases his discussion of the golden age on Boethius. The heavenly Jerusalem is described in the Book of Revelation 21–22; in the *Sterfboeck* (1491), it is described in detail on fol. C2 recto–[C4] recto. Gardiner (1993) gives an overview of sources of medieval vision literature; cf. Aubrun (1980). Cohn (1984) offers a classic study of millenarianism, and Lerner (1972) an excellent study of the heresy of the Free Spirit, especially as regards the Brussels Adamites, on 157–63 and 190–95, and the arrogant Walter and the German Adamites, on 30–31; cf. Pleij (1988b), 159–60, 241–42. Glacken (1967), 213–14, 293–301, 312–13, writes about the completion of Creation as a task entrusted to humankind; regarding the special activities of the Cistercians in this respect, see also van Oostrom (1996), 89. Anna Bijns's refrain in (1902), 243–46, esp. 245. Gerard Zerbolt of Zutphen provided exercises in conjuring up visions of paradise in his treatise *Tractatus de spiritualibus ascensionibus*, written in Latin, but a transliterated Middle Dutch version has also been preserved: Zerbolt (1941), 108–13; cf. Goossens (1952), 229. Rites of inversion in general are treated in Pleij (1992); regarding celebrations in clerical circles, see Bischoff (1967). Exuberant feasting among the nobility is dealt with in detail by Lafortune-Martel (1984). For fountains of drink, see Pleij (1988b), 117–18, 350–51. The excerpt from the prose novel *Die historie van Peeter van Provencen* is taken from the facsimile edition of 1982, fol. [H2] recto. Concerning a renewed interest in nature, see Pleij (1990), 17–78, and regarding zoological gardens in particular, see Pleij (1988b), 249–52. Details of the wonder park at Hesdin are to be found in Brunet (1971). Rapp (1975) treats the general subject of fountains of youth. For the farce *Playerwater*, see Hummelen (1968), 229. Nearly half of the pretentious *'t Scep vol wonders*, printed in 1514 by Thomas van der Noot in Brussels (chs. 102–180) treats the miraculous *quinta essentia*, which supposedly had exceptional healing and rejuvenating powers. For *Die buskenblaser*, see *Buskenblaser* (1968). Hallucinations caused by malnourishment and the eating of alternative foodstuffs such as grass are discussed by Camporesi (1989), 17–20, 120–50. Reports of the Palestinian martyrs appeared in the newspaper *NRC Handelsblad* on 4 March 1996; their stories are reminiscent of the medieval story of the Old Man of the Mountain. The existence of an ancient Greek "Cockaigne" may be deduced from fragments of comedies preserved from the fifth century B.C.: see Poeschel (1878), 391–94; Bonner (1910). Concerning Celtic mariners' tales, see Oskamp (1970), as well as the introduction and commentary to the Middle Dutch version of the voyage of Saint Brendan (*De reis van Sint Brendaan* 1994, hereafter referred to as *Reis*). The passage quoted from the Bible is Mark 13:30; cf. Leupen (1996), 44. Concerning purgatory, see Le Goff (1981).

3. The Power of Literature

Besides source books almost nothing has been written about the Middle Dutch rhyming texts on Cockaigne and the prose text on Luilekkerland. In a critical edition of both rhyming texts, de Keyser (1956) makes several remarks, followed by De Meyer (1962), 432–40, from the perspective of the printmaking inspired by Luilekkerland. Pleij (1991) attempts to link the Cockaigne texts with representations of paradise, travel stories, and heresy.

PART 2. TEXTS AS MAPS

4. Rhyming Texts L and B, Prose Text G

Text L is based on the manuscript preserved in the British Library in London, MS Add. 10286, fol. 135 recto–verso; text B on the manuscript preserved in Brussels, Bibliothèque Royal Albert I, MS II.144, fol. 102 verso–105 recto; text G on the copy in Ghent, University Library, Res. 504, of the *Veelderhande geneuchlycke dichten* (Antwerp, Jan van Ghelen, 1600), fol. G1 recto–G4 recto. The texts have undergone slight adaptation in this edition: abbreviated words are written in full, modern punctuation has been added, and the layout modernized. In the case of text L an attempt has been made to guess the content of the text on the missing corner by choosing from the possibilities offered by text B. Priebsch (1894) offers a synopsis of texts L and B; de Keyser (1956), 33–36, attempts to reconstruct the presumed original of the Cockaigne text, represented by texts L and B. Text G occurs in the edition of *Veelderhande geneuchlycke dichten* (1899), 142–50, and also in de Keyser (1956), 37–38.

5. The Two Rhyming Texts on the Land of Cockaigne

The London manuscript containing text L is briefly described in Jansen-Sieben (1989), no. L 720; the existing editions of the separate texts are also mentioned there. Jean-Marc van Tol has attempted in his thesis (University of Amsterdam, 1995) to typify the manuscript as a whole. Dr. Herman Brinkman made transcriptions of the satirical text containing "Merket hoe die nydighe werlt staet" (fol. 133 recto) and the Latin prose text with a satire on money including "Nvmmus que pars Praeposicio" (fol. 136 recto). Further details have been gleaned from material at the Bibliotheca Neerlandica Manuscripta (BNM) at Leiden. The identification of the snippet bound into the London manuscript was made by van Tol (see above). *Die peregrinacie van iherusalem* is on fol. 137 recto–146 recto and appeared in de Flou et al. (1897) 403–32; the text is a translation of the *Peregrinationes* by Willem van Gouda (see Carasso-Kok 1981, no. 345). Comments on nuances of language have been borrowed from information found in the BNM (see above) and various articles from the *Bouwstoffen* (vol. 10) of the *MNW* that discuss separate editions of texts found in the manuscript. There is a separate edition of the *Sidrac* (1936), for example, though it was based on another manuscript. Parts of the *Lucidarius boeck* (in the MS fol. 115 recto–133 recto) appear in Schorbach (1894), 196–216; the mock doctor's prescription containing "Item hyr mach men vinden eenrehande medicinen" (fol. 134 recto–verso) was published in de Flou et al. (1897), 206–8; *Sesterhande verwen* (fol. 146 verso–148 verso) also appears there, on 193–200. Regarding the relative autonomy of the Middle Dutch texts and the influence exerted on them by the printing press, see Pleij (1995c). Van Tol (see above) remarks on the many mistakes made by the copyist, as well as their correction. The startling mistakes in the pilgrims' guide are to be found on fol. 139 recto and 144 recto. The Brussels manuscript containing text B is briefly described in Jansen-Sieben (1989), no. B 950, where editions of the separate texts are also mentioned. Priebsch (1906 and 1907), who also published many of the texts discussed, offers more detail on this subject. The calendar is on fol. 55 verso–56 verso and reprinted in Priebsch (1906), 443–44. Venlo is named in the song on fol. 82 recto (see Priebsch 1906, 464–65); similar songs not mentioning locations are to be found in *Een schoon liedekensboeck* (1968), nos. 191 and 193; see *Liederen* (1966), nos. 138 and 121. Venlo belonged at that time to the so-called Gelderse Overkwartier (see Alberts 1966, 4); accordingly, the song on fol. 100 recto is attributed to a "dominicus de gelria" (a Dominican from Gelre) (see Priebsch 1907, 164). A parallel text speaks only of a "Dominican brother" (see van Duyse (1903–1907), vol. 3, no. 613. Priebsch (1906 and 1907) also provides insight into the way in which the compiler of the Brussels manuscript treated the texts he collected. The *Carmina Burana* atmosphere is compellingly portrayed in Waddell (1968). The text about wine is on fol. 22 recto–26 recto (see Priebsch 1906, 318–22). A poem in macaronic form is to be found on fol. 39 recto–40 recto; the "Meum est propositum" is on fol. 58 verso; an ode to students is on fol. 68 recto–verso (see Priebsch 1906, 451). Regarding Carnival repertoire, see Pleij (1983b), part 3, and Pleij (1992); the mock doctor's prescription in text L was published by de Flou et al. (1897), 206–8; the one in text B appears in Jansen-Sieben (1987).

6. Recitation and Writing

A detailed overview of the problems surrounding communication between author and public, as well as the genesis of texts in the Middle Ages is given by Green (1994). Concerning oral traditions with regard to Middle Dutch literature, see Spijker (1990), 203–27, and Gerritsen (1992b); Richter (1994), 64–72, points out the existence of strong audience participation. Lying tales are dealt with in greater detail in chapter 27. The improvisation of variations and the attraction this held for the audience is treated by Ortutay (1959), esp. 182; the predilection for lying tales and the competition between reciters is treated in *Verfasserlexikon* (1983), col. 1044; cf. Vasvari (1991), 180; see also Chaucer (1995), lines 13.899–910. The quotation from the Tale of Sir Thopas is taken from Chaucer (1974), 167. Ong (1988), esp. 16–27, gives a concise survey of modern field research among reciters and singers; the establishment of a correspondence is found on 62. Details on the three Old French texts plus a critical edition of the texts with variants are given by Väänänen (1947). The term *narrative skeleton* is a literal translation of the Dutch term *verhaalskelet* adopted from Spijker (1990), 205. An edition of the Middle English text on the Land of Cokaygne appears in Robbins (1959), 121–27 and 317–19; cf. de Caluwé-Dor (1977, 1978, and 1980) and Tigges (1988). References to German texts on Schlaraffenland occur in Bolte (1910), 187–93; texts are reprinted in Brant (1854), cxxii–cxxiii, Richter (1984), 149–52, and Müller (1984), 48–51, 55–58. Regarding oral characteristics in texts meant for reading, see Scholz (1980), 84–90. The quotation is from *De natuurkunde van het geheelal* (1968), 1:275, lines 5–8; commentary, 2:623–30. Caedmon and texts recorded as an aide-mémoire for reciters, as opposed to their learning texts by literal memorization, is treated in Ong (1988), 57–58, and Yates (1988), 27 and passim; see also Carruthers (1994).

7. Oral Structures in Writing

Regarding oral narrative technique and writing things down from memory, cf. Duggan (1975), 74; Ong (1988), 34–40; Spijker (1990) 217, 226. Cf.: text L, line 4, and text B, line 4; text L, line 7, and text B, line 7; text L, line 94, and text B, line 108; text L, line 58, and text B, line 66; the first-person narrator in text L, lines 4, 5, 6, and 98, and text B, lines 4, 5, 6, 108, 117, and 130; the opening lines of text L, lines 1–3, and then lines 4 and 7. For the list of elements used as padding, see text L, lines 83 and 94, and text B, lines 24, 100, 101, and 108. Close correspondences between texts L and B, respectively, include line 10 and line 10; lines 20 and line 18;

line 96 and line 110; line 18 and line 16 and 48; line 40 and line 34; lines 55–56 and lines 63–64. Concerning the proverbs, see Harrebomee (1980), 1:344 and 3:410; Suringar (1873), 125–26, 494; Frank (1991), 317–19, deals with the proverbs found in Bruegel. Repeated key phrases occur in text B, lines 19 and 97 (line 19 occurs almost exactly in text L, line 21), text B, lines 16 and 48, and text B, lines 63 and 125; introductory formulas occur in text B, lines 76, 89, 103, and 114, and, despite reservations regarding their occurrence in text L, owing to loss of text, in lines 12, 46, and 86 there; other repetitions occur in text B, lines 63–64 and lines 125–26, and in line 62 and line 70. For the passage on sex, see text B, lines 103–15. For the closing, see text B, lines 130–32, and text L, lines 99–100. The carbuncles in text B, line 24, are treated in detail in chapter 40. Regarding spontaneous lapses of memory, cf. also Spijker (1990), 217. Class satire is treated in Pleij (1983b), 177–86, where there is also information on *Der sotten ende der narren scip* (Brant 1500). All information on the Old French texts plus a critical edition (text F) with variations is to be found in Väänänen (1947). Concerning charivari, see Rey-Flaud (1985) and Pleij (1989). Correspondences between the roast geese occur in text F, lines 39–42, and text B, line 72; similarities between the increased frequency of holidays occur in text F, lines 80–88, text B, lines 98–101, and text L, lines 77–83.

8. The Existing Potential

Regarding reciters in the Low Countries, see Pleij (1977); Peters (1983), 172–206; Hogenelst (1993); Meder (1996). Hildegaersberch is treated in detail in Meder (1991). Concerning the resistance to street poets, see Boendale (mentioned below). The quotation from the Deventer rules and regulations is in Hogenelst (1993), 97; "Snelryem" (epigrammatist) is in Jonckbloet (1851–1855), 3:600; information on, as well as the text by, Pieter den Brant is to be found in Batselier (1976), 8–11, and de Pauw (1893–1897), 577–80; for Caedmon, see Fry (1975), 42–44. See *Van den IX besten* in *Het Geraardsbergse handschrift* (1994), 146–64, lines 1–3, 14, 23. The Brussels satirical rhyming text appears in Cuvelier (1928); lines 1–3 are quoted here (in translation); cf. Pleij (1988b), 155–58. Boendale's text occurs in his *Der leken spieghel* (1844–1848), vol. 3, ch. 15, esp. lines 119–82; cf. Gerritsen (1992a) and Pleij (1995a), 161–67. The quotation from "Tristan and Isolde" is from the adaptation by Bédier: *Tristan* (1964), 48; in this part he translated a passage from the High German version by Eilhart von Oberge. Chaucer also makes a clear distinction between stories stemming from a written tradition and those from an oral tradition, represented by the "Man of Law" and the "Wife of Bath," respectively, quoted by Mulder-Bakker (1996), 50.

9. The Prose Text on Luilekkerland

See the basic information in chapter 1. Concerning recommendations in the presentation of printed literature, see Vermeulen (1986); cf. Pleij (1995c). In *Veelderhande geneuchlycke dichten* (1899), see 40, 49, 64, 72, 110, 115, 142, 156, 163, 188, 191, 195, and 199. For early (Low German) editions of the Aernout texts, see *Frantzen* (1920) and cf. translation and afterword in *Schelmen* (1985). For an earlier edition of the text on the life of the pseudosaint Laudate, see *Hier beghint 't leven* (ca. 1550). At least three separate, early editions are known of *Jan Splinters testament: Leest hierin wat genoechlicx claer* (ca. 1508), published in De Pauw (1893–1897), I, 684–90; [Splinter] (1584); and [Splinter] (ca. 1600). Regarding mock datings and suchlike in the Carnival repertoire, see Pleij (1983b), part 3; the document dating from 1517 is discussed, with illustrations, in Pleij (1983a). References to the German Carnival play occur in "Der Prozesz gegen Rumpold" (1991), 350–51. For later broadsheets and songs, see de Keyser (1956); de Meyer (1962), 432–40; de Meyer (1970); van Veen (1976), 116–17; see also *Verhael* (1692); *Af-vaaren* (ca. 1700); Kalff (1884), 490–91; Scheltema (1885), 265–66. All information on Hans Sachs's *Schlaraffenland* (hereafter referred to as S) is from Bolte (1910), 187–93; see also Sachs (1893), no. 4, 8–11; cf. Wunderlich (1986). A modern translation in German appears in Müller (1984), 57–58. Sachs's text was also translated into Dutch verse beneath an eighteenth-century print: see De Meyer (1960). Regarding "true tidings" in the sixteenth century, see Mout (1984), 365. For the notion that prose contains more truth than verse, see Scholz (1980), 184–86, and more generally Lie (1994). The phenomenon of "prodigal children" or "white-bread children" as a late-medieval symbol of urban prosperity is treated in Pleij (1983b), 205–10; Pleij (1988b), 148–50; Pleij (1995b), 177. The examples from Sachs are to be found in Müller (1984), 48–51 and 55–57. The humorous translation of "Christmas" occurs in S 3, and text G, line 5; sleeping on cushions and hunting vermin occurs in S 58–60. The elaborations mentioned occur in text G, lines 17, 28–29, 67–70, 70–72, 40–42 52–53, respectively. Earning money is discussed in text G, lines 73–77; debtors in text G, lines 79–90; rewarding drunkards in text G, lines 91–96; rewarding misbehavior in text G, lines 111–129; and whores in text G, lines 100–105. Regarding Antwerp as a city full of whores, see Pleij (1993a), 83–85; on the prodigal children, see S 101–7 and text G, lines 124–131; see also above. For *Das Wachtelmäre*, see *Verfasserlexikon* (1953), col. 729–30, and "Wahtelmaere" (1828). In addition, see chapters 27 and 28 for both rhetoricians' farces.

PART 3. EATING TO FORGET

10. Eating Habits

Regarding positive and negative attitudes to nature, see Pleij (1990), 17–78. The so-called *Kerelslied* and *Van den kaerlen* appear in Komrij (1994), 222–24 and 171–75, respectively; see Stijevoort (1930), nos. 18 and 66; *Een schoon liedekens-boeck* (1968), no. 213; *De middelnederlandse boerden* (1957), 39; Macropedius (1995), 53. For typical peasant fare, see Montanari (1994), 102; Bergner (1990), 47–48. For Hans Weiditz, the Petrarch Master, see Scheidig (1955), 204 (with illus.), and Raupp (1986), 27–28. All references to mock prognostications can be found in *Het zal koud zijn in 't water als 't vriest* (1980), 68, line 162; and Bijns (1902), 335. A richly illustrated overview of depictions of the months of the year in calendars and suchlike is given by Hansen (1984). The notion of monotonous eating habits between 1000 and 1300 is put forward by van Werveke (1967), 5; the ample supply of food thereafter ("carnivorous Europe") is discussed in Montanari (1994), 87–88. See Jansen-Sieben (1993), 161–63; and Salisbury (1994), 58. Regarding the eating habits of the aristocracy, see Montanari (1994), 98–105; Bergner (1990), 47–48; Bumke (1986), 1:241–46; Lafortune-Martel (1984), 97–98; Schotel (1840), 9–14; on the fact that, above all, nobles ate meat, see Salisbury (1994), 57. Wild game in Cockaigne is mentioned in text L, lines 41–45, and text B, lines 39–42. For animals as food for man and meat as consolation, see Thomas (1990), 16, 304–5; Salisbury (1994), 43. On fruit, see de Lorris et al. (1991), lines 8177–88; and de Roovere (1866), 65. For spices in Cockaigne, see text L, lines 67–68; text B, lines 85–86; and text G, lines 17 and 53; see Montanari (1994), 77; Laurioux (1989), 206–7; Maerlant (1857–1863), vol. 3, part 1, ch. 39, lines 37–38; the text by Egidius is reprinted in Verdam (1892), 286; the Carnival play is in Hummelen (1968), No. 1, no. 8, fol. 149 recto; the refrain is in Komrij (1994), 1140; and de Lorris et al. (1991), lines 11.712–21. On luxury peasant fare and variety, see van den Berghe (1950) (for the quotation, see lines 228–29, 343–49, and 354); and de Weert (1915), lines 1308–11.

11. Hunger and Scarcity

Regarding the small number of actual famines, see van Werveke (1967); and Russell (1972), 66. Blockmans el al. (1980), 56, points out the small number of deaths attributable to starvation alone; see also Montanari (1994), 18, 38. For dependence on people in one's immediate surroundings, see Behre (1990), 78–80, 86. The need to seek contrasts with the present, easily to be found in the Middle Ages, is noted in Pleij

(1990), 220–34, and Pleij (1993b), 7–13, 34–35. A monograph on medieval famines does not exist; the surveys of hunger and scarcity during the ancien régime in Torfs (1859–1862) are very unreliable as regards the Middle Ages (1:145–250 and 2:231–53) and not well founded; Curschmann (1900) treats only the period up to 1315 and is, of course, no longer up to date. Concerning the interrelation of causes and consequences, see Blockmans et al. (1980), 56; and Curschmann (1900), 18–23; cf. van Cappel (1906). Many chronicles speak mainly or exclusively of the vindictive hand of God as a cause of famine. For the famine of 1315–1317, Velthem's sequel to Maerlant's *Spiegel historiael* gives a curious mixture of causes, such as God's wrath, natural catastrophes, and economic hardship: see Velthem (1906–1938), vol. 3, part 6, chs. 24–25. The plague in particular obscures our view of deaths from famine, see Curschmann (1900), 60–62; and Montanari (1994), 84; and cf. Verhoeven (1992), 9; Lucas (1930), 358, 364–65; and Rommel (1893), 66. Furthermore, vagueness regarding the definition of the terms *famine* and *scarcity* plays tricks with both the old sources and the modern interpretations thereof. On a plague of grasshoppers in 873, see Curschmann (1900), 22; and cf. van Cappel (1906), 21–22. For an example of weather as the cause of the famine of 1124–1125, see Galbert (1967), 84–89. On usury, see Curschmann (1900), 47–51; cf. a number of Brussels examples of such artificial scarcity in Vanhemelryck (1984), 159–61 and 169; Gregory of Tours (1974), 427, already called usury the cause of famine in Gaul between 584–591; for Hildegaersberch and Lauris Janszoon, see Meder (1991), 131, 594 n. 23; and Marijnissen (1971), 23–24, respectively; regarding Janszoon, cf. Kuttner (1949), 218–27. On war, see Curschmann (1900), 25. Regarding scarcity between 1000–1300 and the three famines during that period, see van Werveke (1967), 5; cf. van Cappel (1906), 35, who points out no fewer than seven famines during the same period; Montanari (1994), 54, names more than twenty-six periods of scarcity in the eleventh century. Agriculture produced only one-half or one-third as much at the beginning of the twentieth century, see van Cappel (1906), 29. On the famine of 1315–1317, see Curschmann (1900), 33 and 208–17 (with survey of sources); Lucas (1930); van Werveke (1960); van Werveke (1967), 6; Frank (1990), 96–97 (for England); *Brabantsche yeesten* (1839), vol. 5, ch. 10, lines 779–850 (the quotation occurs on lines 808–10); Velthem (1906–1938), vol. 3, part 6, chs. 24–25. The anecdote about Louis X is in Torfs (1859–1862), 1:176; whether it is true or not is of no importance: the important thing is that it was told. Russell (1972), 66, describes the social control over the exploitation of agricultural land. For the increasing fear of hunger and scarcity in the fourteenth century, see Montanari (1994), 18, 38, 82, 84, 110–11; and Frank (1990), 88–89. On the serious consequences of this, see van Werveke (1967), 5–7; Curschmann (1900), 27, 62–67; van Cappel (1906), 149; Lucas (1930), 363; and Frank (1990), 95. On the diary of de Doppere, see

Rommel (1893), 66. The mention of the hand of God is almost never lacking in medieval chronicles: see Curschmann (1900), 12–14; van Cappel (1906), 20–21. Famines demonstrate the perversion of Creation resulting from the Fall of Man and are reported as such in the Bible: see, for example, Genesis 12:10, 26:1; Ruth 1:1; II Samuel 21:1; I Kings 18:2; II Kings 6:24–30; and Acts 11:28. According to the gospels, famines more particularly point to the end of time, see Matthew 24:7, Mark 13:8, and especially Luke 21:11. These passages from the Bible provide the model for contemporary interpretations of scarcity: see Galbert (1967), 84–85 (also with a reference to Psalms 105:16); cf. Gregory (1974), 584; Alpertus (1980), 17; Glaber in Duby (1993), 120. *Sidrac* (1936), 64, interprets the late-medieval standpoint of the laity: hunger is the punishment inflicted on humankind for original sin.

12. The Topos of Hunger

See Galbert (1967), 84–89, for the emphasis on fears. For horror stories in chronicles, see Curschmann (1900), 57; cf. Walker Bynum (1987), 2; Montanari (1994), 16, and further examples in this chapter. Regarding terrifying memories of large-scale famines, see also *Handwörterbuch* (1927–1942), s.v. "Hunger." For the model of Jeremiah 14, see Frank (1990), 96. Bunte (1992) gives a complete edition of all Middle Dutch and sixteenth-century sources containing reports of the famine during the siege of Jerusalem in A.D. 70; cf. *Een historische beschryving* (1741), 35–39. Regarding the vengeance God postponed for forty years, see [Boendale] (1994), 13. For the tapestries, see Weigert (1962), 52. Arent Willemszoon's first thoughts upon seeing Jerusalem are recorded in *Bedevaart* (1884), 103–4. The two traditions in Middle Dutch literature are dealt with by Braekman in *Boec van de destructien van Jherusalem* (1984), 6–8. Concerning Maerlant's *Wrake*, see also van Oostrom (1996), 254–55, 263. For the recurring points in such accounts, see the selected passages on the destruction of Jerusalem in Bunte (1992); the mother who butchers and eats her own child is never missing from these accounts; the model for this is found in the Bible, II Kings 6:24–30; this is also a well-known motif in folk tales and legends, see *Handwörterbuch* (1927–1942), s.v., "Hunger," col. 503. For this as a model for other cases of starvation, see Kramer et al. (1971), 100; Maerlant (1857–1863), vol. 3, part 6, ch. 31, lines 13–18, and vol. 4, part 1, ch. 41, lines 41–43; Lucas (1930), 355, 364, 376; Torfs (1859–1862), 1:179; Cohn (1984), 277. Regarding the topos of hunger, see also Montanari (1994), 56. For Glaber, see Duby (1993), 120–23. For bizarre details, see Alpertus (1980), 17; and Glaber in Duby (1993), 121–22. On food surrogates, see van Cappel (1906), 26, 148, 149; Curschmann (1900), 58; Montanari (1994), 17, 55; Lucas (1930), 356, 360; Glaber in Duby (1993), 121, 122; *Een historische beschryving* (1741), 35, 67;

Gregory (1974), 427; and *Proverbes* (1937), 70 and plate 130. On unclean and dead animals, see van Cappel (1906), 148–49; Curschmann (1900), 58; Montanari (1994), 55; *Een historische beschryving* (1741), 67; Glaber in Duby (1993), 121; and Lucas (1930), 355, 370. The punishment of gluttons in hell is described in detail in *Boeck* (1930), 168. On cannibalism as characteristic behavior of marginal peoples, see Curschmann (1900), 59; Camporesi (1989), 48–53; Pagden (1981), 17–18; Mandeville (1908), cols. 154, 213, 244. Regarding the ancient Bacchanalia, see Pagden (1981), 19–20. The quotation is from *Den spieghel der salicheit van Elckerlijc* (1967), lines 26–29. For behavior during times of famine, see Frank (1990), 97; Glaber in Duby (1993), 120–23; *Een historische beschryving* (1741), 36, 39, 53, 56, 61, 66, 67; and Lucas (1930), 355–36, 376; see also the references to Maerlant and Torfs mentioned earlier in the sources for this chapter. Unburied corpses occur as a model in Jeremiah 14:16; see Frank (1990), 96–97; *Boec van de destructien van Jherusalem*(1984), fol. L2 verso; Glaber in Duby (1993), 122–23. On the huge numbers of victims, see Curschmann (1900), 61–62 (for numbers in Metz in 1316); and Lucas (1930), 362; cf. *Een historische beschryving* (1741), 52, 56; Maerlant (1857–1863), vol. 4, part 1, ch. 51, lines 39–42; *Brabantsche yeesten* (1839), vol. 5, ch. 10, lines 832–33; and Lucas (1930), 366.

13. The Intoxicating Effect of Fasting

The fasting practices of the desert fathers are described by Brown (1990), 172–76; and Fox (1986), 19; cf. *Vaderboec* (1480), fol. [A7] recto, G2 recto, G4 recto–verso; cf. in general Walker Bynum (1987). For eating as a sign of decadence, see also the *Sidrac* (1936), 45. Concerning Adam's vegetarianism and the "unnaturalness" of eating meat, see Thomas (1990), 304–5; cf. Bergner (1990), 47–48; models for this are to be found in the Bible, e.g., Daniel 1:8–16; this explains why some monastic orders, such as the Cistercians, embraced vegetarianism as an ideal of the claustral life: see Duby (1989), 67. For discussions of this in Middle Dutch literature with reference to Boethius as the authority, see Boendale (1844–1848), vol. 1, ch. 24, lines 45–48; ch. 31, lines 1–13; cf. de Dene (1978/79), 40, and 56; on meat eaters stinking in their graves, see the Carnival play in Hummelen (1968), 1 N 8, fol. 150 recto. The anecdote about Saint Francis is in Maerlant (1954), lines 2211–28. The madness of fasting and the demonstrative eating sometimes indulged in by hermits is treated in Walker Bynum (1987), 2 and 196. For catering in paradise in Celtic travel stories, see Oskamp (1970), 139; cf. *Reis* (1994), lines 469–75. Concerning the apple sniffers, see Camporesi (1994), 286–96; they are also mentioned in all encyclopedic surveys of marginal peoples. The Camerini are discussed by Boas (1978), 138–39, and occur also in Mandeville. With regard to extreme fasting among nuns and other women, see

Walker Bynum (1987), 73–129. For Lidwina's popular biography with translation, see *Het leven van Liedewij* (1989). Examples of fasting among adherents of the Devotio Moderna (lay sisters) occur in *Hemels verlangen* (1993), 120, 155. The Eucharist is expressed in John 6:48–51. For his sermon, see Brugman (1948), 110–46, esp. 114–15. Augustine's sermon is quoted by Montanari (1994), 30. Ruusbroec's text is taken from his *Van den xij beghinen*, reprinted in *Werken* (1944–1948), vol. 4, ch. 36, 85. The Easter hymn is quoted in Walker Bynum (1987), 49, who also discusses the spiritual consequences of eating His body and drinking His blood (67–68). The accusations of the Romans are treated in Faas (1994), 39–41; for their banqueting traditions, see 93. The Martial quotation is from Martial (1968), 465. The bite taken out of the crusader Jan van Montfoort is noted in Zeebout (1572), 252. The text on Saint Lawrence is taken from *Het Middelnederlandse leerdicht Rinclus* (1893), lines 311–13. Burial customs of marginal peoples in Mandeville are discussed by Greenblatt (1992), 44–45; the quotation is taken from Mandeville (1983), 186–87. There was a great fear in the Middle Ages of dying and being left unburied in the open fields as food for animals to prey on: see Salisbury (1994), 71–72. An example of this in literature is the moving story of Griselda in Chaucer's *Canterbury Tales* (1995), lines 8482–88, 8594–97, 9007–10; her biggest worry as regards the impending execution of her children was the fear that their bodies would remain unburied and be preyed on by carrion eaters. Concerning hallucinations caused by malnourishment, see Camporesi (1989), 127, and Montanari (1994), 150–51. On the visions of delicious food seen by Apollonius et al., see Brown (1990), 174. On drugged Europe, see Camporesi (1989), 14–15 (foreword by R. Porter), 17–20, 122–27; cf. Camporesi (1994), 38–39, 228–36, 275. For the sniffing Folly, see Erasmus (1959), 41, and cf. 29. The subject of Turks getting high is treated in *Een nieu sunderling boeck* (1542), fol. E3 verso; see Mout (1984) in general regarding the picture of the Turks in sixteenth-century scandal sheets. For Job's land, see [Mandeville] (1908), col. 131. For visions in general, see Gardiner (1993) and Aubrun (1980). Walker Bynum (1987) treats the subject of women practicing extreme mortification of the flesh by abstaining from food. For Lidwina of Schiedam, see *Het leven van Liedewij* (1989), esp. 90–91.

14. Gorging in Self-Defense

For proverbs, *Proverbia* (ca. 1484), fol. A1 recto; cf. Kloeke (1959), 42. The "putrid paunch" outburst occurs in de Weert (1915), line 1307; cf. van Delf (1937–1939), 2:209, lines 118–21 (with reference to the First Commandment); see also de Vooys (1902), 362. The Aernout brothers' rule is discussed in *Veelderhande geneuchlycke dichten* (1899), 92. The reproach, often heard, that one worshiped one's belly instead of God is based on

Philippians 3:19 and Romans 16:18. Tertullian is quoted in Faas (1994), 41. Lucas van Leyden's painting is to be found in the Rijksmuseum in Amsterdam. Regarding examples of hedonistic blowouts, see Schmitt (1995), 43 and 144. Panicky gorging is discussed in Galbert (1967), 85–86; *Het volksboek van Ulenspieghel* [Til Eulenspiegel] (1986), 101. Regarding the sacred nature of communal blowouts, see Althoff (1990), 24–25; and Ariès et al. (1987), 344, 352, 354. The names of the various sorts of meals are to be found in Linskens (1976), 110–11. Eating as a victory over death is stressed by Bakhtin (1984), 281–83, 302; cf. Walker Bynum (1987), 2; and Montanari (1994), 111. For wolfish machos among the Franks, see Montanari (1994), 36–37, who describes on 39–40 Charlemagne's fluctuating eating habits; see also Maerlant (1857–1863), vol. 4, part 1, ch. 2, lines 39–50; and van Oostrom (1996), 319. The eating competition between Loki and Logi is described in Montanari (1994), 37, where the *Chanson de Guillaume* is discussed on 71; a contrast to such gluttonous behavior is to be found in courtly romances such as *Erec:* see Bumke (1986), 1:246. On the many fast days, see Montanari (1994), 92; cf. Jansen-Sieben (1993), 159. Regarding the pre-Lenten festivities and the church's Feast of Fools, see in general Pleij (1992) and the literature listed therein. Eating binges and carousing in cloisters are described in Bischoff (1967); *Handwörterbuch* (1927–1942), vol. 4, cols. 745–60; and *MNW* vol. 4, col. 1622; see also Montanari (1994), 37, who treats the incident at Aachen; cf. Lafortune-Martel (1984), 33. Concerning displays of ostentation among the nobility, see Lafortune-Martel (1984), 18, 71, and passim; cf. Duby (1973), 350; Bergner (1990), 47–48; and Bumke (1986), 1:242. Maerlant also found such behavior a necessity for royalty: see van Oostrom (1996), 233–34. Public displays of opulence for the benefit of common folk are treated in Montanari (1994), 107 (Bologna), and in Macropedius (1995), 49. Table fountains spouting drinks are described in Lafortune-Martel (1984), 43–44, 116–17; cf. *The International Style* (1962), no. 126 and plate 107; for other drinking fountains, see Pleij (1988b), 117–18, 350–51; Smit (1995), 318–19; Lafortune-Martel (1984), 49, 116–17 (Brussels 1409); Guenée et al. (1968), 12, 21; Kronyk (1839–1840), 2:109, 110, 111, 225, 230 (Bruges 1440, Ghent 1458); de Roovere (1866), 32 (Bruges 1468); ms Vienna, Austrian National Library, Cod. 2591, fol. 45 verso (Bruges 1515); Dupuys (1515), fol. [E5] recto (Bruges 1515); *De Triumphe* (1515), fol. [C2] verso (idem). Lafortune-Martel (1984) is devoted to the Lille Pheasant Banquet; cf. Jansen-Sieben (1993), 164; something similar also occurred in Bologna in 1487: see Montanari (1994), 107–8.

15. Food in Motion

The subject of spectacular displays of food at banquets is treated by Camporesi (1994), 85–86; cf. a copperplate engraving of 1585 in Jockel (1995), 34. Jansen-Sieben

(1993), 165–75, writes about the surprising dishes made from recipes in cookbooks. Regarding the pig with blood sausages spilling out of it, see also Lafortune-Martel (1984), 40. The whale served at the wedding of Charles the Bold in 1468 is described in de Roovere (1866), 66; Cakes filled with birds are discussed in Lafortune-Martel (1984), 33; and Montanari (1994), 107. The arena of cake containing a fighting snake and dove is described in Lafortune-Martel (1984), 35–37. The siege of Jerusalem served at a banquet in 1378 is reported in van Winter (1976), 50. For the ships at one of the banquets in 1468, see Lafortune-Martel (1984), 53; cf. de Roovere (1866), 40–66, who describes the Tower of Gorcum on 47–48. Concerning the fun and games typical of Roman cuisine, see Faas (1994), 16–18. De Roovere (1866), 40–66, describes banquets at which animals play a role. For entertainment including anthropomorphic animals in an upside-down world, see Pleij (1988b), 135–37. A comprehensive catalog of figural depictions in the margins of medieval illuminated manuscripts is given by Randall (1966); cf. Camille (1992). Weaponry and suchlike made of food is treated in de Dene (1976/77), 122–23, lines 14–18; and *La grande confrarie* (1520–1540), fol. B1 verso–B2 recto. For the divine dispensation of food in paradise, including the eating of animals, see Genesis 1:26, 28, 30. Papias is quoted in Benz (1974), 94. Adam's mastery over the animals and human exploitation of animals is discussed in Thomas (1990), 16, 304–5; and Salisbury (1994), 43. On animals delivered alive to consumers, see Montanari (1994), 74–75. The increasing distaste for butchering is treated in Thomas (1990), 309–10, while the suggestion of the rise of a substitute dream comes from Tamara Bos, a former student at the University of Amsterdam. Regarding the Eucharist, see chapter 13. For the proverb, see Sartorius (1561), fol. K3 verso; cf. Stoett (1981), no. 394. The first quotation from Petronius is taken from the edition of the *Satyricon* translated by William Burnaby (1964), 55; see also Petronius (1988), 64, for the quotation on the roasted pigs. The painting by Mandyn is to be found in the Municipal Museum of Louvain. The biblical text is Exodus 16:13; for other examples of food supplied by divine dispensation, see I Kings 17:16; and John 6:1–13. For typological connections, see van Laarhoven (1992), 126. Biblical models of miraculously supplied food gave rise to contemporary reports of similar occurrences; see Strauss (1975), no. 4; *Wickiana* (1975), 181; cf. Torfs (1859–1862), 1:153. Alexander's upside-down fish are mentioned by Verrycken (1990), 150. For Mandeville's story, see the edition of 1908, col 166–67; the quotation is taken from Mandeville (1983), 133; cf. the example in the story of Odoric, in Mandeville (1964), 337; cf. also Delumeau (1992), 103. The Celtic travel story is treated in Oskamp (1970), esp. 149. For the account of Staden's stay among the cannibals, see Staden (1558), fol. E4 recto, G3 verso–G4 recto. Regarding the spontaneous growth of food, see Mandeville (1908), cols. 163–64, 224; the quotations are taken from

Mandeville (1983), 132 and 165; cf. the so-called bernakes in *Vensters* (1985), 15–16; and Uyttersprot (1989), 243, 247. For the spontaneous dispensation of food in a dreamland, see *La grande confrarie* (1520–1540), fol. B2 verso–B3 recto. For the proverb used to close the text, see Komrij (1994), 112–13.

16. Literary Refreshment

Concerning Carnival customs and repertoire in general, see Pleij (1983b) and Pleij (1992). For kitchen humor, see Bumke (1986), 1:271–74; cf. Camporesi (1989), 81. The texts on gluttons appear in de Dene (1978/79), 95–102, esp. 96 and 97. Regarding mock sermons in general, see Kayser (1983/84). The text on Saint Nobody is quoted in Pleij (1983b), 276–80; the quotations are from lines 47–49 and 133–43; see Komrij (1994), 1047–55, for the Dutch translation. For the roasted swan, see *Carmina Burana* (1930–1971), no. 130, vol. 1, part 2, 215; for a translation, see *Carmina Burana* (1959), 98–101, esp. 101 (the English version in the text is a translation of this Dutch version). Alijt the Goose appears in Kalff (1890), 182–85. The text on the herring is published in de Vreese (1922); cf. Resoort et al. (1975/76), 653. The eighteenth-century mock documents appear in Braekman (1992), 298–322. On the debates and fights between Carnival and Lent, see Bakhtin (1984), 298; *Deux Jeux* (1977), vii–xiv; Lozinski (1933); cf. de la Chesnaye (1991), 9; and Molinet (1936–1939), 2:636–48. The Dutch Carnival play is to be found in Hummelen (1968), 1 N 8; the quotation is on fol. 148 recto. A painting of around 1600 treating this theme is to be found in Utrecht, Catharijnenconvent. A print depicting the fight between fish and meat is preserved in Oxford, Ashmolean Museum; see de Meyer (1970), no. 93. Master Ghybe is discussed by Pleij (1989), 309; cf. Braekman (1992), 13–55; and Wright (1865), 373. On the subject of kitchen implements used as weapons, see also Bakhtin (1984), 184. The painting of the fatso attributed to Bruegel is to be found in Copenhagen, Statens Museum for Kunst; related to it is the painting of 1600 in Antwerp, Museum Mayer van den Bergh; the prints are found in Lebeer (1969), cols. 136–43. Regarding the songs in musical annotation consisting of food, see Pleij (1983a); in a painting with the title *Tavern Scene* dating from the second half of the sixteenth century, a company sings from an open songbook displaying such notation: see Szmodis-Eszláry (1990), no. 15. For grotesque distortions in general, see Bakhtin (1984). The *Gula* drawing of 1557 by Bruegel appears in Münz (1961), no. 128, cat. no. 131; cf. the print in Lebeer (1969), no. 22. For *Ysengrimus*, see the edition of 1987, 30–31. Celtic and Germanic displays of gluttony are found in Van helden (1979), 92–103; and Sturluson (1983), 57–58 and 25; cf. Montanari (1994), 23. Examples taken from early-modern Italian literature and reports from Picardy of autophagia occur in Camporesi (1989), 37–40 (the quotation is found on 40); for other examples of autophagia, see Randall (1966), plate 449; Camille (1992), 64; cf. also the decorations on the capitals in the abbey of Maria Laach in Germany. The Breda play is discussed in Pleij (1996); cf. *Het spel van den heilighen sacramente* (1955). The Turnhout farce appears in van Ballaer (1890). Regarding ironical nicknames, see also the example given in van Oostrom (1996), 90; cf. Pleij (1988b), 112–13. Mock names also occur in many of the texts (including the one about the Aernout brothers) in *Veelderhande geneuchlycke dichten* (1899), 87–88, 89, 92, 93, 103, 110, 122–25, 168, 173–82, 183–85, 186, and 187–88. North America as a Luilekkerland is discussed in Delumeau (1992), 152.

PART 4. PARADISE REFURBISHED

17. The Land of Cockaigne as Paradise

A history of paradise was written by Delumeau (1992). Wading through pig dung is found in the Middle English *Land of Cokaygne*; see Robbins (1959), 127, lines 177–82. Mountains of cheese are discussed in de Keyser (1956), 19–21. The quotation from a description of paradise and other information are to be found in de Vooys (1906), 105–6. Regarding the frugal meals in paradise, see chapter 13. The quotation from the *Land of Cokaygne* is taken from Robbins (1959), 121, lines 1–12. Its similarities to paradise are based on a reading of Genesis 2:8–25. For a picture of the popularity of performances of the Expulsion from Paradise during religious processions, see chapter 1. For a typification of Mandeville, see Deluz (1988). Regarding the subordination of animals, see Genesis 1:26, 28, 30; cf. Isaiah 11:6–10 and 65:25; see also Thomas (1990), 16, 304–5. For correspondences between the Cockaigne texts, see text B, lines 39–42 (possibly also lines 72–75), and text L, lines 42–45; cf. also text G, lines 37–45. The four rivers and precious stones occur in Genesis 2:10–14; the silver plates appear in text B, lines 79–80. The carbuncle occurs in text B, line 24; this is treated in greater detail in chapter 40; cf. Ezekiel 28:13. For allegorical interpretations of the story of paradise, see Augustine (1972), book 13, chap. 21; Kirschbaum (1968–1976), s.v. "Parodies"; cf. Boendale (1844–1848), vol. 1, ch. 21. For the influence of the Song of Songs, see Pearsall (1973), 63; for the influence exerted by the *locus amoenus*, see Raedts (1992), 40, and chapter 5; for that of other dreamworlds, see Delumeau (1992), 24; regarding the furnishing of paradise in general, see also Cioranescu (1971). Bishop Avitus of Vienne is discussed by Raedts (1992), 40–41; Delumeau (1992) discusses Pseudo-Basil, 23. Regarding the furnishing of paradise by the Syrian Christians, see Benz (1974), 99. The contamination of paradise by the

aurea aetas of antiquity is discussed in Delumeau (1992), 24; for examples of intermingling traditions, see Boas (1978), 157–58; Benz (1974), 98, treats Chrysostom.
Deluz (1982), 146, treats Isidore of Seville's codification of paradise; the second stop
is Bartholomaeus Anglicus (1485), book 15, ch. 112. Regarding Enoch and Elijah, see
also de Vooys (1906), 103–4, 120–21, 127–31; cf. van Delf (1937–1939), 2:36. The quotation from the first Middle Dutch description of paradise appears in de Vooys
(1906), 107; for information about the second description, see de Vooys (1906), 117;
cf. similarities between Cockaigne versions: text B, lines 98–102, and text L, lines
77–84. On exotica, see de Vooys (1906), 119; cf. 128. Regarding Bosch's interpretation of paradise in his *Garden of Delights*, see Vandenbroeck (1989). The location of
paradise is given in Genesis 2:8; see in general Verrycken (1990), 46–49, 96–99.
Mandeville's report is taken from the edition of 1908, cols. 261–63; the quotation is
taken from Mandeville (1983), 183–84. Paradise occurs on many medieval maps of
the world: see Delumeau (1992), part 3; other reports of its location occur in de
Vooys (1906), 117, 128; van Delf (1937–1939), 2:36; cf. Delumeau (1992), 74, and,
based on Ezekiel 28:13–19, West (1992), 532. The statement from the *Sidrac* is from
Het boek van Sidrac in de Nederlanden (1936), 43–44: note that a copy of this text also
appears in the London MS containing Cockaigne text L. Petrissa's vision appears in
de Vooys (1906), 128–29; it was clearly inspired by the Song of Songs 4:14, 4:16, and
5:1. Regarding dependence on the weather and the comfort of stable weather, see
Pleij (1988b), part 1. Boendale (1844–1848), vol. 1, chap. 21, lines 30–31, sketches the
constancy of paradisiacal weather. Concerning the "eternal spring" prevailing in
paradise, see Kirschbaum (1968–1976), s.v. "Paradies," col. 381. See Delumeau (1992),
16–18, 23, for the golden age, Islands of the Blessed, and the early Christian authors;
cf. Boas (1978), 157. Mandeville's dread of the abrupt changes in weather in Tartary
is described in the edition of 1908, col. 110–11; the quotation is taken from Mandeville (1983), 103. For examples of weather reports from paradise, see de Vooys
(1906), 105; and *Sterfboeck* (1491), fol. C2 verso. The observations of Columbus are
from the edition of 1991, 83, 106, 110, 112, 115, 118, 157, 168. The ideal month of May
is also discussed in de Vooys (1906), 105, 117; *Van den levene Ons Heren* (1968), line 65;
Boeck (1930), 206; and van Delf (1937–1939), 2:36. The proverb is in Kloeke (1959), 75;
cf. in general Hansen (1984). For eternal springtime and edible precipitation in
Cockaigne and Luilekkerland, see text L, lines 75 and 59–60; text B, lines 94–95 and
67–68; and text G, lines 28–29 and 67–70. For the rivers of drink, see text L, lines
61–66, and text B, lines 77–84; cf. text G, lines 19–22. For milk, honey, wine, and so
forth in paradise and other dreamlands, see the Song of Songs 5:1; Delumeau (1992),
17, 23–24, 103, 112; Endepols (1909), 54; *Pelgrimstocht* (1948), 91; *Reis* (1994), lines
745–49; and Oskamp (1970), 141.

18. Never Say Die

The Jordan is mentioned in text L, line 89. Regarding fountains of youth in general, see Rapp (1975); cf. Camporesi (1989), 31–32, 282–83; Mezger (1991), 357–73. The effects of the Jordan are covered in text L, lines 89–93; the quotation is from lines 91–92. The contents of the text on the Three Kings and on Saint John Chrysostom can be found in *Van den heilighen drien coninghen* (1914), 129; see also the notes on 279. For Mandeville's reckless statement, see Mandeville (1908), col. 146–47; the quotation is taken from Mandeville (1983), 123. For further reports of the miraculous powers of water, see John 5:2–4; cf. *Bedevaart* (1884), 81; Herodotus (1955), 183; Oskamp (1970), 163–64; Stephanus (1877), no. 80; Virgilius (1950), fol. [E3] recto; Willems (1839); Mandeville (1908), cols. 146–47; Mandeville (1983), 123; Penninc et al. (1957), lines 3586–92; *Verzameling* (1851), 69, 70; Leendertz (1896), 98; Sachs (1893), 321–23; also mentioned in the pilgrims' guide in the London MS; see de Flou et al. (1897), 419; cf. Delumeau (1992), 71–72. Immortality in paradise is also mentioned in the Song of Songs 4:15 and John 5:2–4; cf. van Delf (ed. 1937–1939), 2:37; for the heavenly paradise, see Revelation 22:1–2; cf. Boas (1978), 167. For characterizations as early as Babylonian legend, Endepols (1909), 51. The decreasing lifespan of humans on earth is discussed in the *Ridderboek* (1991), 24–25; for Adam's age, see Schorbach (1894), 205. Examples of rejuvenation methods appear in Virgilius (1950), fol. [E3] recto; Hazelzet (1988); Geisberg (1974), G 1584; Strauss (1975), 1100; Hollaar et al. (1980), 421 (Deventer); Boas (1978), 169–70 (Irish island where dying is impossible); *'t Scep* (1514), ch. 163 (*quinta essentia*); cf. also van Gijsen (1993), 134; Bartholomaeus Anglicus (1485), book 15, ch. 112, also mentions this Irish island. Regarding early Christian baptismal rituals, see Leupen (1996), 34–35. The paradisiacal brook in *Huon de Bordeaux* is discussed in Delumeau (1992), 69; the land of Prester John is described in Mandeville (1908), cols. 146–47; cf. Delumeau (1992), 103, 109. Concerning the Nile, see Delumeau (1992), 71; Vanhemelryck (1994), 174–81; and Schama (1995), 263–67. For the ideal age of people, see *Boeck* (1930), 206; and *Sterfboeck* (1491), fol. C3 recto. On the subject of fountains of youth in literature and the applied arts, see also Delumeau (1992), 177–78; the Nuremberg fountain of youth is discussed in Sumberg (1941), 154. The *Elucidarium* is quoted in Delumeau (1992), 33; the Middle Dutch rhymed adaptation appears in *Die Dietsche Lucidarius* (1851), 12, lines 924–28; the quotation is taken from the *Sidrac* (1936), 43–44.

19. Heavenly Rewards

On the earthly paradise as a waiting room, see West (1992), 526. Regarding the heavenly Jerusalem in general, see Kirschbaum (1968–1976), s.v. "Jerusalem, himmlisches";

and Raedts (1991). Quotations are from Isaiah 54:11–12; 66:10–14; the New Jerusalem is discussed in the Book of Revelation 21:9–27; 22:1–5. Carbuncles occur in text B, line 24; dimensions in text B, line 93. References to the willingness to engage in sex occur in text L, line 70, and text B, lines 90–92, 103–7, and 111–14. On the nature of sex in paradise, see Augustine (1972), book 14, chs. 24 and 26; cf. Lerner (1972), 158–59. Text B, line 107, alludes to sleeping with one another "tenderly"; cf. de Roovere (1955), 256–58, esp. 257, lines 49–50; and Pleij (1990), 28–30. The lists with negative comparisons are quoted from *Des coninx summe* (1900), 324; and *Sterfboeck* (1491), fol. C2 verso; cf. *Sinte Augustijns Hantboec* (1962), 1:66–73; and *Boeck* (1930), 204–10. For the merging of the earthly and the heavenly paradise, see in general Kirschbaum (1968–1976), s.v. "Paradies." Van de Velde (1982), 17, points out the Jewish apocalyptic literature. The Egyptian realm of the dead is discussed in Endepols (1909), 51; the quotation is from Ezekiel 28:13. For entangled descriptions of paradise, see Brugman (1948), 137, lines 824–33; *Sterfboeck* (1491), fol. C2 verso; de Vooys (1906), 106–8; *Reis* (1994), lines 705–11, 737–41, 745–49, 814–17, 861–62; cf. Boas (1978), 164–67; and de Vooys (1906), 117–26. Regarding the negative image of the city in general, see Le Goff (1987), 368; Le Goff (1989), 102; Orbán (1987), 74. Tacitus's utterance is found in the *Annals* (1976), 365, book 15, ch. 44. The Bruges text is in *Oudvlaemsche liederen* (1849), 490, 491; cf. negative statements about London and Paris quoted in Camille (1992), 152; and in Duby (1989), 148; cf. also Schlüter (1995), 57–58. Regarding the heavenly blueprints of the city, see Le Goff (1973), 73; for colorful churches, see Pleij (1994), 73–74. A bibliographical overview of medieval visions can be found in Gardiner (1993); concerning descriptions of heaven in visions, see Aubrun (1980); standard characteristics are discussed in Kirschbaum (1968–1976), s.v. "Paradies," col. 376: the inhabitants of heaven are also discussed there. For Papias's furnishing of paradise, see Benz (1974), 94. Lidwina's testimony appears in *Het leven van Liedewij* (1989), 90–91; that of Brugman is in Brugman (1948), 132–33; cf. Matthew 5:6. Regarding divine drunkenness, see also Axters (1967), 119–21; cf. van Delf (ed. 1937–1939), 3B:672. The heavenly blowout indulged in by the dead knight and his living cousin is described in de Vooys (1906), 104–5, 131–39; cf. Tubach (1969), no. 780; and Palmer (1982), 402–3. The music of David is described in Brugman (1948), 133. David's performance is a standard part of receptions in the heavenly paradise; cf. *Een devoot ende profitelyck boecxken* (1889), 48; *Van den levene Ons Heren* (1968), lines 53–54, 60–61, 94; see also *Meditations* (1977), 380–81. Enumerations of musical instruments appear in *Sterfboeck* (1491), fol. [C3] verso. On music in the earthly paradise, see Delumeau (1992), 74; de Vooys (1906), 110, 121–22; van Delf (1937–1939), 2:37. Regarding the pleasure parks of the nobility, see chapter 22. Music in paradise is mentioned in Isaiah 51:3 ("voice of melody"). Regarding music in the *locus amoenus* and the *Romance of the Rose*, see

Vellekoop (1992). For Arent Willemszoon's alarming report, see *Bedevaart* (1884), 17. Concerning the negative associations of music and dance with Mary Magdalene, see Linke (1971), 359; de Vooys (1905a); cf. Pleij (1990), 42–44; in general, see *Boeck* (1930), 171–76; Brant (1500), ch. 58; van der Vet (1902), 140–41; *Die spiegel der sonden* (1900), 22. For music and dance in Cockaigne, see text L, lines 95–97, and text B, lines 38 and 109–10; cf. *Des coninx summe* (1900), variant reading on 324 and notes on 558. The multiplication of holidays is discussed in text L, lines 77–85, and text B, lines 98–102; the passage from the Bible on which the rhyme is based is II Peter 3:8. For the little rhyme, see Priebsch (1906), 447; cf. *Een devoot ende profitelyck boecxken* (1889), 48; Verrycken (1992), 74; de Vooys (1926), 35–39, 314–15. Clothes lying ready for the taking are mentioned in text L, lines 47–51, and text B, lines 53–56; cf. text G, lines 48–50. Regarding Memling's depiction of the angels dressing resurrected souls, see Kirschbaum (1968–1976), s.v. "Paradies"; concerning the shoes, see Dinzelbacher (1986), 71; cf. Vellekoop (1986).

20. Other Paradises

For stories in various cultures concerning the loss of paradise and the promise of its recovery, see Eliade (1959). For Hesiod, see the edition of 1986, 60–62; cf. Strabo's vision of a paradise situated in India in Benz (1974), 98. Poeschel (1878) traces Cockaigne's path from India via Greece to the West. Delumeau (1992) discusses many of the Western dreamworlds. Metlitzki (1977) puts forward strong arguments for a direct relationship between Cockaigne and the Muslim paradise, all basic information also to be found here; see also van Kooy (1992) and Cioranescu (1971), 101. For eroticism in early Christian representations of the heavenly paradise imagined by the Syrians, see Benz (1974), 99. Mael Dúin's experiences are recounted in Oskamp (1970), 155. For the *Romance of the Rose*, see de Lorris et al. (1974), lines 8431–34; cf. Gerritsen (1978), 13; see also the differing standpoint in *Des coninx summe* (1900), 324 and commentary on 556. For further information on the Muslim paradise, see Vanhemelryck (1994), 268. On Syrian Christianity, see Benz (1974), 99. For sex as the main theme in Mandeville, see the edition of 1908, cols. 112–13; quotation is taken from Mandeville (1983), 104. Gruenemberg's account is in *De pelgrimstocht van ridder Gruenemberg* (1948), 90–91; cf. Zeebout (1557), book 1, ch. 3, 22. The imitation of the Old Man of the Mountain is treated in detail in Polo (1988), 70–73; for all sources, see Okken (1987), 160–70; cf. Mandeville (1908), cols. 235–38. The quotation is taken from Mandeville (1983), 172. See also Camporesi (1994), 234, 295–99; Delumeau (1992), 112–13. The pleasure gardens and orchards at Boulac are treated in Zeebout (1572), 127, 174, 205, and 267. Arent Willemszoon's experiences in Venice are found in *Bedevaart* (1884), 245. See *Land of*

Cokaygne in Robbins (1959), 121, lines 1–2. Regarding the Celtic hereafter, see Dillon (1967), 91; Noelle (1974), 218–19; and Endepols (1909), 54; cf. *Van helden* (1979), 208; cf. also the idyllic spots in the travels of Mael Dúin in Oskamp (1970), 113–15, 121, 131, 133, 139, 141, 149, 155, 163, 165, 173. Bartholomaeus Anglicus (1485), book 15, ch. 112, mentions particular features of Ireland. Godfrey of Viterbo's story is found in Verrycken (1992), 74. For the voyage of Saint Brendan, see *Reis* (1994), lines 705–11, 737–41, 745–49, 814–17, 862 (quotation); cf. Boas (1978), 158–60.

21. Lovely Places, Golden Ages

Regarding the antique tradition of the *locus amoenus*, see Wiersma (1992). The quotation from Homer is taken from the *Odyssey*; see Homer (1946), 115. See in general Camporesi (1994), 184–86, 224–28, 236; for the antique tradition in medieval literature, see Kooper (1992); the model appears in Vendôme (1980), 59–60. Paradises for the tribes of Israel are mentioned in Joel 3:18 (quoted in text) and Amos 9:13–15. Regarding the later secularization of the Garden of Eden, see Kirschbaum (1968–1976), s.v. "Paradies," col. 381. For the views of the Benedictines and Peter Damian, see Southern (1970), 230; cf. Raedts (1991), 99–100. Regarding places of relaxation for the middle classes, see Vandenbroeck (1983), Janssen (1990), and de Jong et al. (1996). For the *jardin de plaisance* in Bruges, see *Triumphe* (1515), fol. [B4] verso; and Dupuys (1515), fol. E 1 recto; cf. *Kronyk* (1839–1840), 2:217, for something similar in Ghent in 1458. Albertus Magnus is discussed in Oldenburger-Ebbers (1992); Erasmus is discussed in Schlüter (1995). Regarding the golden age in general, see Cohn (1984), 187–91, 195–96. Hesiod is reported in Delumeau (1992), 15–16; see further, including a discussion of Horace and Virgil, the thesis by L. Nijsten (1979), 4–9; cf. Spann (1977), 75. Regarding Hyperborea and Atlantis, see Cioranescu (1971), 109–11. For Boethius on the golden age, see the edition of 1969, 68–69; the Middle Dutch translation of this by Jacob Vilt appears in de Vooys (1941), 15–16. The Ghent translator's version of Boethius with his detailed commentary on the text can be found in Boethius (1485), fol. 78 verso–81 recto. Basic information on both Boethius adaptations occurs in Goris (1996); cf. Gerritsen (1978), 12–13. Versions after Boethius appear in Boendale (1844–1848), vol. 1, ch. 31; van Aken (1868), lines 8931–9058; and *Fragmenten* (1958), fragment A1, lines 253–404. The extent to which history continued to be described in terms of eras slipping from bad to worse emerges from a long refrain dating from 1527 by Anna Bijns, composed as a *Zeitklage* on the contrast between the present-day Iron Age of decay and the earlier golden age filled with harmony. The closing line of the refrain is "'t Is seer verkeert, dat plach te zijne" (Things aren't what they used to be); see Bijns (1875), no. 70, 461–67. Regarding food offering itself for consumption and subservient beasts, see chapter 15. Communal ownership of property is mentioned in text L, lines 71–74, and text B, lines 49–52. Sex in the golden age is discussed in de Lorris et al. (1974), lines 8431–34. On Germania as a golden age, see Silver (1983); cf. Schama (1995), 75–134. The Batavian myth is treated in depth by Tilmans (1988), 121–66. On Erasmus, see Phillips (1967), 32–33. Tilmans (1993), 115–16, quotes the Italian humanist who wrote under the pseudonym Chrysostomus. For the places mentioned in the Cockaigne texts, see text L, lines 14–15, and text B, lines 12–13. Regarding *petou* or *betouw* as wine from Poitou, see Baudet (1904), 121; *MNW*, s.v. "petauwe"; and *WNT*, s.v. "Betouw."

22. Wonder Gardens and Pleasure Parks

Concerning the marvelous architecture of castles and pleasure parks in the Middle Ages, see the rich collection of material by Okken (1987). Harvengt is quoted in Le Goff (1989), 55; Aymeri is quoted from Le Goff (1973), 73–74. The citadel on Mount Zion (Sion) is described in *Reis* (1994), lines 1656–1791. The heavenly arrangements in the palace of King Wonder is from Penninc et al. (1957), lines 3451–3592; cf. *Torec* (1978), lines 2374–85; cf. also *En toch was ze rond* (1990), 139–41. Mechanical music is discussed in van Delf (1937–1939), 2:37. Regarding the pseudo-tomb of Blancheflur, see van Buuren (1992), 123. For the model book of Villard de Honnecourt, see Camille (1991), 244–48; and Scheller (1995), no. 14, 176–87. The pleasure garden is described in van Assenede (1912), lines 3386–3405; cf. Winkelman (1981) and Gerritsen (1988), 198–99. Magicians in China who could delude one's senses are described in Mandeville (1908), col. 202; in cols. 235–38 he speaks of the tricks played by the Old Man of the Mountain. The wonder garden of Haroun al-Rashid is described in Delumeau (1992), 167–68. For the transport of automated garden architecture to the West via Sicily, see Camille (1991), 244–48. The paradise garden of Albertus Magnus is described by van Oostrom (1996), 184–85. Hesdin is discussed in Brunet (1971) and Okken (1987), 171–87; for Caxton's reaction, see Hittmair (1934), 54. Binche is described in Gachard et al. (1874), 386, 388–89; Alvarez (1964), 109–10; *Binche 1549* (1985), 27–30; van den Boogert et al. (1993), 171–72, 289–90, 310–13. William of Orange was there as well. On the imitation pleasure palace built by Duché, see Favier (1990), 291; cf. Vandenbroeck (1990), 37.

23. Dreams of Immortality

Regarding Alexander's visit to paradise, see Boas (1978), 158–59; cf. *Van den IX besten* in von Kausler (1844–1846), 3:145, lines 117–20. For Seth's visit to the gates of paradise, see *Dat boec van den houte* (1959). The promise of the greatest blessings in heaven as a reward for the worst suffering on earth is discussed in de Vooys (1906), 109, among others. For Zerbolt's instructions, see Zerbolt van Zutphen (1941), 108–13; cf. Goossens (1952), 229. Concerning the nearly divine status in paradise of all people, see de Vooys (1906), 107. For the paradise for children in the guise of Luilekkerland, see Wolf (1974), 743. Regarding interference from the devil, see Schmitt (1995), 31. Breaking the First Commandment and Mount Venus are treated in de Vooys (1902), 362, 369–70; cf. the song "Van heer Danielken" in *Een schoon liedekens-boeck* (1968), no. 160. The exemplum of Stephen of Bourbon is in Schmitt (1995), 142–43. The exemplum from *Der Sielen troest* can be found in the edition of 1479, fol. 124 recto. For the *Biënboec*, see van der Vet (1902), 212–14, where other examples are also given; cf. de Vooys (1926), 174. For the bewitched castle, see *Volksboek van Margarieta* (1952), 7–9; cf. *Die schoone hystorie van Malegijs* (1903), 158.

PART 5. THE IMAGINATION JOURNEYS FORTH

24. Geographical Musings

Regarding visions as travel literature, see Gardiner (1993), xxii–xxiv; the trip to the hereafter is discussed in Dinzelbacher (1986), 71. There is a detailed treatment of medieval maps of the world, on which paradise is often to be found, in Verrycken (1990), 51–136. For Lucian's text in English translation, see Lucian (1968), 249–94. Deluz (1988) treats Mandeville; she attempts to give a new typification of his work and her arguments are inspired. See the Middle Dutch translation of Mandeville (1908); cf. Ganser (1985) and *En toch was ze rond* (1990), 17–41. Concerning the contrasts with exotic peoples, cf. also Delumeau (1992), 112. The Brahmans are mentioned in Mandeville (1908), cols. 250–52; the quotation is taken from Mandeville (1983), 178; cf. Boas (1978), 146–4;, and Bejczy (1990). Regarding the land of Prester John, see Bejczy (1994). The doubts expressed by Rubruck are in *En toch was ze rond* (1990), 126. Basic information on the account of van Ghistele's trip is in Deschamps (1972), no. 101. Before the printed editions dating from 1557 onward, his account was widely distributed in manuscript form, which made it highly popular. The story about Prester John is in Zeebout (1572), 42, 314–15. Concerning the confusion of topographical terms, see Verrycken (1990), 90; cf. Columbus (1991), 144, 156, 159, 173; and *Bedevaart* (1884), 133. Regarding the negative associations evoked by the color black, see Pleij (1994). For the land of Prester John as the exact opposite of the Western world, see Mandeville (1908), cols. 157 and 261; the quotation is taken from

Mandeville (1983), 129; cf. *En toch was ze rond* (1990), 12. For the doubts cast on Marco Polo's expedition, see Wood (1996).

25. Real Dreamworlds

Regarding the accessibility of paradise, see Deluz (1982), 150–52; cf. Verrycken (1992), 74. For paradise as a waiting room, see West (1992), 526. Jan Witte van Hese's testimony is in Verrycken (1990), 97; particulars about his sojourn can be found in Jansen-Sieben (1989), 233, 442, 443. Concerning the rivers of paradise, see Delumeau (1992), 59–65. The passage from the Bible is Genesis 2:10–12. Van Delf (1937–1939), 2:38–41, speaks of healing herbs; for means of increasing one's longevity, see further chapter 25. For Columbus's assignment, his obsession with paradise, and his optimism regarding the natives' convertibility to Christianity, see Raedts (1992), 35; Cook (1977), 32; and West (1992), 521–52; cf. Sweet (1986); see also the entries in his diary in Columbus (1991), 97, 104, 126, 128, 141, 160, 176. Regarding El Dorado, see also Verrycken (1990), 106. The obsession with gold is on nearly every page of Columbus's diary; see Columbus (1991). Pigafetta's excitement is described in Magalhaes (1986), 50 (quotation), 53, 70; cf. also 72–73 and 109; a better edition is Pigafetta (1923). All information about the land of Prester John is from Bejczy (1994); cf. Delumeau (1992), 99–109. Concerning Montezuma's treasures, see Jantz (1976), 93. *Spelen* (1562), fol. Zz 3 verso, describes a Europe glittering with jewels. Visions of the New World in terms of a paradisiacal golden age are discussed by Delumeau (1992), 145–46; cf. Cioranescu (1971), 103–4. Regarding Alexander the Great, see Verrycken (1990), 150. For Marco Polo, see Campbell (1988), 110, and more generally 174–75, 193–97, 213. The Gouda edition of Marco Polo's text published by Gheraert Leeu appeared around 1483/84: see *De vijfhonderdste verjaring* (1973), no. 129. For Columbus's fear of a Cockaigne, see Colomb (1961), 242, 466. Concerning the United States as a Luilekkerland, see Delumeau (1992), 149–52; cf. Boas (1978), 172. For Vespucci and Pigafetta, see Delumeau (1992), 146–51.

26. Wonders of East and West

Concerning Eastern wonders in general, see Le Goff (1977). Campbell (1988), 65, quotes Higden. Maerlant (1857–1863), vol. 1, part 1, ch. 18, treats India. Regarding exotic peoples, see Verrycken (1990), 112–20. For examples of sections of exotica in Middle Dutch encyclopedias, see Maerlant (1878), vol. 1, lines 117–440; Maerlant (1857–1863), vol. 1, part 1, ch. 17–39; *Sidrac* (1936), 73–76. Regarding Atlantis, the

Islands of the Blessed, and the Hesperides, see Cioranescu (1971), 109–11; Verrycken (1990), 106; Boas (1978), 168–69; Bartholomaeus Anglicus (1485), book 15, ch. 62; Maerlant (ed. 1857–1863), vol. 1, part 1, ch. 31. Regarding Celtic pleasure spots and Ireland, see Cioranescu (1971), 101–2; Leerssen (1995); Bartholomaeus Anglicus (1485), book 15, ch. 80. Regarding the island where it is impossible to die, see Boas (1978), 169–70. On the subject of Spain in the Middle Ages, see Bartholomaeus Anglicus (1485), book 15, ch. 79. The comparison with Spain occurs in text L, line 14, and text B, line 12. The proverb about Spain is in van Aken (1868), lines 2432–33. It was apparently jotted down by a contemporary user in the Amsterdam MS: see van der Poel (1994), 112 and 387 n. 37; Bijns (1880), no. 35, 76; Sartorius (1561), fol. [O05] recto; cf. Stoett (1943), no. 1444. The upside-down drinking habits of men and women in India are discussed in Mandeville (1908), col. 148; see also Mandeville (1983), 124. Regarding the changing roles in the West, see Pleij (1988b), 278–87, and the literature cited there. For noble savages in general, see Bejczy (1994), 97, 123; cf. Verrycken (1990), 90–96, 100–5. For the Camerini, see Boas (1978), 138–39. For the Brahmans, see Boas (1978), 146–49; Bejczy (1990); Verrycken (1990), 117; and Mandeville (1908), col. 251–52; see also Mandeville (1983), 178–180; and Maerlant (1857–1863), vol. 1, part 4, ch. 57–62. The religious zealots are discussed in Mandeville (1908), col. 151; the quotation is taken from Mandeville (1983), 125–26. The letter from Transsylvanus to the cardinal is quoted in Magalhaes (1986), 108, 110. Mostaert's painting is discussed in Snyder (1976) and Cuttler (1989). Gog and Magog are to be found in the Bible in the Book of Ezekiel 38:2–39:16, and the Book of Revelation 20:8; cf. Verrycken (1990), 100–3; Bejczy (1994), 125–26. On marginality and culture, see in general Bejczy (1994). Pope Alexander VI and the papal bull regarding the civilizing of the newly discovered lands is discussed by Greenblatt (1992), 66–72. Regarding the Native Americans' superior society, see Cioranescu (1971), 104–6; Jean de Léry's opinions are found in Gilmore (1976), 521. For Vespucci, see *Van der nieuwer werelt* (ca. 1507); cf. Franssen (1990), 62–63; and Jantz (1976), 96–97. For the quotations taken from it, see *Van der nieuwer werelt* (ca. 1507), fol. A4 recto and B1 recto. The quotation from Vasco da Gama's account is taken from Calcoen (1931), 19; cf. ibid., 16. Cf. also the Dutch translation of Balthasar Sprenger's journey in *Die reyse van Lissebone* (1508), fol. [A3] verso; this text is not a sequel to Vespucci's *Nieuwer werelt* as the book itself suggests. For Columbus's optimism about the naked savages, see Columbus (1991), 126, and cf. 96, 159, 167, 176. For the mocking of the Indians, see Pigafetta (1923), 46. The streets paved with spices and overhung with hides are mentioned in Cockaigne text B, lines 85–88; cf. text L, lines 67–68; for a similar street in Bethlehem, see *Van den heilighen drien coninghen* (1914), 95. Covered streets are considered exotic by Westerners; see de Flou et al. (1897),

3:411, as well as the pilgrims' guide in the London MS, which mentions a street covered with stones. Zeebout (1572), 260, records the existence in Tripoli of streets covered as protection from the rain. For marginality in Luilekkerland, see text G, lines 1 and 79–90; cf. Bejczy (1994), 164.

27. Fanciful Destinations

On the subject of lying tales, see Coigneau (1979); Rooth (1983), 127–33; Pleij (1988b), 118–20; cf. also Vasvari (1991) and *Verfasserlexikon* (1983), s.v. "Lügenreden," col. 1039–44. For the Old French texts, see Väänänen (1947). For Diodorus, see Delumeau (1992), 19. On the Cockaigne of Greek antiquity, see Poeschel (1878), 391–94; and Bonner (1910). Roasted pigs are described in Petronius (1988), 64. For the *True History*, see Lucian (1968), 249–94. The Old French *Farce des coquins* is in Vasvari (1991), 189. The *Farce de Jenin Landore* is in Rooth (1983), 188. For *Aucassin and Nicolette*, see Vasvari (1991), 184–85; see also *Aucassin* (1971), 49–50 and 157 n. 13.

28. Virtual Dreamlands

Regarding Rabelais, see Müller (1984), 61–62; cf. correspondences among text L, line 18; text B, lines 16 and 48; and text F, lines 27–30. The *Disciple* (1982) gives the text and all information: see esp. chs. 18–30; on p. xxxvi there is also a discussion of the *Nouvelles admirables* of 1495. Boccaccio's travel parody is in the tenth story of the sixth day, see Boccaccio (1969), 2:106–7. The text on the brotherhood of good-for-nothings is in *Confrarie* (1520–1540). Dr. Jelle Koopmans gave me several worthwhile suggestions as to the meaning of the title; regarding this genre, see further Pleij (1983b), 96–108, 177–86; and discussions of the *Land of Cokaygne* in Robbins (1959), 121–27, 317–19. For similarities to representations of the heavenly paradise, see chapter 19. Both versions of Lauris Janszoon's play are described in Hummelen (1968), 1 R 5 and 1 oI 6, and published in van Vloten (1877), 1:194–205; cf. Kalff (1885), 154; see also Marijnissen et al. (1971), 91, with a quotation from Marcus van Vaernewijck's chronicle, in which the same proverb is used in just as satirical a way. Regarding Italy as an idyllic place in lying literature, see also Coigneau (1979), 55, 70–71; the lying song is taken from *Drie Eenlingen* (1597), fol. [B6] verso–[B7] verso. On the subject of political utopias from Plato onward, see Cioranescu (1971); for *Utopia* of 1516, see the facsimile edition of More (1966). For the *Kaetspel* see Roetert-Frederikse (1915), 69–71, lii–liv. Regarding both German texts, see von Ertzdorff (1989), 49–50; bibliographical information appears in Gotzkowsky (1991), 521–23, 565–69.

PART 6. HERETICAL EXCESSES

29. The Thousand-Year Reign of Peace and Prosperity

God's command to be idle is reported in text L, lines 8–10, and text B, lines 8–10; God's love for that land is mentioned in text B, line 47; "a Jordan" is mentioned in text L, line 89; the Holy Ghost in text L, line 17, and text B, line 15. Regarding the rhetoricians' festival at Ghent in 1539, see Hummelen (1993), and concerning the tense situation at that time as regards literary life in general, see Decavele (1975), 1:193–230. A standard work on millenarianism is Cohn (1984); Jansen (1973) gives a short survey. The thousand-year reign and the New Jerusalem are mentioned in the Book of Revelation 20–22; the passages quoted are taken from Revelation 20:1–10 and Revelation 21:3; Emmerson et al. (1992) affords insight into the numerous medieval commentaries; regarding the heavenly paradise, see chapter 19. On the subject of Old Testament prophecies, see Cohn (1984), 19–20. For the unintentional literal interpretation of the passage from the Book of Revelation, see Raedts (1991), 92. For Augustine's vision as church dogma, see Cohn (1984), 29. On Joachim's views, see Cohn (1984), 108–10, 129; a short survey appears in de Vries (1982), 264–68; a more general overview can be found in Reeves (1969). The *Land of Cokaygne* is discussed in Robbins (1959), 121–27, 317–19. For commentary on Maerlant's text, see Maerlant (1954), 2:359–60, 386–89; the quotation is taken from vol. 1, lines 1–2, 13–19. The passage quoted from the Bible is II Timothy 3:1–4; cf. van Buuren (1991), 244–46. Augustine's views are presented in Frederiksen (1992), 29; and Lerner (1992), 52. Regarding the rebelliousness and impatience of the poor, see Cohn (1984), 13–14. An overview of the medieval mendicant movements appears in de Vries (1982), esp. 241–80. Commodianus is discussed in Cohn (1984), 28, who analyzes on 45–57, 59–60, and 65–95 the underlying causes of the aggressive rebelliousness of the poor and their demands for the establishment of a utopia in Jerusalem; the quotation is from 64.

30. Heresies of the Free Spirit

Regarding the Free Spirit movements, see in general Lerner (1972); Cohn (1984), 148–97; and de Vries (1982), 297–344. On indulging in promiscuity as a matter of principle, see Cohn (1984), 150–51. Regarding Adam and Eve, see Augustine (1972), book 14, chs. 24 and 26. The passage quoted from the Bible is I John 3:9. On the subject of following the dictates of nature in the *Romance of the Rose*, see Le Goff (1989), 160–61; and more generally Duby (1990), 79–112, esp. 92 and 110. Regarding extreme mortification of the flesh, see chapter 13. Willem Cornelis is treated by Lerner (1972), 13; and Cohn (1984), 158; the quotation is from Cohn (1984), 158; see Lampo (1980), 196–99; cf. McDonnell (1969), 488–90. For the quotation attributed to Thomas of Cantimpré, see van der Vet (1902), 211. Regarding Tanchelm, see Lampo (1980), 192–93; cf. de Vries (1982), 229–31. For Marguerite Porete, see Lerner (1972), 1–2; and Passenier (1993); cf. Janssens (1984), 16–17; and Schweitzer (1990). Concerning Meister Eckhart, see Lerner (1972), 185, 211, 215–19, 235; Eckhart (or Pseudo-Eckhart) in the Low Countries is quoted in de Vooys (1905b), esp. 61 (quotation attributed to Eckhart). The condemned Averroists are discussed in Lerner (1972), 24. The influence of the call to track down heretics on their recognition is reported in Lerner (1972), 20, 25, 58, and esp. 82 and 87 (quotation on 82); cf. Passenier (1993), 110, who even speaks of a "slander campaign" within the church. Concerning Beguines, Beghards, and Lollards, see Lerner (1972), 36–41, 82; Grundmann (1978), 47–59; Janssens (1984), 12–23; van Mierlo (1930); and Kurze (1965). For Beguines as drifters, see Hildegaersberch (1870), nos. 9 and 77, line 21. Beguines in particular are suspected of having insatiable sexual appetites; see Enklaar (1956), 101–56; Pleij (1983b), 211–12; and Pleij (1988b), 92–93, 158–60, 241–42, and 284–85. The passage from the Bible is II Corinthians 3:17; cf. Lerner (1972), 82, who speaks on 87 of the inquisition at Strasbourg.

31. Sex Adam-and-Eve Style

Regarding communal possessions, see Cohn (1984), 182–83; the quotation is from 183. Adamites are discussed in Mandeville (1908), cols. 153–54; the quotation is taken from Mandeville (1983), 127, where the second quotation is also to be found. The passage from the Bible is Genesis 1:22. For Adamites, see Lerner (1972), 25–32; see also the overview in Fraenger (1975), 17–29, who maintains that Bosch's *Garden of Delights* portrays the Adamites' teachings; cf. Isidore (1911), vol. 1, book 8, part 5, ch. 14; van Paassen et al. (1993), 11, points out the power of the accepted model, which by itself generates Adamites and other heretics; the inspiration for this view is to be found in II Timothy 3:1–10. The quotation concerning the Homines intelligentiae is taken from Cohn (1984), 168. Regarding the Brussels trial of 1411, see Lerner (1972), 157–63, 190–95; and de Waha (1975); cf. Pleij (1988b), 92–93, 158–60, 241–42, 284–85. Quotations from Papias are in Cohn (1984), 27. Regarding the so-called Crusades of the Shepherds, see Cohn (1984), 94–95. The promise of huge quantities of food and the subject of begging is discussed in Cohn (1984), 119–20 and 182. For the Holy Ghost and the Brussels heretics of 1411, see the literature on the Brussels trial of 1411 listed above; for Hans Becker, see Lerner (1972), 177–80; the quotation is on 178; cf. 79–80, 115, 129, 144, 158, 159. Concerning Columbus's inspiration by the Holy Ghost, see Sweet (1986), 379 and 376. The text by Hildegaersberch is mentioned in the edition of 1870, no. 79, lines 147–55.

32. Low-Country Heterodoxy

Ruusbroec's typification of heretics is in a short text in *Verzameling* (1851), 30; see in general van Mierlo (1932). See Bot (1990), 213, regarding the tendency of women in particular to become adherents of heretical teachings. Regarding Maerlant's difficulties resulting from his translation of the Bible, see de Bruin (1979). For the fundamentalism of the Franciscan Spirituals, see Cohn (1984), 110, 158. The alleged change from hopeful waiting to active restoration of the golden age is treated in Cohn (1984), 198. Concerning the presumed lecherousness of Beguines, see the literature listed at the end of the sources for chapter 30. The saying quoted from the Brussels MS is in Priebsch (1906), 309. Regarding the lecherousness of Beguines, see further *Truwanten* (1978), lines 177–81; van Herwaarden (1994), 313; *Des coninx summe* (1900), 236; de Dene (1978/79), 98, lines 21–22; Bijns (1902), 237, stanza B; Bijns (1875), 157, stanza A; Komrij (1994), 49; Pleij (1983b), 260, lines 134–41; *Veelderhande geneuchlycke dichten* (1899), 77. Bernard of Clairvaux's outburst is reported in Duby (1989), 139. Regarding John of Brünn and the duty of women, see Lerner (1972), 109, 137 (the quotation is on 109). For the passages on sex, see text L, line 16, and text B, lines 14, 103–7, 111–14. For Meister Eckhart, see Lerner (1972), 211, and cf. 219 and 1–2; for texts in Middle Dutch attributed to Eckhart, see de Vooys (1905b). For details of the Brabant heretics, see the literature listed in the sources for chapter 30, as well as Willems (1904); Brabant heretics in England are treated in Map (1983), 119. For Bloemardinne, see Lerner (1972), 191; see also Janssens (1984), 12–13, 20; and *Nationaal Biografisch Woordenboek* (*NBW*), vol. 1 (1964), cols. 207–9. Regarding the hostile attitude of the populace toward the inquisitors and the mocking song, see also Vanhemelryck (1981), 79–80; and Janssens (1984), 20. For the added passage, see *Des coninx summe* (1900), 344–46, esp. 346; see also 568; cf. Janssens (1984), 19. Concerning Ruusbroec's fight against heresy, see Janssens (1984), 12–23; and van Mierlo (1932). For his campaign against Marguerite Porete, see Verdeyen (1992). The remark made by Jan van Schoonhoven is reported in Lerner (1972), 192. For Ruusbroec's typification of heresy, see also *Ruusbroec* (1970), 105–6; cf. *Verzameling* (1851), 26–31. Regarding Geert Grote, see van Zijl (1963), 170–81. Concerning the self-inflicted suffering of the adherents of the Devotio Moderna, see *Hemels verlangen* (1993), 31–32, 59, 82–84, 120–22, 138; for such material in general, see Scheepsma (1996). For the example given by the desert fathers, see Brown (1990), 172–76; cf.

Vaderboec (1480), fol. [A7] recto, G4 recto–verso. For Lidwina, see *Het leven van Liedewij* (1989), 11, 14, 26, 28, 30, 32. The upside-down life of the Brussels heretics is treated in Lerner (1972), 159.

PART 7. LEARNING AS A MATTER OF SURVIVAL

33. Didactic Differences

For the closing passage, see text B, lines 116–22; for the closing verse, see text G, lines 132–139; for the close of the prose text, see text G, lines 124–131. Regarding class satire, see Pleij (1983b), 177–86. For the charivari context of the Old French texts, see chapter 8. Hans Lützelhüpsch is discussed in Vandenbroeck (1989), 102–3. Regarding the celebration of Carnival, see Mezger (1991); Pleij (1983b); and Pleij (1992). On the subject of humor employed in the service of teaching, see Pleij (1980/81). The wedding song is from Moll (1857); cf. Pleij (1988a), 6–7. Regarding divine drunkenness, also in Hadewijch and Ruusbroec, see Mak (1960); cf. Axters (1967), 119–21. In addition to the literature listed above regarding urban rituals of inversion, see also Pleij (1988b), 174–79; and Pleij (1989). Concerning society's three estates, see Duby (1985), esp. 67 as regards the first satire; see also *Carmina* (1930–1971), no. 6, vol. 1, part 1, 7–8; cf. translation in *Carmina* (1959), 110–15. For the development of middle-class morality, see Pleij (1983b), 229–36; and Pleij et al. (1991), 8–51. The upside-down world is treated in Burke (1990), 177–82; Pleij (1988b), 135–40 and passim (see index); and Spierenburg (1988), 93–104. The snowman is in MS K.A. XXXVI, fol. 78 verso, in The Hague, Royal Library; this includes other marginalia as well. Regarding this manuscript and the poem on the *arma Christi*, cf. Oosterman (1995), vol. 2, rhyming prayer no. 167 and MSS no. 76. Regarding snowmen, see Pleij (1988b); an interpretation of Villon's poem is given by Verhuyck (1993). Gaignebet (1985) gives many examples of grotesque caricatures in subject matter having to do with sex and scatology. For the marginalia in illuminated manucripts, see Randall (1966) and Camille (1992); for decorated choir stalls, see also Steppe (1973) and Kraus et al. (1986); for comparable insignia on clothing, see van Beuningen (1993). The decoration on the capital in Toulouse is discussed by Camille (1992), 57. The biblical passage referred to is Matthew 17. Concerning the presentation of religious processions, see Ramakers (1996b). The excesses prevailing at Houthem are described in Foncke (1955); cf. Hermant (1935/36), 267. The warning issued by the town council of Mechelen is in Autenboer (1962), 58. Regarding the metaphorical use of thawing, see Pleij (1988b), 64, 71–73, 84–85; cf. 367–68, lines 349–408, esp. 397–400. The other marginalia in the manuscript are to be found on fol. 69 recto, 98 recto, and 75 verso. As far as the meaning of such marginal depictions is concerned, Bedaux (1994) prefers to typify them as territorial and signposting iconography; this technique of the contrast was heavily and continually criticized by contemporaries, who thought that all those dirty apes, monsters, and fighting knights expressed nothing but a penchant for silliness. Bernard of Clairvaux, in particular, reacted furiously; see Randall (1966), 3–5, who gives a great number of examples under the entry "obscaena"; cf. Camille (1992), 10; see also Hogenelst et al. (1995), 43.

34. Topsy-Turvy Worlds

On the subject of topsy-turvy worlds, see Clark (1980), esp. 106–8; cf. Bejczy (1994), 140–57. For examples of the upside-down world portrayed in the visual arts, see also Falkenburg (1985), 100–101, 121–22; Falkenburg (1990); and Falkenburg (1991/92), esp. 179–80. For examples of topsy-turvy worlds in literature, see Curtius (1963), 94–98. The apocryphal passage quoted by Glaber is to be found in Duby (1993), 60. See Augustine (1972), 449 (book 11, ch. 18; cf. book 14, ch. 28, and book 15, ch. 1); see also Augustine (1930), 24–25 (book 11); the quotation is from Augustine (1968), 3:497. Augustine refers repeatedly to passages in the Bible such as II Corinthians 6:7–10 and Ecclesiasticus (Apocrypha) 33:14–5; the passage quoted from the Bible is Ecclesiastes 3:1–8. For *concordia discors*, see Clark (1980), 106–7; the quotation from the *ars poetica* by Geoffrey of Vinsauf is from Galfredus de Vino Salvo (1971), lines 120–25. Rhetoric is by its very nature antithetical, see Ong (1988), 111. Hadewijch quoted from Komrij (1994), 47–49; Augustine is quoted from *Sinte Augustijns Hantboec* (1962), 1:122–24. For similar instances of antitheses in lying tales, see *Verfasserlexikon* (1983), cols. 1039–44, s.v. "Lügenreden." Regarding the attempts to make a definite typification of the differences between good and evil, see McGinn (1992), 16; Frederiksen (1992), 26; Emmerson (1992), 311; cf. Augustine (1930), 24–31. The statement made by Thomas Aquinas is quoted from Aquinas (1952), 1:261, where question 48 of *the Summa Theologica* (I.q.48) is treated. For the upside-down world and the phenomenon of the *Zeitklage* ("a complaint on the times") in literature, see Curtius (1963), 94–98; this is also very typical of the *Strophische gedichten* by Maerlant (1918). Regarding "earthly" traditions in the visual arts, see Falkenburg (1985), 100–101; cf. Pleij (1990), 17–78. For the woodcuts from Vintler's book, see *The Illustrated Bartsch* (1983), 6:231–2. Adalbero of Lâon is discussed in Duby (1985), 67; cf. *Carmina* (ed. 1930–1971), no. 6, vol. 1, part 1, 7–8; see also the translation in *Carmina* (1959), 110–15. The quotation is from *Liederen* (966), no. 15, lines 1–3. Van der Luere is discussed in Komrij (1994), 156–58; cf. the text from *Het handschrift-Jan Phillipsz* (1995), 139–40; and de Roovere (1955), 302–4, 306–10, 317–18, 322–23, 326–28; cf. also Lievens (1992); de Pauw (1893–1897), 646; Bijns (1902), 309–11; and various texts in Komrij (1994), 671–74, 765, 999. Regarding the contents of the London MS containing Cockaigne version L, see chapter 5; the quotation is on fol. 133 recto. For the Blauwe Schuit (Blue Barge), see Pleij (1983b), with the mock sermon on Saint Nobody on 276–80; the sermon also appears in Komrij (1994), 1047–55. For other similar texts, see Pleij (1983b), 177–86, 250–54; Kayser (1983/84); Pleij (1989); and Pleij (1992). The quotation from the mock sermon is taken from Komrij (1994), 1048. Regarding the Amazons, see Bartholomaeus Anglicus (1485), book 15, ch. 12; cf. Gerritsen (1985). The quotation is from Mandeville (1983), 176. The topsy-turvy world caused by women in control is treated in Moxey (1989); cf. Pleij (1988b), part 8. Mandeville's views of upside-down emotions regarding life and death are reported in Greenblatt (1992), 44. Columbus's statements can be found in Colomb (1961), 242, 466.

35. Hard Times

The *Land of Cockaigne* print with text is reproduced in van der Heiden (1985), no. 14. Regarding acedia and melancholy, see Pleij (1990), 79–100. For the more positive image of work, see Le Goff (1977), 46–65, 66–79, 162–80; cf. Pleij et al. (1991), 30–36. The quotation is from Boendale (ed. 1844–1848), vol. 1, ch. 23, lines 54–59. The reference is to Genesis 2:15; The quotations are from *Spiegel* (1900), 1:110, lines 8650–51; *Die Dietsche Lucidarius* (1851), 3:12, lines 973–78. Thomas Aquinas thought in terms of worsening working conditions; see Aquinas (1945), 948–49. On the corrupting influence of work, see the *Sidrac* (1936), 91, 130–31. Meister Eckhart's text is quoted in de Vooys (1910), 218–19; cf. Pleij et al. (1991), 33–34; see also Boendale (1844–48), vol. 3 ch. 1; de Lorris et al. (1991), lines 11.356–58, 11.373–76; and Brugman (1948), 130–31. The proverb is to be found in *Proverbia* (ca. 1484), fol. [C7] verso. For the triumphant procurement and consumption of food, cf. also Bakhtin (1984), 281–83, 302. The Kampen proverb is quoted in Kloeke (1959), 71; the passage from the pilgrims' allegory is from *Dit is dat boeck van den pelgherym* (1486), fol. F2 recto–verso. The short text from the Brussels MS is quoted in Priebsch (1907), 172.

36. Moderation, Ambition, and Decorum

For gluttony as bestial behavior, see Walker Bynum (1987), 2. Drunkenness was also viewed as a form of gluttony; see Chaucer (1995), 626. Van Kempen is quoted from

Een devoet boecxken (1516), fol. [F7] recto; see also the *Ridderboek* (1991), 100; and *Dit es die historie ende leven* (1903); cf. Tubach (1969), no. 1816; and Deighton (1993); see also *Spiegel* (1900), cols. 25–28; *Des coninx summe* (1900), 281–82; Boccace (1476), book 7, ch. 7; and de Weert (1915), lines 1254–1449. Regarding the saying that the belly is a temple of God, see chapter 14 and the list of sources for that chapter; see also van Delf (1937–1939), 2:209, lines 118–21. For the sumptuary laws imposed by the authorities, see Jansen-Sieben (1993), 164; and Muchembled (1991), 104–5. Regarding the evil nature of the owl, see Vandenbroeck (1985). For the *mât de Cocagne*, see Müller (1984), 25–26. For references to Bruegel's corpulent figures, see the list of sources for chapter 16. For Hans Weiditz, the so-called Petrarch Master, see Scheidig (1955), 204, 302; the engraving of the drunkard is in Geisberg (1974), 1473. Regarding the parasitic character types in plays performed at the Latin schools, see Lazard (1978), 278–96. The quotation from the *Twee bedelaers* is from the edition in van Vloten (1877), 1:195; the other play is quoted from Mak (1950), 35, lines 5–10; cf. also the unpublished play *Van twee personages, den eenen genaemt Grooten Honger and de d'ener genaemt Goeden Appetijt* (Of two characters, one called Great Hunger and the other called Good Appetite), in Hummelen (1968), 1 OI 7. The laid tables are described in Cockaigne text L, lines 53–57, and text B, lines 57–65. For the technique of the caricatural, negative self-image, see Vandenbroeck (1987), 63–116; and Pleij (1988b), 126–35. Concerning appropriate times for meals, see Jansen-Sieben (1993), 13; and Baudet (1904), 1–4. For views expressed in literature, see Boendale (1844–1848), vol. 1, ch. 15, lines 59–66; cf. Jansen-Sieben (1993), 163. It appears from the French parallel that these lines have a proverbial character; see *Renout* (1966), lines 2492–94; and *Boec van het kerstene leven*, ms II.280, fol. 3 recto–80 recto, Brussels, Bibliothèque Royale Albert I. Dr. Geert Warnar at Leiden was so kind as to draw this to my attention; regarding this manuscript, see de Baere (1987); cf. also de Weert (1915), lines 1360–65; *Dat Boeck* (1930), 167, 227; Zerbolt (1941), 104, 283; Brant (1981), fol. X2 recto; *Wech* (1479), fol. [B7] recto–verso; *Oudvlaemsche liederen* (1849), 509; *Een devoet boecxken* (1516), fol. [F6] verso; *Spiegel* (1900), col. 33; *Des coninx summe* (1900), 283–84; and Chaucer (1995), 626. On eating once a day in the land of the Tartars, see Mandeville (1908), col. 110; the quotation is taken from Mandeville (1983), 158; cf. Bejczy (1994), 67. For negative examples in Mandeville, see the edition of 1908, cols. 187 and 213. Anglo-Norman monastic satire can be found in Aspin (1953), 130–42, lines 56–58.

37. Lessons in Pragmatism

Boethius (1485), fol. 78 verso–81 recto, treats the golden age and gluttony. Regarding the provenance of the commentary, see Angenent (1991); it concerns the Epistle of

Paul the Apostle to the Philippians 3:19. The passage quoted from the Bible is Romans 16:18. The quotation from Boethius is from the edition of 1485, fol. 79 verso, col. b. The quotation on urban decadence is from Boendale (1844–1848), vol. 3, ch. 26, lines 83–86. Getting rich while you sleep in Cockaigne is reported in text L, line 18, and text B, lines 16 and 48; the quotation on guzzling is in text G, lines 91–96. On added morals and increasing spiritualization, see Reynaert (1994); cf. Pleij (1995b), 173–74. On the subject of reading aloud to one another, see Pleij (1991/92).

PART 8. DREAMING OF COCKAIGNE: THE END

38. The Name Cockaigne

Ong (1988) gives a concise survey of the characteristics of oral communication. "Beliren" occurs in the London MS, fol. 139 recto. For Kokanje (and also Kokinje), see WNT s.v.; for Luilekkerland, see de Keyser (1956); de Meyer (1962), 432–40; and WNT s.v. On Cocagne as a name in Old French fabliaux, see Väänänen (1947). The passage in *Aymeri* is in the edition of 1884–1887), added to the other manuscript after line 1788; cf. Tobler (1936), cols. 510–11; similar expressions occur in the only manuscript dating from the beginning of the fourteenth century, Joufrois (1972), lines 954, 1009, 1134, 1137, and 1373; see also Adenés (1874), line 5621 (MSS dating from the thirteenth century). For the association with honey cakes and similar delicacies, see Müller (1984), 11; Robert (1985), 673; WNT, s.v. "Kokinje." Väänänen (1947), 5, says the name Cuccagna occurs as early as 1142 in Italian sources, but not to any appreciable extent in narrative texts until the fifteenth century. The Latin song on the loose-living abbot is from *Carmina* (1930–1971), no. 222, vol. 1, part 3, 81–82, where there is also information on the other two texts; the version quoted is taken from *Carmina* (1986), 177–78. The dating "circa 1164" is by Väänänen (1947), 5. The passage in Spanish is to be found in Bolte (1918), 248. The Middle English text is from Robbins (1959), 121–27, 317–19. Regarding Joachim and the thousand-year reign, see Cohn (1984), 108–13, and also chapter 29. The possible connection with Aristophanes' *Birds* was put forward by de Caluwé-Dor (1977). For the Muslim paradise, see chapter 20; Cockaigne as a derivation of *coc* (rooster), the guardian of the Muslim paradise, was suggested by Metlitzki (1977), 213–14. For details on Kokkengen, see Blok (1957), 24; Moerman (1956), 180; van der Linden (1955), 277; Muller (1920–1959), vol. 5, no. 2823; Grevenstuk (1919); and Manten (1987). The tradition of mock toponyms is discussed in Pleij (1983b), 117–25 and passim; cf. *Het zal koud zijn in 't water* (1980), 47–51; and *Van den vos Reynaerde* (1983), lines 298–301, 599, 3016–19. The 1759 description of Kokkengen is from Grevenstuk (1919). The quotation from Boendale is from the edition of 1844–1848), vol. 1, ch. 35, lines 7–9. Cockijn is derived from the Old French *coquin* and Latin *coquus* or *coquinus*; see *MNW*, s.v.; cf. Poeschel (1878), 404–9. The *cockaert* in the farce is in Leendertz (1907), 119–31, line 212. All the words mentioned are to be found in *MNW*, van der Voort van der Kleij (1983), and Mak (1959). Regarding the *mât de Cocagne*, see Müller (1984), 25–26. For Cockaigne's use as a surname, see Cockayne (1990).

39. A Depreciated Cultural Asset

Examples of the interest in Cockaigne from the field of what used to be called folklore (and is now called, among other things, cultural anthropology), as well as from the field of art history, are to be found in de Keyser (1956); de Meyer (1962), 432–40; and Lebeer (1969), no. 63, 152–56. For a political interpretation, see Frank (1991). Regarding Bruegel's painting, see an der Heiden (1985) and Jockel (1995). An Antwerp inventory dating from 1617 lists "een stucxken schilderye on doeck in lyste van d'Luylackerlant" (one painting on canvas of the Land of Cockaigne, in a frame); see Duverger (1984), no. 260; this cannot be the panel of 1567 but is perhaps a copy of it made by one of Bruegel's offspring (Dr. Wim Anrooij was so kind as to draw my attention to this). The Marxists quoted are Kuczynski (1980), 45; and Morton (1952), 24, respectively. The parodic character of the Middle English text of the *Land of Cokaygne*, in any case, as well as that of the French fabliaux, is underscored by Tigges (1988), 99; and Boas (1978), 167–68. Regarding the content of the London and Brussels MSS with Cockaigne texts L and B, see chapter 6. The altarpiece of 1488 is reproduced and discussed in Boockmann (1990), 196 and illus. 197.

40. From Countryside to Town

Regarding the pseudorealism of the caricatures of peasants in literature and the visual arts, see Pleij (1988b), 121–45. Dancing is mentioned in text L, line 96, and text B, lines 38 and 110; cf. Stijevoort (1930), nos. 18 (which is repeated in no. 66) and 55. Gold and silver are mentioned in text L, line 28, and text B, line 80. Concerning the meaning of minuscule details, see Ginzburg (1988), 214–19. The quotation is from text B, lines 23–24. On the carbuncle, see Petronius (1988), 72; Bartholomaeus Anglicus (1485), book 16, ch. 25; and Mandeville (1908), cols.

233–34 (the quotation is taken from Mandeville [1983], 170); *Parthononeus* (1897/98), lines 682–87; *Triumphe* (1514), stanza 168; *Pelgrimstocht* (1948), 18; cf. Camille (1991), 254. For other meanings of *carbuncle*, see *MNW* and *WNT*. The corresponding passage occurs in text G, lines 16–17. A comparable text occurs in the Brussels MS in Priebsch (1906), 466. Regarding marvelous castles made of precious stones, see chapter 20. Carbuncles as building material are mentioned in Ezekiel 28:13. A New Jerusalem furnished in this way is described in Isaiah 54:12; cf. Boeck (1930), 234; *Reis* (1994), line 739; cf. also Delumeau (1992), 104 and 109, with reference to Prester John. The decorated walls are described in *Confrarie* (1520–1540), fol. B1 verso–B2 recto. The *Land of Cokaygne* is treated in detail in de Caluwé-Dor (1978); cf. de Caluwé-Dor (1980); the text is in Robbins (1959), 121–27; German translations occur in Richter (1984), 135–40; and Müller (1984), 43–44; cf. Tigges (1988), 101. Concerning the passion for precious stones among the bourgeoisie, see Favier (1990), 291; and Vandenbroeck (1990), 37. *Dit es die historie ende leven* (1903) warns of one sin leading to another. Tigges (1988), 102, thinks that the sex in the (aristocratic) Middle English text on the Land of Cokaygne is indicative of its popular roots; however, the opposite is more likely to be the case. Regarding obscenities in elite culture, see Pleij (1988b), 99–109; see also Gaignebet (1985). The attitude of the desert fathers to sex is treated in Brown (1990), 172–74. For the dictionary of thieves' slang dating from 1547, see de Meyere and Baekelmans (1914), 9–15; there is a modern translation in *Schelmen* (1985), 38–43; see also the afterword there. On the subject of fairy tales as the oldest traces of ideas, cf. Ginzburg (1988), 214–19. Smells are mentioned in text G, lines 71–72. For nourishing oneself by breathing the air or sniffing an apple, see de Vooys (1906), 123; and Camporesi (1994), 286–96; cf. Aubrun (1980), 118. Corbin (1986), 18, begins his study with the remark that in the eighteenth century people's sensitivity to smells increased drastically, incorrectly giving the impression that odors were hardly a worry before that time. For this reason, Anna Bijns also finds smells decadent and a sign of the decline of humankind: (1875), no. 70. Devils perverting the sense of smell are mentioned in van der Vet (1902), 213; Mandeville (1908), col. 234, on Prester John (quotation taken from Mandeville [1983], 170). For Jesus' cross in Mandeville, see the edition of 1908, col. 8; the quotation is taken from Mandeville (1983), 47. In the *Boec van den houte* (1959) such motivating factors are not mentioned; cf. also Baert (1995). Regarding measures taken by city authorities to combat stench, see Linskens (1976), 31–41. Smells emanating from the theater stage are described in *De Gentse spelen* (1982), 1:34. Smells at the courts of the nobility are discussed in Raue (1996), ch. 2.

41. The Necessity of Fiction

The proverb is to be found in Kloeke (1959), 9. Regarding hunger and scarcity in Europe, see chapter 11. Such simple connections between famine and Cockaigne are made, for example, by Richter (1984), 31. Individualism is apparent in text B, lines 62 and 70. Payen (1984), 437–38, points out the middle-class dimensions of the Old French texts. Cockaigne is described as being not for the rich in text F, lines 184–85. The battle cry at the tournament is quoted in Joufrois (1972), line 1009.

Bibliography

Adenés li Rois. *Les Enfances Ogier*. Ed. A. Scheler. Brussels, 1874.

Het af-vaaren van het vol en zoet geladen Schip Sint Reyn-Uyt, Zeylende met een altyd goede Wind naar de aangename Contreije van Luy-Lekker-Land. N.p., ca. 1700. (Copy: The Hague, Royal Library.)

The Age of Bede. Trans. J. F. Webb. Ed. D. H. Farmer. Harmondsworth, 1998.

Aken, H. van. *Die rose*. Ed. E. Verwijs. The Hague, 1868.

Alberts, W. J. *Geschiedenis van Gelderland van de vroegste tijden tot het einde der middeleeuwen*. The Hague, 1966.

Alpertus van Metz. *Gebeurtenissen van deze tijd*. Trans. H. van Rij. Amsterdam, 1980.

Althoff, G. "Der frieden-, bündnis- und gemeinschaftstiftende Character des Mahles im früheren Mittelalter." In *Essen und Trinken im Mittelalter und Neuzeit*, ed. I. Bitsch et al., 13–25. Sigmaringen, 1990.

Alvarez, V. *Relation du Beau Voyage que fit aux Pays-Bas, en 1548, le prince Philippe d'Espagne*. Ed. M.-T. Dovillée. Brussels, 1964.

Angenent, M. P. "Het Gentse Boethiuscommentaar en Renier van Sint-Truiden." *Tijdschrift voor Nederlandse taal- en letterkunde* 107 (1991): 274–310.

Aquinas, Thomas. *Basic Writings*. 2 vols. Ed. A. C. Pegis. New York, 1945.

——. *The Summa Theologica of Saint Thomas Aquinas*. 2 vols. Trans. Fathers of the English Dominican Province. Chicago, 1952.

Ariès, Ph., et al. *Geschiedenis van het persoonlijk leven*. Vol. 1. Amsterdam, 1987.

Aspin, I. S. T. *Anglo-Norman Political Songs*. Oxford, 1953.

Assenede, Diederic van. *Floris ende Blancefloer*. Ed. P. Leendertz Jr. Leiden, 1912.

Aubrun, M. "Caractères et portée religieuse et sociale des 'Visiones' en Occident du VIe au XIe siècle." *Cahiers de la Civilisation Médiévale* 23 (1980): 109–30.

Aucassin and Nicolette. Trans. P. Matarasso. Harmondsworth, 1971.

Augustine. *Enchiridion*. Trans. C. Bloemen. Roermond, 1930.

——. *The City of God Against the Pagans*. 7 vols. Trans. David S. Wiesen. London, 1968.

——. *Concerning the City of God Against the Pagans*. Trans. H. Bettenson. Harmondsworth, 1972.

Autenboer, E. van. *Volksfeest en rederijkers te Mechelen (1400–1600)*. Ghent, 1962.

Axters, St. G. *Inleiding tot een geschiedenis van de mystiek in de Nederlanden*. Ghent, 1967.

Aymeri de Narbonne. Ed. L. Demaison. Paris, 1884–1887.

Baere, G. de. "Een opvallende tekstgetuige van Ruusbroecs Kersten ghelove: Het handschrift Brussel, Koninklijke Bibliotheek Albert I, II.280." In *Miscellanea Neerlandica* (essays for J. Deschamps), 1:199–205. Leuven, 1987.

Baert, B. *Het "Boec van den Houte."* Brussels, 1995.

Bakhtin, M. *Rabelais and His World.* Trans. H. Iswolsky. Bloomington, Ind., 1984.

[Ballaer, E. V. J. van.] "Het Turnhoutsch Heybloemken op het feest der Violieren te Antwerp 1561." *Kempisch Museum* 1 (1890): 37–46.

Bartholomeus Anglicus. *Van den proprieteyten der dinghen.* Haarlem: J. Bellaert, 1485. (Copy: Amsterdam, University Library.)

Batselier, A. *Kroniek van het toneel en van het letterkundig leven te Geraardsbergen (1416–1808).* Geraardsbergen, 1976.

Baudet, F. E. J. M. *De maaltijd en de keuken in de middeleeuwen.* Leiden, 1904.

Bedaux, J. B. "Functie en betekenis van randdecoratie in middeleeuwse handschriften." *Kunstlicht* 14 (1994): 28–33.

Bedevaart naar Jerusalem in 1525. Ed. C. J. Gonnet. Haarlem, 1884.

Behre, K.-E. "Die Ernährung im Mittelalter." In *Mensch und Umwelt im Mittelalter*, ed. B. Herrmann, 74–87. Frankfurt am Main, 1990.

Bejczy, I. "De bon sauvage in de middeleeuwen: Alexander en de Brahmanen. Het voorbeeld van Maerlant." *De nieuwe taalgids* 83 (1990): 434–45.

———. *Pape Jansland en Utopia: De verbeelding van de beschaving van middeleeuwen en renaissance.* Nijmegen, 1994.

Benz, E. *Das Recht auf Faulheit oder Die friedliche Beendigung des Klassenkampfes.* Stuttgart, 1974.

Berghe, Jan van den. *Dichten en spelen.* Ed. C. Kruyskamp. The Hague, 1950.

Bergner, H. "Das grosze Festmahl in der mittelenglischen Prima Pastorum des Wakefield-Zyklus." In *Essen und Trinken im Mittelalter*, ed. I. Bitsch et al., 45–57. Sigmaringen, 1990.

Beuningen, H. J. E. van, et al. *Heilig en profaan: 1000 laat-middeleeuwse insignes uit de collectie H. J. E. van Beuningen.* Cothen, 1993.

Binche 1549: De blijde intrede van prins Filips, toekomstig koning van Spanje. Brussels, 1985.

Bischoff, B. "Caritas-Lieder." *Mittelalterliche Studien*, 2:56–77. Stuttgart, 1981.

Blockmans, W. P., et al. "Tussen crisis en welvaart: Sociale veranderingen, 1300–1500." In *Algemene Geschiedenis der Nederlanden.* Vol. 4, *Middle Ages*, 42–86. Haarlem, 1980

Blok, D. P. "Naamsveranderingen en modeverschijnselen in de middeleeuwse plaatsnaamgeving in Utrecht en Holland benoorden de Lek." *Mededelingen van de Vereniging voor Naamkunde te Leuven* 33 (1957): 17–26.

Boas, G. *Essays on Primitivism and Related Ideas in the Middle Ages.* New York, 1978.

Boccace [Boccaccio]. *De la ruyne des nobles hommes et femmes.* Bruges: Colard Mansion, 1476. (Copy: Vienna, Austrian National Library.)

Boccaccio, G. *Decamerone.* 2 vols. Trans. A. Schwartz. Amsterdam, 1969.

Dat boec van den houte. Ed. L. Hermodsson. Uppsala, 1959.

Boec van de destructien van Jherusalem (1482). Facsimile ed. Ed. W. L. Braekman. Sint-Niclaas, 1984.

Dat boeck van der voirsienicheit Godes. Ed. A. Burssens. Brussels, 1930.

Het boek van Sidrac in de Nederlanden. Ed. J. F. J. van Tol. Amsterdam, 1936.

Boendale, Jan van. *Der leken spieghel.* 3 vols. Leiden, 1844–1848.

[———.] *Boek van de wraak Gods.* Trans. W. van Anrooij. Amsterdam, 1994.

[Boendale, Jan van, et al.] "Het boec van der wraken." In *Nederlandsche gedichten uit de veertiende eeuw,* ed. F.-A. Snellaert, 287–491. Brussels, 1869.

[Boethius.] *De consolatione philosophie, ten trooste, leeringhe ende confoorte.* Ghent: A. de Keyser, 1485. (Copy: Amsterdam, University Library.)

Boethius. *The Consolation of Philosophy.* Ed. V. E. Watts. Harmondsworth, 1969.

Bolte, J. "Lügenpredigt: Vom packofen." *Zeitschrift für deutsches Altertum* 36 (1892): 150–54.

———. "Bilderbogen des 16. und 17. Jahrhunderts." *Zeitschrift des Vereins für Volkskunde* 20 (1910): 182–202.

Bolte, J., et al. "Das Märchen vom Schlauraffenland." In *Anmerkungen zu den Kinder- und Hausmärchen der Brüder Grimm,* 3:244–58. Leipzig, 1918.

Bonner, C. "Dionysiac Magic and the Greek Land of Cockaigne." *Transactions and proceedings of the American Philological Association* 41 (1910): 175–85.

Boockmann, H. "Das Leben in städtischen Häusern um 1500." In *Mensch und Umwelt in Mittelalter,* ed. B. Herrmann, 194–206. Frankfurt am Main, 1990.

Boogert, B. van den, et al. *Maria van Hongarije (1505–1558): Koningin tussen keizers en kunstenaars.* Zwolle, 1993.

Boonen, W. *Geschiedenis van Leuven, geschreven in de jaren 1593 en 1594.* Ed. E. van Even. Leuven, 1880.

Bot, P. *Tussen verering en verachting: De rol van de vrouw in de middeleeuwse samenleving, 500–1500.* Kampen, 1990.

De Brabantsche yeesten, of rymkronyk van Braband. Ed. J. F. Willems. Brussels, 1839.

Braekman, W. L. *Spel en kwel in vroeger tijd: Verkenningen van charivari, exorcisme, toverij, sport en spel in Vlaanderen.* Ghent, 1992.

[Brant, S.] *Dit is der zotten ende der narren scip.* Paris: Guido Coopman, 1500. (Copy: Paris, Bibliothèque Nationale.)

Brant, S. *Narrenschiff.* Ed. F. Zarncke. Leipzig, 1854.

———. *Der sotten schip. Antwerpen 1548.* Ed. L. Geeraedts. Middelburg, 1981.

Brown, P. *Lichaam en maatschappij: Man, vrouw en seksuele onthouding in het vroege christendom, 50 na C.–450 na C.* Amsterdam, 1990.

Brugman, J. *Onuitgegeven sermoenen.* Ed. P. Grootens. Tielt, 1948.

Bruin, C. C. de. "De prologen van de Eerste Historiebijbel geplaatst in het raam van hun tijd." In *The Bible and Medieval Culture,* ed. W. Lourdaux et al., 190–219. Leuven, 1979.

Brunet, M. "Le parc d'attractions des ducs de Bourgogne à Hesdin." *Gazette des Beaux-Arts* 78 (1971): 331–42.

Bumke, J. *Höfische Kultur: Literatur und Gesellschaft im hohen Mittelalter.* 2 vols. Munich, 1986.

Bunte, W. *Die Zerstörung Jerusalems in der mittelniederländischen Literatur (1100–1600).* Frankfurt am Main, 1992.

Burbure, L. de *De Antwerpsche ommegangen in de XIVe en XVe eeuw.* Antwerp, 1878.

Burke, P. *Volkscultuur in Europa, 1500–1800.* Amsterdam, 1990.

Buskenblaser. In *De abele spelen,* ed. L. van Kammen, 148–59. Amsterdam, 1968.

Buuren, A. M. J. van. " 'Ay hoor van desen abuze.' Enkele dorpers uit de Middelnederlandse literatuur." In *Gewone mensen in de middeleeuwen,* ed. R. E. V. Stuip et al., 137–59. Utrecht, 1987.

———. "Kerk en wereld in de middeleeuwse literatuur: Een Utrechts tweeluik." In *Utrecht tussen kerk en staat,* ed. R. E. V. Stuip et al., 243–62. Hilversum, 1991.

———. "De tuin in het kader van de middeleeuwse natuurbeleving." In *Tuinen in de middeleeuwen,* ed. R. E. V. Stuip et al., 115–30. Hilversum, 1992.

Bijns, A. *Refereinen.* Ed. W. L. van Helten. Rotterdam, 1875.

———. *Nieuwe refereinen.* Ed. W. J. A. Jonckbloet et al. Groningen, 1880.

———. *Nieuwe refereinen.* Ed. W. J. A. Jonckbloet et al. Ghent, 1886.

———. "Onuitgegeven gedichten." *Leuvensche bijdragen* 4 (1902): 199–368.

Calcoen. *Récit flamand du second voyage de Vasco de Gama vers l'Inde, en 1502–1503.* Ed. J. Denucé. Antwerp, 1931.

Caluwé-Dor, J. de. "Cocagne II; ou, L'étymologie et l'étude de la tradition se rejoingent." In *Actes du colloque du Centre d'Etudes médiévales de l'Université de Picardie,* ed. D. Buschinger, 95–104. Amiens, 1977.

———. "L'anti-paradis au *Pays de Cocagne.* Cocagne I. Etude et traduction du poème moyen-anglais." In *Mélanges de philologie et de littérature romanes offerts à J. Wathelet-Wittem,* 103–23. Liège, 1978.

———. "L'élément irlandais dans la version moyen-anglaise de *The Land of Cockaygne.*" In *Mélanges de langue et littérature françaises du moyen age et de la renaissance offerts à C. Foulon,* 1:89–98. Rennes, 1980.

Camille, M. *The Gothic Idol: Ideology and Image-making in Medieval Art*. Cambridge, 1991.

——. *Image on the Edge: The Margins of Medieval Art*. London, 1992.

Campbell, M. B. *The Witness and the Other World: Exotic European Travel Writing*. Ithaca, 1988.

Camporesi, P. *Bread of Dreams: Food and Fantasy in Early Modern Europe*. Trans. D. Gentilcore. Cambridge, 1989.

——. *Het onvergankelijke vlees: Heil en heling in middeleeuwen en vroeg-moderne tijd*. Nijmegen, 1994.

Cappel, E. van. "De hongersnood in de middeleeuwen tot de XIIIe eeuw." *Annales de la Société d'Emulation de Bruges* 56 (1906): 16–40, 143–64.

Carasso-Kok, M. *Repertorium van verhalende-historische bronnen uit de middeleeuwen*. The Hague, 1981.

Carmina Burana. 4 vols. Ed. A. Hilka et al. Heidelberg, 1930–1971.

Carmina Burana: Kleine bloemlezing uit de middeleeuwse vagantenpoëzie. Trans. W. van Elden. The Hague, 1959.

[*Carmina Burana*]. *Selections from the Carmina Burana: A Verse Translation*. Trans. David Parlett. Harmondsworth, 1986.

Carruthers, M. J. *The Book of Memory: A Study of Memory in Medieval Culture*. Cambridge, 1994.

Chaucer, G. *The Canterbury Tales*. Ed. F. N. Robinson. Oxford, 1974.

——. *De Canterbury-verhalen*. Trans. E. van Altena. Baarn, 1995.

Chesnaye, N. de la. *La condemnation de banquet*. Ed. J. Koopmans et al. Geneva, 1991.

Cioranescu, A. "Utopie: Cocagne et âge d'or." *Diogène* 75 (1971): 86–123.

Clark, S. "Inversion, Misrule, and the Meaning of Witchcraft." *Past and Present* 87 (May 1980): 98–127.

Clément-Hémery, A. *Histoire des fêtes civiles et religieuses, des usages anciens et modernes*. 2 vols. Paris, 1834–1846.

Cockayne, R. A. C. "New Thoughts on an Old Pedigree: A Reconsideration of the Cockaynes of Ashbourne in the Early Fifteenth Century." *Derbyshire Archaeological Journal* 110 (1990): 105–33.

Cohn, N. *The Pursuit of the Millennium: Revolutionary Millenarians and Mystical Anarchists of the Middle Ages*. London, 1984.

Coigneau, D. "Het leugenrefrein bij de rederijkers." *Studia Germanica Gandensia* 20 (1979): 31–74.

——. *Refreinen in het zotte bij de rederijkers*. 3 vols. Ghent, 1980–1983.

Colomb [Columbus], C. *Oeuvres*. Ed. A. Cioranescu. Paris, 1961.

Columbus, C. *Het scheepsdagboek*. Ed. R. H. Fuson. Utrecht, 1991.

Des coninx summe. Ed. D. C. Tinbergen. Leiden, 1900.

Cook, H. J. "Ancient Wisdom, the Golden Age, and Atlantis: The New World in Sixteenth Century Cosmography." *Terrae Incognitae* 9, no. 2 (1977): 25–43.

Corbin, A. *Pestdamp en bloesemgeur: Een geschiedenis van de reuk.* Nijmegen, 1986.

Cronycke van Hollandt, Zeelandt ende Vrieslant. Antwerp: J. van Doesborch, 1530. (Copy: Amsterdam, University Library.)

Curschmann, F. *Hungersnöte im Mittelalter: Ein Beitrag zur deutschen Wirtschaftsgeschichte des 8. bis 13. Jahrhunderts.* Leipzig, 1900.

Curtius, E. R. *European Literature and the Latin Middle Ages.* Trans. W. R. Trask. New York, 1963.

Cuttler, Ch. D. "Errata in Netherlandish Art: Jan Mostaert's *New World* Landscape." *Simiolus* 19 (1989): 191–17.

Cuvelier, J. "Eene onbekende rijmkroniek van het begin der XIVe eeuw." *Verslagen en mededelingen van de Koninklijke Vlaamse Akademie voor taal- en letterkunde,* 1928: 1039–53.

Dal, E. *The Ages of Man and the Months of the Year: Poetry, Prose and Pictures Outlining the "Douze mois figurés" Motif, Mainly Found in Shepherds' Calendars and in Livres d'Heures (14th to 17th Century).* Copenhagen, 1980.

Decavele, J. *De dageraad van de Reformatie in Vlaanderen (1520–1565).* 2 vols. Brussels, 1975.

Deighton, A. R. "The Sins of Saint John of Beverley: The Case of the Dutch 'volksboek' *Jan van Beverley.*" *Leuvense Bijdragen* 82 (1993): 227–46.

Delf, D. van. *Tafel van den Kersten Ghelove.* 4 vols. Ed. L. M. Fr. Daniëls. Antwerp, 1937–1939.

Delumeau, J. *Une histoire du paradis: Le jardin des délices.* Paris, 1992.

Deluz, C. "Le paradis terrestre: Image de l'Orient lointain dans quelques documents géographiques médiévaux." *Senefiance* 11 (1982): 143–61.

———. *Le Livre de Jehan de Mandeville: Une "géographie" au XIVe siècle.* Louvain-La-Neuve, 1988.

Dene, E. de. "Testament rhetoricael." In *Jaarboek "De Fonteine,"* ed. W. Waterschoot and D. Coigneau, 26 (1975), vol. 2; 28 (1976/77), vol. 2; 30 (1978/79), vol. 2.

Deschamps, J. *Middelnederlandse handschriften uit Europese en Amerikaanse bibliotheken: Catalogus.* Leiden, 1972.

Deux jeux de Carnaval de la fin du moyen âge. Ed. J.-C. Aubailly. Geneva, 1977.

Een devoet boecxken van den inwendighen navolghen des levens ende des cruces ons heren Ihesu Cristi. Antwerp, 1516. (Copy: Xanten, Stiftstbibliotheek.)

Een devoot ende profitelyck boecxken: Geestelijk liedboek met melodieën van 1539. Ed. D. F. Scheurleer. The Hague, 1889.

Die Dietsche Lucidarius. In P. Blommaert, *Oudvlaemsche gedichten der XIIe, XIIIe en XIVe eeuwen,* 3:1–74. Ghent, 1851.

Dillon, M., et al. *Celtic Realms.* London, 1967.

Dinzelbacher, P. "The Way to the Other World in Medieval Literature and Art." *Folklore* 97 (1986): 70–87.

Le disciple de Pantagruel (Les navigations de Panurge). Ed. G. Demerson et al. Paris, 1982.

Dit es die historie ende leven van den heilyghen heremijt sint Jan van Beverley. Ed. G. J. Boekenoogen. Leiden, 1903.

Dit is dat boeck van den pelgherym. Haarlem: J. Bellaert, 1486. (Copy: The Hague, Royal Library.)

Doesborch, J. van. *De refreinenbundel.* 2 vols. Ed. C. Kruyskamp. Leiden, 1940.

Drie Eenlingen. Delft: B. H. Schinckel, 1597. (Copy: The Hague, Royal Library.)

Duby, G. "La vulgarisation des modèles culturels dans la société féodale." In *Hommes et structures du moyen âge,* 343–52. Paris 1973.

———. *De drie orden: Het zelfbeeld van de feodale maatschappij, 1025–1225.* Trans. B. Raymakers. Amsterdam, 1985.

———. *Bernard van Clairvaux en de Cisterciënzerkunst.* Amsterdam, 1989.

———. *De middeleeuwse liefde en andere essays.* Trans. R. de Roo-Raymakers. Amsterdam, 1990.

———. *Het jaar duizend.* Trans. I. Groothedde. Amsterdam, 1993.

Duggan, J. J. *Oral Literature.* Edinburgh, 1975.

Dupuys, R. *Le triumphante et solemnelle entrée faicte en sa ville de Bruges.* Paris: G. de Gourmont, 1515. (Copy: London, British Library.)

Duverger, E. "Tapisseries de Jan van Tiegem représentant l'histoire des premiers parents." *Bulletin van de Koninklijke Musea voor Kunst en Geschiedenis* 45 (1973): 19–63.

———. *Antwerpse kunstinventarissen uit de zeventiende eeuw.* Vol. 1, *1600–1700.* Brussels, 1984.

Duyse, Fl. van. *Het oude Nederlandsche lied.* 3 vols. The Hague, 1903–1907.

Die eerste bliscap van Maria en Die sevenste bliscap van onser vrouwen. Culemborg, 1973.

Eliade, M. "The Yearning for Paradise." *Daedalus* 88 (1959): 255–67.

Emmerson, R. K. "Introduction: The Apocalypse in Medieval Culture." In *The Apocalypse in the Middle Ages,* ed. R. K. Emmerson et al., 293–332. Ithaca, 1992.

Emmerson, R. K., et al., eds. *The Apocalypse in the Middle Ages.* Ithaca, 1992.

Endepols, H. J. E. "Bijdrage tot de eschatologische voorstellingen in de middeleeuwen." *Tijdschrift voor Nederlandse taal- en letterkunde* 28 (1909): 49–111.

Enklaar, D. Th. *Varende luyden: Studiën over de middeleeuwse groepen van onmaatschappelijken in de Nederlanden.* Assen, 1956.

En toch was ze rond . . . Middeleeuws mens- en wereldbeeld. Exhibition cat. Brussels, 1990.

Erasmus, D. *Moriae encomium, dat is de lof der zotheid.* Amsterdam, 1959.

Erenstein, R. L., main ed. *Een theatergeschiedenis der Nederlanden.* Amsterdam, 1996.

Ertzdorff, X. von. *Romane und Novellen des 15. und 16. Jahrhundert in Deutschland.* Darmstadt, 1989.

Even, E. van. *L'Omgang de Louvain.* Louvain, 1863.

Faas, P. C. P. *Rond de tafel der Romeinen.* Diemen, 1994.

Falkenburg, R. L. *Joachim Patinir: Het landschap als beeld van de levenspelgrimage.* Nijmegen, 1985.

——. "Antithetical Iconography in Early Netherlandish Landscape Painting." *Bruegel and Netherlandish Landscape Painting from the National Gallery, Prague,* 25–36. Tokyo, 1990.

——. "Randfiguren op het toneel en in de schilderkunst in de zestiende eeuw." *Jaarboek "De Fonteine"* 41–2 (1991/92): 177–99.

Favier, J. *In naam van God en des gewins: De wording van de zakenman.* Amsterdam, 1990.

Flou, K. de, et al. *Beschrijving van Middelnederlandsche en andere handschriften die in Engeland bewaard worden.* 3 vols. Ghent, 1895–1897.

Foncke, R. "Het oordeel van een 16e-eeuwse Duitser over de Sint-Lievensprocessie van Gent." *Oostvlaamsche Zanten* 30 (1955): 161–3.

Fox, R. L. *Pagans and Christians.* London, 1986.

Fraenger, W. *Hieronymus Bosch.* Dresden, 1975.

De fragmenten van de Tweede Rose. Ed. K. Heeroma. Zwolle, 1958.

Frank, R. H. "An Interpretation of the Land of Cockaigne (1567) by Pieter Breugel the Elder." *Sixteenth Century Journal* 22 (1991): 299–329.

Frank, R. W. "The 'Hungry Gap.' Crop Failure and Famine: The Fourteenth-Century Agricultural Crisis and Piers Plowman." *Yearbook of Langland Studies* 4 (1990): 87–104.

Franssen, P. J. A. *Tussen tekst en publiek: Jan van Doesborch, drukker-uitgever en literator te Antwerpen en Utrecht in de eerste helft van de zestiende eeuw.* Amsterdam, 1990.

Franssen, P. J. A., et al. "Is de prozatekst over Virgilius de tovenaar oorspronkelijk in het Nederlands geschreven?" *Spektator* 23 (1994): 1–21.

Franssen, P. J. A., et al. "De andere Virgilius of hoogmoed komt voor de val." *De nieuwe taalgids* 88 (1995): 223–35.

Frantzen, J. J. A. A., et al. *Drei Kölner Schwankbücher aus dem XVten Jahrhundert.* Utrecht, 1920.

Frederiksen, P. "Tyconius and Augustine on the Apocalypse." In *The Apocalypse in the Middle Ages,* ed. R. K. Emmerson et al., 20–37. Ithaca, 1992.

Fry, D. K. "Caedmon as a Formulaic Poet." In *Oral Literature,* ed. J. J. Duggan, 41–61. Edinburgh, 1975.

Gachard, L. P., et al. *Collection des voyages des souverains des Pays-Bas.* Brussels, 1874.

Gaignebet, C. *Art profane et religion populaire au moyen âge.* Paris, 1985.

Galbert of Bruges [van Brugge]. *The murder of Charles the Good, Count of Flanders.* Trans. J. B. Ross. New York, 1967.

Galfredus de Vino Salvo. "Poetria Nova." In E. Gallo, *The Poetria Nova and Its Sources in Early Rhetorical Doctrine.* The Hague, 1971.

Ganser, W. G. *Die niederländische Version der Reisebeschreibung Johannes von Mandeville.* Amsterdam, 1985.

Gardiner, E. *Medieval Visions of Heaven and Hell: A Sourcebook.* New York, 1993.

Gassen, H. van. "De ommegang van het Heilig Kruis te Ninove (14e–16e eeuw)." *Het Land van Aalst* 1 (1949): 97–102, 135–38.

Geisberg, M. L. *The German Single-Leafed Woodcut, 1500–1550.* 4 vols. Munich, 1974.

De Gentse spelen van 1539. 2 vols. Ed. B. H. Erné. The Hague, 1982.

Het Geraardsbergse handschrift: Hs. Brussel, Koninklijke Bibliotheek Albert I, 837–845. Ed. M.-J. Govers et al. Hilversum, 1994.

Gerritsen, W. P. *De clepsydra, een tunnel naar de antipoden, en de natuur in een middeleeuwse proeftuin.* Utrecht, 1978.

———. "De omgekeerde wereld van de Amazonen." In *Middeleeuwers over vrouwen,* ed. R. E. V. Stuip, 1:157–76, 204–7. Utrecht, 1985.

———. "Vertalingen van Oudfranse litteraire werken in het Middelnederlands." In *Franse literatuur van de middeleeuwen,* ed. R. E. V. Stuip, 184–207. Muiderberg, 1988.

———. "De dichter en de leugenaars: De oudste poetica in het Nederlands." *De nieuwe taalgids* 85 (1992a): 2–13.

———. "Jan en Jenneken en de mondelinge overlevering van balladen." In *Een zoet akkoord: Middeleeuwse lyriek in de Lage Landen,* ed. F. Willaert et al., 287–302, 417–20. Amsterdam, 1992b.

Gerson, J. *Opera omnia.* 5 vols. Hagae Comitis, 1728.

Gilmore, M. P. "The New World in French and English Historians of the Sixteenth Century." In *First Images of America,* ed. F. Chiappelli, 2:519–270. Berkeley, 1976.

Ginzburg, C. *Omweg als methode: Essays over verborgen geschiedenis, kunst en maatschappelijke herinnering.* Nijmegen, 1988.

Glacken, C. J. *Traces on the Rhodian Shore: Nature and Culture in Western Thought from Ancient Times to the End of the Eighteenth Century.* Berkeley, 1967.

Gnapheus, G. *Acolastus.* Trans. P. Minderaa. Zwolle, 1956.

Goossens, L. A. M. *De meditatie in de eerste tijd van de Moderne Devotie.* Haarlem, 1952.

Goris, M. "Boethius' *De consolatione philosophiae:* Twee Middelnederlandse vertalingen en hun bronnen." In *Verraders en bruggenbouwers: Verkenningen naar de relatie tussen Latinitas en Middelnederlandse letterkunde,* ed. P. Wackers et al., 113–32, 297–301. Amsterdam, 1996.

Gotzkowsky, B. *Volksbücher, Prosaromane, Renaissance-Novellen, Versdichtungen und Schwankbücher: Bibliographie der deutschen Drucke.* Vol. 1. Baden-Baden, 1991.

La grande confrarie des soulx d'ouvrer et enragez de rien faire. Lyons, [1520–1540]. (Copy: Paris, Bibliothèque Nationale.)

Green, D. H. *Medieval Listening and Reading: The Primary Reception of German Literature, 800–1300.* Cambridge, 1994.

Greenblatt, S. *Marvelous Possessions: The Wonder of the New World.* Oxford, 1992.

Gregory of Tours. *The History of the Franks.* Trans. L. Thorpe. London, 1974.

Grevenstuk, J. G. Th. "Het edele lant van Cockaengen." *Jaarboekje van het Oudheidkundig Genootschap "Nifterlake",* 1919: 7–11.

Grundmann, H. *Ketzergeschichte des Mittelalters.* Göttingen, 1978.

Guenée, B., et al. *Les entrées royales françaises de 1328 à 1515.* Paris, 1968.

Guratzsch, H. *Die Auferweckung des Lazarus in der niederländischen Kunst von 1400 bis 1700.* 2 vols. Kortrijk, 1980.

Gijsen, A. van. "17 juni 1514: Thomas van der Noot publiceert *Tscep vol wonders*— de drukker-uitgever als verspreider van artes-teksten." In *Nederlandse literatuur, een geschiedenis,* ed. M. A. Schenkeveld-Van der Dussen, 131–36. Groningen, 1993.

Hand, J. O. *The Saint Anne Altarpiece by Gerard David.* Washington, D.C., 1992.

Het handschrift-Jan Phillipsz. Hs. Berlijn, Staatsbibliothek Preußischer Kulturbesitz, Germ.Qu.557. Ed. H. Brinkman. Hilversum, 1995.

Handwörterbuch des deutschen Aberglaubens. 10 vols. Ed. H. Bächtold-Stäubli. Berlin, 1927–1942.

Hansen, W. *Kalenderminiaturen der Stundenbücher Mittelalterliches Leben im Jahreslauf.* Munich, 1984.

Harrebomee, P. J. *Spreekwoordenboek der Nederlandsche taal.* 3 vols. Amsterdam, 1980.

Hazelzet, K. *Heethoofden, misbaksels en halve garen: De bakker van Eeklo en de burgermoraal.* Zwolle, 1988.

Heiden, R. an der. *Pieter Bruegel der Aeltere: Das Schlaraffenland und der Studienkopf einer Bäuerin in der alten Pinakothek.* Munich, 1985.

Van den heilighen drien coninghen. Ed. T. J. A. Scheepstra. Groningen, 1914.

Van helden, elfen en dichters: De oudste verhalen uit Ierland. Ed. M. Draak et al. Amsterdam, 1979.

Hemels verlangen. Trans. W. Scheepsma. Amsterdam, 1993.

Hermant, P. "De folklore in het werk van Erasmus." *De Brabantsche folklore* 15 (1935/36): 211–81.

Herodotus. *The Histories.* Trans. A. de Selincourt. Harmondsworth, 1955.

Herwaarden, J. van. "Dat scaecspel: Een profaan-ethische verkenning." In *Wat is wijsheid? Lekenethiek in de Middelnederlandse letterkunde*, ed. J. Reynaert, 304–21. Amsterdam, 1994.

Hesiod. *Theogony: Works and Days*. Trans. D. Wender. Harmondsworth, 1986.

Hier beghint 't leven van laudaten der weerdiger vrouwen. Antwerp: Jan van Ghelen, [ca. 1550]. (Copy: private collection.)

Hildegaersberch, W. van. *Gedichten*. Ed. W. Bisschop et al. The Hague, 1870.

Die historie van Peeter van Provencen. Antwerp: W. Vorsterman, ca. 1517. Facsimile ed. Sint Niklaas, 1982.

Een historische beschryving van duure tyden en hongersnoden. Amsterdam: A. van Huissteen, 1741. (Copy: The Hague, Royal Library.)

Hittmair, R. *Aus Caxtons Vorreden und Nachworten*. Leipzig, 1934.

Hogenelst, D. "1418: Verbod in het reglement van het Deventer gasthuis om binnenshuis op te treden met sproken en boerden—Sprooksprekers: Venters in vermaak en vermaan." In *Nederlandse literatuur, een geschiedenis*, ed. M. A. Schenkeveld-Van der Dussen, 97–102. Groningen, 1993.

Hogenelst, D., et al. *Handgeschreven wereld: Nederlandse literatuur en cultuur in de middeleeuwen*. Amsterdam, 1995.

Hollaar, J. M., et al. "Toneelleven in Deventer in de vijftiende en zestiende eeuw." *De nieuwe taalgids* 73 (1980): 412–25.

Homer. *The Odyssey*. Trans. E. V. Rieu. Harmondsworth, 1946.

Hoppenbrouwers, P. C. M. *Een middeleeuwse samenleving: Het Land van Heusden (ca. 1300–ca. 1515)*. 2 vols. Wageningen, 1992.

Hummelen, W. M. H. *Repertorium van het rederijkersdrama, 1500–ca. 1620*. Assen, 1968.

——. "12–23 juni 1539: Negentien rederijkerskamers nemen deel aan een wedstrijd te Gent—Rederijkersdrama en reformatie." In *Nederlandse literatuur, een geschiedenis*, ed. M. A. Schenkeveld-Van der Dussen, 142–46. Groningen, 1993.

The Illustrated Bartsch. Gen. ed. W. L. Strauss. New York, 1978–.

The International Style: The Arts in Europe Around 1400. The Walters Art Gallery. Baltimore, 1962.

Isidore of Seville. *Etymologiarum*. 2 vols. Ed. W. M. Lindsay. Oxford, 1911.

Jansen, H. P. H. "Chiliasme in de middeleeuwen." *Spiegel Historiael* 8 (1973): 210–19, 253.

Jansen-Sieben, R. "Van korte borsten en wassen hoofden (MS. Brussel KB, II.144, 108v–111v)." In *Rapiarijs: Een afscheidsbundel voor H. van Dijk*, ed. S. Buitink et al., 55–57. Utrecht, 1987.

——. *Repertorium van de Middelnederlandse Artes-literatuur*. Utrecht, 1989.

——. "Europa aan tafel in de Zuidelijke Nederlanden (15de eeuw–ca. 1650): Een inleidend overzicht." In *Europa aan tafel: Een verkenning van onze eet- en tafelcultuur*, 146–89. Antwerp, 1993.

Janssen, W. "Mittelalterliche Gartenkultur: Nahrung und Rekreation." In *Mensch und Umwelt in Mittelalter*, ed. B. Herrmann, 224–43. Frankfurt am Main, 1990.

Janssens, J. D. "Jan van Ruusbroec in Brussel (1304–1343); of, Nog maar eens Ruusbroec en Bloemaerdinne." In *De Brabantse mysticus Jan van Ruusbroec, 1293–1381*, 3–33. Brussels, 1984.

Jantz, H. "Images of America in the German Renaissance." In *First Images of America*, ed. F. Chiappelli, 1:91–106. Berkeley, 1976.

Jockel, N. *Pieter Bruegel: Das Schlaraffenland.* Hamburg, 1995.

Jonckbloet, W. J. A. *Geschiedenis der middelnederlandsche dichtkunst.* 3 vols. Amsterdam, 1851–1855.

Jong, E. de et al. *Aardse paradijzen: De tuin in de Nederlandse kunst, 15de tot 18de eeuw.* Ghent, 1996.

Joufrois de Poitiers. *Roman d'aventures du XIIIe siècle.* Ed. P. B. Fay et al. Geneva, 1972.

Kalff, G. *Het lied in de middeleeuwen.* Leiden, 1884.

———. "Wouter Verhee." *Tijdschrift voor Nederlandse taal- en letterkunde* 5 (1885): 137–86.

———. "Handschriften der universiteitsbibliotheek te Amsterdam." *Tijdschrift voor Nederlandse taal- en letterkunde* 9 (1890): 161–89.

Kasper, C. "Das Schlaraffenland zieht in die Stadt: Vom Land des Ueberflusses zum Paradies." *Jahrbuch der Oswald von Wolkenstein Gesellschaft* 7 (1992–1993): 255–91.

Kausler, E. von. *Altniederländische Gedichte vom Schlusse des XIII. bis Anfang des XV. Jahrhunderts.* 3 vols. Tübingen, 1844–1866.

Kayser, D. "Het laatmiddeleeuwse spotsermoen." *Spektator* 13 (1983/84): 105–27.

Keyser, P. de. "De nieuwe reis naar Luilekkerland." In *Ars Folklorica Belgica: Noord- en Zuid-Nederlandse volkskunst*, ed. P. de Keyser, 7–41. Antwerp, 1956.

Kirschbaum, E. *Lexikon der christlichen Ikonographie.* 8 vols. Freiburg, 1968–1976.

Kloeke, G. G. *Kamper spreekwoorden: Naar de uitgave van Warnersen anno 1550.* Assen, 1959.

Komrij, G. *De Nederlandse poëzie van de twaalfde tot en met de zestiende eeuw in duizend en enige bladzijden.* Amsterdam, 1994.

Kooper, E. S. "Het Vogelparlement van Geoffrey Chaucer." In *Tuinen in de middeleeuwen*, ed. R. E. V. Stuip et al., 155–65. Hilversum, 1992.

Kooy, K. R. van. "Tuinen in het islamitische cultuurgebied." In *Tuinen in de middeleeuwen*, ed. R. E. V. Stuip et al., 51–70. Hilversum, 1992.

Kramer, H. et al. *The Malleus Maleficarum.* Trans. M. Summers. New York, 1971.

Kraus, D. et al. *Le monde caché des miséricordes: Suivi du répertoire de 400 stalles d'église en France.* Paris, 1986.

Kronyk van Vlaenderen, van 580 tot 1467. 2 vols. Ed. C. P. Serrure et al. Ghent, 1839–1840.

Bibliography

Kuczynski, P. "Utopie und Satire in *The Land of Cockaygne*." *Zeitschrift für Anglistik und Amerikanistik* 28 (1980): 45–55.

Kurze, D. "Die festländischen Lollarden; Zur Geschichte der religiösen Bewegungen im ausgehenden Mittelalter." *Archiv für Kulturgeschichte* 47 (1965): 48–76.

Kuttner, E. *Het hongerjaar 1566.* Amsterdam, 1949.

Laarhoven, J. van. *De beeldtaal van de christelijke kunst: Geschiedenis van de iconografie.* Nijmegen, 1992.

Lafortune-Martel, A. *Fête noble en Bourgogne au XVe siècle: "Le banquet de Faisan" (1454); Aspects politiques, sociaux et culturels.* Montreal, 1984.

Lampo, J. "De Antwerpse ketters: Een bijdrage tot de studie van de middeleeuwse ketterijen in de Nederlanden." *Handelingen van de Koninklijke Zuidnederlandse Maatschappij voor taal- en letterkunde* 34 (1980): 189–201.

Lantschoot, J. van. *De Ommegang van Dendermonde.* Dendermonde, 1930.

Laurioux, B. "Modes culinaires et mutations du gout à la fin du moyen-age." In *Artes mechanicae in middeleeuws Europa,* ed. R. Jansen-Sieben, 199–222. Brussels, 1989.

Lazard, M. *La comédie humaniste au XVIe siècle et ses personnages.* Vendôme, 1978.

Lebeer, L. *Beredeneerde catalogus van de prenten naar Pieter Bruegel de Oude.* Brussels, 1969.

Leendertz, P., Jr. "Het Zutfensch-Groningsche handschrift." *Tijdschrift voor Nederlandse taal- en letterkunde* 14 (1895): 265–83; 15 (1896): 81–99, 270–76; 16 (1897): 25–43, 129–42.

———. *Middelnederlandse dramatische poëzie.* Leiden, 1907.

Leerssen, J. "Wildness, Wilderness, and Ireland: Medieval and Early-Modern Patterns in the Demarcation of Civility." *Journal of the History of Ideas* 56 (1995): 25–39.

Leest hierin wat genoechlicx claer: Wat in Hollant is geschiet vorwaer. Delft: [A. Hendrickx?], [ca. 1508]. (Copy: Ghent, University Library.)

Le Goff, J. "The Town as an Agent of Civilisation, c. 1200–c. 1500." In *The Fontana Economic History of Europe,* ed. C. M. Cipolla, 71–106. London, 1973.

———. *Pour un autre moyen age: Temps, travail et culture en Occident: 18 essais.* Paris, 1977.

———. *La naissance du purgatoire.* Paris, 1981.

———. *De cultuur van middeleeuws Europa.* Amsterdam, 1987.

———. *De intellectuelen in de middeleeuwen.* Amsterdam, 1989.

Lerner, R. E. *The Heresy of the Free Spirit in the Later Middle Ages.* Berkeley, 1972.

———. "The Medieval Return to the Thousand-Year Sabbath." In *The Apocalypse in the Middle Ages,* ed. R. K. Emmerson et al., 51–71. Ithaca, 1992.

Leupen, P. *Gods stad op aarde: Eenheid van kerk en staat in het eerste millennium na Christus. Een kerkelijke ideologie.* Amsterdam, 1996.

Het leven van Liedewij, de maagd van Schiedam. Trans. L. Jongen et al. Schiedam, 1989.

Van den levene Ons Heren. 2 vols. Ed. W. H. Beuken. Zwolle, 1968.

Lie, O. S. H. "What Is Truth? The Verse-Prose Debate in Medieval Dutch Literature." *Queeste* 1 (1994): 34–65.

Liederen en gedichten uit het Gruuthuse-handschrift. Ed. K. Heeroma. Vol 1. Leiden, 1966.

Lievens, R. "Tegen de tamboers." In *Serta devota in memoriam G. Lourdaux,* 337–81. Leuven, 1992.

Linden, H. van der. *De Cope: Bijdrage tot de rechtsgeschiedenis van de openlegging der Hollands-Utrechtse laagvlakte.* Assen, 1955.

Linke, H. "Zwischen Jammertal und Schlaraffenland: Verteufelung und Verunwirklichung des saeculum im geistlichen Drama des Mittelalters." *Zeitschrift für deutsches Altertum und deutsche Literatur* 100 (1971): 350–70.

Linskens, R. *Wat 'n leven! Deel II: straten en huizen, eten en drinken in de middeleeuwen.* Antwerp, 1976.

Lorris, G. de, et al. *Le Roman de la Rose.* Ed. D. Poirion. Paris, 1974.

———. *De Roman van de Roos.* Trans. E. van Altena. Baarn, 1991.

Lozinski, G. *La Bataille de Caresme et Charnage.* Paris, 1933.

Lucas, H. S. "The Great European Famine of 1315, 1316 and 1317." *Speculum* 5 (1930): 343–77.

Lucian. *Satirical Sketches.* Trans. P. Turner. Harmondsworth, 1968.

Macropedius, G. *Aluta (1535).* Ed. J. Bloemendal et al. Voorthuizen, 1995.

Maerlant, J. van. *Spiegel historiael.* 3 vols. Ed. M. de Vries et al. Leiden, 1857–1863.

———. *Der naturen bloeme.* 2 vols. Ed. E. Verwijs. Groningen, 1878.

———. *Strophische gedichten.* Ed. J. Verdam et al. Leiden, 1918.

———. *Sinte Franciscus leven.* 2 vols. Ed. P. Maximilianus. Zwolle, 1954.

Magalhaes [Magellan], F. de. *De eerste tocht rond de wereld.* Baarn, 1986.

Mak, J. J. *Vier excellente cluchten.* Antwerp, 1950.

———. *Rhetoricaal glossarium.* Assen, 1959.

———. "Heilige en onheilige dronkenschap in de middeleeuwen." *Volkskunde* 61 (1960): 49–70.

[Mandeville, J.] *De reis van Jan van Mandeville.* Ed. N. A. Cramer. Leiden, 1908.

———. *The Travels: With Three Narratives in Illustration of It.* New York, 1964.

———. *The Travels of Sir John Mandeville.* Harmondsworth, 1983.

Manten, A. A. "Gastarbeiders in Breukelen en omgeving in de 10de tot 12de eeuw." *Tijdschrift van de Historische Kring Breukelen* 86 (1987): 11–20 (reaction 107–9).

Map, W. *De nugis curialium.* Ed. C. N. L. Brooke et al. Oxford, 1983.

Maria op de markt: Middeleeuws toneel in Brussel. Trans. W. Kuiper et al. Amsterdam, 1995.

Martial. *Epigrams.* Trans. Walter C. A. Ker. London, 1968.

Marijnissen, R.-H., et al. *Brueghel.* Brussels, 1971.

McDonnell, E. W. *The Beguines and Beghards in Medieval Culture.* New Brunswick, N.J., 1969.

McGinn, B. "Introduction: John's Apocalypse and the Apocalyptic Mentality." In *The Apocalypse in the Middle Ages*, ed. R. K. Emmerson et al., 3–19. Ithaca, 1992.

Meder, T. *Sprookspreker in Holland: Leven en werk van Willem van Hildegaersberch (circa 1400).* Amsterdam, 1991.

Meder, T. "Omstreeks 1266: In Der naturen bloeme worden sprooksprekers en acteurs vergeleken met een Vlaamse gaai—de vroegste bronnen van het wereldlijke theater." In *Een theatergeschiedenis der Nederlanden*, ed. R. L. Erenstein, 16–23. Amsterdam, 1996.

Meditations on the Life of Christ. Ed. I. Ragusa et al. Princeton, 1977.

Metlitzki, D. "The Muslim Paradise as the Land of Cokaygne." In *The Matter of Araby in Medieval England*, 210–19, 295–96. New Haven, 1977.

Meyer, M. de. "Een berijmde vertaling van Hans Sachs Schlauraffenlandt." *Volkskunde* 61 (1960): 145–55.

———. *De volks- en kinderprent in de Nederlanden van de 15e tot de 20e eeuw.* Antwerp, 1962.

———. *Volksprenten in de Nederlanden, 1400–1900.* Amsterdam, 1970.

Meyere, V. de and L. Baekelmans. *Het Boek der rabauwen en naaktridders: Bijdragen tot de studie van het volksleven der 16e en 17e eeuwen.* Antwerp, 1914.

Mezger, W. *Narrenidee und Fastnachtsbrauch: Studien zum Fortleben des Mittelalters in der europäischen Festkultur.* Konstanz, 1991.

De middelnederlandse boerden. Ed. C. Kruyskamp. The Hague, 1957.

Het Middelnederlandse leerdicht Rinclus. Ed. P. Leendertz. Amsterdam, 1893.

Mierlo, J. van. "Het Begardisme." *Verslagen en mededelingen van de Koninklijke Vlaamse Akademie voor taal- en letterkunde*, 1930: 277–305.

———. "Ruusbroecs bestrijding van de ketterij." *Ons geestelijk erf* 6 (1932): 304–46.

MNW. See Verwijs, E. and J. Verdam.

Moerman, H. J. *Nederlandse plaatsnamen.* Leiden, 1956.

Molinet, J. *Les faictz et dictz.* 3 vols. Ed. N. Dupire. Paris, 1936–1939.

Moll, W. *Johannes Brugman en het godsdienstig leven onder vaderen in de vijftiende eeuw.* 2 vols. Amsterdam, 1854.

———. "Een bruilofstlied van de zestiende eeuw." *Kerkhistorisch Archief* 1 (1857): 339–40.

Montanari, M. *Honger en overvloed.* Trans. K. van Liemt. Amsterdam, 1994.

More, Thomas. *Utopia.* 1516. Facsimile ed. Leeds, 1966.

———. *Utopia.* Trans. P. Turner. Harmondsworth, 1968.

Morton, A. L. *The English Utopia.* London, 1952.

Morus, T. *De Utopie.* Antwerp: H. de Laet, 1562. (Copy: Antwerp, Plantijnmuseum.)

Mout, M. E. H. N. "Turken in het nieuws: Beeldvorming en publieke opinie in de zestiende-eeuwse Nederlanden." *Tijdschrift voor geschiedenis* 97 (1984): 362–81.

Moxey, K. "The Battle of the Sexes and the World Upside Down." In *Peasants, Warriors, and Wives: Popular Imagery in the Reformation*, 101–26, 155–60. Chicago, 1989.

Muchembled, R. *De uitvinding van de moderne mens: Collectief gedrag, zeden, gewoonten en gevoelswereld van de middeleeuwen tot de Franse revolutie.* Trans. R. Siblesz et al. Amsterdam, 1991.

Müller, M. *Das Schlaraffenland: Der Traum von Faulheit und Müssiggang. Eine Text-Bild-Dokumentation.* Vienna, 1984.

Münz, L. *Bruegel: The Drawings.* London, 1961.

Mulder-Bakker, A. B. "Met recht van spreken: Johanna van Valois, gravin van Holland, Zeeland en Henegouwen." *Jaarboek voor vrouwengeschiedenis* 16 (1996): 37–56.

Muller, J. W. "Brokstukken van middeleeuwsche meerstemmige liederen." *Tijdschrift voor Nederlandse taal- en letterkunde* 25 (1960): 1–60.

Muller Fzn., S. et al. *Oorkondenboek van het Sticht Utrecht tot 1301.* 5 vols. Utrecht, 1920–1959.

De natuurkunde van het geheelal: Een 13de-eeuws Middelnederlands leerdicht. 2 vols. Ed. R. Jansen-Sieben. Brussels, 1968.

Een nieu sunderling boeck, spreekende van 't gheheel regiment des grooten Turcx. Antwerp: M. Nuyts, 1542. (Copy: Leiden, University Library.)

Het nieuwe testament van de Moderne Devoten. Ed. C. C. de Bruin. Leiden, 1979.

Van der nieuwer werelt oft landtscap. Antwerp: J. van Doesborch, [ca. 1507]. (Copy: Providence, J. C. Brown Library.)

Noelle, H. *Die Kelten.* Bergisch Gladbach, 1974.

Nijsten, L. "De Middelnederlense dichter and het paradijs." Thesis, University of Amsterdam, 1979.

Okken, L. *Das goldene Haus und die goldene Laube: Wie die Poesie ihren Herren das Paradies einrichtete.* Amsterdam, 1987.

Oldenburger-Ebbers, C. "Architectuur en beplanting van middeleeuwse tuinen." In *Tuinen in de middeleeuwen*, ed. R. E. V. Stuip et al., 91–102. Hilversum, 1992.

Ong, W. J. *Orality and Literacy: The Technologizing of the Word.* London, 1988.

Oosterman, J. B. *De gratie van het gebed: Overlevering en functie van Middelnederlandse berijmde gebeden.* 2 vols. Amsterdam, 1995.

Oostrom, F. van. *Maerlants wereld.* Amsterdam, 1996.

Orbán, A. P. "Het spreekwoordelijke beeld van de rusticus, de boer, in de middeleeuwen." In *Gewone mensen in de middeleeuwen*, ed. R. E. V. Stuip et al., 69–87. Utrecht, 1987.

Ortutay, G. "Principles of Oral Transmission in Folkculture." *Acta Ethnographica* 8 (1959): 175–221.

Oskamp, H. P. A. *The Voyage of Mael Dúin: A Study in Early Irish Voyage Literature.* Groningen, 1970.

Het oude testament. 3 vols. Ed. C. C. de Bruin. Leiden, 1977–1978.

Oudvlaemsche liederen en andere gedichten der XIVe en XVe eeuwen. [Ed. C. Carton.] Ghent, 1849.

Paassen, D. van et al. "Inleiding en bronnenkritiek." In *Op zoek naar vrouwen in ketterij en sekte: Een bronnenonderzoek,* ed. D. van Paassen et al., 7–24. Kampen, 1993.

Pagden, A. "The Forbidden Food: Francisco de Vitoria and José de Acosta on Cannibalism." *Terrae incognitae* 13 (1981): 17–29.

Palmer, N. F. *Visio Tnugdali: The German and Dutch Translations and Their Circulation in the Later Middle Ages.* Munich, 1982.

Parthonopeus van Bloys. Ed. A. van Berkum. Leiden, 1897–1898.

Passenier, A. "Heilige Kerk-de-Kleine in de spiegel van Marguerite de Porete." In *Op zoek naar vrouwen in ketterij en sekte: Een bronnenonderzoek,* ed. D. van Paassen et al., 95–115. Kampen, 1993.

Pauw, N. de. *Middelnederlandsche gedichten en fragmenten.* 2 vols. Ghent, 1893–1897.

Payen, J.-C. "Fabliaux et Cocagne: Abondance et fête charnelle dans les contes plaisants du XIIe et XIIIe siècles." In *Epopée animale, fable, fabliau.* ed. G. Bianciotto et al., 435–48. Paris, 1984.

Pearsall, D. *Landscapes and Seasons of the Medieval World.* London, 1973.

De pelgrimstocht van ridder Gruenemberg naar het Heilige Land in 1486. Trans. A. C. J. de Vrankrijker. Amsterdam, 1948.

Penneman, T. "De Ros-Beiaard-Ommegang te Dendermonde, 1377–1789." *Gedenkschriften Oudheidkundige Kring van het Land van Dendermonde,* ser. IV:1, nos. 1–2 (1975): 5–119.

Penninc et al. *De jeeste van Walewein en het schaakbord.* 2 vols. Ed. G. A. van Es. Zwolle, 1957.

Peters, U. *Literatur in der Stadt: Studien zu den sozialen Voraussetzungen und kulturellen Organisationsformen städtischer Literatur im 13. und 14. Jahrhundert.* Tübingen, 1983.

Petronius. *The Satyricon of Petronius.* Trans. William Burnaby. New York, 1964.

———. *The Satyricon.* Trans. J. P. Sullivan. Harmondsworth, 1988.

Petrus Pictaviensis. *Summa de Confessione.* Ed. J. Longère. Turnhout, 1980.

Phillips, M. M. *Erasmus on His Times: A Shortened Version of the "Adages" of Erasmus.* Cambridge, 1967.

Pigafetta, Antonio. *Relation du premier voyage autour du monde par Magellan, 1519–1522.* Ed. J. Denucé. Antwerp, 1923.

Pleij, H. "Volksfeest en toneel in de middeleeuwen. II. Entertainers en akteurs." *De revisor* 4, no. 1 (1977): 34–41.

———. "Over de betekenis van Middelnederlandse teksten." *Spektator* 10 (1980/81): 299–339.

———. "Het gebruik van spotteksten bij volksfeesten." *Spiegel Historiael* 18 (1983a): 562–68.

———. *Het Gilde van de Blauwe Schuit: Literatuur, volksfeest en burgermoraal in de late middeleeuwen.* Amsterdam, 1983b.

———. *Het literaire leven in de middeleeuwen.* Leiden, 1988a.

———. *De sneeuwpoppen van 1511: Literatuur en stadscultuur tussen middeleeuwen en moderne tijd.* Amsterdam, 1988b.

———. "Van keikoppen en droge jonkers: Spotgezelschappen, wijkverenigingen en het jongerengericht in de literatuur en het culturele leven van de late middeleeuwen." *Volkskundig Bulletin* 15 (1989): 297–315.

———. *Nederlandse literatuur van de late middeleeuwen.* Utrecht, 1990.

———. "Van het luie, lekkere leven: Over de doelloze bestudering van de Middelnederlandse letterkunde." In *Misselike tonghe: De Middelnederlandse letterkunde in interdisciplinair verband,* ed. F. P. van Oostrom et al., 25–44. Amsterdam, 1991.

———. "Onvoltooide literatuur: Over dramatisch lezen, spiritueel herkauwen en de emotionele verwerking van gedrukte teksten in het algemeen." *Jaarboek "De Fonteine"* 41–42 (1991/92): 167–75.

———. "Van vastelavond tot carnaval." In *Vastenavond—Carnaval: Feesten van de omgekeerde wereld,* ed. M. Mooij, 10–44, 177–79. Zwolle, 1992.

———. "Antwerpen verhaald." In *Antwerpen, verhaal van een metropool, 16de–17de eeuw,* ed. J. van der Stock, 78–85. Ghent, 1993a.

———. *De toekomst van de middeleeuwen.* Raalte, 1993b.

———. *Kleuren van de middeleeuwen.* Bloemendaal, 1994.

———. "The Despisers of Rhetoric: Origins and Significance of Attacks on the Art of the Rhetoricians (Rederijkers) in the Sixteenth Century." In *Rhetoric-Rhetoriqueurs-Rederijkers,* ed. J. Koopmans et al., 157–74. Amsterdam, 1995a.

———. "Lekenethiek en burgermoraal." *Queeste* 2 (1995b): 170–80.

———. "De onvoltooide middeleeuwen: Over de drukpers en het andere gezicht van de Middelnederlandse literatuur." In *Grote lijnen: Syntheses over Middelnederlandse letterkunde,* 137–55, 217–20. Amsterdam, 1995c.

———. "24 juni 1500: Spectaculaire duivelscènes domineren de opvoering van het mirakelspel Van den heilighen sacramente van der Nyeuwervaert in Breda—De duivel in het middeleeuwse drama en op het toneel." In *Een theatergeschiedenis der Nederlanden,* ed. R. L. Erenstein, 64–69. Amsterdam, 1996.

Pleij, H., et al. *Op belofte van profijt: Stadsliteratuur en burgermoraal in de Nederlandse letterkunde van de middeleeuwen,* 8–51, 347–53. Amsterdam, 1991.

Poel, D. E. van der. "Moderne en middeleeuwse lezers van de Roman van de Roos." In *Wat is wijsheid? Lekenethiek in de Middelnederlandse letterkunde,* ed. J. Reynaert, 101–15. Amsterdam, 1994).

Poeschel, J. "Das Märchen vom Schlaraffenlande." *Beiträge zur Geschichte des deutschen Sprache und Literatur* 5 (1878): 389–427.

Polo, M. *The Travels.* Trans. R. Latham. London, 1988.

Potter, F. de. *Schets eener geschiedenis van de gemeentefeesten in Vlaanderen.* Ghent, 1870.

Priebsch, R. "Noch einmal Van dat edele lant van Cockaengen." *Tijdschrift voor Nederlandse taal- en letterkunde* 13 (1894): 185–91.

———. "Aus deutschen Handschriften der Königlichen Bibliothek zu Brüssel." *Zeitschrift für deutsche Philologie* 38 (1906): 301–33, 436–67; 39 (1907): 156–79.

Proverbes en rime: Text and Illustrations of the Fifteenth Century from a French Manuscript in the Walters Art Gallery, Baltimore. Ed. G. Frank et al. Baltimore, 1937.

Proverbia seriosa theutonico-latina. [Gouda: G. Leeu, ca. 1484.] (Copy: Dublin, Trinity College.)

"Der Prozess gegen Rumpold: Vert. C. Dauven-van Knippenberg e.a." In *Europees toneel van middeleeuwen naar renaissance,* ed. M. Gosman, 303–54. Groningen, 1991.

Raedts, P. G. J. M. "Jeruzalem in tijd en eeuwigheid: Een essay over de verbeelding van het heilige." In *Utrecht,* ed. R. E. V. Stuip et al., 89–102. Hilversum, 1991.

———. "Het aardse paradijs: De tuin als beeld van het geluk." In *Tuinen in de middeleeuwen,* ed. R. E. V. Stuip et al., 35–50. Hilversum, 1992.

Ramakers, B. A. M. "Horen en zien, lezen en beleven: Over toogspelen in opvoering en druk." *Jaarboek "De Fonteine"* 41–42 (1991/92): 129–65.

———. "5 mei 1448: Begin van de traditie van de jaarlijkse opvoering van een van de zeven Bliscappen in Brussel—Toneel en processies in de late middeleeuwen." In *Een theatergeschiedenis der Nederlanden,* ed. R. L. Erenstein, 42–49. Amsterdam, 1996a.

———. *Spelen en figuren: Toneelkunst en processiecultuur in Oudenaarde tussen middeleeuwen en moderne tijd.* Amsterdam, 1996b.

Randall, L. M. C. *Images in the Margins of Gothic Manuscripts.* Berkeley, 1966.

Rapp, A. *Der Jungbrunnen in Literatur und bildender Kunst des Mittelalters.* N.p., 1975.

Raue, S. *Een nauwsluitend keurs: Aard en betekenis van "Den triumphe ende 't palleersel van den vrouwen" (1514).* Amsterdam, 1996.

Raupp, H.-J. *Bauernsatiren: Entstehung und Entwicklung des bäuerlichen Genres in der deutschen und niederländischen Kunst ca. 1470–1570.* Erftstadt, 1986.

Reeves, M. *The Influence of Prophecy in the Later Middle Ages: A Study in Joachimism.* Oxford, 1969.

De reis van Sint Brandaan: Een reisverhaal uit de twaalfde eeuw. Ed. W. P. Gerritsen et al. Trans. W. Wilmink. Amsterdam, 1994.

Renout van Montalbaen. Ed. D. van Maelsaeke. Antwerp, 1966.

Resoort, R. J., et al. "Nieuwe bronnen en gegevens voor de literatuurgeschiedenis van de zestiende eeuw uit Parijse bibliotheken." *Spektator* 5 (1975/76): 637–59.

Rey-Flaud, H. *Le charivari: Les rituels fondamentaux de la sexualité.* Paris, 1985.

Reynaert, J. "Leken, ethiek en moralistisch-didactische literatuur: Ter inleiding." In *Wat is wijsheid? Lekenethiek in de Middelnederlandse letterkunde,* ed. J. Reynaert, 9–36, 353–62. Amsterdam, 1994.

Die reyse van Lissebone om te varen na dat eylandt Naguaria in groot Indien. Antwerp: J. van Doesborch, 1508. (Copy: Providence, J. C. Brown Library.)

Richter, D. *Schlaraffenland: Geschichte einer populären Phantasie.* Cologne, 1984.

Richter, M. *The Oral Tradition in the Early Middle Ages.* Turnhout, 1994.

Ridderboek. Trans. G. Warnar. Amsterdam, 1991.

Robbins, R. H. *Historical Poems of the Fourteenth and Fifteenth Centuries.* New York, 1959.

Robert, P. *Dictionnaire alphabétique et analytique de la langue française.* Ed. A. Roy. Paris, 1985.

Roetert-Frederikse, J. A. *Dat kaetspel ghemoralizeert.* Leiden, 1915.

Rommel, H. "De dagboek van Rombout de Doppere." *Biekorf* 4 (1893): 17–22, 33–38, 65–71, 97–104.

Rooth, A. B. *Fran lögensaga till paradis.* Stockholm, 1983.

Roovere, A. de. "De blyde jncompste van Vrauw Margriete van Yorck; uitg. W. G. Brill." *Kronijk van het Historisch Genootschap,* ser. 5, 22 (1866): 17–71.

———. *De gedichten.* Ed. J. J. Mak. Zwolle, 1955.

Russell, J. C. "Population in Europe, 500–1500." In *The Fontana Economic History of Europe: The Middle Ages,* ed. C. M. Cipolla, 25–70. London, 1972.

Ruusbroec, J. van. *Werken.* 4 vols. Tielt, 1944–1948.

Ruusbroec de wonderbare. Ed. W. H. Beuken. Culemborg, 1970.

Sachs, H. *Sämtliche Fabeln und Schwänke.* Ed. E. Goetze. Halle, 1893.

Salisbury, J. E. *The Beast Within: Animals in the Middle Ages.* New York, 1994.

Sartorius, J. *Adagiorum chiliades tres.* Antwerp: J. van der Loe, 1561. (Copy: Amsterdam, University Library.)

't Scep vol wonders. Brussels: Th. van der Noot, 1514. (Copy: The Hague, Royal Library.)

Schama, S. *Landscape and Memory.* London, 1995.

Scheepsma, W. "Zusterboeken: Bijzondere bronnen voor de Moderne Devotie." *Jaarboek voor Vrouwengeschiedenis* 16 (1996): 153–70.

Scheidig, W. *Die Holzschnitte des Petrarca-Meisters zu Petrarca's Werk "Von der Artzney bayder Glück."* Augsburg, 1532. Reprint. Berlin, 1955.

Scheller, R. W. *Exemplum: Model-Book Drawings and the Practice of Artistic Transmission in the Middle Ages (ca. 900–ca. 1470).* Amsterdam, 1995.

Van schelmen en schavuiten: Laatmiddeleeuwse vagebondteksten. Trans. H. Pleij. Amsterdam, 1985.

Scheltema, J. H. *Nederlandsche liederen uit vroegeren tijd.* Leiden, 1885.

Schlüter, L. L. E. *Niet alleen: Een kunsthistorisch-ethische plaatsbepaling van tuin en woning in het "Convivium religiosum" van Erasmus.* Amsterdam, 1995.

Schmitt, J.-C. *Bijgeloof in de middeleeuwen.* Nijmegen, 1995.

Scholz, M. G. *Hören und Lesen: Studien zur primären Rezeption der Literatur im 12. und 13. Jahrhundert.* Wiesbaden, 1980.

Die schoone hystorie van Malegijs. Ed. E. T. Kuiper. Leiden, 1903.

Een schoon liedekens-boeck. Ed. W. G. Hellinga. The Hague, 1968.

Schotel, G. D. J. *Geschied-, Letter- en Oudheidkundige uitspanningen.* Dordrecht, 1840.

Schweitzer, F.-J. "Marguerite Poréte." In *De minne is al: Negentien portretten van vrouwelijke mystieken uit de middeleeuwen,* ed. J. Thiele, 168–78. The Hague, 1990.

Schorbach, K. *Studien über das deutsche Volksbuch Lucidarius und seine Bearbeitungen in fremden Sprachen.* Strasbourg, 1894.

Sidrac. See *Het boek van Sidrac in de Nederlanden.*

Der Sielen troest. Utrecht: n.p., 1479. (Copy: The Hague, Royal Library.)

Silver, L. "Forest Primeval: Albrecht Altdorfer and the German Wilderness Landscape." *Simiolus* 13 (1983): 5–43.

Sinte Augustijns Hantboec. 2 vols. Ed. J. J. Lub. Assen, 1962.

Smit, J. G. *Vorst en onderdaan: Studies over Holland en Zeeland in de late middeleeuwen.* Leuven, 1995.

Snyder, J. "Jan Mostaert's West Indies Landscape." In *First Images of America,* ed. F. Chiappelli, 1:495–502. Berkeley, 1976.

De Sotslach. In *Klucht uit ca. 1550,* ed. F. Lyna et al. Brussels, 1932.

Southern, R. W. *Western Society and the Church in the Middle Ages.* Harmondsworth, 1970.

Spann, P. O. "Sallust, Plutarch, and the Isles of the Blessed." *Terrae Incognitae* 9, no. 1 (1977): 75–80.

Het spel van den heilighen sacramente van der Nyeuwervaert. Ed. W. J. M. A. Asselbergs et al. Zwolle, 1955.

Spelen van sinne. Antwerp: W. Silvius, 1562. (Copy: Amsterdam, University Library.)

Die spiegel der sonden. 2 vols. Ed. J. Verdam. Leiden, 1900.

Den spieghel der salicheit van Elckerlijc. Ed. R. Vos. Groningen, 1967.

Spierenburg, P. *De verbroken betovering: Mentaliteitsgeschiedenis van preïndustrieel Europa.* Hilversum, 1988.

[Splinter, J.] *Jan Splinters testament.* Rees (Germany): D. W. van Santen, 1584. (Copy: Leiden, University Library.)

[———.] *Testament van Jan Splinter.* Rotterdam: D. Mullem, [ca. 1600]. (Copy: The Hague, Royal Library.)

Spijker, I. *Aymijns kinderen hoog te paard: Een studie over Renout van Montalbaen en de Franse "Renaut"-traditie.* Hilversum, 1990.

[Staden van Homborch (of Homburg), H.] *Warachtige historie ende beschrijvinge eens lants in America ghelegen.* Antwerp: Christoffel Plantijn, 1558. (Copy: Ghent, University Library.)

Stephanus de Bordone. *Anecdotes historiques.* Ed. A. Lecoy de la Marche. Paris, 1877.

Steppe, J. K. *Wereld van vroomheid en satire: Laat-gotische koorbanken in Vlaanderen.* Kasterlee, 1973.

Sterfboeck. Zwolle: P. van Os, 1491. (Copy: The Hague, Royal Library.)

Stiefel, A. L. "Ueber die Quellen der Fabeln, Märchen und Schwänke des Hans Sachs." In *Hans Sachs-Forschungen,* 35–192. Nuremberg, 1894.

Stoett, F. A. *Nederlandse spreekwoorden, spreekwijzen, uitdrukkingen en gezegden.* Zutphen, 1943.

———. *Nederlandse spreekwoorden en gezegden.* Zutphen, 1981.

Strauss, W. L. *The German Single-Leaf Woodcut: 1550–1600.* 3 vols. New York, 1975.

Stuip, R. E. V., et al., eds. *Tuinen in de middeleeuwen.* Hilversum, 1992.

Sturluson, S. *Over de Noordse goden: Verhalen uit Edda en Heimskringla.* Trans. P. Vermeyden. Amsterdam, 1983.

Stijevoort, J. van. *Refereinenbundel anno 1524.* 2 vols. Ed. F. Lyna et al. Antwerp, 1930.

Sumberg, S. L. *The Nuremberg Schembart Carnival.* New York, 1941.

Suringar, W. H. D. *Erasmus over Nederlandsche spreekwoorden en spreekwoordelijke uitdrukkingen van zijnen tijd.* Utrecht, 1873.

Sweet, L. I. "Christopher Columbus and the Millennial Vision of the New World." *Catholic Historical Review* 72 (1986): 369–82.

Szmodis-Eszláry, E., et al. *Middeleeuwse Nederlandse kunst uit Hongarije.* Utrecht, 1990.

Tacitus. *The Annals of Imperial Rome.* Trans. M. Grant. Harmondsworth, 1976.

Thomas, K. *Het verlangen naar de natuur: De veranderende houding tegenover planten en dieren, 1500–1800.* Amsterdam, 1990.

Tigges, W. "*The Land of Cokaygne:* Sophisticated Mirth." In *Companion to Early Middle English Literature,* ed. N. H. G. E. Veldhoen et al., 97–104. Amsterdam, 1988.

Tilmans, K. *Aurelius en de Divisiekroniek van 1517: Historiografie en humanisme in Holland in de tijd van Erasmus.* Hilversum, 1988.

——. "La Grande chronique de la Hollande (1517)." In *Lieux de mémoire*, ed. P. den Boer et al., 113–19. Amsterdam, 1993.

Tobler, A. *Altfranzösisches Wörterbuch.* Ed. E. Lommatzsch. Vol. 2. Berlin, 1936.

Tol, J.-M. van. "Het Londense Handschrift Ms. Add. 10.286." Master's thesis, University of Amsterdam, 1995.

Torec. Ed. M. Hogenhout et al. Abcoude, 1978.

Torfs, L. *Fastes des calamités publiques survenus dans les Pays-Bas.* 2 vols. Paris, 1859–1862.

Tristan en Isolde. Adapt. J. Bédier. Utrecht, 1964.

Den triumphe ende 't palleersel van den vrouwen. Brussels: Th. van der Noot, 1514. (Copy: The Hague, Royal Library.)

De Triumphe ghedaen te Brugghe ten intreye van Caerle. Antwerp: A. van Bergen, 1515. (Copy: The Hague, Royal Library.)

Truwanten. In *Een toneeltekst uit het handschrift-Van Hulthem*, ed. work group of authorities on Dutch from Brussels and Utrecht. Groningen, 1978.

Tubach, F. C. *Index Exemplorum: A Handbook of Medieval Religious Tales.* Helsinki, 1969.

Twispraec der creaturen. Gouda: G. Leeu, 1482. (Copy: Darmstadt, Landesbibliothek.)

Uyttersprot, V. "In de geest van D'Heere." In *Ingenti spiritu: Hulde-album opgedragen aan W. P. F. de Geest*, ed. M. de Clercq et al., 241–49. Brussels, 1989.

Vaderboec. Gouda: G. Leeu, 1480. (Copy: The Hague, Royal Library.)

Väänänen, V. "Le fabliau de Cocagne: Le motif du pays d'abondance dans le folklore occidental." *Neuphilologische Mitteilungen* 48 (1947): 3–36.

Vandenbroeck, P. "Bij het Schuttersfeest (1493) en het Dubbelportret (1496) van de Meester van Frankfurt." *Jaarboek van het Koninklijk Museum voor Schone Kunsten te Antwerpen*, 1983: 15–32.

——. "Bubo significans: Die Eule als Sinnbild von Schlechtigkeit und Torheit." *Jaarboek van het Koninklijk Museum voor Schone Kunsten te Antwerpen*, 1985: 19–135.

——. *Beeld van de andere, vertoog over het zelf: Over wilden en narren, boeren en bedelaars.* Antwerp, 1987.

——. "Jheronimus Bosch' zogenaamde Tuin der Lusten. I." *Jaarboek van het Koninklijk Museum voor Schone Kunsten te Antwerpen*, 1989: 9–210.

——. "Stadscultuur in de Nederlanden, ca. 1400–ca. 1600: Ideologische zwaartepunten, evenwichtsmechanismen, dubbelbinding." *Gemeentekrediet* 44 (1990): 17–41.

Vanhemelryck, F. *De criminaliteit in de ammanie van Brussel van de late middeleeuwen tot het einde van het Ancien Régime (1404–1789).* Brussels, 1981.

——. *Ellendelingen voor galg en rad.* Antwerp, 1984.

——. *Kruis en wassende maan: Pelgrimstochten naar het Heilige Land.* Leuven, 1994.

Vasvari, L. O. "The Geography of Escape and Topsy-turvy Literary Genres." In

Bibliography

Discovering New Worlds: Essays on Mediaeval Exploration and Imagination, ed. S. D. Westrem, 178–92. New York, 1991.

Veelderhande geneuchlycke dichten, tafelspelen ende refereynen. Leiden, 1899.

Veen, C. F. van. *Centsprenten—Catchpennyprints—Nederlandse volks- en kinderprenten*. Amsterdam, 1976.

Velde, C. van de. "Het aards paradijs in de beeldende kunsten." In *Het aards paradijs*, 17–35. Antwerp, 1982.

Vellekoop, C. "Het visioen van boer Gottschalk." In *Visioenen*, ed. R. E. V. Stuip et al., 151–68. Utrecht, 1986.

———. "Muziek en dans in tuinen." In *Tuinen in de middeleeuwen*, ed. R. E. V. Stuip et al., 167–77. Hilversum, 1992.

Velthem, L. van. *Voortzetting van den Spiegel Historiael (1284–1326)*. 3 vols. Ed. H. van der Linden et al. Brussels, 1906–1938.

Vendôme, Matthew of. *The Art of Versification*. Trans. A. E. Galyon. Ames, 1980.

Vensters naar vroeger: Eenentwintig schoolvakken in middeleeuws perspectief. Compiled by a group of university students of Dutch in Utrecht. Amsterdam, 1985.

Verdam, J. "Kleine Middelnederlandsche overblijfselen." *Tijdschrift voor Nederlandse taal- en letterkunde* 11 (1892): 285–305.

Verdeyen, P. "Oordeel van Ruusbroec over de rechtgelovigheid van Margaretha Porete." *Ons geestelijk erf* 66 (1992): 88–96.

Verfasserlexikon: Die deutsche Literatur des Mittelalters. Ed. K. Langosch et al. Vol. 4. Berlin, 1953.

———. Ed. K. Langosch et al. Vol. 5. Berlin 1983.

Verhael met den Almanach van het Luylecker-Landt, daer men den kost crijcht sonder wercken. Antwerp: J. Mesens, 1692. (Copy: Antwerp, Municipal Library.)

Verhoeven, G. *Devotie en negotie: Delft als bedevaartplaats in de late middeleeuwen*. Amsterdam, 1992.

Verhuyck, P. "Villon et les neiges d'antan." In *Villon hier et aujourd'hui*, ed. J. Dérens et al., 177–89. Paris, 1993.

Vermeulen, Y. *"Tot profijt en genoegen": Motiveringen voor de produktie van Nederlandstalige gedrukte teksten, 1477–1540*. Groningen, 1986.

Verrycken, A. *De middeleeuwse wereldverkenning*. Leuven, 1990.

———. "Het geheime stekje: Middeleeuwse ideeën over het aards paradijs." *Madoc* 6 (1992): 66–77.

Verwijs, E. and J. Verdam. *Middelnederlandsch woordenboek*. 10 vols. The Hague, 1885–1952. (Referred to in "Sources" as *MNW*.)

Verzameling van Nederlandsche prozastukken, van 1229–1476. Leiden, 1851.

Vet, W. A. van der. *Het Biënboec van Thomas van Cantimpré en zijn exempelen*. The Hague, 1902.

Virgilius. Facsimile ed. Ed. J. Gessler. Antwerp, 1950.

De vijfhonderdste verjaring van de boekdrukkunst in de Nederlanden. Brussels, 1973.

Vloten, J. van. *Het Nederlandsche kluchtspel van de 14e tot de 18e eeuw.* 2 vols. Haarlem, 1877.

Volksboek van Margarieta van Lymborch (1516). Ed. F. J. Schellart. Antwerp, 1952.

Het volksboek van Ulenspieghel. Ed. L. Geeraedts. Kapellen, 1986.

Voort van der Kleij, J. J. van der. *Middelnederlandsch handwoordenboek: Supplement.* The Hague, 1983.

Vooys, C. G. N. de. "Bijdrage tot de kennis van het middeleeuwse volksgeloof." *Nederlandsch Archief voor Kerkgeschiedenis,* n.s., 1 (1902): 357–85.

———. "De legende Van sinte Maria Magdalena bekeringhe." *Tijdschrift voor Nederlandse taal- en letterkunde* 24 (1905a): 16–44.

———. "Meister Eckhart en de Nederlandse mystiek." *Nederlandsch Archief voor Kerkgeschiedenis,* n.s., 3 (1905b): 50–92, 176–94, 265–90.

———. "Middeleeuwse schilderingen van het aardse paradijs." *Tijdschrift voor Nederlandse taal- en letterkunde* 25 (1906): 81–139.

———. "De dialoog van Meester Eggaert en de onbekende leek." *Nederlandsch Archief voor Kerkgeschiedenis I,* n.s., 7 (1910): 166–226.

———. *Middelnederlandse legenden en exempelen.* Groningen, 1926.

———. "De Middelnederlandse Boethius-vertaling van Jacob Vilt." *Tijdschrift voor Nederlandse taal- en letterkunde* 60 (1941): 1–25.

Van den vos Reynaerde. Ed. F. Lulofs. Groningen, 1983.

Vreese, W. de. "De legende van Sint-Haringus." *Het Boek* 11 (1922): 299–304.

Vries, Th. De. *Ketters: Veertien eeuwen ketterij, volksbeweging en kettergericht.* Amsterdam, 1982.

Waddell, H. *The Wandering Scholars.* London, 1968.

Waha, M. de. "Note sur l'usage des moyens contraceptifs à Bruxelles au début du XVe siècle." *Annales de la Société Belge d'Histoire des Hôpitaux* 13 (1975): 5–28.

"Das Wahtelmaere [Wachtelmäre]." In H. F. Maszmann, *Denkmaeler deutscher Sprache und Literatur,* 105–12. Munich, 1828.

Walker Bynum, C. *Holy Feast and Holy Fast: The Religious Significance of Food to Medieval Women.* Berkeley, 1987.

Die wech der sielen salicheit. Oudenaarde: A. de Keyser, 1479. (Copy: Cambridge, University Library.)

Weert, J. de. *Nieuwe doctrinael of Spieghel van sonden.* Ed. J. H. Jacobs. The Hague, 1915.

Weigert, R.-A. *French Tapestry.* Newton, Mass., 1962.

Werveke, H. van. "Bronnenmateriaal uit de Brugse stadsrekeningen betreffende de hongersnood van 1316." *Bulletin de la Commission Royale d'Histoire* 125 (1960): 431–510.

———. *De middeleeuwse hongersnood.* Brussels, 1967.

West, D. C. "Christopher Columbus, Lost Biblical Sites, and the Last Crusade." *Catholic Historical Review* 78 (1992): 519–41.

Die Wickiana: Johann Jakob Wicks Nachrichtensammlung aus dem 16. Jahrhundert. Ed. M. Senn. Zürich, 1975.

Wiersma, S. "Tuin en landschap in literair-retorische traditie: De locus amoenus." In *Tuinen in de middeleeuwen*, ed. R. E. V. Stuip et al., 21–33. Hilversum, 1992.

Willems, J. F. "Aenteekeningen van eenen pelgrim der XVe eeuw." *Belgisch Museum* 3 (1839): 408–10.

Willems, L. "De ketter Willem van Hildernissem en diens verhouding tot Bloemaerdinne." In *Mélanges P. Frédéricq*, 259–66. Brussels 1904.

Winkelman, J. H. "Het Ptolemeïsche wereldstelsel op een reliëf in de Middelnederlandse Floris ende Blanchefloer van Diederic van Assenede." *De nieuwe taalgids* 74 (1981): 101–20.

Winter, J. M. van. *Van soeter cokene: Recepten uit de oudheid en middeleeuwen.* Haarlem, 1976.

WNT. See *Woordenboek der Nederlandsche Taal.*

Wolf, H. "Erzähltraditionen in homiletischen Quellen." In *Volkserzählung und Reformation*, ed. W. Brückner et al., 705–56. Berlin, 1974.

Van die wonderlicheden ende costelicheden van Pape Jans landen. Antwerp: J. van Doesborch, [ca. 1506]. (Copy: London, British Library.)

Wood, F. *Did Marco Polo Go to China?* London, 1996.

Woordenboek der Nederlandsche Taal. Ed. M. de Vries et al. The Hague, 1864. (Referred to in "Sources" as *WNT.*)

Wright, T. *A History of Caricature and Grotesque in Literature and Art.* London, 1865.

Wunderlich, W. "Das Schlaraffenland in der deutschen Sprache und Literatur: Bibliographischer Überblick über den Forschungsstand." *Fabula* 27 (1986): 54–75.

Yates, F. A. *De geheugenkunst.* Amsterdam, 1988.

Ysengrimus. Trans. J. Mann. Leiden, 1987.

Het zal koud zijn in 't water als 't vriest: Zestiende-eeuwse parodieën op gedrukte jaarvoorspellingen. Ed. H. van Kampen et al. The Hague, 1980.

Zeebout, A. *'t Voyage van mynher Joos van Ghistele.* Ghent: H. van den Keere, 1557. (Copy: Ghent, University Library.)

———. *'t Voyage van mynher Joos van Ghistele.* Ghent: widow of G. van Salenson, 1572. (Copy: Ghent, University Library.)

Zerbolt van Zutphen, G. *Van geestelijke opklimmingen.* Ed. J. Mahieu. Bruges, 1941.

Zijl, Th. P. van. *Gerard Grote, Ascetic and Reformer (1340–1384).* Washington, D.C., 1963.

De Zuidnederlandse vertaling van het Nieuwe Testament. Ed. C. C. de Bruin. 2d part. Leiden, 1971.

Index

"abbas Cucaniensis," *394*, 394-97

Abundia, Lady, 129

Abyssinia, 250

acedia. *See* sloth

Adalbero of Lâon, 356

Adam, 118-19, 141, 256

Adam and Eve, 6-12, 63, 165-68, 263;
     Free Spirit movement and, 311, 318,
     321; time spent in Garden, 193-94;
     as vegetarians, 165-66, 177, 385. *See
     also* Fall of Man

Adamites, 18-19, 319-20

Ad nostrum, 316-17

Adoration of the Golden Calf (Lucas van
     Leyden), 129

Adornes of Bruges, 188

Aegidius Cantor, 323

Aernoutsbroeders (Aernout brothers),
     128, 160

Aertsen, Pieter, *95*

Africa, 250

Albertus Magnus, 218, 233

alchemy, 187

Alcinous, 216

Alexander the Great, 260, 263, 268, 270;
     paradise and, 144, 170, 207, 236,
     255

Alexander VI, 271

Alfonso, Pedro, 210

Alijt the Goose, 149

allegory, 23, 174, 222, 305

All Saints' Day, 71

aloe, 256

Alpertus of Metz, 112

al-Rashid, Haroun, 232

Aluta, 134

Amazons, 362

Ambrose, Saint, 172

Anabaptists, 110

animals, 114, 176, *355*; in paradise, 141-
     46, 168, 174; self-roasting, 3, 38,
     208, 283, 284, 285, 365, 379; servi-
     tude, 34, 37, 168, 226

anorexia nervosa, 127

anorexia sacra, 333

Anthony of Burgundy, 135

antique tradition, 295

Antony, Saint, 144

Antwerp, 84-85, 313, 329, 382, 419

Apocalypse. *See* Bible; millenarianism

Apollonius, 124

apple sniffers, 119-20, 421

Aquinas, Thomas, 141, 354

architecture, edible, 137-40; in Cock-
     aigne, 3, 55, 151, 278, 290, 413, 415,
     419-21; paradise and, 169, 416

Arcimboldo, 285, 286

Aristophanes, 397

arma christi, 347

Armageddon, Battle of, 271

Arnoldus, Saint, 160

ars poetica, 216, 353

Ars versificatoria (Matthew of Vendôme),
216

art, 353-54

Arthur, King, 238

asceticism, 312-13, 332-34, 380, 412;
desert fathers, 118-19, 332; hermits,
196-98, 373

Asia, 250

assassins, 212

Atlantis, 5, 220-21, 264

Atrecht, 345

Attic comedies, 283

Aucassin and Nicolette, 287

Augustine, Saint, 122, 238, 319, 386; on
Adam and Eve, 193-94; *civitas dei*,
352; *civitas terrena*, 352, 354-55; millenarianism and, 18, 305; paradise,
view of, 171, 172

aurea aetas. See golden age

automata, 22-25, 202, 233-34

autophagia, 158-59

Autun, Honoré d', 189

Averroës, 316

Averroists, 316

Avitus of Vienne, 169

Aymeri de Narbonne, 230, 393

B. *See* Rhyming Text B

Bacchanalia, 116

bagpipes, 287-88

Baldung Grien, Hans, *321*

ballade à l'impossible, 281

Balten, Pieter, 406

Bartholomaeus Anglicus, 171-72, 176,
214, 267, 415

Basel, 419

Basil the Great, Saint, 172

Batavia, 64, 227-29

Battle Between Lent and Carnival (after
Bruegel), 153, *153*

Battle Between Lent and Carnival (circle of
Bruegel), *152*, 153

Becker, Hans, 323-24

Bede, Venerable, 172

Beghards, 316-17, 327, 328

Beguines, 151, 313-14, 316-17, 320, 325,
327, 334

Belgium, 399

Bellaert, Jacob, 171-72

Bellum Judaicum (Flavius Josephus), 109

belly worship, 128, 374-75, 384

Berghe, Jan van den, 98, 295-96

Bernard of Clairvaux, 19, 327, 385

Bible, 106, 178; Book of Ecclesiastes,
352-53; Book of Ezekiel, 169, 195;
Book of Isaiah, 192, 203; Book of
Revelation, 16, 112, 192, 231, 239,
271, 302-5, 308, 354, 396; Epistle to
the Romans, 384; First Epistle of
John, 312; Genesis, 8, 141, 168, 174,
366-68; Gospel According to Saint
Mark, 27; Gospel According to
Saint Matthew, 347; Gospel of
Saint John, 120; Kings, 109; Old
Testament, 170, 305, 306; Psalms,
185; Second Epistle to Timothy,
307; Sermon on the Mount, 201;
Song of Songs, 22, 169, 170, 203,
216, 385

Bibliotheca historica (Diodorus Siculus),
282-83

Biënboec, 239, 312-13. *See also Bonum universale de apibus*

Bijns, Anna, 19-20, 73

Binche castle, 234-35

Birds (Aristophanes), 397

Bloemardinne, 329-30

Blue Barge, Guild of the, 69, 292, 358-61, 360

Boccaccio, Giovanni, 291

Boeck van der Voirsienicheit Godes, 114, 188

Dat boec van den houte, 236

Dat boec van den pelgherym, 370

Boec van der wraken, 107-8, 270-71

Boec van het kerstene leven, 380

Boendale, Jan van, 73, 75, 76, 222, 366, 380, 400; *Brabantsche Yeesten*, 104; *Der leken spieghel*, 15-16, 222, 386

Boethius, 15, 222-24, 384-85

Bologna, 134

Bonaventure, Saint, 202

Bonrepas, 399

Bonum universale de apibus (Thomas of Cantimpré), 239

Book of bees. See *Biënboec*

Book of death. See *Sterfboeck*

Book of Hours of Catherine of Cleves, 183

Book of Vices and Virtues, 194

Borneo, 258

Bosch, Hieronymus, 114, 144, 174, 203; *The Garden of Delights*, 175; *The Last Judgment*, 387; *The Ship of Fools*, 375-76, 401

Brabant, 51, 158, 326, 329-31

Brabantsche Yeesten (van Boendale), 104

Brahmans, 249, 268-69

Brant, Pieter den, 73-74

Brant, Sebastian, 69

Brazil, 262, 273

Brendan, Saint, 119, 196, 215, 230, 264. See also *Voyage of Saint Brendan*

Brethren of the Common Life, 332, 410

British-Celtic romances, 74-75, 131

Bronze Age, 224

Bruegel, Pieter the Elder: *Desidia*, 367; *Dulle Griet*, 379; *Fight Between Carnival and Lent*, 151, 152; *Gula*, 156-57; *The Harvest*, 92; *The Kermis at Hoboken*, 282; *Land of Cockaigne*, 66, 151, 152, 405, 405-6; *Netherlandish Proverbs*, 66; *Wedding Meal*, 91

Brueghel, Jan the Elder, *Visit to a Farmstead*, 92, 94

Bruges, 96-97, 105, 135

Bruges Gruuthuse manuscript, 357

Brugman, Johannes, 122, 195, 200-202, 369

Brussels, 10, 135, 320, 329, 330, 334, 345

Brussels Adamites, 18-19, 320

Buch der Chroniken (Schedel), 265

Buch der Tugend, 355-56, 356

Burgundians, 22, 23

burlesques, 403

De Buskenblaser, 25

Butcher's Shop (Aertsen), 95

Cadhilhe (Kao-li), 146

Caedmon, 61, 74

Cain, 196

Calanok, 144-45

Calcoen (da Gama), 277

Cambrai, 399

Camerini, 120, 268

Canary Islands, 125, 220

cannibalism, 109-17, *111*; Christianity and, 120-22, 276-78; foreign peoples and, 109, 116, 123-24, 145, 270, 272, 273, 276-77, 319

Canterbury Tales (Chaucer), 56-57

carbuncles, 36, 169, 196, 414-17, *417*

caricatures, 289

caritas drinking, 20-21, 133

Carmina Burana, 52, 149, 357, 394-97, 408

Carnival, 49, 54, 69, 78-79, 92, 132, 189, 340; contrasting themes, 151-55; fight between Carnival and Lent, 151-53; fight between meat and fish, 150-51; literature on, 147-48; nicknames, 159-60; ritual inversion and, 358-62; songs, 79, 155, 156

Carolingian epic, 131

castle gardens, 23-25, 218-19, 233-35

castles, 198, 215, 340, 415-16

Caxton, William, 194, 233-34

Celtic paradise, 27, 209, 214, 215

Celtic tradition, 157, 187

Celtic travelers' tales, 264-67, 284. *See also Voyage of Saint Brendan*

Chanson de Guillaume, 131

charivari, 58, 70, 338-39

Charlemagne, 75, 131, 133, 230

Charles the Bold, 96-97, 136, 137, 138

Charles V, 136, 138, 218, 234, 259, 375

Chaucer, Geoffrey, 56-57

chiliasm. *See* millenarianism

China, 232

chivalry, epics of, 239-40

Christianity: cannibalism and, 120-22, 276-78; gluttony and, 128-29; savages and, 257, 261, 263, 270-73, 276-78, 319; Syrian Christians, 170, 210; utopias and, 296

Christmas, 35, 39, 71

Chronik des Konstanzer Konzils, 1414-1418 (Richental), *143*

Cistercians, 19

cities, 228, 284; heavenly paradise as, 191-94, 196-98

City of God (Augustine), 18

civitas dei, 352

civitas terrena, 352, 354-55

classical antiquity, 147, 170

class literature, 92

class satire, 69, 84, 338

Clement V, 323

clerical humor, 342-44

cloister gardens, 233

Cluniacensis, 395

Cluny Abbey, 218, 394

cocanha (honey cake), 393-94

Cockaengen, 391, 393

Cockaenien, 392

Cockaigne: biblical paradise and, 167-69; edible architecture, 3, 55, 151, 278, 290, 413, 415, 419-21; location of, 177, 245-47; names, 391-402; as necessity, 423-27; sources, 3-5; weather, 173, 180-81. *See also* Luilekkerland; paradise, earthly; paradise, heavenly

Cockanyngen, 392

Cockenge (Cockange, Kockange), 399, 401

Columbus, Christopher, 13-15, 189, 252, 256-61, 272, 274, 276, 278, 324, 364

Columbus, Ferdinand, 324

comic relief, 28, 30

Commodianus, 308

competition, 382

complaint on the times. *See Zeitklage*

concordia discors, 353

confession manuals, 106, 194, 204, 209, 330, 372, 379

Confrarie. See Grande confrarie des soulx d'ouvrer et enragez de rien faire

convivium, 130-31

Convivium religiosum (Erasmus), 219
copyists, 49-52, 68-69, 391-92
Coquardz, 290
Cornelis, William, 312-13, 329
Cornelius Aurelius, 228
Cortez, Hernán, 259
Coster, André de, 7
Council of Clermont, 192, 310
Council of Vienne, 316-17
courtly literature, 147, 393, 418
courtly society, 373-74, 421-22
Courtrai, 399
Cranach, Lucas the Elder, *221, 223, 225*
crusades, 27, 192, 257, 310, 322
Crusades of the Shepherds, 322
Cucania, 395-97, 401, 417
Cucaniensis, 395
cuckoo (cuculus), 395
cultural milieus, 414-15

dance, 203-4, 213
Daniel (the Glutton), 160
Dante, 199, 248
David, King, 185, 202
Decameron (Boccaccio), 291
De consolatione philosophiae, 222
decorative food, 137-40, 146
Delf, Dirk van, 201, 202, 256, 374-75
Demmerik (Denmark), 399
Dendermonde, 154
Dene, Eduard de, 141, 148
Denmark, 399
De proprietatibus rerum, 171-72
desert fathers, 118-19, 332
Desidia (Bruegel), 367
Deutz, 198
devil, 114-15, 126, 144, 324; deceptive-

ness, 237-39; defeat of, 303-5;
derangement of human senses, 237-39
Devotio Moderna, 20, 120, 236, 332, 410
devotion, 368-69
didacticism, 337-51; in clerical humor, 342-44; in drinking songs, 342-43; in illuminated manuscripts, 347-51; Luilekkerland and, 237, 341-42; in rhyming prayers, 345-47; satire and, 338, 344-45. *See also* confession manuals; moralizing
didactic texts, 16, 28, 147, 295, 372, 380
Didimus, 268
Dietsche Lucidarius, 189, 367, 368. *See also Lucidarius*
Diodorus Siculus, 282-83
Diogenes, 224
Le Disciple de Pantagruel, 289-91
disease, 102, 105, 262
Dit is 't bescrive van den eertschen paradijs, 172-73, 196
Divine Comedy (Dante), 199, 248
Divisiekroniek (Cornelius Aurelius), 228
Doesborch, Jan van, 274, *275, 279*
Dominicans, 110, 313
Doppere, Romboudt de, 106
Draijer, Gorde den, 7
dreamworlds. *See* Cockaigne; Luilekkerland
Drie daghe here, 400
Drie Eenlingen, 293
Drincatibus, Sanctus, 148
drinking, 148, 212, 373, 377, 382; *caritas* drinking, 20-21, 133; drinking songs, 342-43, 394-95; in Prose Text G, 42-43, 84; in Rhyming Text B, 38; in Rhyming Text L, 35

Duché, Jacques, 235
Dulle Griet (Bruegel), *379*
Dürer, Albrecht, 259, *304*
Dutch Revolt, 406

early-modern society, 343, 406
Easter, 35, 38, 71
eating, 26; habits, 89-99; mealtimes,
    380-82; peasant fare, 90-95; in
    Prose Text G, 40-42, 82-83, 89-90,
    365, 382, 415; in Rhyming Text B,
    36-38; in Rhyming Text L, 33-35. *See
    also* food; gluttony
eating disorders, 127, 162, 333
Eckhardt, Meister, 313, 316, 329, 368
edible architecture. *See* architecture, edi-
    ble
Eerste Bliscap van Maria, 10
Egidius, 97
"Ego sum abbas Cucaniensis," *394*,
    394-97
Egypt, 195
Elckerlijc, 116
El Dorado, 5, 26, 257-58
Elijah, 172, 174, 215, 255, 293
Elizabeth of Gorlitz, 135
Elucidarium, 189, 190
Elysian fields, 220
emotions, 362
Emperor of Abstinence, 150
Enchanted Chamber, 235
encyclopedias, 119, 264, 285, 368
End of the Silver Age (Cranach), 225
Enoch, 172, 174, 196, 215, 255, 293
Ephraem Syrus, 210
epics of chivalry, 239-40
Epicurus, 148
epilogues, 67, 69

Episode from the Conquest of America
    (Mostaert), *271*
Erasmus, 219, 228, 284, 293
Erec, 131
Ethiopia, 187, 250
etiquette, 95, 97-98, 382
Eucharist, 120-23, *121*, 142, 186, 201
Eulenspiegel, Till, 129-30
Euphrates river, 217-18, 256
evil, 352, 354
exotic lands, 174, 246-47, 254, 264, 362,
    381, 421; gluttony and, 114-15; para-
    dise and, 145-46, 246-47. *See also*
    savages
explorers, 13-15
The Expulsion from Paradise, 14

fabliaux, 393, 396, 403, 418
Fabri, Felix, 188
fairy tales, 418, 421
Fall of Man, 6-12, 63, 118-19, 167-68,
    248; earthly paradise and, 177, 179
The Fall of Man (van der Goes), 9
Fall of Man and The Expulsion from Paradise
    (Josephus), 10
famine, 100, 102, 103-5, 159, 162, 423-24
Farce des coquins à cinq personnes, 285
Farce de Jenin Landore, 285-86
farces, 25, 159-60, 285-86
fasting, 94, 98, 118-27, 132, 204-5, 328;
    apple sniffers, 119-20; desert
    fathers and, 118-19; Eucharist and,
    120-23; hallucinations and, 118,
    124-27
The Fat Kitchen (van der Heyden after
    Bruegel), 153, *154*, 157, 376
fatrasie, 281
fatso image, 151-53, 376, *377*

Feast of Fools, 20, 132, 149, 292, 417

Feast of Saint John, 35, 71, 132, 133, 158, 173

Feast of Saint Martin, 149

Der Fielen, Rabauwen oft der Schalcken Vocabulaer, 419, 420

Fight Between Carnival and Lent (Bruegel), 151

films, 408, 410

Flanders, 326

Flavius Josephus, 107, 109, 111

floats, 7-10, 168, 218

Flood motifs, 96

Floris ende Blanchefloer, 231, 232

folk culture, 403-4, 413

fons iuventutis. See Fountain of youth

food: availability, 90, 96, 98, 99; decorative, 137-40; etiquette, 95, 97-98, 382; feasts, 20-21, 71, 98; fruit, 96-97; millenarianism and, 112, 320-22; mobile food, 3, 137-46, 208, 283-85, 365, 379; of nobility, 95-98; paradise and, 165-66, 178, 200-201; shortages, 92-93, 100-101; spices, 97, 258, 278. *See also* eating; gluttony; hunger

fools' society, 152, 154

formulaic elements, 55, 59, 62, 68, 71-72, 285

Fortunate Isles, 125

Fortune, 222

fountains, 22, 134-36, 196, 210

fountain of youth, 25, 182-85, 258, 267; in Prose Text G, 41-42; in Rhyming Text L, 35, 68-69

Fountain of Youth, 184

Fra Cipolla, 291

fragrances, 421-22

France, 308-9, 319, 326

Francis, Saint, 119, 307

Franciscans, 119, 226, 307, 326, 328, 342

Franciscan Spirituals, 307, 326

Franks, 131, 133

Frederick II, 232

Free Spirit movement, 18, 311-17, 322-23; clergy and, 329-30; sexuality and, 318-19, 327-29; van Rode on, 330-31

French texts, 58-59, 66, 85, 289, 302, 393, 396, 401, 424; didactic aspects, 338-39; framework, 70-71; *Huon de Bordeaux,* 187; Northern French literature, 151

Friars Minor. *See* Franciscans

fruit, 96-97, 177-78, 189-90

G. *See* Prose Text G

Galbert of Bruges, 106, 107, 129

Gama, Vasco da, 277

games, 141, 160; literary games, 394-95, 397

Ganges river, 256

Garden of Delights (Bosch), 174, *175*

Garden of Eden, 8-12, 165, 184, 196, 213, 246

gargoyles, 347

Gefraess (von Reuenthal), 147

Gelre, duchy of, 51

genre painting, 405

geography, 165, 245-54, 274; reliability of, 250-54. *See also* travel literature

geography books, 248

Geraardsbergen, 74

Geraardsbergen manuscript, 74-75

Germania (Tacitus), 227

Germanic tradition, 157-59, 227, 423

German texts, 59, 80, 81, 147, 313, 393

Gesta Romanorum, 295

Gheliken dorpen, 399

Ghent, 135

Ghistele, Joos van, 123, 213, 250, 252

Ghybe (Gib), 152, 154

Gieltjesdorp, 399

Gilbert of Tournai, 325

Gisbers, Liesbeth, 333

Glaber, Radulfus, 111-12, 352

gluttony, 5, *116*, 118-19, 128-36, *130*, 332, 384, 406, 418, 423; autophagia, 158-59; blowouts, 129-32; Christianity and, 128-29; exotic lands and, 114-15; fountains, 134-36; moderation and, 372-83; nobility and, 133-36; solidarity and, 130-31; in Turnhout farce, 159-60; types, 380-81; visual representations, 152-57

Godfrey of Bouillon, 50, 391

Goes, Hugo van der, 9

Goethe, Johann Wolfgang von, 408

Gog and Magog, 271

golden age, 15, 170-71, 179, 219-22, 284-85, 295, 384-85; Batavia, 227-29; Boethius on, 222-24

The Golden Age (Cranach), 221, 223

Golden Fleece, 233-34

Gottschalk, 205, 206

Graduale (John of Deventer), 21

La Grande confrarie des soulx d'ouvrer et enragez de rien faire, 291-92, 416

Grande Place (Brussels), 10

Great Khan, 381

Great Procession, 10

greed, 384

Greek comedy, 397

Greeks, 27, 170, 207-8, 219

Gregory of Tours, 129

Grote, Geert, 331

Gruenemberg, knight, 211-12

Gugganiensis gulescopus, 395-96

guild, the, 313

Guild of the Blue Barge, 69, 292, 358-61, 360

Gula (van der Heyden after Bruegel), 374

Hadewijch, 342, 353

The Hague, 256

hallucinations, 26, 124-27, 424. *See also* visions

Hanneken Leckertant, 98

Harvengt, Philip van, 230

The Harvest (Bruegel), 92

Have-Not, Saint, 160

heaven, 191, 236-40, 426. *See also* paradise, heavenly

hell, 114-15, *115*, 387

Henry II, 329

heresies, 303, 316-17, 426

hermits, 196-98, 373

Hesdin castle, 23-25, 233-34

Hese, Jan Witte van, 255

Hesiod, 207

Hesperides, 264

Heyden, Pieter van der, 153, *154*, *155*, *219*, 360, 374

Higden, Ranulf, 263

Hildegaersberch, Willem van, 73, 103, 323

Hingene, Rombaut von, 7

historicity, 264

holidays, 35, 38, 204-5. *See also* Carnival

Holy Family, 201

Holy Ghost, 64, 70, 301-4, 306, 320, 331, 334, 396

Holy Land, 68, 182, 211, 248

Holy Trinity, 306, 350

Homines intelligentiae, 320, 323, 329

honey cake, 393-94

Horst, 51

humanists, 378

humor, 134-35, 137, 147, 294, 407, 410; Anglo-Norman, 382; caricature, 155-56; clerical, 342-44; in Italian literature, 158; jokes, 56, 81; mock sermons, 148-50, 155, 285, 358, 361; nicknames, 159-60; place names, 398-400; religious, 301, 382; significance, 408-9

hunger, 100-106; causes, 102-6; in chronicles, 107-12; degeneration process, 113-15; famines, 100, 102, 103-5, 159, 162, 423-24; fear of, 103, 105-6, 107, 114-15, 117, 118, 140, 159, 208, 408; fear of in third world, 161-62; natural disasters as cause, 102, 104; profiteering, 102-3; proverbs on, 113-14, 128; sack of Jerusalem and, 107-9; as topos, 107-17; war and, 103, 110-11. *See also* cannibalism; food; gluttony

Huon de Bordeaux, 187

Hymns of Paradise (Ephraem Syrus), 210

Hyperboreans, 220

Hyspanien, 392

idleness, 26, 55, 64, 365-71, 400, 406, 418; devotion and, 368-69; in Prose Text G, 365-66; in Rhyming Text B, 36, 37, 39; in Rhyming Text L, 33, 34. *See also* sloth

illuminated manuscripts, *346*, 347-51, *349*, *350*, *355*

Image du Monde, 253

Imitatio Christi (Thomas of Kempen), 372

immortality, 25, 182-90, 236-41, 256. *See also* fountain of youth

India, 170, 207, 256-57, 263-64; Brahmans, 249, 268-69

individual, 424-25

Indo-Germanic cultures, 208

Innocent VIII, Pope, 110

inquisition, 317, 325, 329, 330, 334

intoxication. *See* drinking; fasting; hallucinations

inversion, ritual, 343, 358-62

Ireland, 214, 264-67

Iron Age, 224

irony, 70, 273, 340, 358

Isidore of Seville, 171, 176, 319, 414-15

Islamic world, 170, 232. *See also* Muslim paradise

Islands of the Blessed, 5, 172, 179, 220-21, 264, 284-85, 290

Italian literature, 158

Italy, 125, 293

Iter ad Paradisium, 255

Jacob (monk), 322

Janszoon, Lauris, 103, 292-93, 378

Jason (Caxton), 233-34

Jerusalem, 107-9, 138, 183, 192, 230, 309; visual art, *108*, *139*. *See also* New Jerusalem

Jesus, 19, 27, 201, 237, 342, 347, 421; Eucharist and, 120-22, 142

Jewish apocalyptic literature, 195

Jews, 107-8, 270-71, 310, 348. *See also* Jerusalem

Joachim of Fiore, 305-7, 323, 396

Job, land of, 126

Johannesminne, 132

John of Beverley, 373, 418

John of Brünn, 328

John Chrysostom, Saint, 170-71, 182

John of Deventer, 21

John the Divine, Saint, 192

John the Evangelist, 183, 320-22

John of Trokelowe, 107

John XXII, Pope, 191

John of Viktring, 19

Joinville, Jean de, 188

Jordan river, 68-69, 182, 301

Josephus, Flavius, 11

Joufroi of Poitiers, 427

Dat kaetspel ghemoralizeert, 295-96

Kalendrier des Bergiers, 115

"Kerelslied," 91-92

The Kermis at Hoboken (Bruegel), 282

Keysere, Roland de, 222

kockinen (coquin), 400

Kokanje (Kokinje), 393

kokenje (kokinje), 393

Kokkengen, 398-400

Koran, 210

Kraemer, Heinrich, 110

L. *See* Rhyming Text L

Lalebuch, 296

Laleburg, 296

Lamory, 318-19

Land of Cockaigne (Bruegel), *ii*, 66, 151, 152, 405, 405-6

Land of Cockaigne (after Bruegel), 365

Land of Cokaygne (Middle English text), 59, 89, 166-67, 214, 267, 292, 306, 396-97, 406, 416, 425

Las Casas, Bartolomé de, 261

Last Judgment, 6, 18, 106, 172, 191, 344

The Last Judgment (Bosch), 387

Lateran Synod, 133

Latin, 295, 378, 396, 401

Latin satire, 358

Laurel and Hardy, 410

Lawrence, Saint, 123, 287

Lax, Saint, 292

The Lean Kitchen (van der Heyden after Bruegel), 153, *155*, 157, 376

Leeu, Gheraert, 260

Legende van Sinte Haryngus, 149-50

Der Leken spieghel (van Boendale), 15-16, 222, 386

Lent, 71, 79, 100-101, 151-53

Léry, Jean, 273

Liber scalae, 210, 398

Lidwina of Schiedam, 120, 127, 200, 333

Limburg, 51

literary studies, 403-4

Livy, 116

locus amoenus, 22, 169, 170-71, 179, 203, 216-19; castle gardens, 218-19; pleasure gardens, 217, 218. *See also* paradise; paradise, earthly; paradise, heavenly; pleasure gardens

Lollards, *315*, 316-17, 330

London manuscript, 45-50, 190, 358, 367. *See also* Rhyming Text L

Lord's Prayer, 100

Louis X, 105

Louvain, 7-9

Lucas van Leyden, 129

Lucian, 221, 247, 284-85, 291, 397

Lucidarius, 48, 49, 185, 359,411, 412. *See also Dietsche Lucidarius*

Luciferans, 19

Luere, Boudewijn van der, 357

Luilekkerland, 5, 6, 279, 341-42, 426; compared with heavenly paradise, 204, 205; decorative food and, 141; didacticism and, 237, 341-42; eating and, 90; illustrations, *338, 339*, 370, *409*; location, 177, 245; money in, 42, 82, 83, 424; moralizing in, 418; name of, 392, 393; as paradise, 167; text, 28; weather, 180-81, 342; as written tradition, 80. *See also* Prose Text G

Luther, Martin, 237

Luyeleckerlant, 392

lying couplets, 281

lying tales, 75-76, 78, 83, 86, 245, 287, 293, 354, 358; decorative food and, 141, 146

macaronic form, 52

Mac Dathos, 157

Mâcon, 112

Macropedius (Joris van Lancvelt), 134

Mael Dúin, 119, 145, 209

Maerlant, Jacob van, 73, 75, 97, 119, 131, 226; *Dat boec van den boute* (attrib.), 236; *Der naturen bloeme,*266; on India, 263-64; on millennium, 307-8; *Rijmbijbel*, 325; *Spiegel Historiael*, 110, 269; *Wrake van Jerusalem*, 109

Magellan, Ferdinand, 257-58, 262, 269, 278

Malleus maleficarum (Sprenger and Kraemer), 110

Manasses, 313

Mandeville, Sir John, 126, 168, 179, 188, 232, 247-52, 362; on earthly paradise, 174-76, 241; on fountain of youth, 182-85; on India, 268; on Lamory, 318-19; on mobile food, 144-46; parodies of, 285, 291, 293; on Prester John, 123-24, 415, 421; on sexuality, 211, 212

Mandyn, Jan, 144

manuscript fiction, 77

Map, Walter, 329

Marco Polo, 212, 253, 260

Margaret of York, 96, 136

Margarieta van Lymborch, 239-40

marginalia, 345-51, *346, 349, 350*, 355

Martial, 123

martyrs, 26, 148-50, 287

Mary Magdalene, 203

masses for the dead, 191, 246

Master of Hungary, 322

mât de Cocagne, 375-76, 401

Mathesius, Johannes, 237

Matthew, Saint, 347, 374

Matthew of Vendôme, 216

Maximilianus Transsylvanus, 269

Mechelen, 348

Medici, Catherine de', 422

Meditations on the Life of Christ, The (Bonaventure), 202

melancholy, 366, 370

Memling, Hans, 17

mendicant orders, 226, 342. *See also* Franciscans; Franciscan Spirituals

Men of Intelligence. *See* Homines intelligentiae

merchants, 259

Mesopotamia, 217-18

Metz, 117

Meung, Jean de, 209, 312

middle class, 83-85, 177, 204, 372. *See also* urban society

Middle Dutch texts, 48, 59, 173-74, 403; *Floris ende Blanchefloer,* 231, 232; name of Cockaigne and, 392, 393; *Sinte Augustijns hantboec,* 354; *The Voyage of Saint Brendan,* 196, 214, 215, 230, 284. *See also* Prose Text G; Rhyming Text B; Rhyming Text L

Middle English texts. *See Land of Cokaygne*

millenarianism, 18, 302-10, 313, 323, 334, 396; food and, 112, 320-22; moralizing and, 325-26; poverty, 308-10, 326

minnedrinken, 21, 132

mirabilia, 245

miracle plays, 158

mnemonic aids, 60-62, 64, 74

mobile food, 3, 137-46, 208, 283-85, 365, 379

mock doctor's prescription, 47, 48, 49, 52-53, 358, 412

mock documents, 150-51

mock sermons, 78-79, 148-50, 155, 285, 291-92, 358, 361

model peoples, 268-70

moderation, 372-83, 388

modern society, 5, 344-45, 408, 410; paradises, 240, 241; realism, 252-53

Mohammed, 210, 211

Moluccas, 269-70

money, 358, 424; in Prose Text G, 42, 83, 84; in Rhyming Text B, 39; in Rhyming Text L, 34

monks, 20-21, 292, 306, 322, 366, 397

monster races, 264, 265, 266, 282

Montalbaen, Renout van, 380

Montezuma, 259

Montfoort, Jan van, 123

morality plays, 60, 302, 422

moralizing: at end of Middle Ages, 387-88; humor and, 294; millenarianism and, 325-26; in Prose Text G, 81, 83, 85, 260, 337; in Rhyming Text B, 69-70, 260, 337; satire and, 326-27; in travel literature, 248-49, 260; written tradition and, 69-70, 85. *See also* didacticism

More, Thomas, 295, 296

Morre, Jan, 102

Mostaert, Jan, 270, 271

mountain of buckwheat porridge, 165, 177

Mount Venus, 238

Mount Zion, 230-31

mundus inversus. See topsy-turvy world

Münster, 110

Munster, Dirk van, 103

music, 199, 201-4, 287-88, 292

Muslim paradise, 26, 27, 170, 208-13; name of Cockaigne and, 397-98

mysticism, 127, 311, 314-16, 426

Mystic Marriage of Saint Catherine (Memling), *17*

nakedness, 7-8, 318

Narbonne, 230

narcotics, 26, 125

narrator, 62-63

nature, 227-28, 370, 418-19

Der naturen bloeme (Maerlant), 266

Natuurkunde van het geheelal, 60

negative comparisons, 194, 264

Netherlandish Proverbs (Bruegel), 66

Netherlands, 308, 320

New Jerusalem, 16-18, 191-99, 230, 246,
303-5, 309; paintings, *17, 304*
New World, 161, 259-62, 270, 426-27
nicknames, 159-60
Nieuwe Doctrinael (de Weert), 99
Nile river, 188, 256
Nivardus, 157
nobility, gluttony and, 133-36
noble savage. *See* savages
Nobody, Saint, 148, 358, 361
Nonnecourt, Villard de, 232
nonsense verse tradition, 281
nouvelles, 291
Nouvelles admirables, 291
Nuremberg carnival, 189

Odoric of Pordenone, 145
Odyssey, The, 216
oral tradition, 3-4, 27-28, 85-86, 302, 405,
424; closing lines, 67-68; didacticism in, 340; name of Cockaigne
and, 392-93; narrator, 62-63; parody
and, 283; recitation, 55-57; in
Rhyming Text L, 48; suspicion of,
75-76; techniques, 62-65; travelers'
tales and, 284; variants, 56-57
Orff, Carl, 408
Orinoco river, 257

padding, 62, 64, 65, 74
Palestinian martyrs, 26
Papias, 141, 200, 320-22
paradise, 5-6, 18-20, 426; Adam and
Eve's expulsion from, 6-12; animals
in, 141-46, 168, 174; carbuncles in,
415-16; Celtic paradise, 27, 209, 214,
215; exotic lands and, 145-46, 246-
47; Greek, 207-8; Muslim paradise,

26, 27, 170, 208-13, 397-98; as
refuge, 216-18; sexuality in, 208-14.
See also paradise, earthly; paradise,
heavenly; pleasure gardens
paradise, earthly, 6-12, 162, 246; absence
of food, 165-66, 178; exotic countries, 246-47; inaccessibility, 165,
171, 176-77; Mandeville on, 174-76,
241; monotony of, 165-66, 174, 179,
240-41, 416; rivers, 184-85, 255, 256;
stability, 179-80; weather in, 173,
178-81. *See also* paradise, heavenly
paradise, heavenly, 16, 191-206, 303-5;
biblical story of, 167-69; as city,
191-94, 196-98; codification of, 171;
descriptions, 194-95; food in, 200-
201; as New Jerusalem, 191-94;
population, 199-200. *See also* New
Jerusalem; paradise, earthly
Parasite, 378
Paris, 230
parody, 52, 78, 245, 281-83; prayer parodies, 161; of travel literature, 285,
289-93, 354, 378, 406. *See also* satire
Paul, Saint, 128, 307, 369
peasants, 90-95, 308, 413; sexuality and,
418-19
Peeter van Provencen, 22-23
pendants, 153
Pentecost, 324
perfection, 311-12, 313, 317, 328
Peter Comestor, 325
Peter Damian, 172, 218
Peter the Venerable, 210
Petrarch, 120
Petrarch Master. *See* Weiditz, Hans
Petrissa, 177
Petronius, 140, 142-44, 284

Petrus Damascenus, 172
Pheasant Banquet, 136
Pherecrates, 283
Philip the Good, 7, 135, 136
Philippines, 257-58
Philip II, 235
Phillipszoon, Jan, 357
Pigafetta, Antonio, 257-58, 262, 278
pilgrims' guides, 48, 49, 50, 412
Pison river, 256
Plato, 220, 294
playacting, 287
Playerwater, 25
plays, 60, 158, 168, 302, 422
pleasure, 170-71, 303, 353-54
pleasure gardens (pleasances), 202, 213-
    14, 217, 230-35, 425-26; bourgeois
    versions, 235; castle gardens, 23-25,
    218-19, 233-35; cloister gardens,
    232-33; devil's distortion of, 238-39
Pliny, 267
Poitou, 64, 229
Polychronicon (Higden), 263
Pomerius, 329
Pompeii, 140
Poperingen fools' society, 152, 154
popular culture, 403-4, 406-7, 418; rural
    character, 413-14
population increase, 308-9
Porete, Marguerite, 313-14, 316, 331
Portugal, 271
Poseidon, 221
poverty, 368; Free Spirit movement and,
    312-13, 322; millenarianism and,
    308-10, 326
Praise of Folly, The (Erasmus), 125
prayer parodies, 161
precious stones, 141, 168-69, 210, 268,

284, 384; carbuncles, 36, 169, 196,
    414-17, *417;* cultural milieu and,
    414-15; El Dorado and, 257-58; in
    Garden of Eden, 195, 256; in New
    Jerusalem, 192-93, 230
Prester John, land of, 123, 187, 250-52,
    251, 258, 274, 279, 293, 381; pre-
    cious stones, 415
Priapus, 123
pride, 373
primitivism, 15
Procession of the Holy Cross, 348
profiteering, 102-3
property ownership, 226, 294-95
prophets, 305, 322
Prose Text G, 40-44, 204, 279, 281, 302,
    404; on animals, 168; compared
    with Sachs's text, 81-85; decorum
    in, 83-84; descriptive title, 77-79,
    78; didactic aspect, 337-38; drink-
    ing in, 42-43, 84; earthly paradise
    in, 165; eating in, 40-42, 82-83, 89-
    90, 365, 382, 415; fountain of youth
    in, 41-42; fragrances in, 421-22;
    hybridization, 340-41; idleness in,
    365-66; money in, 42, 83, 84; mor-
    alizing in, 81, 83, 85, 260, 337;
    opposites in, 386; sexuality in, 43,
    84-85. *See also* Luilekkerland; Sachs,
    Hans
Provençal dialect, 393
Proverbes en rime, 113
proverbs, 66, 142, 146, 180, 293, 327, 369,
    423; on hunger, 113-14, 128
Pseudo-Basil, 170
publishers, 80, 85, 274, 289, 388; tid-
    ings, 254, 291
puns, 397

purgatory, 191, 199
Pythagoras, 221

quinta essentia, 25, 187

Rabelais, 141, 289-90
reading, 65, 388, 393
reality, 281
recitation, 55-57; mnemonic aids, 60-61,
64, 74-75; rhyming couplets, 60,
66. *See also* storytellers
recitation texts, 80, 103, 287
rederijkers. See rhetoricians
Reformation, 343
Reihenspiel, 159
Reineke Fuchs (Goethe), 408
religious festivals, 7-12, 20-21, 168, 343
Remus, 196
Renaissance, 179
Renier of Sint-Truiden, 222
Reuenthal, Neidhart von, 147
Reynard the Fox, 157
rhetoric, 353
rhetoricians, 60, 281, 302, 378
Rhine valley, 18, 308, 310, 319, 329
rhyming couplets, 60, 66, 392
rhyming prayers, 345-47
Rhyming Text B, 29, 36-39, 46, 50-54,
89, 412; on animals, 168; Batavia
in, 228; carbuncles in, 416-17; contamination of, 414-15; copyist, 51-
52, 392; didactic aspects, 340;
earthly paradise in, 165, 167; eating
in, 36-38; on Holy Ghost, 301; idleness in, 36, 37, 39; language of,
404; location of Cockaigne in,
245; mock doctor's prescription,
52-54, *53;* moralizing in, 69-70,

260, 337; name of Cockaigne in,
400; New Jerusalem in, 193-94;
omissions, 71; opposites in, 386;
oral characteristics in, 65; precious
stones in, 193; satire in, 338; sexuality in, 39, 67, 327, 328; similarities
with L, 55-56, 62, 64, 67; title, 50;
weather in, 180; on work, 370-71
Rhyming Text L, 33-36, 45-50, 54, 60, 85,
89, 412; on animals, 168; Batavia
in, 228; brevity of, 71; copyists, 49-
50, 68, 391-92; didactic aspects,
340; earthly paradise in, 165, 167;
eating in, 33-35; folio, 404; fountain of youth in, 35, 68-69; on
Holy Ghost, 301; idleness in, 33,
34; illustrations, 46, 47; lack of
sex in, 68, 69; location of Cockaigne in, 245; mock doctor's prescription, 47, 48; moralizing in,
337; name of Cockaigne in, 391,
400; oral characteristics in, 65;
precious stones in, 168-69; property ownership in, 226; rejuvenation, 182; satire in, 338; similarities
with B, 55-56, 62, 67; title, 45;
weather in, 180
Richental, Ulrich, *143*
Ridderboeck, 185, 372
Rijmbijbel (Maerlant), 325
ritual inversion, 343, 358-62
rivers, 182, 184-85, 188, 217-18, 255, 256,
257, 399
Rode, Jan van, 330-31
Roermond, 51
The Romance of the Rose, 98, 203, 222, 317,
369; food in, 96, 98; on sexuality,
96, 226-27, 316

The Romance of the Rose (de Meung), 209, 312

Roman Curia, 133

Roman de la Rose, 24, 217

Romans, 123, 140, 170, 219

Rome, 196, 293

Romulus, 196

roosters, 398

Roovere, Anthonis de, 138-39, 194, 357

Royal Book, 194

Rubruck, Willem van, 250

Ruiz, Juan, 396

Rupert of Deutz, 198

Ruusbroec, Jan van, 122, 313, 325, 330, 331, 342-43

Sachs, Hans, 80, 81-86, 339, 382. *See also* Prose Text G

sacraments, 313, 324

Saehrimnir, 157

Saint-Martin abbey, 105

Salvation, 348

Satia, 129

satire, 78, 247, 285; class satire, 69, 84, 338; Latin satire, 358; monastic, 396, 401, 406, 417; moralizing and, 326-27; in Prose Text G, 83; social order and, 356-58; on street poets, 73, 75; topsy-turvy world and, 344-45, 355; of travelers' tales, 281-82, 285, 289-91; on utopias, 294, 296. *See also* parody

Satyricon (Petronius), 144

savages, 252, 270-73, 362, *363*, 364; Christianity and, 257, 261, 263, 270-73, 276-78, 319; noble savage, 257, 262, 269, 276, 277, 319; sexuality and, 260-61, 274-76

scandal sheets, 126

Schedel, Hartmann, 265

Schlaraffenland, 59, 80, 81-85, 82, 340, 392

Das Schlaweraffenland (Hans Sachs), 81

Schockland, 159

Schoen, Erhard, 82

scholars, 52

Schoonhoven, 399

Schoonhoven, Jan van, 331

science, 186-87

Second World War, 161

Sesterhande verwen, 49

Seth, 256

sexuality, 64, 226-27, 318-24; Adamites and, 18-19, 319-20; Free Spirit movement and, 318-19, 327-29; in paradise, 208-14; peasants and, 418-19; in Prose Text G, 43, 84-85; in Rhyming Text B, 39, 67, 327, 328; Rhyming Text L and, 68, 69; in *The Romance of the Rose*, 96, 226-27, 316; savages and, 260-61, 274-76; sex-role swapping, 362

Ship of Fools (Bosch), 375-76, 401

Ship of Fools (Brant), 69

Sidrac, 48, 49, 177, 190, 412

Silver Age, 225

Sinte Augustijns hantboec, 354

Sinte Franciscus leven (Maerlant), 307

Sint Lievens Houthem, 348

Skinnybones, 376

slaughterhouses, 142, 143

sloth, 327, 329, 365, 366, 368, 382. *See also* idleness

Smeken, Jan, 348

Snelryem den spreker, 73

snowmen, 345-47, *346*

social criticism, 281-82, 294, 296; name
of Cockaigne and, 401-2; topsy-
turvy world and, 287-88, 386-88
social order, 343-44, 356-58, 406; Guild
of the Blue Barge, 69, 292, 358-61
Somme le roi, 194, 204, 209, 330
"Song of the Roasted Swan," 149
Song of Roland, The, 230, 393
Sotte Benedicite, 161
Sotte Gratias, 161
sources, 3-5
Spaengen, 392
Spain, 63, 228, 267, 271
Speculum Historiale (Vincent of Beau-
vais), 210-11
Spengen, 399-400
spices, 97, 258, 278
Spiegel Historiael (Maerlant), 110, 269
Spiegel der sonden, 367
spiritual drunkenness, 342-43
spiritual love, 353-54
Sponger, 378
Sprenger, Johann, 110
Spring (van der Heyden), 219
Springer, Bartholomeus, 275, 279
Staden, Hans, 145
Stephen of Bourbon, 238
Sterfboeck, 16, 180, 187, 194-96, 202
Stijevoort, Jan van, 92
stock phrases, 62, 64, 65-66, 74
Stone Heads, 152
storytellers, 73-76, 357. *See also* recitation
Strabo, 207, 264, 288
Strassburg, Gottfried von, 131
street poets, 73, 75-76, 302
Sturluson, Snorri, 131, 157
submotifs, 62, 82, 289
Sumatra, 318

Suriname, 262
Syrian Christians, 170, 210

tableaux vivants, 168, 422, 426
Tacitus, 196, 227
tafelspel, 292-93
"Tale of Sir Thopas" (Chaucer), 56-57
tall tales, 81-82, 285
Tanchelm, 313, 329
Tartary, 179, 381
Teleclides, 283
Ten Commandments, 103, 128, 238, 249,
374
Tertullian, 128-29, 309
Testament rhetoricael (de Dene), 141
texts, 13, 26, 28-30, 345; closing lines,
67-68, 81; contamination of, 28-30,
414-15; copyists, 49-52, 68-69, 391-
92; epilogues, 67, 69; formulaic
elements, 55, 59, 62, 68, 71-72, 285;
hybridization, 340-41; languages
used, 48, 51; lost original (text X),
55-56; padding, 62, 64, 65, 74; pil-
grims' guides in, 48, 49, 50, 412.
See also French texts; Prose Text G;
Rhyming Text B; Rhyming Text L
Thalamass, 145-46
Third Reich, 227
third world, 161-62
Thomas (evangelist), 128
Thomas of Cantimpré, 239, 313
Thomas of Kempen, 372
Thonis, Brother, 333
thousand-year reign. *See* millenarianism
Three Kings, history of the, 278
tidings, 80, 254, 291
Tigris river, 217-18, 256
toponyms, 391

topsy-turvy world, 83-84, 160, 173, 301, 352-64; Alexander the Great and, 260; animals in, 355; *concordia discors,* 353; didactic aspects, 337, 339; golden age and, 224; heavenly *vs.* earthly reality, 352-53; in illuminations, 345-51; irony in, 340; moderation and, 372; *mundus inversus,* 149, 345, 355, 417; Prester John's country as, 252; ritual inversions, 343, 358-62; satire and, 344-45, 355; sex-role swapping, 362; social criticism and, 287-88, 386-88; work and, 365-71. *See also* Carnival

travel literature, 80, 119, 126, 141; on El Dorado, 257-58; by Godfrey of Viterbo, 214-15; moralizing in, 248-49, 260; on Muslim paradise, 211-12; oral tradition and, 284; paradise and, 145-46, 174, 255; parody of, 285, 289-93, 354, 378, 406; reliability in, 250-54. *See also* geography; Mandeville, Sir John

Trimalchio, 142

Tristan and Isolde, 76, 131

Trogus Pompeius, 295

True History (Lucian), 247, 284-85, 397

Turelure, land of, 287

Turks, 125-26

Turnhout farce, 159-60

Twee bedelaers, 292-93, 378

Urban II, Pope, 192, 310

urban society, 340, 382-83, 388, 421

Utopia (More), 295, 296

utopias, 16-18, 273, 294-97, 343, 398,

406; New World as inspiration for, 426-27

Utrecht, 155, 313, 398-400, 401

vagabonds, 73, 106

Valerius Maximus, 295

Van den corencopers, 103

Van den heilighen sacramente van der Nyeuwervaert, 158

Van den IX besten, 74-75

Van den kaerlen, 92

Van der nieuwer werelt, 274

Van Onse Lieven Heers minnevaer, 378

Van 't coren, 103

Van tijtverlies (van der Luere), 357

Van 't Luye-lecker-landt, 59-60, 77. *See also* Prose Text G

Van den zekeren hope, 324

Vecht river, 399

Veelderhande geneuchlycke dichten, tafelspelen ende refereynen, 77, 78, 361-62

vegetarianism, 15, 118-19, 165-66, 177, 226, 385

Velthem, Lodewijk van, 233

Venice, 213

Venlo, 51, 392

vernaculars, 295

Vespucci, Amerigo, 259, 262, 274

Vikings, 399

Villon, François, 345

Vincent of Beauvais, 110, 146, 210-11, 269, 295

Vintler, Hans, 355-56, 356

Virgil, 185-86, 220

Virgin Mary, 19, 222, 313

visions, 16, 20, 205, 426; fasting and, 118, 124-27; of heavenly paradise, 199, 200. *See also* hallucinations

Visit to a Farmstead (Brueghel), 92, *94*

The Voyage of Saint Brendan, 196, 214, 215, 230, 284

Vulgar Latin, 396

Wachtelmäre, Das, 86

Walewein, 231, 232

Walsperger Map of 1448, *197*

war, 159, 161

weather, 195, 282; in Cockaigne, 173, 180-81; in earthly paradise, 173, 178-81; in Luilekkerland, 180-81, 342

Wedding Meal (Bruegel), *91*

Weert, Jan de, 99, 128

Weiditz, Hans, 92, *93, 341, 376, 376-78*

West Flanders, 152

Whitsun, 71

whores, 84-85, 312, 382

Willemszoon, Arent, 108-9, 203, 213-14, 252

William of Auvergne, 129

William of Egmont, 19

William of Hildernissen, 18, 323

William II of Holland, Count, 233

witchcraft, 110, 318

Wonder, King, 231

woodcuts, 254, 355-56, *373*

work, 3, 119, 301, 382, 388, 424; topsy-turvy world and, 365-71

World War II. *See* Second World War

Wrake van Jerusalem (Maerlant), 109

written tradition, 56, 58-59, 291, 302, 340-41, 424; as aid to recitation, 64-65, 74; as authoritative, 75-76; moralizing and, 69-70, 85; name of Cockaigne and, 393; oral elements in, 60, 64-65; process of, 404-5

Younger Edda (Prose Edda), 131, 157

Ypres, 105

Ysengrimus, 157

Ysperia, 267

Zeitklage, 354

Zerbolt of Zutphen, Gerard, 236

Zion, 203